Acclaim for *All Saints:*

"In these short, splendidly wrought profiles, Robert Ellsberg gives us a vigorous cloud of witnesses — mystics, martyrs, social activists, artists, writers, composers — who do what all saints do: mediate the many and surprising ways in which grace makes discipleship possible. John Paul II has called for a millennial martyrology of unofficial witnesses to the faith who died in this century; he should start with this book. The Maritains, Bloy and Bernanos, Mozart, Bach and Barth, Heschel and the Baal Shem Tov — all find their places in this richly imagined collection of mediating figures in a spiritual communion of many faiths."

— KENNETH L. WOODWARD, Religion Editor, *Newsweek,*
author of *Making Saints*

"A wonderfully broad, knowing, and narratively compelling look at human goodness as it has been tested by life. This book will give all of us the very best kind of moral and spiritual education."

— ROBERT COLES, author of *The Moral Life of Children*

"A Calendar of Saints for our time. An invaluable book."

— SALLY FITZGERALD, author of *The Habit of Being:
The Letters of Flannery O'Connor*

"This book should be in every home, on every shelf, in every library. It raises the standards of life. It is the kind of book which, if read to our children, could change the tone of the next generation. *All Saints* is a gift of unusual proportion, a tour de force of both history and insight."

— JOAN CHITTISTER, author of *The Psalms*

"Ellsberg proves that we do not have to search far for heroes and saints. They are in our midst. Some have been canonized, many have not been; many never will be. What brings them all together is love of God and love of neighbor, high ideals, and a willingness to sacrifice self for others. Ellsberg brings all these heroes of our tradition, even those who may seem peripheral to it, to life again."

— MOST REVEREND REMBERT G. WEAKLAND, O.S.B., Archbishop of Milwaukee

"Remember when you read Butler's *Lives of the Saints* and you felt guilty about falling asleep after the third page? Relief is here, thanks to Robert Ellsberg. When you read *All Saints* you will not only stay fully awake but you'll be hyperactively telling everyone you meet to read it. Make a nuisance of yourself. It's not a sin, it's fun."

— COLMAN MCCARTHY, columnist, *The Washington Post*

"Each entry in *All Saints* is as crisp as freshly picked lettuce. Robert Ellsberg has a rare gift for getting a great deal into a small space and always getting to what matters most."

— JIM FOREST, author of *Living with Wisdom: A Life of Thomas Merton*

" 'Take and read,' said the voice reaching St. Augustine from a neighboring house. He took up Scripture and what he read transformed his life. This is one of the accounts in *All Saints,* a book telling of 365 holy ones, compiled by Robert Ellsberg. 'Take and read' these vibrant accounts. You may not be transformed, but you will be enriched, your heart moved and exhilarated, and your mind delighted."
— EILEEN EGAN, author of *Such a Vision of the Street*

"What a rich compendium, a vade mecum for every day of the year! Where else but in this wise and generous book would one find a famed modern theologian side by side with a first-century woman, a Christian Zen monk near a Quaker artist, a mystic of the Holocaust and then a desert hermit? Here we meet the capacities and, yes, the glories of humankind."
— DANIEL BERRIGAN, S.J., author of *Isaiah*

"Well-suited for daily prayerful reading, Robert Ellsberg's reflections help us to enter into the mystery of the communion of saints. These 365 cameos are crafted by a verbal artist who has the vision of a prophet and a scholar's eye for the important details. Because *All Saints* includes those at the margins as well as in the mainstream of the Christian tradition, it offers both invitation and challenge to reexamine our understanding of holiness and to think anew about what it takes to be a saint."
— MICHAEL DOWNEY, editor, *The New Dictionary of Catholic Spirituality*

"Ellsberg makes the biblical 'cloud of witnesses' come alive in these sharply etched portraits. This is a sanctoral cycle for the twenty-first century. Highly recommended."
— LAWRENCE S. CUNNINGHAM, author of *The Catholic Heritage*

"We are essentially imitative creatures. We cannot imagine it until we see it 'in the real.' Robert Ellsberg has put some fine lamps on the lampstand for all of us to see — and catch the light. No theory here, only human lives in all their dignity."   — RICHARD ROHR, author of *Job: The Mystery of Suffering*

"A richly diverse spiritual banquet generously laid before us, offering daily sustenance for the searcher and the pilgrim. Who cannot benefit from this book? I plan to make it part of my individual and family prayer."   — PAUL WILKES, author of *The Good Enough Catholic*

"This book is a great treasure. Though not pious it is spiritually evocative; though untraditional, it is consistent with the larger Catholic tradition. While broadening the traditional vision of sanctity it calls us to explore our own ways of becoming a saint. I consider Robert Ellsberg to be one of the most significant spiritual writers in the United States, and this book puts him right into the center of contemporary spiritual literature."
— HENRI J. M. NOUWEN (in response to proofs of *All Saints;*
after Nouwen's death the author devoted a chapter to his life)

ALL SAINTS

ALL SAINTS

*Daily Reflections on Saints, Prophets,
and Witnesses for Our Time*

With a New Study Guide

ROBERT ELLSBERG

A Crossroad Book
The Crossroad Publishing Company
New York

This printing: 2007

The Crossroad Publishing Company
16 Penn Plaza, 481 Eighth Avenue
New York, NY 10001

Printed in the United States of America

Library of Congress Cataloging-in-Publication Data
Ellsberg, Robert, 1955-
    All saints : Daily reflections on saints, prophets, and witnesses
for our time / Robert Ellsberg.
       p. cm.
    Includes bibliographical references and index.
    ISBN 0-8245-1599-4 (hc). – ISBN 0-8245-1679-6 (pb)
    1. Religious biography.   I. Title.
    BL72.E44 1997
    242'.37–dc21   97-6263

To
Nicholas, Catherine, and Christina

*"There is no way of telling people
that they are all walking around
shining like the sun."*

— THOMAS MERTON

Contents

February

March

April

June

July

August

September

October

November

December

ALL SAINTS

Introduction

Therefore, since we are surrounded by so great a cloud of witnesses, let us also lay aside every weight, and sin which clings so closely, and let us run with perseverance the race that is set before us, looking to Jesus, the pioneer and perfecter of our faith. —Hebrews 12:1

I have spent a good deal of time on Sunday mornings contemplating the stained-glass windows of my parish church. As in many another Catholic church, these windows present a gallery of popular saints. They are a reminder that those who gather to worship God in the name of Jesus are never alone. There is a wider "communion of saints" that unites believers across all boundaries of time and space, even across such a boundary as divides this world from the next.

This communion with those who have "died in the Lord" was a vivid reality to the early Christians. They liked to gather at the graves of the martyrs to remember their heroic witness and to commemorate the anniversaries of their deaths. It was this devotion that gave rise to the cult of the saints.

There was a time when martyrdom was virtually the defining characteristic of sainthood. The men and women who died in the Roman arena had offered a total witness to Christ, not only imitating his death on the cross but proclaiming by this sacrifice their faith in the resurrection. Their blood, as Tertullian said, was the seed of the church. But as the era of martyrdom passed, so it became clear that there were other ways of bearing witness. There were those whose prayer and self-sacrifice were so intense as to constitute a kind of living martyrdom. Such holy men and women did more than set an edifying example. They assumed an aura of transcendence and sacred power. This power even extended beyond their deaths — hence, the miracles associated with their relics and with the invocation of their names. Increasingly this miraculous power itself became a certifying mark of sanctity. But as this became so, the saints served less as ideals of Christian discipleship and more as miracle workers or heavenly patrons. The saints, it seemed, were more to be venerated than imitated.

In the windows in my parish church I see many of the greatest of the canonized saints: Teresa of Avila, Jerome, Augustine, Catherine of Siena, Clare and Francis of Assisi....I wonder if they are widely noticed, or whether these windows are not simply part of the "religious" architecture, easily taken for granted. For many Christians, the saints are little more than legendary figures — "perfect Christians" — who bear little relevance to their own daily struggles and concerns. It does not help that so many of these saints seem to be clothed in religious garb. What do such "special" people have to do with the challenges of ordinary life in "the world"?

In the minds of many people today the legends of the saints reflect an all too stereotypical pattern: They spent their lives in prayer and performing good works. Some of them were martyrs. Others founded religious orders. Others had visions or performed miracles.... All this may be true, but it tends to elide a good many issues. While there are recognizable patterns in the lives of the saints, each one was in his or her own way an "original." They achieved their holiness with the material at hand — material, in many cases, of apparently dubious quality. Many of them struggled hard to invent a new style of Christian witness in response to the needs of their time — not infrequently needs obvious to themselves alone. Even among the canonized saints, it is striking how many of them paid dearly for the originality of their vision. Along with the many certified martyrs there are countless others who suffered persecution or humiliation — not from ostensible "enemies of the faith" but at the hands of their fellow Christians. All this is easily forgotten.

The great Christian apologist Pascal, writing in the seventeenth century, observed how easily veneration of the saints can pass over into a pious trivialization of their challenge. We tend to regard the saints as "crowned with glory and years, judged almost divine before our time." That is how it seems to us, with the passage of time.

> But at the time when he was being persecuted, this great saint was just a man called Athanasius; and St. Teresa just a woman. Elias was a man, subject to like passion as we are, as St. Peter says, to rid Christians of the false idea which makes us reject the example of the saints as bearing no relation to our state. "They were saints," we say. "It is not the same for us."

This is one reason, apart from humility, that holy people are loath to be called saints. As Dorothy Day, founder of the Catholic Worker movement, used to say, "Don't call me a saint. I don't want to be dismissed that easily." By putting saints on a pedestal, we imply that their example poses no personal challenge. But when this happens, the Christian imagination is immeasurably weakened. Describing the function of the saints, Karl Rahner wrote, "They are the initiators and the creative models of the holiness which happens to be right for, and is the task of, their particular age. They create a new style; they prove that a certain form of life and activity is a really genuine possibility; they show experimentally that one can be a Christian even in 'this' way; they make such a type of person believable as a Christian type." The saints are those who, in some partial way, embody — literally incarnate — the challenge of faith in their time and place. In doing so, they open a path that others might follow.

But before we can follow we must know their stories. In this book I have compiled a list of men and women whose lives and message, I believe, speak to the spiritual needs of our day. They are both ancient and contemporary figures, men and women, including those who have been officially canonized or beatified by the church as well as many who have not. In part my goal is to encourage the rediscovery of many familiar figures from Christian history, to show their creativity, courage, and imagination in the face of historical challenges; to highlight aspects of their lives or message that speak to contemporary concerns; and above all to show that their sanctity was not simply a garment they wore but a quality that was expressed through struggle and conflict as they lived their lives. But I have another purpose, as well. By exploring a range of lives far beyond the official canon of saints, I hope to expand the popular understanding of holiness itself.

The church makes no pretense that its list or "canon" exhausts the number of actual saints. There are countless men and women whose holiness is recognized by God alone. Along with the "official saints" they are commemorated by the church on November 1, the feast of All Saints — which has supplied the title for this work. The process of "making saints" has itself undergone considerable evolution in the past two thousand years. In the early centuries, canonization was largely a matter of popular acclamation; it was the people of a local church who proclaimed that a saint had been in their midst. Over time this was replaced by an intensely organized and bureaucratic process centralized in the Vatican. Today, before any persons can be declared "blessed" (beatified) or officially canonized as saints, their lives and writings must be examined for evidence of heroic virtue and doctrinal orthodoxy; finally, they must be credited with the performance of miracles. While this elaborate process underlines the solemnity of the church's declarations, it tends to influence the selection of candidates for canonization. If the canon of saints — especially in modern times — is overly populated by members of religious orders, this reflects in large part the fact that such congregations have had the time and resources to invest in the lengthy process of canonization. The official process has been notoriously weak on promoting examples of lay holiness. It has tended to recognize conventional forms of piety and to avoid the prophetic figures, those who brought discomfort to the religious authorities of their time. Finally, the weight attached to miracles tends to reinforce that sense of "otherness" in the saints that only undermines the power of their example: "They were saints; it is not the same for us."

Nevertheless, most people, I am convinced, possess an instinctive ability to recognize heroic sanctity when they see it. Quite apart from any official process, they recognize that there are certain people whose lives, in some extraordinary fashion, proclaim the mystery of the gospel. Of those included in this book, some are persons who might well be candidates for official canonization: Archbishop Oscar Romero, Thomas Merton, and Dorothy Day are a few examples from recent times. But my list includes others, such as the martyred theologian Dietrich Bonhoeffer, or Albert Schweitzer, or the Methodist John Wesley, who as non-Catholics would never be eligible for formal canonization. It is not hard to argue that such lives present a more vivid inspiration for contemporary Christians than the memory of many long-ago saints.

Then there are non-Christians like Gandhi, or the Jewish prophet Abraham Heschel, or even nonreligious moralists like Albert Camus, whose impact on Christian spirituality and ethics has, arguably, equaled that of any orthodox Christian of our time. By including them in an expanded roster of "saints" my intent is not to dragoon them unwillingly into the Christian fold but to point in the direction of the God who (according to St. John) is "larger than our hearts." As Heschel wrote, "Holiness is not the monopoly of any particular religion or tradition. Wherever a deed is done in accord with the will of God, wherever a human thought is directed toward Him, there is the holy."

The more troubling question, for some readers, will be the inclusion of men and women who do not represent any common standard of holiness. Insofar as this poses a problem, it may arise from our tendency to equate holiness with moral perfection. Such an equation, it is worth noting, was unfamiliar to the authors of Scripture. Most of the biblical heroes — including Abraham, Jacob, Moses, and David — are in many ways deeply flawed. The same must be said for Christ's closest disciples. And yet Christ himself proclaimed that there were those who were blessed simply because they gave a drink of water to a thirsty stranger or visited a prisoner in jail. Surely among the communion of "all saints" there are those whose apparent weaknesses served to disguise the spiritual greatness within, but whose witness, nevertheless, was redeemed by one great deed, by one special gift, or simply the earnestness of their intention. These lives, too, bear some message about the challenge of faithfulness in our time.

And so the procession of figures in this book is a somewhat mixed and motley crew. Doubtless St. Augustine or St. Dominic would be alarmed to find themselves linked with the likes of Vincent van Gogh or Leo Tolstoy. (The obverse is just as likely.) In such a work the selection itself inevitably makes a certain statement. How to choose? Here I have been guided by an insight of Simone Weil: "Today it is not nearly enough merely to be a saint; but we must have the saintliness demanded by the present moment. . . . " I believe that many traditional saints, precisely insofar as they responded to the demands of their own moment, remain a precious resource. But what are the needs of the present moment?

Previous models of sanctity tended to emphasize a world-denying asceticism; today we need examples of discipline and self-denial in service to the world and in solidarity with a suffering humanity. There are countless saints who exhibited the virtue of charity; we need saints who combine charity with a prophetic thirst for justice. Much of Christian history has been written with male hands; we need to recall the example and the gifts of holy and prophetic women. The traditional list of saints has been dominated by the clergy and those in religious life; we need to give special attention to the witness of lay people — those whose vocation is to infuse the "world" with the spirit of the gospel. Church history tends to be written in Western terms; in this era of what Karl Rahner called the "world church" we need to remember the struggle of saints who translated the gospel into the idiom of local, non-Western cultures, who engaged the wisdom of other religious paths, and who tried to understand their faith in terms of new intellectual and cultural horizons. We need examples of holiness beyond the cloister: saints immersed in the worlds of art, literature, scholarship, in political struggle, and in everyday life. We need prophets who challenge the church as well as the world to better reflect the justice and mercy of God. We need the witness of the martyrs, ancient and new, who have laid down their lives for their faith and for their neighbors. We must attend the vision of the mystics, who see through the shade of everydayness and so remind us of the God who is ever-greater than our theologies or our imaginations.

Are there saints who speak to all these concerns? Perhaps a few. But the challenge is to draw on the partial witness of many holy companions for our journey, a journey that begins where each of us stands.

We are formed by what we admire. But it is possible to cultivate one's taste in this regard as in any other pursuit. It is important to learn how to recognize what is good, to train our ears to discern the truth, to pay honor to what is truly honorable, to choose a moral standard that lies beyond our easy grasp. It is especially important to convey such lessons to our children, who are otherwise too easily beguiled by our culture to admire what is merely glib or successful, to honor power, superficial beauty, and the illusion of celebrity.

How are we to learn these things? Did anyone ever become better from reading a handbook on ethics? Yet most of us, at one time or another, have felt our hearts respond to an example of courage, goodness, or spiritual nobility that inspired us to a higher path. It was thus for the saints themselves. One of the recurring motifs in their stories is the importance of an encounter with another saint — sometimes in person, but often through reading a story or hearing a legend. I can truthfully say of my own life that I have learned far less about the gospel from studying theology than I have from the lives of holy people. In part this reflects the narrative structure of the Christian gospel. The truths of Christianity are verified in living witness rather than in logical syllogisms. But the saints do more than offer an edifying example. There is indeed an aura of transcendence and sacred power that surrounds their lives. This has little to do with the display of miracles, in the traditional sense. It has more to do with a quality of mystery that is only reinforced by their human idiosyncrasies. Like the figures in the stained-glass windows, they are illuminated by a source beyond themselves. Thus, they help to awaken us to the realization, if we allow it, that our own lives are illuminated by the same source. As Cardinal Suhard observed, to be a saint means "to live in such a way that one's life would not make sense if God did not exist."

It is easier to explain the logic for combining traditional and unconventional "saints" in this work than it is to explain what all these lives have in common. Readers may discern their own patterns. But I have been struck by the uncompromising character of their commitment, by their willingness to sacrifice everything for the sake of their vocation. Sometimes what now makes them seem heroic or admirable made them, in the eyes of their contemporaries, rather difficult to tolerate. This too must be recognized. Holiness is not the same as "niceness" or even "goodness" in the usual sense.

On the other hand, how human they are. Despite the supernatural effects that may adorn their legends, what comes through again and again is their humanity. They experienced doubt, weakness, loneliness, and fear — just like the rest of us. But ultimately their lives were organized around higher principles — the human capacity for love, for sacrifice, and generosity. "Purity of heart," said Kierkegaard, "is to will one thing." This singleness of intention is one of the characteristics that unites so many of these figures. This does not mean they were free of the ambiguity that makes it difficult to reduce any life to a single meaning or message. But under the gaze of contemplation, there is something that rises to the surface. It is that, and not their faults, weaknesses, or limitations, that is their essential message and legacy.

What did they have in common? They did not apply themselves to being "saints." If anything, they applied themselves seriously to the task of being human, understanding this vocation in the profound sense reflected in the old formulas of the catechism: "*Who made you?* God made me. *Why did God make you?* God made me to know, love, and serve him in this world and to be happy with him in the next."

No, the saints are not perfect humans. But in their own individual fashion they became *authentic* human beings, endowed with the capacity to awaken that vocation in others. Dorothy Day, as I have noted, did not like to be called a saint: "When they call you a saint, basically it means you are not to be taken seriously." This book offers a different argument: that to call someone a saint means that his or her life should be taken with the utmost seriousness. It is a proof that the gospel can be lived.

•

A few final matters:

The assignment of dates in this work is not arbitrary. In the case of beatified or canonized saints I have used an official feast day. Unless otherwise noted, this is the current feast day. In some cases, however, I have used an alternative date of ancient origin. In the case of noncanonized persons, I have used either the date of their death or birth. When these dates were uncertain, as in the case of biblical figures, I felt free to choose any open space. As I completed this work, I found it necessary in a few cases to depart from my rules, usually by moving a name to within a day or two of the "appropriate" date. A close reading of the text should make it evident where this is so.

In writing these reflections I have relied, in most cases, on several primary or secondary sources. Rather than provide an exhaustive bibliography I have listed one or two principal works which may provide a useful starting point for anyone wishing to learn more. An unacknowledged but consistently useful starting point for anyone interested in the saints is *Butler's Lives of the Saints*. As a further assistance to readers, I have noted with an asterisk (*) where references appear to persons otherwise featured in the book.

In a work concerned with contemporary spirituality I believe the prevalence of sexist language deserves a note of apology. The feminist challenge is surely one of the great signs of the Spirit in our age. But most of the figures in this book did not live to experience this challenge. In the interest of honesty I have not altered their noninclusive language.

I am not able to acknowledge properly the many friends who have encouraged me in this project. I am truly grateful for the consistent support of publisher Mike Leach and editor John Eagleson at Crossroad. But I would also like to thank my understanding colleagues at Orbis Books and a number of friends with whom I have discussed the text: in particular, Michael Downey, John Garvey, Rachelle Linner, Judy Anderson, Jim Forest, Joan Chittister, Dan Berrigan, John Dear, Andreas Meier, and the Woodcrest Bruderhof. I had originally intended to commission another author for this book, but I could think of no one sufficiently foolhardy or presumptuous. Special thanks are due to my colleague Patti Gatzke, who posed the irresistible challenge: "Why not do it yourself?"

Throughout this project I have been conscious of my debt to all my teachers, particularly John Padberg, S.J., John O'Malley, S.J., and Stephen Marini, of the Weston School of Theology; the late George MacRae, S.J., Harvey Cox, Margaret Miles, Clarissa Atkinson, and Francis Schüssler Fiorenza, of the Harvard Divinity School; and finally Robert Coles, who long ago encouraged my passionate interest in the lives of "those who are truly great." Their lessons have been elucidated by my own cloud of witnesses, particularly Mev Puleo, John Leary, Henri Nouwen, Penny Lernoux, Fritz Eichenberg, and Dorothy Day.

If there is a particular point of view that I have brought to this project it reflects the diverse influence of my parents. From my mother and her practice of Christian faith I was introduced to the gospel and the communion of saints. From my father I was introduced to the example of Gandhi and the tradition of nonviolent struggle. Their combined, if diverse, influence directed me, more than twenty years ago, to the Catholic Worker movement. Thus, I am indebted to them both not only for my life but also my vocation.

To Peggy, my wife and companion in life, I owe more thanks than words allow. She has ever reminded me of the truth of St. Catherine's words, that "all the way to heaven is heaven."

Finally, I pass this book on as a legacy to my three children, Nicholas, Catherine, and Christina. May they learn to draw light from these holy lives and so become a source of light for others. To them, with love, this work is dedicated.

•

See: Butler's Lives of the Saints, Herbert Thurston, S.J. and Donald Attwater, eds., 4 vols. (London: Burns & Oates, 1956; Westminster, Md.: Christian Classics, 1980); David Hugh Farmer, *The Oxford Dictionary of Saints* (Oxford: Oxford University Press, 1978); Donald Attwater, *A Dictionary of Saints* (New York: Penguin, 1965); Kenneth L. Woodward, *Making Saints* (New York: Simon & Schuster, 1990); Lawrence S. Cunningham, *The Meaning of Saints* (New York: Harper & Row, 1980); Peter Brown, *The Cult of the Saints* (London: SCM, 1981); Karl Rahner, "The Church of the Saints," *Theological Investigations,* vol. 3 (New York: Crossroad, 1982); Elizabeth A. Johnson, "Saints and Mary," in Francis Schüssler Fiorenza and John P. Galvin, eds., *Systematic Theology,* vol. 2 (Minneapolis: Fortress, 1991); Joan Chittister, *A Passion for Life: Fragments of the Face of God* (Maryknoll, N.Y.: Orbis, 1996).

❦ JANUARY ❦

January 1

Mary, Mother of Jesus
(first century)

"Behold the handmaid of the Lord."

Mary, a young Galilean woman of Nazareth, was betrothed to a carpenter named *Joseph. One day, according to the Gospel of *Luke, she was visited by the angel Gabriel, who greeted her with the words, "Hail, O favored one, the Lord is with you!" After calming her fears he announced that she would conceive and bear a son named Jesus, who would be called "the Son of the Most High."

Mary was troubled by this news, for she was as yet unmarried. If she were charged with adultery she could be stoned to death. But the angel told her that she would conceive by the power of the Holy Spirit. "With God nothing will be impossible," he assured her. And so Mary responded in faith: "Let it be done to me according to your word."

It was in the space created by Mary's faith — and not simply in her womb — that the Word became flesh. For this reason she has been called not only the Mother of Jesus but Mother of the Church. In the past it was common to emphasize the ways in which Mary was set apart from and above all other women and the ordinary conditions of humanity. Today there is a new emphasis on her status as a woman of the people and her solidarity with the rest of humanity. A "Mariology from above" emphasized God's initiative in selecting Mary for her part in the divine mystery of redemption. In contrast, a "Mariology from below" begins with the poor woman, Mary of Nazareth, who was rooted in the faith and struggles of her people, subject to the cruelties of the world, and heir to the ancient hope for deliverance and salvation. In this light, Mary is not so much honored for her special nature as for her exceptional faith.

Two stories in the Gospels highlight this point. One time Jesus was told that his "mother and brothers" were looking for him. Gazing at those who were seated around him he answered, "Who are my mother and my brothers? These are my mother and my brothers. Whoever does the will of God is brother and sister and mother to me" (Mark 3:33–35). Another time someone called out from a crowd, "Blessed is the womb that bore you and the breasts that nursed you!" To this Jesus responded, "Rather, blessed are they who hear the word of God and keep it" (Luke 11:27–28).

Neither of these stories reflects a disregard on the part of Jesus toward his mother. But they do show that he rejected the claims of blood or natural kinship in favor of discipleship. In this perspective Mary's preeminence is due to her having exemplified the spirit of true discipleship: attention, reverence, and obedience to the word and will of God.

The Gospel of *John places Mary at the foot of the cross beside "the beloved disciple." According to Luke, she was among the disciples who gathered in the upper room in Jerusalem after Jesus' ascension. She was in effect the first and paradigmatic disciple. She is thus the first to be honored among the saints. In the darkness of faith, she offered her consent to the mysterious plan of God. In the light of grace she responded with her extraordinary song of praise and thanksgiving:

> My soul magnifies the Lord,
> and my spirit rejoices in God my Savior,
> for he has regarded the lowliness of his handmaiden.
> For behold, henceforth all generations will call me blessed;
> for he who is mighty has done great things for me,
> and holy is his name....

See: Elizabeth A. Johnson, "Saints and Mary," in Francis Schüssler Fiorenza and John P. Galvin, eds., *Systematic Theology: Roman Catholic Perspectives,* vol. 2 (Minneapolis: Fortress, 1991).

January 2

St. Seraphim of Sarov
Russian Monk (1759–1833)

"Prayer, fasting, watching may be good in themselves; yet it is not in these practices alone that the goal of our Christian life is found, though they are necessary means for its attainment. The true goal consists in our acquiring the Holy Spirit of God."

St. Seraphim entered the Russian monastery of Sarov when he was twenty. After making his vows and being ordained a priest, he received permission to retire to a hermitage in the forest. There he maintained a life of solitary prayer, tending a small garden, chopping wood, and otherwise observing an austerity reminiscent of the desert fathers. He exposed himself to the cold, deprived himself of food and sleep, and spent long periods perched on a rocky outcrop. For several years he had no contact whatsoever with the monastic community and declined to utter a word. As a reminder of his death to the world, he built a coffin which he kept beside him in his cell.

For fifteen years Seraphim maintained this solitary existence. In the meantime, however, his reputation had spread far and wide. One day he was visited by a rich landowner who was seriously ill and had persuaded his family to carry him to the cell of the holy hermit. When Seraphim had completed his prayers, he emerged and asked his visitors, "What, you have come to look upon poor Seraphim?" After the sick man had explained his condition, Seraphim agreed to pray over him. Instantly the man was healed. In his joy he asked Seraphim for a way to express his gratitude. Deflecting all the credit to God, Seraphim instructed the rich man to give away everything he possessed, free his serfs, and take on holy poverty. With all this the man complied.

Word of this "double miracle" enhanced the celebrity of Seraphim, and from that time on he was forced to entertain a continuous stream of pilgrims, penitents, the sick and poor, and lay people seeking spiritual counsel. Seraphim received them all, freely dispensing his wisdom, counsel, and healing powers. So he became the great model of the Russian *starets*, the holy monk who serves as a spiritual elder or advisor to inquiring lay people. Like his contemporary in France *John Vianney, he was reputed to have the gift of reading souls. He addressed everyone in the same fashion: "My joys," he called them.

The recorded teachings of Father Seraphim are not especially remarkable; they are mostly quotations from Scripture and a few treasured church fathers. Evidently Father Seraphim's impact came from the simple power of his personality, for so long weathered by arduous self-denial. His purified humanity was apparently charged with a supernatural charity. Such is the impression given by one of his visitors, Nicolai Motivilov, whose account of his interview with the holy Seraphim gives the flavor of the monk's intense and charismatic energy.

After advising Nicolai for some time about the simplicity of the spiritual life and finding little comprehension, Seraphim reportedly took his visitor by the shoulders and said, "Look at me."

Nicolai demurred: "I am not able, Father, for there is lightning flashing from your eyes. Your face has grown more radiant than the sun, and my eyes cannot bear the pain." Father Seraphim replied, "Do not be afraid, my good Theophilus, you have also now become as radiant as I. You yourself are now in the fullness of the divine spirit; otherwise you would not be able to perceive me in the exact same state."

On January 2, 1833, St. Seraphim was found dead in his cell, kneeling with hands crossed before an icon of Our Lady of Tenderness. He was canonized by the Russian Orthodox church in 1903.

See: "St. Seraphim: Mystic and Prophet," in G. P. Fedotov, ed., *A Treasury of Russian Spirituality* (London: Sheed & Ward, 1950).

Takashi Nagai
Mystic of Nagasaki (1908–1951)

"Our lives are of great worth if we accept with good grace the situation Providence places us in, and go on living lovingly."

On the morning of August 9, 1945, Dr. Takashi Nagai was working in his office at the medical center in Nagasaki, Japan. At 11 A.M. he saw a flash of blinding light, followed by darkness, and then heard a crashing roar as his concrete building, and his world, collapsed around him. What at first he took to be a direct hit on the medical center was in fact the explosion of a plutonium-fueled atomic bomb five hundred yards over the Urakami Cathedral. After escaping from the rubble and receiving treatment for a severed carotid artery, Nagai joined the rest of the hospital staff in treating the dazed and dying survivors. Given the force and heat of the blast, he imagined that such a big bomb must have killed hundreds of people. Only gradually did the extent of the destruction become clear. The bomb had killed nearly eighty thousand persons, and wounded many more.

In the days ahead Nagai witnessed scenes of horrifying suffering. The intense heat near the epicenter of the blast had vaporized humans, leaving only the outlines of their shadows. Hordes of blackened survivors, the skin hanging from their arms, desperately wandered the streets crying for water. Nagai's own two children had survived. But he found the charred remains of his beloved wife in the ruins of their home, a rosary clasped "among the powdered bones of her right hand."

Such circumstances might naturally prompt a range of reactions — madness, despair, or the hunger for revenge. But in the days following the explosion Nagai, a devout Catholic, instead expressed a most unexpected attitude — namely, gratitude to God that his Catholic city had been chosen to atone for the sins of humanity.

In arriving at this perspective, Nagai undoubtedly tapped into a spirituality deeply rooted in the consciousness of Nagasaki's Christian population. Since the time of the early Jesuit missions the city had been the center of Japanese Catholicism, and consequently the scene of extensive martyrdom. Over time, Japanese Catholics had claimed a deep identification with the cross of Christ and a conviction that atonement must come only at the price of blood. Thus, it seemed natural for Nagai to pose the question: "Was not Nagasaki the chosen victim, the lamb without blemish, slain as a whole burnt offering on an altar of sacrifice, atoning for the sins of all the nations during World War II?"

Nagai was himself a convert. Born on January 3, 1908, he became a Catholic in 1934. His conversion was prompted by several influences, including the example of his fiancée, who belonged to an ancient Catholic family, his reading of the mystic-scientist *Blaise Pascal, and also a period of deep soul-searching after the death of his mother. Nagai pursued a career in medicine, ultimately entering the field of radiology. In 1941 he was found to be suffering from incurable leukemia, induced by his exposure to x-rays. Nevertheless he was able to continue his work, and in 1945 he had become the dean of radiology at the University of Nagasaki.

In the aftermath of the bombing on August 9 Nagai applied himself tirelessly to the medical needs of the survivors. "Each life was precious. For all of these people the body was a precious treasure." But in the face of the enormity of the disaster, he gradually began to see "that if I did not take a comprehensive view of this situation, we would all be engulfed in the flames with the very victims we were bandaging and trying to save." As he carried on his work he struggled to arrive at some understanding of the meaning of this event, a meaning, ultimately, that he could discern only in relation to the cross.

Nagai found it remarkable that as a result of heavy clouds obscuring the originally intended city, the bomb had been dropped that day on Nagasaki, an alternate target. As a further result of clouds, the pilot had not fixed his target on the Mitsubishi iron works, as intended, but instead on the Catholic Cathedral in the Urakami district of the city, home to the majority of Nagasaki's Catholics. He noted that the end of the war came on August 15, feast of the Assumption of Mary, to whom the cathedral was dedicated. All this was deeply meaningful. "We must ask if this convergence of events — the ending of the war and the celebration of her feast — was merely coincidental or if there was here some mysterious providence of God."

Nagai expressed these sentiments at an open-air requiem Mass just days after the bombing. While his views were controversial, he provided consolation to many of the city's Catholic survivors, desperate to find some redemptive meaning in their terrible suffering:

> We have disobeyed the law of love. Joyfully we have hated one another; joyfully we have killed one another. And now at last we have brought this great and evil war to an end. But in order to restore peace to the world it was not sufficient to repent. We had to obtain God's pardon through the offering of a great sacrifice.... Let us give thanks that Nagasaki was chosen for the sacrifice.... May the souls of the faithful departed, through the mercy of God, rest in peace.

The effects of radiation, combined with his previous illness, left Nagai an invalid, barely able to leave his bed. He lived as a contemplative in a small hut near the cathedral ruins in Urakami, writing books and receiving visitors. Increasingly he came to believe that Nagasaki had been chosen not only to atone for the sins of the war, but to bear witness to the cause of international peace.

> Men and women of the world, never again plan war!... From this atomic waste the people of Nagasaki confront the world and cry out: No more war! Let us follow the commandment of love and work together. The people of Nagasaki prostrate themselves before God and pray: Grant that Nagasaki may be the last atomic wilderness in the history of the world.

Dr. Nagai died on May 1, 1951, at the age of forty-three. His tombstone bears a simple epitaph from the Gospel of *Luke: "We are merely servants: we have done no more than our duty."

See: Takashi Nagai, *The Bells of Nagasaki*, trans. William Johnston (Tokyo: Kodansha International, 1984); Rachelle Linner, *City of Silence* (Maryknoll, N.Y.: Orbis, 1995).

January 4

Bd. Angela of Foligno
Franciscan Mystic (1248–1309)

" 'Lord,' I cried, 'tell me what thou dost want of me; I am all thine.'
But there was no answer, and I prayed from Matins till Terce —
and then I saw and heard."

One of the great legacies of *St. Francis was the foundation of his Third Order, a movement of lay followers of the Franciscan rule who chose to remain in the world rather than adopt an enclosed religious life. Its members were attracted from all walks of life — even queens like *Elizabeth of Hungary and *Elizabeth of Portugal. With their spirit of poverty and their zeal for the apostolic life these Franciscan tertiaries had an enormous influence on the religious and social life of the Middle Ages. Angela of Foligno, mystic and theologian, was one of the remarkable members of this spiritual family.

Angela came from a wealthy background. Her early life was given over to worldly frivolity and pleasure-seeking. She married a rich man and had three sons. But it was an existence without higher purpose. By the time she was thirty-seven she found her life such a burden that she prayed to St. Francis for some relief. The next day she went to church and heard an unfamiliar preacher, a Franciscan friar named Brother Arnold, whose sermon made a tremendous impression. She felt impelled to make her confession to him, after which she decided to transform her life.

Before long, the opportunity for a radical change came about through tragic circumstances — the loss of her entire family during an outbreak of plague. Through her loss Angela discerned the hand of God leading her to a life of penance and prayer. While standing before a crucifix she was moved, in a gesture reminiscent of Francis, to strip off all her fine clothing and to offer her life to Christ's service. During a subsequent pilgrimage to Assisi she was overwhelmed by an experience of the love of God. She gave away all her property, joined the Third Order of St. Francis, and resolved to live on alms.

Brother Arnold, who remained her confessor, was initially suspicious of her dramatic conversion and of the extravagant mystical experiences that followed. At some point, however, he became convinced of the divine origin of her wisdom and revelations, and their roles were reversed. Ultimately he became her devoted scribe and disciple. In the verbatim accounts of her discourse, Angela recounts the progress of her spiritual journey, submitting her motivations to careful scrutiny, and describing the constant temptations that assail her on her path. But she also describes in vivid detail a series of experiences in which she witnesses the power, the humility, the justice, and the love of God. Most of all she describes her own sense of having experienced a deep communion with God in the private "cell" of her soul, an experience of such intimacy that it exists beyond the realm of joy and suffering.

And yet Angela's communion with God did not absent her from concern for others. "The world," she said, "is great with God." In time she gathered around herself a family of Franciscan tertiaries, both men and women, for whom she served as spiritual mother. In the spirit of Francis, she maintained a standard of strict poverty. This was a form of identification with Christ, but it was also a constant reminder to remain sensitive to the needs of others.

One Holy Thursday she exhorted her companions, "Let us go and look for Christ our Lord. We will go to the hospital and perhaps among the sick and suffering we shall find Him." She had them beg for food, which they brought to the hospital: "And so we offered food to these poor sick people and then we washed the feet of the women and the men's hands, as they lay lonely and forsaken on their wretched pallets...." Thus, she concluded, they had successfully fulfilled their quest to find Christ on that Holy Thursday.

Angela eventually died peacefully, surrounded by her spiritual children, on January 4, 1309.

See: Paul Lachance, ed., *Angela of Foligno: Complete Works,* Classics of Western Spirituality (New York: Paulist, 1993).

January 5

Lanza del Vasto
Founder of the Community of the Ark (1901–1981)

"Power can be used for any purpose,
but nonviolence or the power of justice can serve only justice."

Lanza del Vasto presented an uncommon sight to the modern eye. With his clothes of handspun wool and his tall staff, his beard and mane of white hair, he looked every bit the part he played — prophet and patriarch, a modern-day *Noah. Indeed, he called his band of followers the Community of the Ark. They joined together to preserve certain values from the deluge of violence and ugliness and efficiency that threatened to make the planet uninhabitable.

He was born into a noble family in Italy in 1901. For many years he studied philosophy, anxiously seeking the meaning of life. But in 1936, having found no satisfaction in his formal studies, he traveled to India. He sensed that there, closer to the source of humanity's spiritual journey, he might discover a wisdom that the West had forgotten. And so it was.

He prayed and fasted with Hindu holy men, traveled to the Himalayan source of the Ganges, and visited innumerable monasteries. But it was finally his meeting with *Mohandas Gandhi, apostle of nonviolence and leader of the Indian independence movement, that changed the course of his life. He lived in Gandhi's ashram long enough to absorb the basic features of his thought, and then returned to Europe determined to make these ideas known in the West.

Gandhi had given him a new name: Shantidas, "Servant of Peace." He was aptly named. For the next forty years, through words and deeds and a way of life, he devoted himself to reconciliation among religions and resistance to violence in all its personal and institutional forms. In 1948 he and his wife, Chanterelle, formed the Community of the Ark in France, a community of families united by a rule, vows, and common prayer, devoted to the aim of applying nonviolence in every corner of life. For the companions of the Ark, nonviolence was a way of acting that derived from a way of being. It meant refusing to exploit others, even as one refused to submit to exploitation. And so they struggled to make themselves as self-sufficient as possible, living on the land, raising their own food, making their own clothes — all without the assistance of electricity or modern machines.

It was not the intention of Shantidas to retreat from the world and its problems. He simply felt that one could not hope to resolve the problems of the world as long as one was part of them. From the base of their community he and his companions launched one campaign after another in defense of peace, the rights of conscience, and the relief of human suffering. He fasted for twenty days in protest of torture during the Algerian war; he protested against concentration camps; he led a successful struggle for recognition of the right of conscientious objection. For these and similar causes he was repeatedly arrested.

Although his community was open to persons of all religious faiths, Shantidas remained rooted in his Catholic tradition, and many of his most personal initiatives focused on efforts to remind the Catholic church of the gospel message of peace. In 1963 he fasted in Rome for forty days in an appeal to the pope to issue a statement on the arms race and the threat to peace. In return he was rewarded with an advance copy of *Pope John XXIII's encyclical *Pacem in Terris*. Two years later he and Chanterelle organized another fast in Rome, this time in prayer that the Vatican Council in progress would speak strongly to the issue of war and the need for spiritual resistance. Sixteen women — among them *Dorothy Day of the Catholic Worker — fasted for ten days. Again, their prayers were answered in the form of the council's vehement condemnation of nuclear weapons. If few were called to imitate Lanza del Vasto's rigorous consistency, there were many touched by the simple truth of his message that "the future must be a future of nonviolence, or else there will be no future."

Again and again, until his death on January 5, 1981, Shantidas emphasized the positive aspect of nonviolence. He was not simply a grim prophet of doom, but a man of "peace, strength, and joy" — the words that became the motto of his community. Rather than simply rail against the evils of the present age, he invited others to join in his efforts to prepare a new age and he offered a means of getting there: he built an Ark.

See: Lanza del Vasto, *Return to the Source* (New York: Schocken, 1972); *Warriors of Peace* (New York: Alfred A. Knopf, 1974).

January 6
Jacques Ellul
Theologian (1912–1994)

*"Having accepted the God of Jesus Christ,
I affirm that he is our only recourse in the face of Technique."*

The French theologian and social critic Jacques Ellul was one of the great Christian prophets of the twentieth century. In scores of books he critiqued the "secular spirituality" reflected in modern technical society and issued a dire forecast for Western civilization. At the same time, he maintained a deep hope in the promises of God, a hope that even embraced the possibility of universal salvation. This tension between denunciation and annunciation, so characteristic of the prophetic vocation, rendered Ellul somewhat aloof from all movements and organizations, whether political or religious. He was, truly, a "voice crying in the wilderness."

Ellul was born on January 6, 1912, in Bordeaux. He was raised in a poor home in which religion was seldom mentioned. He studied law, eventually earning a doctorate. His eventual fame, however, came about through his work in two very different fields, sociology and theology. This conjunction of interests reflected the impact of two great encounters which occurred in close succession — the discoveries of Karl Marx and Jesus Christ. The integration of Marxism and Christianity was, at the time, far from common. Ellul explained that from the Bible he acquired an understanding of the ultimate meaning of history, while Marx provided a theory about the dynamics of social existence.

Later, the discovery of *Karl Barth and his "dialectical" view of the relation between God and humanity left a deep impression on Ellul's social and theological views. In particular, the emphasis in the early Barth on God as the "Wholly Other" influenced Ellul's critique of the idolatrous claims of modern civilization. Like Barth, Ellul was a member of the Reformed church. Though he was ultimately critical of key elements of Calvinist theology, much of his work could be interpreted as a social commentary on Calvin's great themes: the sovereignty of God, the fallenness of humanity, and the need for salvation by faith alone.

In a series of sociological works, including *The Technological Society* and *The Political Illusion,* Ellul offered an apparently pessimistic assessment of modern civilization. According to Ellul, the governing spirit of this civilization, whether under capitalism or communism, was what he called "Technique" — the principle of technical organization or efficiency. In modern society this principle acquired a sacred value, to which all other values were ultimately sacrificed. Ellul's work in this area eventually enjoyed a certain countercultural vogue among readers unfamiliar with his theological works.

Those more widely familiar with Ellul's thought could recognize that what he criticized was not technology per se, but the "powers and principalities" that hold sway over the world. "I do not believe we should reject technology," he wrote; what is necessary is that "we destroy the deified religious character of technology." With regard to the charge of pessimism Ellul answered, "I am not pessimistic, because I am convinced that the history of the human race, no matter how tragic, will ultimately lead to the kingdom of God. I am convinced that all the works of humankind will be reintegrated in the work of God, and that each one of us, no matter how sinful, will ultimately be saved."

Thus, Christian hope, for Ellul, was easily reconciled with an apparent pessimism regarding human schemes and projects in history. For ultimately this hope was grounded in the promises of God. The task of the Christian living out of this hope, he believed, was "to create a new style of life" at odds with the world's expectations. In part this involved preserving a consciousness of the Transcendent. At the same time, the Christian should desacralize the idols of modern society — whether politics, the state, or the marketplace — and create alternative zones of "free life." In other words, Christians should be "troublemakers, creators of uncertainty, agents of a dimension incompatible with society."

Ellul died on May 19, 1994, at the age of eighty-two.

See: Jacques Ellul, *Perspectives on Our Age* (New York: Seabury, 1981); Jacques Ellul, *In Season and Out of Season* (New York: Harper & Row, 1982).

January 7

Felipe and Mary Barreda
Lay Apostles and Martyrs (d. 1983)

"We discovered that faith is not expecting that the Lord will miraculously give us whatever we ask, or feeling the security that we will not be killed and that everything will turn out as we want. We learned that faith is putting ourselves in His hands, whatever happens, good or bad. He will help us somehow."

In December 1982, while taking part in a coffee harvest in northern Nicaragua, Felipe and Mary Barreda were kidnapped by so-called contra rebels. The Barredas were forced to march to a camp in Honduras, all the while subjected to beatings and torture. Mary was repeatedly raped. On January 7, 1983, the couple were executed.

Under normal circumstances, picking coffee would not entail the risk of death, nor would it be construed as a heroic expression of Christian faith. But the risk and the meaning of this work were clearly understood by the Barredas. And to the five thousand people who crowded the cathedral of Estelí for their memorial Mass the connections were equally obvious. The Barredas were acclaimed as Christian martyrs who had not simply died but who had laid down their lives in faithfulness to the gospel and out of their commitment to God and their neighbors.

In their appearance there was nothing to distinguish this middle-aged couple, married for thirty years, from other Latin American families of modestly comfortable means. Felipe was a watchmaker, Mary was a hairdresser, and together they had raised six children and had fifteen grandchildren. But through a long process beginning in the 1970s with their involvement in the renewal movement of Cursillo, and later as leaders in the base community movement in their hometown, Estelí, their lives had come to center around their Christian faith, a faith expressed in service to the poor.

For Christians like the Barredas, living in Nicaragua under the notorious dictatorship of Anastasio Somoza, such an understanding of the gospel had inescapably political implications. The base communities, which brought families together to reflect on their lives and to read the signs of the times in the light of Scripture, provided strong support to the growing Sandinista revolutionary struggle. When victory came in 1979, the Barredas threw themselves into the work of reconstruction and support for Sandinista programs in literacy and health reform.

This revolution was unprecedented in the degree of Christian participation. Those who supported the Sandinistas believed that their program was an expression of the Christian option for the poor. But not all agreed, and in fact the church came to be bitterly divided. By the early 1980s political opposition to the Sandinistas was joined by the military campaign of the "contras," a rebel army sponsored by the United States and formed initially from members of the ousted National Guard. Operating out of bases in Honduras, the contras waged a war of terror, targeting teachers, health workers, and other community leaders identified with the Sandinista cause. Because the government depended heavily on exchange earnings from the sale of coffee, Nicaragua's principal export crop, the contras focused particular terror against coffee harvesters. Scores were killed or wounded in these attacks.

It was in this context, just before Christmas in 1982, that the Barredas volunteered to join the harvest. On December 28 the farm where they were working was surrounded by contras. The Barredas and another fifty-six harvesters were kidnapped, and the coffee harvest was destroyed.

It was many months before their fate was definitely known. Eventually their actual murderers were captured, and they provided testimony regarding the circumstances of the Barredas' captivity and death. Their interrogators had tried in vain to force the Barredas to declare themselves communists. To the end, however, they had responded with prayers and protestations of their Christian faith.

Nevertheless, the social implications of that faith were clearly suggested in a letter that Mary had written to friends, in which she noted:

> The opportunity to go and pick coffee will be converted into health, clothing, homes and roads and food. For this, I am going to pick

coffee with all the love and enthusiasm of which I am capable. Please understand that in every grain that I cut, every bean that I pick, every one of your faces will be present, the faces of your children, and even the faces of those that I don't know.... We wish to ask you to be present with God this Christmastime with a smile, with greater care for one another and for your children. Wherever I may be, I'll be thinking of you in these moments. I love you all very much.

See: Margaret Swedish and Lee Miller, *Like Grains of Wheat* (Washington, D.C.: Religious Task Force on Central America, 1989); James Brockman, S.J., "The Passion and Death of Maria and Felipe," *America* (December 7, 1985).

January 8

Galileo Galilei
Scientist (1564–1642)

"The surest and swiftest way to prove that the Copernican position is not opposed to Scripture would be to show with a multitude of proofs that it is true and the contrary can in no way be maintained. Thus, since no two truths can contradict one another, this and the Bible would be seen to be, of necessity, perfectly harmonious."

The scientist Galileo, who was born in Pisa in 1564, achieved his original fame through his invention of the thermometer, his experiments in physics and mechanics, and his refinement of the telescope. The telescope inspired a passion for astronomy that would lead, eventually, to his condemnation by the church. The issue was Galileo's determination to prove the theory of the Polish scientist Nicholas Copernicus (d. 1543) that the earth revolved around the sun.

Those who challenged the geocentric view of the universe had to contend not only with the ancient authority of Aristotle and Ptolemy but with the evidence of the senses: the sun, after all, clearly appeared to rise and set. More importantly, however, there was the apparent evidence of many scriptural passages that referred to the motion of the sun. For the church this was the most decisive issue. The works of Copernicus and his theories — except insofar as they were presented merely as "hypotheses" — were formally condemned by the Holy Office.

Still, Galileo labored to prove that Copernicus was right. A number of scientists and even interested theologians were sympathetic to his efforts. Many of them, like Galileo, disputed the notion that the authority of Scripture should be extended to scientific matters. In the famous words of Cardinal Baronius, "The Holy Ghost intended to teach us how to go to heaven, not how the heavens go." Nevertheless, Galileo was formally instructed to desist from his work on Copernican astronomy. When he violated this injunction he was summoned to Rome by the Holy Office.

The trial of Galileo occurred in 1633. In light of his advanced age (seventy) and his poor health, he was treated with reasonable courtesy.

Rather than the customary prison cell he was housed in a comfortable room. Nevertheless, he needed little reminder of the perils of his situation. The pope had issued a document threatening him with torture if he did not cheerfully submit to the findings of the court. In the end Galileo was condemned as "vehemently suspected of heresy" for maintaining the doctrine "which is false and contrary to the Sacred and Divine Scriptures, that the sun is the center of the world and does not move from east to west and that the earth moves and is not the center of the world."

Galileo, who throughout his ordeal had maintained his devout faith and firm commitment to the authority of the church, at this point fell on his knees and formally abjured any heretical opinions he may have held. Convinced of his sincere repentance, the court spared him the sentence of imprisonment. Instead he was confined to house arrest in Florence for the rest of his life. There he continued his scientific work. But by 1638 Galileo, the man who had first seen mountains on the moon, was completely blind. On January 8, 1642, he died.

For many centuries Galileo's ordeal remained a blot on the Christian conscience. Only in the 1990s did Pope John Paul II authorize a papal commission to review his trial and condemnation. The result was a papal decree formally absolving Galileo of heresy and acknowledging the error of the church's previous judgment. The error was attributed, in part, to the church's deficient understanding, at that time, of the nature and authority of Scripture.

And so it has come to pass that the Galileo case, long a symbol of ecclesial obscurantism, has become a signal of the church's ability to recognize and repent of its historic failings. There remains a tendency to claim that the church, as it was once said of the earth, cannot move. To this the legendary words ascribed to Galileo remain appropriate. In making his abjuration, he is said to have whispered under his breath, "Nevertheless, it moves."

See: Jerome J. Langford, O.P., *Galileo, Science and the Church* (New York: Desclée, 1966).

January 9

St. Philip of Moscow
Bishop and Martyr (1507–1569)

"God rejects him who does not love his neighbor.
I have to tell you this though I die for it."

St. Philip spent most of his life as a monk and abbot in the Russian monastery of Solovetsk beside the White Sea. This happy phase of his career ended in 1565 when he was elected to serve as bishop of Moscow and primate of the Russian church. It was the era of Tsar Ivan the Terrible, so named for his notorious cruelty. Philip accurately anticipated that to preach the gospel under the rule of such a tyrant would be to court martyrdom.

The test was not long in coming. After Ivan executed one of his periodic massacres of those suspected of disloyalty, Philip lodged a solemn protest. This only had the effect of fueling Ivan's temper. Soon after, when the tsar attended a eucharistic liturgy at the cathedral in Moscow, Philip denounced him to his face: "At this altar we are offering a pure and bloodless sacrifice for men's salvation. Outside this holy temple the blood of innocent Christians is being shed. God rejects him who does not love his neighbor. I have to tell you this though I die for it."

Ivan responded by having Philip first deposed from office and then placed under arrest. On December 23, 1569, while in the custody of the tsar, Philip was murdered. He was canonized by the Russian Orthodox church in 1636. His feast is celebrated on this day.

See: Donald Attwater, *A Dictionary of Saints* (New York: Penguin, 1965).

January 10

Evagrius Ponticus
Desert Father (345–399)

*"If you are a theologian, you truly pray.
If you truly pray, you are a theologian."*

Evagrius was born in 345 in a small town in Pontus (a region in present-day Turkey). He was a friend and disciple of the three great "Cappadocian fathers," *Basil the Great, Gregory Nazianzen, and *Gregory of Nyssa. Gregory of Nyssa ordained him as a deacon, and so he went on to achieve some prominence in the church of Constantinople. Through his learned preaching and writing he was recognized as an effective scourge of the Arian heresy.

Despite his office Evagrius lived a comfortable life. This changed, however, when he found himself in love with the wife of a prominent official. Extremely unsettled by his conflicting desires, he fell into a profound spiritual crisis. This was resolved by a dream in which he was confronted by vague accusations and responded with a vow to leave Constantinople and "watch after his soul." Upon waking he felt himself bound by the oath, though uttered in a dream. And so the next day he boarded a ship for the Holy Land. Eventually Evagrius made his way to the Egyptian desert, where he took up the ascetic life of the early monks. There he spent the rest of his life.

Among the desert fathers, Evagrius was unusual for his learning and his literary gifts. In the course of his life he produced many books, including works of speculative theology, heavily influenced by the work of *Origen, as well as practical manuals on prayer and the ascetic life. After his death the former were subject to harsh criticism and eventual condemnation at the Second Council of Constantinople (553). Evagrius followed

Origen in writing about the preexistence of souls and the eventual return of all creatures to union with God. Fairly or not, it was deemed that in these areas Origen and his disciples had gone too far in adapting the gospel to neo-Platonism. This condemnation, however, resulted in the destruction of most of Evagrius's extant writings, and his name tended to be written out of the history of spirituality. Nevertheless, through his disciple *John Cassian as well as a number of Syriac translations, his works on monasticism and prayer were preserved. Thus, anonymously, he played an enormous role in the foundation of monastic spirituality and Christian mysticism.

Evagrius's most famous work, the *Praktikos,* is a series of a hundred maxims and short counsels on the aims and ordeals of the monastic life. Much of the work is devoted to a diagnosis of the various "demons" who lie in wait to attack the monk through his passions. It shows that Evagrius possessed a keen sensitivity for human psychology:

> When the demons achieve nothing in their struggles against a monk, they withdraw a bit and observe to see which of the virtues he neglects in the meantime. Then all of a sudden they attack him from this point and ravage the poor fellow.

Among the familiar demons treated by Evagrius are lust, gluttony, anger, sloth, and pride (which induces the monk to "get a big head in regard to the brethren, considering them stupid because they do not all have this same [high] opinion of him"). But there are other demons more specific to the monastic life. Of these the one who causes the monk "the most serious trouble of all" is the demon of *acedia* — "also called the noonday demon."

> He presses his attack upon the monk about the fourth hour and besieges the soul until the eighth hour. First of all he makes it seem that the sun barely moves, if at all, and that the day is fifty hours long. Then he constrains the monk to look constantly out the windows, to walk outside the cell, to gaze carefully at the sun to determine how far it stands from the ninth hour, to look now this way and now that to see if perhaps one of the brethren appears from his cell.... He depicts life stretching out for a long period of time, and brings before the mind's eye the toil of the ascetic struggle and, as the saying has it, leaves no leaf unturned to induce the monk to forsake his cell and drop out of the fight.

Evagrius provided many practical hints on the best way to practice the ascetic life. But he never suggested that the main business of the monk was self-denial. All this was merely a means of focusing on his true business, prayer — the path to union with God. Through prayer the monk burnished the "mirror of his soul," the better to reflect the image of God. Evagrius's particular contribution here was in promoting the value of *contemplative prayer,* a state of pure openness to God without words or mental images.

In time Evagrius attracted many disciples, drawn by his wisdom and reputation for holiness. He was in their midst on the feast of the Epiphany in 399 when he became seriously ill. He asked to receive holy communion and died shortly thereafter. It was a death for which he had long prepared. In one of his maxims he wrote, "By true prayer a monk becomes another angel, for he ardently longs to see the face of the Father in heaven."

See: Evagrius Ponticus, *The Praktikos and Chapters on Prayer* (Kalamazoo, Mich.: Cistercian Publications, 1978).

January 11
Brother Lawrence
Carmelite Lay Brother (1611–1691)

"The time of business does not with me differ from the time of prayer; and in the noise and clatter of my kitchen, while several persons are at the same time calling for different things, I possess God in as great tranquility as if I were upon my knees at the Blessed Sacrament."

It is doubtful that anyone seeking a spiritual director in the Carmelite monastery in Paris would have applied to Brother Lawrence. In a community replete with learned souls, all devoted to the love of God, Brother Lawrence, a lay brother assigned to kitchen work, was not apt to attract attention. And yet when a certain M. de Beaufort, a visiting official on the staff of the cardinal of Paris, happened to initiate conversation with Brother Lawrence, he was astonished by the depth of his spiritual wisdom. In successive conversations, and later through a prolonged correspondence, Brother Lawrence did indeed assume the role of spiritual counselor, humbly sharing the fruit of his life of prayer.

An account of these conversations was later published under the title *The Practice of the Presence of God* — a phrase that neatly summarized the substance of Brother Lawrence's spirituality. His method was to cultivate at all times a consciousness of the presence of God. According to Brother Lawrence, wherever we might find ourselves, whatever the task at hand, we should perform our duties with a consciousness of God's loving presence. With such an awareness all our activities were hallowed; we would thus find ourselves in a state of continuous prayer or conversation with God.

In this light there was no special distinction between traditional spiritual disciplines — reciting the Office or kneeling in church — and the daily tasks with which Brother Lawrence was primarily occupied, scrubbing pots and chopping vegetables. It was well to go to church. But it was also well to construct an oratory in one's heart, in which to return and dwell. "Our sanctification," he believed, "did not depend upon *changing* our works, but in doing for God's sake that which we commonly do for our own."

Little was known of Brother Lawrence's early life, beyond what he shared with his amanuensis. He was born Nicholas Herman in French Lorraine in 1611. He came from a humble background and had little or no formal education. He served briefly in the army and saw action in the

Hundred Years War. The most significant spiritual event in his early life occurred outdoors on a cold midwinter day in the presence of a gaunt and leafless tree. The thought that in a little time the bare branches of this tree would again be covered with leaves filled him with "a high view of the providence and power of God." Eventually he found his way to the Carmelites in Paris, where he was admitted as a lay brother and became Brother Lawrence.

He spent the next forty years in the monastery kitchen, and there he died at the age of eighty. He accomplished no great deeds and left no writings beyond a handful of letters. Were it not for the impression he made on de Beaufort, his life would be a total obscurity, one of the anonymous saints of everyday life who, for all we know, are secretly at work redeeming the world. Brother Lawrence made no distinction between great works and small. As he liked to observe, God "regards not the greatness of the work, but the love with which it is performed."

See: Brother Lawrence, *The Practice of the Presence of God* (Old Tappan, N.J.: Fleming H. Revell, 1958).

January 12

Mev Puleo
Witness of Solidarity (1963–1996)

"When I was in my early teens, a thought took hold of me: Jesus didn't die to save us from suffering — he died to teach us how to suffer.... Sometimes I actually mean it. I'd rather die young, having lived a life crammed with meaning, than to die old, even in security, but without meaning."

So wrote Mev Puleo as a college student at St. Louis University. Years later, her words were remembered by a former professor and close friend, Father John Kavanaugh, who presided over her funeral in 1996. He added the comment, "Such are the dangers of our high and holy desires." Her friends understood the obvious: She had indeed died young after having lived a life "crammed with meaning." Under the tutelage of Jesus and the poor she had even learned to suffer. And she had left many others, only remotely touched by her loving spirit, an enduring challenge to recognize and treasure the preciousness of life.

From a young age Mev felt a strong sense of "religious wonder" in the presence of nature and other people. From her parents, devout Catholics, she also learned that the practice of Christian faith should involve service to others. But a turning point in Mev's life came at the age of fourteen when she accompanied her parents on a trip to Brazil. She was riding on a bus up a steep hill to view the famous statue of Christ the Redeemer that overlooks the city of Rio de Janeiro. On one side of the hill she could see the opulent homes, posh hotels, and immaculate beaches enjoyed by the rich. The view on the other side told a different story, of "ramshackle homes, children in rags, young and old begging for our coins."

Certain questions were inevitable: "What does it mean to be a Christian — a follower of the way of Jesus — in a world of contradictions and conflicts? What does it mean to be on the way to Jesus when I view the world of poverty from an air-conditioned tour bus?" Such questions make an impact on the conscience of a sensitive young person. But in Mev's case they laid the foundation for her later vocation. Over time she felt the call to create a bridge between the different worlds she had viewed from that bus.

While a college student she worked at the St. Louis Catholic Worker house. She went on to earn graduate degrees in theology. But her studies only confirmed her belief in the need for a new language of faith, a language addressed not only to the head but to the heart. As she said, "I believe less in theology and more in God, because I believe that in theology there's only so much you can say about God."

Early in her life Mev had discovered a great talent for photography. In trips to Brazil, El Salvador, Haiti, and elsewhere in the Third World, her photographs documented the life, struggles, and humanity of the poor. Her aim was "to revere the human spirit and bridge the distance between persons." She gave much thought to the spiritual aspects of her art. "The camera lens," she wrote, "is the eye of my soul, through which I touch the world and the world touches me." But she also acknowledged the ethical ambiguities of photography. Often, she admitted to having asked herself, " 'Dare I invade their lives, steal this moment?' Yet how can I *not* share these children with the world, bringing them back with me to hearts who might receive them, voices who might speak for them?"

Mev was not simply touched by the suffering of the poor. She also identified with their struggle for justice and liberation. In her travels throughout the Third World she was exposed to a new model of the church arising from the faith of the poor. She conducted scores of interviews with grassroots activists, prophetic bishops, and liberation theologians. She was fully committed to their vision of a church and a world renewed in the light of God's reign. Some of this work was reflected in her book on the church in Brazil, *The Struggle Is One,* but she also carried the message through photo exhibits, lectures, and a video completed in the last months of her life. Her photographs were published widely in the religious press, and they won her several awards.

No summary of these achievements adequately reflects Mev's extraordinary personality — her enthusiasm for life, her capacity for joy. Her photography expressed a profound ability to connect with other people. She had a contemplative eye, a knack for penetrating to the spiritual essence of things and especially people, in whom she saw reflections of the face of God. In 1992 she married Mark Chmiel, a fellow theology student. It was a marriage filled with love and promise.

But in 1994 Mev was found to have a malignant brain tumor. The initial prognosis, after surgery, was that she had six months to live. She was determined to remain fully alive for each day that remained, and her final months were filled with many accomplishments. She published her book, completed her video, and gave numerous lectures. In 1995 she received the U.S. Catholic Award for furthering the cause of women in the Catholic church.

But ultimately she left her friends a deeper gift in the example of her own faith, courage, and hope as she completed her earthly journey. As Father Kavanaugh noted, "She had wanted to give the poor a face, a voice. She always wanted to be identified with them. And so it came to pass: by the time of her last days, you could see them all in her face — the poor of Bosnia, the hungry of Haiti, the powerless of Brazil. She who gave them voice, lost hers. She who helped us see their faces, could finally see no more.... She became the poor she loved."

Mev Puleo died on January 12, 1996, at the age of thirty-two.

See: Mev Puleo, *The Struggle Is One: Voices and Visions of Liberation* (Albany, N.Y.: SUNY Press, 1994); John F. Kavanaugh, with photographs by Mev Puleo, *Faces of Poverty, Faces of Christ* (Maryknoll, N.Y.: Orbis, 1991).

January 13
George Fox
Quaker (1624–1691)

"For the saints, which were to honor all men, they were in that of God, which did reach to that of God in all men."

There are saints and religious geniuses whose gifts, while widely admired, are essentially inimitable. These are the artists of the spiritual life. Then there are the trailblazers — those who are able, through the resolution of their own spiritual dilemmas, to open a path that others might follow. George Fox, founder of the Quakers, was one of the latter company.

Fox was the son of a weaver, born in Leicestershire, England, in 1624. As a lad he received little formal education and was apprenticed to a leather worker. He was, nevertheless, an inquisitive youth, prone to deep questions about the meaning of life. It was the time of the Puritan revival in England, and this doubtless affected the shape of his religious concerns. But his interviews with countless priests and preachers yielded none who "spoke to his condition," and so he passed much time in lonely dejection.

When he had all but given up hope, he heard an inner voice which said, "There is one, even Christ Jesus that can speak to thy condition." When he heard this his heart "at once did leap for joy." For at that moment he "knew experimentally" that he had no need of special guides or mediators. The "Seed of God" was present in his own soul. His mission in life was to attend to that seed, to heed the "inner voice," and to awaken others to a similar consciousness.

Fox was soon impelled to share his vision with other "Friends." Speaking to passersby on open hillsides or standing in church to address challenging "queries" to the presiding minister, Fox managed to convey his message to a wide audience. But the price of this was often scorn and persecution. He was frequently set upon by his angry fellow Christians to be beaten, put in the stocks, or cast into jail. His message was taken as a sweeping rebuke to the institutional Christianity of his time — as so it was. At the same time, his faith compelled him to adopt social attitudes at odds with his more "worldly" contemporaries.

Fox paid no respect to social hierarchy. He prescribed plain clothes and would not tip his hat to passersby. He spoke plainly and addressed all men and women, "without any respect to rich or poor," in the intimate form of "thee" and "thou." He would not swear any oath, believing in the gospel text that an honest "yea" or "nay" should suffice. This in itself was enough to land him in prison for refusing to take the mandatory Oath of Allegiance, a repudiation of papal authority. Fox opposed war and violence as contrary to the Gospels. He was, furthermore, constantly "moved by the Lord" to seek out the rich and powerful to warn them "to take heed of oppressing the poor." Such attitudes and activities fairly invited persecution.

Fox was arrested a total of eight times, spending all told six years in various prisons. His worst experience was in Cornwall, where he spent several months in 1656 in a dreadful place called Doomsdale, a dungeon without windows or toilet facilities, in which prisoners were required to live in the mire of their own excrement. His longest confinement was over two and a half years (1664–1666) at Lancaster. It was one of his magistrates who first coined the term "Quaker," after Fox enjoined him to "tremble before the Lord." The name "Quaker" was intended as an insult, but it was gradually adopted as a mark of honor by Fox and his followers.

And of followers there were many. Within the first decade of his ministry Fox attracted tens of thousands to join what he called the Society of Friends. Many of them also shared his experience of persecution. By 1686 there were fourteen hundred Quakers in jail. And yet the Quakers did not retreat to the self-righteousness or otherworldliness of a persecuted sect. Under all circumstances they maintained a spirit of "friendliness," an eagerness for dialogue, an openness to the promptings of the spirit and a respect for "that of God" in each person which eventually won them toleration and even widespread respect.

Fox traveled throughout England, though his major efforts were in the North. He also traveled to America, where he spent almost two years. Quakers would later travel there in great numbers, with one of Fox's disciples, William Penn, winning a charter to establish the Quaker commonwealth of Pennsylvania.

Fox's life ended after a period of prolonged illness. But neither age nor infirmity dimmed his zeal. On his deathbed he said, "All is well. The Seed of God reigns over all, and over death itself. And though I am weak in body, yet the power of God is over all, and the Seed reigns over disorderly spirits." He died on January 13, 1691, at the age of sixty-seven. Shortly before the end he was heard to exclaim, "Now I am clear, I am fully clear."

See: Douglas Steere, ed., *Quaker Spirituality: Selected Writings,* Classics of Western Spirituality (New York: Paulist, 1984).

Martin Niemoeller
Confessing Pastor (1892–1984)

"When the Nazis came to get the Communists, I was silent, because I was not a Communist. When they came to get the Socialists, I was silent. When they came to get the Catholics, I was silent. When they came to get the Jews, I was silent. And when they came to get me, there was no one left to speak."

In the 1920s Martin Niemoeller wrote a successful autobiography entitled *From U-boat to Pulpit.* In light of the constant testing of his Christian conscience it was necessary in successive editions to revise that title so that it might finally read "From U-boat to Pulpit to Prison to Pacifism."

Niemoeller had served as a highly decorated German U-boat commander during World War I. The casualty rate for U-boat crews was so high that all who survived were revered as exceptional heroes. Like many German officers Niemoeller regarded the war's loss with a deep sense of betrayal, exacerbated by the humiliating terms of the Versailles treaty. Though after the war he decided to pursue his father's career as a Lutheran pastor, he maintained the hope that Germany would one day realize its intended greatness. In such a frame of mind he was an early supporter of National Socialism, believing in Hitler's promise to vindicate German honor.

Nevertheless, within months of Hitler's rise to power in 1933, Niemoeller had begun to feel uneasy with the hateful extremism of the Nazis. He was further disedified by the emergence of the so-called German Christian movement, which virtually identified the gospel with the Nazi ideology. Many distinguished church leaders and theologians felt no such qualms, and Niemoeller began to attract controversy. At first his principal concern was to maintain the independence and freedom of the churches from political manipulation. Like most German Christians he espoused a traditional brand of Christian anti-Semitism, believing the Jewish people were to be condemned for their rejection of Christ. Though he failed to recognize the terrible danger of such a position, he was at the same time strongly opposed to the Nazi condemnation of the Jews on the basis of "race."

The conflict became clear when anti-Jewish legislation was applied even to baptized Christian pastors of "non-Aryan" extraction. Niemoeller believed that to acquiesce in such measures would spell the death of the church. In response he helped organize a petition that collected the signatures of twenty-three hundred pastors pledging their opposition to the Aryan laws. The Pastor's Emergency Committee that Niemoeller founded later fed into the so-called Confessing Church, in which *Karl Barth and *Dietrich Bonhoeffer were also prominent. This movement was founded in 1934 to protest the capitulation of the churches to National Socialism. Its proponents named their historical situation to be a moment of "confession" which called into question the very identity of the true church. Ultimately, the question for Christians was "Which God do we worship:

Christ or Hitler?" Within a few years the Confessing Church would be suppressed, its members having either capitulated or ended up in prison, in exile, or dead.

Niemoeller was arrested on July 1, 1937. In the relative political space which still existed in those days church bells throughout the country rang in protest. He was charged among other things with having "caused unrest among the people" by urging "rebellion against the laws and ordinances of the state." Though he was convicted, the judges could not bring themselves to sentence the war hero to prison. To this Hitler reacted with fury, dismissing the judges and insisting that Niemoeller be remanded to a concentration camp as his "personal prisoner." Thus he was sent to the Sachsenhausen concentration camp north of Berlin. After the outbreak of war he was transferred to Dachau, where he remained until his liberation by Allied troops in 1945.

Niemoeller survived the war with his basic sense of patriotism intact. But as he gradually learned the extent of the Nazi crimes, his attitude changed. Despite his own sufferings, he refused to evade responsibility. While his arrest in 1937 provided an "alibi" for the subsequent years, there was no such excuse, he claimed, for his failure to speak out as effectively as he might have in earlier years — especially on behalf of the Jews. In the sufferings of all who had been persecuted during those years God in Jesus Christ had been saying to him, "Are you prepared to save me?" Sadly, he admitted, "I turned that service down."

Thus Niemoeller parted company with the many Germans who refused to acknowledge any responsibility for the Nazi atrocities. He helped draft a confession of guilt for the churches which emphasized in particular the Christian role in fostering and tolerating a climate of anti-Semitism.

But this was not the end of Niemoeller's conversion. For years after the war he had maintained a sense of pride in his record of military service. But his attitude toward war began to change after the dropping of the atomic bomb. When he later learned of the immense destructive power of the hydrogen bomb, he went home, reread the Sermon on the Mount, and declared that he could no longer justify the use of force. As he described the key to his ethical principles, he said it was easy. In every situation he simply asked himself the question, "What would Jesus do?"

In the 1950s and in subsequent decades he became a prominent figure in the international pacifist movement, traveling the world to speak out against the perils of nuclear war and bearing witness to the cause of peace and human rights. He continued his activity until he was past the age of ninety. Born on January 14, 1892, he died peacefully on March 5, 1984.

See: James Bentley, *Martin Niemoeller* (New York: The Free Press, 1984); "Martin Niemoeller: A Confessional Courage," in Jim Wallis and Joyce Hollyday, eds., *Cloud of Witnesses* (Maryknoll, N.Y.: Orbis, 1991).

January 15

St. Paul the Hermit
(d. 342)

*"Woe to me a sinner, who falsely bear the name of monk!
I have seen Elias, I have seen John in the desert,
and, in truth, I have seen Paul in paradise!"*
— St. Antony

According to his biographer, *St. Jerome, St. Paul — known as "the Hermit" — deserves recognition as the first desert monk. If so, it is an interesting fact that he evidently stumbled upon his vocation by accident. Jerome relates that Paul was a rich young man of Thebes whose parents died when he was sixteen. Soon after, when a storm of persecution swept over the church in Egypt, Paul decided to ride out the troubles from the safe seclusion of a cave in the wilderness. But by the time it was safe to return Paul had come to love his solitary life, and so he decided to stay.

Nearly a hundred years passed, and many others had since discovered the singular attractions of the ascetic life. The greatest of them, *St. Antony, was by this time an old man of ninety when he heard that there was someone in the desert whose lifetime of solitude surpassed his own. Determined to meet this prodigy, he wandered far and wide until he was guided by the Holy Spirit to the cave of Paul. After Antony called out for some time, the ancient monk emerged from his abode. The two immediately recognized each other as kindred spirits and fell into a warm embrace.

Paul asked his visitor for news of the world: How was man faring? Were there new roofs in the ancient cities? Was there still persecution and heresy? While they caught up on such news, a raven arrived with a loaf of bread for their meal. Paul observed matter-of-factly that he had thus been sustained during his many years in the wilderness. Paul felt that he was coming to the end of his race, and he greeted the arrival of Antony as heaven-sent to arrange for his burial. But so that his new friend would not have to witness his passing, he asked Antony to return to his own monastery and fetch him back a cloak that was a gift of St. Athanasius. Antony believed it was only by revelation that Paul could know of this cloak. He promptly did as he was told.

Though he traveled as quickly as he could, Antony arrived only in time to see Paul "shining in snowy whiteness, ascend into heaven amidst a host of angels." Falling on the ground, Antony exclaimed, "Why do you dismiss me, Paul? Why do you go without a farewell? I have known you so late; why do you depart so quickly from me?" But his grief was to no avail. When Antony arrived at the cave he found Paul's lifeless body kneeling in prayer.

Antony fulfilled his debt to his departed friend and buried his body with deep reverence. Paul had left almost no possessions. But Antony kept for himself an old tunic, which afterward he liked to wear on special holy days.

See: St. Jerome, "Life of St. Paul the Hermit," in Roy J. Deferrari, ed., *Early Christian Biographies,* The Fathers of the Church 15 (New York: Fathers of the Church, 1952).

January 16
Roberto de Nobili
Jesuit Missionary and *Sannyasi* (1577–1656)

"Let others struggle for the good things in life; let others enjoy them. As for me, I have decided to spend my days unknown in some obscure corner to sacrifice my wretched life for the salvation of souls."

The Age of Discovery inaugurated a new era in Christian mission. As Spanish and Portuguese explorers and conquerors encircled the globe they were accompanied by Christian missionaries eager to implant the gospel in fields afar. There is no doubting the faith and courage that marked their heroic efforts. But most were oblivious of the extent to which their message was compromised by the association with colonial power and wealth. Even those who defended the native populations were generally blind to the tendency to confuse the gospel with the supposed superiority of European culture.

This ethnocentric tendency was markedly present in the church in southern India, established under Portuguese authority. Converts were forced to adopt Western customs which effectively alienated them from their own culture and their communities. One missionary who attempted to forge a different path was the Jesuit Roberto de Nobili. Like his confrère in China *Matteo Ricci, Nobili attempted to adapt his style of living and his method of evangelization to the local mentality and culture. Thus, he is one of the grand pioneers of what has more recently been termed "inculturation."

Nobili was an Italian Jesuit, born in Rome of a noble family. In 1605 he arrived in south India, living at first in the Portuguese colony of Goa, where he set himself to mastering the Tamil language. Soon, however, he seized the opportunity to travel inland to the city of Madurai, a center of Tamil culture effectively beyond the range of colonial penetration. In Goa Nobili had observed that the Portuguese missionaries were singularly ineffective in making inroads among the higher castes. In fact, as he became more sophisticated in his understanding of Tamil, he realized that the highly caste-conscious Hindus regarded the Christian missionaries and their converts with utter contempt. The Europeans, with their leather shoes, their alcohol, their primitive hygiene, and their diet of meat, appeared to the fastidious Indians to have set themselves outside of any caste. The Indians were further repelled by the missionaries' arrogant disdain for Indian religion and culture and by their demand that converts forsake their caste identity. To the missionaries the marks of the caste, especially the Brahmin thread, were signs of pagan superstition. But to the Indians these were indispensable signs of social identity.

Nobili undertook an intensive study of Hindu religion and culture. He was probably the first Westerner to master Sanskrit and to read the Hindu classics in their original language. He decided that if he were going to bring the gospel to Indians, he must give up his "barbarian" appearance and adopt the dress and customs appropriate to an Indian holy man, or *sannyasi*. With the permission of his superiors he put aside his black soutane and draped himself in a red-ocher robe, wore wooden sandals, and took up the bamboo stick and drinking gourd that were the obligatory accoutrements of the sannyasi. He moved out of his house and into a simple hut. He foreswore the eating of meat and adopted a simple diet of rice and vegetables.

Immediately he attracted the attention of Brahmin scholars. After submitting to their careful examination, he won their respect as a fellow sannyasi. Having established that he had no interest in imposing Western culture, he found the Hindus quite receptive to engaging in philosophical and religious debate. Nobili went far beyond the superficial adoption of Indian language and customs. He attempted to present the Christian gospel itself in terms of Indian thought and culture. This required a very subtle understanding of Hinduism, but also a critical detachment from the Greek philosophical terms with which Christian dogma was historically intertwined. For instance, it was relatively easy for Hindus to conceive of Jesus as an *avatar*, a manifestation of God in human form. But the full meaning of the Incarnation was much harder to comprehend. The way Nobili put it was that Christ was the divine guru come down on earth.

Nobili's methods drew criticism from the local church in Portuguese Goa. He was accused of dressing like a heathen and tolerating pagan idolatry because he permitted Brahmin converts to retain their caste thread. Furthermore, by concentrating his mission on Brahmins and permitting them to maintain their code of cleanliness — even to the point of disdaining worship in the company of untouchables — he was accused of promoting schism in the church. Nobili defended himself by documenting the many ways that the early church had "baptized" and incorporated into itself various pagan customs and rituals. On the charge of elitism, he argued that his was a special mission which did not preclude the evangelization of the poor. But, like Ricci in China, who dressed as a Mandarin scholar, Nobili believed the route to the conversion of India must pass by those with education and influence. The task of converting or reforming the culture itself was a project for the future. A local church conference was unpersuaded and ended with Nobili's condemnation. However, on appeal to Rome he was vindicated by Pope Gregory XV.

Nobili died on January 16, 1656.

See: Vincent Cronin, *A Pearl to India: The Life of Roberto de Nobili* (New York: E. P. Dutton, 1959).

St. Antony of Egypt
Abbot (251–356)

"Let us not look back upon the world and fancy we have given up great things. For the whole of earth is a very little thing compared with the whole of heaven."

St. Antony was an early and celebrated champion of the ascetic life as well as a pioneer of Christian monasticism. He was born in Egypt, the son of wealthy Christian parents. Their death, when he was about eighteen, left him responsible for a considerable estate as well as the care of his younger sister. Soon after, however, he happened to hear a reading in church of the gospel text in which Jesus instructs the rich young man, "Go sell what you possess and give to the poor, and you will have treasure in heaven." It seemed to Antony that this text was addressed personally to him. He immediately sold all his possessions and donated the proceeds to the poor, keeping only what he required for himself and his sister. Later, hearing the gospel verse, "Do not be anxious about tomorrow," he regretted even this minor concession to prudence. After settling his sister in a convent, he gave up all his holdings and dedicated himself entirely to God.

Monasteries were few in those days, though from various solitary holy men Antony found advice and inspiration. Eventually, he set out for the desert to pursue a life of prayerful austerity. Living in a series of small huts and caves, and even for periods sleeping in cemeteries, he divided his days between prayer, study, and work in a small garden. His ascetic disciplines, both self-imposed and those provided by the harsh environment, were extreme. Aside from hunger, thirst, and lack of sleep, there were the dangers of lions, crocodiles, snakes, and scorpions to contend with. But more famous still are the vivid accounts of the many psychological and spiritual ordeals with which Antony was confronted. Constantly he was assailed by demons who appeared to him in various guises — some hideous and others alluring.

In the story of Antony the spiritual life appears to be a matter of psychological warfare, if not hand-to-hand combat. The adversary is not "the world" per se, but the temptation to "worldliness," pleasure, complacency, sloth, and pride. The lesson of Antony is that anything which presents itself as a substitute for total concentration on God may be a disguise behind which the devil is lurking. Of course such an attitude runs the risk of inuring one to the possibility — just as likely — that all those circumstances and obligations that distract us from prayer and fasting may also be disguises behind which God is lurking.

Antony's example does not hold the same appeal as once it had. It is notable, however, that despite the rigors of his solitary campaign Antony's health remained vigorous and his mind unclouded. For ultimately, according to his biographer Athanasius, Antony prevailed over the foe. And after twenty years of solitude not only was he a picture of health ("not a single tooth was missing!"), but his face was illuminated by compassion and joy.

No longer requiring complete isolation, Antony eventually welcomed a community of monks who had been drawn by his magnetic example. He served as abbot of this early monastery and eventually established a network of similar communities. Antony also received a constant stream of pilgrims who came to seek his counsel, or simply to witness the example of a living saint. Throughout, "he maintained utter equilibrium." When he received a letter from Emperor Constantine himself, Antony was not impressed. As he told his monks, "Marvel, instead, that God wrote the law for mankind and has spoken to us through his own Son."

Antony lived to the age of 105. Soon after his death an account of his life was written by his friend St. Athanasius (d. 373), the bishop of Alexandria. This work widely publicized the example of St. Antony as an ideal Christian. As one of the earliest Christian biographies, it also became a prototype for all later hagiography. The purpose of such writing was not to call attention to the wonderful achievements of an individual but to bear witness to the wonderful, ongoing action of God in history. Thus, *St. Augustine (d. 430) describes in his *Confessions* the impact of his own discovery of the life of St. Antony (a mere thirty years after the saint's death). Rather than remark on the holiness of Antony, Augustine notes, "We were astonished to hear of the wonder You had worked so recently, almost in our own times, and witnessed by so many, in the true faith and in the Catholic Church." It was the witness of such stories (and such lives) to the ongoing presence of God in the world that encouraged his own conversion.

See: Athanasius, *The Life of Antony and The Letter to Marcellinus*, trans. Robert C. Gregg, Classics of Western Spirituality (New York: Paulist, 1980).

January 18

St. Prisca
Evangelist and Martyr (first century)

"Salute Prisca and Aquila, and the church which is in their house."
—St. Paul

St. Prisca was one of a number of women who played a prominent role in the early church — not simply as "helpers" to the male apostles, but as evangelists and church administrators in their own right.

Prisca (or Priscilla) and her husband, Aquila, were Jewish tentmakers living in Corinth. Although they were originally from Rome they had been expelled from the imperial capital, along with all Jews, by order of the emperor Claudius. *St. Paul met them soon after his arrival in Corinth, fresh from his preaching mission in Athens (Acts 18). Their common trade — Paul too was a tentmaker — provided the basis of their acquaintance. But soon, through Paul's influence, they also shared a common zeal for the gospel. The house of Prisca and Aquila became Paul's base of operations in Corinth. Before long they were also serving as evangelists, preaching the gospel to their fellow Jews.

When Paul left for Ephesus Prisca and Aquila joined him. There they established a church in their home that included gentile as well as Jewish Christians. It seems they later returned to Rome. They were probably encouraged by news of the installation of a new emperor, Nero, who had no prior record of anti-Christian animus. Once again their house became the meeting place of the local church. There Paul addressed them in his letter to the Romans: "Greet Prisca and Aquila, my co-workers in Christ Jesus, who risked their necks for my life, to whom not only I am grateful but also all the churches of the Gentiles; greet also the church at their house" (Rom. 16:3–5).

In the end their hope of finding tolerance in Nero's Rome was misplaced. According to tradition Prisca and Aquila perished in the general persecution that occurred around the year 64.

January 19

St. Marguerite Bourgeoys
Foundress of the Congregation of Notre Dame of Montreal (1620–1700)

"I want at all costs not only to love my neighbor,
but to keep him in love for me."

St. Marguerite was born in the French town of Troyes in 1620. When she was twenty she applied in turn to the local convent of the Carmelites and then the Poor Clares. Providentially, she was refused by both. Nevertheless, her sense of religious calling remained intact, fortified by a vision of the Holy Child which, she said, "forever turned my eyes from all the beauty of this world." To her local confessor she made private vows of poverty and chastity.

In 1652 Marguerite heard that the governor of the French colony at Montreal was seeking a schoolmistress. She immediately volunteered, recognizing an opportunity to help implant the gospel in the New World. A year later she was in Montreal — at the time no more than a primitive fort, enclosing a settlement of about two hundred persons. There were as yet few children to teach, and it would be several years before the first schoolhouse was constructed. But she occupied herself in the meantime with a range of charitable activities and worked hard to promote the religious life of the colony.

Marguerite endured poverty, cold, hunger, and the persistent perils of war in her early years on the frontier. But as Montreal steadily grew in size, so also the conception of her vocation expanded. Through several trips to France she recruited women to join her in starting a missionary congregation dedicated to education. She had a particular interest in providing schooling for the Indians.

Though her project was warmly supported by the civil authorities, she ran into obstacles from the bishop of Quebec. He thought her small band of postulants should affiliate with the Ursulines. Marguerite, however, was determined that her congregation remain uncloistered. Asked why, her answer was that the Virgin Mary did not live in the cloister: "True it is that the cloister is a protection, but could we find a more powerful guardian than the Mother to whom the Eternal Father confided the Sacred Humanity of his Divine Son?" Finally she prevailed. In 1676 the Congregation of Notre Dame was officially established. It was the first unenclosed foreign-missionary community for women in the church.

Marguerite Bourgeoys was the first superior of the congregation, a post she retained until the age of seventy-three. After much hardship and suffering she had seen her congregation thrive, and now she was content to retire from center stage. On December 31, 1699, she learned that the young novice mistress, Sister Agnes, was deathly ill. She responded by praying, "Dear Lord, why dost thou not take me, a useless member in the house, rather than this poor Sister who could still do so much for Thee?" Almost immediately Sister Agnes rallied, while Mother Marguerite began to fail. She died in 1700 on January 12 (now her feast day).

See: Elizabeth F. Butler, *The Life of Venerable Marguerite Bourgeoys* (New York: P. J. Kenedy & Sons, 1932).

January 20
Alessandro Valignano
Jesuit Missionary (1539–1606)

"As a result of our not adapting ourselves to their customs, two serious evils followed....First, we forfeited the respect and esteem of the Japanese, and second, we remained strangers, so to speak, to the Christians."

The early Jesuit mission to Japan and China represented a remarkably prophetic chapter in the history of the church. While elsewhere at the time, especially in the Americas, the spread of Christianity accompanied a policy of colonial conquest, in Japan and China the Jesuits insisted on a different approach. This involved distinguishing Christianity from any hint of colonial interest and even from European culture. Instead the Jesuits sought as far as possible to root the gospel in the culture and mentality of their hosts. The most famous representative of this strategy was *Matteo Ricci. But its essential architect was the Jesuit Visitor for Asia, Alessandro Valignano.

Valignano came from an aristocratic family in Italy. He entered the Jesuits in 1566 and was ordained in 1571. Only two years later he was entrusted with an extraordinary task. At the age of thirty-four, and with no previous mission experience, he was appointed Jesuit Visitor to the East, the highest authority over a territory stretching from Mozambique to Japan. Many ranking members of the Society questioned the judgment of the Jesuit general in making such a risky appointment. But evidently the general knew what he wanted and knew Valignano to be the right man for the job.

At the time a papal decree had granted the Portuguese and Spanish crowns authority for establishing and administering the church in their territories. The Far East was predominantly in the Portuguese sphere of influence. Valignano, however, was determined to disengage the Jesuit missions from Portuguese control. In part he accomplished this by taking with him a huge contingent of fifty-five Jesuits, almost all of them from Spain and Italy. He was particularly adamant about not accepting any recruits from the American missions who might have been infected with the spirit of conquest.

Valignano believed that the conquest model of evangelization would be absolutely fruitless in penetrating the ancient civilizations of Japan and China. He entirely rejected the idea of Christendom — the assumption that there was an essential identity between Christianity and European society. Rather than insisting that Asian Christians should adopt European culture, he believed it was essential that the church assimilate itself to Japanese and Chinese culture.

Within some years of his arrival in the Far East Valignano compiled a series of books outlining in careful detail the various measures that the Jesuits should take to practice and master the forms and rituals of Japanese etiquette. He insisted on adopting the Japanese diet and standards of cleanliness, mastering the language, and showing deference to all customs. But beyond such superficial forms of adaptation, he believed that the gospel should itself be rooted in the culture of the people. A native clergy must be trained and every effort made to establish a genuinely Japanese church, rather than a European church superficially implanted on Japanese soil.

Valignano spent a good deal of time in Japan, but most of his Asian career was spent in the Portuguese enclaves of Macao, Goa, and southern India. He never realized his dream to penetrate the interior of China. This mission was left to his most famous protégé, Matteo Ricci. It was while planning to visit Ricci in China that Valignano died in Macao on January 20, 1606.

Valignano had believed that a hundred Jesuits, trained in his methods, could convert the whole of Japan. But the experiment he initiated ultimately ran aground — in Japan, because of official persecution, and in China, because of Roman opposition to the principles of cultural adaptation. While today the practice of inculturation or indigenization has wide official support, this was not so in the seventeenth century. Valignano and Ricci were accused of promoting "syncretism." The Jesuit strategy of cultural "accommodation" was officially suppressed by the Vatican in the early eighteenth century. It was centuries before Valignano's insights were properly appreciated by the church.

See: Andrew Ross, *A Vision Betrayed: The Jesuits in Japan and China, 1542–1742* (Maryknoll, N.Y.: Orbis, 1994).

January 21
St. Agnes
Virgin and Martyr (d. 304?)

"You may stain your sword with my blood,
but you will never be able to profane my body, consecrated to Christ."

It is said that Agnes was born to a rich and noble family of Rome and that at a young age her beauty attracted the interest of many prosperous suitors. She rebuffed them all, insisting that she had consecrated her virginity to her true spouse, Jesus Christ. Her suitors denounced her as a Christian, and she was brought before a magistrate. He in turn tried various forms of persuasion, ranging from mild entreaty to the display of instruments of torture. But nothing would compel her to offer incense to the gods. When she remained adamant, the governor had her condemned to a house of prostitution, where every man might have free use of her. It was found, however, that she exuded such a powerful aura of purity that no one could lay a finger on her. Infuriated by this young woman's defiance, the judge then ordered her to be beheaded. Agnes greeted the sentence joyfully and, according to *St. Ambrose, "went to the place of her execution more cheerfully than others go to their wedding." At the time of her death she was thirteen years old.

The fact that the first recorded account of St. Agnes appeared over a hundred years after her death has prompted doubts about the historicity of her "acts," if not the actual existence of this servant of God. Nevertheless she has been one of the most popular of Christian saints. In the past her memory undoubtedly served a tendency to idealize the virgin state. This was reinforced by the appellation "virgin," attached by the church to Agnes and other unmarried women saints. There is no corresponding word to recognize married women saints (except widow), nor is there any corresponding interest in the marital — or sexual — status of male saints. (We know, for instance, that *St. Augustine was no virgin.)

In the story of Agnes, however, the opposition is not between sex and virginity. The conflict is between a young woman's power in Christ to define her own identity versus a patriarchal culture's claim to identify her in terms of her sexuality. According to the view shared by her "suitors" and the state, if she would not be one man's wife, she might as well be every man's whore. Failing these options, she might as well be dead. Agnes did not *choose* death. She *chose* not to worship the gods of her culture. The God she worshiped sets an altogether different value on her body, her identity, and her human worth. Espoused to God, she was beyond the power of any man to "have his way with her." "Virgin" in this case is another way of saying Free Woman.

January 22

Alexander Men
Orthodox Priest and Martyr (1935–1990)

"I have always wanted to be a Christian living not by candlelight,
but in the direct light of the sun."

In the last years of the Soviet Union, visitors were often struck by the evidence of widescale spiritual revival. After so many decades of enforced atheist propaganda, it was remarkable to find young people crowding the ancient churches and clamoring for religious instruction. This was on the one hand a reflection of just how deeply rooted was the Orthodox faith in the hearts of the Russian people. But on the other hand it reflected the serious spiritual void which many people had come to experience, a sign of the moral, as well as practical, failure of the communist experiment.

One of the most dynamic figures in the modern revival of Christianity in Russia was the Orthodox priest Alexander Men. A scholar, pastor, and courageous witness, Men was one of a number of priests who preached the gospel without compromise. Through his writings, preaching, and spiritual direction he had become, by the time of his death, a symbol of the resurgence of spiritual values in the era of *glasnost.*

Men was born on January 22, 1935, in the heart of the Stalinist era. He was ordained a priest in 1960. Most of his career was spent in relatively obscure pastoral assignments. Though subject, like all priests, to the threat of harassment and persecution, he was able to carve out his small zone of operation in several churches in the area of Moscow. Through the 1970s he worked quietly to establish small Christian communities which emphasized prayer and Bible study.

Gradually, however, Men began to assume an increasingly visible role. He was known as the "priest of the intellectuals," a friend of dissidents like Alexander Solzhenitsyn. But he was also a priest who attracted religious seekers and who was responsible for drawing a widening circle of converts into communion with the church. In the early post-Brezhnev years, when it seemed the government was determined to cling more tightly than ever to the "ideals" of communism, Men and other church leaders were subjected to increasing harassment. He was regularly picked up by the KGB for questioning. When friends from abroad asked if it wasn't wise for him to try to leave the country, he couched his response in a thinly veiled code:

> My illness, which is progressing in a menacing manner, is only part of the general epidemic. No remedy exists. To move to another less infested region is impossible, and not something I particularly want

to do. All that can be done is to believe, to hope, and to continue to live.

But then came the regime of Mikhail Gorbachev, who set in motion a process of reform that quickly assumed its own momentum. The year 1988 marked the celebration of the first Christian millennium in Russia. The government authorized the official observation of this occasion, one of the many signs of change. For the first time Men was able openly to publish his spiritual writings and to offer public lectures on Christianity and the Bible. Despite the public thaw, however, he warned of the challenges to come: "The most difficult moment for the church will come when everything is permitted us. Then we will be ashamed because we are not ready to bear witness."

For the time being he worked at a frantic pace, as if aware that his time was limited. He said, "At present I am like the sower in the parable. I have been given a unique chance to spread the seed." His work, however, attracted resentment on the part of the same people who disapproved of the pace of change, who felt that Gorbachev was betraying the ideals of the Revolution by granting liberty to religious zealots like Men.

On September 9, 1990, unknown assailants accosted Father Men on his way to church. They struck him on the head with an axe, killing him instantly. The identity and motives of the killers were never learned.

This was a fate that Men had anticipated. He had accepted it with confidence that those who might take his life were ultimately powerless to suppress the gospel. As he wrote to a friend, shortly before his death: "Do not be worried about me.... I am only an instrument that God is using for the moment. Afterwards, things will be as God wants them."

See: Yves Hamant, *Alexander Men: A Witness for Contemporary Russia* (Torrance, Calif.: Oakwood Publications, 1995).

January 23

Mary Ward
Foundress of the Institute
of the Blessed Virgin Mary (1586–1645)

"I think, dear child, the trouble and the long loneliness you hear me speak of is not far from me, which whensoever it is, happy success will follow.... The pain is great, but very endurable, because He who lays on the burden also carries it."

In the lives of the great founders and reformers of religious orders there is ample record of the obstacles, calumnies, and persecution they endured as the price for charting new waters. Many of these stories end on a seemingly inevitable note of triumph. The story of Mary Ward, however, reminds us of the many others whose lonely struggles failed to surmount the obstacles in their path and whose dreams had to be entrusted to future generations.

Mary Ward's life began against the background of Elizabethan England and the intense persecution of the Catholic religion. Her family was among the landed gentry whose wealth and title allowed some private space to resist the severe anti-Catholic decrees. Her childhood was marked by secret visits from priests — often Jesuits — who had been quickly ordained overseas, smuggled into the country, and secretly passed from house to house, to celebrate their forbidden Masses. This illicit practice of the Catholic religion was an act of treason, which could mean death not only for the priest but for the sheltering family.

Mary was beautiful and clever, and her family urged her to accept one of the marriage proposals that were readily available. But Mary would have none of it. She insisted instead that she was called to become a nun. This was a somewhat fantastic ambition, given that at the time there was not a single convent in England. Nevertheless, with the grudging support of a confessor, she won her family's approval, and so was smuggled out of the country to Catholic Belgium.

When she presented herself there to a bishop, she was disappointed when he instructed her to accept a position as a lay Sister — essentially a servant — to a community of Poor Clares. Though she found this assignment abhorrent, she nevertheless complied obediently, until a visiting superior of the order recognized her special qualities and set her free to pursue her true vocation.

Unfortunately, Mary had difficulty finding such a vocation among the opportunities at hand. Her search led her through a number of false starts and dead ends. She had come to believe that she was not called to conventional enclosed religious life. Instead, inspired by the example of the Jesuits, she conceived of an institute of women living in a non-enclosed community, free of episcopal authority, who could carry out apostolic work in the world. To say the least, it was an idea ahead of its time.

Nevertheless, Mary was able to convince a number of influential church authorities, including a good Jesuit confessor, of the value of her plan. There followed the first of a number of clandestine visits to England to seek recruits for her community. If she did not have to resort to the subterfuge of the underground priests, she still had to be wary of the constant threat of spies. In the disguise of a traveling gentlewoman she made her rounds of the Catholic households, exhorting the faithful, assisting priests in preparing people for baptism and the other sacraments, visiting and comforting priests in prison, and inspiring a half dozen women to take the leap with her into the unknown.

During one of her visits she was finally discovered and thrust into prison. Sentenced to death, she fully expected to meet her end. But as a result of external political factors of the time, she was spared the ultimate punishment and was instead permitted to accept exile. Back in Europe Mary went about forming her band of followers into a religious community as she simultaneously engaged in the labyrinthine pursuit of official approval for her Institute. She traveled to Rome and won an audience with the pope, who gave her tentative permission to develop her project. The formal recognition she sought, however, was not forthcoming.

As she discovered, her enemies were not only in Protestant England. Her devotion to the spiritual vision of *St. Ignatius fed the distrust of secular clergy, who were rivals of the glamorous Society of Jesus. Her Institute was mocked as a house of "Lady Jesuits." But beyond the territorial jealousies of English Catholics, there was the wider resistance, in principle, to the radical program that Mary outlined. While elements of her program were admired — especially her proposal for free schools for Catholic girls — her adamant insistence that the Institute be nonenclosed and that it remain free of episcopal jurisdiction, ran head-on against the prescribed place of women in the church. While some bishops offered polite approval for her plans, most ultimately shared the opinion of one priest who, while admiring the Sisters' fervor, noted, "When all is done they are but women!"

After she had established houses in a number of cities and had won wide admiration for her exemplary schools, notification came from Rome in January 1631 that the Institute was to be suppressed. Within days messengers arrived to take Mary into custody on the charge of being a "heretic, schismatic, and rebel to the Holy Church." Though her imprisonment in a convent was brief, the suppression of the Institute continued in effect, and she remained under a cloud of ecclesial disapprobation.

In broken health she returned to England. The penal laws against Catholics were still in effect, and once again she faced surveillance and the possibility of arrest. She died in York at the age of sixty on January 23, 1645. In 1703 the rule of her Institute was finally confirmed by Pope Clement XI.

See: Mary Oliver, I.B.V.M., *Mary Ward* (New York: Sheed & Ward, 1959).

January 24

St. Francis de Sales
Bishop of Geneva, Doctor of the Church (1567–1622)

"The measure of love, is to love without measure."

The Protestant Reformation evoked a variety of responses on the part of Catholic apologists. Some reacted defensively. Not content with affirming the truth, they felt the church must aggressively denounce error and cause its suppression by any means necessary. But others responded differently. They perceived in the signs of the times a general summons to conversion and to a more intense aspiration for holiness. Among the great saints of this period was Francis de Sales. As a bishop and spiritual director, he expounded a message of love and moderation that had enormous effect in reestablishing the vitality and credibility of the Catholic church. The only complaint against his methods came from rigorist critics who charged that he made it appear all too easy to become a saint.

Francis was born in Savoy in 1567. His wealthy parents wished him to become a lawyer and perhaps a government minister. He obliged their ambition to the point of earning a doctorate in law. But all the while he was convinced that his true vocation lay in the priesthood. This caused him terrible strain until finally he confessed to his tutor, "God does not want me to embrace the life for which my father destines me." With the support of the bishop of Geneva he was eventually ordained a priest in 1593.

The next year Francis accepted a dangerous assignment. The Chablais region around Lake Geneva had become completely Calvinist. Catholic churches had been burned, convents had closed, and all priests had been forced into exile. But in 1594 the Catholic duke of Savoy reconquered the region and requested that the bishop allow priests to return. Given the depth of the local hostility to the church, this was considered a nearly suicidal mission. Nevertheless, Francis volunteered.

For four years he trudged through the region on foot, many times barely escaping assassination. He lived in poverty, relying on alms, suffering through several harsh winters. Rather than simply denouncing Calvinism, he chose instead to proclaim the positive message of the gospel in a way that would overcome the prevailing negative stereotypes of the Catholic faith. Not by force of arms, but by love and self-sacrifice he sought to return the hearts of the people to their ancient faith. He met with surprising success. At least twenty-three hundred families were publicly reconciled with the Catholic church as a result of his mission.

In 1602 he was named bishop of Geneva. As the city remained a Calvinist stronghold which tolerated no dissent, Francis could not actually enter his titular see. Instead he was based in the town of Annecy, some fifty miles to the south. From there he oversaw the administration of his diocese and achieved wide fame as a preacher and spiritual director.

In travels to France he became acquainted with a wealthy young widow, *Jeanne de Chantal. After the tragic death of her husband, which left her with the care of four young children, Jeanne had felt a vocation to devote herself to God. Francis became her spiritual director, and after some years he enlisted her in a plan to devise a new form of religious congregation. Rather than accept a traditional enclosure, these women would combine prayer with a life of charity among the poor. It was part of Francis's plan to rejuvenate the church by elevating the intensity of spiritual devotion. In 1610 the two of them founded the Order of the Visitation, with Jeanne as the first superior.

By this time Francis himself had achieved wide fame through the publication of his book *An Introduction to the Devout Life.* This manual of devotion was quickly translated into many languages and it remains one of the classics of Christian spirituality. Most such handbooks had been addressed to clerics or members of religious orders. What was significant about Francis's book was that it was addressed to Christians in any state of life. The path to holiness, he taught, could be pursued in the world as well as in the cloister. The task of the spiritual director was to adapt the life of devotion to the variety of walks of life: "Devotion is to be practiced differently by the noble, the worker, the servant, the prince, the widow, the young girl, the wife. Even more than this, the practice of devotion has to be adapted to the strength, life-situation, and duties of each individual." In whatever state one occupied, the logic of the devout life was the same; in essence, it was a matter of gradually weaning oneself from sin and enlarging one's capacity for love and the practice of virtue. "Genuine devotion," he wrote, "is simply true love of God."

This tone of moderation and balance accounted for much of Francis's appeal. Rather than impose harsh discipline or force a drastic choice between good and evil, his method was to develop habits of discernment that would incline one's will in the direction of God's light. The test of true progress in the spiritual life was not to be in the rigor of one's self-mortification but in the intensity of one's charity.

Each page of Francis's book is stamped by his characteristic wisdom and his understanding of human psychology: "A single Our Father said with feeling has greater value than many said quickly and hurriedly." "The King of Glory does not reward his servants according to the dignity of the offices they hold but according to the love and humility with which they fulfill their offices." He anticipates that the devout will daily fall short of their ideals. But rather than abase oneself as a worthless sinner, he urges the penitent to say: "Alas, my poor heart, here we are, fallen into the pit we were so firmly resolved to avoid! Well, we must get up again and leave it forever."

Francis de Sales died in 1622. In 1923 Pope Pius XI named him the patron saint of writers.

See: Francis de Sales and Jane de Chantal, *Letters of Spiritual Direction,* Wendy M. Wright and Joseph F. Power, O.S.F.S., eds., Classics of Western Spirituality (New York: Paulist, 1988).

January 25

St. Andrei Rublev
Russian Monk and Iconographer (d. 1430)

"He who venerates the icon ... venerates in it
the person of the one so depicted."
—Second Council of Nicea, 787

The use of icons, highly "spiritualized" depictions of Christ, the Virgin Mary, and the saints, was one of the earliest and most distinctive elements of Byzantine spirituality. As used in worship, icons were not intended to serve as "realistic" portraits, much less as works of decorative art, but rather as a window linking earthly and heavenly realities.

Nevertheless, despite their popularity in the East, the use of icons was the subject of heated controversy in the early church, as vehement as any of the debates surrounding the nature of Christ and the Trinity. Critics charged that the use of icons constituted a kind of idolatrous worship of images. The defenders of icons responded that it was not the icon itself that was worshiped but the spiritual reality it represented. According to one proponent, "The honor shown to the image is conveyed to its prototype." What was really at stake, according to these advocates, was the very mystery of the Incarnation itself, and the question of whether Christ, a true man, was truly the image of the invisible God. By virtue of the Incarnation it was perfectly justified to approach the material world as a point of access to the divine world. As Dionysius the Areopagite observed, "Sensible images do indeed show forth invisible things." According to Theodore the Studite, "Man himself is created after the image and likeness of God; therefore there is something divine in the art of making images."

The matter came to a head when various popes and councils banned the use of icons and mandated their destruction. Eventually however, the issue was finally settled at the Second Council of Nicea in 787 in a decision in favor of icons, renewed definitively in 843. So significant was this decision for the Eastern church that it is commemorated to this day as the "Feast of the Triumph of Orthodoxy."

The production of icons was itself a spiritual work, generally in the hands of monks, and accompanied by intense prayer and fasting. Because the genre stressed the value of traditional themes, composition, and artistic effects, the personal identity of the artist was seldom known. The icon is thus a largely anonymous art form. Nevertheless certain iconographers developed a more or less distinctive style and so achieved a wider personal fame.

Among Russian iconographers Andrei Rublev, a monk of the fifteenth century, is the most widely revered. He brought the icon to a new level of artistic and spiritual depth and inspired a school of faithful imitators. Relatively little is known of his life and, sadly, very few of his works have survived. One of his great icons, a depiction of Christ known as the "Savior of Zvenigorod," was discovered in 1918 on the bottom of a board used as the stairway to a barn.

Rublev's work is characterized by a lightness and delicacy of style, a balance between tradition and innovation, and an unusually creative representation of theological mystery. Certainly his most famous work is his icon of the Holy Trinity painted in honor of his old abbot, *St. Sergius of Radonezh. To represent the Trinity, Rublev used the image of the three mysterious angels who visited the tent of Abraham at the oak of Mamre. Seated around a table, set for a meal, the three angelic figures show the differentiation between the persons of the Trinity while at the same time subtly indicating their identity and interrelationship. It is a stunning vision of the divine community to which, in the Eucharist, the faithful are invited to participate.

Andrei Rublev has been canonized by the Russian Orthodox church. His feast day is observed on January 29.

See: David and Tamar Talbot Rice, *Icons and Their History* (Woodstock, N.Y.: Overlook, 1974); Jim Forest, *Praying with Icons* (Maryknoll, N.Y.: Orbis, 1997).

St. Paula
Widow and Scholar (347–404)

"God is my witness that what I do I do for his sake. My prayer is that I may die a beggar, not leaving a penny to my daughter and indebted to strangers for my winding-sheet."

Paula came from a wealthy and aristocratic family in Rome. She enjoyed a happy marriage to an equally distinguished husband, with whom she bore several children. The death of her husband when she was thirty-two left her bereft. She found consolation from another widow, *St. Marcella. Through this association Paula committed herself to Christ and adopted a life of severe austerity. She also became acquainted with *St. Jerome, a scholar and priest, then in service to Pope Damasus. He became her spiritual director and lifelong friend.

Jerome was better known for his pugnacious personality than for his human warmth. Nevertheless, when Paula's eldest daughter suddenly died, he responded with tenderness and comfort. In 385, after Jerome left Rome for the Holy Land, Paula followed him, accompanied by another devoted daughter, St. Eustochium. There in Bethlehem Paula used her wealth to establish two monasteries with Jerome, one for men and another for women. Paula oversaw the women's community, but her major work was looking after Jerome and helping him with his scholarly work. As a child she had learned Greek, and she joined Jerome in studying Hebrew. Thus she provided assistance with his masterwork, the Latin translation of the Bible from the original languages.

When she died on January 26, 404, Jerome revealed the depth of his feeling in a letter to her daughter, Eustochium.

> If all the members of my body were to be converted into tongues, and if each of my limbs were to be gifted with a human voice, I could still do no justice to the virtues of the holy and venerable Paula. Noble in family, she was nobler still in holiness; rich formerly in this world's goods, she is now more distinguished by the poverty that she has embraced for Christ.

She had wished to be so poor as not to leave a penny for her daughter. In fact, as Jerome notes approvingly, she far exceeded this aim, leaving her daughter with a mountain of unpaid bills.

She was buried in the Church of the Nativity, site of her Savior's birth.

See: Jerome, "Letter to Eustochium," in S. L. Greenslade, ed., *Early Latin Theology* (Philadelphia: Westminster, 1956).

St. Angela Merici
Foundress of the Ursulines (1474–1540)

"Each member of the Company should strive to despoil herself of everything and set all her good, her love, her delight, not in robes, nor in food nor in relatives, but in God alone and in his benign and ineffable Providence."

It is easy to take for granted the scores of religious congregations dedicated to the works of mercy and other apostolates. As their numbers decline, it becomes harder to recall a time when a vast system of schools, orphanages, and hospitals was run by legions of Sisters, each wearing the distinctive habit of her congregation. It is harder still to recall that there was a time before such communities existed when it fell to certain visionaries and their devoted pioneers to imagine a new way of living out the gospel in response to the needs at hand. Many of them consciously sought a new way for women to live a Christian life in the world — apart from the alternatives of marriage or the enclosure of the convent. One of these visionaries was Angela Merici (sometimes called Angela of Brescia).

Angela was born in the town of Desenzano in northern Italy. She was orphaned at an early age and soon thereafter lost a beloved sister. In her grief she was consoled by a vision — the first of many in her life — which offered assurance of her sister's salvation. In thanksgiving she became a Franciscan tertiary and ever after adopted a life of prayerful simplicity. She devoted many years to continuous pilgrimage, visiting the shrines of Italy. Eventually she took up the irresistible challenge for all pilgrims of her day, a trip to the Holy Land. Before arriving, however, she was mysteriously struck blind and consequently saw nothing of the holy shrines. On her return, her eyesight just as miraculously returned.

The motif of sight or vision appears elsewhere in her biography. She had one remarkable vision in which she saw a company of angels and maidens descending from a ladder in the heavens. A voice revealed that she would one day found a new community of women whose members would be as numerous as those maidens thus revealed to her.

In her youth Angela had been moved by the poverty and ignorance of her neighbors and had undertaken to provide simple religious instruction to their children. Over the years, when not traveling, she had made this her regular occupation. Gradually other women were attracted to join her. In 1533, when she was fifty and had settled in Brescia, she set about to formalize a community of these women. Two years later she had a group of twenty-eight women ready to consecrate themselves with her to the service of God. They chose as their patron St. Ursula, a legendary fourth-century martyr who was popularly venerated as a protector of women.

Although she devised a simple rule for her community of Ursulines, Angela did not conceive of them as a religious order. They did not wear habits; they took no vows; they continued to live with their families rather than behind an enclosure. The idea of such an association of religious women was unheard of at the time and it aroused certain concerns. But the work of Angela and her companions, which centered on the education of poor girls, was widely admired.

Angela was elected the association's first superior general, in which position she devoted herself primarily to spiritual formation. By this time she was revered as a living saint of Brescia. Crowds of people would follow her to church, attracted in part by her reputed ability to levitate several inches off the ground while gazing on the Eucharist.

She died on January 27, 1540, after a long illness. Four years later Rome approved a constitution for her religious community, which would in time come to number many tens of thousands of women. She was canonized in 1807.

See: Philip Caraman, *Saint Angela* (New York: Farrar, Straus, 1963).

January 28
St. Thomas Aquinas
Theologian and Doctor of the Church (1225–1274)

*"Every truth without exception — and whoever may utter it —
is from the Holy Spirit."*

Thomas Aquinas was born in southern Italy into a prosperous family of the lower nobility. He was the youngest of four sons, and his parents entrusted his upbringing to the Benedictine monks at the nearby monastery of Monte Cassino. Their hope was that a monastic "career" for the boy, leading perhaps to the office of abbot, would adequately serve the family interests and honor. Religious life, in any case, proved most congenial to Thomas. But after a period of study at the University of Naples he announced his desire to become a Dominican friar. As *Chesterton observed, such an announcement was comparable, for a modern youth of his station, to the casual information that he had decided to marry a gypsy. His family retaliated by kidnapping him and locking him up for a year in their castle. But when this failed to dissuade him, they finally set him free to pursue his vocation. So he assumed the white habit and black scapular of the Order of Preachers.

Thomas was sent for studies to Cologne, where he was taught by St. Albert the Great. Whether he was intimidated by the competitive atmosphere or simply preferred listening to talking, Thomas rarely opened his mouth. As a result, he was taken by his classmates to be something of a simpleton. They called him "The Dumb Ox," a reference, at the same time, to his corpulent figure. Albert, however, eventually recognized Thomas's brilliance and admonished his classmates. He predicted that the lowing of this "dumb ox" would eventually be heard around the world.

Thomas went on to receive a doctorate at the University of Paris, where he also taught. It was there that he published his first works in philosophy, as well as apologetic arguments and commentaries on Scripture. By this time he was recognized as an unparalleled genius, and his services were in wide demand in the Dominican order as well as in the papal court. He was not, however, a stranger to controversy. He was sharply critical of contemporary methods of theological argument, which relied heavily on the appeal to authority. Thomas advanced a much more rigorous approach to theological argument in which he gave equal weight to opposing points of view before deciding where the preponderance of the evidence might lie. Much more controversial, however, was his systematic adaptation of the philosophy of the pagan Aristotle in the service of Christian theology.

In 1266 Thomas began work on his masterpiece, the *Summa theologiae*, the most ambitious and systematic exposition of the Catholic faith ever undertaken. Through a series of interlocking "questions" Thomas endeavored to demonstrate how the truths of the Catholic faith were related in a consistent and logical fashion, and to show the interrelation of reason and revelation. Previous theologians had tended to work on particular theological problems. Aquinas's great contribution was to undertake a view of the "whole."

In the late nineteenth century Thomas's theology was virtually canonized by the church, and for many decades up to Vatican II a handbook version of "Thomism" completely dominated seminary education. Rather than prescribe Thomas's dialectical approach to theological inquiry, church authorities presented his thought as a system of ready-made answers to all questions — an approach utterly out of character with the spirit of Thomas himself. It fell to more innovative theologians like *Karl Rahner to revive the truly creative aspects of Thomas's project and to recall just how open he had been to dialogue with the wisdom and philosophy of his time, even to the point of interpreting Christian theology in terms of pagan (Aristotelian) thought. Those who honored Thomas as "The Angelic Doctor" often forgot just how controversial Thomas was in his time. In 1270 the bishop of Paris drew up a list of eighteen errors and condemnable propositions from his works. This was renewed and expanded in 1277. Only after fifty years did a later bishop of Paris revoke this condemnation. By that time, of course, Thomas was long dead.

In fact, Thomas never completed his massive *Summa.* He abruptly ceased work on the project in December 1273. He was living at this point in a Dominican house of studies in Naples, where the order had assigned him to escape the controversies in Paris. During Mass on the feast of *St. Nicholas he had a strange experience that caused him afterward to hang up his writing instruments, never to resume his great work. When he was asked the reason for this silence, he replied, "I cannot go on.... All that I have written seems to me like so much straw compared to what I have seen and what has been revealed to me."

The meaning of this mysterious pronouncement has been the subject of much speculation. In any case, his time was running short. Three months later, on his way to the Council of Lyons, he fell ill and was taken to the Cistercian abbey of Fossa Nuova. After making his last confession and receiving communion he said: "I am receiving thee, Price of my soul's redemption: all my studies, my vigils, and my labors have been for love of thee. I have taught much and written much of the most sacred body of Jesus Christ; I have taught and written in the faith of Jesus Christ and of the holy Roman Church, to whose judgment I offer and submit everything."

He died two days later on March 7, 1274, at the age of forty-nine. His feast is celebrated on this day.

See: Mary T. Clark, ed., *An Aquinas Reader* (Garden City, N.Y.: Image, 1972); F. C. Copleston, *Aquinas* (New York: Penguin, 1955).

January 29
Père Jacques Bunol
Carmelite Priest (1900–1945)

"The saints have never attached importance to what their hands do;
they did what they had to do but they did it for love."

Even after many years the former students at the Carmelite school in Lille spoke with awe and reverence of their headmaster, a priest whom they called Père Jacques. More than a teacher, he was a friend, a mentor, a spiritual guide, who carefully studied each boy under his charge and found the way to encourage his special gifts.

But of all that he taught them, his students clearly remembered his final lesson best of all. That came on January 13, 1944, when Gestapo officers, tipped off by an informer, burst into the school and seized three Jewish students as well as the priest who had offered them asylum. As Père Jacques, in custody, passed before the assembled students he gave them a jaunty wave, as if leaving for a short holiday: *"Au revoir,* boys, see you soon!" They never saw him again.

Père Jacques was born to a poor working-class family on January 29, 1900. From his early childhood he wanted nothing but to be a priest. After his ordination he served as a schoolteacher. Quite soon, however, he felt a new calling to the contemplative life. This was answered by his decision to enter the Carmelites. Having, with some effort, overcome the resistance of his bishop, he entered the Carmelite monastery in Lille. There, immersed in prayer and study of the Carmelite mystics, he spent the happiest year of his life. But this ended abruptly when his community assigned him to take over administration of their junior school. "You see," he wrote a friend, "I am just one more example of those who flee the world in order to find peace in silent contemplation, and whom God puts back in their former occupation to make supple their will and to mortify their too natural taste for complete solitude. Now I must wait for heaven to enjoy God as I had dreamed of doing in the shadow of the cloister." So he returned to the classroom.

Now, however, girded by the habit of prayer, he found it possible to combine the overwhelming demands of his school work with a deep spiritual discipline. He accepted his assignment as an expression of God's will.

It was also an opportunity to communicate to his students something of his own thirst for life and holiness.

Aside from the catechism and reading of the classics, he offered his instruction through walks in the woods and trips to the museum. As one student recalled, "He taught me to enjoy the sun setting on the countryside weighted down and heavy with the labors of man, the prayer that rises with the night like a song of hope. He showed me God in a small blade of grass that bends under the weight of a ladybird."

But he was not simply an ethereal mystic. He was known as an ardent champion of social justice who always preached the duty of solidarity with the oppressed. After France fell to the Germans, such sentiments became dangerous. Nevertheless, the risks did not prevent Père Jacques from using the resources of the school to aid the underground resistance and to shelter fugitives, including Jewish students, from the Nazis. To those who warned of what might happen if he were caught he answered, "Don't you think that if that happened, and if by chance I were shot, I would thus be leaving my pupils an example that would be worth more to them than all the instructions I could give them?"

The day before he was arrested, he wrote to his brother, "It is very possible that before long something will happen to me. If I am shot, rejoice, for I shall have realized my ideal: to give up my life for those who suffer." Even after his arrest, when there was still some possibility of a reprieve, he discouraged any efforts on his behalf: "Priests are needed in prison."

He was detained in a series of camps. In each one he made a strong impression on his fellow prisoners. While most of them were fully occupied with the business of survival, he put himself tirelessly at the service of others — and not simply Catholics. He sought out the abandoned and neglected and made a special point of befriending Communists. He explained that as the son of workers he felt a particular bond with all those who suffered for the cause of social justice. One of them later said, "One felt the presence of Christ in this priest."

Eventually he ended up in the notorious Mauthausen concentration camp in Austria. There between the starvation rations, the brutality of forced labor, the unchecked disease, and the frequent massacres, over 120,000 human beings perished in three years. Any public display of religion was strictly forbidden. Nevertheless, Père Jacques continued to minister to his fellow prisoners, hearing confessions, counseling the doubtful, praying for the dying. His aim was to build a Christian society within the jaws of hell; even if his success extended little farther than himself, it was a continuous defiance of the spirit of Nazism. While hunger reduced many prisoners to a condition of animal need, Père Jacques constantly bore witness to the sanctity and dignity of life. Often he was seen passing on his precious food rations to those in greater need. In a situation where each morsel of bread might mean another day of existence, such sacrifices represented the literal sharing of his life.

In February 1945 all priests were transferred to Dachau. For some reason Père Jacques was passed over. That Easter he risked his life to say Mass three times. As many prisoners as dared gathered round to receive communion at his hands. He said, "At this time we must rejoice in accomplishing God's will to the very end, to give our lives if He demands it; perhaps it is our vocation." Many of those who survived remembered it as one of the transcendent moments of their lives.

Père Jacques himself survived until the liberation of the camp on May 5, 1945. In the following days, though burning with fever, he worked tirelessly to help reestablish order and oversee the distribution of supplies and medicines. When he collapsed he was finally removed to a hospital in France, where he died on June 2, surrounded by the members of his Carmelite family.

See: Michel Carrouges, *Père Jacques* (New York: Macmillan, 1961).

January 30

Mohandas K. Gandhi
"Great Soul" of India (1869–1948)

"If I have read the Bible correctly, I know many men who have never heard the name of Jesus Christ or have even rejected the official interpretation of Christianity who will, probably, if Jesus came in our midst today in the flesh, be owned by him more than many of us."

Mohandas K. Gandhi, hero of the Indian independence movement, did more than any person in history to advance the theory and practice of nonviolence. Others had embraced nonviolence as a personal or religious code. But it was Gandhi who demonstrated that the same spirit of nonviolence he embraced as a principle of life could be harnessed as a principle of political struggle.

Though his relevance is universal, Gandhi has always presented a special attraction and challenge for Christians. As a young lawyer in South Africa he was pursued by evangelical friends who avidly sought his conversion. Gandhi read the Bible and attended their services, only to be confirmed in the Hindu faith of his birth. But it was a faith always open to a greater truth, a truth larger, as he perceived it, than the capacity of any person, church, or tradition to contain it completely. Later, as he came to regard the personal search for truth as inseparable from the public struggle for freedom and justice, Gandhi posed a different kind of challenge. Here was a Hindu who politely rejected the dogmatic claims of Christianity while embracing, with every ounce of his will, the ethical claims of Christ.

In either case, Gandhi's influence on Christians has owed less to his specific comments on Christianity than to his ability to recall, in his witness, the features of Christ and the gospel commandment of love. Nevertheless, Gandhi's writings document his profound appreciation of Jesus, the influence of Christian ideals, and his devotion to many Christian friends. His frequent recourse to Christian Scripture led spiteful critics to accuse him of being a "secret Christian," a charge Gandhi considered both a libel and a compliment: "a libel because there are men who believe me to be capable of being secretly anything, . . . a compliment in that it is a reluctant acknowledgement of my capacity for appreciating the beauties of Christianity." Indeed, if left with the Sermon on the Mount and his own interpretation of it, he said he would gladly call himself a Christian. But he conceded honestly that his interpretation would fall short of orthodoxy.

Gandhi's difficulties with Christianity were at once theological and ethical. He could not bring himself to regard Jesus Christ as the only Son of God. Nor could he accept that his salvation hinged on such a confession. At the same time, the behavior of Christians left him doubtful that their religion had any superior or unique claim to the truth.

His early childhood impressions of Christianity centered on the belief that Indian converts were required to renounce their cultural heritage, to embrace "beef and brandy." Later experiences in England and South Africa did little to change his opinion. It was his encounter with the writings of *Leo Tolstoy that sparked his discovery of what he called the "true message of Jesus," as represented in the Sermon on the Mount with its emphasis on the "law of love." In Tolstoy Gandhi found a confirmation of his own inclination to distinguish between the message of Jesus and the teachings and practice of the Christian church. Thus, Jesus became for Gandhi an object of reverence and devotion, uncompromised by the failures and betrayals of his Christian followers.

Gandhi returned to India, where he tested and developed his philosophy of nonviolent action in the struggle for Indian independence. In the context of his encounters with Christians Gandhi continued to express his opinions on the subject of Jesus, Christianity, and the missionary enterprise. He confessed his sincere devotion to the figure of Jesus, whom he regarded as an ideal representative of nonviolence. He embraced not only the Sermon on the Mount but Jesus' redemptive suffering unto death, and he cited Jesus' example of loving service as the essence of true religion. At the same time he voiced criticism of orthodox Christianity, both for its dogmatic claims and its ethical shortcomings. Christendom, judging from his experience on the receiving end, appeared to be the very negation of the Sermon on the Mount. On the subject of Christian missionary activity in India he was particularly outspoken. He believed that most missionaries harbored disdain for the traditions and culture of India and were blind to their own identification of the gospel with Western civilization. He rejected the teaching that salvation was available only through Christianity and regarded the pursuit of converts as a form of spiritual imperialism, a violation of his own belief in the equality of all faiths.

Long before his death at the hands of a young Hindu fanatic on January 30, 1948, Gandhi's authority as the Mahatma, or "Great Soul," had spontaneously extended beyond his native country. Although his particular brand of asceticism conformed to Indian cultural norms, he was one of those examples of unquestioned holiness — *St. Francis comes to mind as another — whose challenge transcends the limits of his age and culture. It is the example of someone like Gandhi that makes it impossible for most Christians to maintain the notion that salvation is restricted to the visible church. Indeed, Gandhi is a powerful argument for the capacity of non-Christians to function for Christians as saints — living icons of the invisible God.

This is not to bestow on Gandhi the status of "honorary Christian." He remained a committed Hindu and always resisted, with good humor, the opinion of those Christians who held that "if only he accepted Christ" his example would be complete. Jesus, as Gandhi observed, called human beings not to a new religion but a new life. There are nevertheless many Christians who have become better Christians because of Gandhi, who have rediscovered different emphases in the gospel, and have been led to view the suffering figure of Christ through new eyes.

See: M. K. Gandhi, *An Autobiography: The Story of My Experiments with Truth* (Boston: Beacon, 1957); Robert Ellsberg, ed., *Gandhi on Christianity* (Maryknoll, N.Y.: Orbis, 1991).

January 31

St. Marcella
Widow (325–410)

"By heaven's grace, captivity has found me a poor woman, not made me one.
Now I shall go in want of daily bread, but I shall not feel hunger
since I am full of Christ."

All that we know of Marcella is contained in the many letters which she received from her friend *St. Jerome and especially from an eloquent memorial, in which he called her "the glory of all the saints and particularly of the city of Rome."

Marcella was born to a wealthy and noble family of Rome. After the death of her father she was urged to marry and did so. Her husband was also a wealthy man, but his death left her a widow after only seven months of marriage. Henceforth she resisted all invitations to remarry, happily dedicating herself to a life of chastity. When a ranking — and elderly — consul proposed to leave her all his money if she would marry him, she answered, "If I wished to marry... I should in any case look for a husband, not an inheritance."

After this Marcella's life was occupied by prayer, study of Scripture, and frequent visits to the shrines of the martyrs. She gave away all her fortune, "preferring to store her money in the stomachs of the needy rather than hide it in a purse." At this time she came across an account of the life of *St. Antony and was inspired, as much as her circumstances would allow, to emulate his monastic life. Thus she began to gather a community of like-spirited women, both widows and unmarried maidens, who shared her appetite for holiness. Most were of similar social background, though they conformed to Marcella's voluntary poverty. Though they followed no formal rule, this was perhaps one of the earliest such communities of Christian women.

When Jerome arrived in Rome he was introduced to Marcella's circle of holy women, and he was induced, somewhat reluctantly, to serve as their spiritual director. So impressed was he by their learning and piety that he compared them to the holy women who surrounded Jesus. Marcella, he claimed, was another *Mary Magdalene. A number of these women became his lifelong friends, among them the holy *Paula. So frequent a visitor to this community was Jerome that, in "a slander-loving place...where the triumph of vice was to disparage virtue and to defile all that is pure and clean," his enemies found ample material for gossip. Such an atmosphere contributed to his decision to flee Rome for the Holy Land (with Paula following closely in his wake). Nevertheless, he maintained his close correspondence with Marcella until her death.

She continued her holy life until the sack of Rome in 410. The spectacle of this violence and the ensuing famine made an impact on the entire classical world. As Jerome wrote, "The city which had taken the whole world was itself taken." At one point the invading hordes broke into Marcella's house and beat her savagely in order to discover her hidden treasures. In vain she protested that she owned nothing but the robe she wore, and she had fears lest they would take even that from her. Nevertheless her brave composure arrested the assault, and eventually the shame-faced attackers escorted her to the refuge of a nearby church. At eighty-five, she found it difficult to recover from such a traumatic experience.

Marcella died within a few months. Though her sisters wept, Jerome writes, "she smiled, conscious of having lived a good life and hoping for a reward hereafter."

See: St. Jerome, "Letter CXXVII: To Principia," in *Select Letters of St. Jerome*, trans. F. A. Wright (New York: G. P. Putnam's Sons, 1932).

☞ FEBRUARY ☜

February 1
St. Brigid of Ireland
Abbess of Kildare (c. 450–525)

"I would like a great lake of beer for the King of the kings;
I would like the people of heaven to be drinking it through time eternal."

Brigid lived in the era when traditional Irish religion was giving way to the formal institution of Christianity. The lives and legends of holy Brigid reflect that uneasy ebb and flow. It has been noted that in ancient times Brigid was, in fact, the name of the Celtic sun goddess. This has given rise to the suggestion that in St. Brigid, a nun and abbess of the fifth century, we find the repository of primeval religious memories and traditions. In any case, it seems that with the cult of St. Brigid (called "The Mary of the Gael") the Irish people maintained an image of the maternal face of God with which to complement the more patriarchal religion of *St. Patrick and subsequent missionaries.

As best as can be discerned through the mists of legend, it is believed that Brigid was born into slavery and was later converted to Christianity by St. Patrick sometime in her childhood. She was granted her freedom when it proved impossible to curb her enthusiasm for giving alms; it seems she would otherwise have impoverished her master through such unauthorized largesse.

The themes of generosity and compassion are the feature of miracles without number. Brigid's only desire was "to satisfy the poor, to expel every hardship, to spare every miserable man." (That there remained any miserable souls in Ireland is hard to believe, given the extent of her recorded miracles.) Many of her marvels have a particularly maternal character, reflecting her propensity to nourish and give succor. Thus, "She supplied beer out of her one barrel to eighteen churches, which sufficed from Maundy Thursday to the end of the paschal time. Once a leprous woman asking for milk, there being none at hand she gave her cold water, but the water was turned into milk, and when she had drunk it the woman was healed."

Brigid became a nun and ultimately abbess of Kildare, which was a double monastery, consisting of both men and women. Through her fame as a spiritual teacher the Abbey of Kildare became a center for pilgrims.

So great was the authority of Brigid, it seems, that she even induced a bishop to join her community and to share her leadership. According to legend — which the church, for obvious reasons, has strenuously resisted — the bishop came to ordain Brigid as a fellow bishop.

Some chroniclers cite this in a matter-of-fact way (it is, after all, scarcely less credible than many of the reports of Brigid's career). Others report the story while trying in some way to mitigate the scandal. It is suggested, for instance, that the bishop was so "intoxicated with the grace of God" that he didn't know what he was doing. Whatever the historical facts, the persistence of such a tale says a good deal about Brigid's status in the Irish conscience, and perhaps the effort to rectify the exclusion of such an extraordinary woman from the ranks of apostolic authority.

See: Hugh de Blacam, *The Saints of Ireland* (Milwaukee: Bruce, 1942); Mary Condren, *The Serpent and the Goddess: Women, Religion, and Power in Celtic Ireland* (San Francisco: Harper & Row, 1989).

February 2

Alfred Delp
Jesuit Priest and Martyr (1907–1945)

"The conditions of happiness have nothing whatever to do with outward existence. They are exclusively dependent on man's inner attitude and steadfastness, which enable him, even in the most trying circumstances, to form at least a notion of what life is about."

Alfred Delp was born in Mannheim, Germany, and became a Jesuit in 1926. Among his friends and teachers was the great Jesuit theologian *Karl Rahner. During the Second World War he joined a secret anti-Nazi group that was planning to build a new Christian social order after the war. When the group was exposed in the summer of 1944, Delp was arrested and charged with treason. The Gestapo tried unsuccessfully to link him with a plot against Hitler's life, but settled instead for demonstrating his "defeatist" attitude, evidenced in part by his membership in the Society of Jesus. As Delp noted,

My offense is that I believed in Germany and her eventual emergence from this dark hour of error and distress, that I refused to accept that accumulation of arrogance, pride, and force that is the Nazi way of life, and that I did this as a Christian and a Jesuit.

Confined to a dark cell and held in chains, Delp passed his time in the Advent season of 1944 writing a remarkable series of meditations. His reflections on the meaning of Advent and Christmas, set not only against the darkness of war, but in the face of his own approaching death, provide a penetrating glimpse of faith, not to mention courage, under fire. They also present a disturbing contrast to the pious sentimentality so often evoked by "the holiday season."

For Delp the promise of Christmas, the paradoxical entry of God's love into the dark wilderness of history, is literally a matter of life and death.

The fate of mankind, my own fate, the verdict awaiting me, the significance of the feast, can all be summed up in the sentence *surrender thyself to God and thou shalt find thyself again*. Others have you in their power now; they torture and frighten you, hound you from pillar to post. But the inner law of freedom sings that no death can kill us; life is eternal.

Always watchful for the prison guard, conscious that every day might be his last, Delp strengthened his will by focusing on the ultimate victory of love. In doing so, he left a testament that shows how a person, living in the presence of God, may achieve a quality of self-possession and inner freedom that circumstances are powerless to overcome.

In a final message to his friends, he asked them not to mourn and to be clear in their minds that he was "sacrificed, not conquered." With the same hope that had led him in the first place to imagine a future beyond the Third Reich, that had led to his imprisonment, and that had ultimately sustained him in his cell, he wrote, "If through one man's life there is a little more love and kindness, a little more light and truth in the world, then he will not have lived in vain."

Father Delp was hanged in the Plotzensee prison on February 2, 1945.

See: The Prison Meditations of Father Alfred Delp (New York: Herder and Herder, 1963).

February 3

St. Aelred of Rievaulx
Abbot (1110–1167)

"God is friendship.... He who dwells in friendship dwells in God,
and God in him."

St. Aelred of Rievaulx emerges from a contemporary biography and from his own writings as one of the most attractive personalities of the Middle Ages. He spent his life within the starkly penitential atmosphere of a Cistercian monastery. Yet it might well be said of him, as he said of one of his monks, that he was "friendship's child," for he spent all his energy "in seeking to be loved and to love."

Aelred was born in 1110 in Northumbria and raised in the court of the kings of Scotland. His kind and gentle manner won him much affection, and he would, no doubt, have enjoyed a successful career in the king's service. At the age of twenty-four, however, an errand in Yorkshire brought him to a new Cistercian monastery in Rievaulx. Immediately he felt that he had found his true home. The next day he applied for entry as a monk.

Aelred's rise within the monastic community was as rapid as his success at court. He eventually became abbot of Rievaulx and remained in this office until his death at the age of fifty-seven. During his term the monastery grew to include over six hundred monks, making Rievaulx the largest religious community in England.

No doubt this success owed much to Aelred's distinctive style of leadership. He called the monastery a school of love, and he encouraged the cultivation of true friendship among his monks as a reflection of their friendship with and love for Christ. Traditionally, monks had been warned of the dangers of forming "particular friendships." Aelred, however, believed that a monk who had suppressed his natural capacity for friendship was incapable of truly loving God. As he wrote in his treatise *Spiritual Friendship*,

> I call them more beasts than men who say life should be led so that they need not console anyone nor occasion distress or sorrow to anyone, who take no pleasure in the good of another, nor expect their failures to distress others, seeking to love no one and be loved by none.

For the last ten years of his life Aelred suffered terribly from gout and stone. Much of the time he was unable to leave his cell in the infirmary. Nevertheless, he welcomed large groups of monks, twenty or thirty at a time, to visit him in his cell and even lounge on his bed. While noting his approval, his biographer, a monk named Walter, acknowledged that such affectionate intimacy was not typical of monastic decorum:

> There was nobody to say to them, "Get out, go away, do not touch the Abbot's bed"; they walked and lay about his bed and talked with him as a little child prattles with its mother. He would say to them, "My sons, say what you will; only let no vile word, no detraction of a brother, no blasphemy against God proceed out of your mouth." He did not treat them with the pedantic imbecility habitual in some silly abbots who, if a monk takes a brother's hand in his own, or says anything that they do not like, demand his cowl, strip and expel him. Not so Aelred, not so.

Aelred died on January 12, 1167. His feast is celebrated in Cistercian monasteries on February 3.

See: Aelred of Rievaulx, *Spiritual Friendship*, trans. Mary Eugenia Laker, S.S.N.D. (Kalamazoo, Mich.: Cistercian Publications, 1977).

February 4

St. John de Britto
Jesuit Martyr of Goa (1647–1693)

"I await death and I await it with impatience. It has always been the object of my prayers. It forms today the most precious reward of my labors and my sufferings."

John de Britto was born to a noble family of Lisbon in 1647. From his childhood his imagination was fired by tales of *Francis Xavier and the early Jesuit missionaries. His sole desire was to be one of them, a wish that was fulfilled at the age of fifteen when he was admitted to the Society of Jesus.

After his ordination in 1673 de Britto was sent as part of a Jesuit mission to Goa, a Portuguese colony in southern India. There he adopted a style of mission very much in the tradition of his predecessor, the great *Roberto de Nobili. Thus he conformed as much as possible to the appearance of an Indian holy man, dressing appropriately, abstaining from meat, and translating the gospel message into terms comprehensible to a high-caste Hindu audience.

Unlike de Nobili, whose main opposition came from within his own church, de Britto encountered violent persecution on several occasions. In 1686 he and a group of Indian catechists were seized and subjected to excruciating tortures over a period of days. Upon his release and recovery from this ordeal, he was recalled to Lisbon. His superiors tried to induce him to remain in Europe, but he insisted on returning to his mission in India. Three years later he was arrested by a local prince and sentenced to death. In a letter to his superior he wrote,

> The only crime with which I am charged is that I teach the religion of the true God and do not worship idols. It is indeed glorious to suffer death for such a crime! That is what fills me with happiness and joy in our Lord. My guards are keeping a sharp eye on me, and I can write no more. Farewell, Fathers! I ask your blessing and commend myself to your holy sacrifices.
>
> Your Reverences' very humble servant in Jesus Christ,
> JOHN DE BRITTO

On February 4, 1693, he was presented before a large crowd and beheaded. John de Britto was canonized in 1947.

See: Donald Attwater, *Martyrs: From St. Stephen to John Tung* (New York: Sheed & Ward, 1957).

Pedro Arrupe
Jesuit Superior General (1907–1991)

"Today our prime educational objective must be to form men-for-others; men who will live not for themselves but for God and his Christ — for the God-man who lived and died for all the world; men who cannot even conceive of love of God which does not include love for the least of their neighbors; men completely convinced that love of God which does not issue in justice for men is a farce."

On May 22, 1965, Father Pedro Arrupe was elected superior general of the Society of Jesus, the first Basque to occupy this position since the founder of the Jesuits, *Ignatius of Loyola. Comparisons between the two men, however, extend beyond their common homeland. In the eighteen years of his service as superior general Arrupe oversaw a renewal of the Jesuits so profound that he is revered by many in the Society as a "second founder."

Specifically, Arrupe led the Jesuits through their landmark Thirty-Second Congregation, a meeting of representatives from all over the Jesuit world, held from December 1974 to March 1975. He was instrumental in promoting the famous "fourth decree," which defined the modern mission of the Jesuits in terms of "faith that does justice." In the words of this decree, "Our faith in Christ Jesus and our mission to proclaim the Gospel demand of us a commitment to promote justice and to enter into solidarity with the voiceless and the powerless."

Arrupe's belief that the gospel requires effective solidarity with a suffering world had roots in his early years as a priest. Before entering the Jesuits in 1927 he had studied medicine, but an experience of conversion had set him on a different course. After his ordination in 1936 he was assigned to Japan. On August 6, 1945, Arrupe was serving just four miles from the center of Hiroshima, close enough to be nearly blinded by the flash of the first atomic bomb and to feel the blast that sent the walls of the seminary crashing around him. The memory of that day and the suffering survivors whom he tended in the following weeks was present to him in each Mass he celebrated for the rest of his life.

The compassion evoked by this experience developed over time into a conviction that ministry to oppressed and suffering peoples must not remain on the personal level alone. It was necessary also to promote structural changes in the world to alleviate the sources of oppression and violence. Thus, Arrupe was a pioneer in urging the combination of pastoral concern, biblical reflection, and social analysis.

Arrupe was aware that the Jesuits would suffer consequences for this new understanding of their mission, and he urged them to be prepared for criticism and even persecution. His concern was prophetic. Within three years, five Jesuits had laid down their lives in the pursuit of justice, and the criticism was quick to follow. The Jesuits were accused of substituting politics for the gospel, and Arrupe was personally charged with leading the Society astray.

In 1981, after Arrupe suffered a disabling stroke, Pope John Paul II appointed a personal delegate to serve as interim superior of the Society. Arrupe's own choice of vicar general was passed over, a fact perceived by many in the Society as a criticism of their beloved superior general. Arrupe himself never expressed any resentment. Two years later, with the election of his successor, he tendered his official resignation. Unable to speak without difficulty, he prepared a farewell statement that was read to the assembled brethren:

> In these eighteen years, my one ideal was to serve the Lord and his church....I thank the Lord for the great progress I have witnessed in the Society. Obviously there would be defects too — my own, to begin with — but it remains a fact that there was great progress, in personal conversion, in the apostolate, in concern for the poor, for refugees. And special mention must be made of the attitudes of loyalty and filial obedience shown toward the church and the Holy Father, particularly in these last years. For all of this, thanks be to God.

Arrupe spent his final years entirely dependent on others for his daily care. Whereas he had once served God through bold and prophetic leadership, now it was through prayer and patient suffering. As always he set an example of the Ignatian discipline of "finding God in all things." He died on February 5, 1991.

See: Pedro Arrupe, *Justice with Faith Today* (St. Louis: Institute of Jesuit Sources, 1980); Joe Nangle, O.F.M., "Pedro Arrupe: The Other Basque," *Sojourners* (December 1991).

February 6
St. Paul Miki and Companions
Martyrs of Japan (d. 1597)

"My religion teaches me to pardon my enemies and all who have offended me. I do gladly pardon the emperor and all who have sought my death. I beg them to seek baptism and be Christians themselves."

Christianity arrived in Japan in 1549 with the landing of *St. Francis Xavier, one of the original band of Jesuit missionaries. By the time he left, twenty-seven months later, he had established a small but committed community of Christian converts. Subsequent Jesuit missionaries, concentrating their efforts on influential local rulers, managed within a matter of decades to swell the local church by tens of thousands. By the end of the century the number of Christians numbered as many as three hundred thousand, and Christianity was on the way to achieving a significant social presence, especially in the port city of Nagasaki. The trend, however, was soon to be reversed; indeed, as rapidly as it had spread, the Christian religion would be all but eradicated from sight.

The reasons for the persecution were complex. A major cause was the fear on the part of a succession of powerful rulers, beginning with Hideyoshi, that the missionaries were the advance agents for foreign colonialism. At the very least, these rulers feared that the inroads of foreign cultural influence would threaten their own plans to unify the country under centralized control. In 1587 Hideyoshi suddenly ordered the expulsion of all foreign missionaries on the grounds that they were preachers of a "diabolical" law. Although many did leave, the decree was not immediately enforced and discreet missionary activity by the Jesuits continued. Their style, however, clashed with the more open and aggressive evangelization carried out by Spanish Franciscans. Hideyoshi regarded these activities as a deliberate provocation. In 1597 he condemned twenty-six Christians to death. These included three Japanese Jesuits, of whom the best known was Paul Miki, a convert from a wealthy family who had achieved some renown as a popular preacher. The others were six Franciscans and seventeen Japanese laymen. On February 5, 1597, they were publicly crucified in Nagasaki. (Their feast day is February 6.)

Over the next several years, restrictions on missionary activity continued to be intermittently enforced. From 1601 to 1612 the church enjoyed relative peace. After that, all hell broke loose. Waves of savage persecution were unleashed, as all signs of the foreign mission were systematically eradicated. Thousands of ordinary Christians and dozens of priests were executed — many by the ironic means of crucifixion. Countless others suffered imprisonment. For some time priests continued to be smuggled into the country. But the repression was so thorough that they were inevitably found out and killed, a fate shared with any Japanese known to have assisted them.

As a means of ferreting out believers, the authorities devised a ritualized test. Suspected Christians, sometimes whole villages, were presented with an image of Christ or the Virgin, called an *efumi*. They were required to stamp on the image as a sign of apostasy. Faced with the penalty of death — not only for themselves but for the rest of their family — most submitted. But many others refused and paid the penalty.

Through such experience Japanese Christians acquired a distinctive spirituality. Refined in the forge of martyrdom and suffering, the church in Japan developed a fervent devotion to the crucified Savior and a commitment to the cross as a symbol of endurance and the hope of final victory. Such a spirit helped to preserve the faith in a long underground existence. For by the middle of the seventeenth century, the Christian church in Japan had disappeared, and the country itself remained closed to Westerners for the next two centuries.

Japan's isolation began to end with the arrival of Commodore Perry in Tokyo Bay in 1854. By 1860 the first foreign priest, Father Bernard Petitjean of France, was allowed to serve as a chaplain to the French community in Nagasaki. For five years he worked to build a church in Nagasaki dedicated to the original twenty-six martyrs. In 1865 a group of Japanese approached him in the church and, with trepidation, revealed their identity as Christians: "The hearts of all here are the same as yours."

Astoundingly, it turned out that a secret Christian community numbering tens of thousands had continued to pass along the faith from generation to generation, carefully remembering Latin prayers, feast days, and the ritual of baptism. They had seen no priest in two hundred years.

Thus having emerged from the catacombs, and despite intermittent persecution, the Catholic community of Nagasaki proceeded to thrive. Many churches and a magnificent cathedral arose on the sites of ancient martyrdom. But the memory of the cross remained fixed in the people's hearts. And in this light many of them tried to comprehend the terrible mystery of August 9, 1945. That day an American pilot, finding a break in the clouds over Nagasaki, used the steeple of the Urakami Cathedral as his target before releasing a plutonium-fueled atomic bomb. Seventy-nine thousand people were immediately killed. These included at least ten thousand Catholics, half the Catholic population of this traditional center of Japanese Christianity.

See: Andrew Ross, *A Vision Betrayed: The Jesuits in Japan and China 1542–1742* (Maryknoll, N.Y.: Orbis, 1994); Rachelle Linner, *City of Silence: Listening to Hiroshima* (Maryknoll, N.Y.: Orbis, 1995).

February 7
Dom Helder Camara
Archbishop of Recife (1909–1999)

"We who are charged with announcing the message of Christ need to learn the incomparable lesson that he taught us by his own example. He taught first of all with his life, and only then did he preach."

February 7 is the birthday of Dom Helder Camara who, at eighty-eight, was still alive at the time of this writing. In principle this volume features only those whose earthly pilgrimage is done. And yet it seemed unthinkable, in any list of saints and witnesses for our time, to omit the name of Dom Helder. This courageous and prophetic bishop served as one of the century's great apostles of Christian nonviolence. He embodied the church's "option for the poor" and defined through his actions the intimate relationship between love and justice.

Camara was born in 1909 in Fortaleza, Brazil, the twelfth of his parents' thirteen children. By the time he was eight he had already discerned his vocation. When he informed his father, a masonic freethinker, that he wanted to be a priest, his father told him, "Do you know what it means to be a priest? It means to belong to yourself no more. The priest belongs to God and to others." To this, young Helder brightly responded, "But that is exactly what I want to be!"

Camara was ordained in 1931. At that time the church's principal concerns were combatting communism and religious indifference. Camara joined a conservative political movement, the Integralist Party, which was inspired by Italian fascism. Their motto was "God, Country, Family." Within a few years, however, he had broken with the movement. While engaged in pastoral work in Rio de Janeiro he had become increasingly affected by the poor, the inhabitants of Rio's squalid slums, or *favelas*. In trying to relate the message of the gospel to their sufferings he would undergo a steady and radical conversion until he reached the point where he himself was labeled a communist.

Camara was named a bishop in 1952. Around the same time he was instrumental in founding the National Conference of Brazilian Bishops, the first such body of its kind in Latin America. Camara himself served as its secretary general for twelve years. Under his leadership this body became a vigorous advocate for the poor and defender of human rights. As an auxiliary bishop of Rio, Camara himself organized many social services for the poor. But he came to the conclusion that charity was not enough. What was needed was social justice. This in turn required empowering the poor to be the agents of social transformation. Thus, he began to put more emphasis on grassroots education, or "conscientization."

In 1964 Camara was named archbishop of the archdiocese of Recife and Olinda in the impoverished northeast region of Brazil. His appointment came within weeks of a brutal military coup. Immediately he stepped forward as a champion of democracy and human rights, a role that earned him the sobriquet "the red bishop." His outspoken witness for peace and social justice came many years before such positions were widely shared by his brother bishops. His message was reflected as well in a new style of episcopal leadership. Instead of a pectoral cross of gold or silver, he wore a simple wooden cross. He moved out of the bishop's palace and lived in a humble house. He encouraged the training of lay catechists and opened the seminary doors to lay people and women. His own door was always open to any who sought him, and he presented himself truly as the servant of his people.

Among those who once knocked on his door was a hired assassin. When Dom Helder answered the door and identified himself, the man was so undone by the sight of the frail and diminutive bishop that he abandoned his deadly mission: "I can't kill you," he said. "You are one of the Lord's."

It was not the only time Dom Helder was close to death. His house was sprayed with machine-gun fire. The diocesan offices were repeatedly ransacked. For thirteen years he was banned by the military government from any public speaking, and the newspapers were not even permitted to mention his name. Such persecution did not discourage him. But though his life was spared, he endured a more painful fate. That was to see his friends and colleagues — priests, catechists, and lay people — repeatedly imprisoned, tortured, or killed simply because of their association with him.

The government's fear of this single pastor seemed almost comical in light of his appearance. At just over five feet tall, and weighing no more than 120 pounds in his traditional soutane, Dom Helder hardly looked the part of a dangerous revolutionary. Yet those who underestimated his strength of will were soundly corrected.

For all his anger in the face of injustice, Dom Helder conveyed a deep spirit of interior peace and even joy. He rose every night at two to pray and recite his breviary. His day formally began with Mass at six. Thus rooted in prayer, he was able in each situation or encounter to discern the face of God. Within the body of this frail old man, there beat the ardent heart of a troubadour. Like *St. Francis, he had the habit of speaking to animals and even inanimate objects that crossed his path. Often he interrupted a conversation to wave at a flock of passing birds or even an airplane overhead. Everything he encountered received his blessing.

One of his constant themes was the importance of an "Abrahamic minority," the small community of those in each generation who keep hope alive and who are willing to risk security and comfort to seek the "promised land." From his see in Recife, Dom Helder became an inspiration to that minority, a universal bishop to the poor, a friend and pastor to all who struggled for peace and justice. When he retired as archbishop of Recife his conservative successor reversed nearly all of his initiatives. Thus, he lived on to see much of his work swept away. But in a deeper sense he left an indelible impression on the universal church. Though he died on August 27, 1999, his spirit lives on.

See: Vickie Kemper and Larry Engel, "Dom Helder Camara: Hope against Hope," in Jim Wallis and Joyce Hollyday, eds., *Cloud of Witnesses* (Maryknoll, N.Y.: Orbis, 1991); Mary Hall, *The Impossible Dream: The Spirituality of Dom Helder Camara* (Maryknoll, N.Y.: Orbis, 1980).

February 8

Martin Buber
Jewish Philosopher (1878–1965)

"God's speech to men penetrates what happens in the life of each one of us, and all that happens in the world around us, biographical and historical, and makes it for you and me into instruction, message, demand."

Martin Buber, a Jewish philosopher and theologian, was one of the great religious thinkers of the twentieth century. Among Jewish thinkers he had a particular impact on many Christians, stimulating an appreciation for the Jewish origins of Christianity. But on an even wider scale he came to embody the humanistic ideal of dialogue and understanding between peoples of different faiths and conflicting interests, thus suggesting the positive role that faith might play in promoting a more human world.

Buber was born in Vienna on February 8, 1878. When he was three his parents were divorced, and he was sent to live with his grandparents, devout Jews, on their farm in the country. Buber himself soon strayed from religious practice. At the University of Vienna he studied philosophy and literature and married a German Catholic woman (who later converted to Judaism). Nevertheless, in reacting to the anti-Semitic culture of central Europe Buber was attracted to the early Zionist movement. It was thus that he began to explore and rediscover his religious roots. In 1904 he took a leave from his teaching position and other responsibilities to undertake a serious study of Hasidism. This period of withdrawal lasted five years and marked the great turning point in his life.

Hasidism, a movement of Jewish renewal initiated by the *Baal Shem Tov in Eastern Europe in the eighteenth century, emphasized the awareness and celebration of holiness in everyday life. As Buber summarized its essential message: "God is to be seen in every thing, and reached by every pure deed." Buber did not personally embrace the Hasidic life. But he believed that Hasidism reflected an essential dimension of Judaism. At the same time, he believed it presented a vital religious message for the modern world, precisely because it represented a "worldly holiness," an attention to those sparks of the divine that lay hidden within the challenges and responsibilities of the present moment. He wrote, "The task of each man is to affirm for God's sake the world and himself, and by this very means to transform them both."

In 1909 Buber returned to teaching and at the same time undertook his lifelong project of collecting and popularizing the legends and orally transmitted stories of the Hasidim. Through his friendship with the German anarchist *Gustav Landauer, he further developed his commitment to communitarian socialism as the social expression of his religious convictions. When Landauer was murdered during the Bavarian Revolution in 1919, it was for Buber a shattering blow that foreshadowed a season of even greater violence to come.

In 1923 Buber assumed a chair in Jewish religious history at the University of Frankfurt. That year he also published his most influential book, *I and Thou*. Its central theme was the relational nature of human existence, the fact that human beings are ultimately constituted as subjects by the quality of their relationship to others — whether nature, other people, or the Eternal Thou. Thus, our own humanity, according to Buber, is diminished to the extent that we encounter others as objects rather than other subjects. As popularized by countless interpreters, this work achieved almost instant recognition as a modern "classic." It was in many ways his most personal book, outlining the spirit that underlay his own commitment to the "life of dialogue."

With the Nazi rise to power in 1933 Buber was dismissed from his job. In the coming years he engaged in a courageous struggle to defend Jewish rights and culture. But by 1938 he had been effectively silenced. With luck he managed to escape Germany to accept a chair at the Hebrew University in Jerusalem. Though he was sixty at the time, he still had another quarter century of his most productive work ahead of him.

In settling in Palestine Buber had fulfilled the Zionist ideal of his youth. Yet he expressed severe disagreements with much of the Zionist leadership. He believed it was a mistake to define the Zionist goal simply in terms of establishing a Jewish state. He bitterly opposed "the disease of nationalism" and instead promoted what he termed a "Hebrew Humanism." On the basis of their common love for the land, he believed that a just and cooperative arrangement could be worked out between Jews and Palestinian Arabs. Instead, the war that accompanied the establishment of Israel in 1948 came as a bitter fulfillment of his worst fears.

Among modern Jewish religious thinkers, none had so great an impact on Christian theology as Martin Buber. This reflected not only the influence of *I and Thou*, but also the impact of his biblical reflections and his popularization of Jewish spirituality and mysticism. Buber himself wrote extensively on Jesus and Christianity. While of course rejecting Christian claims for the divinity of Christ, he extended affectionate recognition to the Jewishness of Jesus. Jesus, he believed, had exemplified the highest ethical and spiritual ideals of Judaism.

Ultimately, he believed there were matters of irreconcilable difference between the beliefs of Jews and Christians. But he remained a tireless believer in the virtue of dialogue. "Whenever we both, Christian and Jew, care more for God Himself than for our images of God, we are united in the feeling that our Father's house is differently constructed than our human models take it to be."

Buber died in Jerusalem on June 13, 1965, at the age of eighty-seven.

See: Martin Buber, *The Way of Response*, ed. Nahum N. Glatzer (New York: Schocken, 1966); Stephen M. Panko, *Martin Buber* (Waco, Tex.: Word, 1976).

February 9

St. Caedmon
Poet (d. 680)

"My children, I am in charity with all the servants of God."

Caedmon, the first poet of record in the English language, was a monk of the abbey of Whitby in Northumbria. His story appears in the history of *Bede, who lived in the nearby monastery at Jarrow and wrote a mere fifty years after Caedmon's death.

According to Bede, Caedmon was an unlettered cowherd who had no training or natural gift for verse. He was embarrassed at feasts when his fellows would entertain one another by passing the harp and stepping forward to sing. On these occasions Caedmon liked to sneak outdoors and seek refuge among the cows.

On one such occasion he was sleeping soundly when, in a dream, he saw a man standing beside him who called him by name and bid him, "Caedmon, sing me a song." When he demurred, the voice persisted: "But you *shall* sing to me." When Caedmon asked what he should sing, he was told, "Sing about the Creation of all things."

"Immediately," in the English language, "Caedmon began to sing verses in praise of God the Creator." Bede renders a stanza in Latin, the only form, ironically, in which Caedmon's verse survives:

Now must we praise the Maker of the heavenly kingdom,
the might of God and the thought of his mind,
the glorious Father of men,
How he, the Lord everlasting, wrought the beginning of all wonders.
He, the holy Creator, first fashioned
the heavens as a roof for the children of earth;

then this middle-earth the Master of mankind,
the Lord eternal, afterwards adorned,
the earth for men, the Ruler almighty.

Upon awakening, Caedmon remembered these lines and found that he was able to continue the poem. His newfound eloquence astonished his friends who, suspecting divine intervention, brought Caedmon to see the holy *Hilda, abbess of Whitby. She presented him with several texts from Scripture and asked him to render these passages in verse. With this request he readily complied. This was enough to convince the abbess and other witnesses that Caedmon's poetic skills were a gift of grace. She advised him to give up his life as a herdsman and to devote himself to the service of God. And so he became a monk of Whitby.

Caedmon's vocation as a monk progressed in tandem with his growth as a poet. As he was instructed in Christian doctrine he responded with such melodious verse that "his instructors became his audience." As Bede writes, Caedmon sang "of the creation of the world, the origin of the human race, and the whole story of Genesis. He sang of Israel's departure from Egypt, their entry into the land of promise, and many other events of scriptural history. He sang of the Lord's Incarnation, Passion, Resurrection, and Ascension into heaven." He also composed poems on the terrors of hell and joys of heaven, "by which he sought to turn his hearers from delight in wickedness and to inspire them to love and do good."

As Bede notes, "Caedmon was a deeply religious man, who humbly submitted to regular discipline, and firmly resisted all who tried to do evil, thus winning a happy death." He died peacefully in his monastery bed, surrounded by his brothers. "His tongue, which had sung so many noble verses in praise of his Maker, uttered its last words in His praise as he signed himself with the Cross and commended his soul into His hands."

It is significant that Bede, who devotes most of his attention to the lives of kings and bishops, shows such interest in the story of this simple poet-monk. But for him, the miracle that allowed a simple herdsman to translate sacred history into his native language is on a par with the acts of the great missionary bishops. In Caedmon the English tongue was truly baptized. In returning praise to their Creator, a new people in a new language found the true reason for which they were created. The feast of St. Caedmon is observed on February 11.

See Bede, *A History of the English Church and People,* trans. Leo Sherley-Price (Baltimore: Penguin, 1955).

St. Scholastica
Nun (d. 543)

"I asked my Lord, and He listened to me."

This holy woman was the twin sister of *St. Benedict, founder of Western monasticism. Our knowledge of her story depends on two chapters in the famous life of Benedict by *St. Gregory the Great. There we learn that she entered religious life at an early age and apparently rose to the office of abbess in a convent near her brother's monastery at Monte Cassino. Gregory's account of Scholastica is largely given over to a story of her last days. It illustrates the affectionate and yet somewhat competitive relationship between the siblings. More importantly, it provides a monastic parable about the power and virtue of love versus a rigid devotion to rules.

It seems that Benedict and Scholastica had a custom of meeting once a year in a house somewhere between their respective monasteries. There they would spend the whole day "praising God and talking of spiritual matters." One year they met as usual. But when, as dusk began to fall, Benedict made preparations to leave, his sister begged him to spend the night that they might "talk until morning about the joys of life in heaven." Benedict refused, citing the rules of his monastery from which it was "impossible" to deviate. To this answer Scholastica responded by simply lowering her head in prayer. Immediately the heavens erupted in thunder and released such a flood of rain that travel was obviously impossible. "May almighty God spare you, sister," Benedict cried in alarm. "What have you done?" Scholastica answered simply, "I asked you, but you were unwilling to listen to me. I asked my Lord and He listened to me."

And so Scholastica had her desire: "They spent the whole night awake, and had their fill of talk about spiritual matters." St. Gregory comments thus on Scholastica's victory over her brother in this case: "As John says, 'God is love,' and she justly overcame him by the greater strength of her love."

It was to be their last meeting. Three days later, as Benedict stood in his cell, he had a vision of his sister's soul leaving her body and rising to heaven in the form of a dove. Without delay he dispatched several monks to retrieve her body. They found her dead, just as Benedict had foreseen. Her body was carried to the monastery and placed in a tomb which Benedict had prepared for himself. There, in time, he joined her.

See: Gregory the Great, *Dialogues, Book II: Saint Benedict,* Myra Uhlfelder, trans. (Indianapolis: Bobbs-Merrill Educational Publishing, 1967).

A. J. Muste
Peacemaker (1885–1967)

"The way of peace is really a seamless garment that must cover the whole of life and must be applied in all its relationships."

A. J. Muste was arguably the outstanding American exponent of Christian nonviolence in the twentieth century. In season and out, in a career that spanned resistance to both World War I and Vietnam, he stood upon his conscience and his convictions. An indefatigable activist into his eighties, he was esteemed by a generation otherwise distrustful of anyone over thirty. At the same time, his civility and integrity won respect even from members of the establishment he opposed.

Abraham Johannes Muste was born in Holland on January 8, 1885, immigrating to America with his family at the age of six. Though trained as a minister in the Dutch Reformed church, he migrated through a number of denominations during the course of his long career. He was expelled from his first congregation when he proclaimed himself a pacifist in opposition to World War I. For years afterward he eschewed the institutional church altogether, working instead in the radical labor movement. For over a decade he was a dedicated Marxist-Leninist. By 1936, however, he had become disillusioned with sectarian politics, convinced that the Sermon on the Mount contained the most truly radical program for social transformation. With this insight he returned both to active church ministry and to the organized pacifist movement. As he wrote, "Pacifism — life — is built upon a central truth and the experience of that truth.... That truth is: God is love, love is of God. Love is the central thing in the universe."

In 1940 he became executive secretary of the Fellowship of Reconciliation, the leading religious pacifist organization. He occupied this position for thirteen years. These were not especially receptive years for the FOR's message. Nevertheless, the advent of the era of total war confirmed Muste's belief that the principles of the gospel were not simply a utopian ideal but a practical imperative: "Mankind has to find a way into a radically new world. Mankind has to become 'a new humanity' or perish."

Muste became a particularly eloquent opponent of the Cold War and a critic of those theologians who, in the name of "realism," justified the resort to nuclear threats and the encroaching militarization of American culture. In an essay counseling young men to resist conscription, he wrote,

> Nonconformity, Holy Disobedience, becomes a virtue, indeed a necessary and indispensable measure of spiritual self-preservation, in a day when the impulse to conform, to acquiesce, to go along is used as an instrument to subject men to totalitarian rule and involve them in permanent war. To create the impression of at least outward

unanimity, the impression that there is no "real" opposition is something for which all dictators and military leaders strive. The more it seems that there is no opposition, the less worthwhile it seems to an ever larger number of people to cherish even the thought of opposition.

In the era of bomb shelters and civil defense drills, it seemed to Muste that the world was entering a new Dark Age in which the responsibility of the Christian was to nourish small oases of sanity and conscience amid the encircling gloom. When asked by a reporter what good it did for him to maintain a vigil outside a nuclear weapons base, Muste replied, "I don't do this to change the world. I do it to keep the world from changing me."

When he retired from his position at the FOR at the age of sixty-eight, Muste might well have rested from his considerable labors. Instead, the following years were marked by his most courageous activism. He was repeatedly arrested for protests at nuclear weapons sites. In the 1960s he was a key architect of the broad antiwar coalition that emerged in response to the Vietnam War. In 1966, then eighty-one, he was arrested in Saigon after attempting to demonstrate in front of the U.S. embassy. He died the following year on February 11, 1967, weeks after returning from a trip to North Vietnam to witness firsthand the effects of American bombing.

In the annals of Christian radicalism there are few to rival Muste for sheer endurance. Long past the age when most activists grow weary with frustration, Muste displayed a vitality that was not fed by the need for tangible results. As he wrote, "Joy and growth come from following our deepest impulses, however foolish they may seem to some, or dangerous, and even though the apparent outcome may be defeat." His belief in the identity of means and ends encouraged his persistent witness in the face of all discouragement and implacable odds. As he noted in his most oft-quoted line, "There is no way to peace, peace itself being the way."

See: Danny Collum et al., "A. J. Muste: Pilgrim for Peace through a Century of Wars," *Sojourners* (December 1984); Nat Hentoff, ed., *The Essays of A. J. Muste* (New York: Simon and Schuster, 1967).

February 12

C. F. Andrews
"Christ's Faithful Apostle" (1871–1940)

"Christ seeks from us deeds not words. Devotion to him is in the first place not sentimental but practical.... If [the Christian faith] has no power to restore or recreate the human will leading one to deeds of unselfish service, then it stands self-condemned."

In his many years of service to India, the Englishman C. F. Andrews earned many honorific titles. He was called Deenabandhu — the "Friend of the Poor." To his friend *Mohandas Gandhi, who otherwise simply called him "Charlie," he was Brother of the Humble. But perhaps the most apposite title was suggested by the initials of his name: C. F. A. Much to his embarrassment, he was stuck with the title "Christ's Faithful Apostle."

Andrews was born on February 12, 1871, in Birmingham, England. His father was a minister in the minuscule Catholic Apostolic church. While at Cambridge, however, he converted to the Anglican church and was ultimately ordained a priest. From the moment of his conversion Andrews's faith was infused with a commitment to service. For years he combined teaching at Cambridge with ministry among "the most neglected of London's poor." This call to service eventually inspired him to volunteer for a teaching position at St. Stephen's College in India. His arrival there in 1904 marked the great turning point in his life.

Andrews felt an immediate bond with the people of India. So deeply did he respond to their culture and aspirations that he quickly identified with the emerging struggle for independence. In 1912 he met the Bengali poet Rabindranath Tagore, whose ashram, Shantinaketan, would become his principal home. Another important association came two years later when he traveled to South Africa to support the civil rights struggle being waged by an as yet obscure Indian lawyer named Mohandas Gandhi. The intimate rapport between Gandhi and Andrews was immediate, and it lasted until the latter's death. As Gandhi said, "We simply met as brothers and remained as such to the end. . . . It was an unbreakable bond between two seekers and servants."

Andrews was one of the first Westerners fully to recognize Gandhi's greatness as a spiritual leader and the universal significance of his experiments in nonviolence. To Andrews, the Hindu Gandhi embodied the spirit of Christian love in a way that put other Christians to shame. Gandhi in turn recognized in Andrews a kindred spirit who exemplified the most authentic type of Christian missionary. This meant that Andrews's mission was not focused on proselytizing or winning converts but instead on bearing witness to the gospel through deeds. Later, when Gandhi was asked what he desired of Christian missionaries, he would simply answer, "Copy Charlie Andrews."

Andrews returned with Gandhi to India, and he remained at his side during many of the most critical hours of the independence struggle. It was Andrews who nursed Gandhi during his famous "fasts unto death." Inevitably his deep engagement in the freedom struggle caused him some tension with the Church of England. His experience in South Africa had made him acutely sensitive to the scandal of racial division — a reality, unfortunately, even in the Christian church. At the same time Andrews began to feel that his identity as a priest tended to separate him from the rest of humanity. Consequently he notified his bishop that he wished to resign from active ministry. At the same time he renounced any interest in his family's property or any other income, and so embraced a life of voluntary poverty. He was convinced that "the true ministry for which I was fitted and prepared by God was prophetic rather than priestly."

Though he had grown to accept a more universal perspective on the presence of truth in all religions, Andrews remained rooted in a personal commitment to Christ, and he continued to be a communicant in the Anglican church. In his appreciation for the religions of the East he found that, for himself, "Christ has become not less central but more central and universal; not less divine to me but more so, because more universally human. I can see him as the pattern of all that is best in Asia as well as in Europe." If he recognized Christ in the best of other religions, he especially recognized Christ in the poor. In India, he said, "it is as if I saw Christ in the faces of those I met."

In service to the poor of India, Andrews spent many years in Fiji, the South Pacific, and other parts of colonial Africa, wherever there were Indian indentured workers. He was instrumental in the eventual abolition of this system throughout the British empire.

Andrews died in India on April 4, 1940. Among his many published books, he left behind a completed manuscript on the Sermon on the Mount, a text which expresses the spirit of joy that was one of Andrews's most striking characteristics: "My strong conviction is this, that what is needed most of all in our modern world is the recovery of that first radiance and joy of the Way of Life, whereby the earliest disciples were able recklessly and gladly and with singleness of heart to give up everything for Christ's sake in order to bring in His Kingdom."

His death was mourned throughout India.

See: C. F. Andrews, *The Sermon on the Mount* (New York: Collier, 1962); Nicol MacNicol, "C. F. Andrews," in Donald Attwater, ed., *Modern Christian Revolutionaries* (New York: Devin-Adair, 1947).

February 13

Georges Rouault
Artist (1871–1958)

"My only ambition is to be able one day to paint Christ so movingly that those who see Him will be converted."

The French painter Georges Rouault exemplifies the difference between a religious artist and a painter of religious subjects. Many of his paintings did depict the life and suffering of Christ. But his artistic vision was so infused with spiritual depth that he was able, even through such seemingly secular subjects as prostitutes, clowns, and judges, to impart a sense of the sacred and of the religious dimension of human existence.

Rouault was born in Paris on May 27, 1871. His career as an artist began with an apprenticeship in a studio of stained glass restoration. Later this experience would influence his painting style, which is easily recognized by the use of color and the distinctive black outlines surrounding his figures. In the 1890s he studied at the École des Beaux-Arts, where his fellow students included Henri Matisse. Rouault was recognized as an accomplished and promising student. But for all his skills, he came to believe there was something lacking. As he later wrote, "I knew nothing of suffering."

This insight preceded a dramatic change in both his artistic and religious perspectives. At the age of thirty, he wrote, "I was seized with a sort of madness, or of grace, depending on one's perspective. The face of the world changed for me. I saw everything that I had seen before but in a different form and with a different harmony." Artistically, his discovery of Cézanne liberated him from realism, freeing him to express a more personal vision through the bold use of color. But the personal vision itself was informed by his discovery of Christ.

The first decades of the twentieth century were a time of great conversions in France. A veritable renaissance in religious literature and intellectual life was associated with such figures as Charles Péguy, *Georges Bernanos, *François Mauriac, *Jacques and Raïssa Maritain, and *Léon Bloy. Rouault was to give visual expression to this disparate movement. The Maritains were particularly close friends. But the greatest influence was the novelist Léon Bloy, whom he met in 1904. Bloy was the declared enemy of bourgeois religion. He despised the hypocrisy and moral mediocrity of the rich while celebrating the presence of Christ among the poor, the suffering, and sinners.

Rouault tried to communicate a similar message through his paintings. Aside from those with an explicitly religious theme, Rouault was endlessly fascinated with three settings: the brothel, the circus, and the courtroom. Each offered an opportunity to reflect on the themes of sin, hypocrisy, judgment, and thus, in the pathos of the human condition, to suggest a symbolic link with the passion of Christ. "All of my work is religious," he said, "for those who know how to look at it."

But not all knew how to look at it nor did they appreciate what they saw. Léon Bloy himself despised Rouault's work. In a scathing letter to the artist he charged, "You are attracted solely by what is ugly; you appear to have a sort of vertigo of hideousness. . . . If you were a man who prayed, a religious man, a communicant, you could not paint those horrible pictures. It is time for you to stop."

He did not stop, nor could he. Painting for Rouault was in fact a form of prayer, a spiritual dialogue that he maintained for his own sake and for God, and not, ultimately, for the sake of any public audience. Nevertheless in 1948 he shared with the public his most personal work, the fruit of twenty years of labor. Entitled *Miserere,* it is a series of fifty-eight engravings based on the passion and death of Christ. Through scenes like the *Ecce Homo,* and the mocking of the crowd, Rouault stresses the humanity of Jesus in contrast to the shocking inhumanity of his persecutors. So great is the emotional power of this work that it must be reckoned not only an important artistic achievement but as one of the great christological statements of the century.

Nevertheless recognition by the church of Rouault's importance as a religious artist was slow to arrive. Just as he stood apart from the secularized culture of the contemporary art world, so his dark and rough-hewn style of painting had little to do with the saccharine aesthetic then dominating the taste in French religious art. Only toward the very end of his life did Rouault receive one church commission for three stained-glass windows in Assy, France. He refused any payment for this work.

In 1953, at the age of eighty-two, he was named a papal knight by Pope Pius XII. He died five years later, on February 13, 1958.

See: Robert Michael McAuley, "The Faith of Georges Rouault in Jesus Christ as Seen through His Life and His Art," M.S.T. thesis, Yale Divinity School, 1986.

February 14

St. Valentine
Martyr (d. 269)

> *"Greater love hath no man than that he lay down his life*
> *for his friends."*   —John 15:13

The association of St. Valentine with pink hearts, boxes of chocolates, and the exchange of romantic fancies has no intrinsic source in the character or life of the saint. The origin of "St. Valentine's Day" — a day beloved of greeting card companies — is not entirely clear, but it seems to have taken root in England, a cold country where the signs of spring are eagerly anticipated. As far back as Chaucer it was commonly observed that birds began to pair and mate around the feast of St. Valentine, that is, from the middle of February.

In any case, the Valentine whose name is oddly commemorated was apparently a Christian priest in Rome who assisted martyrs during the persecution under Emperor Claudius II. He was eventually arrested and sent before the prefect of Rome. When he refused to renounce his faith he was beaten and beheaded.

Thus, by offering his heart, he proved himself a true devotee of the God of Love.

February 15

Ben Salmon
Catholic Pacifist (1889–1932)

> *"If Christians would have the same faith in their God that non-Christians*
> *have in a mere materialistic idea, 'Thy Kingdom come' would shortly be a*
> *reality in this world of sorrow and travail."*

In 1917 President Woodrow Wilson led America into the Great War in Europe. For many who had voted for Wilson precisely on the basis of his promise to keep America out of the war, this came as a surprise. Nevertheless, most citizens accepted the president's vow "to make the world safe for democracy," and so rallied to the cause with patriotic fervor. Most, but not all. There were Socialists and other radicals who claimed that this was not a "war to end all wars," but a capitalist war. There were isolationists, who believed that if foreigners wanted to kill each other that was no concern of Americans. And then there were pacifists, who believed that all killing, whatever the cause, was to be opposed. Ben Salmon was one of the pacifists, one of several hundred who refused even to accept noncombatant status in the military, and so endured brutal imprisonment. But in one important respect Salmon was different from the others — different from virtually every other man in America. He based his pacifism on his Roman Catholic faith.

Salmon was born to a working-class Catholic family in Denver in 1889. Growing up in an era of bitter labor struggles in Colorado, he quickly acquired a keen commitment to social justice. As a young man he became known in Denver as something of a rebel, active in union organizing and other agitation. But despite his radical social views, he remained a devout Catholic who often attended Mass and who took pride in his membership in the Knights of Columbus. In 1917 he married his longtime sweetheart. By this point, however, the war had been declared, and Salmon received notification to report for military service.

Salmon applied for recognition as a conscientious objector on the basis of his religious convictions. The government made provision for conscientious objectors belonging to historic "peace churches" like the Quakers or Mennonites. But Roman Catholics, whose church supposedly disavowed pacifism in favor of the traditional "just war theory," were not recognized as candidates for C.O. status. In any case even recognized C.O.'s were required to accept "noncombatant status," an option that Salmon definitely rejected. He believed that any cooperation with the military system would represent a violation of his conscience, a compromise with Satan. And so he was arrested in January 1918.

Salmon was given a military court martial and sentenced to death, a sentence subsequently reduced to twenty-five years in prison. He was incarcerated in Leavenworth and a series of federal penitentiaries, much of his time spent in solitary confinement as a punishment for his refusal to perform prison labor. For six months he was kept in a windowless, vermin-infested cell above the prison sewer. In that hot and fetid air he was allowed no visitors or mail and fed nothing but bread and water. Within months of his imprisonment the war in Europe ended. And still his confinement continued. Finally after two years in prison Salmon announced that he would no longer cooperate with the system and began an indefinite hunger strike. After several weeks, the authorities forced milk down his throat. They kept this up for months, while meantime he grew steadily weaker. Claiming his fast was a symptom of mental illness, the authorities transferred Salmon to St. Elizabeth's Hospital for the Insane in Washington, D.C. Finally, when it was clear that they could not indefinitely keep him alive on a diet of milk, they released him from prison in 1920.

Salmon was one of hundreds of resisters imprisoned during the war. But he was one of only four Catholics. Of these, he was alone in attributing his resistance to his Catholic faith. It was a solitary stand that evoked nothing but incomprehension if not the open contempt of his fellow citizens. His hometown newspaper called him "the slacker, the pacifist, the man with a yellow streak down his spine as broad as a country highway,...who loves the German flag more than the Stars and Stripes." When he began his hunger strike the headline read, "Slacker starves himself in cell: Denver's 'yellowist draft dodger' plans to cheat justice." He fared little better among his fellow Catholics. Prison chaplains tried to convince him that he was setting himself up in opposition to the pope, that his duty as a Christian was to defend his country, to obey the law, and to support his family. Some priests refused to offer him the sacraments, accusing him of heresy for his uncompromising pacifism.

Although his pacifism contradicted the wisdom of most Catholic moral theologians, Salmon was able to mount a spirited defense of his witness and beliefs. Armed with nothing but the Bible and the *Catholic Encyclopedia* and weakened by his hunger strike, Salmon managed to write a two-hundred-page manuscript critiquing the church's just war teaching and justifying his commitment to nonviolence. Under any circumstances it was a remarkable achievement for a man with no formal education beyond the eighth grade. Nevertheless, in this work Salmon was the first American Catholic to mount a systematic critique of just war teaching.

Salmon argued that in the modern era it was no longer sensible to imagine a war that could satisfy all the criteria of the just war. In any case, this tradition was impossible to square with the clear teaching of Jesus with regard to the love of enemies. "The justice of man cannot dethrone the justice of God," he wrote. "There is no such animal as a 'just war.'" In enduring his imprisonment, Salmon identified with the early Christian martyrs who offered the witness of their lives to oppose the idolatry of the Roman empire. The name of the new idolatry was militarism.

Upon his release Salmon led a relatively quiet life with his family. Nevertheless, his prison ordeal had permanently affected his health, contributing to his early death at the age of forty-three on February 15, 1932. He remained a devout Catholic to the end of his life. Of his three children, one became a priest and another a Maryknoll Sister.

See: Torin R. T. Finney, *Unsung Hero of the Great War* (New York: Paulist, 1989).

February 16

Janani Luwum
Anglican Archbishop of Uganda, Martyr (1924–1977)

*"Even if I have to die for my convictions,
I can never lower the standards God has set me."*

Uganda was the site of the heroic martyrdom of a number of Christian youths in 1886. Charles Lwanga and his companions, some of them young boys, were cruelly murdered by a wicked ruler for refusing to deny their faith. These celebrated Martyrs of Uganda were canonized in 1964. But the era of martyrdom in Uganda was not then complete. Uganda had yet to experience the notorious reign of General Idi Amin.

In the 1970s, after seizing power from an elected government, Amin introduced a reign of terror, dispatching critics and potential enemies with astonishing cruelty. Estimates of the number of his victims range conservatively in the tens of thousands. Amin was famous for his paranoid wrath, and there were few who dared to provoke him.

Janani Luwum was the Anglican primate of Uganda. He was, by all accounts, a fairly traditional prelate, not by temperament suited to the role of prophet. He had drawn criticism from some members of his church for his efforts to maintain friendly relations with the dictator. Biting his tongue, the archbishop would frequently say, "We are with you, your Excellency, with all that you do that is good." As Luwum saw it, his job was to steer clear of "politics" and look after the welfare of his church.

By 1977 Luwum could no longer pretend that such a neutral course was possible. Amin himself would not permit it. He began to circulate rumors that the bishops were plotting violence against him. Luwum responded in angry denial and with a demand for proof. In early February, government troops surrounded his residence and searched for "incriminating evidence," while holding the archbishop himself at gunpoint. The bishops responded with their most outspoken denunciation of conditions in the country. If this was how the archbishop was treated, there was clearly no protection for anyone else.

On February 16 the Anglican bishops and other religious leaders were summoned to the presidential palace where Amin unveiled a cache of weapons, supposedly confiscated from the archbishop and his confederates. The charges were clearly absurd, but there was no doubting the likely consequences of this charade. Eventually the bishops were dismissed, all except for Luwum. He was told that the president wanted to speak to him personally. Luwum was never again seen alive.

Early the next morning it was announced that the archbishop had died in a tragic car accident. The government refused to release the body. Later the story was revised: the archbishop had been shot while trying to overcome the soldiers transporting him to detention. Only after some weeks was the bullet-riddled body of Luwum quietly released to his family. According to the later testimony of witnesses, Luwum was shot by Amin himself, after he had refused to sign a confession. Instead, realizing that his hour was at hand, Luwum had proceeded to pray. This, it is said, had provoked Amin to a rage, and he had drawn his pistol and shot him in the mouth.

Before the release of the body and in defiance of government orders, a funeral service for the archbishop was conducted in his cathedral. Standing over an empty grave, Luwum's predecessor, Archbishop Erica Sabiti, repeated the message of the angels on Easter Sunday: "He is not here.... He is risen."

See: Diana Dewar, *All for Christ* (Oxford: Oxford University Press, 1980).

Giordano Bruno
Cosmologist and Martyr (1548–1600)

"The wise soul fears not death; rather she sometimes strives for death, so goes beyond to meet her. Yet eternity maintains her substance throughout time, immensity throughout space, universal form throughout motion."

Giordano Bruno was one of the first human beings to intuit and thus consciously occupy the universe in its full immensity. Thus, he seemed to his contemporaries to be like an alien from a different world. And so they killed him.

Bruno was born in the town of Nola, near Naples, Italy. He entered the Dominican order at the age of seventeen and proceeded through the usual course of studies and preparation for final vows. In the Dominicans he received an eclectic education in the classics, philosophy, and theology, the subject in which he eventually earned a doctorate. He acquired a reputation as a brilliant scholar, widely envied for his extraordinary powers of memory. But he was also reputed to be something of an iconoclast, attracted to suspect philosophical and scientific speculations, and insufficiently deferential to authority. After eleven years he found the mental constraints of the monastery too oppressive. So he put off his religious habit and became an itinerant scholar.

In the next years Bruno traveled widely and published extensively on such themes as logic, the science of memory, mathematics, and philosophy. He lectured in England, Paris, and other parts of the Continent. His most controversial work was in the area of cosmology. It was only a few years since Copernicus had published his work challenging the ancient view of the earth as the center of the universe. Bruno believed that Copernicus had not developed the full cosmological implications of this insight. He postulated the idea of an infinite universe with an infinity of worlds, many of them, perhaps, populated with creatures as intelligent as ourselves. He suggested furthermore that in the future human beings might develop means of traveling through space and visiting these other worlds. Such opinions generated a good deal of ridicule. But there were church authorities who took Bruno's views much more seriously.

In 1592 while visiting in Venice, Bruno was denounced as a heretic before the local Inquisition. He found himself under arrest. No doubt he hoped the matter would be quickly resolved; he had, after all, never engaged in theological controversy. Instead, he entered into a Kafkaesque ordeal of endlessly repeated interrogations that lasted for eight years. During this time he was eventually consigned to the Inquisition in Rome, and so spent much of this period confined to a dank dungeon. A series of alleged heretical propositions was drawn from Bruno's writings. He persistently denied the meaning attached to these sentences, taken out of context from his work. The charge that most seriously outraged the court was his idea of an infinite universe.

On February 8, 1600, Bruno was declared to be "an impenitent and pertinacious heretic and therefore to have incurred all the ecclesiastical censures and pains of the Holy Canon, the laws and the constitutions, both general and particular, imposed on such confessed impertinent pertinacious and obstinate heretics." His books and papers were publicly burned in the square of St. Peter. And he was then turned over to the "secular arm" for punishment. Before his execution Bruno addressed his judges: "Perchance you who pronounce my sentence are in greater fear than I who receive it." On February 17, he was publicly burned before a cheering mob.

In later centuries Bruno was acclaimed as a champion of intellectual freedom against the forces of intolerance. In a deliberate snub to the Vatican, the republican government of Rome erected a statue in his honor in the square where he was burned. Bruno did not regard himself as a "free thinker," but as a devout Christian who believed there was no disrespect to the Creator in trying to fathom the infinite mysteries of creation.

See: Dorothea Waley Singer, *Bruno: His Life and Thought* (New York: Henry Schuman, 1950).

February 18

Bd. Fra Angelico
Dominican Artist (1395?–1455)

"He often commented that ... the man who occupies himself
with the things of Christ should live with Christ."   —Vasari

Fra Angelico, born Guido di Piero sometime between 1395 and 1400, was a Dominican friar and artist who lived in the community of San Domenico da Fiesole near Florence. His religious name was Fra Giovanni, but he became better known to his brothers as Fra Angelico — a tribute both to his angelic piety and to his artistic talents. He occupied a number of offices within his community but otherwise declined any higher ecclesiastical calling, feeling that complete dedication to painting was the true expression of his religious vocation.

Fra Angelico was one of the great early precursors of the Florentine Renaissance. His frescos and paintings featured vivid color, startlingly lifelike portraits, an ingenious use of perspective, and realistic backgrounds. But for all their stunning beauty and technical virtuosity, the artist's primary end was not the aesthetic but the religious impact of his work. What makes his paintings religious is not the subject matter but their intended purpose in exciting the viewer to feelings of religious devotion.

The frescos that Fra Angelico painted in the Florentine monastery of San Marco are among his most famous. They include scenes from the lives of Mary and Christ. Nearly all of them include Dominican saints — dressed identically to the friars who would be viewing the paintings. The message was plain. The viewer was to place himself imaginatively in the scene before him and identify with the attitude of devotion as displayed in the painting itself.

In one picture of the crucifixion *St. Dominic himself kneels at the foot of the cross, his eyes fixed in grief-stricken adoration of the Holy Wounds. Likewise, in a painting of the heavenly Coronation of the Virgin, the scene is embraced by a cloud of holy witnesses, all kneeling with arms raised in an attitude of prayer. In a particularly haunting depiction of the mocking of Christ, the blindfolded Savior is beset by a swarm of disembodied hands, while in the foreground sit the Blessed Mother, lost in private meditation, and St. Dominic, contemplating an open book in his lap.

In these paintings the distances of time and place are collapsed. The figures are dressed in contemporary clothes and set against backgrounds familiar to the time. For Fra Angelico the religious life was a life lived in the presence of Christ and emotionally engaged in the ongoing drama of redemption. It was this mystical vision that was communicated in his paintings with such angelic purity.

Fra Angelico was beatified in 1982 by Pope John Paul II, who also named him patron of artists.

See: Jacqueline and Maurice Guillaud, *Fra Angelico: The Light of the Soul* (New York: Clarkson N. Potter, 1986); Giorgio Vasari, *Lives of the Artists* (Baltimore: Penguin, 1965).

February 19

Hagar the Egyptian
Slave Woman

"Thou art a God of seeing."

In the biblical narrative in Genesis, Hagar was an Egyptian slave who belonged to Sarah, the wife of Abraham. When Sarah was unable to provide Abraham with a child, she proposed that her husband beget a child with her slave. It was a solution permitted under the law. Presumably Hagar had no choice in the matter. So she served as a surrogate mother for her mistress. But by the time she was pregnant Sarah apparently regretted the arrangement. Sarah treated her so harshly that she tried to flee. But an angel of Yahweh appeared to her and urged her to return and bear her child. She was promised, like Abraham, descendants so numerous that "they cannot be numbered for multitude." And she was told that she should name her child Ishmael, which means "God hears." Hagar in wonder named the source of this annunciation: "Thou art a God of seeing.... Have I really seen God and remained alive after seeing him?"

Ishmael, the son of Hagar and Abraham, was duly born. But after many years another child of God's promise was born to Sarah and Abraham. Sarah was now displeased at the thought that her son, Isaac, should be an equal heir with the son of her bondswoman. At her insistence Abraham sent Hagar and her son alone into the wilderness — a shocking deed, even if mitigated, in the text, by God's assurance that no harm would come to them.

Hagar and Ishmael wandered in the desert heat until their water supply was finished. Then Hagar put the boy under a bush and wandered off alone, unable to bear the sight of her child's death. But God heard the tears of Ishmael and comforted Hagar, assuring her that her son would be the father of a great nation. "Then God opened her eyes, and she saw a well of water; and she went and filled the skin with water, and gave the lad a drink."

Though Hagar is not the main protagonist in the story of Abraham and Sarah, she plays an important role in the characterization of God. Though she is an outsider, a foreigner, a woman of no account, a discarded slave in the wilderness, it is yet she who "sees" God and names him in turn as the God who sees. Her experience discloses furthermore that Yahweh is a God of life and liberation who hears the voice of the oppressed. Thus, her deliverance in the desert prefigures the later deliverance of Abraham's descendants from slavery in Egypt. Hagar is a witness to the power of God who "makes a way out of no way."

See: Genesis 16:1–15, 21:1–21; Delores S. Williams, *Sisters in the Wilderness: The Challenge of Womanist God-Talk* (Maryknoll, N.Y.: Orbis, 1993).

February 20

Cardinal Henri de Lubac
Theologian (1896–1991)

"The finest and boldest Christian effort, the freshest and most enduring, has always flourished from the roots of tradition."

Henri de Lubac, who died in 1991 at the age of ninety-five, was among the generation of theological giants who fashioned the Catholic renewal at Vatican II. Born on February 20, 1896, in northern France, he joined the Society of Jesus in 1913 and spent nearly his entire career on the Catholic faculty at the University of Lyons. As a young theologian de Lubac resisted the domination of Catholic theology by the practitioners of a rationalistic neo-scholasticism. In his own writings he sought to recover an older and more spiritually rich tradition, represented by the early church fathers. His *Catholicism*, first published in 1938, remains a classic expression of this approach.

His most famous work, *Surnaturel*, posed a critical challenge to the neo-scholastic tendency to differentiate between the "natural" and "supernatural" destinies of human beings. Such a scheme presented human existence as self-contained with no intrinsic orientation to transcendence. On the basis of an older patristic tradition and the work of philosophers like *Blondel, de Lubac held that human beings were created with a natural openness and desire for the supernatural. Union with God was the true vocation of humanity.

De Lubac's work suffered a serious setback in 1950 with the issuance of a papal condemnation, *Humani Generis*. The target of the decree was "the new theology," an ironic epithet for those theologians who were actually questioning modern church teaching from the standpoint of more ancient traditions of the church. De Lubac was forbidden to teach or write on theology without submitting to prior censorship. In these years of "silence" he turned to explorations of literature and Buddhism.

Nevertheless, when *Pope John XXIII convoked the Second Vatican Council, de Lubac was one of the theologians he appointed to serve as experts. In this capacity he played a vital role in writing several of the council documents, including the Constitution on Revelation and the Pastoral Constitution on the Church in the Modern World.

Despite his sufferings, de Lubac remained a loyal and devout son of the church. While in the 1950s his theological stance had marked him as a liberal, in the postconciliar era he was often seen as a conservative. Neither label accurately accounted for his spiritual vision. At heart he represented a confidence in the ancient wisdom and tradition of the church and its ability, under the influence of the Spirit, to speak to the challenges of history. In 1983, in recognition of his many contributions to the church Pope John Paul II named him a cardinal.

See: Henri de Lubac, *Catholicism* (New York: Sheed & Ward, 1950); Avery Dulles, "Henri de Lubac: In Appreciation," *America* (September 28, 1991).

February 21
Cardinal John Henry Newman
Theologian (1801–1890)

"Lead, kindly light, amid the encircling gloom."

John Henry Newman, born on February 21, 1801, was one of the most eminent and attractive figures of the Victorian era. As a priest, a theologian, and a writer, he affirmed the value of tradition while engaging in dialogue with the modern world. Though often scorned by the church he loved, he was vindicated in his own lifetime when, at the age of seventy-eight, he was named a cardinal. He chose as his motto: "Heart speaks to heart."

The first half of Newman's life is identified with Oxford, where he studied and taught, and which ever remained a kind of spiritual home. After ordination as an Anglican priest he assumed the prestigious post of Vicar of the University Church of St. Mary. During the 1830s he achieved wide fame as one of the leaders of the Tractarian, or Oxford, movement, a conservative effort to restore the Church of England to holiness and catholicity. In 1841 Newman published Tract 90, which seemed to offer a Catholic interpretation of the Anglican 39 Articles. It was denounced by the church and the university, causing Newman to resign from his post. Retiring to a religious community outside of Oxford, he labored over a massive study of the development of Christian doctrine. His aim was to show that the Anglican church had maintained the authentic deposit of faith in contrast to the distortions in the Catholic church. But his studies led him to the opposite conclusion. He came to believe that the development of doctrine in the Roman church was not a distortion of the faith but an unfolding of its potentiality in response to new questions. Thus convinced that the Roman Catholic church was faithful to its primitive origins, he accepted the inevitable conclusion that he should become a Catholic.

His conversion in 1845 was greeted with horror by his Anglican confreres. And yet among the conservative and basically anti-intellectual leadership of the Roman church in England, his conversion was not entirely a cause for celebration. The very reason for his conversion, rooted as it was in an appreciation for the "development of doctrine," contradicted the church's conviction that its teachings were what "everyone, everywhere, and at all times had always believed."

Nevertheless, Newman was allowed to pursue ordination as a Catholic priest. To this end he was sent for a term of study in Rome. There, meekly, he sat on a bench with little boys applying himself to the rigors of scholastic method. He did not find it congenial. Later he would write *A Grammar of Assent*, arguing against the idea that Christian faith can be proved through logic.

With his ordination in 1847 Newman became a priest of the Oratory of *St. Philip Neri. Returning to England he established an Oratory in working-class Birmingham. In 1851 he was invited to Dublin to establish a Catholic university. His views on "liberal education" were presented in his classic work *The Idea of a University*. Through his publications, preaching, and a number of public disputes with hostile critics of the church, Newman emerged as the most distinguished Catholic churchman of his day. For a wave of converts he was an inspiration. And yet Newman continued to evoke suspicions on the part of his own church leadership. It was his misfortune to live in a time when the English church was deeply rent between liberal and extreme papalist (Ultramontane) factions. Despite his innately conservative nature, Newman was associated with the liberals through his basic independence of mind and his distaste for the authoritarian and triumphalistic tone that prevailed among the hierarchy.

In 1859 his article "On Consulting the Laity in Matters of Faith" was delated to Rome, casting a shadow over his name that would endure for decades. Similar disapproval attended his criticism of papal claims to temporal power and his apologetic efforts to soften the reactionary reputation of the church. "Are they not doing the Holy See a grave disservice," he asked, "who will not let a zealous man defend it *in his own way*, but insist on his doing it *their* way or not at all?"

Newman was grieved by the increasing factionalism within the church. His own cautious temperament resisted confrontation. After 1864 when Pius IX issued his *Syllabus of Errors*, Newman hoped for no more than to moderate the most extreme claims of the Ultramontanes and to hold open the door for future dialogue. He regarded the definition of papal infallibility at Vatican I as inopportune. And yet he mounted a spirited defense of the church against critics in England who charged that now a Catholic could not be a loyal subject. He argued that no obedience due papal authority could rob the individual of his or her own moral responsibility.

In his own time Newman was recognized for his critical role in the reestablishment of Catholicism in England. Today he is remembered as one who struggled to keep the mind of the church open to what was good and valuable in the modern world. His understanding of the historicity of doctrine, his defense of the laity, his nonscholastic approach to theology, his spirit of tolerance, his belief in separation of church and state, his appreciation for the spiritual integrity of the intellectual life, and his celebration of the rights of conscience — all these values are consonant with the modern Catholic sensibility. They were not so in the nineteenth century.

When Newman was named a cardinal — the first such appointment by *Pope Leo XIII — it was said that this only showed how Rome had not read any of his writings. And yet he was not a "liberal Catholic" in the factional sense of the time. What was and remains interesting about Newman was his effort to stand in two worlds, modern and traditional. This accounts both for his courage and the tension in his life. Because what passed for conservatism in his age was so often intemperate, close-minded, and extreme, it appeared to many that Newman was a liberal. According to his own sense, he was a conservative, committed to preserving the old truth while remaining open to new questions.

If he was anything he was a realist. Thus, he preserved his optimism by counting on the long run. One of his favorite mottoes was "Everything in its time." *Pope Paul VI must have recognized the truth of this saying when he called Vatican II "Newman's Council."

See: Louis Bouyer, *Newman: His Life and Spirituality* (New York: P. J. Kenedy & Sons, 1958); Brian Martin, *John Henry Newman: His Life and Work* (New York: Oxford University Press, 1982).

February 22

Hans and Sophie Scholl
Martyrs of the White Rose (d. 1943)

"We will not be silent. We are your bad conscience."

In the summer and fall of 1942 the citizens of Munich were astonished by a series of leaflets that began to circulate throughout the city. Slipped into mailboxes by unknown hands, left in empty bus stops or on park benches, the leaflets contained a sweeping indictment of the Nazi regime and enjoined readers to work for the defeat of their own nation. At a time when the merest hint of private dissent was a treasonable offense, the audacity of this open call to resistance threw the Gestapo into a rage.

Contrary to the suspicions of the authorities, the authors of these leaflets, who called themselves simply "The White Rose," were not members of any sophisticated organization. They were in fact a few dozen university students who had been inspired by Christian faith and the uncorrupted idealism of youth to challenge the edifice of tyranny. At the center of the group were a brother and sister, Hans and Sophie Scholl, only twenty-four and twenty-one years old. Hans was a medical student who had served on the Russian front. Sophie studied philosophy. Discerning with uncommon clarity the depth of Nazi depravity, they had decided to wage a spiritual war against the system, armed with no other weapons than courage, the power of truth, and an illegal duplicating machine. Their strategy was simple. At the very least they hoped to shatter the illusion of unanimous consent and to defy the Nazis' claim to omnipotence. Beyond that, they dared hope that by proclaiming the truth they might break the spell in which all Germany was enthralled and inspire those with doubts to move toward active resistance.

Hans and Sophie were devout Christians. They believed that the struggle against Hitler was a battle for the soul of Germany, and thus a duty for all Christians. As one of their leaflets read, "Everywhere and at all times of greatest trial men have appeared, prophets and saints who cherished their freedom, who preached the One God and who with His help brought the people to a reversal of their downward course. Man is free, to be sure, but without the true God he is defenseless against the principle of evil.... We must attack evil where it is strongest, and it is strongest in the power of Hitler.... We will not be silent. We are your bad conscience. The White Rose will not leave you in peace."

Emboldened by the furor caused by their leaflets, members of the White Rose began to make other dangerous gestures, such as writing "Down with Hitler" on street signs and the walls of buildings. It was perhaps inevitable that the circle of amateurs would be discovered. The end began on February 18, 1943, when Hans and Sophie were caught distributing leaflets outside a lecture hall in the university. Under arrest and realizing that their fates were sealed, they proceeded to confess to all the actions of the White Rose, thus hoping to spare other conspirators from discovery. Despite their efforts, however, the Gestapo quickly rounded up the rest of the circle, both in Munich and in Hamburg, where an allied cell had formed.

Hans and Sophie Scholl along with their fellow conspirator Christoph Probst, a twenty-three-year-old medical student, were quickly convicted of treason and sentenced to death. All witnesses attest to the extraordinary poise with which Hans and Sophie met their fate. Their bravery was based not just on a confidence in the verdict of history, but on a deep faith that the executioner's block was the entryway to freedom and eternal life. They were beheaded on February 22.

See: Inge Scholl, *The White Rose: Munich 1942–43* (Middletown, Conn.: Wesleyan University Press, 1983).

St. Polycarp
Bishop of Smyrna, Martyr (70–155?)

*"He who has given me strength to face the flames
will also enable me to stay unflinching at the stake."*

Polycarp was one of the most revered of the Apostolic fathers, that generation of bishops who received their faith from the original apostles. According to tradition, Polycarp was a disciple of *St. John the Evangelist. As a young man he kissed the chains of *St. Ignatius of Antioch when the latter passed through Smyrna on his way to martyrdom in Rome. In a letter to Polycarp, Ignatius counseled, "A Christian does not control his own life, but gives his whole time to God." Years later, as an old man, Polycarp met his own death as a martyr. The account of his death, circulated in a letter from the church of Smyrna, is the oldest account of Christian martyrdom outside the New Testament. According to this document, martyrs are not simply those who suffer for their beliefs. The narrator emphasizes the fact that Polycarp's death was "a martyrdom conformable to the gospel." In other words, the death of the holy bishop was a mystical reenactment of the passion of Christ, who lived and died to save the world.

At the time of his arrest in Smyrna in 155, Polycarp was eighty-six years old, having served as bishop for many decades. When the Roman proconsul ordered him to declare that "Caesar is Lord" and to curse Christ, Polycarp refused, saying, "Eighty-six years I have served him and he never did me any wrong. How can I blaspheme my King who saved me?"

The proconsul then threatened to have him burned. But Polycarp replied: "The fire you threaten burns but an hour and is quenched after a little; for you do not know the fire of the coming judgment and everlasting punishment that is laid up for the impious. But why do you delay? Come, do what you will."

When he was readied for the flame, Polycarp offered a prayer to heaven:

Lord God Almighty,...I bless thee, because thou hast deemed me worthy of this day and hour, to take my part in the number of the martyrs, in the cup of thy Christ, for resurrection to eternal life of soul and body in the immortality of the Holy Spirit, among whom may I be received in thy presence this day as a rich and acceptable sacrifice.

Upon concluding his prayer the sentence was carried out. But the narrator goes on to record a miraculous sign: "For the fire made the shape of a vaulted chamber like a ship's sail filled by the wind, and made a wall around the body of the martyr. And he was in the midst, not as burning flesh, but as bread baking or as gold and silver refined in a furnace." Seeing that he remained alive amid the flames, the executioner stabbed him in the heart, which issued in such a quantity of blood "that the fire was quenched and the whole crowd marveled."

See: "The Martyrdom of Polycarp," in Cyril C. Richardson, ed., *Early Christian Fathers* (New York: Macmillan, 1970).

February 24
St. Montanus and Companions
Martyrs (d. 259)

"Let us love and cherish union with all our might. Let us be of one mind here in imitation of what shall be hereafter. As we hope to share in the rewards promised to the just, . . . let us do those things which will lead us to him and to his heavenly kingdom."

The early martyrs believed they were bearing witness not only to their own faith but to the faith of the church. This doubtless contributed to the courage they invariably displayed at the moment of death. Nevertheless, as the story of St. Montanus and his companions demonstrates, the martyrs were not immune to fear. They craved constant reassurance that they were not deluded. In this they were fortified by dreams and visions but also by their exhortation to one another to finish the race.

St. Montanus was a deacon in Carthage who, along with seven other Christians, was martyred during a persecution under the emperor Valerian. Imprisoned over a period of many months, regularly deprived of food and water for days at a time, the prisoners relied on one another for support.

> We have all one and the same spirit, and this unites and cements us together in prayer. . . . These are the ties which link hearts together, and which make men the children of God. To be heirs of His kingdom we must be His children and to be His children we must love one another.

According to the Acts of these martyrs, each one of them was comforted before death by a reassuring vision. A priest named Victor beheld "a child whose countenance was of a wonderful brightness enter the prison." The child promised him a glorious crown. When Victor asked for a sign for his friends, the child answered, "Give them the sign of Jacob, that is, his mystical ladder reaching to the heavens." Victor's vision, which he related to his companions, filled them with joy. After many months in prison, Montanus was finally taken out to be executed. The night before his death he was visited in a vision by St. Cyprian, the martyred bishop of Carthage. He asked him whether death was painful. Cyprian answered: "The body feels no pain when the soul gives herself entirely to God."

Montanus was followed to the place of execution by a great crowd, which included many priests and his own mother. There he prayed for the peace and unity of the church. Then he knelt, lowered his head, and received the death-stroke of the executioner.

February 25

Felix Varela
Cuban Priest and Patriot (1788–1853)

*"I have always concluded that Christianity and liberty
are inseparable."*

Felix Varela, a Catholic priest and theologian, was one of the most remarkable figures of the early nineteenth-century church. In his native Cuba, he has long been revered as a champion of liberty and social justice. In the United States, in contrast, his name has remained virtually unknown, despite the fact that most of his career was spent in exile in New York City. There he served an important role in the leadership of the archdiocese, published the first Catholic literary journal, and became the first Hispanic theologian in the United States.

Varela was born in Havana in 1788. He was ordained a priest and served for many years as professor of philosophy at San Carlos College. With the publication of several scholarly works, he earned a reputation as one of the most distinguished figures in Latin American philosophy. In 1821 he was elected as a delegate to the Spanish Cortes in Madrid. There he introduced two significant bills, one calling for Cuban independence from Spain and the other for the abolition of slavery in Cuba. As he wrote, "Constitution, liberty, equality are synonymous; and their very names repudiate slavery and inequality of rights." As a result of such seditious talk he was forced to flee Spain in 1823 and go into exile. He never returned to Cuba.

Varela settled in New York City, where he spent many years in pastoral work among the city's poor Irish immigrants. Still passionately loyal to his homeland, he began a Spanish-language newspaper that became an effective voice for the cause of Cuban independence. His efforts proved so threatening to the Spanish government that an assassination plot was mounted. (Confronted by his assassin, Varela was able to disarm him with an appeal to faith and honor.) Meanwhile, he earned a doctorate in theology (the next Hispanic theologian in the United States would not come for over a century) and served as vicar general of the archdiocese of New York.

Varela's major work, published in two volumes in Spanish, was entitled *Letters to Elpidio,* a name derived from the Greek word for hope. Addressed to his former students in Cuba, the work is a subtle expression of political theology, an attempt to integrate faith and the cause of liberty in such a way as to avoid the extremes of "irreligiosity" on the one hand and superstition or fanaticism on the other hand.

In his book Varela examined the forms and causes of unbelief in the modern world, but argued that in the end "irreligiosity" undermined the moral fabric of a society and so proved inimical to the cause of freedom. "Once irreligiosity is spread throughout the social body, it destroys all links of appreciation, and like poison, it corrupts and kills the body. Honor becomes a vain word; patriotism a political mask; and virtue a fancy." The inevitable result was tyranny. Thus, he argued, religion was not the enemy of human freedom but its guardian.

At the same time, Varela criticized the church and those of his fellow Catholics who opposed the spirit of liberty and democracy. Thus, the second part of his book addressed the spirit of "superstition" — his word for the misuse of religious sentiment and the manipulation of people in the name of God. Where liberty was suppressed, the result was dogmatism and fanaticism. On the other hand, "Where the Spirit is," he proclaimed, "there is liberty."

Impoverished by his extensive forays in publishing and propaganda and exhausted by his tireless ministry, Varela died on February 25, 1853, in St. Augustine, Florida. In the United States his name was quickly forgotten. Not so in Cuba. In 1892 José Martí, the father of Cuban independence, visited Varela's tomb and called him "the Cuban saint." In 1911 the bishop of St. Augustine allowed Varela's remains to be removed to Cuba. There his grave is honored to this day by Cuban patriots, whether Catholic or communist.

See: Felix Varela, *Letters to Elpidio* (New York: Paulist, 1989).

February 26

Antonio Valdivieso
Bishop of Nicaragua and Martyr (d. 1550)

*"I write these letters hurriedly in order that Your Majesty might be aware . . .
of the great need that exists in these parts for justice."*

Antonio Valdivieso, a Spanish Dominican assigned to Nicaragua, was the first bishop in the Americas to die for the cause of justice and the defense of the Indians. From the moment he arrived in Nicaragua in 1544 he vigorously opposed the cruel oppression of the native Indians by the Spanish — including, in particular, the governor and his family. He departed for Spain to present his complaints directly to King Charles V. The king in turn named him bishop of Nicaragua. Valdivieso returned with trepidation, convinced that his new appointment was the equivalent of a death sentence.

When he landed in Central America Spanish soldiers tried unsuccessfully to prevent his return to the capital in Léon. Once in the cathedral he resumed his prophetic preaching. Before long plans for his assassination were being openly discussed. On February 26, 1550, the governor's son and several of his henchmen forced their way into the bishop's home and stabbed him, along with two other Dominicans.

See: Enrique Dussel, *A History of the Church in Latin America* (Grand Rapids: Eerdmans, 1981).

February 27
Luis de Leon
Augustinian Theologian (1527–1591)

"In Jesus we find condensed as in a vast ocean the whole being and substance of the world."

In 1561 Luis de Leon, an Augustinian priest and theologian from Castile, was elected to an important chair at the conservative University of Salamanca. He was responsible for teaching an advanced course on the theology of *Thomas Aquinas. But Leon was not satisfied to remain within the enclosed world of scholastic thought. In the spirit of Renaissance humanism he hungrily explored all areas of human wisdom and culture, including Platonic and Arabic philosophy as well as Jewish mystical writings and biblical interpretation. In order to pursue his own critical study of the Scriptures he mastered Hebrew. When word circulated that he had privately acknowledged errors of translation in the official Vulgate (Latin) Bible, he was denounced to the dreaded Inquisition.

In March 1572 Leon was arrested and imprisoned in a dark cell of the Valladolid Inquisition. There he remained for five years, deprived of the sacraments and provided with little food or fresh air. Despite interminable interrogations he was never informed of the charges against him or confronted with his accusers. At the conclusion of this Kafkaesque ordeal in December 1576, he was declared innocent of heresy and released.

Despite his sufferings Leon felt no bitterness for his own sake. But his experience of injustice inspired a certain contempt toward all centers of absolute power. His theological writings provided an opportunity for social criticism, such as when he compared the arrogance of earthly princes with the sweetness and humility of Jesus, Prince of Princes. "What can we say about kings and princes who not only lower and despise some of their subjects but think that this is the only way they themselves can feel important and try their best so that the groups they have lowered and despised will be held down and despised generation after generation?"

In 1583 Leon published his masterwork, *The Names of God,* a vast series of meditations on the various biblical appellations for Christ: Face of God, Way, Arm of God, Prince of Peace, Son of God, Lamb, Beloved, and finally Jesus. Each of these names becomes a window through which to view the relation between God and the cosmos, a prism in which the light of faith is refracted.

Despite his ordeals with the Inquisition, Leon's genius was recognized by the university. In addition to theology he went on to win additional chairs in Scripture and moral philosophy. He was also honored by his order when in 1591 he was elected provincial for the Augustinians of Castile. He died later that year.

See: Luis de Leon, *The Names of God,* trans. Manuel Durán and William Kluback, Classics of Western Spirituality (New York: Paulist, 1984).

February 28
Martyrs in the Plague of Alexandria
(d. 261)

"Many who had healed others fell victims themselves. The best of our brethren have been taken from us in this manner: some were priests, other deacons, and some laity of great worth. This death, with the faith which accompanied it, appears to be little inferior to martyrdom itself."

The quoted words are from the bishop of Alexandria, St. Dionysius, recounting the heroic charity of his fellow Christians during an outbreak of plague in that Egyptian city in 261. So virulent was the disease that every house in the city was affected. The bodies of the dead and even the dying, of whom there was general dread, were cast into the streets, contributing to the stench of pestilence.

At this point a wonderful thing happened. Christians of the city, who had been forced by persecution to hide themselves and conduct their meetings in secret, now emerged from their homes to attend to the dead and dying. At great risk to themselves — both from infection and from the possibility of arrest — they nursed the sick, washed the bodies of the dead, and saw to their burial. For many of these Christians, as their bishop observed, this service entailed the laying down of their own lives for their neighbors. Those who died were recognized by the church as true martyrs of charity and were added to the calendar of the saints.

❧ MARCH ❧

George Herbert
Anglican Vicar and Poet (1593–1633)

"Teach me thy love to know;
That this new light, which now I see,
May both the work and workman show:
Then by a sunne-beam I will climbe to thee."

George Herbert was the fifth son of a distinguished Welsh family. He received a superb education at Westminster School and Trinity College, Cambridge, where he excelled in the classics as well as modern languages. In 1620 he was named Public Orator of the university, a prestigious post that required him to compose eloquent speeches for university occasions. The post was often a stepping stone to high political office, and it appears that Herbert cultivated ambitions in that direction. In the early 1620s he served a term as member of Parliament. All the signs in his life pointed toward a brilliant career. But all the while this worldly success was in tension with a very different ambition.

In 1626 Herbert resigned his position and announced his desire to seek holy orders in the Anglican church. His friends tried to persuade him that this was a terrible waste of his talents and opportunities. But his mind was set. In 1629 he married Jane Danvers. The following year he was ordained a priest and accepted the position of rector of the church in Bemerton, a tiny rural parish in Salisbury Plain.

He found the impoverished church half in ruins. The rectory was nearly uninhabitable. Surely his country parishioners wondered how long this highborn gentleman from the university would last. But Herbert's sincere faith and genuine love quickly won their hearts. By all accounts he was a model priest who found genuine happiness and fulfillment in serving the spiritual needs of his humble parish. Sadly, his ministry lasted only three years. He died of consumption on March 1, 1633, at the age of forty. So his name might have vanished into the obscurity he willingly accepted. But before dying he entrusted to a friend a manuscript of poems. Their publication after his death eventually established the reputation of George Herbert, vicar of Bemerton, as one of the greatest poets in the English language.

All his poems deal with the religious life. They are written in a simple but fresh style that seems to reflect the virtues of balance and moderation so prized in Anglican spirituality. As a priest, Herbert valued the rich language of the Book of Common Prayer, the loveliness of church hymns, and the beauty of stained glass. Indeed, in one of his poems he likens the role of a preacher to a window through which God's grace may shine. Similarly, Herbert's poetry has a light and transparent quality. But the simplicity of his style is deceptive. In his poems Herbert did not shrink from laying bare his own soul. Writing verse was a form of prayer, a way of contemplating God, of offering praise and giving thanks, but also a way of questioning and even arguing with his Creator. So personal is his poetic voice that it is impossible to respond to his poems without also forming an impression of the character and virtue of their author, the man his parishioners called "Holy Mr. Herbert."

One of his most moving poems, "Prayer," consists of nothing but concise images, piled one upon the other:

> Prayer the Churches banquet, Angels age,
> God's breath in man returning to his birth,
> The soul in paraphrase, heart in pilgrimage,
> The Christian plummet sounding heav'n and earth.

Each and every succeeding image — "Reversed thunder," "Heaven in or-dinarie" — almost constitutes a sermon in itself, until the poem rises to a breathless whisper: "The land of spices; something understood."

His most famous metaphysical poem, "Love," employs the courtly language of courtesy to describe the encounter between Love and the soul: "Love bade me welcome: yet my soul drew back / Guiltie of dust and sinne." Feeling unworthy, the soul shrinks from the invitation to partake of Love's banquet. But Love persists, noting that we have been created worthy to receive him and that he himself has taken on the blame for our sins: "You must sit down, sayes Love, and taste my meat: / So I did sit and eat."

At the time of Herbert's death, there were doubtless many friends from former days who regretted that such a promising career had ended with so little accomplishment. Herbert would have smiled on their incomprehension. In his short life he had discovered the secret of happiness: "Heaven in ordinarie."

See: W. H. Auden, ed., *Herbert: Poems and Prose* (New York: Penguin, 1973).

Father Engelmar Unzeitig
Priest and Martyr (1911–1945)

*"We feel ourselves well protected in the hand of God,
as St. Paul says: Whether we live or die, we are the Lord's!"*

Engelmar Unzeitig was born in a German district of Czechoslovakia in 1911. As a boy he dreamed of becoming a missionary priest — to travel to foreign lands, to dedicate his life "to the conversion of pagans," and perhaps to offer his life for the salvation of souls. So at the age of seventeen he entered the seminary of the Marianhill missionary order. His eventual ordination, however, came on August 15, 1939, just two weeks before the outbreak of World War II. Within two years he was under arrest by the Gestapo, charged with making "insidious expressions" and defending the Jews in his sermons. In June 1941 he was conveyed to the notorious concentration camp at Dachau, passing through the entryway under the famous motto, "Work Makes You Free." So he encountered a far different mission field than he had ever imagined possible.

Situated in scenic Bavaria, Dachau was one of the original Nazi concentration camps, founded in 1933 to house political prisoners. During the war its population swelled to two hundred thousand inmates from nearly forty countries. These included an unusual number of priests and other clergy, nearly three thousand all told, of whom three-quarters were Catholic. Held in special contempt by the SS, the clergy were segregated in their own quarters, known as the "priests' barracks." With good reason Dachau was called "the largest monastery in the world." There amid the filth, degradation, starvation, and the atmosphere of death, the priests and pastors pursued their ministry. They prayed together, Catholics with Protestants. They composed hymns, celebrated clandestine Masses, and otherwise tried to be of pastoral service to their fellow prisoners.

For the newly ordained Father Engelmar, Dachau was virtually the only posting he had experienced as a priest. Despite the hellish circumstances, he tried to regard it as a school for holiness. In a letter smuggled out to his sister he wrote, "What sometimes appears as misfortune is often the greatest fortune. How much a person learns only through experience in the school of life. We should feel and experience for others, I think, the lack of peace in the world and help them to true peace. Then we are not surprised if God takes from us some things which are dear and precious to us."

When not engaged in forced labor, he spent his time consoling and encouraging others and quietly witnessing to the power of faith. He undertook a special mission to the Russian prisoners. Though most of them were communists, he earned their trust and friendship and with them enjoyed many long hours discussing the meaning of life and their common suffering.

Engelmar managed to survive for nearly four years in the camp — four years of famine, when grass and weeds were a coveted meal, years of back-breaking labor, arbitrary beatings, epidemics, and freezing exposure to the elements. He survived all this and he most likely would have survived the war entirely, had it not been for a terrible outbreak of typhoid that hit the camp in the winter of 1945. In January alone twenty-eight hundred prisoners died of the disease. Those who were infected were confined to a special barracks where they were left to die in horrible squalor with no one to tend or care for them. A call went out for volunteer orderlies. Twenty priests stepped forward. Father Engelmar was one of them.

The meaning of this gesture was clear to all. The priest-volunteers entered the quarantined barracks with no expectation of ever emerging. Conditions in the barracks were appalling. Disease-carrying lice and fleas were everywhere; the floor was awash with the blood, spit, and waste of the dying. Within the hell of Dachau this was surely the inner sanctum. Yet into this void the priests brought their love and faith, making the best of the weeks that were available to them to bring some order and dignity to the place. There was endless work to be done simply caring for the sick — washing their fevered and wasting bodies, cleaning their filthy pallets, trying to get some nourishment into them. But the priests also heard confessions, offered the last rites, and recited the prayers for the dead. The SS would not enter the barracks, and so there was probably no other place in the camp where the priests were so free to exercise their faith.

According to witnesses who survived to testify, Father Engelmar was an angel of mercy, who poured himself out in tireless service to his companions. Here at last was the mission to which he had consecrated himself. Of the twenty priest-volunteers in the typhoid barracks, only two survived. Father Engelmar was not one of them. Within six weeks his body was burning with fever. Still he continued to hear confessions and perform the sacraments as long as he was able. He died on March 2, 1945, the day after his thirty-fourth birthday and only a few weeks before the liberation of the camp by American troops.

In a letter written days before his death, he wrote: "The Good is undying and victory must remain with God, even if it sometimes seems useless for us to spread love in the world. Nevertheless, one sees again and again that the human heart is attuned to love, and it cannot withstand its power in the long run, if it is truly based on God and not on creatures. We want to continue to do and offer everything so that love and peace may soon reign again."

See: Adalbert Ludwig Balling and Reinhard Abeln, *Martyr of Brotherly Love: Father Engelmar Unzeitig and the Priests' Barracks at Dachau* (New York: Crossroad, 1992).

St. Katherine Drexel
Foundress of the Sisters of the Blessed Sacrament
(1858–1955)

"Resolve: Generously and with no half-hearted, timorous dread of the opinions of Church and men to manifest my mission.... You have no time to occupy your thoughts with that complacency or consideration of what others will think. Your business is simply, 'What will my Father in heaven think?' "

Katherine Drexel came from one of the wealthiest families in America. Her father was an extremely successful banker, a Catholic of Austrian descent. Katherine did not know her mother, who died five weeks after her birth. But a year later her father was remarried to another eminent Catholic, Emma Bouvier, who exerted a strong influence on Katherine and her two sisters. When Frances Drexel died he established a trust for his three daughters of $14,000,000. Inspired by their Catholic faith, they all three regarded this fortune as an opportunity to glorify God through the service of others.

This was the great era of Catholic immigration, as American cities stretched to accommodate new arrivals from Europe. The church responded with an extraordinary system of schools, hospitals, orphanages, and other charitable institutions, proving to the world that Catholics knew how to "look after their own." There were certainly plenty of claims on the generosity of a young Catholic heiress. But Katherine Drexel's concern extended to those outside the church, indeed to those all but excluded from American society — namely, Indians and blacks. She began by endowing scores of schools on Indian reservations across the country. In 1878 during a private audience with *Pope Leo XIII she begged the pope to send priests to serve the Indians. He responded, "Why not become a missionary yourself?"

At this point Katherine realized that it was not enough to share her wealth. God was calling her to give everything. Consequently she embarked on a long search to find a religious order corresponding to her own sense of mission. But when none could be found, she received the support of her bishop to establish her own religious congregation. In 1891 she was professed as the first member of the Sisters of the Blessed Sacrament for Indians and Colored People. Within the year ten other women had joined her order.

Though Katherine embraced a vow of personal poverty, she continued to administer the income from her trust — the enormous sum of $400,000 a year. She might well have spent the money to endow the establishments of her own congregation, but she insisted that her own Sisters rely on alms. The money would continue to be used to support other projects of service to Indians and blacks. Among her gifts, over time, were a total of a million dollars to the Bureau of Catholic Indian Missions and $100,000 a year to the support of mission schools on the reservations. In the 1920s she contributed $750,000 toward the founding of Xavier University in New Orleans, the first Catholic college established for blacks. All told she was personally responsible for establishing 145 Catholic missions and 12 schools for Indians, and 50 schools for black students.

Mother Drexel died on March 3, 1955, at the age of ninety-six, her life having spanned the era of slavery and the Indian wars to the dawn of the modern civil rights movement. It was a period in which blacks and Indians, the communities to which Mother Drexel devoted her life, were far from the consciousness of most American Catholics. Her charitable works did little directly to challenge the structures of racism and discrimination. But in the era of rigidly enforced racial segregation her work had a profound "witness value." The exceptional character of her commitment is reflected in a letter from her contemporary, *Father Augustus Tolton, at that time the sole black priest in America:

> In the whole history of the Church in America we cannot find one person that has sworn to give her treasure for the sole benefit of the Colored and Indians. As I stand alone as the first Negro priest of America, so you, Mother Katherine, stand alone as the first one to make such a sacrifice for the cause of a downtrodden race.

Katherine Drexel was canonized by Pope John Paul II in 2000.

See: Sister Consuela Marie Duffy, S.B.S., *Katherine Drexel: A Biography* (Cornwell Heights, Pa.: Sisters of the Blessed Sacrament, 1966); Kenneth L. Woodward, *Making Saints* (New York: Simon & Schuster, 1990).

March 4

Bd. Henry Suso
Dominican Mystic (1300–1365)

"Asked to supply the key to eternal happiness, he replied: 'To die to self in perfect detachment, to receive everything as from God, and to maintain unruffled patience with all men, however wolfish they may be.'"

Henry Suso was born in Constance around the year 1300. He entered a Dominican priory at the age of thirteen and was professed some years later. His spiritual life, throughout most of his youth, was characterized by an extreme and almost morbid asceticism. In his intense identification with the sufferings of Christ he experienced moments of rapture as well as terrifying visions of the torments of hell. After many years of this and feeling that he was tottering on the brink of madness, he sought counsel from the holy Dominican mystic *Meister Eckhart. Whatever the master's advice, "it set him free from the hell in which he had so long dwelt." Suso gave up his mortifications, convinced that he was no longer meant to concentrate on his own soul but to "go forth to save his neighbor." No longer would his sufferings be self-imposed; rather, they would come to him in the form of slander, misunderstanding, and abuse from the world. For as Christ revealed to him, "No one can attain to divine heights or to unusual sweetness unless he be first drawn through the example of my human bitterness."

Suso took to the roads as a wandering preacher. His sermons and writings reflected his passionate and poetic devotion to Christ in the form of Eternal Wisdom, "a gentle loving Mistress." Everything sweet and beautiful reminded him of "his loveliest Love." Writing about himself as "the Servant," he observed,

> It were impossible to tell how often with weeping eyes, from out the unfathomable depth of his outspread heart, he embraced this lovely form, and pressed it tenderly to his heart. And thus it fared with him as with a sucking child, which lies encircled by its mother's arms upon her breast.... Even so his heart many a time leapt up within his body toward the delightful presence of the Eternal Wisdom, and melted away in sensible affections.

Suso was driven by a desire to enkindle hearts with the love of God. He was responsible for many conversions and attracted a good number of disciples. But he was also regularly beset by humiliating exterior trials. He was at various points accused of theft, fraud, and attempted poisoning. In the Netherlands he was charged with heresy. A woman he had been advising once accused him, falsely, of fathering her child. Despite his innocence in the matter, he raised the child, whom its mother had abandoned, until another home could be found. These scandals finally prompted an investigation by the Dominican master general, with the result that Suso was completely vindicated.

Toward the end of his life, Suso enjoyed a deep friendship with a Swiss nun, Elizabeth Stäglin, with whom he corresponded about spiritual matters. When she asked him about the nature of God, he responded with a rhapsody on God's reflection in creation. After describing the loveliness of the heavens and of all nature below, he wrote:

> Ah, gentle God, if Thou art so lovely in Thy creatures, how exceeding beautiful and ravishing Thou must be in Thyself!... See, daughter, how, by gazing on this mirror, there springs up speedily, in a soul susceptible of such impressions, an intense inward jubilee; for by jubilee is meant a joy which no tongue can tell, but which pours itself with might through heart and soul.

Suso died on January 25, 1365. He was beatified in 1831 with a feast assigned to March 2.

See: Henry Suso, *The Exemplar,* Classics of Western Spirituality (New York: Paulist, 1989).

Karl Rahner
Theologian (1904-1984)

"The real and total and comprehensive task of a Christian...is to be a human being, a human being of course whose depths are divine.... To this extent Christian life is the acceptance of human existence as such."

Karl Rahner was the foremost Catholic theologian of the twentieth century. His life passed externally in a fairly monotonous course of teaching and writing. But in his quiet and methodical way he did more than any other theologian to overcome the gulf between Catholic theology and the critical reason of the Enlightenment. His chief aim was to make Christian faith intelligible to human beings living in the modern world — a situation characterized by doubt, pluralism, science, and historical consciousness. Most but not all of his work was addressed to a theological audience. But he was never motivated by purely intellectual interests. He remained first of all a priest concerned with the pastoral needs of the Christian people and the importance of dialogue with all people of good will.

Rahner was born on March 5, 1904, in Freiburg, Germany, to a traditional Catholic family. His older brother, Hugo, entered the Jesuits in 1918, and Karl followed three years later. He was ordained in 1932 and was sent to the University of Freiburg to study philosophy. There he found the professor in Catholic philosophy to be a fairly narrow-minded champion of neo-Thomism. Rahner found it more interesting to attend the seminars of Martin Heidegger. From this exposure he conceived of the possibility of reconciling the thought of Thomas Aquinas with modern philosophy, in particular the "transcendental" philosophy of Immanuel Kant.

Kant had signaled the famous "turn to the subject" in modern philosophy. He was interested in exploring the a priori — or transcendental — conditions within the human subject that enable us to *know* something. Rahner went further, to explore the a priori conditions in the human subject which make it possible to receive divine revelation. For Rahner it was not sufficient to study dogma or the content of revelation in a purely objective fashion. It was necessary to understand the relation between this content and the subjective condition of human existence that makes a person open to revelation in the first place. He called this method of theology "transcendental anthropology."

Rahner's principal genre was the essay, and his most substantial work is contained in the more than twenty volumes of his collected "Theological Investigations." The range of his concerns covered nearly every topic in theology and is thus not easily summarized. But Rahner was an unusually systematic thinker. Nearly any point of entry into his work affords a glimpse of his entire vision.

In essence, Rahner believed that all of human existence is rooted in the holy and infinite mystery of God. Religious experience is thus not a separate category of our existence; it is the potential for a certain quality or depth available in all our everyday life. Grace, which is the self-communication of God, is not something utterly extrinsic to our human nature. Rather, human nature is supernaturally ordained in such a way as to be open to receiving this communication. At the heart of the human being is a dynamism driving us toward union with an infinite horizon that lies beyond the objects of our knowing or loving. That infinite horizon is God, a Holy Mystery, who is forever reaching out to us in every situation of our lives. To the extent that we open ourselves to this gift — offered freely to all people in all situations of life — that is the way of salvation.

From his early writings in the 1950s Rahner showed his determination to liberate Catholic theology from the stultifying constraints of neo-scholasticism. But to conservative officials it seemed that he was simply intent on demolition. Increasingly he was instructed to refrain from writing on one topic after another, until an order was imposed that he submit all his writings to a Vatican censor.

All this changed with the convocation of the Second Vatican Council in 1962. *Pope John XXIII personally named Rahner as a *peritus* (theological expert) to the council. He went on to serve on commissions that drafted the vital documents on revelation, the church, and the church in the modern world. Many theologians and bishops played a role in this vital council of reform and renewal. There is no doubt, however, that Rahner's influence was felt in almost every contribution of the council.

Rahner believed the council marked the arrival of a new era in Christianity, the beginning of a genuinely "world church." And yet he often felt discouragement over developments that seemed in his view to violate the spirit of the council. Invariably, when faced with disappointments, he spoke wistfully of the future and evinced his ultimate confidence in the Holy Spirit. By the end of his life Rahner had become the most widely read and respected theologian in the church, his influence extended by the vast numbers of his students and his own efforts to write in a more popular vein. Although he remained the consummate church theologian, he continued to invite criticism from conservatives for "reducing" theology to anthropology and for erasing the boundaries between the church and nonbelievers. Far more numerous were the number of those who credited Rahner with deepening or even preserving their faith.

His own self-assessment was characteristically modest: "I do not know what's happened to my life. I did not lead a life; I worked, wrote, taught, tried to do my duty and earn my living. I tried in this ordinary everyday way to serve God — that's it."

Rahner died on March 30, 1984, at the age of eighty.

See: Karl Rahner, *Foundations of Christian Faith* (New York: Crossroad, 1978); Herbert Vorgrimler, *Understanding Karl Rahner: An Introduction to His Life and Thought* (New York: Crossroad, 1986).

March 6

Jean-Pierre de Caussade
Spiritual Director (1675–1751)

*"Every moment we live through is like an ambassador
who declares the will of God."*

Little is known of this French Jesuit, whose priestly life was spent in a series of relatively obscure assignments. For one year he served as spiritual director to a community of Visitation nuns in Nancy. To them he addressed a series of letters and conferences on which his reputation rests. *Abandonment to Divine Providence,* which was first published only a century after his death, was soon translated into many languages and quickly achieved the status of a spiritual classic.

The theme of de Caussade's book is easily summarized. In brief, it outlines the path to holiness that lies in the performance of our everyday tasks and duties. Every moment, according to Caussade, is given to us from God and thus bears God's will for us. When we "accept what we cannot avoid, and endure with love and resignation things which could cause us weariness and disgust," we are thus following the path to sanctification.

This was the attitude of Mary, when she uttered the prayer of abandonment, "May it be done unto me according to your will." It is the spirit which Jesus expressed in the Garden: "Not my will, but yours be done." These were extreme moments of decision. But the capacity to make such heroic sacrifices is prepared by the daily exercise of faith and by the willingness to abandon ourselves to God's will in all the small tasks and duties that are revealed in the present moment.

These words, "the present moment," are central in de Caussade's work. It is even legitimate, he claims, to speak of the "sacrament of the present moment." Just as Christ, in the Eucharist, is visible to the eyes of faith under the aspect of bread, so to the faithful Christian it should be evident that God's will is truly present, though disguised, in what might otherwise be dismissed as the ordinary and everyday.

It is very likely that de Caussade's book inspired *St. Therese of Lisieux with her spirituality of the "little way." His book was also a favorite of *Dorothy Day, and one finds echoes of his insights in the work of many other spiritual writers. But apart from written texts, de Caussade suggests that by living in this spirit of mindfulness and abandonment, our own lives become *texts:* "The Holy Spirit writes no more Gospels except in our hearts. All we do from moment to moment is live this new gospel of the Holy Spirit. We, if we are holy, are the paper; our sufferings and our actions are the ink. The workings of the Holy Spirit are his pen, and with it he writes a living gospel."

Father de Caussade died on March 6, 1751.

See: Jean-Pierre de Caussade, *Abandonment to Divine Providence,* trans. John Beevers (New York: Image, 1975).

Sts. Perpetua and Felicity
Martyrs (d. 203)

*"Stand fast in the faith, and love ye one another;
and be not offended because of our passion."*

There are few more poignant documents of the early church than "The Passion of Sts. Perpetua and Felicity." Indeed, the story of these two early martyrs was so popular in the North African church that *St. Augustine complained that it was more widely read than the Gospels. Perpetua was a prosperous young woman, married and the mother of a newborn son, who lived in Carthage in the late second century. At the age of twenty-two she was arrested with her servant Felicity and several male companions, apparently for violating a prohibition against conversion to Christianity.

Part of the striking power of this narrative derives from the fact that it purports to represent the voice of Perpetua herself, as she languished in prison under sentence of death. It is thus a uniquely personal document, filled with painfully intimate details, and strikingly free of the stereotypical conventions of later hagiography. Perpetua emerges not simply as a "type," but as a fully realized person, subject to hunger, fears, and even — as a nursing mother, separated from her child — the pain of swollen breasts.

The last detail points to the other obvious distinction of the narrative. This is not the disembodied voice of a generic Christian — but a Christian *woman.* The modern reader can hardly ignore the pervasive significance of gender throughout the narrative. While the overall "plot" focuses on Perpetua's approaching passion, she is called throughout to negotiate a series of complications arising from her status as a woman — daughter, mother, and spouse (though interestingly her husband is never mentioned). Throughout we sense the struggle of a woman to claim her own identity and vocation amid the various competing claims imposed by society. Even at her trial the proconsul appeals to her sense of duty toward her aged father and her infant son. Perpetua answers the court with the simple declaration, "I am a Christian." One senses that in Christ she has found the power and freedom to name herself and the courage to accept the consequences.

And yet there is no suggestion that Perpetua scorns motherhood or the bonds of family. The narrative describes in touching detail the sufferings caused by the separation from her infant. But when he is restored to her and she is able to nurse him, "straightway I became well, and was lightened of my labor and care for the child; and suddenly the prison was made a palace for me, so that I would sooner be there than anywhere else." The main torture for Perpetua comes from the pleading of her aged father, who resorts to bullying threats as well as abject tears in an effort to dissuade her from her path. Perpetua looks upon him with genuine pity for his "unhappy old age," but also with sadness at the thought that he, as a non-Christian, cannot rejoice in the prospect of her passion.

Perpetua herself does not relish the prospect of death. But in a series of prophetic visions she finds the conviction that her fate is ordained and that her brief suffering will lead to eternal reward. She is consoled finally to be able to entrust her son to safe hands, and so receives the grace to bear whatever may come. She is undeterred when, at their trial, she and her companions receive the most terrifying sentence — to fight with wild beasts in the amphitheater. For in another dream she perceives that she will be fighting "not with beasts, but against the devil; and I knew that mine was the victory."

Her portion of the narrative ends on a haunting note — the actual words of a prisoner on the eve of her death: "Thus far have I written this, till the day before the games; but the deed of the games themselves let him write who will."

Eyewitnesses did complete her narrative. And so we also learn something about her companion and servant Felicity. Eight months pregnant at the time of her imprisonment, Felicity was fearful that because of her condition she would be separated from the fate of her companions. But after a night of ardent prayer, she went into labor and gave birth to a daughter, whom she was able to entrust to Christian friends.

On their last day of life the prisoners celebrated a "Love Feast," attended by many local Christians. The next morning, "the day of their victory," the prisoners went forth from the darkness of their prison into the glaring amphitheater, "as it were to heaven, cheerful and bright of countenance." Perpetua wore the expression of a "true spouse of Christ," while Felicity, rejoicing that her child was born in safety, "came now from blood to blood, from the midwife to the gladiator, to wash after her travail in a second baptism."

Once more Perpetua was urged to abjure her faith. But she refused. We hear her voice a final time — now with a conviction that resounds through the ages: "For this cause came we willingly unto this, that our liberty might not be obscured. For this cause have we devoted our lives."

Perpetua and Felicity were set in the arena together. At first they were stripped, causing the crowd to shudder "seeing one a tender girl, the other her breasts yet dropping from her late childbearing." And so in a final ironic concession to their womanhood they were permitted to cover themselves. They were then exposed to a savage cow which tossed them about on its horns. When they had survived this ordeal the executioner was ordered to put them to the sword. But the swordsman was apparently a novice, and had trouble striking a true blow. The narrator relates that Perpetua, in the final mark of mastery over her fate, directed the sword to her own neck: "Perhaps so great a woman could not else have been slain had she not herself so willed it."

A final poignant image remains. The narrator notes that before meeting the sword the two young women, formerly mistress and servant, now sisters in Christ, turned to one another before the jeering crowd and exchanged a kiss.

See: "The Passion of SS. Perpetua and Felicity," Walter Shewring, trans., in F. J. Sheed, ed., *Saints Are Not Sad* (New York: Sheed & Ward, 1949).

St. John of God
Founder of the Brothers Hospitallers (1495–1550)

*"I know of no bad person in my hospital except myself alone,
who am indeed unworthy to eat the bread of the poor."*

The journey of the man who became known as St. John of God was clouded by sadness and a remorse, it seemed, which no amount of self-abnegation or charity could ever fully expunge. Perhaps the roots of this lay in a strange childhood misfortune, whose circumstances he could never explain. He was born in Portugal and raised in a happy and loving home. But at the age of eight he disappeared from his family and somehow turned up on the other side of Spain as a homeless waif in the kingdom of Castile. Whether he was kidnapped or otherwise induced to run away, it seems that the experience implanted in his life an abyss so wide that happiness and contentment remained forever beyond his reach.

He survived his youth by whatever means he could, and at the age of twenty-two enlisted in the army. While fighting the French he was captured and spent some time as a prisoner. After his release he went on to battle the Turks in Hungary. He had long since abandoned the faith of his childhood, and he had readily accepted the swaggering depravity that was the common standard of his companions. But all the while, amid the death, hardship, and debauchery of his life, he retained some memory of long-lost innocence, associated with the image of his home and his loving parents and the faith in which he had been raised.

Filled with increasing regret for what his life had become, he finally left the army at the age of forty. He made a pilgrimage on foot to the shrine of Santiago de Compostela, made his confession, and resolved to live a life of penitence. Only after making this purpose of amendment did he feel ready to seek out his hometown in Portugal to find out what had become of his family. There he made the sad discovery that his mother had died soon after his disappearance — of a broken heart, it was said — while his father, who had entered a Franciscan monastery, had also long since died. Now John's remorse for all the suffering he had caused was compounded by the sense that he was in some way responsible for his parents' death.

Back in Spain, with no education and no trade, he worked for a time as a shepherd. Then he conceived the idea of traveling to North Africa to offer himself as a substitute for Christian slaves held by the Moors. He got as far as Gibraltar, where a confessor persuaded him to abandon the plan. He ended up in Granada, supporting himself by hawking holy cards and devotional manuals. It was there that he chanced to hear a sermon by the famous preacher John of Avila, which inspired him to take to the streets to proclaim his sins to the world. So well did he play the role of a fool for Christ that he was taken for a lunatic and confined in the local asylum. There he gladly submitted to the daily scourging that was the prescribed treatment for mental disorders. When John of Avila went to interview him, he determined that John was not mad at all but that he had invited this cruel treatment as a form of penance. He urged John to express his love for God in a way more useful to his neighbors. This John immediately resolved to do.

He began methodically to offer shelter and hospitality to all the poor, the sick, and the homeless he could gather from the streets of Granada. With the income from a small shop for religious books and devotional articles he was able to rent a small house. Later his work of hospitality became a full-time occupation, and he accepted alms from interested benefactors for his support. Ex-prisoners, prostitutes, cripples, the sick and dying outcasts of the town — all were welcome to find a warm corner in his house. There he would care for their wounds, bathe their bodies, and treat them with infinite tenderness and respect.

By so doing John began to attract public attention. The bishop visited and conferred his approbation by clothing John in a religious habit and giving him the title John of God. The town expressed appreciation by providing him with a hospital, which he operated with professional care. Still, he received abuse from many quarters — not least from many of his broken and derelict guests. When he was denounced as a hypocrite or a fool, he welcomed the insults as further opportunities for penance. Once when a prostitute was railing against him and his failings he thrust two silver coins into her hand and urged her to share her vilification of his name with the world.

Unworthy though he felt himself to be, John experienced many mystical visions. In one case, as he was washing the wounded feet of a beggar he had carried home, he was astonished to see that the man appeared transfigured, bathed in a radiant light which seemed to envelop John himself, so that when he appeared in the hallway some of the guests thought that he was on fire. On another occasion, he heard a celestial voice saying, "John, all you do for the poor in my name is done for me. It is my hand that receives your alms; it is my body that you clothe, my feet that you wash."

His days and nights were divided between prayer and his ministrations to the needs of a raucous, demanding household. His own needs for rest, sleep, and proper food were ignored. But through it all, eventually, he discovered that he was at peace. In the face of the poor he had found not only the face of Christ, but the features of his own family. All the care he could not offer his mother and father he lavished on those who came to him.

One day, after jumping into a river to save a drowning man, he came down with a terrible chill. Though he struggled to continue his work, his health was broken. When he knew that death was near, he asked those gathered round his bed to leave him alone for a few minutes. When they returned after a short while, they found his lifeless body, kneeling on the floor before a crucifix. He died on March 8, 1550, at the age of fifty-five.

Many of the men he had rescued had by this time joined him in his work. They later became the nucleus of the Brothers Hospitallers, recognized in 1571 by Pope Pius V as an officially approved religious congregation. Their motto is "Caritas."

See: Alban Goodier, S.J., "St. John of God," in F. J. Sheed, ed., *Saints Are Not Sad* (New York: Sheed & Ward, 1949).

March 9

St. Gregory of Nyssa
Bishop (c. 330–c. 395)

"He who applies himself to prayer, having taken the Spirit for guide and support, burns with the love of the Lord and is enkindled with desire, not finding satiety in prayer but being always enflamed with the desire of the Good."

Gregory of Nyssa was one of ten children born in Cappadocia (now Asia Minor) to a remarkable Christian family. Both his parents, Peter and Macrina, were later canonized as saints, as were his brothers *St. Basil the Great and St. Peter of Sebastea, and a sister, *St. Macrina. With Basil and their friend St. Gregory Nazianzen, Gregory is known as one of the great "Cappadocian fathers" who were largely responsible for the formulation of orthodox teaching on the Trinity and on the nature of Christ.

Gregory at first pursued a secular path. He studied rhetoric and philosophy in Athens and was married. Eventually, however, he was persuaded by his countryman Gregory Nazianzen to renounce "the ignoble glory" of secular knowledge and to seek ordination. It is not certain whether Gregory's wife was still living at this point or whether, as some have supposed, she had entered into a monastery. Clerical celibacy was not, at that time, a universal requirement for ordination, but judging from Gregory's panegyrics on the virtue of virginity it seems likely, at the least, that he and his wife had adopted a chaste relationship.

In 372, at the insistence of his brother Basil, bishop of Caesarea, Gregory was chosen as bishop of the small Cappadocian outpost of Nyssa. It was a time of bitter rivalry between the orthodox bishops and the proponents of Arianism, a heresy which denied the identity of being between the three Persons of the Trinity. Although the matter had supposedly been decided at the Council of Nicea (325), large areas of the church continued to hold to some version of Arian belief. The contest between opposing sides was pursued by means fair and foul. At first Gregory proved unequal to the challenge, and Arian enemies contrived to have him arrested on charges of embezzlement. He managed to escape but had to endure some years of exile before he was vindicated and restored to his see in 378.

By this time Basil had died, and Gregory stepped forward to assume the mantle of leadership. Through prolific writing, vigorous preaching, and his contributions at the Council of Constantinople (381) Gregory emerged as one of the most effective champions of orthodoxy. He helped to provide the language that affirmed the simultaneous unity of being and differentiation among the Persons of the Trinity. He also defended the presence of divine and human wills in Christ, thus affirming his identity, at the same time, as God and human.

Aside from these doctrinal questions, Gregory was highly influential in the area of ascetical and mystical theology. Gregory prepared many texts on the theme of the soul's journey to union with God. His "Life of Moses" presented the story of *Moses, his communion with God in the burning bush, and his wanderings in the desert as a symbolic account of the spiritual life. For Gregory the purpose of prayer was to withdraw the soul from sin so that in its original purity it might serve as a mirror of the divine glory.

> God has imprinted the image of the good things of His own nature on creation. But sin, in spreading out over the divine likeness, has caused this good to disappear, covering it with shameful garments. But if, by life rightly led, you wash away the mud that has been put on your heart, the Godlike beauty will again shine out in you.

See: Louis Bouyer, *The Spirituality of the New Testament and the Fathers* (London: Burns & Oates, 1963).

March 10

Marie Joseph Lagrange
Dominican Founder of the École Biblique
(1855–1938)

"It appears that the moment has come when we can no longer remain inactive without endangering the salvation of souls, and without banishing the intellectual strength which is bound up with it; it appears that by moving forward we can win many more souls."

Père Lagrange, as he was widely known, was a French Dominican priest and one of the most outstanding Scripture scholars in the Catholic church. In 1890 the Dominicans sent him to Jerusalem to found the École Biblique, the first modern Catholic school of biblical and archeological research. Under the leadership of Lagrange, the École became a haven for the renewal of biblical studies in the church. It was there that the groundwork was laid for the eventual acceptance of modern biblical criticism.

Despite his wide influence, Lagrange faced relentless criticism, occasional censorship, and the frequent threat of official condemnation. This was the razor's edge on which any serious Catholic biblical scholar was forced to walk in those days. Some fell over the edge and ended in scorn for a church that seemed to love authority more than the truth.

Others, like Lagrange, believed it was not necessary to make a choice. They worked away quietly, their minds as well as their faith at the service of the church they loved, hoping to avoid condemnation while widening a path that others might one day follow.

The critical methods of the École were moderate, bringing archeological evidence to bear on such questions as the sources of the Pentateuch. Lagrange was greatly encouraged by the publication in 1893 of *Pope Leo XIII's encyclical *Providentissimus Deus,* the first modest encouragement to modern biblical scholarship in the Catholic church. Leo encouraged Catholic scholars to become proficient in ancient languages and the skills of textual analysis. Ultimately it was a conservative document, aimed at enlisting the help of scholars in justifying church doctrine and countering the enemy of rationalism.

But Lagrange found support in Leo's teaching for his own investigations into such subjects as the authorship and dating of the Pentateuch and the book of Daniel. The tricky question was whether genuine scholarship could subject itself to predetermined dogmatic conclusions. It was the teaching of the church, for example, that *Moses was the sole author of the Pentateuch. Lagrange prepared a study disputing this tradition. Some of his colleagues urged him not to publish his findings. Silence was the prudent course. But, he asked, "is this really how truth is served? Is it not the task of the present to prepare for the future? Can we ever move forward without taking steps?" He published the book, and it set off a torrent of criticism.

In the next years biblical criticism became the storm center of Catholic theology, much of it centering on the work of the French priest and scholar, Alfred Loisy (d. 1940). Loisy was the foremost Catholic champion of modern biblical criticism, and Lagrange admired his work and his courage. Unlike Lagrange, however, Loisy applied the conclusions of his exegesis to such theological topics as the foundation of the church and the evolution of doctrine. His work was officially condemned in 1907 by Pope Pius X as the central focus of what the Vatican called the heresy of "Modernism."

Unlike Loisy, who ultimately left the church, Lagrange continued to believe that the opening of Leo XIII left room for honest scholarship, and he remained convinced that such work was ultimately at the service of the church. Nevertheless, in 1912, he was forced under bitter attack to leave the École altogether. He continued for many years to endure the charges from conservative prelates that he was a traitor, a crypto-modernist. Untroubled in his conscience, Lagrange carried on with his scholarly work, producing commentaries on the Gospels of Luke, Matthew, and John, as well as many other articles and monographs; his complete bibliography contains 1,786 items.

The quiet and faithful work of Lagrange maintained the honor of Catholic scholarship and helped to facilitate the reconciliation between Catholic faith and modern biblical criticism. He did not live to see his work vindicated by the encyclical *Divino Afflante Spiritus* (1943) of Pope Pius XII, and later by the Second Vatican Council. But apart from his biblical studies, he stands as a heroic example of the Catholic scholar, equally committed to tradition, the community of faith, and the pursuit of truth.

Père Lagrange died on March 10, 1938.

See: Père Lagrange: Personal Reflections and Memoirs, trans. Rev. Henry Wansbrough (New York: Paulist, 1985).

March 11
St. Maximilian
Martyr (d. 295)

"My army is the army of God, and I cannot fight for this world."

St. Maximilian, a third-century martyr in North Africa, was killed for refusing to serve in the Roman army. Maximilian at the time was twenty-one when he was brought before the court of the Roman proconsul Dion and charged with refusing conscription. Maximilian explained: "I cannot enlist for I am a Christian. I cannot serve, I cannot do evil." To this the proconsul replied, "You must serve or die."

MAXIMILIAN: I will never serve. You can cut off my head, but I will not be a soldier of this world, for I am a soldier of Christ.

DION: What has put these ideas into your head?

MAXIMILIAN: My conscience and He who has called me...

DION: Be a soldier and accept the emperor's badge.

MAXIMILIAN: Not at all. I carry the mark of Christ my God already.

DION: I shall send you to your Christ at once.

MAXIMILIAN: I ask nothing better. Do it quickly, for there is my glory....

DION: Write his name down.... Your impiety makes you refuse military service, and you shall be punished accordingly as a warning to others.

The sentence was then read: "Maximilian has refused the military oath through impiety. He is to be beheaded."

MAXIMILIAN: God liveth!

The sentence was carried out immediately. His feast day is observed on March 12.

See: The complete *passio* of St. Maximilian, included in *Butler's Lives of the Saints.*

Rutilio Grande
Martyr of El Salvador (1928–1977)

"It is a dangerous thing to be a Christian in our world."

In the annals of the suffering church of Latin America, El Salvador has earned a special chapter. Beginning in the 1970s, it fell to this tiny, impoverished country, named for the Savior, to represent most dramatically the ongoing crucifixion of Christ in his people. The poor had always suffered under the weight of an oppressive oligarchy. But in the 1970s the struggle for justice was joined by an awakened church. Priests and Sisters, having immersed themselves in the world of the poor, had come to identify with their cause, as well. But to share the cause of the poor, as *Archbishop Romero put it, meant risking "the same fate as the poor,... to disappear, to be tortured, to be captive, and to be found dead." This became the fate of dozens of priests, religious, and the archbishop himself, joining tens of thousands of the faithful poor of El Salvador. The first of them was Father Rutilio Grande.

He was born into a poor family from the small town of El Paisnal. He announced his desire to become a priest at the age of twelve, and five years later entered the Jesuits. Despite his earnest piety, there was nothing in Grande's early years to anticipate his later role as a fearless prophet of justice. He was by all accounts a rather callow seminarian, given to debilitating scrupulosity and a sense of unworthiness that plagued him right up to his ordination in 1959. It was only in the mid-1960s that Grande seemed to undergo a second conversion. In the new atmosphere following Vatican II, he acquired a different understanding of his vocation. Previously he had felt a priest was called to set an example of perfection. Now, as he came to believe, what was demanded was an example of self-sacrifice and loving service. From that time he seemed to exude a new confidence and joy in his priesthood.

In 1965, after studies abroad, Grande returned to the seminary in San Salvador as director of social action projects. In the nine years he spent in this position he had an enormous effect on the formation of all the clergy in El Salvador. Whereas in the past priests had carried an exalted status in society, patronized by the wealthy, Grande encouraged the seminarians to spend time living among the peasants in the countryside, learning to understand their struggles and their faith.

Increasingly Grande began to exemplify a new church in El Salvador, committed to awakening in the poor a sense of their dignity and rights as children of God. This was a time when the social contradictions in El Salvador were building to a violent crisis. In this atmosphere, Grande acquired a reputation as a "radical" priest, an enemy of the system. With the bishops facing pressure to "do something" about this troublesome influence, Grande resigned from his position in the seminary and took up an assignment as pastor of Aguilares, a small town near his birthplace. There he established a vigorous pastoral ministry, training lay catechists to insert the gospel message throughout the community. In base communities peasants studied the Word of God and in that light raised critical questions about the sources of their oppression. Grande's sermons on social justice were infamous among the town's elite, and once again the pressure mounted to have him silenced.

On February 13, 1977, Grande preached the sermon of his life. The occasion was a Mass in honor of Father Mario Bernal, a Colombian-born priest who had recently been arrested and deported without charges. Denouncing the sham of democracy in El Salvador, the feudal enslavement of the masses, and the hypocrisy of those who called themselves Christians while tolerating such conditions, Grande stated:

> I'm quite aware that very soon the Bible and the gospel won't be allowed to cross our borders. We'll get only the bindings, because all the pages are subversive. And I think that if Jesus himself came across the border at Chalatenango, they wouldn't let him in. They would accuse the Man-God, the prototype of man, of being a rabble-rouser, a foreign Jew, one who confused the people with exotic and foreign ideas, ideas against democracy — that is, against the wealthy minority, the clan of Cains! Brothers, without any doubt, they would crucify him again. And God forbid that I be one of the crucifiers!

These were dangerous words, and they did not go unnoticed. On March 12, while driving on the road to El Paisnal, Grande's van was sprayed with gunfire. He was killed instantly, along with an old campesino and a teenage boy who were accompanying him.

His death marked a stunning turning point for El Salvador, the first but not the last time that a priest would be exposed to violence. Among those touched by this event was the new archbishop of San Salvador, Oscar Romero. Grande, a longtime friend, had pressed Romero to understand and speak out against the social crisis in El Salvador. It was Grande's death that forced him to understand, and it proved the catalyst that prompted his own journey on the road to Calvary.

See: William J. O'Malley, S.J., *The Voice of Blood: Five Christian Martyrs of Our Time* (Maryknoll, N.Y.: Orbis, 1980).

March 13

Cardinal Yves Congar
Dominican Theologian (1904–1995)

*"The future is prepared in the waiting when the seed,
once deposited, puts forth a shoot and grows.
What is essential is to have sown the seed."*

Yves Congar was by any measure one of the towering figures in twentieth-century Catholic theology. Altogether, he published over fifteen hundred books and articles. In the area of ecclesiology, the theology of the church, he was probably the most significant figure since the Council of Trent. Although he laid the foundations for Vatican II, he was for many years the target of carping critics in Rome. Nevertheless by his later years he enjoyed universal esteem. Few of his peers possessed such a combination of brilliance, loyalty to the church, and personal holiness.

Born in France on March 13, 1904, Congar decided at the age of seventeen to become a priest, a decision partly influenced by the great suffering he had witnessed during World War I. Eventually he entered the Dominican order and studied in their seminary in Belgium. By the 1930s he had begun to explore the problem of ecumenism, a topic that would occupy his attention for the rest of his career. Congar was always concerned with overcoming the divisions in the Body of Christ. This earned him criticism from conservatives in the church who preferred to consider Protestants as schismatic heretics rather than as "separated brethren."

In 1939, with the outbreak of war, Congar was called up to serve as a military chaplain. Within a year he was captured by the Germans and spent the next several years as a prisoner-of-war at the infamous Colditz fortress. As a result of his wartime service he was later awarded the Croix de Guerre. But despite the hardships of prison life, he considered this a vital training ground in his formation as a theologian. Struck by the general contempt of his fellow soldiers for the Roman Catholic church, he was confirmed in his commitment to ecumenical dialogue and to the need for a greater openness to the secular world.

In these years Catholic theology, following the condemnation of Modernism earlier in the century, was dominated by a fairly rigid and insular neo-scholasticism. Many of the French Dominicans of Congar's day turned in the direction of historical theology, either returning to the original innovative spirit of *Thomas Aquinas or to the earlier church fathers. Congar shared this tendency, emphasizing the need to "return to the sources." Thus he pursued in-depth studies of such issues as the development of doctrine, the principle of reform, the sources of Christian division, and the principle of authority in the church. His historical research surfaced resources for a more spiritual understanding of the church, thus opposing the dominant tendency to give exclusive emphasis to the church's juridical, hierarchical, and institutional elements. Consistently, Congar emphasized the distinction between Tradition and traditionalism. The latter was an unyielding commitment to the past. The former was a living principle of commitment to the Beginning, a process that required creativity, inspiration, and a spirit of openness to the present as well as respect for the past.

Two of Congar's works, on reform in the church and on the theology of the laity, proved especially controversial (though ultimately influential). Congar believed that reform was a vital and necessary dimension of the church. This was rooted in the distinction between the church and the kingdom of God and in the intermingling in the church of both divine and human elements. In light of the church's constant temptation to revert to institutionalism it was always necessary to allow room for the prophetic voice, issuing from the margins, even though this might mean attending to uncomfortable truths.

Equally challenging was Congar's groundbreaking work on the role of the laity. The tendency of the time was virtually to identify the church with the hierarchy or to consign the laity to a merely passive role in the life of the church. In contrast, Congar emphasized the vital role of the laity in the mission of the church. Their vocation was not simply to "listen and obey" but to link the sacred and the profane, to transform the world according to the values of the kingdom of God.

In the 1950s Congar was closely associated with the worker priests (see *Henri Perrin), a missionary movement that encouraged priests to enter the world of the working class by taking up factory jobs. Congar believed this was a vital effort to overcome the growing gulf between the church and the secular world. But the movement was ultimately suppressed, and Congar himself was harshly criticized. For several years he was forbidden to write or teach. He accepted these sanctions in a spirit of faithful obedience. Among his criteria for reform he had always believed one must be guided by charity, infused with a desire "to remain in the communion of the Whole," and committed to the virtue of patience.

In the end Congar was recalled from his internal exile by *Pope John XXIII, who asked him to serve on the preparatory committee for Vatican II. Ultimately he served on a number of council committees and became one of the chief architects of the documents on revelation, the church, mission, ecumenism, and the church in the modern world. Congar's influence in all these areas was enormous. It can be recognized in the council's extreme sensitivity to ecumenical issues, in the famous definition of the church as "the People of God," and in the respectful attention given to the role of the laity. Above all it can be seen in the council's acknowledgment of ecclesial frailty, as witnessed in the unprecedented confession of the church as being "at once holy and always in need of reformation."

By the 1980s Congar was gradually overcome by a painful and paralyzing disorder that left him unable to work. He accepted this suffering with typical grace. In 1985 John Paul II honored him by naming him a cardinal. He died on June 22, 1995, at the age of ninety-one.

See: Aidan Nichols, O.P., *Yves Congar* (London: Geoffrey Chapman, 1989); *Fifty Years of Catholic Theology: Conversations with Yves Congar,* ed. Bernard Lauret (Philadelphia: Fortress, 1988).

March 14

Fannie Lou Hamer
Prophet of Freedom (1917–1977)

"I am sick and tired of being sick and tired."

Fannie Lou Hamer was born the daughter of sharecroppers in the Mississippi Delta, a poor black woman in the poorest region of America. And yet she rose up from obscurity to challenge the mighty rulers of her day, a towering prophet whose eloquence and courage helped guide and inspire the struggle for freedom.

Until 1962 her life was little different from other poor black women in rural Mississippi. One of twenty children in her family, she was educated to the fourth grade and, like her parents before her, fell into the life of sharecropping. This system allowed poor farmers to work a piece of the plantation owner's land in exchange for payment of a share of their crop. In practice, it was a system of debt slavery that combined with segregation and brute force to keep the black population poor and powerless. Looking back on her own twenty years of sharecropping, Hamer later said, "Sometimes I be working in the fields and I get so tired, I say to the people picking cotton with us, 'Hard as we have to work for nothing, there must be some way we can change this.'"

The way opened up for Hamer when she attended a civil rights rally in 1962 and heard a preacher issue a call for blacks to register to vote. At the age of forty-five Hamer answered the call, though it meant overcoming numerous threats and obstacles and resulted in the eviction of her family from their plantation home. Hamer took this as a sign to commit herself to full-time work for the freedom movement, serving as a field secretary for the Student Nonviolent Coordinating Committee, and quickly rising to a position of leadership.

For a black person in 1963 to challenge the system of segregation in Mississippi was literally to court death. Hamer, like other activists in the movement, faced this reality on a daily basis. In the summer of 1963 she was part of a group arrested in Charleston, South Carolina, after they illegally entered the side of a bus terminal reserved for whites. While in jail she was savagely beaten, emerging with a damaged kidney and her eyesight permanently impaired.

In 1964 Hamer led a "Freedom Delegation" from Mississippi to the National Convention of the Democratic Party in Atlantic City. There they tried unsuccessfully to challenge the credentials of the official white delegation. President Lyndon Johnson would tolerate no such embarrassment to the party bosses of the South, and the Freedom Delegation was evicted. But Hamer touched the conscience of the nation with her eloquent account of the oppression of blacks in the segregated South and their nonviolent struggle to affirm their dignity and their rights.

In later years, Hamer's concerns grew beyond civil rights to include early opposition to the Vietnam War and efforts to forge a coalition among all poor and working people in America — the Poor People's Campaign that *Martin Luther King left uncompleted. In all these endeavors, Hamer was sustained by her deep biblical faith in the God of the oppressed. "We have to realize," she once observed,

> just how grave the problem is in the United States today, and I think the sixth chapter of Ephesians, the eleventh and twelfth verses help us to know ... what it is we are up against. It says, "Put on the whole armor of God, that ye may be able to stand against the wiles of the devil. For we wrestle not against flesh and blood but against principalities, against powers, against the rulers of the darkness of this

world, against spiritual wickedness in high places." This is what I think about when I think of my own work in the fight for freedom.

In the nonviolent freedom struggle of the 1960s ordinary people — men, women, and children — became saints and prophets. Inspired by a vision of justice and freedom, sustained by faith, they found the strength to confront their fears and stand up to dogs, fire hoses, clubs, and bombs. In the ranks of this extraordinary movement Hamer was a rock who did as much as anyone of her time to redeem the promise of the gospel and the ideals of America. She said,

> Christianity is being concerned about your fellow man, not building a million-dollar church while people are starving right around the corner. Christ was a revolutionary person, out there where it was happening. That's what God is all about, and that's where I get my strength.

Hamer died of breast cancer on March 14, 1977.

See: Danny Collum et al., "Fannie Lou Hamer: Prophet of Freedom," *Sojourners* (December 1982).

March 15

St. Louise de Marillac
Co-Foundress of the Daughters of Charity
(1591–1660)

"Love the poor, honor them, as you would honor Christ."

Louise de Marillac was raised and educated by her widowed father, a distinguished country gentleman. His death, when she was fifteen, left her in desperate social straits, a situation alleviated only by her consent to marry a gentleman named Antony Le Gras, secretary to the household of the French queen. With him she bore a son, Michel. It was evidently a happy marriage. Nevertheless, she was visited periodically with anxious regrets that she had suppressed a vocation to religious life. When her husband was struck by a debilitating illness, Louise nursed him with great devotion. Even before his death, however, she privately vowed that she would not remarry, but would instead devote her life to the service of God.

After the death of Le Gras Louise withdrew from public life, awaiting some sign of her vocation. This came with her introduction in 1623 to *Father Vincent de Paul, who consented to become her spiritual director and with whom she went on to form one of the great partnerships in the history of religious life.

Monsieur Vincent, as he was widely known, had organized an extraordinary range of charitable projects. These included a circle of aristocratic ladies who joined to work in the Parisian slums among the sick and destitute. Louise readily committed herself to this work. But with time it became clear that the needs of the poor required more effective service than could be provided by such well-intentioned but part-time volunteers. Vincent and Louise formed the notion of a community of women completely committed to loving service to the poor. Thus were born the Daughters of Charity.

From the beginning, Vincent did not conceive of the community as a religious congregation. "Your convent," he wrote, "will be the house of the sick; your cell, a hired room; your chapel, the parish church; your cloister, the streets of the city or the wards of the hospital; your enclosure, obedience; your grating, the fear of God; your veil, holy modesty." Nevertheless, the Daughters were later recognized by Rome as a religious congregation, with members annually renewing vows of poverty, chastity, and obedience. Such recognition of a congregation of women living outside of an enclosed convent and engaged in apostolic work in the world was a novel and remarkable achievement. Although the gray habits and white headdresses later became a distinctive emblem of the Sisters of Charity, at the time their dress was indistinguishable from the garb of contemporary peasant women. In their spiritual formation the Sisters were constantly reminded that the poor were their masters. In them they would encounter the face of Christ. And so they should never hesitate to leave off from other spiritual obligations should they be summoned by those in need. They should realize that in leaving off their prayers or even the Mass to go to the poor they would be going, as it were, "from God to God."

The numbers and works of the Daughters expanded quickly. Soon their communities had spread throughout France and other parts of Europe. With members drawn particularly from among the peasant class, they could be found administering hospitals, orphanages, and schools for the poor, as well as ministering to prisoners and galley slaves and visiting the poor in their squalid hovels. Louise herself cared for the victims of the plague during an epidemic in Paris.

Louise de Marillac was by all accounts a valiant and inspired leader, whose voluminous correspondence with her beloved friend and mentor reveals at the same time her refinement and acute spiritual wisdom. One source of anxiety was her slow-witted son, Michel, to whom, naively, she attributed a vocation to the priesthood. Vincent gently persuaded her that the boy felt no such calling. Michel eventually married and went on to become a civil servant. Years later Louise was happy to receive him with his wife and child at her deathbed. She was deprived, however, of the consoling presence of her friend, Monsieur Vincent, whose age and infirmity kept him from her side. He sent her word that they would soon be reunited in heaven.

Toward the close of her life Louise worried about the future of her congregation. She was afraid in particular that the Sisters would lose touch with the radical spirit of service in the world and become "institutionalized," like so many other religious communities. Vincent shared this concern. Whereas the aim of most religious was their own perfection, he conceived that "these Daughters are used...for the salvation and comfort of the neighbor." Repeatedly, Louise admonished her Sisters to be "diligent in serving the poor...to love the poor, honor them, my children, as you would honor Christ Himself."

She died on March 15, 1660. Vincent de Paul followed her six months later. Louise was canonized in 1934, by which time the Sisters of Charity numbered more than fifty thousand around the world.

See: J. Calvet, *Louise de Marillac: A Portrait* (New York: P. J. Kenedy & Sons, 1959); Joseph I. Dirvin, C.M., *Louise de Marillac* (New York: Farrar, Straus & Giroux, 1970).

March 16

St. Abraham Kidunaia
Hermit (sixth century)

"It is not new to fall; what is wrong is to lie down when you have fallen. Remember where you stood before you fell. The devil once mocked you, but now he will know that you can rise stronger than ever before.... Do not draw back from the mercy of God."

As a wealthy young man, St. Abraham felt irresistibly drawn to a life of prayer. His parents, unfortunately, had planned otherwise; they arranged for him to be married. On his very wedding day Abraham stole off to become a desert hermit. Afterward he lived for many years in a small cell with no possessions but a bowl for his food and drink, a mat on which he slept, and a goatskin garment in which he clothed himself. Despite his vocation to solitude, he had at least two occasions to return to the world — once on a mission for the church, and another time on a personal errand of mercy.

At one point the local bishop asked him to leave his cell and make an effort to convert the residents of a nearby pagan settlement. These people had no interest in Abraham's message, and they harshly beat him for his troubles. When he returned again, denouncing their idolatry and proclaiming the gospel, they nearly stoned him to death. Still he kept returning, enduring continuous abuse and insults. After three years of this campaign, however, his efforts were rewarded. The people asked to be baptized, and they became his devoted disciples. Thus, Abraham felt himself acquitted of further responsibilities and happily returned to his cell.

Another extraordinary chapter in the life of St. Abraham concerns his relationship with an orphaned niece, Mary, who was sent to live with him at the age of seven after her parents died. Abraham built her an adjoining cell, and there she was raised in the holy atmosphere of prayer and monastic discipline.

Twenty years passed. A visiting monk, struck by Mary's beauty, waited until Abraham was out and then raped her. Feeling polluted and shamed, the innocent young woman was unable to face her uncle. She fled in despair to a distant city and there found shelter in a brothel. After two years Abraham learned of her location, though he knew nothing of the circumstances of her flight. He borrowed a horse and the dress of a soldier and made his way to the brothel. Though his heart nearly broke at the sight of his niece, dressed and made up as a harlot, he played the part of an eager customer and waited until they were alone together before disclosing his identity.

Tears filled his eyes as Abraham pleaded with her to explain how she could have fallen to such depths. But Mary, "overcome with shame and fear," made no answer. Finally he exclaimed, "Why do you not speak to me, my heart? Have I not come to take you home, my child? On me be your sin, my daughter, and on the day of judgment I will render an account of it for you to the Lord; it is I who will be responsible for this to God."

She insisted that her sin was too great for her ever to return to her old life. But Abraham continued to talk of God's infinite mercy. "To you, your sins seem like mountains," he said, "but God has spread his mercy over all that He has made....If sparks could set fire to the ocean, then indeed your sins could defile the purity of God." Throughout the night he counseled and cajoled her thus. "Sin is only part of being human; it happened to you very quickly and now by the help of God you are coming out of it even more quickly, for He does not will the death of sinners, but rather that they may live."

Finally her heart was melted by her uncle's great love. She spoke to him: "If you know of any penance I can do which God will receive from me, command me and look I will do it. Go first and I will follow and I will kiss your footprints as I go. For you have so grieved for me that you came down even into this pit of filth in order to bring me out." And so she spent the rest of the night weeping at his feet: "What can I give to You, O Lord, to repay all that you have done for me?"

Afterward Mary and Abraham returned to their cells. Mary's prayer was now more ardent than ever. Abraham lived on for another ten years, finally dying at the age of seventy. His biographer takes note of his many years spent battling the devil, but remarks, "the greatest and most wonderful fight he ever undertook was for the most blessed Mary."

See: St. Ephraem of Edessa, "The Life of St. Mary the Harlot," in Helen Waddel, *The Desert Fathers* (Ann Arbor: University of Michigan Press, 1957).

March 17

St. Patrick
Apostle to Ireland (389–461)

"Christ be with me,
Christ before me,
Christ behind me....
Christ in the heart of everyone who thinks of me,

Christ in the mouth of everyone who speaks of me,
Christ in every eye that sees me,
Christ in every ear that hears me."

Thanks to the Irish diaspora, the feast of St. Patrick is widely celebrated in many parts of the world. Admittedly, this celebration is more often an occasion for national pride than for reflection on the cause to which the saint dedicated his life. Ironically, St. Patrick is much better known for his apocryphal achievement — having rid the Emerald Isle of snakes — than for his actual accomplishments as a missionary. But even his great achievement, having established the Christian church in Ireland, tends to overshadow some of the more personal and poignant aspects of his life.

Patrick's mission to Ireland and its successful outcome is justly celebrated. But it is often forgotten that Patrick's first introduction to Ireland was involuntary. At the age of sixteen he was kidnapped by Irish raiders, stolen from his home, a village somewhere along the western coast of Roman Britain, and taken to Ireland as a slave. Previously he had lived a relatively comfortable life as the son of a petty Roman official. This violent change in his life, as may well be supposed, was a shocking experience. He found himself sold to a local king who employed him in a variety of menial occupations, such as herding livestock on the desolate mountains of the north. As a slave, his life was not valued more highly than the beasts he tended. As he later wrote, "I was chastened exceedingly and humbled every day in hunger and nakedness."

At the same time, far from home and with little prospect of ever seeing his family again, he remembered who he was and where he came from. In particular, he clung fast to his faith as a Christian. Whereas previously he had been relatively indifferent in his faith, now he liked to spend his long days among the flocks reciting endlessly the prayers impressed on his memory since childhood. All the while he dreamed of escape. Eventually, after six years of captivity, an opportunity arose and he seized it. His flight involved a risky journey of two hundred miles to the sea, where he found a place on a boat sailing for the Continent. Thus, eventually, after many further adventures, he made his way back to his home village.

The scene of his family reunion can scarcely be imagined. But the young man who had now returned from the dead was no longer the carefree adolescent of before. He bore the scars of a terrible ordeal, but also the zeal of a profound faith. In the light of this faith he was convinced that both his sufferings and his deliverance had been ordained for some divine purpose.

It was some years hence that this purpose became plain. While living in Gaul, where he had traveled to study for the priesthood, he had a series of dreams in which Irish voices, the voices of those who had stolen his youth, cried out to him, "We beseech thee to come and walk once more among us." At first his superiors resisted the idea of his return to Ireland, judging among other things that he lacked the learning and skills for such a dangerous mission. But he overcame their objections, and so in 432, by this time a consecrated bishop, he returned to the island from which providence had once aided his escape.

Patrick's thirty years as a wandering bishop in Ireland are wrapped in legend, but the scope of his achievements is a matter of historical record. Within ten years he had established the primatial see of Armagh and a network of churches and monasteries throughout the country, all in the hands of a native clergy. He personally baptized tens of thousands of the faithful and ordained hundreds of priests. Although he was not all alone in his work of evangelization, his stature as patron of Ireland is well deserved.

But in a land that has been rent asunder by the memory of ancient crimes and injustices, it should be remembered that St. Patrick was himself the victim of Irish injustice before he ever became the symbol of Irish pride. His extraordinary return to the site of his oppression — not to wreak his vengeance, but to implant the reconciling seeds of his own hard-won faith — deserves appropriate commemoration. The gospel drove Patrick to return to his oppressors that he might devote his life to their peaceful conversion and the cause of their salvation. But the spiritual conquest of Ireland followed the prior victory of love over the anger and bitterness in his own heart. If the memory of this dimension of St. Patrick's life had long ago become a feature of his feast day celebration, it might be truly said that there are no serpents left in Ireland.

See: Maisie Ward, *Saints Who Made History* (New York: Sheed & Ward, 1959); *The Confession of St. Patrick* (New York: Triumph, 1996).

March 18

St. Cyril of Jerusalem
Doctor of the Church (c. 315–386)

"The way of godliness consists of these two parts, pious doctrines and good works. Neither are the doctrines acceptable to God without good works, nor does God accept works accomplished otherwise than as linked with pious doctrines."

St. Cyril was known for his moderate and conciliatory temperament. He deplored the intrusion of politics into the body of Christ and regretted the tendency of theological differences to end in bitter factionalism. Unfortunately, he had the ill fortune to live in a time of violent controversy when, among his fellow bishops, compromise was reckoned as treason and it seemed that one's own orthodoxy could be affirmed only by the condemnation of another's error.

Born in Jerusalem around the year 315, Cyril was later ordained a priest and became bishop in 349. Almost immediately he found himself embroiled in controversies inherited from his predecessor. Further jurisdictional disputes with the bishop of Caesarea resulted in Cyril's formal investigation by a local synod. Among the gravest accusations was that Cyril had sold church property — namely, gifts from the emperor — to give alms to the famine-stricken poor. Cyril was condemned and forced to go into exile. He returned after some years, only to find himself caught up in battles between proponents and opponents of Arianism. Cyril was accused by members of each side of being too sympathetic to the other. He died in 386 at the age of seventy. Of his thirty-five years as a bishop nearly sixteen were spent in exile.

In 1882 Cyril was named a Doctor of the Church, largely on the basis of his principal surviving work, *The Catechetical Lectures*. These talks were delivered to instruct adult catechumens in the Catholic faith, prior to baptism. They represent one of the first systematic accounts of Christian theology, centered around the articles of the creed. While reflecting Cyril's firm orthodoxy, they also underline his determination to present Christian faith in a positive light and to maintain a balance between correct belief and holy action. Even with the passage of many centuries, Cyril's lectures retain a fresh and attractive appeal:

> Let us, then, my brethren, endure in hope. Let us devote ourselves, side by side with our hoping, so that the God of all the universe, as he beholds our intention, may cleanse us from our sins, fill us with high hopes from what we have in hand, and grant us the change of heart that saves. God has called you, and you have your calling.

See: William Telfer, ed., *Cyril of Jerusalem and Nemesius of Emesa*, Library of Christian Classics, vol. 4 (Philadelphia: Westminster, 1960).

March 19

St. Joseph
(first century)

> *"Joseph, son of David, do not fear to take Mary your wife,*
> *for that which is conceived in her is of the Holy Spirit;*
> *she will bear a son, and you shall call his name Jesus,*
> *for he will save his people from their sins."*
> —Matthew 1:20

St. Joseph's part in the Nativity story is a familiar feature of every Christmas pageant. But for many centuries the church paid him scant attention. This is especially obvious compared with the extraordinary concern for the role of *Mary in the economy of salvation. So eager was the church to emphasize Jesus' divine paternity that Joseph, the surrogate father, was consigned to the shadowlands. It was only in the sixteenth century that any official encouragement was extended to his cult. Around that time St. Joseph, in a somewhat romanticized image of the Holy Family, began to figure more widely in popular preaching as the ideal "provider and protector." In 1870 Pius IX declared him Patron of the Universal Church.

Joseph appears in the Gospels of *Matthew and *Luke, both of which contain accounts of the Nativity of Jesus. Significant differences between the two versions reflect the theological interests of the two evangelists.

Nevertheless, both agree that Mary and Joseph were betrothed to be married when Mary was discovered to be pregnant. Luke's version emphasizes the perspective of Mary. When an angel informs her that she will bear a child by the Holy Spirit, she responds, "Behold, I am the handmaid of the Lord; let it be done to me according to your word." Thus, it has been said that the salvation of the world was rooted in Mary's *fiat* to God's plan.

But in Matthew's Gospel we receive the story from Joseph's perspective. Here the discovery of Mary's pregnancy precedes any divine reassurance, thus presenting Joseph with a terrible dilemma. Nevertheless, "her husband Joseph, being a just man and unwilling to put her to shame, resolved to divorce her quietly." (The text delicately avoids the alternative, namely, that she be stoned to death for adultery.) But when an angel appears to him in his sleep and explains the source of Mary's condition, he is apparently satisfied.

A silent figure throughout the Gospel, Joseph utters no words to correspond to Mary's heartfelt prayer. His actions, however, reflect the same pious consent to a plan beyond his understanding. "When Joseph woke from sleep, he did as the angel of the Lord commanded him; he took his wife, but knew her not until she had borne a son, and he called his name Jesus" (Matt. 2:18).

Aside from his virtues as a father or a man of faith, it is also worthwhile to note Joseph's status as a poor working man — a detail not without significance in the gospel. Although he is linked to the house of King David, Joseph remains a carpenter from a Galilean town so miniscule that it serves as the butt of jokes. His wife gives birth in a stable. In presenting their infant in the Temple, he and Mary can only afford to sacrifice pigeons. Soon after, again warned in a dream of King Herod's murderous intentions, Joseph must lead his family into exile in Egypt. Every one of these details emphasizes the distance between Jesus and the centers of power in his world.

And then, having returned the family to the town of Nazareth, Joseph effectively disappears from the story. By receding before the inauguration of Jesus' public ministry he does not interfere with Jesus' privileged relationship with the one he calls "Abba-Father." Joseph remains in the text only as a reminder of Jesus' humble origins and thus, in the eyes of sceptics, a cause for doubting his authority. "Can anything good come from Nazareth?" "Is this not Jesus, the carpenter's son?" Through the history of faith such mocking jests, rather than denigrating Jesus, have only rebounded to the credit of the faithful Joseph.

Besides his feast day on March 19 an additional feast, for St. Joseph the Worker, was assigned by Pope Pius XII on May 1.

See: Andrew Doze, *Discovering St. Joseph* (Slough, U.K.: St. Paul Publications, 1991).

March 20

Sebastian Castellio
Prophet of Religious Liberty (1515–1563)

"To kill a man is not to defend a doctrine, but to kill a man."

With the unfolding of the Reformation Christendom was increasingly rent by a profusion of doctrinal confessions. One side's orthodoxy was another's heresy. Amid this controversy there were a few who raised their voices to affirm one simple truth: that no doctrine of Christ should be a cause to inflict torture or death. Among the clearest of these voices was a French scholar, Sebastian Castellio.

As a young man in Lyons in January 1540 Castellio witnessed the public execution of three Lutheran heretics. He was profoundly shaken by the experience — so much so that he forsook his country and his Catholic faith. Declaring himself for the Protestant cause, he made his way to Geneva, where John Calvin appointed him as schoolmaster. He proved himself a creative scholar and a man of deep faith and courage. He put the city's ministers to shame when he volunteered, as they would not, to minister to the victims of the plague. Yet his own request for ordination was denied on the grounds of his liberal exegesis and doctrinal disagreements. Among other things, he refused to accept Calvin's notion that some people — the reprobate — are predestined to damnation. He believed this to be a monstrous doctrine. Thus discouraged, he moved to Basel where, after some years of poverty, he found a position as a professor of Greek.

In 1553, at Calvin's instigation, an amateur theologian named Michael Servetus was burned at the stake in Geneva for denying the doctrine of the Trinity. To Calvin it was the responsibility of the magistrate to defend true doctrine, and thus to maintain the honor of God. For Castellio this was a defining moment that called for immediate response. The message of Jesus was mercy and forgiveness. He believed there could be no greater blasphemy than to kill a human being in the name of God. He responded with a major book, *On Heretics: Whether They Should Be Punished by the Magistrate*, and several other impassioned works.

Castellio observed that Christ called his followers to put on the white dress of a pure and holy life. "But what instead occupies our thoughts? We do not dispute concerning the way to Christ, but on his relationship to God the Father, on the Trinity, predestination, freedom of the will, the nature of God, the angels, the state of the soul after death — on a multitude of things which are not essential to salvation; things which, in truth, we can never know unless our hearts are pure, for these things must be comprehended spiritually."

One's first duty as a Christian was to love one's neighbor as oneself. But how could one love one's neighbors while killing them over differences about "sound doctrine"? "Oh their sound doctrine!" he exclaimed of the theologians. "How Christ will despise them on the Day of Judgment for this sound doctrine!"

126 ~

Castellio noted that all sects are certain that their religious views are based on the Word of God. "Calvin says that his are certain and they theirs. He says they are wrong and wishes to be the judge and so do they. Who shall be judge? Who made Calvin the judge of all the sects, that he alone should kill?" What, after all, is a heretic? he asked. "After diligent investigation... I can discover no more than this, that we regard those as heretics with whom we disagree."

At a time when nearly all his contemporaries held to the view that "error has no rights," Castellio's plea for toleration and respect for the rights of conscience was certainly exceptional. "To force conscience is worse than cruelly to kill a man," he wrote, "because I must be saved by my own faith and not by that of another.... Religion resides not in the body but in the heart, which cannot be reached by the sword of kings and princes. The Church can no more be constructed by persecution and violence than walls can be built by cannon blasts." When Calvin asked how then was the true church to be recognized, Castellio answered, "By an assured faith concerning things which are hoped for, not known, by love which is better than faith and may be clearly discerned, by the doctrine of piety which is to love your enemies, bless those who curse you, to hunger and thirst after righteousness and endure persecution for righteousness' sake."

Castellio published his works using a pseudonym. Nevertheless, the authorities had little difficulty tracing them to his pen. Legal proceedings were initiated which might, presumably, have led to his imprisonment or exile, had he not died before they could be concluded in 1563. At that time the wars of religion in Europe had barely begun. Centuries were to pass before Castellio's position won widespread respect. His name deserves similar honor.

See: Roland Bainton, ed., *Concerning Heretics: An Anonymous Work Attributed to Sebastian Castellio* (New York: Octagon Books, 1965); Roland Bainton, *The Travails of Religious Liberty* (New York: Harper & Brothers, 1951).

March 21

Johann Sebastian Bach
Composer (1685–1750)

"Where there is devotional music,
God is always at hand with His gracious presence."

Despite his fantastic output as a composer, J. S. Bach was better known in his day as an organist. Only ten of his works — out of thousands — were published in his lifetime. Despite other opportunities he chose to spend most of his career as an organist and choir director in various churches in his native Germany. Only after his death did his renown as a composer — indeed one of the greatest and most popular composers of all time — become firmly established.

Although he composed music of nearly every type, most of Bach's compositions were written for use in church. These include his dramatic works, *The Passions* of St. Matthew and St. John, his *Mass in B Minor, The Magnificat,* and the many hundreds of his chorales. Bach was a devout Lutheran. His work was the perfect artistic reflection of Luther's conviction that the ear — attuned to the Word of God — rather than the eye, was the ideal "Christian sense." Bach's chorales were the Protestant counterpart to the stained-glass windows that adorned the medieval cathedrals or the Baroque paintings that filled the Catholic churches of his day: they engaged the minds and hearts of the worshiping congregation in the mystery and challenge of the gospel.

It seems plain that for Bach music was not simply a form of creative expression but an act of praise and devotion. He described his vocation as the creation of "well-regulated church music to the glory of God." In setting down his compositions he began each manuscript page with the initials "J. J." (*Jesu Juva,* "Help me, Jesus"), or "I.N.J." (*In Nomine Jesu,* "In the name of Jesus"). At the end of the composition he would set the initials "S.D.G." (*Solo Deo Gloria,* "To God alone the glory").

Bach was steeped in the Bible, a text, he believed, which illuminated not only the Christian faith but all of life with its sufferings and joys. Bach himself seems to have had a great capacity for enjoyment, both in his work and in his extensive family (he was the father of twenty children). Bach's spirituality, reflected in his music, is not for the cloister but for the world. Consequently, it is a remarkable fact that any place his music is performed seems instantly to be transformed into a sacred space.

Born on March 21, 1685, Bach died on July 28, 1750, at the age of sixty-five. From his deathbed, virtually blind, he dictated his final work, a chorale entitled "Before Thy Throne I Come." He was buried in an unmarked grave.

See: Gerald R. Cragg, *The Church and the Age of Reason* (New York: Penguin, 1970).

March 22

Emmanuel Mounier
Personalist Philosopher (1905–1950)

> *"On the altar of this sad world there is but one god, smiling and hideous: the Bourgeois. He has lost the true sense of being....He is a man without love, a Christian without conscience, an unbeliever without passion....Comfort is to the bourgeois world what heroism was to the Renaissance and sanctity to medieval Christianity — the ultimate value, the ultimate motive for all action."*

Emmanuel Mounier was born in Grenoble in 1905. He originally studied at the University of Grenoble for a degree in medicine but switched to philosophy and continued his studies at the Sorbonne in Paris. As a devout Catholic, Mounier found his faith challenged and ultimately strengthened by the defiantly secularist atmosphere of the university. But while he opposed the materialism of secular culture he became equally disdainful of the individualistic and complacent "spiritualism" of the established church. His hero was *Charles Péguy (d. 1916), the Catholic poet and activist who had struggled to define a brand of religious socialism capable of integrating the "political" and the "mystical."

Mounier called his own philosophical attitude Personalism, a perspective which accorded the highest value to the human person. As persons, so Mounier maintained, we possess both a temporal and spiritual dimension; we exist in history, in relationship with others, but open to transcendence and ultimately to God. This concept of the person, he believed, was denied as much by an atheistic totalitarianism of the Left as by the bourgeois materialism of capitalist society. To the extent that Christianity had become infected by the bourgeois spirit it had become a prop in what he called "the established disorder." Opposing this "disorder" became the central motive of his life.

In 1932, having abandoned an academic career, Mounier founded *L'Esprit,* a journal dedicated to the personalist cause. Launched in the ideologically polarized environment of the Depression, *L'Esprit* challenged the church to take a stand against injustice and to oppose the soulless culture of capitalism. At the same time it criticized the Marxists for promoting a spirit of class warfare and for denying the spiritual dimension of human existence. Above all it opposed "the bourgeois spirit," a mentality that valued only egoism, greed, and complacency and that was fundamentally opposed to the spirit of the gospel. Only by disassociating themselves from such a culture could Christians "restore Christian values to their full stature and recover their revolutionary potential."

After the Nazi occupation of Paris Mounier moved his operations to Vichy-controlled Lyons. There he entered into clandestine work for the Resistance. In January 1942 he was arrested for subversive activities and spent eleven months in prison. He managed to continue his philosophical studies in jail and was released in November, resolute in spirit, though physically debilitated.

After the war he quickly resumed the publication of *L'Esprit.* The journal played an important role in the rejuvenation of religious and intellectual life in the postwar years. Mounier vigorously opposed the spirit of revenge that threatened to overshadow the Liberation. At the same time he challenged the church to become engaged in the struggle for social reconstruction. To this end, he supported the worker priests who left their parish life to work alongside the factory workers. "I am very concerned," he wrote, "that we discover a means of entering into the suffering and struggle of the workers.... We have vainly tried to work for truth and justice, but we are not entirely with Christ so long as we do not take our place alongside those outcasts."

Mounier's effort to define an independent style of spiritual and social engagement brought criticism from both the Left and Right. To many Catholics his criticism of the church and society made him sound like some kind of communist. At the same time he was denounced in the Communist journal *L'Humanité* as "an idealistic mystic in league with fascists." Mounier defined his own position as one of "tragic optimism" —

a Christian attitude of absolute engagement in the struggles of history, despite the fact that the Absolute cannot be attained in history.

In 1950 Mounier published *Personalism,* the final distillation of his philosophical position. By that time political battles and the exhausting demands of his journalistic work had taken their toll. "Submitting to events" as he would to a spiritual director, he turned over the journal to other hands. Nevertheless, he died shortly afterward of a heart attack on March 22. He was forty-five.

See: Emmanuel Mounier, *Personalism* (Notre Dame, Ind.: University of Notre Dame Press, 1952); Eileen Cantin, *Mounier: A Personalist View of History* (New York: Paulist, 1973).

March 23

Nicolai Berdyaev
Philosopher (1874–1948)

"Always oriented to the future, the prophet is always dissatisfied with the present, denounces the evil in the life about him and awaits the future triumph of higher spiritual elements which are revealed to him in prophetic visions."

Nicolai Berdyaev was born in Kiev to a distinguished Russian family. As a boy he felt "alone and rootless in this world," a feeling which propelled him toward the study of philosophy. As a student at the University of Kiev he became sensitized to social injustice and rebelled against his privileged class. In 1898, after engaging in clandestine revolutionary activities among his fellow students, he was arrested. He was sentenced to three years of exile in the province of Vologda, during which period he continued his studies. Aided in part by his reading of *Dostoevsky he began to look critically at materialist philosophy. By the time he returned to Kiev he had embraced Orthodox Christianity.

For some years Berdyaev moved within a circle of intellectuals and artists who shared his interest in relating Christianity to the movement for social change. His critical and independent spirit ran him afoul of the Orthodox church as it had previously with the government. "I never pretended that my religious thought had a churchly character," he wrote. "I sought the truth and experienced as truth that which was revealed to me." In 1913, after publishing an article challenging the Holy Governing Synod for its identification with the tsarist state, he was arrested and charged with blasphemy — an offense that carried an obligatory sentence of exile for life to Siberia. Only the outbreak of World War I and the subsequent revolutionary turmoil allowed him to escape punishment.

Though he had remained critical of the tsarist regime, he was forthright in his rejection of the Bolshevik revolution: "a consistent application to life of Russian nihilism, atheism, and materialism," he called it. He continued to teach and wrote a number of remarkably outspoken books.

But in 1922 he was again arrested and banished from the Soviet Union on pain of death. He made his way first to Berlin and eventually to Paris, where he participated in ecumenical discussions and wrote a score of works on philosophical and religious themes. He died on March 23, 1948, at the age of seventy-four.

Berdyaev's particular concern was to affirm the spiritual dimension of the human person. This dimension was clearly denied in the collectivist and materialist doctrines of communism. But he was equally opposed to the godless materialism of capitalism and the progressive rise of the "bourgeois" spirit. All around him he witnessed a steady process of dehumanization. Both communism and capitalism reduced the human person to an object, a commodity, whether a machine or a consumer. The worst thing of all, he believed, was the capitulation of Christianity to this spirit. This occurred wherever Christianity substituted institutional security for the radical, subversive image of Christ, who forever confronts history with the eschatological challenge of the kingdom of God.

Berdyaev's hero was not so much the saint as the prophet who "visions a free and spiritual world and awaits its penetration into this stifling world." In the meantime the world was thirsting for a new type of Christian spirituality: "It cannot be an abstract form, retirement from the world and from mankind. The new Christian man...shares the suffering of the world, bears in his body the tragedy of man. He strives to bring the liberating, spiritual element into all of human life."

Throughout his life Berdyaev experienced a sense of lonely exile, a sense of standing apart from the religious and political values of his various milieux. His message was not calculated to win a warm reception. But there were many who appreciated his critique of a soulless world and found in his writings the voice of a true religious prophet.

See: Nicolai Berdyaev, *Christian Existentialism: A Berdyaev Anthology,* ed. Donald A. Lowrie (New York: Harper & Row, 1965).

March 24

Oscar Arnulfo Romero
Archbishop and Martyr of San Salvador (1917–1980)

"I rejoice, brothers and sisters, that our church is persecuted precisely for its preferential option for the poor and for seeking to become incarnate in the interests of the poor.... How sad it would be in a country where such horrible murders are being committed if there were no priests among the victims."

The selection in 1977 of Oscar Romero as archbishop of San Salvador delighted the country's oligarchy as much as it disappointed the activist clergy of the archdiocese. Known as a pious and relatively conservative bishop, there was nothing in his background to suggest that he was a man to challenge the status quo. No one could have predicted that in three short years he would be renowned as the outstanding embodiment of the prophetic church, a "voice for the voiceless," or, as one theologian called him, "a gospel for El Salvador." Nor could one foresee that he would be denounced by his fellow bishops, earn the hatred of the rich and powerful of El Salvador, and generate such enmity that he would be targeted for assassination — the first bishop slain at the altar since *Thomas Becket in the twelfth century.

Something changed him. Within weeks of his consecration he found himself officiating at the funeral of his friend *Rutilio Grande, a Jesuit priest of the archdiocese, who was assassinated as a result of his commitment to social justice. Romero was deeply shaken by this event, which marked a new level in the frenzy of violence overtaking the country. In the weeks and months following Grande's death Romero underwent a profound transformation. Some would speak of a conversion — as astonishing to his new friends as it was to his foes. From a once timid and conventional cleric, there emerged a fearless and outspoken champion of justice. His weekly sermons, broadcast by radio throughout the country, featured an inventory of the week's violations of human rights, casting the glaring light of the gospel on the realities of the day. His increasingly public role as the conscience of the nation earned him not only the bitter enmity of the country's oligarchy, but also the resentment of many of his conservative fellow bishops. There were those among them who muttered that Romero was talking like a subversive.

The church in El Salvador was not the first church to suffer persecution. The anomaly was that here the persecutors dared to call themselves Christians. Their victims did not die simply for clinging to the faith, but for clinging, like Jesus, to the poor. It was this insight that marked a new theological depth in Romero's message. For Romero, the church's option for the poor was not just a matter of pastoral priorities. It was a defining characteristic of Christian faith: "A church that does not unite itself to the poor in order to denounce from the place of the poor the injustice committed against them is not truly the Church of Jesus Christ," he wrote. On another occasion he said, "On this point there is no possible neutrality. We either serve the life of Salvadorans or we are accomplices in their death.... We either believe in a God of life or we serve the idols of death."

Once his course was set, Romero followed his path with courageous consistency. Privately he acknowledged his fears and loneliness, especially the pain he felt from the opposition of his fellow bishops and the apparent distrust of Rome. Constantly he was accused of subordinating the gospel to politics. At the same time he seemed to draw strength and courage from the poor campesinos, who embraced him with affection and understanding. "With this people," he said, "it is not hard to be a good shepherd."

The social contradictions in El Salvador were rapidly reaching the point of explosion. Coups, countercoups, and fraudulent elections brought forth a succession of governments, each promising reform, while leaving the military and the death squads free to suppress the popular demand for justice. As avenues for peaceful change were systematically thwarted, full-scale civil war became inevitable. In 1980, weeks before his death, Romero sent a letter to President Jimmy Carter appealing for a halt to further U.S. military assistance to the junta, "thus avoiding greater bloodshed in this suffering country." On March 23, 1980, the day before his death, he appealed directly to members of the military, calling on them to refuse illegal orders:

> We are your people. The peasants you kill are your own brothers and sisters. When you hear the voice of the man commanding you to kill, remember instead the voice of God. Thou Shalt Not Kill.... In the name of God, in the name of our tormented people whose cries rise up to heaven, I beseech you, I beg you, I command you, *stop the repression.*

The next day, as he was saying Mass in the chapel of the Carmelite Sisters' cancer hospital where he lived, a single rifle shot was fired from the rear of the chapel. Romero was struck in the heart and died within minutes.

Romero was immediately acclaimed by the people of El Salvador, and indeed by the poor throughout Latin America, as a true martyr and saint. For Romero, who clearly anticipated his fate, there was never any doubt as to the meaning of such a death. In an interview two weeks before his assassination, he said:

> I have frequently been threatened with death. I must say that, as a Christian, I do not believe in death but in the resurrection. If they kill me, I shall rise again in the Salvadoran people.
>
> Martyrdom is a great gift from God that I do not believe I have earned. But if God accepts the sacrifice of my life then may my blood be the seed of liberty, and a sign of the hope that will soon become a reality.... A bishop will die, but the church of God — the people — will never die.

See: Oscar Romero, *Voice of the Voiceless* (Maryknoll, N.Y.: Orbis, 1985); James R. Brockman, *Romero: A Life* (Maryknoll, N.Y.: Orbis, 1989).

March 25

St. Margaret Clitherow
English Martyr (d. 1586)

"Jesu, have mercy on me."

Margaret Clitherow was the first woman martyr for the Catholic faith in England during the reign of Queen Elizabeth. The daughter of a wealthy wax merchant of York, she married John Clitherow, a prosperous butcher, at the age of sixteen. Though raised as a Protestant, Margaret converted to the Catholic faith some years after her marriage, apparently inspired by the sufferings of so many Catholics under the repressive penal laws of the time. John Clitherow did not share his wife's new faith, but he placed no obstacles in her way, even when her public reputation as a Catholic incurred fines and other penalties. At one point Margaret was imprisoned for almost two years. She welcomed this as a period of retreat and put her time to good use by learning to read.

Despite the proven risks, Margaret offered a safe haven in her home for fugitive priests, housing them in a specially hidden room where she and other underground Catholics could attend Mass. Her husband turned a blind eye to these goings-on, though she made little secret of her faith. Often she was seen praying at the site of the gallows where many priests had offered their lives. On March 10, 1586, she was arrested. A search of her house uncovered the secret room along with vestments and other vessels and books obviously intended for Mass. Charged with sponsoring illegal religious services, she refused to enter a plea, hoping thus to spare her family and friends the risks of testifying in a trial. She knew, however, that this would automatically incur a judgment against her and the terrible penalty of death by pressing.

In vain the judge urged her to seek the mercy of the court, entreating her to consider her obligations to her husband and children. "I do honor my husband and love my children, according as duty and nature bindeth me," she replied with stalwart conviction, "but I am so far from seeking to help them by yielding unto your desires as that I wish both husband and children might suffer death with me in this good cause." While she was imprisoned she was not permitted to see her children, and only once saw her husband in the presence of the jailer. When he heard of her sentencing, John Clitherow "was like a man distracted, crying out that they would murder the best wife within the kingdom and the best Catholic."

She spent the last night of her life in prayer, accompanied by the jailer's wife, whose company she had requested ("Not that I fear death, for that is comfort; but the flesh is frail"). The next morning, March 25, she was taken to the site of her execution. Aside from her executioners there were a number of persons present, including several women. The sentence required that she be stripped naked for execution. The sheriff refused her request to forego this humiliation, but he and the men agreed to avert their eyes while the women undressed her.

Urged to beg the queen's forgiveness and also that of her husband, she replied, "If ever I have offended him, I do ask him for forgiveness from the bottom of my heart." Then she was placed on a sharp stone with a board laid over her on which steadily increasing weights were applied. She endured this punishment for only fifteen minutes before her ribs were shattered. Her last words were "Jesu, Jesu, Jesu, have mercy on me."

She was canonized in 1970 by *Pope Paul VI. Her feast is celebrated on October 25 among the "Forty Martyrs of England and Wales."

See: Father John Mush, "Bl. Margaret Clitherow," in Donald Attwater, ed., Martyrs: From St. Stephen to John Tung (New York: Sheed & Ward, 1957).

Harriet Tubman
Abolitionist (1820?–1913)

"Go down Moses,
Way down in Egypt land.
Tell ole Pharaoh,
Let my people Go!"

— Negro Spiritual

Harriet Tubman was born into slavery on a plantation in Maryland, sometime around 1820. The exact date is unknown, since the birth of slaves was not recorded. As she grew up, she experienced the typical cruelties of slave life, the beatings, insults, and daily indignities. Like other slaves she became skilled in the art of passive resistance — working slowly, breaking tools, adopting a false mask of simple-minded contentment — while struggling to maintain an inner conviction that she was indeed worth more than a thing. But Tubman was not content merely to survive with her inner dignity intact. She was convinced that God intended her to be free.

It is one of the miracles of Christian history that African slaves, having received a false gospel from their "Christian" slavemasters, nevertheless heard in the biblical story a message of life and liberation. The slavemasters' catechism stressed the virtue of obedience and counseled slaves to be content with their lot. But the slaves heard a different message. The God of the Bible was the God who led *Moses and the Hebrew slaves out of bondage in Egypt, who inspired the prophets, and who was incarnate in Jesus Christ. This was not the god of the slavemasters, but the God of the oppressed.

It was with this God that Harriet Tubman enjoyed a special relationship. From the time she was a child she was subject to deep trances in which she heard the voice of the Lord. In one of these visionary experiences in 1849 she saw "a line, and on the other side of that line were green fields, and lovely flowers, and beautiful white ladies, who stretched out their arms to me over the line, but I couldn't reach them no how. I always fell before I got to the line." When she awoke she took this vision as a signal for her to begin her escape.

Though small in stature, Tubman was a strong woman. She had spurned the housework coveted by most slaves in favor of backbreaking field work. She had trained herself over the years to move quietly, to be at home in nature, and to find her way in the dark. All these skills now came into play as she made her break. Traveling by night, following the North Star, she passed through swamps and forests, sleeping by day in the shelter of caves or hidden in a leafy treetop.

When she finally crossed into the free state of Pennsylvania, she looked at her hands "to see if I was the same person. There was such a glory over everything; the sun came like gold through the trees and over the fields, and I felt like I was in heaven." But at once she was seized by a sense of wider mission. "I had crossed the line. I was FREE; but there was no one to welcome me to the land of freedom. I was a stranger in a strange land; and my home, after all, was down in Maryland.... But I was free and THEY should be free. I would make a home in the North and bring them there, God helping me."

And so, having made her perilous way to freedom, Tubman chose to return to the South to assist in the escape of others still in bondage. Over the next twelve years she returned a total of nineteen times to "Pharaoh's Land," in the process rescuing at least three hundred slaves, including her parents. These trips were fraught with danger at every step. It was one thing to travel alone, but quite another to move twenty or thirty people, including children, across hundreds of miles of open country. She was aided over time by a well-organized network of safehouses and supporters, the so-called Underground Railroad. After passage of the Fugitive Slave Act in 1850 it was no longer sufficient to bring slaves to the North. Her trips extended all the way to Canada.

Though armed bounty hunters roamed the countryside, Tubman never lost a single one of her charges. A fantastic price was put on her head and wanted posters were widely circulated. Among whites she was one of the most hated figures in the South. But among slaves she was known as "Moses."

During the Civil War Tubman worked for the Union Army, first as a nurse, then as a scout and spy. She made numerous trips behind Confederate lines. More than once, her cunning and her unassuming appearance saved her from detection. The "Moses" of the wanted posters was imagined to be a person — probably even a man — of remarkable features, certainly not a scrawny, gap-toothed old woman.

After the war Tubman retired to a small house in Auburn, New York. She was worn out and penniless, but still she devoted herself to providing shelter and care to poor blacks. She supported herself by selling vegetables from her garden. In 1869 a white admirer published *Scenes of the Life of Harriet Tubman* as a means of earning her some money. But she was used to poverty, and so she quickly dispersed her income to those in greater need. When the book was published, Frederick Douglass, the great abolitionist and himself a former slave, wrote to her:

> Most that I have done and suffered in the service of our cause has been in public, and I have received much encouragement at every step of the way. You, on the other hand, have labored in a private way.... I have had the applause of the crowd ... while the most that you have done has been witnessed by a few trembling, scared, and foot-sore bondsmen and women, whom you have led out of the house of bondage, and whose heartfelt "God Bless You" has been your only reward.

Tubman lived into her nineties and died peacefully on March 10, 1913.

See: Sarah H. Bradford, *Harriet Tubman: The Moses of Her People* (Gloucester, Mass.: Peter Smith, 1981).

Meister Eckhart
Dominican Theologian and Mystic (1260–1329)

"Do not think that saintliness comes from occupation; it depends rather on what one is. The kind of work we do does not make us holy, but we may make it holy."

Meister Eckhart, a Dominican theologian, was the greatest of the Rhineland mystics who flourished in the early fourteenth century. Though he achieved renown as a preacher and scholar, his life ended under the shadow of condemnation. Henceforth his distinctive voice was largely lost to the church. In the last century, however, this neglect has been rectified. Increasingly, Eckhart is cited as a prophet whose vision supports the renewal of contemporary spirituality.

Eckhart was born in Hocheim in the German province of Thuringia in 1260. He joined the Dominicans in his teens and studied in Cologne and later in Paris, where he received his licentiate in theology. He twice held the prestigious Dominican chair at the University of Paris, previously held by *Thomas Aquinas. Otherwise, his career was spent in various positions of responsibility in the Dominican order.

In 1326, despite his status as an eminent scholar and a popular preacher, Eckhart found himself accused of heresy by the archbishop of Cologne, where he was then living. He insisted on his right to a hearing at the Holy See, then in Avignon. There he was presented with a list of supposedly heretical propositions extracted from his works. Eckhart presented a vigorous defense. "I may err, but I am not a heretic," he proclaimed, "for the first has to do with the mind and the second with the will." Nevertheless a list of twenty-eight propositions was condemned by the pope. Whether Eckhart ever learned of this is not known. The bull of Pope John XXII, issued on March 27, 1329, speaks of him as already dead.

Modern scholars have disputed the fairness of Eckhart's conviction, and careful study of his writings leaves little doubt of his sincere faith and loyalty to the church. And yet there is no mystery as to why his sermons and writings should have aroused suspicions. Eckhart was a profoundly mystical theologian who tried by means of paradoxical and sometimes disturbing language to describe the ineffable union of the soul with God. When his thoughts were taken out of context and converted into discrete propositional formulas they were inevitably misunderstood.

In Eckhart's world the goal of the spiritual life is an intense awareness of God's presence in the soul. His emphasis is entirely on achieving the correct interior consciousness. Outward devotions or works are of no account in themselves. That is, good works inevitably proceed from a good spirit; it is the latter that is all-important: "People ought not to consider so much what they are to do as what they *are;* let them but *be* good and their ways and deeds will shine brightly." And yet Eckhart was not scornful of charity. "If a person were in such a rapturous state as *St. Paul once entered, and he knew of a sick man who wanted a cup of soup, it would be far better to withdraw from the rapture for love's sake and serve him who is in need."

But the path that leads to this inner God-consciousness is the path of emptying and detachment. We must become detached from our concepts, even our inadequate and therefore idolatrous concepts of God; we must let go of our illusions and all the finite objects onto which we project our longing for the Absolute. Ultimately the detachment required is not from things but from our selves: "Let everyone begin by denying self and in so doing he will have denied all else. Indeed, if a man gave up a kingdom, or even the whole world, and still was selfish, he would have given up nothing." Only in the interior solitude of our souls will we create a space for our Savior to be born and, thus, once again, to take on flesh.

Many admirers of Eckhart, including *Thomas Merton, have remarked on the similarity of his thought to the spirituality of Zen Buddhism. Although Eckhart's spirituality was obviously centered on Christ, his emphasis on mindfulness and on the path of self-emptying, his concern for the power of illusion, his pursuit of the God beyond "god" (the false religious images that impede our access to Reality), and his playful love of paradox all bring to mind the teaching of the Zen masters: "Do not cling to the symbols, but get to the inner truth!" he liked to exclaim.

In relation to that tradition it is easy to comprehend such a statement as the following: "The shell must be cracked apart if what is in it is to come out, for if you want the kernel you must break the shell. And therefore if you want to discover nature's nakedness you must destroy its symbols, and the farther you get in the nearer you come to its essence. When you come to the One that gathers all things up into itself, there you must stay."

Unfortunately, it seemed to church authorities of his time that "the shell" that Eckhart wanted to crack was exactly what they otherwise preferred to call Catholic doctrine and authority. And what were they supposed to make of such a statement as this: "Seek God and you shall find him and all good with him. Indeed, with such an attitude, you might step on a stone and it would be a more pious act than to receive the body of our Lord, thinking of yourself."

Such a perspective got Eckhart condemned, as it might under other circumstances have got him killed, had natural causes not intervened. According to the pope, Eckhart "wished to know more than he should, and not in accordance with sobriety and the measure of faith, because he turned his ear from the truth and followed fables. The man was led astray by the Father of Lies who often turns himself into an angel of light."

Exactly what happened to Eckhart is not known. Before dying, however, he apparently issued a statement in which he "revoked and also deplored the twenty-six articles ... *insofar as* they could generate in the minds of the faithful a heretical opinion." And so Eckhart died in good standing with the church. And yet one cannot fail to note the significance of that careful qualification, *"insofar as . . . ,"* added no doubt by some mischievous Angel of Light.

See: Meister Eckhart: A Modern Translation, trans. Raymond Blakney (New York: Harper & Row, 1941); *Meister Eckhart,* trans. Edmund Colledge and Bernard McGinn, Classics of Western Spirituality (New York: Paulist, 1981).

March 28

Amos
Prophet (eighth century B.C.E.)

"Prepare to meet your God, O Israel!"

In his great study of the prophets, *Abraham Heschel writes, "The prophet's word is a scream in the night. While the world is at ease and asleep, the prophet feels the blast from heaven." These words apply especially well to the prophet Amos, a classic disturber of the false peace, who prophesied in the northern kingdom of Israel in the eighth century B.C.E.

The word "prophesy" is commonly confused with fortune telling. But the principal concern of the classical Hebrew prophets was the present moment. If they foresaw events in the future it was because of their acute sense of the moral and spiritual laws of cause and effect. They judged their age in the light of God's will. Thus, where their contemporaries saw piety and prosperity the prophets saw idolatry and ruin. The elite of Israel liked to invoke God's promises as an unconditional guarantee of their wealth and happiness. But the prophets remembered the terms of the covenant: God's faithfulness was conditioned on the faithfulness of the nation. The elite measured this faithfulness by the volume of their prayers and the value of their burnt offerings. But for the prophets — for Amos, in particular — the crucial measure was the degree of mercy toward the weak and justice for the poor and oppressed. Where this was lacking they forecast disaster.

Amos came from the southern kingdom of Judah in a village called Tekoa. There he was employed as a peasant, tending sheep and dressing sycamore trees, when he received a powerful call from God to be a prophet. He took his message to the northern kingdom, then under Jeroboam II (786–746 B.C.E.) enjoying a complacent period of security and affluence.

In blistering language Amos heaped coals upon the rich and self-satisfied elite of Israel:

> They sell the righteous for silver
> and the needy for a pair of shoes —
> they that trample the head of the poor into the dust of the earth,
> and turn aside the way of the afflicted. . . .

He was equally scornful of their claims to piety:

Thus says the Lord . . .
I hate, I despise your feasts,
and I take no delight in your solemn assemblies. . . .
But let justice roll down like waters
and righteousness like an ever-flowing stream.

Amos's shrill message evoked an angry response. Eventually he was denounced by Amaziah, priest of the shrine at Bethel, for conspiring against the king. He was expelled from Israel and forced to return to his native Judah. Nevertheless he persisted in delivering his unwelcome oracles: death, exile, and destruction for those who disregarded the covenant. His message was taken up by later prophets, and it continues to resonate in the preaching and witness of all who link the true worship of God with the cause of justice.

See: Abraham Heschel, *The Prophets* (New York: Harper & Row, 1962).

March 29
John Donne
Anglican Priest and Poet (1572–1631)

"Death be not proud, though some have called thee
Mighty and dreadfull, for, thou art not soe,
For, those, whom thou think'st, thou dost overthrow,
Die not, poore death, nor yet canst thou kill me. . . .
One short sleepe past, wee wake eternally,
And death shall be no more; death, thou shalt die."

John Donne is often linked with a fellow Anglican priest and "Metaphysical poet," his contemporary *George Herbert. The two were well acquainted and died within two years of one another. But in temperament and poetic style they were far apart. Herbert's poetry, with its lightness and balance, was an apt reflection of its author's temperament and his confidence in God's providence and promises. For Donne, on the other hand, it seems that nothing ever came easily. His poetry was marked by stress and strain, a fit commentary on his preoccupation with death and the struggle for salvation. But in this his writing, no less than for Herbert, reflected the contours of his personality and the peculiar tensions of his life.

Donne was born sometime in 1572 to a prominent family of Recusants — Catholics, that is, who defiantly maintained their faith against the laws of Protestant England. Two of his uncles became Jesuits abroad. One of them returned to England, where he was captured and died in the Tower of London when Donne was eleven. Some years later one of his own brothers was arrested for harboring a priest and died of the plague while incarcerated in Newgate prison.

One can only speculate on the effect of these circumstances on Donne. He grew up in an atmosphere where the practice of faith — or at least the wrong kind of faith — could lead to death. His response was to recoil from his family's religion, turning instead toward a secular career. He studied for the law, served as a courtier, and sought the patronage of wealthy peers, doing his best to penetrate the higher echelons of a world from which Catholics were excluded. As for religion, he embraced the official Anglican church.

For some years Donne seemed to advance rapidly on the path of worldly success. He attained the post of secretary to Lord Egerton, Keeper of the Great Seal of England. But then he made a curiously fateful misstep. He fell in love with Anne More, the fourteen-year-old daughter of a prominent Lord. In 1601 they eloped, leading the girl's enraged father to have Donne imprisoned for a time and to cause his dismissal from his job. Donne and his wife were eventually reunited, and they went on to enjoy a happy and devoted marriage. But the price of their elopement was dismal poverty and for Donne an end to any hopes of social advancement.

For some time Donne had been inclined to seek ordination in the Anglican church. He was ordained in 1614 at the age of forty-two. His wife died in childbirth in 1617, a crushing loss from which he never fully recovered. But it left him more determined than ever in his religious vocation. In 1621 his fortunes turned when he was appointed by King James as dean of St. Paul's Cathedral. Ironically, this was a more distinguished position than any secular post to which he might previously have aspired. Despite the newfound security of his life, however, Donne continued to wrestle with old demons. His public sermons and devotional writings, as well as his private poetry, reflect the intense turmoil of his spiritual life. In one of his most famous poems he wrote,

> Batter my heart, three person'd God; for, you
> As yet but knocke, breathe, shine, and seeke to mend;
> That I may rise, and stand, o'erthrow mee, and bend
> Your force, to breake, blowe, burn and make me new....
> Take mee to you, imprison mee, for I
> Except you enthrall mee, never shall be free,
> Nor ever chast, except you ravish mee.

If in Herbert's poems the encounter with God took the form of a gentle caress, a shared confidence, "something understood" — in Donne it was a wrestling match such as Jacob experienced in his encounter with the angel, a match he must pray to lose:

> Burne off my rusts, and my deformity
> Restore thine Image, so much, by thy grace,
> That thou may'st know mee, and I'll turne my face.

For Donne the soul must be conformed to God, a painful ordeal often accomplished only through suffering and impending death. In 1623 Donne came down with an illness that left him wracked with fever. For the rest of his life illness and the thought of death became a constant partner. It was during this time that he wrote such poems as his "Hymne to God My God, in My Sickenesse." In these and other works he reflected increasingly on death as a passage to eternal life.

So, in his purple wrapp'd receive mee Lord,
  By these his thornes give me his owhter Crowne;
And as to others soules I preache'd thy word,
  Be this my Text, my Sermon to mine owne,
  Therefore that he may raise the Lord throws down.

In February 1631, seriously ill, Donne preached a sermon called "Death's Duel," of which a friend later observed that he had "preach't his own Funeral Sermon." In fact, he died soon after on March 31, 1631, and was buried in St. Paul's Cathedral. So was his battle won. In his final sermon he had concluded with words that expressed his ultimate hope, that by sharing the cross of Christ we might also have a share in his resurrection:

> There [in the hands of God] we leave you in that blessed dependency, to hang upon him that hangs upon the cross, there bathe in his tears, there suck at his wounds, and lie down in peace in his grave, til he vouchsafe you a resurrection, and an ascension into that Kingdom, which he has purchased for you with the inestimable price of his incorruptible blood.

See: John Donne: Selections from Divine Poems, Sermons, Devotions, and Prayers, ed. John Booty, Classics of Western Spirituality (New York: Paulist, 1990).

March 30

Sister Thea Bowman
African-American Franciscan (1937–1990)

"Maybe I'm not making big changes in the world, but if I have somehow helped or encouraged somebody along the journey then I've done what I'm called to do."

Thea Bowman was one of the great treasures of the American Catholic church. As a Franciscan Sister, she managed, in her manifold witness to the gospel, to integrate the resources of her Catholic faith with her identity as an African-American woman. Ablaze with the spirit of love, the memory of struggle, and a faith in God's promises, she impressed her many audiences not just with her message but with her nobility of spirit. No one she encountered, whether school children, college students, cynical journalists, or a convention hall of bishops, could fail to catch a measure of her joy and gratitude for the gift of life. She was a particular inspiration to the black Catholic community, helping them to assert their pride of place among the People of God, while also encouraging them to enrich the wider church with the gifts of their distinctive culture and spirituality.

She was born Bertha Bowman in rural Mississippi in 1937. While attending a parochial school she was baptized as a Catholic at the age of ten. The most formative experience of her childhood came when her parents switched her to a new school run by the Franciscan Sisters of Perpetual

Adoration. There she found her love of learning but also her vocation to become a nun. To her family and friends it was an astonishing decision. Nevertheless, she entered the convent when she was sixteen and took the name Sister Thea ("of God").

As the only black face in a white religious order she tended to stand out. But whatever the expectations of her community, she had no desire to "blend in." She brought with her a strong sense of her identity as a black Catholic woman, and over time she came to believe that this identity entailed a very special vocation. She was committed to asserting a black way of being Catholic. Previously black Catholics were expected to conform to the spirituality of the white Euro-American church. The gospel hymns, the spirituals, the dancing, the testifying in the spirit — all features of the Protestant black churches — were foreign in the Catholic church. But for black Catholics, Sister Thea believed, this accounted for a sense of cultural marginality. Not only should there be room in the Catholic church for the spiritual traditions of African Americans, but their experience had much to contribute to the wider church. Part of this experience was the history of slavery and oppression. But part of it also was a spirituality of survival and resistance reflected in the tradition of the spirituals, the importance of family, community, celebration, and remembrance.

"What does it mean to be black and Catholic?" she asked. "It means that I come to my church fully functioning. I bring myself, my black self, all that I am, all that I have, all that I hope to become. I bring my whole history, my traditions, my experience, my culture, my African-American song and dance and gesture and movement and teaching and preaching and healing and responsibility as gift to the Church."

After earning a doctorate in English, Thea returned to the South to work with the church in Mississippi and Louisiana. In 1980 she helped to found the Institute of Black Catholic Studies at Xavier University in New Orleans. This became the base for her ministry as a speaker and evangelist. Thea was an extraordinary, spellbinding speaker. A combination storyteller, preacher, and performer, she brought to her lectures the atmosphere of a revival meeting. Punctuating her speaking with renditions of the spirituals, she generally had her audiences, black or white, singing along with her before she was finished.

She was invited to speak before hundreds of groups, including the U.S. Catholic bishops at their annual meeting in 1989. In one speech she noted that women were not allowed to preach in the Catholic church. But this shouldn't stop them from preaching everywhere else! "God has called to us to speak the word that is Christ, that is truth, that is salvation. And if we speak that word in love and faith, with patience and prayer and perseverance, it will take root. It does have power to save us. Call one another! Testify! Teach! Act on the Word! Witness!"

By this time Sister Thea was compelled to bear witness in a different way. She was diagnosed in 1984 as suffering from breast cancer. Though increasingly ill, Thea continued her extensive travels and speaking, even when she was confined to a wheelchair. With her bright African robes and her now-bald head, she was, as always, a striking figure. But now when she sang the spirituals — "Sometimes I feel like a motherless child / A long way from home" — her audience detected an even more personal and poignant confession of faith.

The faith that had sustained the slaves, the hope expressed in the spirituals, the love embodied by *St. Francis, now sustained her in her personal way of the cross. And to her other mighty gifts to the church she now added the witness of her courage and trust in God:

> When I first found out I had cancer, I didn't know what to pray for. I didn't know if I should pray for healing or life or death. Then I found peace in praying for what my folks call "God's perfect will." As it evolved, my prayer has become, "Lord, let me live until I die." By that I mean I want to live, love, and serve fully until death comes. If that prayer is answered... how long really doesn't matter. Whether it's just a few months or a few years is really immaterial.

Asked how she made sense out of her suffering, she answered, "I don't make sense of suffering. I try to make sense of life.... I try each day to see God's will.... I console myself with the old Negro spiritual: 'Sooner will be done the troubles of this world. I'm going home to live with God.'"

Sister Thea died on March 30, 1990, at the age of fifty-three.

See: Celestine Cepress, ed., *Thea Bowman: Shooting Star* (Winona, Minn.: Saint Mary's, 1993).

March 31

Mother Maria Skobtsova
Orthodox Nun and Martyr (1891–1945)

"I am your message, Lord. Throw me like a blazing torch into the night, that all may see and understand what it means to be a disciple."

The story of Mother Maria Skobtsova is like a tale in three acts, each with its own drama and each revealing different dimensions of her extraordinary personality. In the first act, she was born Lisa Pilenko into a prosperous aristocratic family in Russia. In this life she was a distinguished poet and a committed political activist who married twice, first to a Bolshevik whom she eventually divorced, later to an anti-Bolshevik, from whom she was later separated. During the revolutionary upheaval, she served as mayor of her hometown, in the process risking persecution from both the Left and the Right. In 1923, with her three young children she joined the throng of refugees uprooted by revolution and civil war and made her way to Paris. Soon after her arrival, her youngest daughter, Nastia, died of meningitis. The impact of this loss initiated a profound conversion. She emerged from her mourning with a determination to seek "a more authentic and purified life." She felt she saw a "new road before me and a new meaning in life,... to be a mother for all, for all who need maternal care, assistance, or protection."

In Paris she became deeply immersed in social work among the destitute Russian refugees. She sought them out in prisons, hospitals, mental asylums, and in the back streets of the slums. Increasingly she empha-sized the religious dimension of this work, the insight that "each person is the very icon of God incarnate in the world." With this recognition came the need "to accept this awesome revelation of God unconditionally, to venerate the image of God" in her brothers and sisters.

She was encouraged by her bishop to become a nun, but she would take this step only on the assurance that she would be free to develop a new type of monasticism, engaged in the world and marked by the "complete absence of even the subtlest barrier which might separate the heart from the world and its wounds."

In 1932 she made her monastic profession and became Mother Maria Skobtsova, thus beginning the "second act" in her drama. Instead of con-fining herself to a monastic enclosure, she took a lease on a house in Paris, large enough to include a chapel, a soup kitchen, and a shelter for desti-tute refugees. Her "cell" was a cot in the basement beside the boiler. As she wrote, "At the Last Judgment I shall not be asked whether I was suc-cessful in my ascetic exercises, nor how many bows and prostrations I made. Instead I shall be asked, Did I feed the hungry, clothe the naked, visit the sick and the prisoners."

Her house became a center not only for the works of mercy but for the renewal of Orthodoxy. While her kitchen was crowded with the down and out, her drawing room was the scene of spirited discussions among the leading emigré intellectuals of Paris. Out of these discussions a new movement was born, Orthodox Action, committed to realizing the social implications of the gospel. As Mother Maria explained, "The meaning of the liturgy must be translated into life. It is why Christ came into the world and why he gave us our liturgy."

The third and shortest act of Mother Maria's life began with the Ger-man occupation of Paris in 1940. In the context of Nazi racism, her commitment to seek out and revere each person as the icon of God as-sumed a deliberately subversive meaning. Aside from her usual work of hospitality, she was aided by her chaplain, Father Dimitri Klepinin, in rescuing Jews and other political refugees. These efforts, linked to the organized Resistance, continued until they were arrested by the Gestapo in 1943. Father Dimitri and Maria's son Yuri died in Buchenwald. Maria was sent to Ravensbruck concentration camp, where she managed to live for almost two years under conditions of indescribable cruelty and hor-ror. Though stripped of her religious habit, she remained the nurturing mother, strengthening the faith and courage of her fellow prisoners and helping to keep alive the flame of humanity in the face of every calculated assault.

In becoming a nun Maria had said, "I think service to the world is simply the giving of one's own soul in order to save others." Now in her hunger, illness, and exposure to the elements, she found the ultimate des-tination of her vocation. In light of the redemptive suffering of Christ she found a meaning to her own suffering. As she wrote in a message smug-gled out of the camp, "My state at present is such that I completely accept suffering in the knowledge that this is how things ought to be for me, and if I am to die I see in this a blessing from on high."

As she hovered close to death, she composed a final mute expression of her spirituality. With a needle and thread, purchased at the price of her precious bread ration, she embroidered an icon of Mary holding the infant Jesus, the child already bearing the wounds of the cross. On the eve of Easter, March 31, 1945, days before the liberation of the camp by Russian troops, Mother Maria perished in the gas chamber of Ravensbruck.

See: S. Stratton Smith, *The Rebel Nun* (Springfield, Ill.: Templegate, 1965); Sergei Hackel, *Pearl of Great Price: The Life of Mother Maria Skobtsova* (Crestwood, N.Y.: St. Vladimir's Seminary Press, 1981).

❧ APRIL ❧

April 1

Moses
Liberator and Mystic

"Let my people go."

The Exodus from Egypt is the foundational "myth" of Israel. At the heart of that story is the figure of Moses, one of the great and mysterious figures of the Bible. Over the centuries, Christians have plumbed various meanings from his story. In his *Life of Moses* *St. Gregory of Nyssa read the story of Moses as a symbolic treatise on mystical prayer. More recently liberation theologians have fastened on the social and political dimensions of the Exodus. Moses is the paradigmatic liberator, the human agent of God's desire to bring people out of bondage and into new life. Perhaps it is possible to reconcile both views of Moses — both the mystic and liberator.

What is certain is that Moses' role in the Exodus story is rooted in his unique and privileged relationship with God. Their first encounter occurs on Mt. Horeb when God speaks to him from the midst of a burning bush. God discloses himself as "the God of your father, the God of Abraham, the God of Isaac, and the God of Jacob." In doing so God also discloses Moses' true identity — heretofore he has represented himself as an Egyptian. God goes on to reveal his own name as Yahweh, "I AM WHO I AM." But most importantly Yahweh reveals himself as the one who hears the cry of the oppressed and who wills their deliverance.

Moses' mission, to secure the deliverance of the Hebrew slaves and to lead them to the promised land, is inseparable from his intimate communion and dialogue with God: "The Lord used to speak to Moses face to face, as a man speaks to his friend" (Exod. 33:11). After his dialogues with Yahweh on Mt. Sinai, "Moses did not know that the skin of his face shone because he had been talking with God."

Scripture maintains some ambiguity as to whether Moses actually saw the face of God. When Moses asks to see the glory of Yahweh, he is told, "You cannot see my face; for man shall not see me and live." (Only a glimpse of the back of Yahweh's glory is permitted.) Later Christian mystics took great interest in such mysteries and the fact that Moses often entered into a cloud to speak with God. Was this not another way of describing the "cloud of unknowing," the "dark night" when one achieves a level of prayer beyond the realm of senses, images, or concepts? Nevertheless, in another verse Yahweh describes his intimate relationship with Moses as being quite unlike his communication with any other: "With him I speak mouth to mouth, clearly, and not in dark speech; and he beholds the form of the Lord."

In the end, however, the significant issue is not simply that Yahweh spoke to Moses; it matters what was said. The topic was not simply God's glory, but the liberation of an oppressed people and God's will to make of them a nation renowned for holiness and justice. Thus, Moses reflects the paradigmatic fusion of the mystical and the political.

Following Yahweh's lead, Moses led the children of Israel for forty years in the wilderness. According to the last verses of Deuteronomy Moses lived only to look over the promised land from the heights of Mt. Nebo. There Moses died, alone except for Yahweh. And there Yahweh performed the last rites of friendship by burying Moses in a place known only to the Lord.

See: George Pixley, *Exodus* (Maryknoll, N.Y.: Orbis, 1987); William Johnston, *Christian Mysticism Today* (San Francisco: Harper & Row, 1984).

April 2
Carlo Carretto
Little Brother (1910–1988)

*"The desert is always the same, the sky is always beautiful,
the road deserted.... The only thing which is always new is God."*

Carlo Carretto was born on April 2, 1910, in northern Italy. He studied to become a teacher, but political difficulties under the fascists curtailed his career. Instead he immersed himself in the dynamic youth movement of Catholic Action, which sought to mobilize the laity in advancing the religious and social message of the church. Rising to a position of leadership in the movement, he spent nearly twenty years immersed in a blur of meetings, conferences, and public organizing. All of this came to an abrupt halt in 1954 when he surprised his friends by resigning from Catholic Action and announcing his intention to join the Little Brothers of Jesus, the community of desert contemplatives inspired by the spirituality of *Charles de Foucauld. In explaining his decision, Carretto could say only that he felt summoned by a call from God: "Leave everything and come with me into the desert. It is not your acts and deeds that I want: I want your prayer, your love."

In December 1954, at the age of forty-four, Carretto arrived in El Abiodh, a remote oasis in the Saharan desert of Algeria, to enter the novitiate of the Little Brothers. He remained there for ten years. As it turned out, the flight to solitude hardly led to obscurity. Twenty years later the publication of his *Letters from the Desert* established his reputation as one of the most popular spiritual teachers in the world. Although he went on to publish a dozen books, it was this first book that best captured his message. It described the desert spirituality of Foucauld, who had sought to emulate Jesus during his anonymous years in Nazareth. The Son of God had lived out a presence of divine love in the midst of his poor neighbors, and Foucauld had envisioned in this model a new kind of contemplative life in the world.

For Carretto the desert was a place of encounter with God and testing of faith. But ultimately he believed that the search for God in the desert must lead us back to the midst of our fellow human beings. Accordingly, in 1964 Carretto returned to Europe and settled the next year in a new experimental community in Spello, Italy. There lay people were invited to share in the fraternity's life of prayer and reflection. In the next decades, through his retreats and publications, Carretto's reputation spread around the world. He earned a certain notoriety in Italy and the displeasure of many ecclesiastical authorities because of his criticisms of certain aspects of the church — especially the temptations of triumphalism, juridicism, and clericalism. But for all his criticisms, there was never any doubt about his loyalty to and love for the church: "No, I shall not leave this church, founded on so frail a rock, because I should be founding another one on an even frailer rock: myself."

Carretto's message had much in common with *St. Francis of Assisi, whose spirit was reflected in the Umbrian countryside around him. In his playfulness, his appreciation for natural beauty, his commitment to poverty and nonviolence, and his anarchistic suspicion of large structures and institutions, he clearly identified with the Poverello. Indeed, one of his most popular books was called *I, Francis,* a personal diagnosis of the church and the world delivered in the "voice" of St. Francis. Despite Carretto's critique of nearly every feature of modern life, the book is marked by an immense spirit of hope and an ingenuous vitality, undiminished by age, illness, or even the approach of death. Appropriately, Carretto passed from this life on the feast of St. Francis, October 4, 1988.

It is not hard to understand the source of Carretto's immense attraction. He represented an ascetic, yet joy-filled spirituality available to lay people in the midst of pressing obligations, the noise of the city, or even poverty and suffering. (Carretto was no stranger to loss. An accident in the desert during his novitiate had left him crippled for life.) He showed that a life of prayer was consistent with a passion for social justice. At the same time he reminded social activists of the need to preserve a place of stillness, to listen to the word of God and to find renewal. Essentially, he showed that it was possible to live a contemplative life in the midst of the world, in the desert that is ultimately everywhere. The challenge of the gospel, according to Carretto, was to make an oasis of love in whatever desert we might find ourselves.

See: Carlo Carretto, *Letters from the Desert* (Maryknoll, N.Y.: Orbis, 1972); Robert Ellsberg, ed., *Carlo Carretto: Selected Writings* (Maryknoll, N.Y.: Orbis, 1994).

Marc Sangnier
Founder of the *Sillon* Movement (1873 – 1950)

"The truth must be sought with all one's soul. . . .
Love is stronger than hate."

Marc Sangnier was one of a long line of French Catholics who tried to heal the rift between Catholicism and the ideals of liberty and democracy. As with others before him his efforts were crushed. But they enriched the soil from which new initiatives would later bloom.

Born on April 3, 1873 into a wealthy family, Sangnier became determined in his youth to apply his Catholic faith to the social problems of his day. With fellow Catholic students he formed a study circle which examined social reality — especially the condition of the workers — in the light of Catholic teaching. Not content with abstract ideas, they entered the world of the workers and sought to establish personal contacts and friendship. These efforts found encouragement in the first great social encyclical, *Rerum Novarum* (1891) of *Pope Leo XIII.

In 1894 Sangnier founded a newspaper, *Le Sillon* ("The Furrow"), which aimed at reconciling the principles of Catholicism with democracy and social justice. This became the foundation of a lay movement of the same name that attracted a corps of idealistic youth, united as much in their traditional faith as in their zeal for justice. By 1899 the Sillonists had organized a number of study centers for workers in Paris and other cities.

Many of the bishops were at first positively disposed to the movement, recognizing the apostolic commitment of its members and their ability to carry the gospel into the anticlerical world of the working class. Sangnier insisted that the movement did not have a systematic program. It was intended, he claimed, as a kind of leaven, to elevate the level of spiritual as well as social consciousness in French society. The Sillonists were received several times in audiences with Pope Pius X, who also offered encouragement to the movement.

Nevertheless, with the growth of the movement, opposition and criticism also began to coalesce. This intensified as the movement began to depart from its evangelical roots and to become more identified with a political program. In 1905 Sangnier founded a new journal, *Eveil démocratique,* which focused more directly on the promotion of democracy. Sangnier defined democracy as "a social organization that tends toward the maximum development of individual conscience and civic responsibility." Although Sangnier and the core of the Sillon remained devout Catholics, in 1907 they called for the formation of a wider group, "the greater Sillon," that would be open to non-Catholics who supported the democratic and pluralistic principles of the movement. This was at a time when the more conservative leadership of the French church continued to harken back to the glorious pre-Republican union of church and crown. These "integralists" pressed for the condemnation of the Sillon.

The condemnation, in the form of a letter from Pope Pius X, was issued on August 25, 1910. In some ways this letter was a companion to his earlier condemnation of "Modernism." Again, beneath the surface of this social movement, the pope detected a set of assumptions that supposedly threatened the principle of divine authority. This apparently was the inference drawn from the Sillon's avoidance of episcopal direction. The Sillonists were charged with claiming that democracy was the only form of government compatible with Christianity. They were furthermore charged with seeking, ultimately, to introduce democracy into the church itself.

A sample of the pope's letter reflects the tone which the papacy (before the time of *John XXIII) typically reserved for addressing the world and its pitiful errors. Regarding the separation of church and state, the pope wrote:

> No, Venerable Brethren — We must again emphatically declare in these days of social and intellectual anarchy when everyone poses as a teacher and legislator — the State is not to be built otherwise than as God has built it; society will not be built up unless the Church lay the foundations and direct the works; no, civilization is not now to be invented nor the new State to be established in the clouds. It has long existed, it exists still; it is Christian civilization, the Catholic State.... The true friends of the people are neither revolutionaries nor innovators, but traditionalists.

News of the condemnation was extremely dispiriting to the thousands of young people who had enlisted in the movement's cause. At the same time it was greeted by the integralists as their latest victory in the campaign to root out all signs of liberalism in the church.

After the condemnation many of Sangnier's supporters on the Left urged him to defy the pope. But instead he obediently complied with the Vatican decree. As he wrote to his supporters,

> I do not regret having to suffer for my faith, and I hope that God will accept the offering of my grief, since I shall be happy if by this sacrifice I may still serve the cause to which I have devoted my life, and I hope to give to the Republic a moral inspiration and to the democracy a Christian spirit. Since I am, and intend to remain, above all a Roman Catholic, the question does not even arise whether I shall or shall not submit to the discipline of the Church.

The dispersed membership of the Sillon went on to take a leading role as activists, journalists, and lay apostles in scores of other Catholic social movements and organizations. One of these alumni was *Peter Maurin, later co-founder of the Catholic Worker movement in New York. As for Sangnier, he remained devoted to the church and to the cause of democracy and social justice, but he never again achieved great social prominence. He died in 1950.

See: Alec Vidler, *A Variety of Catholic Modernists* (Cambridge: Cambridge University Press, 1970).

Martin Luther King
Apostle of Freedom (1929–1968)

"The cross is something that you bear and ultimately that you die on."

In a church in Montgomery, Alabama, on December 2, 1955, a young Baptist minister named Martin Luther King, Jr., at the time only twenty-six and fresh from graduate school in Boston, stood up before a packed audience of protesters. The previous day Mrs. Rosa Parks, a black seamstress, had been arrested after refusing to yield her seat on a bus to a white man. The incident immediately sparked a bus boycott by the city's black population. King, only newly arrived in Montgomery for his first pastoral assignment, had been drafted to lead the protest committee. As he faced the expectant crowd before him that evening he began, "As you know, my friends, there comes a time when people get tired of being trampled over by the iron feet of oppression." The church erupted with applause and cries of "Yes!" "If we are wrong—God Almighty is wrong! If we are wrong," he continued, "Jesus of Nazareth was merely a utopian dreamer and never came down to Earth! If we are wrong, justice is a lie!"

It was an extraordinary speech that galvanized the struggle in Montgomery as surely as it launched King's career as a leader of the black freedom struggle in America. When at last the campaign in Montgomery was won, the tactics of nonviolent resistance tested there were applied and extended throughout the South. King proved to be a gifted political strategist, as well as a brilliant orator. But he was more. He was a prophet, in the truest biblical sense, who proclaimed to his generation the justice and mercy of God, remaining true to his mission even to the laying down of his life.

A critical moment of doubt came early in his journey. One night in 1957 a death threat was delivered over the phone. He had already faced plenty of violence and hatred. But somehow the strain of the moment and the implicit threat not only to himself but to his family brought him to the limit of his strength. He went into the kitchen and as he sat there with a cup of coffee he turned himself over to God. "Almost out of nowhere I heard a voice. 'Martin Luther, stand up for righteousness. Stand up for justice. Stand up for truth. And lo, I will be with you, even until the end of the world.'" Afterward, he said, "I was ready to face anything."

His house was bombed. He was repeatedly jailed. On one occasion he was nearly fatally stabbed. But he was never again tempted by doubt or despair. All the while he continued to grow in his commitment to nonviolence, not simply as a political tactic, but as a thoroughgoing principle of life, a means appropriate to his constant goal — what he called the Beloved Community. In 1963 at the Lincoln Memorial in Washington, D.C., he delivered his famous "I Have a Dream Speech." That speech summarized his most hopeful image of an America redeemed by the transforming power of love: "When we allow freedom to ring, when we let it ring from every village and every hamlet, from every state and every city, we will be able to speed up that day when all of God's children, black men and white men, Jews and Gentiles, Protestants and Catholics, will be able to join hands and sing in the words of the old Negro spiritual: 'Free at last. Free at last. Thank God Almighty, we are free at last.'"

King's popularity was never higher. Within a year he had won the Nobel Peace Prize. But he did not cling to the safety of honor. Instead he continued to grow, to delve deeper into the roots of American racism and violence, to plumb deeper into the challenge of his vocation as a minister of God. In 1967 he broke with many of his colleagues and supporters by publicly speaking out against the Vietnam War. He became increasingly critical of the structures of power in the United States, and he began to forge the bonds of a radical alliance that would unite poor people of all colors in the struggle for social change. J. Edgar Hoover, director of the FBI, who had for many years waged a covert effort to destroy King, publicly called him the most dangerous man in America.

But the roots of King's challenge and hope lay not in any political philosophy. They were based on his faith in the promise of God — the faith, expressed in his maiden speech, that God is not a liar. As he said in 1965,

Truth crushed to earth will rise again. How long? Not long! Because no lie can live forever. How long? Not long! . . . Truth forever on the scaffold, wrong forever on the throne. Yet that scaffold sways the future and behind the dim unknown standeth God within the shadow, keeping watch over his own. How long? Not long! Because the arc of the moral universe is long but it bends toward justice.

By that time King's days were already numbered. In April 1968 he was in Memphis to lend support to the city's striking sanitation workers. He seemed increasingly to anticipate his appointment with destiny. On the evening of April 3 he addressed a rally and ended with these words:

Well, I don't know what will happen now. We've got some difficult days ahead. But it doesn't matter with me now. Because I've been to the mountaintop. And I don't mind. Like anybody, I would like to live a long life. Longevity has its place. But I'm not concerned about that now. I just want to do God's will. And he's allowed me to go up to the mountain. And I've looked over. And I've seen the promised land. I may not get there with you. But I want you to know tonight that we, as a people, will get to the promised land. And I'm happy tonight. I'm not worried about anything. I'm not fearing any man. Mine eyes have seen the glory of the coming of the Lord.

He was assassinated the next day.

King did not represent himself as a saint. Posthumous revelations of some of his weaknesses underscored the fact that King, at the time of his death, was still evolving, still on the way to reconciling the logic of his faith with his personal conduct. But nothing detracts from his role as a "drum major of freedom." He said of himself, "I want you to know . . . that I am a sinner like all God's children. But I want to be a good man. And I want to hear a voice saying to me one day, 'I take you in and I bless you, because you tried.'" King struggled to be more than his weakest qualities. He challenged the church and all Americans to do the same.

See: James M. Washington, ed., *The Testament of Hope: The Essential Writings of Martin Luther King, Jr.* (San Francisco: Harper & Row, 1986); James H. Cone, *Martin and Malcolm and America: A Dream or a Nightmare* (Maryknoll, N.Y.: Orbis, 1991).

April 5
Pandita Ramabai
Indian Christian and Reformer (1858–1922)

"People must not only hear about the kingdom of God, but must see it in actual operation, on a small scale perhaps and in imperfect form, but a real demonstration nevertheless."

Pandita Ramabai, a poet, scholar, and champion of the rights of women, has been acclaimed as a "mother of modern India." In her own time she struggled hard, as a Christian convert, to define her own identity and spiritual path, in the process drawing criticism from Hindus and fellow Christians alike. She remains an intriguing example of the effort to bridge the spiritual traditions of the East and West; both sides felt the challenge posed by this courageous and independent woman.

Ramabai was born in Karnataka in 1858. She was the daughter of a wealthy Brahmin scholar and his much younger wife. Though her father was a devout and orthodox Hindu he scandalized his high-caste friends by teaching his wife and later his daughters to read the Sanskrit classics. This talent later stood her well, when her family perished during a great famine. At the age of sixteen, Ramabai walked across India, visiting the holy Hindu shrines and attracting astonished audiences to her recitation of Sanskrit poetry. Her knowledge of Sanskrit, the sacred language of Hinduism, eventually won her fame and honor. She was given the honorific title "Pandita," mistress of wisdom.

She married at the age of twenty-two, but her husband died of cholera after only sixteen months, leaving her alone with an infant daughter, Manorama. Her travels in India and now her present circumstances sensitized her to the bleak plight of widows and orphans. The practice among higher castes of betrothing young girls to much older men (her own mother had been nine, her father over forty, at the time of their marriage) had contributed to the vast number of widows, women without status or protection. Ramabai set out to do something about this social problem, establishing centers for widows and orphans in Poona and later Bombay, where the women were given basic education and training in marketable skills. Soon Ramabai had become the leading advocate for the rights and welfare of women in India.

Her work brought her into contact with Christian missionaries. In 1883 she accepted an invitation by a congregation of Anglican nuns to visit England. For some time Ramabai had felt a distance from her Hindu upbringing, both on spiritual grounds and on the basis of her perception of the status of women in India. While in England she undertook a serious study of the Bible and eventually asked to be baptized.

News of her conversion provoked angry public controversy in India. Ramabai herself wrestled with her strong aversion to the cultural imperialism of foreign missionaries in India. She was determined that becoming a Christian should not be construed as a denial of her Indian culture and roots. The gospel of Christ represented for her the purest expression of her own spiritual intuitions, in particular her growing belief that to serve women and the poor was a religious and not simply a social work.

She returned to India and continued her charitable work, among other things founding a center for unwed mothers, a program for famine relief, and a series of schools for poor girls. Now, ironically, it was her fellow Christians who became her public critics. They charged that because she made no effort to convert the poor women in her centers her own conversion was only superficial. They also pressed for proof of her doctrinal orthodoxy. Ramabai refused to be drawn into theological or confessional debates. "I am, it is true, a member of the Church of Christ, but I am not bound to accept every word that falls down from the lips of priests or bishops.... I have just with great efforts freed myself from the yoke of the Indian priestly tribe, so I am not at present willing to place myself under another similar yoke."

Ramabai criticized the profusion of Christian denominations, a fact, she believed, that was bewildering to the poor. The spirit of Christ as reflected in the Bible sufficed to satisfy her own religious questions. From that source she learned that the heart of true religion was the love of God and the love of one's neighbor as oneself. That she live by this creed, she insisted, was all that anyone had a right to ask of her. In later years she prayed not for the conversion of Hindus but for the conversion of Indian Christians.

She died on April 5, 1922, at the age of sixty-four.

See: S. M. Adhav, *Pandita Ramabai* (Madras: Christian Literature Society, 1979).

Hadewijch of Brabant
Beguine Mystic (thirteenth century)

"Make haste to virtue in veritable Love; and take care that God be honored by you and by all those whom you can help, with effort, with self-sacrifice, with counsel, and with all that you can do unremittingly."

Almost nothing is known of the life of Hadewijch, a Flemish mystic who lived sometime in the middle of the thirteenth century. Although a prolific author, she inspired no contemporary biography; all that is known of her story must be inferred from her letters and other extant writings. She was apparently a Beguine. This fascinating movement, which flourished in the Low Countries in the thirteenth and fourteenth centuries, attracted women to a new form of community-based religious life, distinct from the alternatives of marriage or traditional enclosure. The Beguines stressed the value of prayer, the works of mercy, simplicity of life, and an affective spirituality focused on the humanity of Jesus. It seems that Hadewijch may have occupied a position of leadership in one such community.

Hadewijch's teachings are contained in letters of spiritual counsel, a great body of poetry, and a series of recorded "visions." The visions describe a number of revelations in which she was afforded particular insights into spiritual realities: "Once on Pentecost Sunday I received the Holy Spirit in such a manner that I understood all the will of Love in all . . . "; "After one Easter Sunday I had gone to God; and he embraced me in my interior senses and took me away in spirit."

The central theme of Hadewijch's writings is Love, a word that dominates nearly every page. Indeed she has been described as a "love-mystic." Everywhere she turned, whether in creation, in community, or in her inner depths, she encountered the love of God. No subject failed to ignite her passion: "Once I heard a sermon in which *St. Augustine was spoken of. No sooner had I heard it than I became inwardly so on fire that it seemed to me everyone on earth must be set ablaze by the flame I felt within me. Love is all!" Insofar as she responded to this reality with love she felt herself plunged into the most profound communion with God.

Hadewijch's love was not a warm inner glow; it was fire, passion, burning desire, the agony and ecstasy of courtly romance. At the conclusion of one of her visions she remarked, "Then I returned into myself, and I understood all I have just said; and I remained to gaze fixedly upon my delightful sweet Love."

Hadewijch's letters, apparently addressed to various of her spiritual daughters, reflect a receptive and nurturing personality. Her spiritual discourse is interspersed with expressions of personal affection, and exhortations to virtue, simplicity, and faithfulness: "O sweet dear child, be wise in God!" As a spiritual director Hadewijch did not place much stress on prayer, fasting, or external discipline. Instead, her emphasis was on love as the essential key to the knowledge and service of God: "Do everything with reliance on Love. . . . Let us live in sweet love. Live for God; let his life be yours, and let yours be ours."

The sweetness of Hadewijch's spiritual discourse gives no evidence of the pressures and criticism that surrounded the Beguine movement. At some point Hadewijch was evicted from her community; under what circumstances we cannot know. Her last letters reflect the pain of this experience, but also the enduring power of her faith:

> O sweet child, your sadness, dejection, and grief give me pain! And this I entreat you urgently, and exhort you, and counsel you, and command you as a mother commands her dear child, whom she loves for the supreme honor and sweetest dignity of Love, to cast away from all alien grief, and to grieve for my sake as little as you can. What happens to me, whether I am wandering in the country or put in prison — however it turns out, it is the work of Love.

"Wandering in the country or put in prison"? Exactly what peril Hadewijch faced is unknown, but these and worse fates befell other Beguine mystics. Whatever her fate, there was no circumstance that could separate Hadewijch from her love of God.

> In love I have experienced all these attributes, and I have acted with justice toward these persons, however much they have failed me. But if I possess this in love with my eternal being, I do not possess it yet in fruition of Love in my own being. And I remain a human being, who must suffer to the death with Christ in Love; for whoever lives in veritable Love will suffer opprobrium from all aliens, until Love comes to herself, and until she is full-grown within us in virtues, whereby Love becomes one with men.

And so Hadewijch vanished from history, leaving behind her love poems, a handful of letters, and a final exhortation: "Farewell and live a beautiful life."

See: Hadewijch: The Complete Works, Classics of Western Spirituality (New York: Paulist, 1980).

April 7
André Trocmé
Pastor of Le Chambon (1901–1971)

"Nonviolence was not a theory superimposed upon reality; it was an itinerary that we explored day after day in communal prayer and in obedience to the commands of the Spirit."

In Israel there are trees planted in honor of the "righteous gentiles" who risked their lives to save Jews during the "epoch of extermination." One of them bears the name of André Trocmé, Protestant pastor of a small French village called Le Chambon. During the years of the Nazi occupation the citizens of Le Chambon quietly organized to offer a haven to thousands of Jewish refugees who were thus saved from certain death.

Just as remarkable as the courage and generosity of the people of Le Chambon was the fact that they themselves did not regard their own actions to be in any way remarkable; they were simply the most obvious expression of human decency. The full story of Le Chambon must give credit to the many hundreds of persons who took part in this "conspiracy of goodness," but there is little doubt of the key part played by Pastor Trocmé.

He was born on April 7, 1901, to an ancient family of Huguenots. The sense of belonging to a once-embattled minority in Catholic France was an element in Trocmé's character, just as the experience of having been an impoverished refugee during World War I helped him identify with the downtrodden. But at the core of Trocmé's ministry was a literal commitment to the Sermon on the Mount and a conviction that the essence of the gospel lay in the love of God and neighbor. From the time in 1934 when he arrived in Le Chambon with his wife, Magda, and their four children, these were the principles Trocmé labored to instill in his flock. Within a few years he had succeeded to a remarkable degree.

The test came with the fall of France in 1940. Though Le Chambon fell within the formally independent domain of Vichy France, it was not long before the values of ultranationalism and chauvinism were insinuated throughout the countryside. From the beginning, through small acts of defiance, Pastor Trocmé made it clear that his village would not submit to the spirit of fear and hatred. As word of the village spread, Le Chambon became a magnet for refugees of the war and others fleeing the net of persecution.

When in 1942 the order came to deliver all Jews for deportation, the village entered into a much more momentous and dangerous form of resistance. In an organization centered around the presbytery and a core of church elders, the village became a safe haven for Jewish refugees, operating under the noses of the Vichy police and, later, of the Gestapo themselves. Trocmé himself was at one point detained and later went into hiding. Still the sheltering of Jews continued.

During the years of war and occupation it is estimated that as many as twenty-five hundred Jews were protected in the village and its surrounding farms. Beside the vast slaughter of those years — even beside the twenty-eight thousand Jews deported from Paris alone in the summer of 1942 — the numbers of persons rescued in Le Chambon are modest. But the achievement is extraordinary when one considers that for Jews in those years this small village in France was perhaps the safest place in all of occupied Europe.

The lives of those twenty-five hundred and their descendants are the legacy of one man. Trocmé so invigorated the faith and conscience of his flock that they willingly risked their own lives to protect the lives of persons who had been labeled disposable "outsiders."

Trocmé died in 1971. The following year his wife, Magda, attended the ceremony in Israel in which her husband was posthumously awarded the Medal of Righteousness. At the top of the citation there appears a saying from the *Baal Shem Tov, "In remembrance resides the secret of redemption."

See: Philip Hallie, *Lest Innocent Blood Be Shed: The Story of Le Chambon and How Goodness Happened There* (New York: Harper & Row, 1979).

St. Julie Billiart
Co-Foundress of the Institute of
Notre Dame de Namur (1751–1816)

"The good God likes me to grope my way along."

Julie Billiart was born in 1751 to a peasant family in Picardy, France. By the time she was seven she was teaching the catechism to other small children of the town. At fourteen she took a vow of chastity and devoted herself to works of mercy and the religious instruction of her poor neighbors. Thus far, her religious vocation progressed along fairly typical lines. Her life took an unexpected turn, however, when a strange malady left her virtually paralyzed. Confined to her bed and unable to move her limbs she still found ways to maintain her evangelical witness. Gradually, she acquired considerable influence and spiritual authority in her town.

During the French Revolution she got into trouble for harboring illegal priests. Amid threats against her life, she had to be smuggled out of her house and taken to Compiègne. Still her pursuers sought her from one refuge to another until she was forced to exclaim, "Dear Lord, will you not find me a corner in paradise, since there is no room for me on earth?" Under the stress of her ordeal she temporarily lost the power of speech.

Once she was out of harm's way and able to rest and recuperate, Julie's speech eventually returned and she resumed her work of religious instruction. Soon, with the encouragement of her confessor, she undertook the foundation of a new congregation, the Institute of Notre Dame, devoted to the Christian education of the poor and the training of religious teachers. The work prospered, and many women were attracted to her community. In 1804, Mother Julie was miraculously freed from her mysterious illness. After twenty-two years as an invalid she was suddenly able to walk once more.

Her newfound mobility was heavily taxed in the expansion and consolidation of the Institute. She made as many as 120 journeys on behalf of her mission. Fifteen new convents were established during her lifetime, including the motherhouse in Namur. On her deathbed, as a Sister read to her from *The Imitation of Christ,* she put her finger on the page and said, "That is the part you must read." The passage read: "If thou carry the cross willingly, it will carry thee, and bring thee to thy desired end, to that place where there will be no end." Julie Billiart died on April 8, 1816, at the age of sixty-five. She was canonized in 1969.

See: Roseanne Murphy, *Julie Billiart: Woman of Courage* (New York: Paulist, 1995).

April 9
Dietrich Bonhoeffer
Theologian and Confessor (1906–1945)

"[The church's] task is not simply to bind the wounds of the victim beneath the wheel, but also to put a spoke in the wheel itself."

Dietrich Bonhoeffer spent the month of June 1939 in New York City in a state of anxious soul-searching. "I do not know why I am here," he wrote. He was there because his American friends, eager to protect the young Lutheran theologian from the clutches of the Gestapo, had arranged for him to serve as a visiting professor at Union Theological Seminary. As a leading figure in the Confessing Church, Bonhoeffer was an avowed enemy of the Nazis. Certainly the escape to New York had saved his life. But Bonhoeffer was not content to remain in safety. After only a few weeks in New York he disappointed and alarmed his friends by announcing his decision to return to Germany. As he wrote, "I will have no right to participate in the reconstruction of Christian life in Germany after the war if I do not share the tribulations of this time with my people."

But though he was unwilling to accept the luxury of security, Bonhoeffer did not deliberately court martyrdom. In fact, many colleagues were astounded when, upon his return to Germany, he used family connections to obtain a position in the *Abwehr* — German Military Intelligence. His brother-in-law, Hans Dohnanyi, was a high-ranking member of the *Abwehr*. He was also, as Bonhoeffer knew, a key figure in the clandestine military conspiracy to overthrow Hitler. Bonhoeffer was immediately inducted into this conspiracy.

In 1943 as the plot began to unravel Bonhoeffer and Dohnanyi were both arrested. Even then, the extent of their activities — which included plans to assassinate Hitler — remained undetected. Pending further investigation, Bonhoeffer was remanded to a military prison in Tegel, where he was held for eighteen months. Despite spartan conditions, he was nevertheless spared the cruelty of a concentration camp and was able to receive books and smuggle out uncensored letters.

In July 1944, after the assassination plot ended in failure, an intensified investigation by the Gestapo uncovered the full extent of the *Abwehr* treachery. From then on the fate of the conspirators was sealed. Bonhoeffer's trail led to Gestapo headquarters in Berlin, then to Buchenwald, and finally to Flossenburg prison camp. There on April 9 he conducted a prayer service for his fellow prisoners, following which he received the summons: "Prisoner Bonhoeffer, get ready and come with us." To a fellow prisoner he hastily entrusted a final message: "This is the end, for me the beginning of life...." The next day he was hanged with five other members of the resistance group.

Bonhoeffer was thirty-nine at the time of his death; the world was left, through his prison writings, only a sketchy outline of the direction of his theology. Nevertheless, the impact of his short life and his scattered writings has left an indelible mark on the postwar church. He is the rare theologian whose biography is studied as carefully as his written work for clues about the challenge of faith in our time.

Bonhoeffer's impact has been felt on at least three levels. First, his witness has inspired other Christians wrestling with the ethical dilemmas of responsible action in the face of oppression. Through most of his career Bonhoeffer had espoused a pacifist position, and he never ceased to believe that violence was inconsistent with the ideals of the gospel. In the end, however, he believed that the crisis of the times was so grave as to require that certain Christians willingly compromise their purity of conscience for the sake of others. "The ultimate question for a responsible man to ask is not how he is to extricate himself heroically from the affair, but how the coming generation is to live."

As a theologian, Bonhoeffer's reputation rests largely on the vision forged in the confinement of his last years and disclosed in letters smuggled to his friend, Eberhard Bethge. Here he outlined the need for a new "religionless Christianity," a way of talking about God in a secular language appropriate for a "world come of age." Traditional religious language tended to posit a stop-gap deity occupying a "religious" realm on the boundaries of day-to-day life. Instead, Bonhoeffer wrote,

> I should like to speak of God not on the boundaries but at the center, not in weaknesses but in strength, and therefore not in death and guilt but in man's life and goodness. God is beyond in the midst of our life. The church stands, not at the boundaries where human powers give out, but in the midst of the village.

In the postwar decades these writings helped inspire a broad range of Christians seeking to overcome the gulf between the churches and the secular world. More recently Third World theologians have highlighted a more radical insight in Bonhoeffer's writings: "We have for once learnt to see the great events of world history from below, from the perspective of the outcast, the suspects, the maltreated, the powerless, the oppressed, the reviled — in short, from the perspective of those who suffer."

And it is perhaps in this light, in which he came to see the identity between the cross of Jesus and solidarity with the oppressed, that Bonhoeffer offers such a poignant model of contemporary holiness. After the war some German Christians were reluctant to call him a martyr, since he had been executed for political rather than "religious" charges. This attitude, which would set the "holy life" apart from the world and its concrete demands, exemplified the religious mentality that Bonhoeffer rejected. For him, following Christ was a matter of engagement in this world, "living unreservedly in life's duties, problems, successes and failures, experiences and perplexities. In so doing we throw ourselves completely into the arms of God, taking seriously not our own sufferings, but those of God in the world — watching with Christ in Gethsemane. That, I think is faith; that is metanoia."

See: Dietrich Bonhoeffer, *Letters and Papers from Prison* (New York: Macmillan, 1972); Eberhard Bethge, *Costly Grace: An Illustrated Biography of Dietrich Bonhoeffer* (San Francisco: Harper & Row, 1979).

Pierre Teilhard de Chardin
Mystic and Scientist (1881–1955)

"I want to teach people how to see God everywhere, to see Him in all that is most hidden, most solid, and most ultimate in the world."

The work of the French Jesuit Pierre Teilhard de Chardin lies behind many of the most creative movements in contemporary theology and spirituality. He was a prophet who labored hard to reconcile the language of science and the language of religion. He was a mystic, afire with a vision of the divine mystery at the heart of the cosmos. He was also a man of profound faith who epitomized a spirituality of engagement in the world and its deepest questions.

Yet little of this was recognized in his life. Throughout his career he was denied permission by Rome and his religious superiors to publish any of his theological or philosophical writings, to lecture publicly, or even to accept any significant academic appointments. Such treatment caused him severe frustration and suffering. Yet he submitted in obedience, convinced that he served Christ best by faithfulness to his vocation. "The more the years pass, the more I begin to think that my function is probably simply that...of *John the Baptist, that is, of one who presages what is to come. Or perhaps what I am called on to do is simply to help in the birth of a new soul in that which already is."

Teilhard was born on May 1, 1881, to a large family of noble lineage. The volcanic hills that surrounded his home in the Auvergne region of France stimulated a childhood fascination with rocks and fossils. He maintained this enthusiasm after entering the Jesuits at the age of eighteen. Thereafter his theological studies were pursued in tandem with research in geology and paleontology.

Teilhard went on to become a scientist of the first rank. He published over a hundred scholarly articles and took part in excavations on three continents. He was part of the team that discovered the remains of "Peking Man," at that time the oldest human ancestor on record. But all the while he was working out a profound theological synthesis, integrating the theory of evolution with his own cosmic vision of Christianity.

According to Teilhard the history of the earth reflected a gradual unfolding of the potentialities of matter and energy. Inanimate matter gave way to life; simple life forms gave way to ever-more complex organisms. All this culminated in human consciousness. But was this the final terminus of evolution? Teilhard believed the process must continue, though now across the threshold of consciousness. Where was the destination of this process? Teilhard called it the Omega Point — the horizon in which spirit and matter must eventually converge. As a Christian, he identified this Omega with Christ, the beginning and end of history. In Jesus, God-made-flesh, we had a guarantee of our ultimate destiny. Here the spirit of God and the principle of matter were definitively joined.

Teilhard's spirituality was marked by a strong apprehension of the Incarnation. With a mystic's eye he perceived the face of the divine in all of creation. In part this vision was forged in the midst of death, while he served courageously as a stretcher-bearer during World War I. He later described an experience that had occurred as he sat in a chapel near the battlefield of Verdun, meditating on the consecrated host. It seemed as if the energy of God's incarnate love expanded to fill the room, and ultimately to encompass the battlefield and the entire universe. For Teilhard, as for the Jesuit *Gerard Manley Hopkins, the world was "charged with the grandeur of God." Similarly, in a "Hymn to Matter," he wrote:

> Blessed be you, harsh matter, barren soil, stubborn rock: you who yield only to violence, you would force us to work if we would eat. ...Blessed be you, mortal matter! Without you, without your onslaughts, without your uprootings of us, we should remain ignorant of ourselves and of God.

Teilhard spent the years 1923 to 1946 doing research and field work in China. The assignment was a kind of exile, the result of his superiors' desire to keep him far from the theological limelight in Europe. But it was there that he worked out his most mature thought. He was thrilled with the idea that through work in the world human beings were participating in the ongoing extension and consecration of God's creation. This insight was especially nourished by his devotion to the Eucharist. But many times while on the road he lacked the requirements for Mass. Thus, he was inspired to write his "Mass on the World."

> Since once again, Lord, ...I have neither bread nor wine nor altar I will raise myself beyond these symbols, up to the pure majesty of the real itself; I, your priest, will make the whole earth my altar and on it will offer you all the labors and suffering of the world.

Copies of Teilhard's writings were passed from hand to hand among a select audience of friends and fellow Jesuits. But he was repeatedly denied permission to have them published. Although he was never formally condemned, his career was continuously frustrated and clouded by the disapproval of Rome. His work might have disappeared altogether if Teilhard had not taken the mildly rebellious precaution of naming a laywoman friend as his literary executor. To this initiative was due Teilhard's posthumous fame and influence.

Teilhard's last "exile" was to the United States, where he spent his final years in New York. He once noted, "I should like to die on the day of the Resurrection." So it came to pass. He was felled by a heart attack and died on April 10, 1955 — Easter Sunday. In dying, his vision was at last released to the world:

> The day will come when, after harnessing the ether, the winds, the tides, and gravitation, we shall harness for God the energies of love. And, on that day, for the second time in the history of the world, man will have discovered fire.

See: Pierre Teilhard de Chardin, *The Divine Milieu* (New York: Harper & Row, 1957); Ursula King, *Spirit of Fire: The Life and Vision of Teilhard de Chardin* (Maryknoll, N.Y.: Orbis, 1996).

April 11

St. Leo the Great

Pope and Doctor of the Church (400?–461)

"It is one and the same Son of God Who exists in both natures, taking what is ours to Himself without losing what is His own."

St. Leo was born to a Tuscan family in Rome around 400. After serving the church in various capacities, he was elected pope in 440. His pontificate coincided with a period of crisis. The once glorious Roman empire was in a state of collapse. Heretical doctrines of all sorts were circulating freely. Barbarian armies were pressing at the gates. Under such circumstances the church might well have disintegrated had it not been for Leo's forceful leadership and bold vision.

As the successor to *Peter, Leo had a deep sense of his responsibility to lead the church and uphold its discipline and order. At the same time, he had the strength of personality necessary to back up his claims of authority. His famous "Tome," addressed to the Council of Chalcedon (451), supplied the language to settle the long-protracted dispute over the dual natures of Christ. Leo taught that Christ is one Person, the Divine Word, in whom two natures, human and divine, are permanently united without confusion or mixture. When Leo's letter was read to the council the bishops cried, "Peter has spoken by Leo." His teaching was adopted as the official doctrine of the church.

Soon after the council Leo met a different kind of threat when the armies of Attila the Hun advanced on Rome. Unarmed, Leo went out to meet the notorious warrior and somehow persuaded him to withdraw his armies. He was less successful in 455 when he tried to exert a similar influence on the Vandal Gaiseric. The best he could obtain was an assurance that the Vandals would merely pillage Rome without burning it. For fourteen days the Vandals ransacked the city. When they left for North Africa they took many captives with them. Much of Leo's effort in succeeding years was spent in ministering to the broken victims left behind.

Leo died in 461. Thanks to him the church not only survived the collapse of Rome but was able to emerge as one of the strongest institutions of the medieval world. Thus he earned the title "the Great," one of only three popes (along with *Gregory I and Nicholas I) to be so honored. In 1754 he was also named a Doctor of the Church. (Leo's feast, long observed on April 11, is now celebrated on November 10.)

See: St. Leo the Great: Letters, trans. Bro. Edmund Hunt, C.S.C., Fathers of the Church 34 (New York: Fathers of the Church, 1957).

St. Guthlac
Hermit (d. 714)

*"My spirit has run the course in the race of his life
and is impatient to be borne to those joys whose course has no ending."*

An eighth-century life of St. Guthlac by his fellow monk Felix relates the story of this Anglo-Saxon hero of the spiritual life. He was born of a noble family and spent his early life as a warrior, engaging in constant battle against Welsh enemies. One day, however, when he was twenty-four, "a spiritual flame began to kindle the heart" of Guthlac. Reflecting on the vanity and fleeting duration of human existence, he vowed to become "Christ's man." The next day he laid down his arms, bade farewell to his comrades and family, and set off on his new life.

He entered a monastery at Repton, where he spent two years. At first his austerity — particularly his disdain for "any intoxicating liquor" — provoked the bitter resentment of his fellow monks. But eventually he won their affection by his good nature and sincere piety. By this time, however, Guthlac was already dreaming of new adventures. Whenever he read about "the solitary life of the monks of olden times, then his heart burned with a hungry longing to seek solitude in the wilderness."

With the consent of his community he set out for a deserted fen country in East Anglia, so forlorn and (according to rumors) populated by monsters, that it was thought to be uninhabitable. In this marshy "desert" Guthlac made his abode. He wore only rough animal skins and lived on a meager diet of barley bread and muddy water, a meal he consumed only after sundown.

Monsters, spiritual or otherwise, quickly beat a trail to his cell. Guthlac was regularly besieged by Satan, who sent him "arrows of despair" and other temptations. Like *St. Antony he was forced to battle terrible spirits — sometimes whole armies of them — who assumed the appearance of frightening beasts or other more alluring figures. But protected by the armor of faith, Guthlac eventually won the day and was troubled no more.

Over time Guthlac's reputation as a prophet and healer attracted visitors and supplicants to his remote hermitage. Despite his solitary existence, Guthlac was no misanthrope. As Felix observes,

> From Guthlac no sick man went away without relief; no one distressed, without assistance; no one sad, without joy; no one weary, without encouragement; no one sorrowing, without comfort; no one worried, without counsel. So strong was Guthlac in real love that he bore the burdens of one and all alike.

One day a visiting bishop, impressed by his holiness, asked if he might confer holy orders on the aged hermit. When Guthlac agreed, the bishop ordained him on the spot.

Guthlac enjoyed great familiarity with the creatures around him. Even fish and birds seemed to respond to his commands. One time a visitor was surprised when two swallows flew into his house, perched on Guthlac's shoulders, and began to sing. When he was asked how it came that these birds were so trusting, Guthlac answered, "Have you not read that with him who is united with God in a pure spirit all things are joined together in God, and that he who forsakes the companionship of men, seeks the companionship of animals and the friendship of angels?"

He apparently meant this quite literally. In his final illness he was attended by a young monk named Beccel. When it was obvious that death was near, Beccel asked Guthlac to tell him who it was with whom he appeared to converse every day. Guthlac revealed that "from the second year that I began to dwell in this hermitage the Lord has sent an angel to be my consolation and to speak with me every morning and evening." On the evening when Guthlac died, according to Beccel, his hermitage was illuminated by a dazzling light "compared with whose brilliance the sun ...seemed pale as a lamp in daylight." (St. Guthlac's feast is celebrated on April 11.)

See: Felix, "The Life of St. Guthlac," in Clinton Albertson, S.J., ed., *Anglo-Saxon Saints and Heroes* (New York: Fordham University Press, 1967).

April 13

Henri Perrin
Worker and Priest (1914–1954)

"The presence of priests really living among the masses seems to me a necessary condition of reform and progress."

In Paris in the 1940s a group of idealistic priests embarked on a new field of mission. Like traditional missionaries, they wished to implant the gospel in a "foreign land" — though in this case in the midst of "Catholic" France. Their aim was to cross the threshold of the Catholic ghetto and enter the world of the working class, for so long estranged from the church. Swapping their soutanes for overalls, they applied for factory jobs, and so began the extraordinary, though sadly short-lived, experiment of the worker priests.

Henri Perrin was one of these pioneers. He was born on April 13, 1914. During World War II he and a number of young priests volunteered to accompany French workers who had been conscripted to do factory work in Germany. There he worked alongside his countrymen while also serving as a clandestine chaplain. He lasted less than a year before his identity was discovered. After a short imprisonment, he was sent back to France. But the impact of this experience never left him. In the factory he had discovered just how wide was the gulf between the church and the workers. For them, the church was an irrelevant artifact, if not simply an ally of the propertied class.

Back in Paris, Perrin and others of a similar mind dreamed of a new apostolate aimed at breaking down these barriers. The church should not exist in some marginal "religious" world, they believed, but should take root in the life and experience of the masses. But this could not be achieved through preaching alone. What was needed were priests willing to leave the insulated world of parish life and enter fully into the world of the poor.

In 1947 Perrin and a number of priests received support from their bishops and religious superiors to implement this program. Perrin himself initially found work in a plastics factory. He was cautious about revealing his identity to his co-workers, but as it became known that he was a priest he was rewarded with an experience of respect and fellowship that he had never known in parish life. Many workers confessed that his presence was the first reason they had ever had to take an interest in the church.

Although the French bishops were largely pleased with this experiment, concerns from the Vatican were not slow to arrive. One of the problems was that the unions were largely dominated by Communists. In 1949 the Vatican issued a decree condemning Catholics who either belonged to or collaborated with the Communist Party. This posed an insoluble dilemma for the worker priests. They could not work without belonging to a union, and many of them had in fact risen to positions of leadership in their unions — a reflection of their co-workers' esteem. The priests felt that their effective presence required not just that they work in the factories but that they participate in the workers' struggles. Some, including Perrin, were actively involved in a series of bitter strikes and so were susceptible to the charge of allowing their priestly apostolate to be submerged in their identity as labor militants. For his part, Perrin expressed frustration with the fact that church authorities "draw back as soon as they reach the threshold of the problems raised by the worker's world. . . . One thing is certain: The voice of the poor is not listened to."

In early 1954 the bishops, under strong pressure from Rome, called a halt to the experiment. To Perrin and his confreres, the decree was a devastating blow: "Everything we've been doing for the last ten years has been repudiated and chucked away." While personally hurt, their suffering, Perrin wrote, "is nothing compared with that of the millions of workers who feel they have been abandoned and betrayed by the Church of Christ." For many of the priests the decree presented an "impossible choice." While most submitted to the church, others felt such a step would represent a betrayal of their comrades which they were unwilling to make. They remained in their posts and accepted the ecclesiastical penalties of disobedience.

Perrin himself struggled in lonely solitude over the appropriate response. He had spoken so often in the past of the importance of leaving the "Catholic ghetto" and "the desire to live frankly among other men." Now only one thing was certain: "It is impossible that I should go back to the ghetto." But the choices were bleak. One option was to resign from the priesthood, but something made him shrink from the decision. In his case the dilemma remained unresolved, for on October 25, 1954, he was killed in a motorbike accident.

The challenge of the worker priests was not forgotten. Surely it was present ten years later when the bishops at Vatican II issued their famous pronouncement: "The joys and hope, the grief and anguish of the men and women of our time, especially of those who are poor or afflicted in any way, are the joy and hope, the grief and anguish of the followers of Christ as well." During the dark night of faith, as he struggled with his conscience, Perrin had never doubted that others would one day take up the struggle to bridge the gulf between the church and the poor. As he wrote, "With us, or without us, or in spite of us, God will fill that gulf — if only we don't put too many spokes in the wheels."

See: Priest and Worker: The Autobiography of Henri Perrin, translated with an introduction by Bernard Wall (New York: Holt, Rinehart and Winston, 1964).

April 14

St. Justin
Philosopher and Martyr (100?–165)

"You can kill us but you cannot do us any real harm."

St. Justin was born of gentile parents in Samaria at the turn of the first century. As a young man he devoted himself to philosophy, exploring in turn the major schools of Greek thought in his quest for religious truth. After many years of searching he was introduced to the Hebrew Scriptures and the early Christian writings. In these texts he found his way to the church. In becoming a Christian, however, he saw no need to renounce philosophy. He regarded Christianity as the "true philosophy," the goal toward which Plato and other philosophers had been groping. From then on, Justin committed his talents as a philosopher and teacher to expounding the Christian faith and engaging in debate with other religious seekers. Wearing the "philosopher's cloak," he remained a layman, traveling throughout the Greek world before settling in Rome.

Justin was the author of several apologetic works, defending the Christian religion against the charges and suspicions circulating in the Greek world, especially those of immorality and godlessness. In his principle work, his *Apology,* he offered a spirited argument for the truth of Christianity and its superiority over pagan religion and philosophy. In doing so he stressed the continuity between Christianity and the glimmering of truth which was accessible to all people of good will. Just as the prophecies of the Old Testament were realized in Christ, so, he argued, the philosopher's search for truth was fulfilled in Christianity.

Justin's *Apology* contains the early basis for an "inclusive" understanding of the salvation of those outside the church:

> We have been taught that Christ is the First-begotten of God, and have previously testified that he is the Reason [Logos] of which every race of man partakes. Those who lived in accordance with Reason are Christians, even though they were called godless, such as, among the Greeks, Socrates and Heraclitus and others like them.

What distinguishes Christianity from these other philosophies, according to Justin, is the fact that in Christ the Logos has entered history and become a human being.

Though he stressed the reasonableness and higher morality of Christianity, Justin's letter of Apology, addressed to Emperor Antoninus Pius, was written in the context of persecution. Justin himself was eventually arrested and tried before the prefect of Rome. When asked what teaching he followed, Justin replied, "I have studied all in turn, but have given my adhesion to the teaching of the Christians, however displeasing it may be to those who follow error." When he refused the order to sacrifice to the gods he was scourged and beheaded. (The feast of St. Justin, long observed on April 14, is now celebrated on June 1.)

See: "The First Apology of Justin, the Martyr," in Cyril C. Richardson, ed., *Early Christian Fathers* (New York: Macmillan, 1970).

April 15

Bd. Damien of Molokai
Priest and Leper (1840–1899)

"I make myself a leper with the lepers to gain all for Christ."

Damien De Veuster, a young Belgian priest, had served nine years as a missioner in the Hawaiian Islands when he felt called to request a perilous assignment. He asked his superiors to be allowed to serve on the island of Molokai, the notorious leper colony.

Westerners had arrived in the Hawaiian Islands only late in the eighteenth century, finding a native population of about three hundred thousand. Within a hundred years the ravages of disease had reduced this number to fifty thousand. Among many illnesses, the most dreaded scourge was leprosy. The first case appeared only in 1840, but within thirty years it had reached epidemic proportions. Helpless to control its spread and unable at that time to offer any remedy, the authorities responded in 1868 by establishing a leper settlement on the remote and inaccessible island of Molokai. By law, Hawaiians found to be suffering from the disease were snatched by force from their families and communities and sent to this island exile to perish.

Conditions on the island were horrific. Patients were literally dumped in the surf and left to make their way ashore, seek shelter in caves or squalid shacks, and cling to life as best they could, beyond the pale of any civil or moral law.

It was to this island that Father Damien was assigned. From the beginning he sought to instill in the members of his "parish" a sense of self-worth and dignity. His first task was to restore dignity to death. Where previously the deceased were tossed into shallow graves to be consumed by pigs and dogs, he designed a clean and fenced-in cemetery and established a proper burial society. He constructed a church and worked alongside the people building clean new houses. Within several years of his arrival the island was utterly transformed; no longer a way-station to death, it had become a proud and joyful community.

As part of his effort to uplift the self-esteem of his flock, Damien realized from the beginning that he must not shrink from contact with the people. Despite the horrid physical effects of the disease, he insisted on intimate contact with them. When he preached, he made a habit of referring to his flock not as "my brothers and sisters," but as "we lepers."

One day this reference assumed a new meaning, as Damien recognized in himself the unmistakable symptoms of the disease. Now he was truly one with the suffering of his people, literally confined, as they were, to the island of Molokai. Despite the advancing illness, which eventually ravaged his body, he redoubled his efforts, working tirelessly in his building projects and his pastoral responsibilities.

In his last years he suffered terrible bouts of loneliness, feeling keenly the lack of a religious community of support, and even the opportunity to receive absolution. On one occasion a visiting bishop refused to disembark from his ship. Damien rowed out to meet him and suffered the humiliation of shouting up his confession. Because of fear of contagion he was even forbidden to visit the mission headquarters of his order in Honolulu.

Damien died of leprosy on April 15, 1889. By that time his fame had spread widely throughout the world. He was beatified in 1995 by Pope John Paul II.

See: Gavan Dawes, *Holy Man, Fr. Damien of Molokai* (New York: Harper & Row, 1973).

April 16

St. Benedict Joseph Labre
Poor Man of God (1748–1783)

"I am only a poor, ignorant beggar."

Benedict Joseph Labre was a religious vagabond, a "holy fool for Christ" of a type familiar in the traditions of the East, but less so in the West. He was born in a village near Boulogne in the south of France, the son of a shopkeeper, the eldest of fifteen children. When he was twelve his family sent him to live with an uncle who was a parish priest. There he received some rudimentary education. When his uncle died in an outbreak of plague, Benedict briefly returned to his family. But he had decided by this time to devote his life entirely to God. He was turned away from the Trappists on account of his youth. He was likewise refused by a series of other religious communities. Thus discouraged, he divined that his true vocation was to seek a cloister within the world. Accordingly he set off on foot on a pilgrimage that lasted several years, wandering thousands of miles across Europe, all the while praying and visiting shrines and churches.

Benedict dressed in rags and never bathed. This helped to discourage human contact and thus contributed to the prayerful isolation which he relished. He declined to beg, though occasionally passersby were moved to offer him alms. Often he would pass these along to others he felt were in greater need. When food was not offered, he lived off of what was discarded by the roadside.

His appearance was as likely to evoke contempt as pity, and he was frequently harassed and shooed along his way by more fastidious citizens. Nevertheless, he accepted all rebukes in a penitential spirit. When a priest in the confessional, struck by his theological knowledge, asked him if he had ever studied divinity, he replied, "I, Father? I am only a poor ignorant beggar." But those who were able to see beneath his disheveled appearance — including, eventually, his confessor — recognized the saint in their midst.

Eventually he settled in Rome, where he spent his nights sleeping in the ruins of the Coliseum — site of ancient martyrdom — and his days praying in the various churches of the city. When his health began to fail, he consented to sleep in a hospice for the destitute. But this belated concession to human frailty could not reverse the toll of his ascetic existence. At the age of thirty-five he collapsed on the steps of a church and was carried to the house of a nearby butcher. There he died on April 16, 1783. Almost immediately, children of the neighborhood began calling through the streets, "The Saint is dead, the Saint is dead!" His reputation quickly spread across the city, and before long throughout Europe. Biographies were published in many languages. Through one of these accounts his parents, still alive in the village of his birth, learned what had become of their long-missing son. He was canonized in 1883.

See: Alban Goodier, S.J., "St. Benedict Joseph Labre," in F. J. Sheed, ed., *Saints Are Not Sad* (New York: Sheed & Ward, 1949).

April 17

Max Josef Metzger
Priest and Martyr (1887–1944)

*"Only a great venture of faith, humility, and love
can solve the problem of the fate of Christendom."*

Max Josef Metzger was born on February 3, 1887, in the German village of Schopfheim. Early in his life he decided on a vocation to the priesthood. He was ordained shortly before the outbreak of World War I, during which he served as an army chaplain. His experience at the front filled him with a deep revulsion for war and formed his determination to devote his life to the cause of peace and reconciliation.

After the war Metzger worked with a number of organizations, including the White Cross, an apostolic mission among the down and out. He also founded the World Peace League and the World Congress of Christ the King, a movement dedicated to Christian unity and international peace. In a speech in France he declared, "Only the realization of what is the dream of us all can bring peace: a true league of nations, a coalition of all nations in a genuine Christian family of nations worthy of man." Metzger was also an early pioneer in the ecumenical movement, actively working to promote dialogue and cooperation between Catholics and Protestants in a movement called Una Sancta.

From the beginning of the Nazi reign, Metzger had regular conflicts with the state. He was arrested on several occasions, the first time in January 1934. In each case the Gestapo failed to find grounds for charging him. His final arrest came in June 1943 after the interception of secret letters he had sent to foreign bishops begging their help in promoting a negotiated end to the war. Metzger was charged with treason and giving comfort to the enemy. He was convicted and sentenced to death, a sentence he greeted with disdain: "I knew there was no shame, only honor, in being declared dishonorable by such a court." Afterward he told his friends, "Now it has happened, I am calm. I have offered my life to God for the peace of the world and the unity of the church. If God takes it I will be happy; if He grants me a still longer life I will also be thankful. As God wills!"

He spent most of a year incarcerated in a series of Berlin jails. Much of the time he was kept in irons. He suffered from not being able to say Mass. Nevertheless, he managed to send hopeful messages to friends on the outside, and he inspired his fellow prisoners with his extreme courage and stalwart faith. One of them later recalled, "I had often observed [Father Metzger] walking and looked to see if I could not make out a halo.... In the last weeks he impressed me as a saint, and that he was, in my deepest conviction — he is so in all eternity."

On April 17, 1944, Metzger was told to prepare himself for death. He knelt and said a prayer: "Now, Lord Jesus, I come quickly." Without faltering, he calmly walked to the place of execution, and there he was beheaded.

See: Leonard Swidler, *Bloodwitness for Peace and Unity* (Philadelphia: Ecumenical Press, 1977).

April 18

Cornelia Connelly
Foundress of the Society of the Holy Child Jesus (1809–1879)

"Is not our faith a sword of strength? I feel it so, my Lord."

Through much of her life Cornelia Connelly struggled hard to discern her vocation amid the claims and demands which others made on her. But when she was certain she had heard God's voice she stood firm, despite the terrible sacrifices this entailed.

She was born in 1809 to a wealthy Philadelphia family. In 1831 she married an Episcopal priest named Pierce Connelly. When his studies convinced him that Catholicism was the true religion, he renounced his Anglican orders and entered the Catholic church. Cornelia joined him. Although in her conversion, as in many subsequent decisions, Cornelia was to some extent carried along by the tide of her husband's strong will, she too felt a call to holiness. She hoped to discover this in the setting of family life; circumstances dictated that it should come instead through suffering and sacrifice.

In 1839 Cornelia and Pierce, with their three children, were living in rural Louisiana, where they both taught in Catholic schools. A fourth child, Mary Magdalene, died after only seven weeks. Five months later, while this wound was still fresh, their two-year-old, John Henry, was pushed by a dog into a vat of boiling sugar cane juice. He died forty-three hours later. During that time, as all the while she held his scalded body, Cornelia experienced a deep identification with the sorrows of Mary. When the child died on February 2, the feast of the Presentation, Cornelia wrote in her diary, "He was taken into the Temple of the Lord."

Later that year Pierce confided that he wished to seek ordination as a Catholic priest. Cornelia was stricken. It would mean the breakup of the family and, for her, a lifelong commitment to celibacy. To her spiritual advisor she asked, "Is it necessary for Pierce to make this sacrifice and *sacrifice me? I love my husband; I love my darling children; why must I give them up?"* Still, the dutiful wife, she tried to believe in the coincidence between her husband's wishes and the will of God. So she agreed to co-operate with her husband's plan. She accepted the trial of the celibate life and remained behind, pregnant with her fifth child, Adeline, while Pierce went off to Rome to explore the possibilities for his vocation.

Eventually Pierce summoned the family to join him. He had secured an audience with Pope Gregory XVI, who accepted his vocation and cleared the way to his ordination, provided Cornelia would make a vow of chastity. While Pierce pursued his studies, Cornelia lived with her children in the Sacred Heart convent on Trinità de Monte. Though Pierce visited once a week she was, for all practical purposes, quite alone. Prayer offered little consolation. She wrote, "Incapable of listening or understanding or thinking...I forced my will to rejoice in the greatness of God."

In 1845 Cornelia made the requisite vow and Pierce was ordained. It was not clear what she was now supposed to do. She supposed she would return to America. At this point, however, several bishops and priests urged her to go to England. There the struggling Catholic church, emerging from long suppression, was undergoing a period of expansion and renewal. It was suggested to Cornelia that her true calling was to establish a religious congregation in England for the education of girls. Cornelia accepted the challenge, provided she could keep her children with her. And so in 1846 she arrived in England to take over a newly built convent school in Derby.

There were numerous twists and turns in the foundation of this school and the community that attended it. But within a few years Cornelia had achieved some eminence within the English Catholic church. In 1847 she took religious vows, and Bishop Wiseman formally installed her as superior of her congregation, the Society of the Holy Child Jesus. The name reflected her profound devotion to the Incarnation, specifically to the "humbled God" who had revealed himself in the form of a helpless infant. In this spirit she instructed her Sisters, "As you step through the muddy streets, love God with your feet; and when your hands toil, love Him with your hands; and when you teach the little children, love Him in His little ones." Her toil at this point was only beginning.

After only three years of her new life a new round of trials began. By this time Pierce had grown restless and dissatisfied with the priesthood. At first he tried to interfere with and take over Cornelia's congregation. After she asked him please to stay away from her convent, he announced that he was leaving the priesthood and wished her to resume her marital duties. Once again Cornelia was appalled. Though her husband's will had led her to the religious habit, now that she wore it it was her own, and she would no longer accept his word as the word of God. When she refused his demand he brought a suit against her in a high ecclesiastical (Anglican) court. Now a professional anti-Catholic, Pierce painted a lurid picture of his wife being held captive by agents of Rome. Nevertheless, the court decided in Cornelia's favor. Enraged, Pierce retaliated by kidnapping her children and taking them out of the country. She was never to see them again.

Cornelia remained the superior of her congregation for over thirty years. During those years she saw new schools established in England, America, and France. Her congregation did much to promote the advancement and education of young women, especially the poor. Nevertheless, Mother Cornelia always bore the weight of her many sorrows. Toward the end of her life she suffered from an excruciating case of eczema that gave her the appearance of a leper — as though, it was said, "she had been scalded from head to foot." It seemed she was revisiting in her illness the experience of her greatest sorrow as well as her deepest identification with the Holy Child. Now it was she who was to be offered in the Temple. On the day before she died, on April 18, 1879, she turned to the nursing Sister and exclaimed, "In this flesh I shall see my God!"

See: Mary Andrew Armour, *Cornelia* (Society of the Holy Child Jesus, 1979); Juliana Wadham, *The Case of Cornelia Connelly* (New York: Pantheon, 1957).

April 19

St. Alphege
Archbishop of Canterbury, Martyr (953–1012)

"Then was he captive · who had been the head
Of the English race · and of Christendom.
There was misery to be seen · where bliss had been before

In that unhappy city · whence came to us first
Christendom and happiness · in the sight of God and man."
— Anglo-Saxon Chronicle

The great Cathedral of Canterbury will forever be associated with the murder of *Thomas Becket in 1170. But Thomas was not the first archbishop of Canterbury to fall a victim of violence. His martyrdom was preceded by that of the Anglo-Saxon St. Alphege, 150 years before.

Alphege was a monk and later bishop of Winchester. He lived in a time when England was subject to the periodic terror of Danish marauders. In 994, at the behest of King Ethelred the Unready, Alphege undertook a peacekeeping mission to several Danish warlords. In the process he converted them to Christianity while winning assurance, henceforth, of their peaceful intentions.

In 1005 Alphege was named archbishop of Canterbury. But in the meantime the Danish terror had returned to southern England. In 1010 the Danes laid siege to Canterbury. Despite the payment of tribute, the invaders overran the city and held the archbishop and many other prominent citizens hostage. The others were released on the payment of ransom, but an exorbitant sum — three thousand gold crowns — was demanded for the release of Alphege. He forbade his people to pay such a sum. In retaliation he was brutally murdered.

Alphege was afterward revered as a martyr as well as a national hero. A later archbishop of Canterbury, Lanfranc (d. 1089), came to question whether, given the circumstances of his death, the sainted Alphege should properly be regarded as a martyr. But he was satisfied by the answer of his protégé, *St. Anselm (d. 1109), that to die for justice was martyrdom indeed.

See: J. R. H. Moorman, *A History of the Church in England* (New York: Morehouse-Barlow, 1973).

April 20

St. Hildegund
Monk and Virgin (d. 1188)

"If I were to dress as a woman they would think of me as a woman, and then what would become of me?" — St. Joan of Arc

St. Hildegund was the daughter of a German knight. After her mother died she accompanied her father on a pilgrimage to the Holy Land. For protection along the way she was disguised as a boy called Joseph. On the way home her father died, leaving Hildegund / "Joseph" to undergo a series of extraordinary adventures before making it back to Germany. All the while and over many years, she maintained her identity as a boy and then a man. Finally, back home, she was admitted to the Cistercian monastery in Schönau, where she remained until her death. Only then was the secret of her sex discovered.

Despite its fabulous qualities, the story of St. Hildegund is attested by many contemporary sources. It is interesting to note, however, that such stories of women passing as men in religious life are far from uncommon in the annals of the saints. Most of these are undoubtedly apocryphal, with little more historical foundation than the fantastic legend of "Pope Joan." Still they remain in the official calendar of saints.

They include St. Eugenia, a supposed martyr of the early church. It is claimed that she dressed as a man and passed some years as the abbot of a monastery in Egypt. Eventually she was forced to reveal her sex as the only way of clearing herself of charges of misconduct. She then fled to Rome where she died as a martyr.

St. Pelagia the Penitent was supposedly a dancing girl in Antioch who, after her conversion, disguised herself as a man and lived as a hermit on the Mount of Olives in Jerusalem.

St. Marina, the daughter of a monk in Bithynia, lived with her father disguised as a boy. After her father died she lived on in the monastery. She silently endured a false accusation and subsequent punishment for fathering the child of an innkeeper's daughter. After her death, her true sex, and also her innocence, were proved to the wonder and shame of her accusers.

What is the lesson of such stories? Perhaps they serve as parabolic reminders of the ideal that "in Christ," if not yet in the world or the church, "there is no male or female."

April 21

St. Anselm
Archbishop of Canterbury and Doctor of the Church
(1033–1109)

"There can be no doubt at all that something than which a greater cannot be thought exists both in the understanding and in reality."

St. Anselm, who was born in Burgundy, spent the better part of his life, from the age of seventeen until he was fifty-nine, in the Benedictine abbey of Bec in Normandy. He attained the office of abbot, and there he might happily and productively have lived out the remainder of his days. In 1092, however, during a visit to England, he was compelled, much against his desires, to accept the vacant see of Canterbury. As archbishop of Canterbury and primate of the British Isles, Anselm displayed the same gifts for leadership and pastoral discernment he had displayed in his years as abbot. His tenure was marked, however, by continuous tensions with the reigning monarch, William Rufus, as well as his successor Henry I, over the independence of the church from lay political control. Twice he was compelled to go into exile, while the Vatican applied pressure on his behalf. He returned to England for a final time in 1106 and achieved a reconciliation with King Henry, but his death followed three years later.

Despite his ecclesiastical accomplishments, Anselm's place in history owes far more to his contributions as a theologian. He is renowned, in fact, as the "father of scholasticism." In his *Proslogion* he defined the task of theology as "faith seeking understanding" — a definition that has ever since justified the application of reason to the mystery of Christian faith. He was not, however, a proponent of "natural theology." Theological understanding, for Anselm, was ultimately rooted in the gift of faith, and not in unassisted reason.

This remained so, even as he offered his so-called ontological "proof" for the existence of God. God is "that than which nothing greater can be conceived." Thus, in conceiving of God it is necessary that existence be predicated of such a being; otherwise it would be possible to conceive of something greater. It is doubtful that anyone was ever converted by such an argument. But that was not the point. For Anselm the purpose of theology is to exercise the understanding of the believer, and not to persuade the skeptic.

Anselm's masterpiece was his *Cur Deus Homo* (Why God Became Human). His effort here was to explain why it was necessary that Christ our Redeemer combine the natures of God and humanity. His reflection on the Incarnation turned on the doctrine of atonement. According to Anselm, humanity, in the person of Adam, had infinitely offended God (the infinite degree of the offense reflecting the infinite dignity of the one offended). Such an infinite offense required infinite satisfaction — something that only God himself could supply. But the satisfaction would not be effective unless it were the guilty party — humanity itself — which paid the price. Therefore, our Redeemer must be one who combined the natures of God and human being. This was the meaning and purpose of the Incarnation.

Anselm's solution was extremely influential for centuries. For many reasons it no longer holds the same appeal. For one thing, it makes God into a kind of cold-blooded executioner. Thus, Jesus did not die as a result of sin or as an expression of infinite love, but in order to satisfy the offended honor of God. Not a few people today find such a doctrine more horrible than consoling. What is notable, however, is Anselm's attempt to understand the mystery of salvation in terms borrowed from the social and political values of his time — namely, the code of feudal honor. Such a perspective is no longer convincing. But Anselm's effort gives support to those who today struggle to understand the gospel in light of contemporary concerns.

Apart from his other contributions Anselm is also distinguished by his personal character. A winsome portrait by his fellow monk, Eadmer, puts less emphasis on Anselm's miracles than on his fully redeemed humanity. Eadmer dwells with particular affection on Anselm's tenderness as an abbot who always preferred to lead his flock by loving exhortation and wise example rather than by punishment or harsh discipline. He documents Anselm's tears over a wayward youth, and describes his habit of nursing sick brothers by his own hand:

And so, while he was a father to those who were well, he was a mother to the sick: or rather, he was both father and mother to the sick and the sound alike. Hence any of them with any private trouble hastened to unburden himself to him, as if to the gentlest of mothers, and this was particularly the case with earnest and zealous young men.

See: *St. Anselm: Basic Writings* (La Salle, Ill.: Open Court, 1962); *The Life of St. Anselm, Archbishop of Canterbury by Eadmer,* ed. R. W. Southern (London: Oxford University Press, 1962).

April 22
Käthe Kollwitz
Artist (1867–1945)

"One day, a new idea will arise and there will be an end to all wars. I die convinced of this. It will need much hard work, but it will be achieved."

Käthe Kollwitz, one of the great artists of the twentieth century, was an avowed socialist and pacifist. In her artistic vision these words were not mere ideological labels. They represented a moral and spiritual affirmation of the preciousness of human life and a spirit of resistance to all the idols of death.

She was born in Konigsburg in East Prussia in 1867, the daughter of a minister. She lived most of her life in Berlin, where she married Karl Kollwitz, a doctor who practiced medicine in a working-class section of the city. She drew on his patients as models for many of her drawings and lithographs. Few other artists have been so committed to representing the private struggles and suffering of the poor. Her depictions of hunger, unemployment, domestic violence, and the oppressive burden of despair are among the most poignant images in all of twentieth-century art.

Kollwitz was particularly sensitive to the experience of women, especially the aspects of maternal love. Many of her drawings depict mothers delighting in the presence of their children. But she also depicted a mother's fierce determination to protect her young, and the corresponding potential for devastating loss. Kollwitz herself was no stranger to such loss. In World War I her youngest son, Peter, was killed at the front. His death struck "like a thunderbolt," for a long time crippling her ability to work. "Peter," she wrote, "was seed for the planting that should not have been ground." Eventually she transformed her grief into a passionate commitment to peace and the struggle against all the causes of war.

She had sympathized with the communist revolution in Russia as well as the parallel revolutionary struggles in Germany. In a powerful sequence of engravings she celebrated the doomed Peasants' Revolt of the sixteenth century and its mythic embodiment in the peasant mother, Black Anna. But with the death of her son her commitment to socialism became intertwined with a resolute pacifism.

After the war she was commissioned to design a war memorial at the Soldiers Cemetery near Dixmuiden. She worked on the statue for many years. When it was finally unveiled in 1932, it revealed a scene entitled "Mourning Parents," its figures plainly modeled after herself and her husband, Karl. It remains a devastating image of sorrow over the waste of life.

In the years to come Kollwitz continued to put her art at the service of her conscience and her spiritual vision. With the rise of the Nazis, however, her work was banned and could not be publicly shown. She managed to remain in Berlin throughout the Nazi era and the devastation of the war. Her husband died in 1940. Two years later, her grandson, another Peter, was killed in action.

Still, driven by her sense of personal responsibility, she continued to draw as long as health permitted. As she wrote, "Culture arises only when the individual fulfills his cycle of obligations. If everyone recognizes and fulfills his cycle of obligations, genuineness emerges. The culture of a whole nation can in the final analysis be built upon nothing else."

In April 1945 her granddaughter asked her if she was a pacifist. "Yes," she answered, "if you understand by pacifism more than just antiwar. It is a new idea — that of the brotherhood of man."

She died on April 22, a few days before the Armistice.

See: Renate Hinz, ed., *Käthe Kollwitz: Graphics, Posters, Drawings* (New York: Pantheon, 1981); Mina C. Klein and H. Arthur Klein, *Käthe Kollwitz: Life in Art* (New York: Schocken, 1975).

April 23

Cesar Chavez
Farmworker (1927–1993)

"When you sacrifice, you force others to sacrifice.
It's an extremely powerful weapon."

In the early 1960s Cesar Chavez wrote a new chapter in the history of the American labor movement by organizing the first successful union of farmworkers. Through his commitment to nonviolence and his deep faith in the justice of his cause, he transformed a local labor struggle into a moral cause that brought hope to the hopeless and aroused the conscience of the nation.

Chavez was born in 1927 to a Mexican-American family in the Southwest. During the Depression his family lost their small farm and were forced to join the tide of migrant farmworkers traveling up and down the West Coast. As a child Chavez himself performed stoop labor in the fields as his family followed the crops. Though he attended thirty-seven schools, he never advanced beyond the seventh grade. Farmworkers were notoriously the poorest and most exploited of American workers, unorganized and deliberately excluded from the protection of most labor laws.

By the time Chavez was a young man with a wife and a growing family, he was eager to move as far away as possible from the poverty of his upbringing. But he was influenced by a priest who instilled in him a passion for social justice, and later by a community activist who trained him in the techniques of organization. Chavez moved to Delano, California, with the determination to organize the farmworkers. This was the beginning of what would become the United Farmworkers Union (UFW).

To start with, Chavez believed it was necessary to impart a sense of dignity and community to the farmworkers. This union would not rely on outside funding but on the basic principles of sacrifice and solidarity. All who signed up with the union would pay $3.50 a month in dues — a small amount that nevertheless represented a real hardship for many struggling families. Furthermore, those who worked for the union would make a commitment to voluntary poverty. Chavez himself, like the humblest organizer, lived on a salary of $5 a week plus basic expenses. The second nonnegotiable principle was a commitment to nonviolence, a refusal to respond in kind no matter what the provocation. The strength of the movement, ultimately, would rely on the moral character of its efforts.

Throughout the 1960s support for the UFW cause spread across the country as Chavez added a consumer boycott of table grapes to the strikes and picket lines that were the basic tools of the struggle. Marches by the UFW often had a religious character, reinforced by public prayer, banners of Our Lady of Guadalupe, and the presence of the many clergy and religious who identified with the cause. In 1968 Chavez undertook a twenty-five-day fast, an effort to strengthen the discipline and morale of the movement. When he ended the fast, Robert F. Kennedy, a strong supporter, was there to break bread with him. Another early and loyal supporter was *Dorothy Day, who in 1973 was arrested at the age of seventy-five while walking on a UFW picket line in California.

The nonviolence of the UFW was sorely tested over the years; at times the growers and rival unions resorted to brutal tactics in their effort to intimidate the farmworkers. The movement had its martyrs. But over and over again, when faced with defeat, Chavez drew on the power of his personal commitment and charisma to breath new life into the struggle.

At the time of his death on April 23, 1993, the United Farmworkers had passed the crest of their success of a decade before. The number of unionized workers was down and many contracts had been lost. To some extent this reflected a certain "compassion fatigue" on the part of the public, who could no longer be counted on to provide support for the cause. Nevertheless, thanks to Chavez's lifetime of efforts and the protective legislation he inspired, the farmworkers of America, although still poor, were less powerless, less hopeless. And he had left behind a remarkable witness to the power of nonviolence and the cause of justice. When he broke his long fast in 1968, he expressed the convictions and faith that underlay his life:

> When we are really honest with ourselves we must admit that our lives are all that really belong to us. So it is how we use our lives that determines what kind of men we are. It is my deepest belief that only by giving our lives do we find life. I am convinced that

the truest act of courage, the strongest act of manliness is to sacrifice ourselves for others in totally nonviolent struggle for justice. To be a man is to suffer for others. God help us to be men!

See: Ronald B. Taylor, *Chavez and the Farm Workers* (Boston: Beacon, 1975); Marjorie Hope and James Young, *The Struggle for Humanity* (Maryknoll, N.Y.: Orbis, 1979).

April 24
St. Apollonius the Apologist
Martyr (d. 185)

"Yes, I am a Christian. I worship and I fear the God
who made heaven, earth, the sea and all that is in them."

Though Apollonius was a philosopher and a member of the Roman Senate, his status offered no protection when he was denounced as a secret Christian. He was brought before the Senate for judgment and interviewed by the proconsul Perennis.

The account of his trial is marked by a surprising civility. It apparently pained Perennis to have to apply the law to someone as learned and high-born as Apollonius. Apollonius, for his part, responded to his questioning with poise and eloquence, willing to pay respect to the emperor in all things permissible, save to grant him the deference due to God alone.

Like a friend offering legal advice, Perennis repeatedly "advises" Apollonius to "honor and worship our gods like all of us here and you will continue to live among us." When Apollonius demurs, Perennis gently reminds him, "The decree of the Senate prohibits people from being Christians."

Apollonius answers: "The decree of man does not prevail over the decree of God. The more you kill these innocent faithful, mocking justice and the laws, the more God will increase their number." Death must come for all, and after death, judgment; "but the ways of dying are not the same." Christians prepare for death each day by controlling their passions and living in conformity with God's laws.

In that case, Perennis asks, "Does death give you pleasure?"

"It is life that I love, Perennis, but this love does not make me fear death. For the life which I prefer to all else is eternal life, which awaits those who have lived faithfully in this world."

"I do not know what you are saying," Perennis answers.

"How you and I misunderstand each other! You do not want to be open to the beauties of grace. The word of the Lord, Perennis, bestows itself only on the heart which sees light as the eyes do. Preaching to fools is as vain as pointing out dawn to the blind."

Apollonius goes on to present a very beautiful summary of the gospel and the life and teachings of Jesus Christ, who likewise faced condemnation by uncomprehending men. "If it is folly to believe in the immortal soul, that after death we shall receive judgment, and at the resurrection, reward for our courage, and that God is our judge, we shall willingly take with us such an illusion which has helped us to live."

To all this, Perennis answers sadly, "I thought, Apollonius, that you would bid farewell to your whims and worship the gods with us."

"I hoped, proconsul," replies Apollonius, "that these few words which I have spoken to you about my faith would help you and that my plea would open the eyes of your soul. I hoped that your heart would bear fruit, that you would worship all your days the God who created the world, that you would lift up your prayer only to him without forgetting alms or charity, and that this would be the pure and bloodless sacrifice that you would offer to God."

"I would like to release you, Apollonius," says Perennis, "but the decree of the emperor forbids me. At least I want your death to be gentle."

"I give thanks to my God, proconsul Perennis, with all those who confess the omnipotent God and Jesus Christ, his only Son, and the Holy Spirit, for the sentence you have just given and which brings me eternal life."

According to Perennis's wish that the martyr's death be gentle, Apollonius was spared any torture and was forthwith beheaded.

As this dialogue shows, not all martyrs meet their fate in an atmosphere of sadistic odium. As often as not they are condemned by world-weary bureaucrats, simply intent on doing their duty, scarcely comprehending that they are thus passing judgment on themselves. One wonders, though, whether Perennis ever thought back on this brief encounter, and whether he ever met the face of Apollonius in his dreams.

The feast of St. Apollonius is observed on April 18.

See: "The Acts of Apollonius," in Bruno Chenu et al., eds., *The Book of Christian Martyrs* (New York: Crossroad, 1990).

April 25

St. Mark
Evangelist (first century)

"And a young man followed him, with nothing but a linen cloth about his body; and they seized him, but he left the linen cloth and ran away naked." —Mark 14:51

If, as some commentators believe, the "young man" cited above is none other than the evangelist himself, that would make Mark a disciple of Jesus and thus to some extent a direct witness to the story recounted in his Gospel. Others have suggested that Mark received the gospel from *St. Peter, if he was not the John Mark who appears in the book of Acts as a companion to *Barnabas and *Paul on their missionary journey. Regardless of his sources or his identity there is no doubt that in writing the first Gospel narrative, sometime around the year 70, Mark had a decisive influence on the subsequent development of Christianity. Before Mark's

Gospel the teachings of Jesus circulated in the form of sayings. Paul's letters contain almost no reference to the actual life story of Jesus. But for Mark the authority of Jesus' message was rooted in his paradoxical identity as the suffering and crucified Messiah. This message could be properly understood only in light of his completed ministry and passion. For Mark this was best communicated in the form of a story.

In the first half of Mark's Gospel Jesus reveals his authority through miraculous and astonishing displays of authority: healing the sick, forgiving sins, casting out demons, silencing storms, and raising the dead. The crux of the narrative comes in chapter 8 when Jesus asks his disciples, "Who do you say that I am?" and Peter answers, "You are the Christ." Immediately Jesus begins to predict his passion and death, thus challenging the disciples' understanding of what it means to be the Christ. When Peter rejects this scenario Jesus firmly rebukes him and goes on to explain that discipleship too will require faithfulness unto death: "If any man would come after me, let him deny himself and take up his cross and follow me. For whoever would save his life will lose it; and whoever loses his life for my sake and the gospel's will save it."

And so Mark's Gospel, ostensibly concerned with the story of Jesus, is gradually revealed as a handbook of discipleship. To be a Christian is not simply a matter of saying that Jesus is the Christ. It is a matter of patterning one's own life on Jesus' example of self-sacrificing love. And in a world dominated by the powers of sin the Gospel makes it clear where such discipleship is likely to lead.

Mark's Gospel ends on a curiously dynamic and open-ended note. In place of an explicit account of Jesus' resurrection, Mark's story simply ends with the arrival of three women at the empty tomb and the words of an angel: "Do not be amazed; you seek Jesus of Nazareth, who was crucified. He has risen, he is not here.... Go, tell his disciples and Peter that he is going before you to Galilee; there you will see him, as he told you."

Thus Mark addresses contemporary disciples. Jesus is no longer in the past nor is he confined to Mark's story. Rather, he has gone ahead to Galilee. Mark's readers must write their own conclusion to Jesus' story by taking up the cross of discipleship and going forth to meet him for themselves.

April 26

William Stringfellow
Theologian and Social Critic (1928–1985)

"I believe biography (and history)...is inherently theological in the sense that it contains already — literally by virtue of the Incarnation — the news of the gospel whether or not anyone discerns that. We are each one of us parables."

On a trip to the United States in the early 1960s the famous theologian *Karl Barth encountered a young lawyer whose pointed questions reflected a profound biblical sensitivity to the signs of the times. Afterward Barth remarked, "This is the man America should be listening to." The man in question was William Stringfellow, a lawyer by training, a theologian and prophet by calling, who, in his many books, applied the Word of God to the moral issues of his age: poverty, war, racism, sexism, the abuse of political and ecclesial authority.

Stringfellow was born on April 26, 1928. Raised in the Episcopal church, he was negatively goaded toward his vocation by the suggestion of a parish priest that he think about becoming a minister. Repelled by the implication that ordination made one a superior Christian, he immersed himself in the international Christian student movement, attempting to prove that one could be a "professional Christian" without the certificate of ordination. Later he acknowledged the "phariseeism" behind this attitude, admitting that for all his activity, "I was no Christian as such at the time." Nevertheless, he maintained his conviction that no special vocation divides one class of Christians from another. "Vocation means being a human being; every decision is a vocational event."

After being drafted into the army and serving a term in Germany, Stringfellow attended Harvard Law School. Emerging as "someone virtually opposite" of what a Harvard Law School graduate was expected to be, he settled into a vermin-ridden apartment in Harlem to practice poverty law. From this vantage point he acquired a particular perspective on the world that informed his later writing on the "powers and principalities." He remained fascinated with the capacity of impersonal institutions — the state, the law, medicine, or the church itself — to invest themselves with an ersatz spiritual authority. But while his Harlem experience brought many encounters with the powers of death, it was there that he also encountered the power of grace and the triumph of life. This, as he later wrote, enabled him to survive his own battles with illness and death.

In the late 1960s Stringfellow was found to be suffering from a life-threatening metabolic disorder that led to diabetes and a host of attendant ills. With little expectation of long life, Stringfellow retired with a friend, the poet Anthony Towne, to a house on Block Island that they named "Eschaton."

Certainly Stringfellow's bad health contributed to a tendency to view the world in the light of Eternity and a willingness to risk unpopular stands. He came into conflict with his own Episcopal church for being an early advocate of the ordination of women. He was also an early and outspoken critic of the war in Vietnam. One of his closest friends was the Jesuit priest Daniel Berrigan, who was convicted along with eight others for destroying draft files in an antiwar protest. When Berrigan failed to surrender to authorities to begin his prison term, he became a fugitive, infuriating the FBI by popping up in churches and rallies around the country. In the end, tipped off by an informer, a hundred FBI agents descended on Stringfellow's house, where they found their quarry. Stringfellow and Towne were themselves arrested and charged with harboring a fugitive. The charges were ultimately dismissed.

In the books that followed, Stringfellow continued to define what he called an American moral theology, seeking "to relate the American experience of society and nationhood to the biblical saga and social witness." It was, he observed, "a pitifully neglected realm." His great theme was the Constantinian compromise, the accommodation of Christianity to the values of the empire and the preservation of the status quo. In one of his books he wrote, "My concern is to understand America biblically." This was counter to the opposite and all too common tendency, namely, to understand the Bible "Americanly."

His friend Anthony Towne died in 1980. Stringfellow mourned his passing but he endured. "Vocation," he wrote, "has to do with recognizing life as a gift and honoring the gift in living." And so he honored also the Giver of life until his own death on March 2, 1985. At his funeral Dan Berrigan said: "For thousands of us, he became the honored keeper and guardian of the Word of God."

In the years that followed others reflected on Stringfellow's life in the light of his own words:

> Being holy...does not mean being perfect but being whole; it does not mean being exceptionally religious or being religious at all; it means being liberated from religiosity and religious pietism of any sort; it does not mean being morally better, it means being exemplary; it does not mean being godly, but rather being truly human.

See: Bill Wylie Kellermann, ed., *A Keeper of the Word: Selected Writings of William Stringfellow* (Grand Rapids: Eerdmans, 1994); "William Stringfellow: Keeper of the Word," special issue of *Sojourners* (December 1985).

April 27

St. Turibius of Lima
Archbishop (1538–1606)

"Time is not our own. We will have to give a strict account of it."

St. Turibius was one of the first declared saints of the Americas. Born in Spain in 1538, he was a professor of law and later served as an ecclesiastical judge before receiving the surprising news that he had been selected as the new archbishop of Lima, Peru. In vain, he protested this appointment, which was unusual indeed for a layman. Nevertheless, upon his acquiescence, he was promptly ordained a priest, consecrated a bishop, and put on a ship for Peru. He took up his residence in Lima in 1581.

Turibius found his assignment extremely challenging. Geographically, the diocese covered an enormous and barely traversable area. The local church was lax and corrupt. The Spaniards were nominally Catholic, but their greater devotion was to the pursuit of wealth. The Indian population was horribly exploited and treated with contempt.

Turibius methodically applied himself to all these challenges. He made a point of conducting regular pastoral tours throughout the archdiocese. He cleaned up abuses among the local clergy and established the first seminary in the New World. He was vigorous in denouncing social sins and equally zealous in his charity toward the poor and his defense of the Indians. He studied their languages so that he might preach the gospel more effectively. He was determined that they see a different side of Christianity than that represented by their colonial overlords.

Turibius's forthright leadership earned him enemies among the powerful. They defied his directives, spread vicious rumors about him, and even petitioned Rome to have him removed. But he remained, loved by the poor and supported by such holy friends as *Martin de Porres and *Rose of Lima, both of whom he confirmed. He died in 1606, and was canonized in 1726. (His feast day, long celebrated on April 27, is now assigned to March 23, the day of his death.)

April 28
Oskar Schindler
"Righteous Gentile" (1908–1974)

"He was our father, he was our mother, he was our only faith.
He never let us down." —Testimony of a survivor

If the Holocaust represents the mystery of iniquity then the story of Oskar Schindler, born on April 28, 1908, may be said to represent the mystery of goodness. The mystery in his case is not simply why he did his good work of rescuing Jews from the Nazis while others did not. The mystery is also why *he* did this good work. For, noble as his deeds undoubtedly were, they appeared oddly out of character with everything else about the man.

Schindler was a German industrialist who recognized in the war and particularly the Nazi occupation of Poland a lucrative business opportunity. In Cracow he established an enamel-goods factory employing Jewish workers from the ghetto. In the beginning there was little to distinguish Schindler from many similar entrepreneurs. Over time, however, it became clear that this was no ordinary German factory. It was a haven, an oasis of life. Those lucky enough to be assigned to Schindler's factory were preserved under a unique canopy of protection from the raging storm of annihilation.

Even while he lavished "unnecessary" food and resources on his workers, Schindler still managed to make his fortune. But as the Nazis tightened their noose around the Jews Schindler's occupation steadily changed. Before long the rescue and preservation of "his Jews" became, in fact, his only real business. Running a factory was simply a pretext for saving lives.

To this end he bargained, cajoled, bribed, and even gambled to win concessions from his Nazi "friends" — anything to widen the tenuous circle of life. At every step there was the danger that he would go too far, that he would call too much attention to his enterprise of mercy and thus jeopardize everything. Twice he was arrested by the Gestapo and interrogated — the first time, after he was denounced for having kissed one of his Jewish employees. In both cases highly placed friends vouched for him and won his release. But rather than retreat, each threat of personal danger served simply to embolden him in his single-minded crusade.

The most audacious venture came toward the end of the war. With the rising prospect of Nazi defeat, Polish factories began to close. Their labor no longer needed, Jewish workers were simply fed into the ovens of Auschwitz. Schindler won permission to transfer his entire workforce of eleven hundred men, women, and children to a new site in Czechoslovakia. When the train carrying the women was inadvertently diverted to Auschwitz Schindler raced to the camp, armed with a sack of diamonds and gold, to win their rescue. His new factory, ostensibly devoted to weapons production, was actually an enormous confidence game. Though guarded by SS troops and run with apparent efficiency, the factory produced nothing. Schindler was determined not to contribute in any way to the Nazi war effort. While waiting out the end of the war he spent his entire savings to keep the camp in operation, all the time managing to convince the Nazis of his industry and good faith.

Finally in May 1945 the war ended. The guards fled, shamed by Schindler into disobeying their orders to exterminate the surviving workers. Within hours of the armistice Schindler and his wife also fled, disguised in the uniforms of camp inmates, lest he be captured and lynched as a German industrialist. The prisoners sent him off in an emotional ceremony. They presented Oskar with a ring, fashioned from gold dental work which was donated by one of the grateful prisoners. Inscribed on the ring were words from the Talmud: "He who saves one life saves the entire world."

No one, least of all "Schindler's Jews," doubts that what he did was an unqualified good. But no one is quite sure *why* he did it. His Catholic upbringing is no explanation; he never seems to have had any religious impulse. He was an opportunist and profiteer, a gambler, a drinker, and a faithless husband. Arguably it was precisely the fact that he was the last man anyone would suspect of heroism that allowed him to get away with it. Still the mystery remains. From somewhere in the depths of his own morally complicated character Schindler found the resources to wage a private contest with the devil. The mystery of Schindler is a reminder of the audacity that distinguishes genuine heroism from merely conventional virtue, goodness, or even piety.

Schindler survived the postwar chaos, though he was totally impoverished by his wartime enterprise. He never again found a metier for his unusual talents. But as his story became more widely known he was inducted into the list of the Righteous Gentiles in Israel. When he died in October 1974 he was buried, according to his request, in Jerusalem.

See: Thomas Kenneally, *Schindler's List* (New York: Simon and Schuster, 1982).

St. Catherine of Siena
Doctor of the Church (1347–1380)

"All the way to heaven is heaven, because He said, 'I am the way.' "

St. Catherine of Siena was one of the greatest saints of a tumultuous era. While the Black Death wreaked its devastation, mercenary armies roamed the countryside, waging protracted warfare on behalf of their client-cities. Avoiding the chaos and dangers of Rome, the papacy had decamped to a palace in Avignon, France, leaving administration of the church in the hands of corrupt and high-handed legates. This was the world into which Catherine was born. Like other great mystics, she enjoyed an intimate relationship with Christ. This was certified by a dazzling array of miraculous signs, which even in her lifetime made her something of a celebrity. What was distinctive about the holiness of Catherine was the way she mediated through her own heart the burning love of Christ and the needs of her time.

The daughter of a prosperous wool dyer, she was the twenty-fourth of twenty-five children. Her parents had hopes that Catherine would serve the family well by making an advantageous marriage. But she adamantly resisted this plan, insisting that she was called to betrothal with Christ. As a sign, she cut off her beautiful golden hair. Her family retaliated by treating her as a servant. But with Christ's help she constructed within herself "a secret cell" to which she happily retreated from her daily drudgery. In the end her father was won over. All it took was the sight of a dove hovering over Catherine's head as she knelt in prayer. Afterward he consented to her vocation, noting that Christ would not make such a bad son-in-law.

Rather than enter a formal religious order, Catherine put on the habit of a Dominican tertiary. "My cell," she said, "will not be one of stone or wood, but of self-knowledge." In what did this self-knowledge consist? She received the answer in a vision of Christ: "Know daughter that I am He who is, and thou art that which is not." From this simple formula, Catherine would develop her whole understanding of the spiritual life and her vocation.

For three years she remained enclosed in her room. During much of this period she was besieged by doubts, demonic visions, and taunting voices, until she finally banished them with laughter. Immediately Christ appeared to her. "And where were *you* when all this was happening?" she asked, reproachfully. "I was in your heart," came the reply. After this, according to her biographer, she received daily visitations by Christ, sometimes in the company of *Mary Magdalene and other saints. The climax of this period came during Shrove Tuesday 1367, while all the town celebrated, and Catherine remained praying in her room. In a mystical betrothal Christ appeared to her and placed a ring on her finger, visible only to herself.

This was the signal for Catherine to begin the second great phase of her career. She emerged from her room, rejoined her family, and set about serving her neighbors. Again, the move was prompted by the command of Jesus: "The service you cannot do me you must render your neighbors." The next several years found her nursing the sick, distributing alms to the poor, and ministering to prisoners and plague victims. Through miraculous healings and her air of spiritual authority, she began to attract disciples — the so-called Caterinata — including both men and women, even friars and priests. Affectionately, they called her Mamma.

In 1374 there came another turning point. After praying for a long time in an ecstatic state, Catherine appeared for a matter of hours to have died. Afterward she described an excruciating experience of union with God: "My heart could bear it no longer, and the love became as strong as death; then the heart broke in two." Now Christ commanded her to return to the world "for the good of souls." But it was the wider world and the universal church that claimed her attention. She commenced her role as a public figure, dictating hundreds of letters to the pope, monarchs, and other persons of note, counseling them on the performance of their duties. She also wrote her great work, *The Dialogue*, describing the contents of her mystical conversations with Christ.

For some years Catherine had served as a local peacemaker, mediating between feuding families in Siena. Now she took up a more difficult challenge: mediating in an armed conflict between the city of Florence and the Avignon-based papacy. With her retinue of followers, she traveled across Italy to meet with the contending parties. Everywhere she went she was greeted by enthusiastic crowds. Finally she journeyed all the way to Avignon to meet personally with Pope Gregory XI. While honoring the pope as her "sweet Christ on earth," she was blunt and uncompromising in her insistence that he return to Rome. The court in Avignon, she claimed, stank of sin. The pope's place was beside the bones of the martyrs.

The mission was a surprising success. Affected by her appeal, the pope did in fact return to Rome. But the victory was not all that Catherine had hoped for. Soon after his return, Gregory died. He was succeeded, disastrously, by Urban VI, a pope who exemplified the expression "to be driven mad by power." Before long the college of cardinals, regretting their decision, elected a second pope. But having failed first to persuade Urban to abdicate, the church was now saddled with two rival, and soon-to-be warring, pontiffs, a scandalous condition that would last for several decades.

Catherine remained adamantly loyal to the unworthy Urban, judging that for all his faults he had been duly consecrated. But she could not help feeling that the wound in the Body of Christ could be healed only by tremendous sacrifice. After praying that she might atone for the sins of the church, she experienced her final vision. It seemed as if the church, like a mighty ship, was placed on her back. She collapsed to the ground in terrible pain and paralysis. After several weeks she died on April 29, 1380, at the age of thirty-three. Upon her death the marks of the stigmata and her "wedding band" were clearly visible on her body. In 1970 St. Catherine was named a Doctor of the Church.

See: Catherine of Siena, *The Dialogue,* Classics of Western Spirituality (New York: Paulist, 1980); Carol Lee Flinders, *Enduring Grace* (San Francisco: HarperSan-Francisco, 1993).

April 30

Bishop James E. Walsh
Confessor to the Chinese (1891–1981)

"Prayer is so powerful. I am a living example of what prayer can do."

On July 10, 1970, a frail and elderly man left the company of the Red Guards and walked across the bridge linking mainland China and the island of Hong Kong. On the other side he was embraced by a crowd of friends and fellow Maryknoll missioners who, forewarned of his arrival, had gathered to welcome him to freedom. After twelve years in prison, Bishop James E. Walsh, the last foreign missionary in communist China, was on his way home.

Walsh was born on April 30, 1891, in Cumberland, Maryland. After graduating from college he became one of the original pioneers of Maryknoll, the Catholic Foreign Mission Society of America, established in 1912. Maryknoll had been founded with the grand vision of sending American missionary priests to China, and Father Walsh was among the first departing team. He worked for eighteen years in Yeungkong in southern China, where he quickly developed a deep respect for the culture of China and a love for its people. In 1927 he was named a bishop.

For ten years (1936–1946) Walsh was recalled to the United States to serve as the second superior general of Maryknoll. During that time he worked hard to instill in the Maryknollers a keen sense of the spirituality of mission and a willingness to "give everything for Christ." But in 1948 he was back in Shanghai, serving as director of a board overseeing the work of Catholic foreign missionaries in China. Two years later the communist Revolution reached Shanghai. Walsh's activities were increasingly restricted and he experienced various forms of harassment, but he continued for some years to operate in relative freedom. In the meantime many other foreigners were either expelled or detained, if they did not leave voluntarily. His classmate from Maryknoll, Bishop Francis Ford, died in a Communist prison in 1952.

Walsh, however, insisted that he would never voluntarily leave his assigned field of mission. In a moving article written in 1951 he explained his reasons:

> At a time when the Catholic Religion is being traduced and persecuted with the design of eliminating it from China, I think it is the plain duty of all Catholic missionaries...to remain where they are

until prevented from doing so by physical force. If internment should intervene in the case of some, or even death, I think it should simply be regarded as a normal risk that is inherent in our state of life... and as a small price to pay for carrying out our duty.... In our particular case I think that such an eventuality would be a privilege, too, because it would associate us a little more intimately in the Cross of Christ.

Walsh believed that the vocation of a priest was not simply represented in his occupational work — whether teaching, preaching, or performing pastoral duties. The vocation remained the same, even when all these activities were stripped away. Part of it was a matter of remaining at all times open to divine providence. "If we start to pick and choose for ourselves, it is very hard to tell if we are carrying out our vocation or running away from it."

As for the danger that arrest would mean "enforced inactivity" and thus a waste of one's gifts, he observed that "suffering patiently borne is activity, so is prayer, so is any kind of mental work — things which can be done, one would think, in prison as well as anywhere.... A priest and a father does as much for his flock by suffering for them — and maybe he does even more."

Walsh eventually had occasion to test these convictions. He was finally arrested in 1958 and charged with conspiracy and espionage. For the first two years he was held in solitary confinement and subjected to endless interrogation sessions. He was finally "convicted" and sentenced to twenty years in prison.

Walsh accepted his situation with remarkable serenity. He later observed, "My twelve years of prison life went by without too much difficulty. The experience was not pleasant. Life seemed rather wearisome at times. But I was not despondent at all nor even unhappy." He spent much of the time saying the rosary and studying a Chinese dictionary, convinced that by such quiet witness he was serving the gospel as faithfully as he could. Finally in 1970, at the age of seventy-nine, he was taken to the border and freed.

Walsh returned to Maryknoll, where he lived on for more than a decade. He rarely spoke of his ordeal and never expressed bitterness or resentment toward his captors. He spent much of his remaining time in prayer, though he was always eager to encourage young missioners and to share with them his own sense of the spirit of Maryknoll. As he once said, "That spirit is charity, and if there is any other spirit, Maryknoll does not want it and could not conceivably profit by it."

He was revered by Maryknollers and others around the world as a heroic and holy confessor. But he always disclaimed any special recognition. When he was awarded the prestigious Cardinal Gibbons Award from Catholic University in Washington he said,

I am not aware that I ever did anything to deserve such an honor. True, I did spend twelve years in prison in China, and that is something unusual, no doubt. But in my case, the experience was just a routine part of my profession, and therefore, I consider it no great credit to myself. I was a Catholic priest and my people were in trouble. So, I simply stayed with them as all priests should at such times.

Bishop Walsh died at Maryknoll on July 29, 1981, at the age of ninety.

See: Bishop James E. Walsh, *Zeal for Your House* (Maryknoll, N.Y.: Maryknoll Publications, 1976); Jean-Paul Wiest, *Maryknoll in China* (Armonk, N.Y.: M. E. Sharpe, 1988).

❧ MAY ❧

May 1

Thomas à Kempis
Spiritual Master (1380–1471)

"If you seek Jesus in all things you will surely find Jesus. And if you seek yourself you will surely find yourself, but only to your ruin."

Thomas à Kempis was born in 1380 in the town of Kempen, near Düsseldorf. His early spiritual formation came in the Brethren of the Common Life, with whom he and his brother John lived for a number of years. This society, formed in 1376 by *Geert Groote, sought to gather lay people and clergy in a religious brotherhood committed to living in the spirit of the gospel. The Brethren were bound by no permanent vows, but they lived under a common rule, shared all things in common, and supported themselves by simple labor.

In 1399 Thomas entered an Augustinian monastery in Zwolle, where he was professed a monk in 1406 and was ordained a priest in 1413. His life as a monk was unremarkable. He occupied a number of offices in the monastery, copied manuscripts, and wrote various spiritual treatises. He died on May 1, 1471, at the age of ninety-two. Thomas was by all accounts a holy monk. But he is less remembered for his biography than for his book *The Imitation of Christ*, probably the most influential handbook of spiritual devotion ever written. Although addressed chiefly to his brother monks, it essentially epitomized the spirituality of Groote and his lay brethren, showing how a life of religious devotion could be lived in the world and not just in a monastery or convent.

For Thomas the imitation of Christ does not mean emulating his external deeds but adopting the inner pattern of his piety: humility, detachment from the world, prayer, and obedience to the will of God. Though it is an exacting manual of spiritual perfection, *The Imitation* suggests that the path to perfection is available to everyone, requiring no particular setting, occupation, or station in life. Indeed, throughout, Thomas emphasizes that the spiritual life is concerned not with one's outward activities but with the spirit that underlies them. The world sees and judges according to appearances; God sees what is in the heart. Thus, "God regards the greatness of the love that prompts a man, rather than the greatness of his achievement."

Thomas is particularly scathing with regard to those who seek to substitute knowledge or learning for true devotion: "A humble countryman who serves God is more pleasing to Him than a conceited intellectual who knows the course of the stars, but neglects his own soul." Holiness is more important than learning: "A humble knowledge of oneself is a surer road to God than a deep searching of the sciences."

Modern readers may recoil from Thomas's apparent contempt for the world. With harsh language he exhorts his readers to kill their natural desires and to withdraw their love from visible things. But it is not the world of God's creation that he so vehemently condemns. What he rejects is a set of values that renders the world opaque. When we become detached from things as ends in themselves they become transparent; we see them and love them in reference to their Creator, the source of all that is good and beautiful. When we look with the eyes of faith, we see God all around us. Otherwise, we see nothing but ourselves.

The Imitation of Christ has appealed equally to Catholics and Protestants. Its devoted readers have included *Thomas More, *Ignatius Loyola, *John Wesley, and *George Herbert. The popularity of the work owes much to the simple, lapidary directness of its style: "I would far rather feel contrition than be able to define it." But ultimately its power rests in its classic definition of the spiritual life as an effort to conform to Christ. For this effort we should never deceive ourselves into believing that reading books about spirituality is an adequate substitute. As Thomas notes: "At the Day of Judgment we shall not be asked what we have read, but what we have done."

See: Thomas à Kempis, *The Imitation of Christ,* trans. Leo Sherley-Price (New York: Penguin, 1952).

May 2

Gustav Landauer
Revolutionary (1870–1919)

"Whoever kills, dies himself. Whoever wants to create life must live anew and be reborn again from within.... Only from within to without can the world be formed."

Gustav Landauer lived in an age of revolution. But among German revolutionaries of his time he was something of an anomaly — as much a mystic and poet as a political activist. He combined the anarchist ideal of freedom with the socialist commitment to community. But his actions were rooted in a moral and spiritual vision that tended to invite scorn from more pragmatic comrades. To friends like *Martin Buber, he was another *Amos or *Jeremiah — a prophet who combined righteous denunciation of injustice with the annunciation of something totally new.

Landauer was born on April 7, 1870, into a middle-class Jewish family. From an early age he became immersed in the revolutionary movements of his day. But he put little stock in political parties. He particularly abhorred the authoritarian tendencies of Marxism, with its obsession with seizing political power. As a self-described Anarchist-Socialist, Landauer sought a revolution from below. It involved the transformation of relationships — whether by cooperatives, trusts, or unions — from a spirit of power to a spirit of community. His strategy was to build a new world within the shell of the old. "The State," he wrote, "is a condition, a certain relationship between human beings, a mode of human behavior; we destroy it by contracting other relationships, by behaving differently." At the same time he bitterly opposed the tendency of fellow anarchists to resort to violence or the romance of terrorism. "Every act of force is dictatorship.... The anarchists must realize that a goal can be reached only if the means to this goal are already bathed in the color of it."

Landauer served several prison terms as a result of his political activities. In 1899 he spent six months in prison for having written a "libelous" attack on the Berlin commissioner of police. While in prison he studied and translated the writings of *Meister Eckhart, the fourteenth-century German mystic. He was much taken by Eckhart's exhortation to discover God in one's soul. From this Landauer derived the insight that by delving deep into our souls we might find the roots of a universal community. He later edited Eckhart's writings, a work he considered the critical bridge between his spiritual vision and political convictions.

Anticipating the coming World War, Landauer worked tirelessly to prevent it. He hoped the workers would resist the tide of nationalism and militarism. But in this he was disappointed and found himself almost entirely alone.

Landauer was a moralist in a dark age. He was a poet and mystic who believed no lasting human society could be established that did not draw upon the image of God, a sense of the unity of life, memorized deep within the human soul. His voice might have added a note of humanity to a world on the edge of chaos. But his voice could not be heard.

In Munich in the aftermath of the First World War Landauer briefly served as minister of education in a short-lived revolutionary republic. On May 2, 1919, he was arrested by German troops and beaten to death. His last words were, "Kill me then! To think that you are human."

See: Eugene Lunn, *Prophet of Community: The Romantic Socialism of Gustav Landauer* (Berkeley: University of California Press, 1973); Martin Buber, *Paths in Utopia* (Boston: Beacon, 1958).

May 3

St. James

Apostle (first century)

*"As the body apart from the spirit is dead,
so faith apart from works is dead."*

Two of the original twelve apostles were named James. One was the son
of Zebedee, the brother of *St. John, who appears in many gospel stories
and who, according to Acts, was the first of the apostles to die as a martyr. Then there is the James whose feast is celebrated on this day. He is
identified as the son of Alphaeus, but it has been suggested that he is the
same man known as "the brother of the Lord," who saw the risen Christ
and became the first bishop of Jerusalem. According to the chronicles of
Josephus he was stoned to death in the year 61.

This apostle is traditionally identified as the author of the Epistle of
James. Although his letter is short, it reveals much about the problems
facing the local church at that time. For one thing, James was very concerned about the intrusion of class divisions within the community of
faith. Apparently he observed that "a man with gold rings and in fine
clothing" was treated with greater respect in the assembly than "a poor
man in shabby clothing." This was a violation of the gospel:

> Has not God chosen those who are poor in the world to be rich
> in faith and heirs of the kingdom which he has promised to those
> who love him? But you have dishonored the poor man. Is it not the
> rich who oppress you, is it not they who drag you into court? Is
> it not they who blaspheme the honorable name which was invoked
> over you?

James was also concerned with the tendency of some Christians —
perhaps inspired by Paul's preaching on salvation by faith — to dismiss
entirely the value of "works." For James true faith is revealed in righteous
works — especially works of mercy toward the poor and justice toward
the oppressed.

> What does it profit, my brethren, if a man says he has faith but has
> not works? Can his faith save him? If a brother or sister is ill-clad
> and in lack of daily food, and one of you says to them, "Go in peace,
> be warmed and filled," without giving them the things needed for
> the body, what does it profit? So faith by itself, if it has not works
> is dead.

To Martin Luther such passages reeked of "works righteousness," violating his own insistence on the primacy of faith. Thus, he disdained the
Epistle of James as a "straw epistle," unworthy of the New Testament
canon. Nevertheless, the Epistle of James continues to preserve a vital dimension of the gospel message of "good news to the poor." It is James

who reminds the church that Christians must be "doers and not simply hearers of the word."

See: Elsa Tamez, *The Scandalous Message of James* (New York: Crossroad, 1992).

May 4

The Woman with a Flow of Blood
(first century)

"If I touch even his garments, I shall be made well."

One day as Jesus passed through a crowd, a woman pressed her way unnoticed through the protective circle of disciples and touched his garment. Immediately Jesus perceived that "power had gone forth from him." He stopped. Facing the crowd, he asked, "Who touched my garments?" With fear and trembling the woman stepped forward, fell before him, and told her story. She had suffered for twelve years from a "flow of blood."

In making this humiliating confession she might well have braced herself against the revulsion of the crowd. More than a simple physical infirmity, such a condition would have rendered her unclean in the eyes of the law. She was an outcast, an untouchable; her very touch had the power of defilement. And yet having heard reports of Jesus' healing miracles she had dared to touch his garment, trusting that this alone would heal her. By this action she had understood, in a way that the disciples as yet did not, that the power of Jesus was at the service of love. And in touching his garment she had immediately felt herself to be healed.

There was no special saving power in physical proximity to Christ. Among those who heard him preach were the ones who plotted his death. Judas dipped his hand into the same bowl as Jesus before he went out to betray him. It was not enough to touch him, for so did the many others who jostled against him in the crowd, and so did those others who later stripped and scourged him and nailed him to a cross.

Christ was present in that crowd in all his love and power. But it was the faith of a poor, frightened, sick, untouchable woman who had recognized that power and so awakened it with a touch and brought it into full view.

Jesus listened to her story. According to the codes of ritual purity he should have been shocked. But he was not. He was able to distinguish in this woman's presumptuous gesture the authentic act of faith. "Daughter," he said, "it is your faith that has made you well."

See: Mark 5:25–34; Hisako Kinukawa, *Women and Jesus in Mark: A Japanese Feminist Perspective* (Maryknoll, N.Y.: Orbis, 1994).

May 5
Friedrich von Hügel
Catholic Philosopher (1852–1925)

"The lonely, new, and daring (if but faithful, reverent, and loving) outgoing of the discoverer and investigator are as truly acts of . . . the church and her life as his coming back to the Christian love and community."

As a scholar and man of letters Friedrich von Hügel played an immensely important role in the Catholic intellectual world of his time. On many fronts — in biblical criticism, historical theology, and the study of the mystical tradition — he attempted to open the mind of the church both to neglected currents of modern thought as well as to forgotten spiritual resources of the past. His name was vitally linked to that network of scholars and theologians encompassed in the Vatican condemnation of "Modernism." Von Hügel was indeed a friend to most of the protagonists in that affair. And yet while others left the church or were driven out, von Hügel remained. Both to conservatives and liberals of the time his combination of traditional piety and intellectual independence presented something of an enigma. It may be, however, that this was his most enduring contribution.

Von Hügel came from a privileged, aristocratic family. He was born on May 5, 1852, in Florence, where his father was the Austrian ambassador to Tuscany. After living in a number of European cities, the family settled in England, which would remain Friedrich's adopted country. Though raised in a deeply Catholic home, von Hügel dated his own mature faith to an experience of conversion at the age of eighteen. With financial independence and a passion for the intellectual life, he determined to pursue a vocation as an independent Catholic scholar.

While in Paris in 1884 he met Alfred Loisy, a French priest who was at the time the foremost Catholic champion of modern biblical criticism. Von Hügel and Loisy became close friends and collaborators. It was by this route that von Hügel came to play a critical part in the Modernist controversy. The Modernists were a loosely connected network of scholars and theologians who sought to reconcile Catholic faith with the principles of modern philosophy, critical methods of biblical interpretation, and historical consciousness. Above all they advocated a greater freedom in the church to explore theological alternatives to what they regarded as the monolithic and outdated system of scholasticism.

To the extent that these thinkers constituted any kind of "movement" von Hügel was in many ways the connecting thread. He had a gift for what today might be called "networking." It was he who put Loisy in touch with the English Jesuit *George Tyrrell, and he likewise facilitated many other introductions among the key figures in several countries. Although he remained somewhat in the background, he was among those cited by the prefect of the Congregation of the Index who "apparently seek to arrogate to themselves control of the church and desire to teach the pope himself."

Some of the Modernists, Loisy and Tyrrell in particular, displayed an appetite for controversy. When the Vatican condemnation of Modernism was pronounced in 1907, the two priests were singled out and ultimately excommunicated. Loisy became an embittered foe of the church, while Tyrrell, who died soon after, continued to profess his loyalty. Though von Hügel shared many of his friends' principles, he did not share their passion for confrontation. After the death of Tyrrell he tended to pull back from the controversy, a move which some of his allies found hard to understand. He insisted, however, that the church was much deeper than the institutional dimension and that one's disappointment with the exercise of authority (which was very often "cruel and unjust") was no reason to cut oneself off from the spiritual and sacramental life of the church. To the end of his life he continued to go to weekly confession, to say the rosary, and to spend frequent hours in contemplation of the Blessed Sacrament.

After 1907 von Hügel shifted the direction of his work. Rather than directly address the sensitive areas of exegesis or theology, he turned to the study of spirituality and mysticism, a necessary balance, he believed, to the church's overemphasis on the institutional element. The result was his scholarly masterpiece *The Mystical Element in Religion*, a two-volume study of mysticism, focusing on *St. Catherine of Genoa.

As for Modernism, he later distinguished between two meanings. He distanced himself from the set of propositions condemned by Pius X, "a strictly circumscribed affair, one that is really over and done." To another meaning, however, he continued, without apology, to give support: This he called "a permanent, never quite finished, always sooner or later, more or less, re-beginning set of attempts to express the old Faith and its permanent truths and helps — to interpret it according to what appears the best and most abiding elements in the philosophy and the scholarship and the science of the later and latest times. Such work never ceases for long, and to it I shall try to contribute my little share."

Von Hügel died on January 27, 1925, at the age of seventy-two.

See: Maurice Nédoncelle, *Baron Friedrich von Hügel: A Study of His Life and Thought* (London: Longman, Green, 1937); Meriol Trevor, *Prophets and Guardians: Renewal and Tradition in the Church* (Garden City, N.Y.: Doubleday, 1969).

May 6

Henry David Thoreau
Naturalist and Social Critic (1817–1862)

"If a man does not keep pace with his companions, perhaps it is because he hears a different drummer. Let him step to the music which he hears, however measured or far away."

Henry David Thoreau was born in Concord, Massachusetts, in 1817. He studied at Harvard College and worked for a time as a schoolteacher. He published two books, both of them virtually ignored in his lifetime. One of these, *Walden,* an account of his two years of elected solitude at Walden Pond, was subsequently acclaimed as an American classic. But in a sense Henry David Thoreau was himself an American classic. He embodied the spirit of nonconformity, the impulse to seek renewal in nature, and the will to stand firm by his convictions. Like the fictional Huckleberry Finn, afire with the urge to "light out for the territories," Thoreau continuously sought to slip the bonds of social hypocrisy as well as the servitude that passed for civilized life. In the pursuit of truth he preferred to follow his own compass reading, indifferent as to whether it might lead him to solitude, to jail, or the ridicule of his neighbors.

Although he subscribed to no organized religion, there was in Thoreau something of the Taoist sage and the desert father. He too felt an intense need to dispense with socially defined values and instead to experience life "first-hand." It was this desire that led him in 1845 to his famous retreat to Walden Pond, near Concord. There he sought to escape a world in which "the mass of men lead lives of quiet desperation." Like the early ascetics who fled to the desert, Thoreau was not so much renouncing "the world" as the "deadness" of life in the world. As he wrote, "I went to the woods because I wished to live deliberately, to front only the essential facts of life and see if I could not learn what it had to teach, and not, when I came to die, discover that I had not lived."

In his book Thoreau provides a meticulous account of the details of his life, the construction of his house, the supply of his food, and his attention both to the world of nature around him and to his own inner world. He did not feel lonely, surrounded as he was by the company of Nature. Sitting in the rain, "Every little pine needle expanded and swelled with sympathy and befriended me."

Walden describes a kind of mystical rapture in the communion with Nature that speaks directly to the concerns of an ecological age. But for Thoreau, as for the desert fathers, the wilderness provides the setting for a journey of inner discovery: "There are continents and seas in the moral world to which every man is an isthmus or an inlet, yet unexplored by him."

In undertaking this moral exploration, Thoreau was not simply a "nature mystic," rejecting the ugliness and stress of modern society. There was also a deeply ethical dimension to his flight. With his profound commitment to personal freedom he found it intolerable to live in a country in which slavery was permitted. The fact that Massachusetts was a "free state" was no salve to his offended conscience.

> How does it become a man to behave toward this American government today? I answer that he cannot without disgrace be associated with it. I cannot for an instant recognize that political organization as *my* government which is the *slave*'s government also.

Many of his friends supported the abolitionist cause. But Thoreau was not content with words alone. In 1845, the same year as his retreat to Walden, he was arrested for refusing to pay a poll tax that was intended to finance the war with Mexico. Thoreau believed that this was an imperialist war that also served the extension of slavery. To the extent that the tax provided oil for the machine of injustice, Thoreau resolved to refuse the tax and to apply his small weight as a "counter-friction" to the machine.

It was no more than a gesture. After a night in jail his relatives paid the tax for him and won his release. But the experience inspired his essay "On the Duty of Civil Disobedience," one of the most eloquent arguments ever written on the authority of conscience and the duty to resist legally sanctioned injustice. "Under a government which imprisons any unjustly," he wrote, "the true place for a just man is also a prison."

Thoreau's message had little immediate impact in his own country. Most of his neighbors regarded him as a harmless crank, if not a social deviant. But by the end of the century his essay on civil disobedience had been discovered by the Russian novelist and moralist *Leo Tolstoy. From Tolstoy it was discovered by the Indian *Mahatma Gandhi. From Gandhi it was discovered by *Martin Luther King, Jr., leader of the nonviolent freedom struggle in the United States. So, by this route, the spirit of Thoreau returned to his native land.

All this was unforeseen when Thoreau died of tuberculosis on May 6, 1862. Yet for all his years as a social critic, Thoreau had lived in a state of hope, "an infinite expectation of the dawn, which does not forsake us in our soundest sleep." That hopeful note was sounded in the last lines of *Walden:* "The light which puts out our eyes is darkness to us. Only that day dawns to which we are awake. There is more day to dawn. The sun is but a morning star."

See Henry David Thoreau, *Walden and "Civil Disobedience"* (New York: New American Library, 1960).

May 7

St. Stanislaus
Bishop of Cracow and Martyr (1030–1079)

The story of the Polish church and its role in hastening the downfall of communism has been widely told. But in their stand against tyranny and injustice the present generation of Catholics was upholding an ancient Polish tradition. One of the most revered saints in Poland is St. Stanislaus, a bishop of Cracow, who died as a martyr in the eleventh century.

Among the bishops of his day, Stanislaus was the only one with the courage to stand up to the tyrannical king Boleslaus II and to denounce his cruelty and abuse of power. The last straw came when Boleslaus abducted the beautiful wife of one of his noblemen and carried her away to his castle. Upon hearing of this outrage, Stanislaus went to rebuke the king and to threaten him with excommunication if he did not amend his ways. When all other methods of persuasion failed, Stanislaus carried through on his threat. Thus, when Boleslaus and his retinue arrived at the cathedral for Mass, he was turned away at the door.

Enraged, Boleslaus ordered his guards to kill the bishop. When they balked at this command, Boleslaus drew his sword and performed the bloody deed himself. Stanislaus was immediately acclaimed as a martyr. Pope Gregory VII put the country under an interdict, which endured until the death of the unrepentant Boleslaus. St. Stanislaus was canonized in 1253. His feast day, formerly celebrated on May 7, is now assigned to April 11.

May 8

Peter Waldo
Poor Man of Lyons (d. 1209?)

"Friends, I am not out of my mind, as you may think. Rather I am avenging myself upon these enemies of my life who have enslaved me, so that I cared more for gold pieces than for God and served the creature more than the Creator."

Peter Waldo was a wealthy merchant of Lyons, whose fortune was amassed by lending money at interest. In about 1170, concerned for the welfare of his soul, he sought out a master of theology and asked him what was the most perfect way of attaining to God. He heard the text from Scripture, "If thou wilt be perfect, go sell what thou hast...." Waldo was amazed. He had never heard this text before. He set out to pay a couple of priests to translate the Gospels into the vernacular. After studying these texts and nearly committing them to memory he turned over a good portion of his property to his wife and daughters and distributed the rest to the poor. He took to the streets, proclaiming his deliverance from the bondage of money and preaching the gospel to any who would listen. He began to gather associates in his way of life. According to an early chronicle, "They followed his example in giving their all to the poor and became devotees of voluntary poverty. Little by little, both publicly and privately, they began to declaim against their own sins and those of others."

After being banned by the archbishop of Lyons, Waldo sought Vatican approval for his movement. In 1179 he was warmly embraced by Pope Alexander III, who approved his vow of voluntary poverty but forbade his preaching. Most of the assembled clergy were appalled at the effrontery of these unlettered paupers who nevertheless dared to assume the mantle of the apostles. Waldo tried to comply with the pope's decree but he could not put from his mind the words of Christ, "Preach the gospel to every creature." Finally, resolving that "we ought to obey God, rather than men," he resumed his preaching. The "Poor Men of Lyons," or Waldensians, as they came to be known, based their life on the Sermon on the Mount. They embraced poverty, refused to take oaths, and rejected any excuse for taking life. Otherwise, on all doctrinal matters, Waldo remained entirely orthodox, as even his enemies conceded. Nevertheless, for violating a papal decree Waldo was charged with heresy. He and his followers were subsequently excommunicated.

Though subjected to terrible persecution the Waldensians managed to survive. Waldo himself faded from the pages of history. He died around 1209, about the same time another Poor Man — this time from Assisi, and with happier results — was petitioning the pope for approval of his mendicant brotherhood.

See: Walter L. Wakefield and Austin P. Evans, eds., *Heresies of the High Middle Ages* (New York: Columbia University Press, 1969); Walter Nigg, *The Heretics* (New York: Alfred A. Knopf, 1962).

May 9

Peter Maurin
Co-founder of the Catholic Worker (1877–1949)

*"The future will be different
if we make the present different."*

Peter Maurin was born on May 9, 1877, in the ancient Languedoc region of southern France. He was one of twenty-three children, born to a peasant family who could boast of a claim to the land they farmed dating back fifteen hundred years. Educated by the Christian Brothers, he had breathed in the atmosphere of Catholic populism, then in ferment in France, before sailing for North America in 1909. For twenty years he drifted through America performing various kinds of hard manual labor. Like *St. Francis, he embraced Holy Poverty as his bride, dining in skid-row beaneries and sleeping wherever he could find a bed. What little money he earned he either spent on books or gave away to those in greater need. His mind was elsewhere. As he roamed the country, breaking rocks and mending roads, he was all the while engaged in his true work, an effort to devise a synthesis in the area of Catholic social philosophy.

The main problem with society, as Maurin saw it, was that sociology, economics, and politics had all been separated from the gospel. In the process, society had lost any sense of the ultimate, transcendent purpose of human activity. Social life had come to be organized around the drive for production and the search for profits, rather than the full development of persons. Human beings, rather than co-creators with God, had become alienated cogs in a machine. The church, in Maurin's view, had an answer to all this, but it had failed to act on it. There was "dynamite" in the Gospels, but the clergy preferred to keep it under lock and key. What was necessary was to "blow the lid" off that dynamite.

Maurin's program was a "personalist revolution," which called for "building a new world within the shell of the old." Rather than waiting for the correct "objective circumstances," one should begin at once to live by a new set of values. "The future will be different," he said, "if we make the present different."

He had set his ideas into "Easy Essays," designed for street-corner declamation:

The world would become better off
if people tried to become better.
And people would become better
if they stopped trying to become better off.

But with his thick French accent, shabby appearance, and visionary gleam, Maurin was considerably more successful at formulating principles than translating them into actions on a scale larger than himself.

All this changed in 1932, however, when he was directed to meet a young journalist, *Dorothy Day, a Catholic convert with a history of involvement in radical social movements. She had been seeking a sign as to how to combine her religious faith with her social vision. In Peter Maurin, who began to indoctrinate her within minutes of their first meeting, she believed she had found the answer to her prayers.

Maurin had a three-part program, which involved starting a newspaper "for the clarification of thought"; organizing "houses of hospitality" for the practice of the works of mercy (feeding the hungry, clothing the naked, etc.); and the organization of farming communes as the first step toward a decentralized, communitarian economy, the kind of society "where it would be easier to be good."

With her background in journalism, Day immediately responded to the first suggestion. The result was the *Catholic Worker,* first distributed in Union Square on May 1, 1933. The newspaper gradually evolved into a movement based in rural and urban communities across the land. Imbued with the radical spirit of the Beatitudes, the *Catholic Worker* promoted such themes as voluntary poverty, community, solidarity with the poor and oppressed, and gospel nonviolence. As a prophetic voice in the American church, the Catholic Worker movement exerted an enormous influence beyond the numbers of its subscribers and its committed activists.

Though the message of the movement came to be identified more with Dorothy Day, she always credited Maurin with its inspiration. In later years she would say, "If he had said, 'Go to Madison Square Garden and speak these ideas,' I would have overcome all sense of fear and would have attempted such a folly, convinced that though it was the 'folly of the Cross' and doomed to failure, God Himself would take this failure and turn it into victory."

Peter Maurin lived to see his ideas put in action at last. But his years of activity in the Catholic Worker were limited. He died in 1949 at the age of seventy-two. In his last five years he had been mute and feeble, disabled by a stroke that impaired his mind and left him, in his own words, "unable to think." Day considered the manner of his death instructive. Peter had been the poor man of his day. He had stripped himself of everything else, and finally he was stripped of the one thing he cherished. This man of vision had, in the end, to be dressed and fed like a child. Yet he never complained. He accepted his condition with grace and patience. Some years before his death, he gave the community a fright by disappearing for several days. When at last he returned, confused but apparently pleased with himself, he explained that he had felt like going for a ride on a bus. Thereafter, a note was pinned on his suit: "I am Peter Maurin, founder of the Catholic Worker movement."

See: Peter Maurin, *Easy Essays* (Chicago: Franciscan Herald, 1977); Dorothy Day, *The Long Loneliness* (New York: Harper & Row, 1952); Marc H. Ellis, *Peter Maurin: Prophet in the Twentieth Century* (New York: Paulist, 1981).

May 10
Karl Barth
Theologian (1886–1968)

"Jesus Christ, such as Scripture bears witness of Him for us, is the one word of God that we must hear, that we must trust, and that we must obey in life and death."

In the scope of his work and his impact on the church and theology, Karl Barth was certainly the most significant Protestant theologian of the twentieth century. Many would go further, adding him to the list, among such figures as *Augustine, *Thomas Aquinas, and Calvin, of the greatest theologians of all time. Such a status was far from his mind when he started out as the pastor of a Reformed church in a small parish in his native Switzerland. His journey as a theologian began with the realization that he did not know how to preach the gospel to his simple flock.

Born on May 10, 1886, Barth had studied in Germany with the great names of liberal Protestant theology, including Hermann and Harnack. Their theology had reflected the optimistic and anthropocentric spirit of their age, a confidence in progress and a belief that Christianity was another way of talking about the highest human ideals. To all those who espoused such a faith and who had welcomed the twentieth century as the dawn of a new era of civilization, the outbreak of World War I in 1914 came as a devastating rejoinder. For Barth it also represented the failure of his formation as a theologian. The moment of this insight was engraved on his memory. It was the day in August 1914 when he read a manifesto signed by ninety-three German intellectuals, including all his theology professors, supporting the kaiser's war efforts.

Shocked at what he regarded as the grave ethical collapse of liberal theology, Barth went back to the Bible to discover the source of the error. He concluded that liberal theology had lost sight of its true subject — God — opting instead to talk about "man in a loud voice." The first task of theology, according to Barth, was to recognize (in *Kierkegaard's phrase) the "infinite qualitative distinction" between God and human beings. God, he argued, is the "Wholly Other" who cannot be tamed or domesticated in the service of human desires, ideologies, or religion. From this it follows that our only basis for talking about God is provided by God's own revelation in his Word, Jesus Christ. Thus, Barth's rejection of liberal theology extended also to rationalistic efforts at "natural theology," and even to the claims of "religion," as such, to get a handle on God. All this was a new version of what *St. Paul had termed the slavery of the law. In its place Barth wished to recover the radical meaning of faith — attention and obedience to the sovereign Word of God.

In 1919 Barth published the first edition of his historic commentary on the Epistle to the Romans. Into the quiet and self-satisfied world of academic theology Barth's book landed with the impact of a meteor. Once the dust had cleared, it was evident that Barth had dramatically changed the theological agenda of the church and the academy. The success of his book brought Barth instant fame and an invitation to teach theology in Bonn. There he commenced his work on an extraordinarily ambitious project which would occupy his efforts for the rest of his life. This was his colossal *Church Dogmatics,* a complete exposition of the doctrines of creation, reconciliation, and eschatology, rooted in his theology of the Word of God. Thirteen massive volumes were published by the time of his death, though the project remained unfinished.

The first volume of the *Dogmatics* appeared in 1932. It was followed within a year by the rise of Adolf Hitler, the most significant possible test of Barth's theology. Immediately Hitler tried to coopt the churches to endorse his racist and ultranationalistic policies. This gave rise to the so-called German Christian movement. For Barth this was the apotheosis of the kind of manipulation of God he most detested. He was the prime author of the Barmen Declaration, the charter of what became known as the Confessing Church. According to this historic manifesto, the present situation called into question the very "confession" of the church: did Christians ultimately worship God or Hitler? The Confessing Church courageously opted for Christ, and thus placed itself in jeopardy before the Nazi state. In the years to come many members of the Confessing Church would suffer persecution. As a foreign national Barth himself was merely dismissed from his university position and deported, in 1935, to Switzerland.

In later life Barth softened the dialectical starkness of his earlier theology. In the early years, he said, it had been necessary to compensate for the weakness of liberal theology by emphasizing the "Deity of God." In retrospect he felt it was not adequate, from a Christian point of view, to speak of God as the Wholly Other, a distant and complete stranger to human existence. In a short book entitled *The Humanity of God* he wrote,

> In Jesus Christ, there is no isolation of man from God or of God from man. Rather, in Him we encounter the history, the dialogue, in which God and man meet together and are together.... Jesus Christ reveals that God does not exist without man.

This softening was also reflected in the later volumes of his *Dogmatics.* As he approached the great themes of reconciliation and salvation he seemed increasingly to assume a more hopeful attitude. Far from the dark judgmental tones of his book on Romans, he now seemed to evince an optimistic expectation of universal salvation for all human beings. Characteristically, however, this optimism was not based on the progressive destiny of humanity but on the fact that the Sovereign Lord was also the God of Love.

Karl Barth died on December 10, 1968.

See: Karl Barth, *The Epistle to the Romans* (London: Oxford University, 1933); Herbert Hartwell, *The Theology of Karl Barth* (London: Duckworth, 1964).

May 11

Matteo Ricci

Jesuit Missionary to China (1552–1610)

"Those who adore heaven instead of the Lord of heaven are like a man who, desiring to pay the emperor homage, prostrates himself before the imperial palace at Peking and venerates its beauty."

Matteo Ricci, an Italian Jesuit, is an extraordinary figure in the history of Christian mission. He was one of the first Westerners to win entry into the closed and xenophobic society of sixteenth-century China. Having mastered the Chinese language and the literary classics of the Confucian literati he succeeded in transcending his status as a foreigner and won recognition from the educated elite and the imperial court as a scholar of the highest distinction. The work of Matteo Ricci and the Jesuits who followed him showed great promise of establishing an authentically Chinese Christianity. In the end, their efforts were undone by Vatican officials whose philosophy was, in effect, "When in China do as the Romans."

Ricci first entered China in 1583 after spending some time in the Portuguese colony of Macao at the mouth of the Canton river. After intensive study of Chinese and immersion in the classic texts of Confucianism, Ricci was able to present himself as a scholar, a status that was eventually confirmed by the respect of his Chinese peers. He dressed appropriately in elaborate silk dresses and published works on such topics as astronomy, science, and philosophy. He won particular admiration for his map-making skills and for his accomplishments as a teacher of mnemonic techniques.

Ricci's mission strategy was based on the view that before Christianity could make any progress in China it must win the acquiescence of the educated elite. To do this it must eschew any taint of foreign imperialism and present itself in terms of Chinese culture. Ricci was not concerned about the number of conversions. He conceived of his work as laying the foundation for future mission. Once Christianity was an accepted part of Chinese society, others might work to spread the gospel among the masses.

By the time Ricci won permission to live in the imperial city of Beijing, he had achieved renown as a Confucian scholar. His study had convinced him that the ethical precepts of Confucianism — the dominant religious underpinning of Chinese culture — were reconcilable with Christian morality. Furthermore, he argued that in its origins Confucianism recognized a supreme Creator, who could be identified with the Christian God. In his mind the work of assimilating Confucianism with Christianity was little different from what *Thomas Aquinas had accomplished with the philosophy of Aristotle.

Remarkably, Ricci's interpretation of Confucianism, though it contradicted the consensus of most scholars, won general respect and even the agreement of some of his Chinese peers. Among these he was able to count many significant conversions. At the time of his death on May 11, 1610, his body "lay in state," with hundreds of mandarins joining Christians in paying their final respects. By imperial decree, Ricci was buried in a special tomb, a rare honor for any Chinese, and unheard of for a foreigner.

It is impossible to know what effect Ricci's efforts might have had over time. Regrettably, his project was stillborn. Within a hundred years his project was condemned by the Vatican, a casualty of the so-called Rites Controversy. Ricci had recognized the important role in Chinese culture played by the veneration of family ancestors. His intimate knowledge of Chinese culture convinced him that such expressions of filial piety need not represent a conflict with Christian faith and morality. Furthermore, to deny participation in such rites to Chinese Christians was instantly to excommunicate them from their society, an outcome that would render any mission effort moot.

Ricci had won provisional acceptance from Rome for this policy. However, the matter was ultimately decided otherwise. A papal decree of 1704, renewed in even stronger terms in 1742, vehemently condemned the Christian toleration of ancestor rites as idolatrous and superstitious and utterly rejected Ricci's efforts to reconcile the gospel with Confucianism.

This was a fateful decision for the fledgling Christian community in China. Henceforth that ancient society would remain effectively closed to evangelization, and Christianity would never make the inroads for which Ricci had prepared the way. It was also a fateful decision for the church, which was deprived for another two hundred years of the wisdom of non-Western paths to God.

See: Andrew Ross, *A Vision Betrayed: The Jesuits in Japan and China, 1542–1742* (Maryknoll, N.Y.: Orbis, 1994); Jonathan Spence, *The Memory Palace of Matteo Ricci* (New York: Viking, 1984).

May 12

Henri Dominique Lacordaire
Dominican (1802–1861)

"I am a citizen of the future."

Henri Lacordaire devoted his life to the spiritual renewal of France, a task, he believed, that could not be achieved without overcoming the mutual hostility between the church and the forces of liberty.

He was born on May 12, 1802. Trained as a lawyer, he underwent a conversion in his youth that caused him to abandon his Deist outlook and return to the church. At the same time he decided to become a priest. He was accepted into the seminary of Saint-Sulpice, but his "independent spirit" was a source of concern to his tradition-minded superiors. For his part, he was equally uncomfortable with the "ecclesiastical spirit" that struck him as sadly out of touch with the times. While French society was divided in two, the church maintained its pious nostalgia for a bygone era and hoped for some future restoration. Lacordaire urged a more forward-looking strategy.

"The business of this century," he wrote, "is to save religion and the only means, apart from divine intervention, is to be found in religious education." By this he was not referring simply to catechesis. What was needed, he believed, was a complete renewal in the presentation of the faith. The church could not survive on the loyalty of the aristocracy; it must be able to present the gospel in terms of modern experience.

Lacordaire's superiors didn't know quite what to do with him. The prospect of being able to implement his bold mission seemed remote, and Lacordaire was on the verge of emigrating to the United States. But he decided to remain and fight for his convictions. With his fellow priest Felicité Lamennais and a young layman, Charles Montalembert, he launched a journal, *L'Avenir,* dedicated to the rapprochement between Catholicism and the positive features of the Revolution. These included the principles of liberty, democracy, and the separation of church and state. The latter, they maintained, was particularly necessary to enable the church to carry out its spiritual mission in society.

The journal lasted only thirteen months. In the face of bitter opposition from the French bishops, Lacordaire naively suggested that they ought to put their case directly to the pope. In retrospect this was a bad idea. At the time, the Vatican was waging its own battles in defense of the Papal States, and there was no reason to suppose that the pope held any sympathy for the ideas of *L'Avenir.* In fact, Lacordaire's appeal prompted Pope Gregory XVI to issue a general condemnation of the liberal Catholics in his encyclical *Mirari Vos* (1832). The editors obediently submitted to this ruling — Lamennais with an ill-concealed bitterness that eventually drove him from the church; Lacordaire with sadness, but considerable grace. Despite his loyal submission, he would continue to be shadowed by the taint of Roman condemnation and by his association with the more radical Lamennais.

At the same time, however, there were many French Catholics, including *Frédéric Ozanam, who realized the importance of Lacordaire's approach and believed it held the future for the church of France. They induced the conservative archbishop of Paris to allow Lacordaire to deliver a series of Lenten sermons at Notre Dame Cathedral. In 1835 he delivered his first sermon to a packed audience, one of the largest religious gatherings since the Revolution. Aside from devout Christians, the audience drew in a considerable number of skeptics, radicals, and intellectuals, curious about the message of this avant-garde priest. To such an audience Lacordaire believed it was important to preach in an entirely new style, improvised and from the heart. As it turned out, the audience was electrified, and the Lenten series became a *succès fou*. Simply speaking, it represented a turning point in the life of the French church.

From then on Lacordaire was in constant demand as a preacher. But his very success convinced him of the need for a more ambitious strategy. His aim was to bring the church out of the shadows and back into the public light. Thus he announced his decision to become a Dominican and to reintroduce the Dominican order to France. He accomplished this goal in 1840. After undergoing a Dominican novitiate in Rome and making his solemn vows he returned to France in his Dominican habit — the first time this garb had been seen in France in fifty years. It was not many years since such a sight would have provoked a riot. But Lacordaire had judged correctly that the times were changing. When he preached at Notre Dame Cathedral, the crowds turned out in even greater numbers than before.

While working for spiritual renewal and acceptance of the church in French society, Lacordaire maintained his commitment to the principles of political and religious liberty. In 1848 he was elected to the Constituent Assembly as a deputy for Marseilles. But he resigned after only eleven days, overcome by second thoughts about whether his religious vocation was compatible with such a blatantly political role. His scruples contrasted ironically with the pope's own claims to temporal sovereignty. On the subject of the Papal States, Lacordaire wrote with scorn of the pope's supposed spiritual independence, guaranteed by the foreign bayonets required to defend him against his unwilling subjects. "When I was in Rome in 1846 Gregory XVI used to bless and shoot down his subjects in turns. Pius IX puts them in prison.... I sincerely hope that Providence will put an end to this scandal."

By this time the ancient divisions within French society had entered increasingly into the church as well. Lacordaire's outspoken views provided ample ammunition for his enemies. He remained content to exist on the margins of toleration, scorned by most of the hierarchy, while continuing to serve his dual project: to maintain a space for liberty in the church, and a space for religion in the Republic. He died on November 20, 1861.

See: Lancelot C. Sheppard, *Lacordaire: A Biographical Essay* (New York: Macmillan, 1964).

May 13

Bd. Julian of Norwich
Mystic (1342–1416)

"As truly as God is our Father, so truly is God our Mother.
Our Father wills, our Mother works,
our good Lord the Holy Spirit confirms."

The late fourteenth century was a time of terrible upheaval. With the Black Plague, the Hundred Years War, and the crisis of church authority occasioned by the long papal schism, Europe was burdened by an atmosphere of anxiety. Intense concern about the prospects for personal salvation, coupled with doubts about the efficacy of the church and its prescribed channels of spirituality, led to a proliferation of new forms of religious expression. Much of the new spirituality emerged from lay people aspiring to lives of holiness outside of conventional religious orders.

The yearning for a personal, experiential faith contributed to a flowering of nonmonastic Christian mysticism. Fourteenth-century England produced a significant number of mystical classics, written in the vernacular, often by lay people living as solitaries, and addressed to other lay people seeking a more intimate relationship with God. The *Showings* of Julian of Norwich is one — and perhaps the greatest — of these works.

We know little of Julian's biography; her name itself is uncertain, possibly being taken from the church of St. Julian in Norwich, to which she attached herself in her later life as an enclosed anchoress. As an anchoress, she would have been literally sealed in a dwelling attached to the wall of a church. Her cell would have allowed a view of the church interior, as well as an outside window for the delivery of food and the reception of visitors seeking spiritual counsel. She may also have enjoyed a garden and the companionship of a cat. Otherwise, her life was devoted to prayer and reflection.

What may today seem like an extreme form of rejection of the world was recognized in her own time as serving an important social function. In any case, her writings testify to the profound love and compassion that were the fruit of her solitary existence. As for other details of her life we are entirely dependent on the testimony of her *Showings*.

Thus we learn that she was born in 1342. At some point in her youth she prayed that she might be granted three graces: recollection of Christ's passion; bodily sickness; and "three wounds" of contrition, compassion, and longing for God. Her prayer was answered at the age of thirty when she fell so seriously ill that she was given the last rites of the church. She did not die, but as she lay gazing on a crucifix, she experienced sixteen distinct revelations concerning Christ's passion, after which her sickness left her completely. She recorded these revelations in two versions written some twenty years apart.

In Julian's first revelation she beholds Christ's crown of thorns, the effects of which are described with clinical exactness: "the red blood running down from under the crown, hot and flowing freely and copiously, a living stream." Yet this vision, while "hideous and fearful," is also "sweet and lovely." This unexpected conjunction of adjectives underlines the most distinctive quality of Julian's work. For her the cross becomes a source not of terror and anguish but of consolation, a sign of Christ's "friendliness" and extreme "courtesy." In that the one who is highest has assumed the point reserved for the lowest, God pays the honor of a king who condescends to familiarity with a servant. Physically she sees a bleeding head. Spiritually she sees into the depth of God's love and goodness.

This single vision proves an extraordinarily rich soil, yielding reflection on a range of theological issues, including the value of creation, the power of atonement, and the impotence of evil. Creation amounts to no more than a hazelnut in the hand of God. Physically it is nothing. But spiritually its value is measured against God's love and the price God has paid for it in blood. Thus, to gaze into the heart of darkness itself is to enter the mysterious immensity of God's goodness. The smaller our value the greater is God's love. For all its weakness and sin, God suffered for this world; Christ's blood was its price. And in the end God's suffering is turned to joy. For our Creator, who is also our Protector, is also our Lover, working good through all manner of things. The logic of joy and mercy is predetermined ever before Christ suffered his crown of thorns. We are "soul and body, clad and enclosed in the goodness of God."

There are many themes in Julian's writings that speak directly to the heart of contemporary spirituality. Among these is her frequent recourse to feminine images of God. Jesus, she says, is our true Mother, who bears us in the womb of his love and nourishes us with his own flesh. Throughout her writings, the affirmation of the goodness of creation and her stress on the beauty, friendliness, and love of God contrast sharply with a theology that lays stress on the anger and omnipotent judgment of God over a sinful world.

Julian did not directly address the major political and ecclesial crises. But it cannot be said that she was remote from the concerns of her day. In an age of anxious uncertainty, Christians were desperate to seek assurances of salvation, of the meaning of suffering, and of the power and goodness of God. Julian's answers spoke directly to these issues. Her central insight was that the God who created us out of love and who redeemed us by suffering love, also sustains us and wills to be united with us in the end. This love, and not sin, fundamentally determines our existence. Evil has no independent status; whatever we may suffer, God has already suffered. "The worst," as she noted, "has already happened and been repaired." As for our suffering in this life, insofar as we share Christ's passion we may look forward as well to sharing his joy in heaven. Thus she could say, in her most famous and characteristic words, "All shall be well, all shall be well, and all manner of things shall be well."

See: Julian of Norwich, *Showings,* trans. James Walsh, S.J., Classics of Western Spirituality (New York: Paulist, 1978).

May 14

Brother Juniper
Franciscan Lay Brother (d. 1258)

"My dear man, I have nothing to give you except my habit — and my superior has told me under obedience not to give it or part of it away to anyone. But if you pull it off my back, I certainly will not prevent you."

Brother Juniper was one of the original companions of *St. Francis and "a man of such unshakable humility, patience, and self-contempt that the rising waves of temptation and tribulation could not move him." Brother Juniper evidently attained such a degree of holiness that he was quite indifferent to the opinion or regard of others. This was fortunate, since "he was considered stupid and foolish by those who did not know how perfect he was."

Apart from the stories in his brief "Life," little is known of the biography of Brother Juniper. In these stories, Brother Juniper appears to function among the early Franciscans as a kind of living parable. Francis and his followers were regarded, by the world, as "fools for Christ." Just so, the exasperating foolishness of Juniper served among the friars as a standard by which to test their own degree of compromise with the wisdom of the world.

Once when a sick brother expressed his longing to eat a pig's foot, Brother Juniper exclaimed, "Leave that to me!" Immediately he went out and found a pig. He cut off its foot and promptly cooked and "served it with great kindness to the sick friar." This led to an altercation with the irate owner of the pig and caused great embarrassment to the rest of the brothers. But in the end Brother Juniper's guilelessness won the day; even the pig's owner was moved to acknowledge the edifying power of the simple friar's charity.

At the sight of the poor Brother Juniper was filled with such compassion that he would immediately hand them his garments, or even rip off a sleeve or a cowl to give them. Not content with giving away his own habit, he would freely dispense with books, altar vestments, or anything else at hand. As a result, "when poor people came to Brother Juniper to beg, the friars used to take and hide the things they wanted to keep."

Over and over again Juniper tested the patience of his brothers. And not infrequently, after one of his escapades, "the friars were very much shocked and scandalized, and they rebuked him forcefully, calling him a lunatic and a fool and a disgrace to the order of St. Francis, and declaring that he should be put in chains as a madman." But in each case his foolishness ultimately bore a lesson in charity, faith, or humility, so that Francis himself was moved to observe on one occasion, "My Brothers, if only I had a great forest of such junipers!"

Brother Juniper was sent by Francis to found friaries in Viterbo and Gualdo Tadino. He was present at the death of *St. Clare in 1253 and died in Rome in 1258.

See: "The Life of Brother Juniper," in *The Little Flowers of St. Francis,* trans. Raphael Brown (Garden City, N.Y.: Image, 1958).

May 15
St. Isidore the Farmer
(1070–1130)

In March 1622 five great saints were canonized together. They included four of the giant figures of the Catholic Reformation: *St. Ignatius,

*St. Francis Xavier, *St. Teresa, and *St. Philip Neri. The fifth, St. Isidore, stood apart. He founded no order, he accomplished no great deeds (apart from tilling the land); he neither left any teachings, nor inspired any disciples. He was, in fact, a simple farmworker, born in Madrid, who spent his entire working life in the service of the same wealthy landowner. With his good wife, Maria, he bore one son, who died in childhood. He knew the hardships, the toil, and the sorrows of all farmworkers then and since. And he displayed the simple though profound faith so common to *campesinos* the world over. He attended Mass daily and prayed continuously as he worked the fields. In Isidore's case, however, his faith was attended by visible signs and wonders. It was reported, for example, that angels were seen assisting him as he ploughed. He was famous for his generosity toward those even poorer than himself. His table was always open to the indigent, while he was content to live on the scraps left over. His kindness extended to animals. One winter day he was so moved by the sorrowful noise of some hungry birds that he opened the sack of corn he was carrying and poured out half its contents. Though witnesses scoffed at this prodigality, later, at the mill, the bag was found miraculously to be full.

Other similar stories are told of this holy peasant, who died on May 15, 1130. Yet for all the miraculous legends, what most stands out is the very ordinariness of his life. He is simply one of the "little ones" so beloved of God. Though not a monk he passed his life in "work and prayer." Though poor himself he poured himself out in charity. Though happily married he communed with angels. In the list of canonized saints his type is surprisingly rare; in heaven, presumably, less so.

May 16

Heloise
Abbess of the Convent of the Paraclete (1100–1164)

"You know, beloved, as the whole world knows,
how much I have lost in you."

The story of Heloise, inseparable from that of her beloved Abelard, is one of the most memorable episodes in medieval literature. Though it has been frequently recounted, the story retains its poignant mystery.

Heloise, a beautiful and exceptionally intelligent girl, was raised by her uncle Fulbert, a canon of the cathedral in Paris. Such was her brilliance that Fulbert hired the most famous scholar in France, the renowned Peter Abelard, to be her tutor. Heloise was about seventeen, while Abelard, then at the peak of his powers, was in his mid-thirties. In his later account of their affair, Abelard blamed himself for seducing Heloise. Nevertheless, however ignoble his initial intentions, the two were soon passionate lovers. Their lack of discretion led to tragic consequences.

Heloise became pregnant and bore a son. Fulbert was enraged, and he was not appeased by the couple's secret marriage. Hoping to resolve the conflict, Abelard sent Heloise to a convent. In the meantime, however, Fulbert's men broke into Abelard's chamber one night and violently castrated him. In agony and shame Abelard retired quickly to a monastery, intending never again to see his wife or the son she had borne.

Years passed. Abelard had suffered much, both from his public humiliation and a series of bruising theological controversies. But as a monk he had gradually regained a good deal of his former renown. He had even had some indirect contact with Heloise. Having learned that her religious community was without a home he established them in the Oratory of the Paraclete, which he had founded. There remained, however, much unresolved business between them.

In 1132 Abelard wrote a letter to a fellow monk, a "History of My Misfortunes," in which he recounted in intimate detail the story of his relationship with Heloise and its tragic denouement. The text found its way to Heloise, now abbess of the convent in which she had so long lived. It was many years since she had taken her final vows as a nun, but the wounds of her abandonment by Abelard had never healed. In his self-centered "History" she was shocked to find another betrayal of their relationship, and so at long last she was moved to break her silence.

In a long letter she addressed him with blunt irony: "To her master, or rather her father, husband, or rather brother; his handmaid, or rather his daughter, wife, or rather sister; to Abelard, Heloise." She described her emotions upon reading his letter — pity for all his sufferings, mixed, however, with a certain resentment. What of *her* sufferings?

> Why, after our entry into religion, which was your decision alone, have I been so neglected and forgotten by you? . . . It was not any sense of vocation which brought me as a young girl to accept the austerities of the cloister, but your bidding alone, and if I deserve no gratitude from you, you may judge for yourself how my labors are in vain. I can expect no reward for this from God, for it is certain that I have done nothing as yet for love of him.

In responding Abelard tried to turn her bitter thoughts to some spiritual resolution. Their love could not be. She should try to love him in Christ. Heloise in turn accused herself of hypocrisy. The world thought her devout and chaste when all the while her body burned with the memory of their illicit union. It was for love of him that she had taken the veil: "Look at the unhappy life I lead, pitiable beyond any other, if in this world I must endure so much in vain, with no hope of future reward." Abelard urged her still to accept their condition as a fact, and to seek in suffering the path to sanctification.

At this point Heloise abruptly changed course. She gave up her personal appeals and asked him instead to give her a rule and instruction for her monastic community. Obviously relieved, Abelard responded with several long treatises. They never again referred to their common history.

Abelard died in 1142 in the midst of a theological dispute that brought him close to official condemnation. His abbot arranged for him to be buried in the abbey church of Heloise's community. She lived on for another twenty-one years and died on May 16, 1164. Her body was placed beside her husband's.

Over the centuries Heloise and Abelard have attracted their respective champions. Certainly Heloise was one of the great women intellectuals and writers of the Middle Ages. Was she also, as some have suggested, a kind of saint? The answer depends to some extent on whether one accepts, at face value, her own assessment of her condition. Did she ever achieve the peace of mind to which Abelard had urged her? Is that the best criterion of holiness?

Under her administration the Paraclete became one of the great religious communities of Europe, and Heloise was widely revered as a wise and holy abbess. Is it possible, as Etienne Gilson has said, that "Heloise did not know everything about her own situation"? Because she would not renounce her human love for the love of God she believed herself a hypocrite. But who can say whether God desired such renunciation? Perhaps it was her insistence on the integrity of her love — even at the cost of great suffering — that was her own path to sanctification. In any case it was sufficient to sustain her through a lifetime of prayer and service.

In returning Abelard's body to the Paraclete, Peter the Venerable offered a touching acknowledgment of Heloise's claims, both in this world and in the light of eternity: "Christ cherishes him in your place, indeed as a second you, and he will restore him to you of his grace on the day that the Lord shall come down from heaven. "

See: *The Letters of Abelard and Heloise* (New York: Penguin, 1974); Elizabeth Hamilton, *Heloise* (Garden City, N.Y.: Doubleday, 1967); Etienne Gilson, *Heloise and Abelard* (Ann Arbor: University of Michigan Press, 1960).

May 17
St. Josephine Bakhita
Ex-Slave and Nun (1869–1947)

"Seeing the sun, the moon, and the stars, I said to myself: Who could be the Master of these beautiful things? And I felt a great desire to see him, to know him, and to pay him homage."

Among the distinctive features of the pontificate of John Paul II has been his keen interest in enlarging the field of canonized saints. In his first eighteen years as pope he canonized and beatified nearly a thousand saints — more than in the several previous centuries since the Council of Trent. Apart from his belief in the teaching value of holy lives, he has been particularly interested in recognizing "local saints" — persons whose lives bear a special meaning for the churches he has made a point of visiting around the world. Typical of these new saints is Sister Josephine Bakhita of Sudan, beatified on May 17, 1992.

Bakhita ("the fortunate one") was born in a village in the southern Sudan in 1869. When she was nine she was kidnapped and sold into slavery. Transferred from one master to another over a period of years, she experienced brutality in many forms. A turning point came in 1883 when she was sold to an Italian family who treated her with relative kindness and brought her back to Italy to work as a maid and nursemaid to their baby, Mimmina. Bakhita became devoted to the child. When Mimmina was old enough to be sent to a boarding school in Venice Bakhita accompanied her. The school was run by the Daughters of Charity, or "Canossian Sisters." It was there that Bakhita first heard the gospel and divined that it was God's will that she be free.

When, after nine months, Bakhita's mistress announced that they were returning to the Sudan, Bakhita expressed her intention to remain. The Signora professed to be hurt. Hadn't they always treated her as a member of the family? How could she now be so ungrateful? As difficult as it was to resist these entreaties, Bakhita remained firm in her resolution: "I am sure the Lord gave me strength at that moment," she later wrote, "because he wanted me for himself alone."

When pleading did not work the Signora tried another tack: she sued in court for the return of her "property." But the superior of the Canossian Sisters and the cardinal of Venice intervened and came to her defense. It was only thus that Bakhita discovered what no one had bothered to inform her, namely, that slavery was illegal in Italy. She had been free all along.

And so Bakhita remained in Italy. On January 9, 1890, she was baptized, taking the name Josephine Bakhita. By this time she heard "more and more clearly the gentle voice of the Lord from the bottom of my heart, urging me to consecrate myself to God." She was accepted into the novitiate of the congregation that had sheltered her. Finally, in 1896 she made her religious vows.

Sister Josephine lived to the age of seventy-eight. She spent her life in simple tasks, cooking, sewing, serving as sacristan and doorkeeper. No work was unimportant when performed for "the Master" — her favorite word for God. She became famous for her quiet faith and the care she brought to assignments big and small. It was said that she had a gift for making the ordinary extraordinary. To those Sisters who were schoolteachers she said, "You teach catechism; I will stay in the chapel to pray for you that you may teach well."

She lived on through World War I and then World War II. By this time her reputation for holiness was so widespread in the town of Schio where she lived that she was invoked as a protection against falling bombs. She had assured the people that no bomb would damage the town, a promise that was fulfilled.

In her last years she became ill and could not leave her wheelchair. When a visiting bishop asked her what she did all day in her wheelchair, she replied, "What do I do? Exactly what you are doing — the will of God." Sister Josephine Bakhita died on February 8, 1947. She was canonized in 2000, the first native of the Sudan to be so recognized.

See: Alicia von Stamwitz, "Blessed Josephine Bakhita: Woman of Faith and Forgiveness," *Liguorian* (February 1993).

Origen
Theologian (186–253?)

"It is likely that we shall both be reproached by our neighbors and scorned by those who surround us and shake their heads at us as fools. . . . But when all this happens, it is blessed to speak to God the word uttered by the prophet in his boldness, 'All this has come upon us, and we have not forgotten you, and we have not been false to your covenant, and our heart has not turned back' (Ps. 44:17–18)."

Origen, the greatest theologian of the early Greek church, was born in the cosmopolitan city of Alexandria, Egypt. He was the son of devout and educated Christian parents. His father, Leonidas, died as a martyr during a wave of persecution in 202. It was said that Origen — fifteen at the time — was prevented from embracing a similar fate only when his mother hid his garments. So he survived, though permanently marked by this experience and the consciousness of belonging to a church of martyrs.

As a teenager, Origen had already acquired a reputation as an outstanding philosopher and student of Scripture. At the age of sixteen he was appointed as catechist for the church in Alexandria, a position he occupied for many years. His position was somewhat compromised by his penchant for extreme asceticism, reflected especially in his literal response to the text of Matthew 19:12. After reflecting on this text — "There are some who have made themselves eunuchs for the kingdom of heaven's sake" — Origen was inspired to castrate himself. Such mutilation had yet to be condemned by the church — perhaps because no one had anticipated the error. But it was deemed by his local bishop, Demetrius, to be at the very least an impediment to ordination.

Nevertheless, during an eventful trip to Palestine in 230 Origen was ordained a presbyter by the local church. Demetrius took offense at this flouting of his directives. He convened a synod in which Origen's ordination was disavowed, and he was permanently banned from his native city. Consequently he remained in Caesarea in Palestine for the rest of his life.

Origen was an incredibly prolific writer. His scholarly industry earned him the nickname "man of steel." For some time, thanks to the arrangement of a wealthy patron, he employed the services of a team of secretaries to take down his dictation. It is said that he produced no less than six thousand works in his life, though only a small number have survived. *St. Jerome, who compiled a critical edition of his works, observed, "Who can read all the works of Origen?" Among his surviving works are his *First Principles,* one of the first systematic expositions of the Christian faith, employing the language of Hellenistic thought; his "Exhortation to Martyrdom"; several treatises on prayer; and scores of biblical commentaries.

Origen's speculative theology brought him under suspicion. He was accused of having adapted the gospel to neo-Platonic philosophy rather than the other way around. Evidence was drawn from his writings on the preexistence of souls and his apparently optimistic eschatology. Based on *St. Paul, who had described the terminus of history in which God will be "all in all," Origen affirmed the possibility of universal salvation, even for the devil. These and other Origenist positions — some taken to extremes by his later disciples — generated fierce controversy, leading to the formal condemnation of "Origenism" in the sixth century.

Nevertheless, it is in the area of biblical studies that Origen made his most substantial contribution. He was first of all a textual scholar, concerned to establish the most accurate and reliable edition of the Holy Scriptures. He compiled a work in which the entire Old Testament was written in six columns, including Hebrew, a Greek transliteration of the Hebrew, and four different Greek versions.

Secondly, he devised a method of interpreting Scripture that would lay the foundation for all medieval exegesis. Origen believed that Scripture could be read on several levels, corresponding to the human dimensions of body, soul, and spirit. In simple terms, it was important to understand not just the "letter" of the text but its "spiritual" meaning. Beyond the literal, historical meaning of the text one should seek to uncover the additional typological and symbolic meanings. For Origen Christ and his spiritual teaching were the key to interpreting Scripture. Thus, virtually any text in the Old Testament could also be seen as a "type" or foreshadowing of the New Testament and by extension a foreshadowing of our heavenly destination.

For example, the story of *Noah's Ark recounted a supposedly historical event. But the Ark was also a figure of the Christian church. And this, in turn, prefigured the communion of saints in heaven. Origen's interpretation of Scripture was laid out in full-scale commentaries on most of the books of the Bible, as well as hundreds of learned sermons. His commentary on the Song of Songs, which Origen read as a symbolic discourse on the marriage between the soul and God, was particularly influential, opening an immensely rich fount of later mystical theology.

Origen's method of interpretation avoided the danger of a literalist approach to Scripture and theology. He opened the church to the spiritual riches of Holy Scripture, allowing Christians to find meaning and interest in even the most obscure or prosaic scriptural texts. On the other hand, his approach had the danger of encouraging fanciful interpretations and of minimizing the significance of history in favor of ideal spiritual archetypes.

Origen served the church faithfully as a scholar and apologist. Nevertheless, his poetic and mystical style of theology aroused doubts about his orthodoxy that nagged him throughout his life and only gained force in the centuries after his death. In 250 he was arrested during a persecution of the church and underwent savage torture aimed at forcing his apostasy. Nothing would induce him to renounce his faith, and he was released in an amnesty upon the death of the emperor. He never fully recovered, however, and lived on for only a few short years.

See: Origen, trans. Rowan A. Greer, Classics of Western Spirituality (New York: Paulist, 1979).

St. Celestine V
Pope (1209?–1296)

"I wanted nothing in the world but a cell, and a cell they have given me."

In the two-thousand-year history of the church, the office of the pope has not always been synonymous with holiness. There have been popes whose election seemed to owe more to nepotism and political influence than the inspiration of the Holy Spirit. There have been others whose gifts were more readily employed in aggrandizing the powers of the papacy than in witnessing to Christ in the world. There is no such thing as *ex officio* sanctity. At the same time, many popes have appeared among the list of canonized saints. Some, like *St. Peter, the first bishop of Rome, were martyrs. Others, like *St. Gregory the Great, were towering figures who brought credit to the church through their vision and bold leadership. And then there is the remarkable story of Celestine V, a simple monk who experienced great tensions between the office of pope and the call to holiness, and resolved them by abdicating.

He began life as Pietro di Morone, the eleventh of twelve children born to a peasant family in the wild Abruzzi. As a young man he showed a penchant for prayer and solitude and spent some time in a Benedictine monastery, where he received a rudimentary education. At the age of twenty he retired to a mountain cell to live as a hermit. But despite his wish for solitude, his reputation for holiness drew many visitors and later disciples to his cell. He was finally persuaded to seek holy orders, and soon thereafter became the head of a community of hermits on Mt. Morone. They adopted the Rule of *St. Benedict, but otherwise they were close in spirit to the Franciscan Spirituals, a controversial movement in the Franciscan family which sought to maintain the ideal of radical poverty.

After the death of Pope Nicholas IV in 1292, the papal throne remained vacant for twenty-seven months. The cardinals were bitterly divided by family rivalries and political interests that left them unable to agree on a successor. At this time they received a message from the holy hermit Pietro di Morone, threatening them with the wrath of God should they fail in their duty. Without hesitating, the conclave responded by electing Pietro himself. The hermit was by this time an old man of eighty-four. Nevertheless, he accepted the charge and returned to Aquila, riding on a donkey.

News of the selection of this holy man inspired wild enthusiasm among the public. It is said that two hundred thousand people crowded the streets of Aquila to welcome the new pope, who chose the name Celestine V. There were those who saw in the consecration of Celestine the fulfillment of the prophecy of Joachim of Fiore, inaugurating the new age of the Holy Spirit. But the selection of Celestine was equally appealing to ambitious job-seekers and power-hungry intriguers who sought to manipulate the unworldly pope into favoring their interests.

Celestine, bewildered by the affairs of the papal court, soon became convinced that his piety was no match for the duties of office. After five months he was miserable with longing for the solitude of his cell. And so, on December 13, 1294, Celestine read a solemn declaration of abdication. He laid aside his pontifical robes, resumed his religious habit, and returned to his monastic community.

The next pope was Boniface VIII, a man whose character was in every sense a contrast with his predecessor: gifted in political intrigue where Celestine was innocent; cruel and contemptuous toward his rivals where his predecessor was self-effacing. Boniface is chiefly famous for promulgating the bull *Unam Sanctam,* one of the most extreme statements of papal supremacy ever issued. The concluding sentence affirms that the salvation of every creature depends on subjection to the Roman pontiff. Boniface's enthusiasm for statecraft and his autocratic personality left him with few friends and many enemies. Fearing that the still-popular Celestine might serve as a beacon for opposition to his own reign, he had the former pontiff arrested and imprisoned in a fortress in Fumone. Celestine responded to this turn of events with characteristic resignation: "I wanted nothing in the world but a cell, and a cell they have given me." There, after ten months, Celestine died on May 19, 1296. In 1313 he was canonized by Pope Clement V (as a confessor, not as a martyr, despite public suspicions that he was assassinated by Boniface).

Opinions of Celestine's abdication have varied. *Dante, charging him with "the great refusal," placed Celestine in the vestibule of the *Inferno.* So he punished Celestine for having saddled the church with Boniface. More recently, another Italian, *Ignazio Silone, made him the hero of a play, in which the story of the saintly pope dramatizes the conflict between the spirit of the gospel and the principle of power.

See: Ignazio Silone, *The Story of a Humble Christian* (New York: Harper & Row, 1970); J. N. D. Kelly, *The Oxford Dictionary of Popes* (Oxford: Oxford University Press, 1986).

May 20

Rose Hawthorne
Founder of the Servants of Relief for Incurable Cancer (1851–1926)

"I tried to acquire a fondness for the very poor, and I finally came to like them very much if they were rather good. But I was not satisfied with liking them; I wanted to love all the poor whom I met."

Rose Hawthorne was born on May 20, 1851. She was the third and favorite child of Nathaniel Hawthorne, the great American writer and author of *The Scarlet Letter.* Her father died when Rose was thirteen, and her mother's death followed only a few years later. Bereft with this loss, Rose accepted the marriage proposal of George Lathrop, a young American writer she had met in Europe. They were married in 1871, soon after her twentieth birthday. They had one son, who died at the age of four. This sorrow was compounded by the gradual deterioration of her marriage, largely as a result of Lathrop's alcoholism. For a time a common attraction to Catholicism held promise of restoring the marriage. In 1891 they were both received into the Catholic church. But two years later they formally separated.

Rose at this time was in her forties. Her life had been spent in devotion to her husband and in the frivolous obligations of what was called "society." Now finding herself alone in New York City with no family responsibilities, she felt that she was called to some more heroic expression of her faith.

She had become aware of the terrible plight of the impoverished victims of cancer, a disease for which there was little available treatment. Once diagnosed, such cases were not permitted to remain in New York hospitals. Those without family or other means were banished to die in bleak isolation on Blackwell's Island. Rose became convinced that her vocation was to provide an alternative to this fate.

Immediately she took a nursing course and then found lodging in the squalid immigrant quarter of the Lower East Side. At first she set about visiting cancer patients in their homes. But eventually she began inviting them into her own apartment, where she offered them loving care and companionship until they died. For support she relied on contributions from friends, for she adamantly refused any payment or gift in exchange for her services. For a woman of refined taste and fastidious habits, it was not an easy or natural adjustment to this new life. Day after day she spent washing the cancerous sores and changing the dressings and bedclothes of her impoverished guests. But rather than simply providing nursing care, Rose was determined to extend friendship and respect, to convey a sense of dignity to those who had become outcasts. Inspired by the example of *St. Vincent de Paul she borrowed his motto to describe her mission: "I am for God and the poor."

After the death of George Lathrop, Rose believed she ought to formalize her vocation by entering religious life. In 1900 she and a companion in her work, Alice Huber, were received into the Dominican order. Six years later her own Dominican congregation, the Servants of Relief for Incurable Cancer, was formally established, and she became known as Mother Alphonsa.

She died at the age of seventy-five on July 9, 1926, at the motherhouse of her congregation in Hawthorne, New York. The work of her congregation continues today in a number of homes around the country. According to the strict rule she established, no money is accepted from patients, their families, or even from the state.

This trust in providence later inspired *Dorothy Day, who was reading the biography of Rose Hawthorne when she decided to launch the *Catholic Worker.* Hawthorne, Day observed, had not waited for official authorization or financial backing before beginning her charitable mission, working out of her tenement apartment and trusting that if it were God's work, money and support would follow.

So the influence of Rose Hawthorne has extended in many directions. The modern hospice movement was begun without reference to her example. But she may fairly be credited with pioneering this new attitude toward "death and dying." In her ministry she affirmed the sanctity of life, even in its most distressing guise, even in its final moments.

See: Diana Culbertson, O.P., ed., *Rose Hawthorne Lathrop: Selected Writings* (New York: Paulist, 1993); Katherine Burton, *Sorrow Built a Bridge: A Daughter of Hawthorne* (New York: Longman, Green, 1937).

May 21
Christian de Chergé and Companions
Trappist Martyrs of Algeria (d. 1996)

"If it were ever to happen . . . that I should be the victim of the terrorism that seems to be engulfing all the foreigners now living in Algeria, I would like my community, my church, my family to remember that my life was given to God and to this country."

With these words Father Christian de Chergé, prior of a Trappist monastery in Algeria, began a letter to his family which he sealed with the notation, "To be opened in the event of my death." The letter was opened three years later after de Chergé and six of his fellow Trappists were murdered by fundamentalist rebels in 1996. In their deaths they joined a long procession of past victims — both Christians and Muslims — sacrificed to one another's conception of the glory of God. But unlike many Christian martyrs of the past these Trappists did not offer their lives for the conversion of their Muslim neighbors, but as a witness to the One God of all, and for the cause of friendship among all God's people. For Father de Chergé, at least, it was the repayment of an ancient debt.

In 1958, as a young man of twenty-one, he had served as a French soldier fighting Algerian rebels in the war of independence. It was a war marked on both sides by exceptional brutality. But one day, during an ambush, his life was saved when a friend — who happened to be a devout Muslim — shielded him with his own body. This man's sacrifice, which de Chergé believed was motivated by religious faith, prompted his own conversion — a process that led him to the priesthood and ultimately to the Trappists. After studies in Rome he asked to be assigned to Our Lady of Atlas monastery in the highlands near Algiers. Many French religious and missionaries had fled the country after independence in 1962. But, at the urging of the Catholic archbishop, the Trappists had stayed on to offer a contemplative Christian presence among their Muslim neighbors.

The monks lived a traditional Trappist life of prayer and work. But they made a point of offering a place where Christians and Muslims could pray and talk together. De Chergé himself was an avid student of the Qur'an. A building in the monastery enclosure had been offered for use as a mosque. Thus, "the sound of chapel bells mixed with the Muslim call to prayer."

To many of their neighbors the monks were trusted men of God. But to others — fundamentalists, who felt increasing resentment toward the secular policies of Algeria's military government — the French Trappists were foreign infidels. As a later rebel dispatch put it, "They live with the people and draw them away from the divine path, inciting them to follow the Gospel."

By 1993 the country was on the verge of a violent rebellion. An ultimatum, issued by the rebels, warned all foreigners to leave the country. But the monks decided to stay. They also declined an offer of military protection. It was then that Father de Chergé wrote his last testament and mailed it to his family in France. In the following years a number of priests and women religious were killed. But still the monks remained. As de Chergé wrote, "For us it is a journey of faith into the future and of sharing the present with our neighbors, who have always been very closely bound to us." In putting on the Trappist habit they had all left their families and their country to follow Christ. "Now all that is left for us is to give our blood to follow Christ to the end."

The end came in 1996 when rebels invaded the monastery and seized Father de Chergé and six other brothers and marched them into the mountains. Several weeks later, on May 23, the rebels announced, "We have cut the throats of the seven monks....Glory to God!" The heads of the monks were discovered the next day. They were buried in the small cemetery of the monastery.

At this point, remembering his sealed letter, de Chergé's family discovered his prayer of forgiveness for his murderers and hopes that their action would not contribute to negative stereotypes about Islam or Algeria. "For me, Islam and Algeria...are body and soul." He offered thanks for all his friends and family. But he reserved his final words for his murderer, "You too, my last-minute friend, you who know not what you do. Yes, for you, too, I wish this thank you, and this *adieu* which is of your planning. May we be granted to meet each other again, happy thieves, in paradise, should it please God, the Father of both of us. Amen! *In sh' Allah!*"

See: Rick Hampson, "A Martyr's Testament," Associated Press (April 4, 1997); Christian de Chergé, "Amen! In sh' Allah!" *Commonweal* (January 31, 1997).

May 22

Baal Shem Tov
Founder of Hasidism (1700–1760)

"I came into the world to show another way,
to cultivate love of God, of Israel, and of the Torah,
and there is no need for fasting and mortification."

The Baal Shem Tov — "Master of the Good Name" — was the title given to Rabbi Israel ben Eliezer of Mezbizk, the founder of Hasidic Judaism.

Rather than providing a set of teachings the Baal Shem Tov — or the Besht, as his name was commonly abbreviated — communicated his lessons through a certain attitude, a spirit of joy, an instinct for the holiness of existence, that would ultimately inspire a following far beyond the Hasidim, or "pious ones," as his followers came to be called.

He was born in a small town in the Ukraine in 1700. For Jews of that time and place the memory of savage persecution was still fresh. A series of pogroms in the latter half of the seventeenth century cost the lives of more than a hundred thousand Jews. In such an atmosphere of catastrophe there arose a number of messianic and mystical movements, of which Hasidism was ultimately the most successful. Nevertheless, the first part of the Besht's life was spent in quiet obscurity. Only midway through his life did he suddenly take to wandering from village to village, performing wonders and imparting his vision and wisdom. The Besht proclaimed a mysticism of the everyday. Within each task and each moment there was a spark of the divine. The responsibility for each person was to discover and to fulfill the potential holiness imbedded within ordinary existence. This responsibility, furthermore, should be discharged in a spirit of joy. He opposed obsessive asceticism and self-mortification, just as he opposed a preoccupation with the law. Much more important was the spirit in which one lived. The religious life, according to the Besht, was not a matter of performing religious duties; the essential thing was the piety that one brought to daily life. He spoke of prayer as a window to heaven and called the entire world a prayer house. Thus, "A man needs no fixed place to say his prayers, no synagogues; among the trees of the forest, everywhere one can pray."

*Martin Buber, the twentieth-century Jewish philosopher, was the first to popularize the tales and legends of the Baal Shem Tov and the early Hasidic masters, thus helping to carry their message far beyond their original home in Eastern Europe. Though not himself a Hasid, Buber believed that Hasidic spirituality had a universal message especially relevant to the secularized West. He summarized this message as the consecration of everyday life to God: "For there is no rung of being on which we cannot find the holiness of God everywhere and at all times." Elsewhere he noted, "The task of man, of every man, according to Hasidic teaching, is to affirm for God's sake the world and himself and by this very means to transform both."

The large Hasidic community in Eastern Europe was largely extinguished by the Nazis. But vibrant communities, especially in the United States and Israel, continue to live out the joyful and compassionate vision of the Baal Shem Tov. As he lay dying, surrounded by his family and followers, the Besht said, "I am not worried at all for I know that I am leaving through one door and entering through another door."

He died on May 22, 1760.

See: Martin Buber, *Tales of the Hasidim* (New York: Schocken, 1966); Dan Ben-Amos and Jerome R. Mintz, eds., *In Praise of the Baal Shem Tov* (Bloomington, Ind.: Indiana University Press, 1970).

May 23

Girolamo Savonarola

Dominican Reformer (1452–1498)

"I want no [cardinal's] hats, no miters great or small.
I only want the one You, O Lord, gave to your saints, death.
A red hat, a hat of blood, that is what I want."

Girolamo Savonarola was a Dominican preacher who gained a wide following in Florence in the late fifteenth century as a result of his fiery sermons. These sermons, strongly influenced by the prophetical and apocalyptic texts of the Bible, combined a strong moral appeal with sweeping condemnations of social injustice and religious corruption. Savonarola prophesied that God's judgment on Italy was at hand, a prediction that seemed to be fulfilled in 1494 when the French army of Charles VIII closed in and prepared to lay siege to Florence. Savonarola was commissioned to meet with the French king and negotiate a surrender.

He was successful in this mission, winning assurance from Charles that there would be no plundering of the city. In the meantime, however, the city rose up to overthrow the ruling Medici family. Savonarola's passionate preaching inspired the city to declare itself a republic and to institute various democratic reforms.

During a period of over a year Savonarola, through his sermons, was the guiding light of a remarkable experiment in social reform. Florence, he believed, was to be "the watchtower of Italy," the center of a movement of renewal that would gradually spread and realize the kingdom of God on earth. With time, however, his zeal aroused bitter opposition, both from the ruling circles of Florence and even more from the papal court in Rome.

As his vision drew energy, Savonarola felt increasingly free to direct his criticism at the papal curia and at the scandalous behavior of Pope Alexander VI, a man who, even by the lax standards of the Renaissance papacy, set a standard for venality, nepotism, and overall corruption. Beginning in 1495 Savonarola and Alexander became locked in a deadly duel. It began when Alexander commanded Savonarola to appear in Rome to explain his preaching. Savonarola responded by sending a copy of his book. This was followed by a papal order that he abandon his preaching ministry. When Savonarola disobeyed, he was excommunicated. The last straw for the pope came when Savonarola issued a letter to the rulers of Europe exhorting them to summon a general council to depose the unworthy pope and to reform the church.

By 1498 the rulers of Florence had tired of protecting the troublesome friar, and the populace too had lost heart for his moralistic appeals. Thus, he was arrested and put to torture. Until the end he maintained his faith in Christ and the justice of his cause. On May 23 he was publicly hanged and then burned in the Piazza della Signoria. Nevertheless, there were many at the time, as there have been since, who believed that Florence had killed a saint.

See: Roberto Ridolfi, *The Life of Girolamo Savonarola* (London: Routledge and Kegan Paul, 1959); *Apocalyptic Spirituality,* trans. Bernard McGinn, Classics of Western Spirituality (New York: Paulist, 1979).

May 24
Job
The Poor Man

"Naked I came from my mother's womb,
naked I shall return again.
Yahweh gave, Yahweh has taken back.
Blessed be the name of Yahweh!"

The book of Job begins with a cruel wager between God and Satan. At issue is the question whether there is such a thing as disinterested faith. The occasion is God's pleasure in one of his faithful servants, a man named Job, renowned for his virtue and piety. Satan taunts that such faith comes easily to Job, given his worldly happiness and success. "But put forth thy hand now, and touch all that he has, and he will curse thee to thy face." God accepts the challenge and so puts his unfortunate servant into Satan's hands. In quick succession Job proceeds to lose his family, his fortune, and ultimately his health. He is left a loathsome pauper, sitting amid the ashes, scraping his sores with a potsherd.

Many have read the book of Job as a meditation on the mystery of suffering or the mystery of a God who permits such suffering. Thus, the theme of Job is commonly summarized in the popular phrase: "Why do bad things happen to good people?"

This is certainly a question posed by the character of Job. To be sure, it *is* answered by a trio of Job's self-appointed "comforters." Each in his own way is concerned to justify the power and righteousness of God at Job's expense. In this they reflect the common assumption of their time that virtue is directly linked to worldly reward. According to this view, if Job has suffered then the fault must ultimately lie with himself. Job himself had shared this assumption until his own *experience* introduced him to the reality of *innocent suffering.* In light of this reality, the book of Job addresses a different question, namely, how are we to talk about God from within the situation of the suffering of the innocent?

This is the approach to Job taken by the Peruvian theologian Gustavo Gutiérrez. Gutiérrez himself writes from a situation of massive injustice, violence, and the suffering of the poor. He is well acquainted with theologies or ideologies which try either to reconcile the poor to their suffering ("It is the will of God") or to blame them for their own fate. Such theologies may be more or less sophisticated. But their proponents share in common with the comforters of Job that they don't know what they are talking about. At least, they do not know what Job knows. According to Gutiérrez, "Job's words are a criticism of every theology that lacks human compassion and contact with reality." Job is often characterized as "patient." But in Gutiérrez's words, Job is rather a rebellious believer: "His rebellion is against the suffering of the innocent, against a theology that justifies, and even against the depiction of God that such a theology conveys."

Job begins simply by lamenting his miserable existence. But eventually, provoked by the empty prattle of his "friends," he gradually rises to heroic heights, rejecting the design of a universe that consigns the poor to suffering, and challenging God to give an account. In a mysterious flight of faith he even seems to invoke one image of God — as Redeemer, defender of the innocent — against another image, the God who is the author of his suffering.

> For I know that my Redeemer lives
> and at last he will stand upon the earth;
> and after my skin has been thus destroyed,
>   then from my flesh I shall see God.

Job's scandalized friends accuse him of blasphemy. But in the end God responds to Job's challenge and speaks to him from the whirlwind. In a long peroration on the immensity and mystery of creation, God makes little direct response to Job's agonized questions. But that the Creator of the universe has been willing to meet with this poor servant and to affirm his innocence is enough to satisfy Job. So he responds with a humble profession of faith. Referring not only to this but to Job's previous discourses God observes that Job has "spoken right." In contrast, God expresses rage at Job's friends. In claiming to speak in the name of God while neglecting the duty of compassion and practical solidarity it appears that they are the true blasphemers. Now, according to God, their own salvation depends on the prayers of the poor man, Job.

The book of Job is clearly a literary work which makes no pretense of describing a historical personage. The framework of the story was probably derived from an ancient folktale which circulated for centuries before it was written in its present form by an anonymous Jewish poet during the Babylonian exile (sixth century B.C.E.).

Is it proper to include a fictional character in a calendar of saints? The fact that Job was not a historical figure does not mean he did not — does not — exist. Job's features may be discerned in the face of all who suffer. But in a special way Job lives on "anonymously" in the residents of countless hovels and shantytowns. According to Gutiérrez, they are the objects of God's special love, not "because they are necessarily better than others, morally or religiously, but simply because they are poor and living in an inhuman situation that is contrary to God's will." Such "saints" invite neither veneration nor imitation but solidarity and love.

See: The Book of Job; Gustavo Gutiérrez, *On Job: God-Talk and the Suffering of the Innocent* (Maryknoll, N.Y.: Orbis, 1987).

St. Bede the Venerable
Doctor of the Church (673–735)

"I earnestly request all who may hear or read this history of our nation to ask God's mercy on my many failings of mind and body, and . . . grant me the favor of frequent mention in their devout prayers."

St. Bede was a true product of the monastery. At the age of seven he was entrusted by his parents to a local abbot, who saw to his education and upbringing. Later he was transferred to the nearby monastery at Jarrow, where he remained a monk for the rest of his days. He rarely emerged from his monastery, and he probably never traveled beyond his native Northumbria. And yet, from his obscure monastic perch, he was able to take the measure of his world to a degree shared by few of his contemporaries.

Bede's was a long and uneventful life. His story is unadorned by fabulous acts of asceticism, mystical visions, or miracles. As he described himself, "My chief delight has always been in study, teaching, and writing." But it was precisely his passion for study and writing that were his path to sanctity. He left behind many books, the most famous being his charming *History of the English Church and People.* Rather than simply recording names and events, Bede tried to compose a coherent narrative encompassing the arrival of Christianity in the British Isles, the progress of its great early saints and missionaries, and the gradual role of Christianity in pulling together the disparate tribes and races of Britain into a unified nation.

It is a story abounding in heroes: there is the legendary *St. Alban, protomartyr of the English church, killed by the Romans for sheltering an illegal priest; St. Augustine, the first archbishop of Canterbury, sent to Britain by *Pope Gregory the Great; King Edwin, who convened the first church council in 627 with the result that he and his nobility embraced the Catholic faith; Bishop Aiden, founder of the see of Lindisfarne; Oswald, the Christian king of Northumbria; *Abbess Hilda of Whitby; the sainted cowherd-poet *Caedmon; and various other monks, bishops, kings, and warlords.

The story of Christianity is told largely through the interaction between these key actors, especially saints and kings. The saints bear the gospel, while the kings determine the people's response. In one famous scene Bede recounts the story of the holy monk Paulinus, who brings the gospel to King Edwin of Northumbria. The king assembles his advisers — including his pagan priests — to discuss the pros and cons of the proposed faith. One of his advisers reflects that the present life of a man is like "the swift flight of a lone sparrow" through a banquet hall. While he is inside he is safe from the winter storms, but then "he vanishes from sight into the darkness whence he came." So with a man, "we know nothing of what went before this life, and what follows. Therefore if this new teaching can reveal any more certain knowledge, it seems only right that we should follow it." One by one the high priests submit before the wisdom of Paulinus and agree to adopt the new religion. Thus Bede recounts the origins of Christianity in his own Northumbria.

Through this and similar stories, Bede depicts the gradual knitting together of many kingdoms and peoples into a common history, thereby linking the primitive civilization of Britain with the ancient church of Rome and the faith of the apostles.

In 735 Bede fell seriously ill. Still he labored strenuously to complete his works in progress, including an English-language translation of the Gospel of John. He dictated the final passages of his translation before expiring on May 25, 735.

There is a resemblance in Bede's work to the Acts of the Apostles. Just as *Luke relates the movement of the church from Jerusalem to Rome, so Bede continues the story from Rome to his own "fair and pleasant land." He believed that it was not only in Scripture but in the history of his own people and the stories of holy lives that the handwriting of God could be discerned. Reading this handwriting was his own path to sanctity. He is an inspiration to all who follow that path.

See: Bede, *A History of the English Church and Its People,* trans. Leo Sherley-Price (Baltimore: Penguin, 1955).

May 26

St. Philip Neri
Founder of the Congregation of the Oratory
(1515–1595)

"No bond but the bond of love."

Philip Neri, the "Apostle of Rome," was one of the great figures of the Catholic Reformation. His influence is the more remarkable for the fact that he wrote no books, proposed no original theology, and inspired no school of spirituality. He simply radiated a spirit of joy and holiness, and so managed to elevate the spiritual level of his time.

Neri was born in Florence in 1515. Though his family was of modest means he faced the prospect of a significant inheritance from a rich relative. Nevertheless, following a dramatic conversion he spurned all worldly success and set off for Rome. Traveling without money, he had no special plan aside from a general desire to serve God. For some years he lived in a garret, earning enough from part-time tutoring to subsist on bread and olives. It was a time of prayer and preparation for some work which he had yet to discover.

The city of Rome at that time had fallen into a state of moral and spiritual disrepair. With a few exceptions the Renaissance popes were more distinguished for their patronage of art and their talent for intrigue and statecraft than for their spiritual example. The appointment of cardinals was determined by politics if not by nepotism. Altogether the city was in the sway of a deep cynicism with regard to the Christian message. Nevertheless, it was precisely in this atmosphere that Philip Neri gradually conceived of his vocation: nothing less than the reevangelization of Rome.

This was a fairly audacious undertaking. But with characteristic impulsiveness Neri decided to begin at once. To start with he would stand about on street corners striking up conversations with whomever he chanced to meet. Wherever he went, in shops or markets, he would widen his circle of acquaintances, finding a way in every conversation to introduce the topic of religion and to inquire about the state of his new friend's soul. So guileless was his personality and, as it turned out, so uncannily gifted was he at reading souls that his casual overtures frequently resulted in lifelong friendships. Such conversations often continued during a walk to a local church or to a hospital to visit the sick. Before long his reputation had spread and all types of people began to seek his company.

In 1550, when he was thirty-five, Philip acceded to the urging of his confessor that he become a priest. Instantly, he acquired a sizeable following of penitents who formed long lines outside his confessional. He began the practice of leading them on walking tours of the city, discoursing on spiritual matters, while stopping in at the seven great basilicas of Rome. Hundreds of people eventually flocked to these pilgrimages, and they began to take on the characteristics of a public spectacle. Many church officials scowled at the sight. But Philip acquired his share of friends in the Vatican who sensed that something important was at work. When Neri at one point felt inspired by the example of the Jesuits to join the overseas mission he was persuaded by his confessor that Rome would be his Indies. And so there he remained.

In an attic room above the church where he lived Philip used to entertain mixed groups of clergy and laity (predominantly laymen) for an evening of prayer and spiritual reflection. One of the group would be invited to stand up and give a presentation on some spiritual theme, to which the others would respond. They called themselves Oratorians, and this would be the genesis, ultimately, of a new congregation. The example of such "mixed" gatherings in which lay people were invited to "preach" aroused the suspicion of the Inquisition. Was Neri possibly propagating some kind of Protestant deviation right in the heart of Rome?

Philip emerged unscathed from his investigation. Eventually in 1575 his congregation received the endorsement of Pope Gregory XIII, who also provided the site for a new church. The constitutions of the Oratorians very much reflected Philip's preference for personal rather than juridical authority. His priests took no vows. They were to be bound by personal loyalty and a spirit of brotherhood. "If you want to be obeyed," he said, "don't give commands."

Countless miracles of healing and clairvoyance are credited to Philip in his life. On the feast of Pentecost 1544 he had experienced a strange mystical ecstasy in which it seemed that his heart was expanded by a sudden infusion of divine love. After this he was prone to extended periods of mystical communion, especially during Mass, in which his face seemed to shine with a supernatural quality.

He was widely revered as a saint, and like all saints Neri disdained such acclaim, but he had his own way of coping with it. He liked to dress in comical outfits, assume outlandish disguises, go about with only one side of his face shaved, or indulge in elaborate practical jokes. This was part of a deliberate campaign to keep people from putting him on a pedestal. At the same time it reflected his genuine playfulness and the joy he discovered in the spiritual life.

By the end of his life Neri was in many ways the spiritual heart of Rome. Not only his family of priests but bishops and cardinals — many of them alumni of his Oratory — made their way to his small room for spiritual counsel. His charitable works, especially in providing chaplains to the city hospitals, were well known to the people of Rome. On May 25, 1595, he spent a normal day of hearing confessions and receiving visitors. Before retiring, he simply said, "Last of all, we must die." He died that night.

The Oratory continued. One of its most famous sons was the English convert *John Henry Newman, who surprised many at the time by choosing the congregation of St. Philip Neri over the better-known Jesuits or Dominicans. Newman went on to establish the first English Oratories in Birmingham and London. But to anyone familiar with Newman's personality the attraction to Neri is unsurprising. Neri would certainly have appreciated the personal motto that Newman adopted for himself: "Heart speaks to heart."

See: Meriol Trevor, *Apostle of Rome: St. Philip Neri* (London: Macmillan, 1966).

May 27

Rahab
Faithful Prostitute

"I know that Yahweh, your God, has given this land to you. . . .
The news has frightened us, and everyone has lost courage because of you,
for Yahweh, your God, is God in heaven above as he is on earth below."
—Joshua 2:9–11

The name of Rahab, a Canaanite prostitute, is an unlikely addition to the list of biblical saints and heroes. And yet *St. James singles her out with Abraham as a model of faith in action. The author of Hebrews includes Rahab among the "mighty cloud of witnesses." *St. Matthew even includes her name in the genealogy of Jesus.

Rahab's story appears in the book of Joshua in connection with the siege of Jericho. We are told that when Joshua sent spies to look over the Canaanite city the two men sought shelter in the house of "a harlot whose name was Rahab." Apparently her house, which abutted the walls of Jericho, afforded a useful view of the city and its defenses. When the king's own informants detected the arrival of the men of Israel, he commanded Rahab to deliver them. Instead she hid the spies and lied about their presence. But before doing so she struck a deal with the fugitives. She had heard of the escape of Israel from Egypt and of the prior victories in Canaan. She confessed her fear of Yahweh and expressed her belief that "Yahweh is he who is God in heaven above and on earth below." In exchange for sheltering these spies she exacted a promise that they would protect the lives of her family and herself. And so the two men survived to make their report. Joshua in turn remembered the oath and made certain that Rahab and her family were delivered from the town before it was destroyed. She lived out the rest of her life among the people of Israel.

Evidently the authors of Scripture were able to draw various meanings from the story of Rahab. According to James, Rahab illustrates his point about salvation by works: "Was she not justified by her works when she harbored the messengers and sent them out by a different route? Be assured, then, that faith without works is as dead as a body without breath" (James 2:25–26). But there are, as well, other lessons to be drawn from the story of Rahab. Rahab was not a penitent or "reformed prostitute" when she stepped forward to betray her social world and to identify with its enemies. Nevertheless, as one whose profession placed her among the outcasts of society, she had responded with special interest to the story of the Exodus and of the covenant Yahweh had formed with the runaway Hebrew slaves. She chose to defect, to change sides, to worship the God who led slaves to freedom.

Rahab's is the story of a marginalized "outsider" who, by her courageous deeds and faith in the promises of Yahweh, the Lord of history, was raised to a place of honor among God's special servants.

See: Joshua 2; Judette A. Gallares, *Images of Faith: Spirituality of Women in the Old Testament* (Maryknoll, N.Y.: Orbis, 1992).

May 28

Walker Percy
Novelist (1916–1990)

"The search is what anyone would undertake if he were not sunk in the everydayness of his own life.... To become aware of the possibility of the search is to be onto something. Not to be onto something is to be in despair."

The two great vocational decisions in Walker Percy's life were to become a Catholic and to be a writer. Although the two decisions were not formally related, his religious conversion had a good deal to do with the kind of writer he became. He did not write "religious" novels in the usual sense. But his novels were crucially shaped by a certain Catholic understanding of reality and of the meaning and destiny of human existence.

Percy was born in Birmingham, Alabama, on May 28, 1916, to a distinguished southern family. When he was twelve his father committed suicide. His mother died soon after in an accident, and Percy was adopted and raised by his uncle, a lawyer and poet. After college he went north and studied medicine at Columbia. In 1942, during a residency in pathology, he contracted tuberculosis and had to spend the next five years confined to bed in a series of sanataria. While all the world was plunged in war, Percy lay on his back, reading and thinking intensely about the paradoxes and absurdities of the modern world. He read everything he could get his hands on by *Kierkegaard, as well as novelists like *Dostoevsky, Kafka, and *Tolstoy. Ultimately he believed the Catholic doctrines of sin, grace, and redemption offered the best explanation of human existence. In 1946, after his release from the sanatarium, he became a Catholic.

This left many questions open about what to do with his life. The one thing he was sure of was that he had no interest in practicing medicine. Fortunately, an inheritance spared him the immediate necessity of earning a living. Instead he married and settled in New Orleans and continued to devote himself to serious reading. As his children were born and went on to school it became something of an embarrassment to explain what their father did. He read. But his reading was directed to a purpose. He was, as he later wrote of one of his characters, "onto something."

Percy was obsessed by those characteristics which one of his heroes, *Pascal, ascribed to modern humans: boredom, anxiety, and dread.

> Why does man feel so sad in the twentieth century? Why does man feel so bad in the very age when, more than in any other age, he has succeeded in satisfying his needs and making over the world for his own use?... Why is it that the only time I ever saw my uncle happy during his entire life was the afternoon of December 7, 1941, when the Japanese bombed Pearl Harbor?

In 1954 Percy began to publish his first writings, dense philosophical essays in obscure professional journals. But he began to think about the possibility of writing about his ideas in a more popular form. The result was his first novel, *The Moviegoer*, which appeared in 1961 when he was forty-four. It won the National Book Award. A massively entertaining story of a young man, Binx Bolling, and his difficulty in deciding what to do with his life, *The Moviegoer* dealt with themes that would surface in all his subsequent novels. In particular, it explored the difficult human challenge of remaining fully *alive* while avoiding the lure of everydayness, routine, and despair.

Subsequent novels assumed an increasingly comic and sometimes cynical tone. Percy was an astute social critic. Among the targets on which he trained his fire were social scientists who seek to reduce the mystery of human beings to the status of "an organism in an environment"; the culture of consumerism with its idolatry of the self and its ultimate capacity to empty the self of any meaning; the hubris of scientists who claim to fathom the logic of the universe, and yet have no explanation for the human heart; and the sentimental pieties of those liberals who, in the name of "quality of life," are willing to countenance euthanasia and abortion. To his critics he often sounded like an angry curmudgeon. To his admirers he was a modern prophet — in many ways out of step with his culture and thus able to see it with uncommon clarity. "Is it too much to say that the novelist...is one of the few remaining witnesses to the doctrine of original sin, the imminence of catastrophe in paradise?"

Though he wrote from a Christian perspective, Percy was convinced that it would no longer do simply to repeat traditional verities. One of the problems was the "devaluation" of Christian language. "The old words of grace are worn smooth as poker chips." Another matter was the moral failure of Christianity. In his own region he saw this especially in the churches' lack of appropriate response to the scandal of racial oppression. The challenge of the Christian writer, he believed, was first to help contemporary people to name their condition as one of alienation or despair. Secondly, the task was to point in the direction of an explanation: the fact that we are not in fact living in our true home. "The worst of all despairs is to imagine one is at home when one is really homeless."

Percy saw the greatest danger of our times to be the "devaluation of human life." Human beings, as he wished to show, were far from angels. They were, nonetheless, endowed with a sacred identity and destiny as "pilgrims, wayfarers on a journey." Their challenge was to recover their true humanity, to break loose from abstractions, ideologies, and the soul-deadening allure of self-gratification, and so to "reenter the lovely, ordinary world."

Percy died of cancer on May 10, 1990.

See: Walker Percy, *The Message in the Bottle* (New York: Farrar, Straus and Giroux, 1975); Robert Coles, *Walker Percy: An American Search* (Boston: Little, Brown, 1978).

May 29

G. K. Chesterton
Apologist (1874–1936)

"A characteristic of the great saints is their power of levity. Angels can fly because they can take themselves lightly."

G. K. Chesterton, born in Kensington, England, on May 29, 1874, was an imposing figure — over six feet tall, wide of girth, excitable, opinionated, and drawn to controversy. His friend George Bernard Shaw (with whom friendship was unimpeded by their disagreement on virtually every subject) described him affectionately as "a large abounding gigantically cherubic person who...seems to be growing larger as you look at him." Apart from his size, the most notable characteristic of G. K. Chesterton was his ability to combine gaiety and humor with a kind of deadly seriousness about the things that mattered.

Trained as an artist, Chesterton devoted his life instead to writing. He was a fantastically prolific author and editor, turning out poems, essays, editorials, and books of every sort. In one two-year period he published nine books. He was particularly popular for his successful detective series, the "Father Brown" stories. But he also wrote popular books on

*Blake, *St. Francis, and *Thomas Aquinas, as well as on social issues and religion.

Although famous as a Catholic apologist, Chesterton's formal conversion to Catholicism came only in 1922 when he was forty-eight. But he had been traveling in this direction for many years. One of his most famous books, *Orthodoxy,* a defense of traditional Christianity, was published in 1908. The book was inspired by the remark of a reader of his previous book, *Heretics,* who challenged him to state the standpoint from which he dismissed the views of everyone else. So he had set out to define his own religion, only to realize that a definition already existed in the creeds of Christianity. He compared this discovery to the embarrassment of an English yachtsman who miscalculated his course and "discovered England under the impression that it was a new island in the South Seas.... I am that man in a yacht. I discovered England."

One of the principles of orthodoxy that Chesterton affirmed was the value of Tradition. Though this principle was often regarded as contrary to the spirit of democracy, Chesterton argued otherwise: "Tradition is only democracy extended through time," he said.

> Tradition means giving votes to the most obscure of all classes, our ancestors. It is the democracy of the dead. Tradition refuses to submit to the small and arrogant oligarchy of those who merely happen to be walking about. All democrats object to men being disqualified by the accident of birth; tradition objects to their being disqualified by the accident of death.

Chesterton's populist views also extended to the social realm. He was an outspoken critic of capitalism and the modern culture of industrialism. An ardent patriot he was by the same principle a bitter opponent of imperialism. He called the annexation of the Transvaal in South Africa "a crime committed against the European virtue of patriotism. For a man has clearly no more right to say that his British patriotism obliges him to destroy the Boer nation than he has to say that his sense of the sanctity of marriage makes him run away with his neighbor's wife."

In his own journal, *G. K.'s Weekly,* Chesterton was a champion of what he called Distributism. This represented a kind of economic democracy, based on principles of decentralization of property and power. The popularity of Chesterton's journal, however, rested less on the acceptance of his ideas than on the attractiveness of his "voice" and his witty, epigrammatic style:

> Solemnity flows out of men naturally; but laughter is a leap. It is easy to be heavy: hard to be light. Satan fell by the force of gravity.

> The morality of a great writer is not the morality he teaches, but the morality he takes for granted.

> Despair does not lie in being weary of suffering, but in being weary of joy.

Chesterton never wearied of joy nor of the enjoyment of life, his friends, the love of his devoted wife, or his causes. But a body could endure only so much enjoyment. Chesterton died on June 14, 1936. Throughout his life, his views on religion, politics, and most public issues had set him among a small minority in his native land. And yet there were few literary figures of his day more widely admired, indeed beloved. In words that might have served as his own fitting epitaph Chesterton had described the saint as "a medicine because he is an antidote.... He will generally be found restoring the world to sanity by exaggerating whatever the world neglects."

See: Nigel Forte, ed., *A Motley Wisdom: The Best of G. K. Chesterton* (London: Hodder & Stoughton, 1995); Margaret Canovan, *G. K. Chesterton: Radical Populist* (New York: Harcourt Brace Jovanovich, 1977).

May 30
St. Joan of Arc
Maid of Orleans (1412?–1431)

"On being asked whether she did not believe that she was subject to the church which is on earth, namely, our Holy Father the Pope, cardinals, archbishops, bishops, and prelates of the church, she replied: Yes, but our Lord must be served first.*"*

Joan of Arc is one of the most attractive and intriguing heroes of history. Her life has been the subject of countless studies, as well as the inspiration for films, plays, novels, and poems. She has been claimed, variously, as a symbol of patriotism, military valor, and feminism, and as a martyr of conscience. At least since 1920, when she was formally canonized, she has also been claimed as a Christian saint. Just what kind of a saint remains the subject of debate. But among canonized saints she enjoys what is probably the unique distinction of having been previously condemned by the church and executed as a heretic. She thus may be legitimately claimed not only as a patron of France, but of all those holy men and women who have been vilified in their own time in the hope of eventual vindication.

Her familiar story remains compelling. As a young peasant girl in southern France, she claimed to hear the voices of the Archangel Michael, later joined by *St. Catherine of Alexandria and St. Margaret, charging her with a mission to save France by restoring the Dauphin to his rightful throne and driving the English enemy from French soil. It was partly a reflection of the desperate times that she managed to convince the Dauphin and his advisors to put her in command of his faltering army. She turned the tide of the war by successfully breaking the English siege on Orleans. Dressed in soldier's attire and brandishing the standard, she inspired the French troops to valor and managed a string of military victories which paved the way for the crowning of the Dauphin as Charles VII, King of France.

But from this pinnacle the wheel of fortune quickly turned. In a subsequent battle she was captured by Burgundian troops who sold her to their English allies. She was imprisoned for a year and subjected to an interminable interrogation by an ecclesiastical court sympathetic to the English cause. Though her fate was never in doubt, the court sought desperately to discredit her by finding evidence of heresy or witchcraft. Joan deflected their questions with guileless wit and impressed many with her evident faith and purity of heart. Throughout she held adamantly to the authority of her "voices," and she would not give up her male clothing. These were the bases on which she was eventually convicted.

On May 30, 1431, Joan was publicly burned at the stake. Her ashes were thrown in the Seine. She was nineteen years old.

In 1455 an official ecclesiastical investigation examined Joan's court proceedings and found her innocent of the charges against her. She was canonized 450 years later, a testimony to the longstanding interest in her cause. Even then, however, there was a certain vagueness about the kind of holiness she represented. Not wanting to call her a martyr, the church emphasized instead her piety and virginity.

There is no gainsaying Joan's purity and ardent faith. This accounts in part for the perennial fascination with her story: she epitomizes the confrontation between purity and the corruptions of power. But unlike traditional saints, she employed her piety not so much in the service of the church but in the cause of national liberation. She represents a kind of political holiness, not a "church" piety or the mystical rapture of the convent, but a mysticism expressed in commitment to the world and engagement in the events of history. In this, she was more like the Maccabean martyrs of Israel than her virginal patrons Sts. Catherine and Margaret. It is useless to speculate what supposed interest these saints might have had in the dynastic fortunes of France. But for us that is not the issue; Joan's "voices" spoke to her alone, and what is important is the courage of her response. Thus she inspires us to attend to the voices of our own angels and to respond with equal faith.

An illiterate peasant girl, a shepherd, a "nobody," she heeded a religious call to save her country when all the "somebodies" of her time proved unable or unwilling to meet the challenge. She stood up before princes of the church and state and the most learned authorities of her world and refused to compromise her conscience or deny her special vocation. She paid the ultimate price for her stand. And in doing so she won a prize far more valuable than the gratitude of the Dauphin or the keys of Orleans.

See: Marina Warner, *Joan of Arc: The Image of Female Heroism* (New York: Alfred A. Knopf, 1981).

Mary and Elizabeth
Feast of the Visitation

"In those days Mary arose and went with haste into the hill country, to a city of Judah, and she entered the house of Zechariah and greeted Elizabeth."

This day is unique. It does not commemorate a saint but an extraordinary meeting between two pregnant saints: *Mary, the mother of Jesus, and her kinswoman Elizabeth, the mother of *John the Baptist.

As recounted in *Luke's Gospel it was Mary who took the initiative for this "visitation," a journey of some distance from Nazareth. From the angel who had announced her own miraculous conception, Mary had learned that Elizabeth — "she who was called barren" — had also conceived a son "in her old age." The story suggests that Elizabeth's miraculous conception was a kind of guarantee of the promises made to Mary: "For with God nothing will be impossible." That might explain why Mary's first impulse was to visit Elizabeth, to see for herself the woman to whom she was strangely linked in God's mysterious plan.

When Elizabeth hears Mary's greeting she feels the babe in her womb leap for joy. "Blessed are you among women," she exclaims, "and blessed is the fruit of your womb."

Upon receiving this blessing Mary suddenly experiences a sudden insight into her own part in the unfolding and realization of all God's promises, especially as these relate to the poor and oppressed. She responds with an extraordinary prayer, the "Magnificat":

> My soul magnifies the Lord,
> and my spirit rejoices in God my Savior,
> for he has regarded the lowliness of his handmaiden....
> He has shown might with his arm,
> he has scattered the proud in the conceit of their hearts,
> he has put down the mighty from their thrones,
> and exalted the lowly;
> he has filled the hungry with good things
> and the rich he has sent empty away.

It is a remarkable and subversive vision in which the favor of God to two humble women is seen to presage a thoroughgoing process of social reversal: victory to the poor! defeat to their enemies!

The joy of that encounter is unclouded by any foreshadowing of the price to be paid. There is no hint that the kind of vision evinced in Mary's prayer will one day lead to the death of these two leaping babes. But that day will be a long way off. For now the feast of the Visitation remembers only the joy and celebrates the sisterhood of two women joined by their faith in the God of the Impossible.

See: Luke 1:39–56.

✥ JUNE ✥

June 1
Marguerite Porete
Beguine Martyr (d. 1310)

"I beg you, those who read these words, try to understand them inwardly, in the innermost depths of your understanding, with all the subtle powers at your command, or else you run the risk of failing to understand them at all."

It is hard to imagine any greater betrayal of the spirit of Christ than the impulse to crucify and burn one's enemies. Sadly, it is an impulse that the church itself, through a good part of its history, has found hard to resist. One such victim was the Beguine mystic and preacher Marguerite Porete.

What little we know of Marguerite Porete is preserved in the proceedings of the Inquisitorial court in Paris which condemned her as a heretic in 1310. The record and her writings suggests that, whatever her errors, she was a holy woman whose heart burned with the love of God. Of the men who condemned her, whatever may be said of their good intentions, it is hard to conclude otherwise than that they loved orthodoxy more than they loved Christ.

Marguerite was identified as a Beguine, that is, a member of a loosely organized religious movement of women popular in the Lowlands of her time. The origin of the term "Beguine" is disputed; among its opponents it served as a term of contempt, like the label of "heretic" itself or, more recently, "communist." Strictly speaking it referred to a network of small communities of Christian laywomen united in a life devoted to prayer and charity. These women sought to live quiet lives of devotion without taking religious vows, thus basically opting out of the economic and ecclesiastical structures of their society.

As religious women attempting to define a spiritual identity in the world without recourse to ecclesiastical approbation, the Beguines were subject to waves of persecution. But they also had their protectors. A number of well-known mystics were associated with the Beguines, including *Mechthild of Magdeburg and *Hadewijch, whose writings were widely read and admired.

Marguerite Porete was somewhat outside the usual mold in that she was apparently not based in a particular community, but chose to travel and publicly preach her spiritual message. She also wrote a book, *A Mirror* for *Simple Souls,* that describes her mystical spirituality. It was because of these ideas and her persistence in preaching that she was arrested by the Inquisition in Paris.

A Mirror for Simple Souls is a mystical discourse on divine charity, written in the form of a dialogue between the Soul and Reason. The aim of the book is to encourage the pursuit of spiritual perfection in a state of loving communion with God and one's neighbors. Addressed to "simple souls" it is anything but a simple work. The Inquisitors who examined her writing converted her poetic language into a series of propositions which were deemed heretical. As was often the case with mystics, she was accused of propagating a spirituality that dispensed with the church in favor of direct communion with God.

On April 11, 1310, a team of canon lawyers proclaimed her guilty of heresy. Her writings were publicly burned. On June 1, after being turned over to the secular arm for punishment, she was herself burned at the stake as an unrepentant heretic. Her death began a new wave of official persecution of the Beguines. Two years later the movement was formally suppressed.

See: A Mirror for Simple Souls: The Mystical Work of Marguerite Porete (New York: Crossroad, 1990).

June 2
Anthony de Mello
Priest and Spiritual Guide (1932–1987)

"Total presence in the now. Holiness!"

Anthony de Mello was an Indian Jesuit who achieved international fame for his writings and spiritual retreats. From his reading of the Gospels he discerned that Christ was not so much concerned with imparting doctrines to his listeners as in awakening them to new life and the offer of salvation that was in their midst. Through parables, symbolic actions, and teachings, Jesus constantly startled people out of their preconceived notions of religion. "Wake up!" — that was his message. It was a challenging message, and one that led him to the cross.

De Mello's own method of spiritual direction followed a similar style. Drawing on an eclectic fund of stories — borrowed from Hasidic, Zen, and Sufi masters, as well as from Jesus and the mystics of the West — he tried to awaken his listeners to the presence of God in their midst. The fact that his audience consisted of spiritual seekers did not make his task any easier. Most seekers were like the man who traveled all over the world on the back of a buffalo, seeking the definition of "buffalo"; or the fish who constantly sought to discover the meaning of the ocean. Just so, the person who constantly attended retreats and conferences to discover God.

De Mello's teaching was often expressed in simple definitions. *Theology:* "The art of telling stories about the Divine." *Mysticism:* "The art of tasting and feeling in your heart the inner meaning of such stories to the point that they transform you." But someone who preferred to memorize such definitions was like a ravenous person in a restaurant who devoured the menu instead of the meal. Christian doctrines were simply a finger pointing to the moon; they were misunderstood if they became the final object of our attention. The gospel, for de Mello, pointed us to the Truth that lies behind words, concepts, and images — to what the mystics liked to call "the God beyond god."

Enlightenment could not be received at second hand. The most eloquent report of the taste of a peach was no substitute for one's own experience of tasting the fruit. "In the land of the spirit, you cannot walk by the light of someone else's lamp," he said. "You want to borrow mine. I'd rather teach you how to make your own." True knowledge, saving knowledge, was in any case "to be transformed by what one knows."

DISCIPLE: "What's the difference between knowledge and enlightenment?"

MASTER: "When you have knowledge you use a torch to show the way. When you are enlightened, you become a torch."

De Mello was director of the Sadhana Institute of Pastoral Counseling in Poona, India. His books were originally published in India, and for many years he was little known outside of Jesuit circles. In the 1980s, however, foreign editions of his books began to appear, and he was in much demand as a retreat leader and spiritual director. Those who experienced his retreats often spoke of his authority, his extraordinary combination of peacefulness and energy, and his ability to make the familiar lessons of the gospel appear like startling revelations.

Among his writings, de Mello left many meditations on the theme of his own death. Such thoughts encouraged, simultaneously, a spirit of detachment and an appreciation for the preciousness of earthly existence. Thus, he was well prepared when he died suddenly of a heart attack on June 2, 1987, while preparing to deliver a series of conferences in New York. He was fifty-six.

To a disciple who was obsessed with the thought of life after death the Master said, "Why waste a single moment thinking of the hereafter?" "But is it possible not to?" "Yes." "How?" "By living in heaven here and now." "And where is this heaven?" "In the here and now."

See: Anthony de Mello, *The Song of the Bird* (New York: Image, 1984); *One Minute Wisdom* (New York: Doubleday, 1986); Thomas H. Stahel, "An Appreciation of Tony de Mello, S.J.," *America* (December 12, 1987).

Bd. John XXIII
Pope (1881–1963)

"The substance of the ancient deposit of faith is one thing,
and the way in which it is presented is another."

On October 28, 1958, a new pope greeted the church from the balcony overlooking St. Peter's Square. There stood the smiling, rotund figure of Angelo Giuseppe Roncalli, the son of peasants and recently the patriarch of Venice. "I am called John," he said.

In appearance and in almost every other respect Pope John XXIII stood in contrast with his predecessor. Whereas the late Pius XII had seemed gaunt and otherworldly, John was gregarious and open. He exuded an enthusiasm for life and an enjoyment for human company that in itself set a positive tone for his pontificate and raised hopes for a season of change. But hopes were modest. At seventy-seven, it was widely supposed that Pope John would be no more than a transitional pope, filling the chair of Peter until the next papal conclave. In the end he proved to be transitional in quite a different sense. In four and a half years he managed to bridge two utterly different eras in the history of the church. He broke with the fortress mentality of what *Karl Rahner called the "Pian era" and initiated a new era of openness and positive dialogue between the church and the modern world.

The decisive initiative came only three months after his election when Pope John casually mentioned his intention to convene an ecumenical council at the Vatican, the first such council since 1870 and only the second since the sixteenth-century Council of Trent. Despite the novelty of this announcement (which caught the Vatican curia off guard), there was little expectation of just how significant this event would be. But Pope John spoke of the need to "open the windows" of the church, to let in fresh air. The church was badly in need of what he called *aggiornamento,* or "updating."

In October 1962 Pope John addressed an assembly of twenty-five hundred bishops from around the world in words that set the tone for the sessions to come.

> In the daily exercise of our pastoral office, we sometimes have to listen — much to our regret — to voices of persons who, though burning with religious zeal, are not endowed with too much sense of discretion or measure. In these modern times they can see nothing but prevarication and ruin.... We feel we must disagree with these prophets of gloom. In the present order of things, divine providence is leading us to a new order of human relations which, by human effort and even beyond human expectation, are directed toward the fulfillment of God's higher and inscrutable designs; and everything, even human differences, leads to the greater good of the Church.

Unfortunately, it was the curial "prophets of gloom" who were largely responsible for setting the council's agenda. These Vatican bureaucrats, long accustomed to running the church, had prepared a series of documents that simply reiterated the standard Catholic "truths" in the age-old language of ecclesial documents. Conservative bishops, meanwhile, were eager to pronounce the condemnation of a whole new syllabus of modern errors.

But Pope John, as he made it clear, had a different agenda. "The Church has always opposed...errors," he said. "Nowadays, however, the Spouse of Christ prefers to make use of the medicine of mercy rather than that of severity." What he envisioned was a pastoral council, especially concerned with the cause of Christian unity, the promotion of peace, and his hope that the church might realize its true identity and vocation as a "church of the poor."

Otherwise, Pope John spoke little during the opening session. But he did intervene at what became a critical point in the proceedings. The first proposed document on Revelation was rejected by a majority of the bishops, but not by a sufficient number to table it definitively. Pope John personally directed that the document be returned for complete revision. This strengthened the resolve of the progressive majority of bishops to set aside the entire set of draft documents and start from scratch. They were aided by a team of theological experts, many of whom had only recently been subject to Vatican censorship, including Karl Rahner, *Yves Congar, *Henri de Lubac, and *John Courtney Murray.

Having launched the council, Pope John did not live to see it completed. Already he was suffering from a terminal cancer. His final months were spent in terrible agony. Nevertheless, he retained until the end his gracious humor and humility: "My bags are packed," he said, "and I am ready to go."

From his deathbed he dictated a final message to the church he loved:

Now more than ever, certainly more than in past centuries, our intention is to serve people as such and not only Catholics; to defend above all and everywhere the rights of the human person and not only those of the Catholic Church; it is not the Gospel that changes; it is we who begin to understand it better.... The moment has arrived when we must recognize the signs of the times, seize the opportunity, and look far abroad.

Pope John XXIII died on June 3, 1963. In a few brief years he had won the hearts of the world, and his passing was universally mourned. His beatification followed in 2000.

See: Peter Hebblethwaite, *Pope John XXIII: Shepherd of the Modern World* (Garden City, N.Y.: Doubleday, 1985).

Maurice Blondel
Catholic Philosopher (1861–1949)

"I propose to study action, because it seems to me that the Gospel attributes to action alone the power to manifest love and to attain God! Action is the abundance of the heart."

Maurice Blondel was a French Catholic philosopher who initiated a fresh approach to the relation between Christian faith and human existence. His work coincided with the so-called Modernist heresy, which was harshly condemned by the Vatican in 1907. Although Blondel's perspective was quite different from the Modernists, he was in his own way sharply critical of the dominant scholastic method in Catholic philosophy, with the result that he was often lumped in the category of suspect thinkers. But as a layman and a philosopher, Blondel fell outside the main sights of the Vatican censors, and his work escaped condemnation. In time, his insights were appreciatively received by *Karl Rahner and many of the Catholic theologians who reshaped the religious consciousness of the church at Vatican II.

Blondel's particular concern was what he called the "extrincism" of Catholic apologetics. The church tended to present revelation as God's communication of a set of "heavenly" truths. The church's main apologetic method was to establish the divine origin of this revelation, as certified by such miracles as the resurrection of Christ. Thus, the credibility of revelation depended entirely on its divine origin rather than on its actual content or its intrinsic relevance to human existence.

Blondel differed sharply with this approach. The very definition of saving truth, he believed, was that it must correspond to questions and yearnings rooted in the human heart. Thus, instead of "extrincism," he proposed a "method of immanence." This was an effort to show how the logic of human existence itself pointed to the presence of the transcendent in human life.

This method was the focus of Blondel's dissertation and major work, *L'Action.* By action Blondel referred to the whole range of human willing, choosing, and doing through which human beings affirm and determine their identity in history. He believed that in each of our actions there is an implicit reference to the absolute and infinite reality in which existence is grounded. Ultimately our lives are characterized by a choice — whether to open ourselves to the dimension of infinite being or to become closed in on ourselves. This choice is offered to all human beings. The Christian gospel names it explicitly in the life, death, and resurrection of Jesus. Thus, Christianity does not deal with a foreign and extrinsic message, but with Good News that resonates with the meaning of our deepest experience.

Blondel's argument bore far-reaching implications. It implied that faith did not concern simply some special "religious" aspect of life but referred to a dimension of all human experience. It suggested that revelation was not a communication of "divine truths" but a matter of God's self-disclosure and the invitation to participate in the divine life. Blondel's work definitely suggested that grace and salvation were not enclosed within the church, but were freely available everywhere. To the extent that these and other insights were reflected in the documents of Vatican II, Blondel deserves to be recognized as one of the seminal Catholic thinkers of the twentieth century.

By 1927 Blondel had become virtually blind. This ended his career as a professor at Aix-en-Provence. Nevertheless he went on to dictate ten major volumes over the next twenty years. As his health allowed, he attended daily Mass throughout his life. In 1945 he received a letter from Pope Pius XII congratulating him on his philosophical work, which "you have carried on with a talent equalled only by your faith."

Blondel died on June 4, 1949. At his funeral the archbishop of Aix said: "It is in seeing Maurice Blondel that I have understood what it means to be in the Church."

See: Maurice Blondel, *The Letter of Apologetics and History and Dogma,* trans. Alexander Dru and Illtyd Trethowan (Grand Rapids: Eerdmans, 1994); Gregory Baum, *Man Becoming* (New York: Seabury, 1970).

June 5

St. Boniface
Missionary and Martyr (c. 675–754)

"This now is that very day we have long dreamed of. That moment of freedom we have yearned for is right here. So be heroic in the Lord and suffer this royal grace of his will gladly. Keep your trust in him and he will set your souls free."

St. Boniface, one of the great figures in the annals of Christian mission, spent the first half of his life as a monk in England. When he was about forty, however, he was seized by a missionary fervor. Unlike the Irish monks, for whom mission was largely a vehicle to the ascetic discipline of pilgrimage, Boniface's primary interest was in evangelization. An Anglo-Saxon by birth, he felt a keen desire to return to his family roots and to convey the gospel to the Saxon people, still unpersuaded by the spreading Christian religion. After a first mission to the Continent, where he preached to the non-Christian peoples of Frisia, Boniface traveled to Rome to present his mission to Pope Gregory II. From the pope he received a commission to return to Germany, to go forth "to those peoples who are still in the bonds of infidelity...to teach them the service of the kingdom of God by persuasion of the truth in the name of Christ, the Lord our God."

Boniface traveled widely in Hesse and Thuringia and soon achieved extraordinary results. Before long he was writing back to the English people, asking for their prayers and help in the conversion of those who "are of one blood and bone with you."

Though he sought to adapt Christianity as far as possible to the local culture, Boniface was adamant in opposing idolatry. In particular he deplored the worship of trees, a common feature of German folk religion. In 723, in a famous incident, Boniface took an ax to a tree dedicated to the god Thor. Such an action would not normally be an effective opening to dialogue. But apparently the deed was taken in its intended meaning — not so much as an act of wanton violence but as a contest to determine who had the more powerful god. A crowd of onlookers was aghast, expecting lightning bolts to rain down on Boniface for his sacrilege. But when he remained unscathed his act inspired a wave of conversions.

Boniface was eventually named a bishop and later archbishop of Mainz. Though he was a skilled administrator, Boniface's heart remained set on spreading the gospel. Nearing eighty, he received permission to leave administration of his cathedral in the hands of an assistant and to return to Frisia, his original mission field. There, with a group of followers, he was attacked by hostile non-Christians and brutally killed on June 5, 754. His dying words are cited above.

See: "The Life of St. Boniface," in Clinton Albertson, S.J., ed., *Anglo-Saxon Saints and Heroes* (New York: Fordham University Press, 1967).

June 6

St. Philip the Deacon
(first century)

"And the multitudes with one accord gave heed to what was said by Philip, when they heard him and saw the signs which he did."

According to the Acts of the Apostles, St. Philip, along with *St. Stephen and five others, was among the first deacons in the church, appointed to serve at table and to attend to the needs of widows and the poor. Little is known of Philip's career, but in his brief appearance in the New Testament he is associated with a critical moment in the church's expansion.

Following the martyrdom of Stephen and the ensuing persecution, the church in Jerusalem scattered. Philip crossed over into Samaria to preach the gospel. Among the Samaritans, a people despised by the Jews, he found a surprisingly receptive audience. So great was the response to Philip's preaching that *Peter and *John were sent to confirm his work. Meanwhile an angel instructed Philip to travel south toward Gaza. On the road he encountered an Ethiopian eunuch, a servant of the queen of Ethiopia, who was returning home from Jerusalem. When he discovered that the Ethiopian was reading the book of Isaiah, he asked, "Do you understand what you are reading?" "How can I, unless someone guides me?" replied the Ethiopian.

The text before them was about the Suffering Servant, a providential entry to the story of Jesus. As the two men traveled together the Ethiopian pointed out a body of water and asked whether he couldn't be baptized there on the spot. So "they both went down into the water, Philip and the eunuch, and he baptized him. And when they came up out of the water, the Spirit of the Lord caught up Philip; and the eunuch saw him no more, and went on his way rejoicing." Even if it may be surmised that the Ethiopian was a Jewish proselyte, this striking story foreshadows the subsequent spread of the gospel beyond the confines of Israel. Through Philip and his Ethiopian convert Africa is represented in the infancy of the universal church.

See: Acts 8:4–40.

June 7

Seattle
Chief of the Suquamish (1786?–1866)

"Humankind did not weave the web of life. We are but one strand within it. Whatever we do to the web we do to ourselves."

Seattle was born in a Suquamish village along the Puget Sound, sometime around 1786. As a child he witnessed the arrival of the first whites in the Northwest. They were trappers and traders who did not come to stay. But for Seattle and his people, it was the beginning of irrevocable change.

In his early twenties Seattle was named the chief of his tribe. By this time the early white visitors had opened the way for an ever-increasing stream of settlers. It fell to Seattle to set a strategy for dealing with these invaders and their insatiable claims. Seattle rejected the option of violent resistance and put his trust in the possibilities of peaceful dialogue. But as the full intentions of the whites became clear his goal was reduced simply to ensuring the survival of his people.

In 1830 Seattle and many of the Indians in Puget Sound converted to Christianity. As a leader of his people he tried to integrate the principles of his faith with the beliefs of his ancestors. But with each passing year it seemed that his traditional world was growing smaller. Ultimately, Seattle came to believe that the struggle with the whites really represented the contrast between conflicting spiritual values. In particular the Indians and the whites held to completely different understandings of the relationship between human beings and the earth.

The whites considered the land something to be bought and sold. As Seattle observed, "How can you buy or sell the sky, the warmth of the land? The idea is strange to us.... Every part of this earth is sacred to my people. Every shining pine needle, every sandy shore, every mist in the dark woods, every clearing and humming insect is holy in the memory and experience of my people.... We are part of the earth and it is part of us."

In 1855 Seattle signed the Port Elliott Treaty, which transferred ances-
tral Indian lands to the federal government and established a reservation
for Native American tribes in the Northwest region. The alternative, he
believed, was the extinction of his people. But he took the opportunity
to address a letter to President Franklin Pierce. It is a haunting and
prophetic document, often cited today by the proponents of ecology. It
certainly does reflect Seattle's profound ecological imagination, as well as
the spiritual vision in which it was rooted:

> We know that the White Man does not understand our ways. One
> portion of the land is the same to him as the next, for he is a
> stranger who comes in the night and takes from the land whatever
> he needs. The earth is not his brother, but his enemy, and when he
> has conquered it, he moves on.
>
> One thing we know, which the White Man may one day discover —
> our God is the same God. You may think now that you own Him
> as you wish to own our land; but you cannot. He is the God of hu-
> manity, and his compassion is equal for the red man and the white.
> The earth is precious to him, and to harm the earth is to heap con-
> tempt on its Creator.... Even the white man cannot be exempt from
> the common destiny. We may be brothers after all. We shall see.

Chief Seattle died on June 7, 1866, on the Port Madison Reservation near
the city which today bears his name.

See: "Chief Seattle's Message," in Robert Cooney and Helen Michalowski, eds.,
The Power of the People: Active Nonviolence in the United States (Philadelphia: New
Society Publishers, 1987).

June 8

Gerard Manley Hopkins
Jesuit Priest and Poet (1844–1889)

"The world is charged with the grandeur of God ... "

Gerard Manley Hopkins was born in England in 1844 into a prosperous
High Anglican family. He received a superb education, culminating in
studies at Oxford, where he was called "the star of Balliol" College. It
seemed he was destined for a brilliant and successful career, if not in the
family insurance business, then certainly as a scholar or man of letters.
But all these great expectations were dashed when he announced his decision in 1866 to become a Roman Catholic. In October he was received
into the church by *John Henry Newman.

It was over a generation since Newman had himself pursued the logic
of the Anglican renewal — the Oxford movement — into the church of
Rome. Yet the social stigma attached to Catholicism remained in force.
Catholics were not allowed to graduate from Oxford or Cambridge. And

so just a matter of months after receiving his Double First, Hopkins withdrew from the university.

Having thus stunned his friends and family Hopkins went for broke and entered the Society of Jesus — a move tantamount, in polite society, to joining a bizarre and foreign cult. Evidently Hopkins believed that in becoming a Jesuit he must entirely subordinate his literary interests to his religious vocation. And so he privately burned all his poetry.

It was nearly ten years before he wrote again. In 1875, as he was studying theology in Wales, he read a newspaper account of a terrible shipwreck off the coast of Kent. The *Deutschland* had been carrying a group of German Franciscan nuns who were escaping anti-Catholic persecution in their native land. As the ship foundered on rocks one of the nuns had been heard to cry, "Christ, come quickly!" When Hopkins's superior mentioned casually that the event ought to be memorialized, Hopkins took this as an authorization to resume his writing. The result was his epic poem "The Wreck of the *Deutschland*," one of the most remarkable poems in the English language. In compressed, highly charged language, he used the event of the nuns' death to describe the mysterious victory which Christ wrought by his passion and resurrection. The poem also displayed the distinctive and utterly original poetic voice that would characterize all of his subsequent verse:

> Thou mastering me
> God! giver of breath and bread;
> World's strand, sway of the sea;
> Lord of living and dead;
> Thou has bound bones and veins in me, fastened me flesh,
> And after it almost unmade, what with dread,
> Thy doing: and dost thou touch me afresh?
> Over again I feel thy finger and find thee.

Neither this nor any of his poems was published in his lifetime. Those friends with whom he shared his poems found them virtually unreadable, with their strange syntax and compressed rhythm.

Hopkins's life was spent in obscure religious assignments for which he displayed no particular aptitude. In 1884 he was sent to Dublin to teach classics at the Catholic University. He found it pure drudgery. Possessed of a nervous and hypersensitive constitution, he was frequently ill. At the same time he suffered wracking doubts about his abilities and the accomplishments of his life. All this — both his capacity for exhilaration and wonder in the face of creation and his tendency to desolation — was reflected in his poetry.

Hopkins had a profound appreciation for the sacramental character of the created world and its capacity to shine forth in witness to its Creator. Created things, simply by being what they were meant to be, gave praise to God. For human beings this was more complicated. The task of realizing our true vocation and identity did not come naturally; it required that our hearts, under the influence of grace, be conformed to the supernatural charity of Christ.

Each mortal thing does one thing and the same:
　　Deals out that being indoors each one dwells;
　　Selves — goes itself; *myself* it speaks and spells,
Crying *What I do is me: for that I came....*
　　...For Christ plays in ten thousand places,
Lovely in limbs, and lovely in eyes not his
　　To the Father through the features of men's faces.

Toward the end of his life, however, it was the voice of desolation that seemed to prevail. In a series of "Terrible Sonnets," poems that came "written in blood," "unbidden and against my will," Hopkins poured out his private sufferings. He was tormented by a sense of the utter waste and sterility of his life.

　　...birds build — but not I build; no but strain
　　Time's eunuch, and not breed one work that wakes.
　　Mine, O thou Lord of Life, send my roots rain.

For all his struggles, however, one thing was certain. The old doubts about the compatibility of his vocations as priest and poet were resolved. Poetry, his means of naming and replicating the sacramental nature of existence, was precisely his way of expressing his true being, and thus of returning praise to his Creator. Hopkins himself seemed to realize this in the end, when he wrote of "that year / Of now done darkness I wretch lay wrestling with (my God!) / my God."

　　Hopkins died of typhoid on June 8, 1889. His last words were, "I am so happy!"

See: *Poems and Prose of Gerard Manley Hopkins,* ed. W. H. Gardner (New York: Penguin, 1953); Margaret R. Ellsberg, *Created to Praise: The Language of Gerard Manley Hopkins* (New York: Oxford University Press, 1987).

June 9

St. Columba
Abbot of Iona (521–597)

"Unto this place, small and mean though it be, great homage shall yet be paid, not only by the kings and peoples of the Scots, but by the rulers of barbarous and distant nations with their peoples. The saints, also, of other churches shall regard it with no common reverence."

The early Irish church produced a host of great missionaries, monks who combined ascetic zeal with a penchant for the wandering life. Their travels were themselves a form of mortification, a reminder that as Christians they were exiled from their true home, and so should pass as strangers and sojourners in this world. St. Columba was one of these missionaries. In his case, however, the sojourn was not entirely voluntary.

　　Columba was born to a royal family in Donegal. He entered the monastic life as a boy and rose to become the abbot and founder of several important monasteries, including Derry and Kells. Tall and commanding, with a voice "so loud and melodious it could be heard a mile off," Columba combined natural charisma with monastic gifts for prayer and scholarship. He was also, it seems, endowed with a quick and violent temper. This was to play a role in his ultimate destiny.

Columba's troubles stemmed from his love of books. When his former master, St. Finnian, returned from a trip to Rome with a rare copy of *Jerome's psalter, Columba sought access to the precious book and took advantage of the opportunity to make a copy in his own hand. When Finnian learned of this he claimed that the copy by rights should also belong to him. The dispute was brought to King Diarmaid, overlord of Ireland, who ruled in favor of Finnian. "To every cow her calf," said the king, "and to every book its son-book."

Columba did not accept the judgment with grace. His anger was increased when a fellow clansman, sought by Diarmaid for killing one of his men during a hurling match, fled to Columba for asylum. Violating the monk's protective sanctuary, Diarmaid's soldiers seized the unfortunate renegade and slew him on the spot. There followed a bloody war between Columba's clan and the followers of Diarmaid, culminating in a battle in which three thousand lives were lost. Columba's role in encouraging this bloodshed is not clear, but the church held him to blame, and he certainly accepted moral responsibility: "Ill have I served the heavenly kingdom, and ill have I served Ireland in that I have caused the men of Ireland to shed one another's blood. Men lie dead through the pride of a man of peace." As restitution Columba uttered a public oath: "I will not rest till I have won for God the souls of as many men as have fallen in this battle."

And so in the spring of 593 Columba and a band of twelve monks set to sea in an open boat, a kind of wicker basket covered with leather. Their destination was unknown — some place out of sight of their beloved country. Columba was moved to tears as he bade farewell to the friends and followers who gathered on the shore: "It is like the parting of soul and body for me to leave my kinsmen and my fatherland, and go from them into strange and distant places in everlasting exile."

Their boat finally landed on Iona, a remote and barren island off the coast of Scotland. There Columba established a monastery that would, in time, achieve wide fame throughout Europe as one of the vital fonts of Celtic spirituality. It also played an important role in the evangelization of Scotland and northern England. Columba proved as good as his oath, making countless missionary journeys among the northern Picts. His great prize came in 574 when he converted King Brude of Inverness, and so brought a great number of his people into the church.

Columba lived in Iona for over thirty years. It seems that time and the austerity of his life had a soothing influence on his temper. Among his monks he was revered as a wise and holy father, a man of powerful prayer, and a scholar avidly devoted to the copying of manuscripts. In the wider church he was known as a tireless apostle and miracle worker. Though Ireland remained fixed in his heart and his prayers he found peace in his island exile. As Adamnan, his successor and biographer, observed: "In the midst of all his toils, he appeared loving unto all, serene and holy, rejoicing in the joy of the Holy Spirit in his inmost heart."

He died on Iona on June 9, 597, at the age of seventy-six.

See: Ian Bradley, *Columba: Pilgrim and Penitent* (Glasgow: Wild Goose Publications, 1996).

June 10

St. Margaret
Queen of Scotland (1046–1093)

"So thoroughly did her outward bearing correspond with the staidness of her character that it seemed as if she had been born the pattern of a virtuous life. I may say, in short, every word that she uttered, every act that she performed, showed that she was meditating on the things of heaven."

— Turgot

St. Margaret was one of the last members of the Anglo-Saxon royal family. After the Norman Conquest in 1066 she and her family took refuge in Scotland, where she found particular favor with her host, King Malcolm. They were married three years later when she was twenty-four. Margaret and Malcolm enjoyed an exceptionally happy union, resulting in eight children. It was happy also for the nation, for the queen used her influence to promote the virtues of faith, charity, and justice that she held dear. Malcolm especially came to honor her piety, and he gave her free rein to promote the practice of Christianity in his kingdom. Together they founded churches, monasteries, hospices, and almshouses throughout the land. As the monk Turgot, her admiring biographer, wrote of Malcolm: "He saw that Christ truly dwelt in her heart;... what she rejected he rejected;... what she loved, he for love of her loved too."

Margaret was particularly famous for her love of the poor. She spent much of her time personally attending to the sick. Each night she invited several dozen beggars to dine at her table, and she never sat down to eat before she had served her guests and washed their feet. During Advent and Lent the royal dining hall was crowded with three hundred poor men and women.

Aside from such works of charity, Margaret attended to the institutional life of the church. At her instigation the church in Scotland convened its first synod. Its purpose was to examine abuses and indifference among the clergy and to reconcile discrepancies between the liturgical calendar in Scotland and the rest of the Western church. Margaret herself played an important role in the discussions, sharing her interpretation of Scripture as well as principles of faith.

Margaret worked hard to curb the feuding and warlike proclivities of her people. But she was not able to prevent the frequent recurrence of conflict between Scotland and England. In 1093 Malcolm and their eldest son were killed in battle. Margaret was already on her deathbed. When she heard the news, she cried out, "I thank thee, Almighty God, that in sending me so great an affliction in the last hour of my life, thou wouldst purify me from my sins, as I hope, by thy mercy." She died soon afterward on November 16 (her official feast day). She was canonized in 1250 and, in 1673, named patron of Scotland (where the translation of her relics was long celebrated on this day).

See: G. Scott-Moncrief, *The Mirror and the Cross: Scotland and the Catholic Faith* (Baltimore: Helicon, 1960).

June 11
St. Barnabas
Apostle (first century)

"We are also men, of like nature with you, and bring you good news,
that you should turn from these vain things to a living God
who made the heaven and the earth and the sea and all that is in them."

St. Barnabas, one of the earliest missionaries in the church, played a vital role in spreading and translating the gospel to a gentile audience. His story appears in the Acts of the Apostles. There he is originally introduced as a Cypriot Jew named Joseph, whom the apostles renamed Barnabas ("Son of encouragement") after he sold his property and donated the proceeds to the church.

Though Barnabas was not one of the original Twelve, *St. Luke terms him an apostle on account of his having received a special commission from the Holy Spirit. One of his first and most fruitful contributions was to vouch for *St. Paul, the recent convert, who was still feared by the other apostles for his previous persecution of the church. Later Barnabas was sent on a preaching mission to Antioch. As his labors there bore fruit he sent for Paul to join him; together they implanted a thriving church. According to Acts, it was in Antioch that "the disciples were for the first time called Christians."

It was to this worshiping community that "the Holy Spirit said, 'Set apart for me Barnabas and Saul [Paul] for the work to which I have called them.' Then after fasting and praying they laid their hands on them and sent them off." So Barnabas and Paul set off on the first formal overseas missionary journey, first to Cyprus (where they converted a Roman proconsul) and then to the mainland of Asia Minor. They first preached to the Jews, but where they were rebuffed they began reaching out successfully to gentile audiences. In one town their Greek audience was so impressed with the missionaries that they worshiped Barnabas and Paul as the gods Zeus and Hermes. Only with difficulty did the two apostles prevent the crowd from offering them sacrifices.

The successful mission to the gentiles raised the question of whether these new converts must first be circumcised according to the Jewish law.

Paul and Barnabas opposed this practice and their argument carried the day at the Council of Jerusalem.

Barnabas and Paul planned to continue their mission, but on the eve of their departure a disagreement arose over whether to include another disciple, John Mark, in their party. Over this the two apostles parted. Paul, accompanied by Silas, went on to dominate the narrative of Acts, while Barnabas slipped off the pages of history.

Though positive knowledge is lacking, it seems that Barnabas, accompanied by John Mark, returned to Cyprus. There, according to legend, he was martyred in the year 61.

See: Acts of the Apostles 4–15.

June 12

Anne Frank
Witness of the Holocaust (1929–1945)

*"Who would ever think that so much can go on
in the soul of a young girl?"*

There are some persons whose great gift, in a dark age, is simply to maintain a candlelight of humanity and so to guarantee that darkness should not have the final word. Anne Frank, a Jewish child who perished during the Holocaust, was surely one of these. Her life was extinguished at the age of fifteen — thus contributing to the Nazi dream of a Jewish-free Europe. But her light continued to burn, thus fulfilling her own dream: "I want to go on living after my death."

Anne's story is well known. She was born on June 12, 1929. During the Nazi occupation of Holland, her family and another family, the Van Daams, took shelter in a "secret annex" in her father's office in the center of Amsterdam. They remained sequestered for two years. Keeping still all day, never able to leave their hidden quarters, they relied on the support of Dutch friends to preserve their secret, to bring them supplies and news of the outside world. Anne was thirteen when she entered the annex in July 1942. Besides her schoolbooks and her treasured scrapbook of Hollywood stars, Anne brought along with her a diary she had received for her thirteenth birthday. Addressing her daily entries to an imaginary girlfriend, "Kitty," Anne faithfully kept her diary throughout the course of her captivity. This diary was published after the war and was quickly acclaimed as one of the most deeply affecting artifacts of the Holocaust. But because of Anne's unusual gifts as a writer and because of the extraordinary qualities of her personality, her work merits recognition as a literary classic in its own right and as one of the great moral documents of the twentieth century.

For Anne herself keeping a diary was not simply a distraction but a duty, a responsibility to render her experience and her feelings in the most accurate possible terms. "I want to write, but more than that, I want to bring out all kinds of things that lie buried deep in my heart," she writes in the early pages. With remarkable skill Anne manages to describe the personalities and atmosphere in the annex — the strain of captivity and close quarters and the brave efforts to carry on with life. All this takes place against the backdrop of fear and the constant danger of discovery.

> I see the eight of us with our "Secret Annex" as if we were a little piece of blue heaven, surrounded by heavy black rain clouds. The round, clearly defined spot where we stand is still safe, but the clouds gather more closely about us and the circle which separates us from the approaching danger closes more and more tightly.

The diary is mostly a sharply recorded chronicle of the everyday trials and the modest joys of a young girl's life "underground." But it also contains Anne's remarkably unchildlike reflections on the meaning of life and faith in the face of adversity.

> The best remedy for those who are afraid, lonely, or unhappy is to go outside, somewhere where they can be quiet alone with the heavens, nature, and God. Because only then does one feel that all is as it should be and that God wishes to see people happy, amidst the simple beauty of nature. As long as this exists...I know that there will always be comfort for every sorrow, whatever the circumstances may be.

Lying in bed, she says she ends her evening prayers with the words, "I thank you, God, for all that is good and dear and beautiful," and adds, "I am filled with joy.... I don't think of all the misery, but of the beauty that still remains."

Aside from acknowledging the terror that prowls beyond her hiding place, the diary also reflects the mysterious unfolding of Anne's personality, her emergence from childhood, and her growing sense of herself as a person with a future and a task in the world.

> I know what I want, I have a goal, an opinion, I have a religion and love. Let me be myself and then I am satisfied. I know that I'm a woman, a woman with inward strength and plenty of courage. If God lets me live...I shall not remain insignificant, I shall work in the world and for mankind! And now I know that first and foremost I shall require courage and cheerfulness.

Rarely has anyone so well defined the virtues required by our age — "courage and cheerfulness" — as this fourteen-year-old girl already living under sentence of death.

In August 1944, soon after Anne's fifteenth birthday, the secret annex was betrayed and all its eight inhabitants were dispersed among the factories of death. Only Otto Frank, Anne's father, survived the war and returned to the old house in Amsterdam. He learned that his wife had died in January 1945 in Auschwitz, while Anne and her sister Margot had died of typhus in Bergen-Belsen in early March. Then he was presented with the diaries of his daughter, lovingly preserved by friends in hopes of her eventual return.

In light of her death it is excruciating to read Anne's intimate confidences, her account of the homey details of life in hiding. But through the girlish record of quarrels with her mother, worries about her studies, and the possibilities for finding romantic happiness with the Van Daams' teenage son, Otto Frank was the first to recognize in his daughter's diary a profound witness to the value of life and the virtue of hope. Words written days before her arrest only gain additional power in the light of her fate:

> In spite of everything I still believe that people are really good at heart....I see the world gradually being turned into a wilderness, I hear the ever-approaching thunder, which will destroy us too, I can feel the sufferings of millions and yet, if I look up into the heavens, I think that it will all come right....In the meantime, I must uphold my ideals, for perhaps the time will come when I shall be able to carry them out.

See: The Diary of Anne Frank (London: Pan, 1954).

June 13

St. Anthony of Padua
Doctor of the Church (1195–1231)

"O Sweet Jesus: what is there sweeter than Thee?
Sweet is Thy memory, sweeter than that of honey or any other object.
Thy very name is a Name of sweetness, a Name of Salvation.
For what does the name Jesus signify, if not Savior?
Therefore good Jesus, for Thy own sake be to us a Jesus."

St. Anthony is among the most popular of all saints. This has less to do with the memory of his spellbinding preaching than with his posthumous career as a miracle-worker. Throughout the centuries Anthony's intercession has been piously sought in matters great and small, with particular homage accorded his knack for locating lost objects. Lost amid this devotion has been much recollection of who St. Anthony was, apart from the fact (important to many of those who most honor his name) that he was Italian. (Actually, Portuguese.)

Anthony was born in Lisbon in 1195 and first entered religious life as an Augustinian canon in Coimbra. There one day he had occasion to wait on a group of five visiting Franciscans who were on the way to Morocco. Anthony was greatly impressed by these courageous missionaries, the more so when news came of their martyrdom and when their remains returned by way of his monastery.

At once Anthony was inspired to apply to the Franciscans. He was accepted and was even granted his wish to follow in the footsteps of the martyrs. But no sooner had he arrived in Morocco than he became so ill that he was forced to turn around. In Italy he attended the famous Franciscan chapter of 1221, the last one held during the lifetime of *St. Francis. It was also the last Chapter to which all Friars were invited and was thus, with three thousand brothers in attendance, a considerable jamboree. Afterward Anthony was assigned to a small hospice for lay brothers at Monte Paolo. It was a lowly assignment, befitting a brother who, up to this time, had shown no remarkable talents.

But soon Anthony's star would shine. When, on an important religious occasion, there was found to be no available preacher, Anthony was asked to extemporize. He proceeded to astonish his audience with the unexpected elegance, conviction, and profound learning of his sermon. Word quickly spread, and Anthony soon received a letter from Francis himself authorizing him to preach and to teach theology to the friars.

Eventually Anthony was sent on a preaching mission that covered all of Italy. Thousands flocked to hear his open-air sermons, and his visits had the impact of a spiritual revival. It was said that men gave up gambling and drinking at the sound of his melodious voice. Criminals were reformed. Feuding enemies were reconciled. For these effects, quite apart from the miracles that adorn his legend, Anthony earned his reputation as the "Wonder Worker."

Anthony's sermons integrated a message of spiritual uplift with a bold challenge to the social vices of the day, especially greed and the practice of usury. He attacked the tyranny of the powerful and was unsparing when it came to the failings of the clergy. "You there, with the mitre!" he addressed one visiting archbishop, apparently in particular need of a prophetic word. He volunteered for hazardous mission tours among the Catharist heretics in southern France. And so successful were his exhortations to charity wherever he preached that he was also well known by the title, "Friend of the Poor."

Weary from his exhausting mission, Anthony died on June 13, 1231, at the age of thirty-six. He was buried in Padua, the city where he had spent the last years of his life. It is a measure of his popularity that Anthony's canonization followed only one year after his death. In 1946 Pope Pius XII declared him also a Doctor of the Church.

See:: Raphael M. Huber, *St. Anthony of Padua* (Milwaukee: Bruce, 1948).

June 14

St. Basil the Great
Bishop and Doctor of the Church (330?–379)

> *"Are you not a robber, you who consider your own*
> *that which has been given you solely to distribute to others?*
> *This bread which you have set aside is the bread of the hungry;*
> *this garment you have locked away is the clothing of the naked;*

those shoes which you let rot are the shoes of him who is barefoot;
those riches you have hoarded are the riches of the poor."

St. Basil was raised in a family of saints. His grandmother, his parents, his brothers and sister (including *St. Gregory of Nyssa and *St. Macrina) all came to be canonized. And yet there was nothing inevitable about his religious vocation. Though his family was pious they were also quite wealthy. By his own account Basil's early life was given over to "vanity." He received a classical education in Constantinople and Athens, studying philosophy and rhetoric. He was nearly thirty when he experienced a conversion, which he described as "waking from a profound sleep." As he wrote, "I opened my eyes to the wonderful life of the evangelical truth." Immediately he resolved to abandon worldly ambitions and devote himself to God.

Basil made a tour of the monastic communities in Egypt, the Holy Land, Syria, and Mesopotamia, before settling into a monastery near his hometown of Caesarea. He spent five years there — long enough to devise a rule that had a revolutionary influence on the development of monasticism. Unlike the early monks whose spirituality focused on individual feats of asceticism, Basil stressed the importance of community. The monastery was more like an ideal society, a place in which the love of God and the love of neighbor could be cultivated in tandem. As he wrote, "A community of brothers is a stadium in which athletes are exercised.... Its end is the glory of God according to the commandments of God."

At the same time, he believed the monastery should be clearly integrated into the life of the church and the society. Rather than existing in isolation, the monastery should welcome guests; it should include orphanages and schools; it should be a center of service and the works of mercy. For Basil the monastery did not exist for the sanctification of its members alone, but for the wider community.

In order to better serve the church Basil agreed to be ordained. Afterward he divided his time between monastic life and priestly duties. In 370 he was elected bishop of Caesarea. In this office he served as a pastoral leader to the local church while also emerging as one of the most important champions of theological orthodoxy. With his brother *Gregory of Nyssa and his lifelong friend Gregory of Nazianzus he became known as one of the Cappadocian fathers. Together they effectively countered the Arian heresy by their persistent teaching on the theology of the Trinity.

As a trained rhetorician, Basil became famous for his preaching and exposition of the Scriptures. But as a bishop he was even more distinctive for his heavy emphasis on the social aspects of the gospel. During times of famine he organized soup kitchens, personally donning an apron to wait on the hungry. He established a hospital for the sick poor that was described as one of the wonders of the world. Constantly he referred to the teaching of Christ, who so united the precepts of love of God and neighbor "that He refers to Himself the good deeds of which our neighbor is the object: 'For I was hungry, and you gave me to eat.'"

Basil, however, went beyond the usual exhortation to charity, calling for a basic redistribution of wealth as a demand of justice. In effect, he taught that the needs of the poor held a social mortgage on the superfluous holdings of the rich. Thus he challenged the well-to-do in unusually outspoken terms:

> You refuse to give on the pretext that you haven't got enough for your own needs. But while your tongue makes excuses, your hand convicts you — that ring shining on your finger silently declares you to be a liar! How many debtors could be released from prison with one of those rings?

Exhausted by his own labors and austerities, Basil died on January 1, 379, at the age of forty-nine. He was quickly acclaimed as a saint and later named a Doctor of the Church. (St. Basil's feast day, formerly celebrated on June 14, has moved to January 2.)

See: Louis Bouyer, *A History of Christian Spirituality,* vol. 1 (New York: Seabury, 1963).

June 15

St. Germaine Cousin
Shepherdess (1579–1602)

"I have what God wished me to have, and I want no more."

St. Germaine was a peasant girl from the village of Pibrac, near Toulouse. Her mother died in childbirth, and she was raised by an unloving father and a stepmother who made no effort to conceal her positive dislike for the girl. To keep Germaine away from her own children her stepmother forced Germaine to sleep in the stable or under the stairs, kept her busy with chores, and fed her on table scraps.

Despite the drudgery and injustice of her life, Germaine accepted every insult with cheerfulness and love. She especially welcomed the task of tending her father's sheep, as this afforded an opportunity for undisturbed prayer and communion with God. As she stood watch in the fields, God "spoke to her soul as He speaks to the humble and clean of heart, and she lived ever consciously in His presence."

Germaine was faithful in attending daily Mass. When she heard the bells ringing she would plant her crook in the ground and hasten to church, entrusting the flock to her guardian angel. Invariably she found them safe and sound.

In time Germaine acquired a reputation for holiness among her neighbors. This won her no special privileges at home. Indeed, she was harshly punished for sharing her table scraps with more unfortunate beggars. Even her stepmother was caught short, however, when she confronted Germaine on a winter's day and forced her to open her apron, expecting to find there some missing bread. Instead there fell a cascade of spring flowers.

Afterward her family grudgingly invited Germaine to accept a proper bed in the home. But this real-life Cinderella preferred her humble place beneath the stairs. There one morning she was found dead at the age of twenty-two. Her grave soon became a popular object of pilgrimage. She was canonized by Pope Pius IX.

See: Henri Ghéon, *St. Germaine of the Wolf Country* (New York: Longman, Green, 1932).

June 16
John Howard Griffin
Author of *Black Like Me* (1920–1980)

"I go to live on the other side of the river, hoping to find that it is no different from this side, and that we can no longer justify demonizing man for such false reasons."

In 1959 John Howard Griffin traveled to New Orleans. There, with the help of drugs, dyes, and radiation, he darkened his skin, shaved his head, and "crossed the line into a country of hate, fear, and hopelessness — the country of the American Negro." For two months he traveled through the Deep South, later publishing his observations in a magazine series and the widely acclaimed book *Black Like Me.* Griffin's effort to cross the color line was the most dramatic gesture in a life devoted to radical empathy. But for Griffin it was simply another exploration of the concern that preoccupied him throughout his life — the struggle to discover what it means, finally, to be a human being.

Born in Texas on June 16, 1920, Griffin was educated in France, where he studied medicine and music until the outbreak of World War II. After the German occupation he helped run a network smuggling Jews out of the country and narrowly escaped arrest by the Gestapo. He spent most of the war in military service in the South Pacific. Toward the end of the war a nearby explosion impaired his vision and eventually left him completely blind. The experience of blindness and severe illnesses that visited him throughout his life imposed a stark choice — either to give in to despair or to trust in some higher purpose. "Tragedy," he wrote, "is not in the condition but in man's perception of the condition." Despite his handicap, Griffin went on to study music, married and raised a family, tried his hand at ranching, and wrote two novels. The year his second novel was published he entered the Roman Catholic church.

Then in 1957 something miraculous happened. A blockage of the circulation of blood to the optic nerve suddenly opened, restoring his sight. He saw his wife and two young children for the first time. For some years he had been studying theology, and in his journal he described the joy he felt in being able to read the Divine Office: "The soul's nourishment, the soul's normalcy, sinking beyond the words to their innermost meaning, seeking and thirsting for it.... This morning, then, the tired brain, the battered brain conceived the idea of reading the clear black type of the Office. And therein found full reason and justification for seeing again."

With the return of his sight Griffin became aware of how much we do not see, of the way superficial appearances can serve as obstacles to true perception — especially in the illusion that allows us to regard our fellow humans as "the intrinsic other." Nowhere did this seem so true as in the case of American racism. Yet Griffin was struck by the frequent challenge from black friends: "The only way you can know what it's like is to wake up in my skin." He took these words to heart. The result was the journey recorded in *Black Like Me*.

The book received and sustained enormous attention, though not all readers recognized it as a deeply spiritual work. Griffin's concerns went beyond a set of social conditions to the underlying disease of the soul. His book was really a meditation on the effects of dehumanization, both for the persecuted and the persecutors themselves. As he described it, he had changed nothing but the color of his skin — and yet that was everything. Suddenly doors closed, smiles became frowns — or worse. He discovered the hateful face that white Americans reserved for blacks; it was a devastating experience. "Future historians," he wrote later, "will be mystified that generations of us could stand in the midst of this sickness and never see it, never really feel how our System distorted and dwarfed human lives because these lives happened to inhabit bodies encased in a darker skin; and how, in cooperating with this System, it distorted and dwarfed our own lives in a subtle and terrible way."

After his story was published, Griffin was exposed to a more personal form of hostility. His body was hung in effigy on the main street of his town. His life was repeatedly threatened. Nevertheless he threw himself into a decade of tireless work on behalf of the growing civil rights movement. Necessity forced him, much against his nature, into the role of activist. "One hopes," he wrote, "that if one acts from a thirst for justice and suffers the consequences, then others who share one's thirst may be spared the terror of disesteem and persecution." And so he persevered with those who shared "the harsh and terrible understanding that somehow they must pit the quality of their love against the quantity of hate roaming the world."

For years Griffin suffered from a range of afflictions, some possibly induced by the skin treatments he had undergone years before. He died (of "everything," according to his wife) on September 8, 1980.

What finally was the meaning of his life? "The world," he once wrote, "has always been saved by an Abrahamic minority.... There have always been a few who, in times of great trouble, became keenly aware of the underlying tragedy: the needless destruction of humanity."

See: Robert Bonazzi, *Man in the Mirror: John Howard Griffin and the Story of Black Like Me* (Maryknoll, N.Y.: Orbis, 1997); Bradford Daniel, ed., *The John Howard Griffin Reader* (Boston: Houghton Mifflin, 1967).

June 17

John Wesley
Founder of Methodism (1703–1791)

"How far is love, even with many wrong opinions, to be preferred before truth itself without love? We may die without the knowledge of many truths and yet be carried into Abraham's bosom. But if we die without love, what will knowledge avail? Just as much as it avails the devil and his angels."

In January 1738, as he returned to England from a bleak stint as an Anglican missionary in the colony of Georgia, John Wesley fell to examining his conscience. Sadly he confessed "that I, who went to America to convert others, was never myself converted to God." It was a dismal insight for the thirty-four-year-old cleric, and one that would have puzzled all those who had known him, since his youth, to be exceptionally pious and determined in his religious practice. Wesley had prayed and fasted and studied and sacrificed for the gospel. But all the time, dogging his efforts, there was the sense that he lacked "one thing necessary."

He was born on June 17, 1703, to a deeply religious family. His father was a high-church Anglican priest, and his mother, Susanna, was also famed for her devotion. John and his brother Charles both studied at Oxford and received holy orders. There, dissatisfied with a merely formal adherence to the faith, they had formed a study circle of zealous Christians who were known by such mocking sobriquets as the Bible Moths or, on account of their strict and methodical piety, "Methodists."

Rather than go in for parish work, John felt called to become a missionary and preacher. So he responded eagerly to an opportunity to travel to the colony of Georgia under the auspices of the Society for the Propagation of the Gospel. His ostensible mission was to preach among the Indians, but he never ventured far from the English colony in Savannah. He was a singularly ineffective preacher, and within months his Anglican flock had virtually booted him out of the colony.

Back home, he continued doggedly to pursue his calling as an itinerant preacher, but with little more success. With depressing frequency, as his journals record, his efforts were rewarded with the warning, "Sir, you must preach here no more."

Wesley was convinced of his calling to serve in the vineyard of the Lord. But the tepid reception that he encountered echoed a private sense of his own unworthiness. The turning point for Wesley came in a famous experience at a mission on Aldersgate Street on the evening of May 24, 1738. There, as he listened to someone reading Luther's "Preface to the Epistle to the Romans" — a text concerning the change God works in the heart through faith in Christ — he wrote that "I felt my heart strangely warmed. I felt I did trust in Christ, Christ alone for salvation; and an assurance was given me that he had taken away *my* sins, even *mine,* and saved *me* from the law of sin and death."

In this experience Wesley was infused with the love of God. This literally "heart-warming" assurance brought a new dimension to his faith and his preaching that enabled him in turn to warm the hearts of countless others. Thus, Wesley found his voice as an evangelist and preacher, imparting to those who heard him the perception that Christianity was not so much a religion of laws and doctrines but of love. This message was particularly welcomed by the poor, who flocked in fantastic numbers to his outdoor sermons. He was said to have addressed crowds of as many as twenty thousand people, an impressive accomplishment in the era before loudspeakers. Over his life he traveled a quarter of a million miles on horseback, covering the length and breadth of England on his preaching missions. "The whole world," so he liked to say, "is my parish."

The Methodists, as his followers were known, remained for many years a revival movement within the Anglican church. The relationship suffered strain, however, and eventually came to separation when Wesley undertook to ordain clergy for the North American colonies. The spirit of Methodism, as it took root in the lower classes, combined an affective piety with earnest morality. This extended also to issues of social reform; Wesley himself was an ardent opponent of slavery and a champion of prison reform.

Although Wesley staked out a distinct theological position on such issues as free will, the relation between faith and good works, and the salvation of all believers, he remained exceptional for his open-mindedness toward other churches and denominations. Indeed, he might well be regarded as a prophet of the ecumenical movement. As he wrote, "Though we cannot think alike, may we not love alike? May we not be of one heart, though we are not of one opinion?" In meeting a Christian of a different denomination, his first question was not about doctrine or polity, but only this: "Is thine heart right, as my heart is with thy heart?...If it be, give me thy hand."

After many hard years laboring in the vineyard, John Wesley died on March 2, 1791, at the age of eighty-eight.

See: Albert C. Outler, ed., *John Wesley* (New York: Oxford University Press, 1964).

June 18

St. Ephrem the Syrian
Doctor of the Church (306?–373)

"The Lord Himself became true altar, priest, and bread and chalice of salvation. He alone sufficeth for all, yet none for Him sufficeth. Altar He is and lamb, victim and sacrificer, priest as well as food."

St. Ephrem was born in Nisibis in Mesopotamia around 306. As a young man he was baptized as a Christian and later ordained a deacon. He apparently declined any further advancement, even feigning madness as a way of avoiding episcopal consecration. In 363, when Nisibis fell to the Persians, Ephrem, along with the rest of the Christian population, took flight. He settled in Edessa (in present-day Iraq), where he lived in a remote cave and spent the rest of his life in monastic seclusion.

Despite his retirement from the world, Ephrem made an important contribution to the church through his writings and musical compositions. He was largely responsible for demonstrating that poetry and hymns could be a mode of theological discourse. Though not greatly learned, he was skilled in translating orthodox theology into liturgical hymns, sometimes borrowing melodies from popular songs of the day. Aside from hymns extolling such mysteries as the Incarnation, the Virgin Birth, and the Immaculate Conception of Mary, Ephrem wrote hymns against various heresies of the day. One of his favorite topics was death and the Last Judgment. His vivid depictions of heaven and hell later influenced the writings of *Dante. For his hymns Ephrem became known as "the Harp of the Holy Ghost."

Shortly before his death he left his cave to administer relief to the victims of a terrible famine. In this role he combined effective leadership with acute compassion, so that it was said by one of his contemporaries, "God gave him this occasion to win the crown in the close of his life." He survived the ordeal by only a month and died in 373. (His feast day, formerly June 18, is now celebrated on June 9.)

See: Ephrem the Syrian, *Hymns,* Classics of Western Spirituality (New York: Paulist, 1989).

June 19
John Lord Acton
English Catholic Historian (1834–1902)

"Power tends to corrupt, and absolute power corrupts absolutely."

Lord Acton was one of the outstanding historians of the Victorian Age. A pious Catholic, fiercely loyal to the doctrines of the church, he was also a staunch liberal, equally committed to the principles of truth, liberty, and the rights of conscience. Much of his career was spent in an effort to reconcile these values, an effort that was ill-appreciated by most of his contemporaries in the church, and similarly misunderstood by most of his secular allies.

Acton was born in 1834, a scion of the minor Catholic aristocracy in England. Since Catholics were not permitted to study at the great universities of Cambridge or Oxford, he was sent in 1850 to Munich, where he became the protégé and longtime friend of Father Ignaz von Dollinger — at the time the most distinguished Catholic historian in Europe. Dollinger was also at the center of a liberal movement seeking to infuse the church with a more historical consciousness. Acton became his eager disciple, inspired by his study of the historicity of dogma and the evolution of church institutions like the papacy.

In 1858 he returned to England, where the Catholic church lagged far behind the critical spirit at loose on the Continent. Acton took it upon himself to raise the intellectual standards of his native church. To this end he became involved in editing a series of liberal Catholic journals, beginning with *The Rambler*. At a time when there was great suspicion about the political agenda of Catholics in England, Acton became an eloquent apologist for the rapprochement between Catholicism and liberty. His slogan was "A free Church in a free State." At the same time, his tendency to sarcasm and his evident disdain for those church authorities whom he deemed guilty of ignorance and obscurantism undermined potential support for his projects.

There was little precedent or tolerance in the church for the role of loyal critic, and Acton's self-assurance in speaking his mind was a source of astonished irritation to the hierarchy. He constantly criticized the alliance between the church and reactionary political causes; he challenged the church's claims to the Papal States and urged the pope to renounce all temporal power, the source, he believed, of much corruption. These positions were such a provocation to conservatives that he was eventually forced to suspend publication of his journals or else face condemnation.

That same year, 1864, Pope Pius IX issued the *Syllabus of Errors,* an inventory of propositions to be condemned. Among these were the opinion that the church should renounce its temporal power and rely upon spiritual rather than coercive authority; that it was desirable that there should be a separation of church and state, freedom of the press, and freedom of worship; and finally that "the Roman Pontiff can and ought to reconcile himself to and agree with progress, liberalism, and modern civilization."

Rather than yield quietly to this challenge, Acton set himself to writing a series of essays chronicling such stains on the Catholic conscience as the violence of the Inquisition and the church-authorized massacre of French Huguenots on St. Bartholomew's Day in 1572. Resolutely opposed to the idea that the end justifies the means, Acton found it abominable that the church should have allowed the faith to be defended by means of murder. All theorists, divines, or historians who justified these acts were no better than the original culprits. And this corruption, he believed, was the inevitable fruit of the marriage of sacred and temporal power.

In 1870 when Pius IX convened the Vatican Council — apparently with the intention of defining the dogma of papal infallibility — Acton went to Rome to lobby and rally opposition to what he believed was a dangerous tendency to authoritarianism. Through his aristocratic connections, he was able to gain wide access to the secret proceedings. He infuriated conservatives by sending out anonymous letters documenting the crude pressures and flagrant manipulation being applied to guarantee the cause of the infallibilists.

Even after the decree was issued, Acton believed it was still possible to rally opposition on the part of bishops and theologians. But this proved fruitless. One by one the bishops affirmed their consent to the decree. Theologians who resisted, like Dollinger, were excommunicated. As a layman Acton enjoyed a certain freedom of operation. Nevertheless, he feared that his own condemnation was inevitable.

Finally the archbishop of Westminster publicly challenged him to declare one way or the other on infallibility. Acton's equivocal response, which emphasized his utter loyalty to the doctrines of the church, satisfied his own bishop, and the crisis passed. He was never sanctioned. Nevertheless, at the age of forty-one, his career as a public figure in the church was ended.

Thus was he freed to pursue his career as a historian, a pursuit that was capped in 1895 when he was named to the prestigious Regius Professorship of Modern History at Cambridge. This was both an extraordinary recognition of his scholarship as well as a sign of the social advancement of English Catholics since the time of his youth. He held this position until his death on June 19, 1902.

Acton was a complicated and in some respects unattractive personality. Furious in his disdain for hypocrisy or any compromise with deceit, he could be unforgiving toward friends who fell short of his high standards. Certainly his positions were out of step with the church of his time. Yet few recognized that his zeal in exposing the historical sins of the church was in fact an expression of deep piety. His violent speech represented the extreme tension of a man who desired nothing more than to love with equal passion both the church and the truth.

See: Gertrude Himmelfarb, *Lord Acton* (London: Routledge & Kegan Paul, 1952); H. A. MacDougall, *Lord Acton on Papal Power* (London: Sheed & Ward, 1973).

June 20

St. Alban
Martyr (third century)

"My name is Alban, and I worship and adore the living and true God, who created all things."

St. Alban was a prominent citizen — possibly a soldier — who lived in Roman-occupied Britain sometime in the third century. According to the legend recounted in *Bede's history of the English church, Alban gave shelter to a priest fleeing persecution. Although Alban was a non-Christian, he was touched by the piety of his guest, and after several days he asked to receive instruction and to be baptized in the Christian faith. Aware that soldiers were in close pursuit, Alban contrived to assist the priest's escape by exchanging clothes. When the soldiers arrived at his house they seized Alban, dressed in the priest's cloak, and led him bound to the judge. Upon discovering his identity, the enraged judge declared, "Since you have chosen to conceal a sacrilegious rebel rather than surrender him to my soldiers to pay the well-deserved penalty for his blasphemy against our gods, you shall undergo all the tortures due to him if you dare to abandon the practice of our religion." Alban declared himself to be a Christian and willingly submitted to the judgment of the court. He was flogged and beheaded.

Bede records that Alban's executioner was so moved by the courage and fate of the condemned that he in turn confessed the faith and was "baptized" in the blood of his own martyrdom. And so the principle of mercy, once enacted by Alban, set in motion an endless chain reaction, continued in the memory and the telling of his story.

See: Bede, *A History of the English Church and People,* trans. Leo Sherley-Price (Baltimore: Penguin, 1965).

June 21

Bd. Osanna of Mantua
Mystic (1449–1505)

"Child, life and death consist in loving God."

From a mysterious voice Bd. Osanna heard the words above, as she wandered, a child of five, beside the river Po. Immediately she fell into a mystical rapture in which she was led by an angel to behold the company of the blessed in paradise. It was an experience that marked her forever.

Osanna was born in 1449 to a noble family of Mantua. She was the eldest of many children, and her family hoped for an advantageous marriage. But in light of her childhood ecstasy, and many others which followed, she begged to be allowed to join the Dominicans. Eventually her family relented, and she put on the habit of a Dominican tertiary.

Osanna continued to live in her family home, but she spent most of her time in church or praying silently in her room. Her reputation for holiness attracted wide attention. The duke of Mantua, to whom she was related, relied on her not only for spiritual counsel but also for her opinion on affairs of state. When not in prayer she was busy with works of mercy, whether nursing the sick, visiting prisoners, or serving the poor and afflicted. She made use of her well-placed connections to advocate the cause of many victims of injustice.

Osanna maintained a personal devotion to the Dominican prophet *Savonarola of Florence (d. 1498), who ultimately was burned at the stake after running afoul of the notorious Borgia pope Alexander VI. In the spirit of his apocalyptic preaching Osanna foresaw much suffering and ruin hanging over Italy on account of the sins of Christians — particularly the rampant corruption in Rome. She tended to share Savonarola's opinion of Pope Alexander VI. So grave were the pope's sins that Bd. Osanna, who otherwise held out hope for the salvation of all, could sustain little hope in his case. Though she prayed mightily on his behalf, her appeals fell on deaf ears. "Alas, wretched sinner that I am! God ever kept motionless, with aspect and countenance of wrath; and He gave no reply to anyone who prayed; not to the Madonna, nor to the apostles, nor to my soul."

Osanna died on June 20 (her feast day), 1505, at the age of fifty-six.

St. Thomas More
Martyr (1478–1535)

*"Little as I meddle in the conscience of others, I am certain that my con-
science belongs to me alone. It is the last thing that a man can do for his
salvation: to be at one with himself."*

Thomas More was one of the most highly respected men of his time. A
successful barrister, a judge known for his scrupulous integrity, a scholar,
famous for his wit and learning, he rose by sheer merit to the highest
status of any commoner in England. After a series of important public
offices he was in 1529 appointed by King Henry VIII to the post of lord
chancellor of England. To this his friend *Erasmus, the Continental hu-
manist, remarked, "Happy the commonwealth where kings appoint such
officials."

Despite his achievements, More had little ambition for worldly success.
As he later wrote, "Reputation, honor, fame, what is all that but a breath
of air from another person's mouth, no sooner spoken but gone? Thus
whoever finds his delight in them is feeding on wind." More was a man
of deep and demanding faith. In his youth he had considered a monastic
vocation before deciding instead that he was called to serve God in the
world. While outwardly he enjoyed a life of comfort, in the privacy of his
spiritual life he wore a hair shirt, attended daily Mass, and practiced a
strict discipline of prayer.

More maintained a large household and took special delight in his children. His role in overseeing the education of his daughters, especially
Margaret, his eldest and favorite, was considered remarkable for the time.
After the death of his beloved first wife, he quickly married an older
widow, Alice. She proved a loyal wife and a good stepmother, though she
was prone to exasperation with her husband's scholarly friends, his sense
of humor, and his costly scruples.

King Henry had reckoned wisely on his chancellor's brilliance and
honesty. In all matters of his office More served with loyalty and distinction. But circumstances were to evolve to the point that Henry required a
more absolute loyalty than More could offer. For some years the court of
Henry had been moving toward a fateful collision with the authority of
the Catholic church. The issue was the king's desire to annul his marriage
to Catherine of Aragon so that he might marry Anne Boleyn. Catherine
refused to acquiesce in this scheme, and the pope upheld the inviolability
of their marriage. When Henry made clear his intention to have his way,
regardless of the church's ruling, More resigned his office rather than publicly oppose the position of the king. He retired to his country home and
endeavored to ignore the raging controversy. Nevertheless, it was widely
remarked that he declined to attend the coronation of Queen Anne. In 1534
an Act of Succession was proclaimed. All the king's subjects were required
to take an oath recognizing the offspring of Henry and Anne as true successors to the throne. More had no problem with this. As far as he was

concerned the king was free to declare any successor he liked. However, the oath also required an avowal that the king's marriage with Catherine had been no true marriage and a repudiation of "any foreign authority, prince or potentate." Such an oath represented a decisive break with the authority of the pope. This oath More refused to take. Consequently, on April 13 he was arrested and imprisoned in the Tower of London.

He remained there for fifteen months. All the while the court pressured him either to take the oath or to state his reasons for withholding his assent. More would do neither, believing that as long as he kept his opinions to himself he could not be convicted of treason. He was presented with a parade of clergy and bishops who all (save Bishop John Fisher) had signed the oath. More maintained that others must abide by their own conscience, as he must be true to his own. Meanwhile, the miseries of prison life, including cold, hunger, and vermin, were compounded by pressure from his family. When his wife tried to coax him to alter his course, he responded, "My good woman, you are no good at doing business. Do you really want me to exchange eternity for twenty years?"

On February 1, 1535, Parliament passed the Acts of Supremacy, which proclaimed the king "only supreme head of the Church of England." Thomas continued to maintain his silence. Finally in June he was brought to trial. On the basis of perjured evidence, he was convicted of having spoken against the Acts and sentenced to death. Now, with his fate settled, Thomas at last broke his silence. He denied that Parliament had the authority to set up a temporal lord as head of the church. No more could the English Parliament overrule the law of the universal church, he declared, than the City of London could make a law against an act of Parliament. Finally, he addressed the lords who condemned him, noting that while *St. Paul had persecuted *St. Stephen, "and yet be they now both twin holy saints in Heaven...so I verily trust, and shall therefore right heartily pray, that though your lordships have now here on earth been judges of my condemnation, we may yet hereafter in Heaven merrily all meet together to everlasting salvation."

He spoke in similar terms as he bade farewell to his loyal daughter Margaret: "I will pray for us all with my whole heart, that we may meet one day in heaven, where we shall forever be gay and have no more pains."

On July 6 he was taken to the site of execution. Though he had grown weak and haggard in his months in confinement, he was not abandoned by his famous wit. Attempting to make his way up the scaffold he addressed his guard, "I pray you, master Lieutenant, see me safe up, and as for my coming down, let me shift for myself." Addressing those gathered about he made brief remarks before laying his head on the executioner's block: "I die in and for the faith of the holy Catholic Church. Pray for me in this world, and I shall pray for you in that world. Pray for the king that it please God to send him good counsellors. I die as the king's true servant, but God's first." His feast and that of his fellow martyr John Fisher are celebrated on this day.

See: Anthony Kenny, *Thomas More* (Oxford: Oxford University Press, 1983); Christian Feldman, *God's Gentle Rebels* (New York: Crossroad, 1995).

June 23

Bd. Mary of Oignies
Mystic (d. 1213)

"As her thirst for the life-giving Blood of her Lord was so great that she could not bear it, she sometimes entreated that, at least, the bare chalice might be left on the altar after Mass, that she might feast her sight with it."
—James de Vitry

Bd. Mary of Oignies was born to a wealthy family of Brabant, in Belgium. Despite her yearning for religious life, she was forced into marriage at the age of fourteen with another well-born young man. She persuaded him not only to respect her desire for chastity but to turn their house into a hospital for lepers. There they personally nursed the invalids under their care.

Soon Mary's reputation for holiness began to attract considerable attention. She was particularly famous for her "gift of tears," a sign of her extraordinary sorrow over the sufferings of Christ in the world. When she was asked why her tears and constant fasting did not make her ill, she replied, "These tears are my feast; they are my bread day and night; they feed my mind; rather than emptying and afflicting my head they bring satiety to my soul."

When the stream of pilgrims to her door became too oppressive, Mary received permission from her husband to enter a convent at Oignies. There her mystical visions increased in number, especially when she was in the presence of the Eucharist. The sight of the crucifix would cause her to faint. Often in an ecstatic state she would sing or speak in verse. She said that when she received communion the host had the taste of honey.

Mary died on June 23, 1213, at the age of thirty-eight. Her biography was written by her confessor and disciple, Cardinal James de Vitry, who attributed his vocation to her influence and intercession.

See: Caroline Walker Bynum, *Holy Feast and Holy Famine* (Berkeley: University of California Press, 1987).

June 24

Père Vincent Lebbe
Apostle to the Chinese (1877–1940)

"I believe that we owe it to the Christians here, and even to the non-Christians, to be to them what the Church is wherever it exists — the last refuge of what is right and proper, where justice need never fear to make its voice heard."

Vincent Lebbe was born in Belgium in 1877. At the age of eleven he resolved that his vocation was to be a missionary priest, to go to China, and there to lay down his life. From this plan he never deviated, and his ambitions were ultimately fulfilled.

Lebbe first arrived in China in 1901. He was twenty-three and a priest of the Congregation of the Missions (the Vincentians). Even before his arrival in China Lebbe was fired by a passionate love for the Chinese and a desire to be one with them. His fellow missionaries, however, quickly sought to erase such notions. "What are you doing?" one of them asked him when he tried to carry his suitcase off the boat. "In China no missionary ever carries his own case."

Lebbe quickly observed among his fellow missionaries a strong sense of superiority toward the Chinese. Many French priests and even bishops remained ignorant of the Chinese language, culture, and history. Although a good number of Chinese priests had been ordained, they served only as assistants to their European counterparts. The church, meanwhile, existed under the "protection" of the French government. Many missioners could scarcely distinguish between their loyalty to Christ and their loyalty to the French tricolor. Nor could they perceive how such attitudes alienated them from the hearts of most Chinese. Because of them, Christianity was widely perceived as a foreign religion and the church in China as no more than a spiritual colony of France. To Lebbe this approach to mission was incomprehensible. "I myself am a Chinese with all my heart and soul and strength," he wrote. "China is my destiny, my country, and the people here are my brothers and children."

Instead of traditional parish work, Lebbe propagated the gospel by every means he could devise. He organized public lectures and preached on street corners. He reached out to civic leaders and prominent non-Christians, working hard for their friendship and respect. He organized charitable organizations, schools, and associations of lay Catholics. He even established the first Catholic press in China. The response was extraordinary. Within a few years he had become one of the most visible and highly respected foreigners in China. His devotion to the Chinese was obvious, not only in his mastery of their language, but in his dress. Instead of a traditional soutane he dressed like a poor Chinese laborer, even down to his traditional pigtail. Though he was mocked by fellow missioners, to whom such conduct was unbecoming a priest, he answered that *St. Paul had become a Greek to the Greeks. "If I tried to go on being a European I should be no better than a corpse. We get to know people only by becoming one with them; we win them only by giving ourselves."

Despite his success, Lebbe's methods were a source of increasing irritation to his superiors. The heart of the problem was Lebbe's conviction that the future of the church in China required the development of a truly Chinese church. The church must overcome its identification with European culture and its dependence on foreign personnel. Among the most important first steps, he believed, would be the consecration of native-born Chinese bishops. This flew directly against the wisdom of his superiors. It would be a hundred years, they claimed, before there would be suitable candidates among the Chinese clergy. In the meantime they began to see Lebbe as a troublemaker.

Henceforth Lebbe was subjected to incredible harassment. Despite his effectiveness and popularity as a missioner, he was treated by his own superiors as a pariah, stripped of responsibility, and shunted from one backwater assignment to another. He submitted to these humiliations with obedience and dignity, though it cost him much suffering. Indeed, he wondered if this was not the martyrdom he had envisioned as a child.

It became clear to Lebbe that the future of the Chinese church lay in Rome. And so he returned to Europe. There he worked as an unofficial chaplain to Chinese university students, all the while pressuring the Vatican to look into the situation in China. He finally won an audience with Pope Pius XI and handed him a list of Chinese priests who would make suitable bishops. The French bishops now regarded him as an open traitor. Not a single bishop would allow him to return to China.

But this was to change. In 1926 Pope Pius XI personally consecrated six Chinese bishops, all of them recommended by Lebbe. He himself was present in the front row at St. Peter's, blinded by tears of happiness as he witnessed the realization of his long dream. Now he had at least six sponsors eager for his services. Upon returning he immediately became a naturalized Chinese citizen. No one could ever force him to leave China again. Lebbe continued his old apostolates. But he took up new ones as well. He organized a community of Chinese priests into a monastic community, the Little Brothers of St. John the Baptist. In 1929 he resigned from the Vincentians to become the superior of this new congregation. But even this was not the end of his activities. With the outbreak of war with Japan Lebbe organized a team of stretcher-bearers that went into the heat of battle to rescue lives. His courageous actions sealed his place of honor in the hearts of all Chinese. While many other missionaries adopted an attitude of neutrality, Lebbe, as always, was passionate in his loyalties. "I would rather die than go on living as a neutral, not daring to call good and evil by their proper names, not daring to give my last ounce of blood for the oppressed."

Under the stress of his exhausting duties his body finally gave out. He died on June 24, 1940. In declaring a day of mourning, the Chinese government honored him both as a great Christian and as a Chinese patriot. They called him only by his Chinese name: Lei-Ming-Yuan ("the thunder that sings in the distance").

See: Jacques Leclercq, *Thunder in the Distance: The Life of Père Lebbe* (New York: Sheed & Ward, 1958).

Sadhu Sundar Singh
Indian Mystic (1889–1929)

"Diamonds do not dazzle with beauty unless they are cut. When cut, the rays of the sun fall on them and make them shine with wonderful colors. So when we are cut by the cross we shall shine as jewels in the kingdom of God."

Sadhu Sundar Singh, who wore the robes of an Indian holy man to preach the gospel of Jesus Christ, was one of the most fascinating and enigmatic figures of modern Christianity. Though sensationally famous in his own time, he was largely forgotten after his mysterious death. He has a special relevance today as someone who found in the model of Jesus a bridge between the spiritual wisdom of the East and West.

Sundar Singh was born in 1889 to a wealthy Sikh family in the village of Rampur in northern India. While growing up he was strongly influenced by his mother, a deeply religious woman. By the time Sundar was seven she had trained him to recite the entire *Bhagavadgita* in Sanskrit. She also encouraged him in the notion that service to God was the highest pursuit in life. His father, a rich landowner, had other plans for his son. After Sundar's mother died when he was fourteen, he enrolled the boy in a local mission school to receive a modern education. This had unintended effects.

At first Sundar rebelled against the Christian teaching of the school. He even burned a copy of the New Testament in protest. Confused and anguished about the proper spiritual path, Sundar prayed one night that God would reveal himself by morning — otherwise he would commit suicide. That night he experienced a strange mystical vision in which the figure of Christ appeared and addressed him in Hindustani: "Why do you persecute me? Remember I gave my life for you upon the cross."

When Sundar informed his father that he was now a Christian, the old man responded with horror. He tried all kinds of threats and inducements to force his son to change his mind. When these proved fruitless, he banished him from his home. And so Sundar was driven out into the streets with no idea as to his future, except that from now on he would obey only one master, the Living Christ.

Sundar was baptized in the Anglican church at the age of sixteen. The Indian Christians whom he knew tended to adopt the dress and culture of Europeans. But Sundar was determined to demonstrate an Indian way of following Christ. Thus, he put off his old clothes and donned the saffron robe and turban of an Indian sadhu, a holy man consecrated to the service of God. Henceforth he would be a Christian sadhu, a pilgrim with no fixed abode, no possessions, living on alms while preaching and bearing witness to Christ through his life of prayer and poverty.

For years he wandered across India on foot, sleeping outdoors, enduring hunger, cold, and exposure to the elements and the hazards of the open country. While his status as a sadhu won him a hearing wherever he went, his audience often reacted violently when they discovered that he was a Christian. His way of life was profoundly Indian, but it was also inspired by his reading of the Gospels. Jesus too had lived like a sadhu, and he had encouraged his disciples to go forth without staff or purse while bearing witness to the ends of the earth. Like Jesus, Sundar taught in parables. On the necessity of suffering:

> A silkworm was struggling out of the cocoon and an ignorant man saw it battling as if in pain, so he went and helped it to get free, but very soon after it fluttered and died. The other silkworms that struggle out without help suffered, but they came out into full life and beauty, with wings made strong for flight by their battle for fresh existence.

Growing up in the Punjab Sundar had lived in the shadow of the Himalayas. To the north was Nepal and Tibet. At some point he felt called to carry the gospel to these remote lands, and in years to come he managed several times to make the perilous journey. In Tibet he experienced his most violent opposition. One time he was arrested, tossed into a dry well, and left to die amid the remains of previous victims. Sometime during the night a rope was lowered, though on surfacing he found no one in sight. For his escape from death on this and other occasions he had no explanation other than divine providence.

Back in India Sundar began to attract enormous attention. Crowds of people often gathered to hear him preach. Many were drawn by his reputation as a miracle worker or divine-man, an image that he labored hard to dispel. His message was not about himself but only about Jesus Christ. Sundar maintained friendly relations with Christians of many denominations, and he frequently received communion in the Anglican church. But he rejected the suggestion that he seek ordination. He was called to the solitary life, bearing witness among non-Christians.

His witness earned him critics as well as admirers. Many prominent Christians objected to his life as an itinerant evangelist and his lack of accountability to any church or higher authority. Some publicly doubted the accounts of his own fantastic adventures, accusing him, in effect, of being a fraud. To others, he was a treasure, a truly inspired man of God who seemed in his words and appearance virtually to embody the spirit of the gospel.

Friends arranged for him to undertake extensive speaking tours in England and America. His unusual appearance, as well as his charismatic appeal, attracted wide interest. For his part Sundar was disturbed by the materialism of the West and what he perceived, for all the evident interest in religion, to be a profound absence of prayer. "Without daily intercourse with God there is no piety, no Christianity, no real life."

In April 1929 Sundar made his last journey to Tibet. He was last seen in his saffron robe walking into the distance. When by July no word had been received, his friends sent an expedition to follow his trail, but they could discover nothing. He may have been killed by bandits or others hostile to his faith or simply succumbed to illness, cold, or the perils of the road, but no clue was ever found concerning his fate.

See: Janet Lynch-Watson, *The Saffron Robe* (Grand Rapids, Mich.: Zondervan Publishing House, 1975); Mrs. Arthur Parker, *Sadhu Sundar Singh* (New York: Fleming H. Revell, 1920).

June 26
Dom Virgil Michel
Leader of the Liturgical Movement (1890–1938)

"Liturgy is essentially the Christian faith prayed;
it is dogma set to prayer."

Virgil Michel, a Benedictine monk from St. John's Abbey in Collegeville, Minnesota, was the pioneer of the liturgical movement in the United States. Through his prolific writings Michel struggled tirelessly to promote a proper understanding of the Mass in the life of the church and, by extension, the place of the church in the life of the world.

In the 1920s, when Michel initiated these efforts, most lay Catholics tended to be passive spectators at the Mass. Conducted in Latin, with scant opportunity for participation by the congregation, the Mass often seemed more like a private transaction between the priest and God than a corporate act of worship and sacrifice. Michel felt it was vitally important to recover a sense of the Mass as the central expression of the living church. But this also required a reform of the liturgy to restore the participation of the people. This in turn involved a shift from a "clericalized" view of the church toward a recovery of the ancient image of the church as the Mystical Body of Christ. In all these concerns he anticipated by several decades the dramatic reforms of Vatican II.

But Michel's concerns did not end with the quality of liturgical celebration. Ultimately he regarded the whole purpose of liturgical renewal as a means of advancing the penetration of Christian values into the world. Michel believed there was an intimate connection between the quality of worship and the effectiveness of Christian witness. "The entire life of the true Christian," he wrote, "must be a reflection and a further expression of his life at the altar of God. If he is predominantly a passive Christian there, can we expect him to be an active Christian in his daily life out in the world?"

Michel believed firmly in the role of lay people as a spiritual leaven, carrying the "healing and sanctifying presence and power of Christ into the whole temporal order." The loss of an authentic liturgical spirit contributed to the loss of a lay apostolate. To the extent that the liturgy was thoroughly clericalized, it contributed to the gap between the religious realm and the everyday world. This in turn contributed to the spirit of individualism, materialism, and secularism so rampant in the modern age. The liturgical spirit, in contrast, represented the spirit of community and the vital interpenetration of the realms of nature and grace. It was thus, he believed, an antidote to the spiritual ills facing the world.

Michel's major work took place against the backdrop of the Depression as well as the rise of fascist and communist totalitarianism. This provided immediate incentive for him to explicate the connections between liturgical renewal and social justice. Among those particularly receptive to his message was *Dorothy Day, whose Catholic Worker movement was then emerging. Day drew inspiration from Michel's call to ground the message of social justice in a deep liturgical spirit. She especially welcomed his emphasis on the Mystical Body of Christ, a doctrine from which she drew broad social implications. Michel, for his part, recognized in movements like the Catholic Worker and *Catherine de Hueck's Friendship House the best expression of his vision of a liturgically rooted lay apostolate.

In all, Michel was a pioneer in promoting the importance of lay spirituality. If previous models of holiness emphasized flight from the world, now, he believed, there was need for a new model of holiness, immersed in the daily routines of life and showing how the whole natural order could be sanctified. As he wrote,

If the first purpose of the liturgical movement is to lead the faithful into more intimate participation in the liturgy of the Church, then the further objective must also be that of getting the liturgical spirit to radiate forth from the altar of Christ into every aspect of the daily life of the Christian.

Born on June 26, 1890, Michel died on November 26, 1938, at the age of forty-eight.

See: Paul Marx, O.S.B., *Virgil Michel and the Liturgical Movement* (Collegeville, Minn.: Liturgical Press, 1957).

June 27
John Gerard
Underground Priest (1564–1637)

"With God's help I shall never do anything that is unjust or act against my conscience or the Catholic faith. You have me in your power. You can do with me what God allows you to do — more you cannot do."

In the late sixteenth century Jesuit missionaries spanned the globe bearing witness to the gospel injunction to "make disciples of all nations." Whether in Japan, Canada, India, or Latin America, they gladly faced every type of peril, privation, and danger — even to the risk of their lives. Yet for English Jesuits there was nowhere that they faced any greater danger than when they traveled in their own country — England under the reign of Queen Elizabeth.

Since the Reformation initiated by King Henry VIII the Catholic religion in England had been formally suppressed. Religious orders were abolished, all churches were appropriated by the Church of England, and all clergy were required to take the Oath of Supremacy (conceding the supreme ecclesial authority of the English monarch). Nevertheless, Catholicism remained alive, sustained by a number of underground priests, a network of lay Catholics, and a steady stream of missionaries smuggled in from the Continent.

Among the latter, the Jesuits figured prominently. Their mission was to seek out and serve the "recusant" Catholic population and where possible to encourage wavering "schismatics" to return to the church. Failing any other accomplishment, they were prepared to bear witness by the laying down of their lives. This was no idle possibility. The priests were regarded not simply as representatives of an outlaw religion but as agents of foreign powers intent on fostering "sedition, rebellion, and open hostility." Torture and death awaited them in custody. So likely was their eventual discovery and capture that in embarking for England it was as though they were setting forth on the way of the cross.

The first challenge was to come ashore and escape detection by the agents who kept watch in all the port towns. The next task was to find refuge among a network of Catholic households, mostly of the gentry, whose wealth and privilege allowed them space to maintain their traditional faith. Their homes included secret chapels equipped with ingeniously disguised hiding places wherein visiting priests and incriminating materials could be safely hidden in the event of a search. Such precautions were the only defense against the informers, spies, and professional bounty hunters — or "pursuivants" — whose job was to apprehend underground priests and their supporters.

This history is the background of one of the most remarkable documents of the period, *The Diary of a Hunted Priest,* by the English Jesuit John Gerard. In his memoir he describes in gripping detail the story of how in 1588, a newly ordained priest at the age of twenty-four, he was smuggled ashore in his native England and underwent the perilous adventures that attended his itinerant ministry. With his cultivated background and his knowledge of such matters as falconry and hunting, he was able to pass as a country gentleman. So he made the rounds of the Catholic gentry, preaching and saying Mass wherever he stopped — always, it seems, just a few steps ahead of the zealous pursuers close on his trail. Once he was cornered in a house and had to remain literally holed up in a wall for four days without food or water while a team of pursuivants tore up the floorboards and stripped the plaster off the walls around him.

Although on that and similar occasions he eluded his captors, he was eventually betrayed and taken into custody in 1594. In the first of several prisons he was kept much of the time in leg irons and subjected to other harsh treatment. All the while he maintained his spirits by repeating — as well as he could remember — the entire Spiritual Exercises of *St. Ignatius. Later, under less oppressive circumstances, he found himself among other imprisoned Catholics, and thus was able to resume his priestly ministry behind bars. In 1597 he was transferred to the Tower of London, the equivalent of a maximum security prison, where he was subjected to cruel tortures. Nevertheless, by means of invisible messages written in orange juice and smuggled to the outside, he was able to organize a daring escape.

Immediately he resumed his underground ministry, aware, however, that he was now one of the most wanted criminals in England and that recapture would mean certain death. Nevertheless he remained safe for a number of years until 1605, when discovery of the foiled Gunpowder Plot — an ill-conceived conspiracy to blow up Parliament — led to a wholesale crackdown on Catholics and their sympathizers. Though he was ignorant of the plot, many of Gerard's friends were implicated in the affair, and Gerard himself was named in an arrest warrant. His Jesuit superiors ordered him to escape.

Gerard's narrative is filled with references to the martyrs who preceded, surrounded, and followed in his wake. These included lay people like *Margaret Clitherow, the famous "Little John," who designed most of the hiding places used by the hunted priests, and Jesuits like Robert Southwell and *Edmund Campion. In the end, it was not Gerard's destiny to be counted among them. On May 3, 1606, after eighteen years in England, he slipped back across the Channel, disguised as a retainer to the Spanish ambassador. He lived on as a Jesuit superior in Flanders and later served as a confessor to the English College in Rome. He was a particular advocate for the cause of *Mary Ward and her Institute of the Blessed Virgin Mary. He died on June 27, 1637.

See: John Gerard, *The Autobiography of a Hunted Priest,* trans. Philip Caraman (Garden City, N.Y.: Image, 1955).

June 28

St. Irenaeus
Bishop of Lyons and Theologian (c. 130–200)

"The glory of God is the living human being."

Little is known of the life of Irenaeus, the first systematic theologian in the church. He was apparently born in Asia Minor, where as a boy he encountered *Polycarp, the saintly (and eventually martyred) bishop of Smyrna. At some point Irenaeus made his way to Lyons, a major Roman outpost in Gaul, where he was ordained a presbyter. In 177, while he was in Rome on a church mission, a savage wave of persecution swept over the church in Lyons. Upon his return he found that his bishop, Pothinus, was among the martyrs. Irenaeus was chosen to succeed him.

As a bishop Irenaeus came to believe the church faced a greater threat than that posed by Roman persecution. This came from the rapid proliferation of gnostic sects, each propagating a truncated version of the gospel. One of the typical features of gnosticism was a sharply dualistic understanding of matter and spirit. It was impossible for the gnostics to imagine any direct interaction between these two realms, either in terms of the Christian doctrine of creation or in terms of the Incarnation. The goal of salvation, according to the gnostics, was to be liberated from the bonds of matter and to enter into the refined dimension of the spirit.

Irenaeus wrote his principal work, *Adversus Haereses,* to counter these ideas. To do this he underscored the links between the Old and New Testaments, insisting on the identity between the God of creation and the God of salvation. There was nothing inherently corrupt in creation; it was only through the distortion of sin that human beings lost their "likeness to God." This was restored through the obedience of Christ, the "second Adam," who "recapitulated" and corrected the story of the first Adam. Only the God who created us could also save us; and only that which was truly assumed (in the Incarnation) could also be redeemed.

According to legend, Irenaeus died as a martyr sometime around the year 200.

See: Irenaeus, "An Exposition of the Faith," in Cyril C. Richardson, ed., *Early Christian Fathers* (New York: Macmillan, 1970).

June 29

St. Peter
Apostle (first century)

"You are the Christ."

All four Gospels agree on the preeminence of St. Peter among the original twelve apostles. A Galilean fisherman and the brother of Andrew, Peter was in fact one of the first apostles to be called by Christ, and he is cited as a witness to many of the most significant events in the gospel story.

Though Peter was originally named Simon it seems that Jesus gave him an Aramaic name, Cephas, which has the meaning of "Rock." From its Greek form it is rendered Peter. This provided Jesus with a memorable pun when he addressed the disciple with the fateful words "You are Peter, and upon this *rock* I will build my church." Upon this text the Catholic church has built a formidable claim for the primacy of the pope as successor to Peter. For understandable reasons, the church draws less attention to the subsequent verse, also addressed by Jesus to the first pope: "Get behind me, Satan! You are a stumbling block; for you are not on the side of God, but of men."

Both declarations reflect the complex characterization of Peter as a man torn between his better and his weaker qualities. As a leader and a spokesperson for the Twelve, he is in many ways not only the preeminent but the paradigmatic disciple. And yet Peter is far from an idealized figure; the Gospels go to great lengths to stress his weakness, fear, and failures. What distinguishes him from his companions is not his infallible judgment but his articulation of their common faith — "You are the Christ" — and his zealous determination, after repeatedly falling, to get back up and rejoin the struggle.

Apart from Jesus himself, Peter is surely the most fully articulated character in the New Testament. His appearances in the Gospels consistently highlight the competing elements of his personality: a bold impetuosity, a tendency to act or speak first and think later, accompanied by a capacity for fear, doubt, and childlike meekness.

As a spokesman for the disciples Peter had his good days. But it was also Peter who was so fearful upon witnessing the transfiguration that he babbled on about building tents for *Moses and Elijah. He asked whether we should forgive as many as seven times seven; he tried to walk on water, but lost faith and almost drowned. He won full marks after Jesus asked them, "Who do you say I am?" and he answered, "You are the Christ." This was one of his grandest moments. But he instantly failed the test and earned a stinging rebuke when he disputed Christ's words about his coming passion and exclaimed, "God forbid, Lord! This shall never happen to you."

At the Last Supper Peter made a bold claim: "Even though they all fall away, I will not." But then before the night was over he had denied his master three times. None of the subsequent sins of the church can be any more scandalous than that betrayal. Yet Peter was also the one who spoke for the disciples when Jesus asked if they too planned to desert him: "Lord, who shall we go to? You have the message of eternal life and we believe." He wept after his betrayal of Jesus, and when on Easter morning he heard that the Lord was risen he ran to the tomb to see for himself. And on this "rock" the church was founded. What could this mean but that if the gospel was to be carried forward in time it would be upon the foundation of faith and grace and not by the natural strength, wisdom, or virtue of any ecclesiastical authority.

John's Gospel ends on a touching note that defines the "petrine" ministry in memorable terms. It is not a matter of preeminence in authority or power. What Jesus seeks is preeminence in love, expressed in service and self-sacrifice. Three times — echoing Peter's triple denial — the risen Christ asks him: "Do you love me?" Each time, when Peter answers, "Yes, Lord, you know that I love you," Jesus commands him, "Feed my sheep." Finally, he says, "Truly, truly, I say to you, when you were young, you girded yourself and walked where you would; but when you are old, you will stretch out your hands, and another will gird you and carry you where you do not wish to go."

According to the book of Acts, Peter continued to serve as a leader of the early church in Jerusalem. He preached the first sermon after Pentecost, performed the first healing, and authorized the extension of the Christian mission unto the gentiles (though he would be publicly rebuked by *Paul for vacillating on this crucial policy). More than once he would be arrested and imprisoned, only to be delivered by miraculous means. After the final incident we are simply told that "he departed and went to another place." He is mentioned no more.

According to ancient tradition Peter became the first bishop of Rome and was there martyred during the reign of Nero (c. 54–68). Eusebius, on the authority of *Origen, records that Peter was crucified. He notes, furthermore, that Peter — believing himself unworthy of emulating his master — requested to be hung upside down.

June 30

St. Paul

Apostle to the Gentiles (c. 64)

"I have been crucified with Christ; it is no longer I who live,
but Christ who lives in me."

According to *Kierkegaard, there are only two appropriate responses to Christ: either scandal or discipleship. For Saul (or Paul as he became known), a devout Jew of Tarsus, the terms of this dilemma were perfectly obvious. Either the claims of Jesus' disciples were true or they constituted blasphemy. If the latter, then his movement should be suppressed with all the force of the law. But if they were true, then one had no choice but to give up everything and follow him. Paul was no believer in half-measures.

His first appearance in the Acts of the Apostles finds him on the edge of a crowd that is stoning *St. Stephen to death. In the heat of their exertion the murderous mob had laid their garments at Saul's feet. Luke notes that "Saul was consenting" to the deed. In the next verse he is no longer a passive witness but a zealous leader in the persecution of the church, even traversing the countryside in search of Christians to denounce.

It was on such an errand to Damascus that his life was suddenly changed. It came about with a flash of light that threw him to the ground and a voice that cried, "Saul, Saul, why do you persecute me?" When he asked for the identity of the voice he heard, "I am Jesus whom you are persecuting." Now convinced that Jesus was indeed the Christ, Saul asked to be baptized and went on to devote the remainder of his life to the service of the gospel.

Saul made his way to Jerusalem and met the original disciples. With some difficulty he overcame their doubts and was eventually commissioned to join *Barnabas in serving the Christian community in Antioch. The local church there, in turn, commissioned the two to undertake the first of many missionary journeys. Henceforth Saul would become completely identified with his service as a missionary. His strategy was first to approach the local synagogue. Frequently this provoked violent persecution. As a result, he found himself turning instead — and with considerable success — to a receptive gentile audience. Appropriate to his new mission, he now preferred to go by a more Hellenized version of his name: Paul.

At a council in Jerusalem around 50 Paul and Barnabas — with the support of *Peter — successfully argued the case for the mission to the gentiles, arguing furthermore that gentile converts need not first be circumcised as Jews. Paul worked out a profound theological rationale for this decision. He argued that by his death and resurrection Jesus had substituted faith in place of obedience to the law as the sole condition for salvation. This position would become the cornerstone of the Christian church as it quickly took on the character of a predominantly gentile religion.

Paul's journeys took him through much of the Mediterranean world. In many towns he was responsible for implanting the seeds of the gospel, and toward these communities he felt special pride and responsibility. As often, however, he met with bitter opposition. He was frequently beaten, stoned, and imprisoned. He endured shipwreck, hunger, and humiliation. But he was sustained by a sense of the invincible power of the Risen Christ: "If God is for us, who is against us?"

In his letters to the Christian communities he reflected at length on the "folly" of Christ who proved victorious by means of failure on the cross. "God chose what is foolish in the world to shame the wise; God chose what is weak in the world to shame the strong; God chose what is low and despised in the world, even things that are not, to bring to nothing things that are."

When Paul was arrested by the Roman authorities in Jerusalem he claimed the privilege of a Roman citizen and was transported to Rome for trial. Along the way he continued to write to the communities, exhorting them to courage, faith, and love toward one another. As he anticipated his fate in Rome, he felt satisfied with his life: "I have fought the good fight, I have finished the race, I have kept the faith."

According to early church tradition Paul was beheaded in Rome under the emperor Nero in the year 64. His letters, which continued to circulate, became foundational documents for the early church. The example of his courageous witness underscored the credibility of his faith:

> For I am sure that neither death, nor life, nor angels, nor principalities, nor things present, nor things to come, nor powers, nor height, nor depth, nor anything else in all creation will be able to separate us from the love of God in Christ Jesus our Lord.

See: Neil Elliot, *Liberating Paul: The Justice of God and the Politics of the Apostle* (Maryknoll, N.Y.: Orbis, 1994).

❧ JULY ❧

Antonio Rosmini
Founder of the Institute of Charity (1797–1855)

"Pray that God in his mercy may give me patience to carry my cross though it be to the end of my life, and that I may never think hardly of those who have brought it on me."

Antonio Rosmini was one of the most eminent Italian priests of the nineteenth century. Through his personal piety, his contributions as a scholar, and his insights into the realm of politics, he endeavored to raise the level of Catholic culture and to enhance the church's leadership with respect to the moral and social questions of his day. Many of his ideas were later claimed by the church. But through much of his career he had to suffer libelous aspersions from prelates for whom the word "modern" remained a fearful epithet.

Rosmini was by all accounts a man of profound spiritual depth. He founded the Institute of Charity, a congregation of priests committed to the pursuit of holiness in the service of the church. One of his particular interests was the revival of Catholicism in England; his Institute sent many Italian priests to work in a number of English cities. (They were responsible for popularizing the "Roman collar" as a distinguishing mark of the Catholic clergy.) Rosmini achieved equal renown as a philosopher. There was probably no other Catholic theologian in Europe with a more comprehensive and sympathetic understanding of modern philosophy, and he eagerly promoted the dialogue between the church and contemporary thought. Rosmini himself wrote scores of scholarly books; the posthumous edition of his collected works ran to sixty volumes.

At the same time Rosmini was an Italian patriot and supporter of the Risorgimento — the cause of Italian unification. This ran counter to Vatican interests since it entailed opposition to Austria (a strong ally of the church), which occupied a great part of the Italian peninsula. The Vatican feared that ultimately the Italian nationalists would turn their gaze on the extensive Vatican states.

Nevertheless, the election in 1846 of Pope Pius IX was regarded by Italian liberals as a cause for optimism. Pius quickly earned a reputation as a progressive reformer after introducing a series of modernizing reforms in the administration of his territories. These included support for the railroad and gas-lighting in the streets of Rome, freedom of the press, and even a hint that constitutional government might soon be permitted. So popular was the new pope, Pio Nono as he was called, that it was said, only half in jest, that he could easily win election as the first president of a unified Italian republic. During this brief papal spring, Rosmini enjoyed cordial relations with the Vatican. As an official representative of the Risorgimento Rosmini met with the pope in an effort to persuade him to join the alliance against Austria. Pius actually informed Rosmini of his desire to name him a cardinal. But as word of the plan leaked out to Vatican officials the pope was besieged with warnings about Rosmini's radical ideas. The red hat was never formally extended.

In the meantime the overall mood in the Vatican was shifting dramatically. The catalyst was a short-lived revolutionary uprising in 1848 that caused the pope to flee Rome in fear of his life. He returned some months later, supported by Austrian troops. But he was now a very different man, convinced of the utter incompatibility between Catholicism and liberal ideals. Henceforth he assumed the reactionary stance that would characterize his long (thirty-two-year) pontificate.

Earlier in 1848, before this ominous turn of events, Rosmini had felt the time was ripe to publish two of his most critical works, *A Constitution Based on Social Justice* and *Five Wounds of the Church*. The first book outlined a program of Catholic social teaching that in many ways anticipated by fifty years the positions of *Pope Leo XIII. But in *Five Wounds* he laid out an extensive critique of the church and the self-imposed afflictions that prevented it from assuming its rightful leadership in the world. These wounds were: (1) the division of the people from the clergy in worship; (2) the defective education of the clergy; (3) the disunity among the bishops; (4) the nomination of bishops by the secular powers; and (5) the enslavement of the church by riches.

Under these headings, he called for such reforms as the use of the vernacular in worship: "The people should be actors in the liturgy as well as hearers, while in fact they are mostly present at Mass like the columns and statues of the building." He decried the corruption and worldliness introduced by wealth and power and the all too close relationship between the church and state. He went so far as to suggest that in those revolutionary movements that targeted the temporal powers of the church there was expressed a vague need "for a religion free to speak to the hearts of the people without the intervention of the State; perhaps in the designs of Providence the revolutions are designed to free the Church of Christ, in whose hand are all things."

But in speaking so freely Rosmini had seriously misjudged the signs of the times. His two books were placed on the Index of proscribed works, and Rosmini was subjected to vicious personal attacks. These were contained in anonymous pamphlets in which he was accused of every type of heresy and immorality. Although he was never formally charged with any particular error, he remained for the rest of his life under a cloud. Vocations to his Institute sharply dropped, and he was unable to exercise any further significant role within the church.

Rosmini submitted gracefully to this repression, satisfied by the knowledge that if he were not in error his message would eventually be heard and received by future generations. He died on July 1, 1855.

See: Claude Leetham, *Rosmini: Priest and Philosopher* (New York: New City, 1982).

July 2
The *Cloud* Author
Mystic (fourteenth century)

"It is not what you are or have been that God looks at with his merciful eyes, but what you would be."

Nothing is known about the English mystic identified simply as the author of *The Cloud of Unknowing*. This classic text was written in the late fourteenth century — the time of Chaucer — in a vernacular English that betrays a hint of the East Midlands. Otherwise the identity of its author — whether a priest or a religious, a hermit or perhaps a Carthusian, as some have argued — has eluded discovery. Not even the gender of its author can be definitively ascertained. Nevertheless, it can be safely asserted that the author of the *Cloud* was one of the great spiritual masters of all time.

This is not to say that the *Cloud* is for all readers. It is intended for a fairly narrow and specific audience, those called to the contemplative life. Indeed, in a passage that well reflects the author's distinctive voice, the reader is begged "not to let anyone see this book unless he is in your judgment able to benefit from it" in the proper way. This excludes the "loud-mouthed, or flatterers, or mock-modest, or busybodies, or tale-bearers, or cantankerous," or the merely "curious," whom the author "would rather that they did not hear it." To all these, in any case, the book will mean "nothing."

That is appropriate, given that "nothing" is precisely the author's principal theme. The *Cloud* is a representative of that tradition of spirituality known as the *via negativa*, which claims that we can more reliably say what God is not than what God is. According to the *Cloud* the hidden and ineffable nature of God is shielded from human understanding by "a sort of cloud of unknowing." This "cloud," as the author insists, "is always between you and your God, no matter what you do, and it prevents you from seeing him clearly by the light of understanding in your reason."

But though God eludes the intellect, this does not mean that God is unknowable. It means, rather, that God is not a concept. What cannot be *thought* may yet be *known* by love. Through the sharp arrows of love directed toward God in contemplative prayer, it is possible to pierce the "cloud of unknowing" and attain blessed union with God. This, however, requires that we wrap ourselves in a "cloud of forgetting," abandoning all images and concepts of the divinity and at the same time overcoming our attachments to worldly creatures. With the help of short words like

"God," or "Love," we may empty our minds and fix our will in the direction of God. This is hard work and it is only the preliminary stage of union with God. But, fortunately, God does the rest.

If this sounds perplexing or mysterious the reader has been well warned that this path is not intended for everyone. The *Cloud*'s teaching is specifically not intended to supplant the value of charitable works or attention to the teachings of the church. But as with the mind-twisting riddles of the Zen master, the *Cloud* delights in confounding paradoxes:

> "Well," you will say, "where am I to be? Nowhere, according to you!" And you will be quite right! "Nowhere" is where I want you! Why, when you are "nowhere" physically, you are "everywhere" spiritually.

It is equally appropriate to say that the author of the *Cloud* is "no one," so effectively did the author submerge his or her identity in the cloud of holy wisdom.

See: *The Cloud of Unknowing and Other Works,* trans. Clifton Wolters (New York: Penguin, 1978).

July 3

St. Thomas
Apostle (first century)

"My Lord and my God!"

From a few verses in the Gospel of John, St. Thomas the Apostle emerges as one of the most vivid characters in the New Testament. When Jesus announces his desire to proceed toward Jerusalem, it is Thomas who issues the bold challenge, "Let us also go, that we may die with him" (11:16). Later, at the Last Supper, when Jesus speaks in a cryptic fashion about the way he is going, Thomas asks, "Lord, we do not know where you are going; how can we know the way?" This evokes the famous response: "I am the way, and the truth, and the life; no one comes to the Father, but by me" (14:5).

But it is for his famous "doubt" that Thomas is chiefly remembered. After Easter, Thomas reacts incredulously to the report of his fellow apostles that they have seen the Risen Lord. He will never believe, he insists, unless he can feel for himself the marks of the nails and place his hand in Christ's wounded side.

Eight days later Christ appears to all of them in the "upper room" where they are hiding. Addressing Thomas by name he invites the doubting disciple to touch his wounds, to place his hand in his side. To this invitation Thomas simply exclaims, "My Lord and my God!" So Jesus responds, "Have you believed because you have seen me? Blessed are those who have not seen and yet believe" (20:24–30).

The activities of Thomas following Pentecost are not known. According to early legends, however, St. Thomas engaged in a great missionary venture that took him as far as the south of India. There he was reportedly martyred. Whatever the truth of this story it is a fact that when Portuguese explorers in the sixteenth century first landed on the Malabar Coast of southern India they found already awaiting them a Christian community that attributed its origins to the direct evangelization of St. Thomas. To this day the descendants of this community refer to themselves as St. Thomas Christians.

July 4

St. Martin of Tours
Bishop (d. 397)

"I am a soldier of Christ and it is not lawful for me to fight."

Martin was born in Sabaria in what is now Hungary. As the son of a military tribune, he was required by law to enter the Roman army at the age of fifteen. Apparently he resisted this fate and had to be inducted in chains. His conversion to Christianity came some years later. While he was serving in Amiens in France there occurred an incident for which he is famous. During a cold winter day he encountered a shivering beggar, dressed in rags, who was begging for alms from passersby. Having no money to offer, Martin removed his own cloak. With his sword he cut the garment in two, giving one piece to the beggar and wrapping himself in the remaining half. That night he dreamed he saw Jesus wearing that part of the cloak he had given away. The next morning he resolved to be baptized.

The story of Martin's conversion is striking for its combination of two themes: the encounter with Christ in the form of the poor, and the conviction that the way of Christ is the way of nonviolence. This insight prompted Martin to present himself to his superiors to request a discharge from the army. "I am a soldier of Christ and it is not lawful for me to fight," he said. At the time his regiment was preparing to go into battle against barbarian invaders. When he was accused of cowardice Martin volunteered to go into battle the next day at the front of the line, unarmed, to meet the enemy in the name of Christ.

His offer was declined. Instead he was imprisoned. But upon the conclusion of hostilities, he won his release and discharge. He then traveled to Poitiers, where he became a disciple of the holy bishop St. Hilary, and later joined the monastery at Solesmes. But after ten years he was called out of solitude to become bishop of Tours, in which office he served for over twenty-five years until his death in 397. His biographer, Sulpicius Severus, describes the many ways Martin brought a commitment to Christian peacemaking to his ministry as bishop. In particular, he opposed the use of violence against heretics, even when this left him susceptible to the charge of heretical sympathies. (The feast on this day commemorates the translation of St. Martin's relics. His official feast day is November 11.)

See: F. R. Hoare, trans. and ed., *Sulpicius Severus et al.: The Western Fathers* (New York: Harper & Row, 1965).

July 5
Georges Bernanos
French Novelist (1888–1948)

*"I am between the Angel of light and the Angel of darkness,
looking at them each in turn with the same hunger for the absolute."*

Georges Bernanos was one of the most ardently Catholic of modern French writers. As a young student at the Sorbonne he became a militant of the Action Française, a right-wing movement that championed the royalist heritage of France. He was among a group of students arrested for attacking a professor who had dared to insult the memory of *St. Joan of Arc. By such methods the Action Française loudly defended the honor of the church and presented itself as the staunch champion of orthodoxy. But for most of its members the church as a symbol of tradition and order took precedence over the spirit of Christ. This ultimately caused Bernanos to break with the movement, some time before it was formally condemned by the Vatican.

Bernanos published his first novel, *The Star of Satan*, in the early 1920s. It was a relative success, convincing him that he should devote himself full time to writing. The theme of the novel was the confrontation between good and evil in the soul of a parish priest. It was a theme that would recur in several of his subsequent novels, thus earning him the reputation of being a "priest's novelist." By this time Bernanos was married and trying to support a family on his income as a writer. (He was delighted by the fact that his wife was a descendent of the brother of Joan of Arc!) Many times they were in desperate straits. His situation became still more difficult when a car accident in 1933 left him partially crippled and forced to walk with a pair of canes for the rest of his life. Only with the success of his great novel, *The Diary of a Country Priest*, was he ever to find relative financial security.

The novel had taken shape in his mind over a period of years. In 1935 he had written to a friend of his desire to write, in the form of a diary, the story of a country priest who "will have served God in exact proportion to his belief that he has served Him badly." Upon its publication in 1937 *The Diary of a Country Priest* was quickly recognized as both a literary and spiritual classic, the one novel by which Bernanos would always be remembered. It was also his most deeply personal work, forged out of his own faith and his constant concern for the intermingling of sanctity and mediocrity in the church.

"Mine is a parish like all the rest." So begins the diary of an unnamed priest assigned to a country parish. Through the diary we follow the priest's struggles to convey the mystery of faith to his flock. It seems that everything he does meets with failure and misunderstanding. Painfully aware of his limitations the priest is entirely unaware of his underlying sanctity. It becomes clear that the fate of his parishioners is being fought out in the depths of his own soul, that he is pouring himself out for their salvation. And ultimately, when we discover that the sickly priest is dying, we sense that he has literally offered himself as a victim soul. His dying words are, "Does it matter? Grace is everywhere."

After the publication of *The Diary of a Country Priest* Bernanos moved his family to the Spanish island of Majorca, where he lived through the horrors of the Spanish Civil War. Bernanos was inclined at first to sympathize with General Franco; the Falangists, after all, were supposedly fighting for the cause of the church. Few Catholic voices, either in Spain or anywhere else in Europe, publicly disputed this claim. But as the war dragged on Bernanos became increasingly disillusioned by the atrocities committed on both sides. Those committed by Franco impressed him as especially reprehensible, since they were committed in the name of Christ. It seemed scandalous to him that the church not only failed to denounce this bloodbath but even seemed to bless it as a Holy Crusade. In 1938 he published a scathing account of the war, *Cemeteries under the Moon,* which was welcomed by many members of the Left, while it was denounced as a betrayal by his usual political and religious allies.

There was in Bernanos a pugnacious side, easily drawn to feuds and public controversies. To his friends, however, he revealed another side — sensitive, easily wounded, hungry for affection. Throughout his restless journey he was haunted by the conviction that there was only one happiness: to be a saint. Sanctity, he insisted furthermore, was the true goal and measure of the church. Without the saints the church was a soulless institution that would be the first to join in crucifying its Savior. As he once wrote, "God did not create the Church to ensure the prosperity of the saints, but in order that she should transmit their memory.... They lived and suffered as we do. They were tempted as we are. The man who dares not yet accept what is sacred and divine in their example will at least learn from it the lesson of heroism and honor."

Bernanos's last project, left unfinished, was a life of Jesus. He died on July 5, 1948.

See: Georges Bernanos, *The Diary of a Country Priest* (New York: Macmillan, 1937); Robert Speaight, *Georges Bernanos* (London: Collins & Harvill, 1973).

Jan Hus
Catholic Reformer, Martyr (1372–1415)

*"Lord, Jesus Christ, it is for the sake of the gospel and the preaching
of the word that I undergo, with patience and humility, this terrifying,
ignominious, cruel death."*

The life of Jan Hus, Czech priest and reformer, was almost exactly
coterminous with one of the most serious crises in the history of Christendom — the Great Schism of the papacy (1378–1417). For nearly forty years,
the church was rent between the rival claims of two and ultimately three
popes. Although Hus's theological works did not directly address this crisis, in an ironic way history made them inseparable. It was at the Council
of Constance (1414–1417), summoned to resolve the papal schism, that
Hus was burned as a heretic.

Hus was a master at the University of Prague and preacher at the
University Chapel. There, through the popularity of his sermons before
enormous crowds, he emerged as the leader of a vigorous movement
of church reform. He attacked corruption among his fellow clergy and
strongly advocated lay spirituality through knowledge of Scripture and
frequent communion. Among his accomplishments was a vernacular
translation of the New Testament.

When one of the contending popes authorized the sale of indulgences
to raise money for a crusade against his rival, Hus spoke out with prophetic indignation. In his view the shameless commercialization of the
sacrament of penance was compounded by the fact that it served an exhortation to bloodshed. His stand alienated not only the archbishop of Prague
but the emperor, who stood to share in the proceeds of this commerce.

The story of Hus's trials and betrayals at the hands of princes, rival
popes, and sometimes friends is exceedingly complex and not easily summarized. Scholars have tended to exonerate Hus of the charges brought
against him. (It is reported that Pope John Paul II is among the supporters
of his rehabilitation.) There is little doubt that his positions were misrep-
resented by critics less interested in the truth than in their own political
and ecclesial agendas.

To be sure, the stakes were high, for the papal schism threatened the
entire social order of Europe. But in the face of this crisis, Hus advanced
a position different from the two principal contending camps. On the one
hand there were those who insisted on the monarchical authority of the
papacy as the basis of church unity. On the other hand there were the
so-called conciliarists who pointed out that papal authority — in a situation of rival pontiffs — was a less-than-ideal basis for unity. Instead, they
sought to resolve the crisis by appeal to the higher authority of church
councils.

Hus pursued a more mystical and evangelical approach. Christ alone
was head of the church. The only sure basis for reform and unity was to
be found not in any juridical conception of power but in an understanding

of communion rooted in moral conversion and holiness. To partisans on either side, Hus's position sounded at best unrealistic, and at worst a kind of dreamy anarchism.

Hus was issued a promise of safe conduct to defend his views at the Council of Constance, which had been convened to resolve the schism. Upon his arrival, however, he was arrested and imprisoned. After a shamelessly biased inquiry — closer to a canonical lynching — he was convicted of heresy and turned over to the secular arm for punishment. On July 6, 1415, he was publicly burned.

The courage and serenity with which Hus met his fate, insisting on his innocence while forgiving his enemies, left many witnesses wondering whether the condemned heretic was not in fact a saint. Like the early Luther, to whom he is often compared, Hus combined a deep loyalty to the church with an outspoken discernment of its various pathologies. He represented a bridge between a rigidly institutional model of the church and a freer, spiritual model. In burning that bridge, the council fathers resolved one crisis only to prepare the way for the far greater upheavals of the following century.

As for Hus, who might have escaped death had he willingly renounced his theology, he wrote his own epitaph: "It is better to die well than to live wickedly. One should not sin in order to avoid the punishment of death. Truth conquers all things."

See: Matthew Spinka, *John Hus: A Biography* (Princeton: Princeton University Press, 1968).

July 7

Sts. Cyril and Methodius
Apostles to the Slavs (d. 869, 885)

"The Slavs were happy because they listened to the great deeds of God in their own tongue."

Cyril and Methodius were brothers born in Thessalonica in the early ninth century. Cyril, the younger, studied philosophy at the imperial university in Constantinople and was ordained a priest. His older brother, Methodius, remained a monk in Greece. Both had participated in cultural and diplomatic missions among the Slavs and had some knowledge of their language. Thus, when the emperor received a request for Christian missionaries from Ratislav, the ruler of Moravia, he offered the commission to the two Greek brothers. They set off in 863.

German missionaries had been operating in the East for some while, but they were hampered by their refusal to instruct the people in any language except Latin. Cyril and Methodius, in contrast, preached in the vernacular. They also set about inventing a written Slavonic alphabet — later the basis of "Cyrillic" script — into which they translated the Scriptures. As a result, they are remembered among other things as founders of Slavonic literature. They also introduced the Slavonic language into the liturgy (where it remains to this day the official liturgical language in many churches of the East).

Their mission was a huge success, but their innovations led to conflicts with the German bishops. To shore up their authority they returned to Rome to present their mission strategy to the pope. After hearing their report he gave them his full support. Cyril in the meantime became a monk, only to die shortly after. He was buried in Rome. But Methodius, now consecrated an archbishop, returned to Moravia. Despite his papal support, he continued to encounter opposition from his rival missionaries and ended up spending two years in prison. He was released upon the intervention of the pope, but once again he had to return to Rome to answer charges of heterodoxy. Again he was vindicated and again he returned to Moravia. He died on April 6, 885.

Cyril and Methodius are celebrated in the calendars of the East and the West. (Their feast day, long observed on July 7, is now assigned to February 14). They are honored as the apostles to the Slavic peoples and as innovative missionaries who pioneered a form of inculturation. In their use of the vernacular they not only respected the local culture but helped to promote and elevate it. They are also revered as patron saints of ecumenism — especially by those who mourn the tragic gulf between the churches of the East and West. These include Pope John Paul II, the first Slavic pontiff of the Roman Catholic church, who dedicated one of his encyclicals to their honor.

See: Michael Lacko, *Sts. Cyril and Methodius* (Rome: Slovak Editions, 1963); Pope John Paul II, *The Apostles of the Slavs* (The Vatican, 1985).

July 8

St. Elizabeth of Portugal
Queen (1271–1336)

"Do not forget that when sovereigns are at war they can no longer busy themselves with their administration; justice is not distributed; no care is taken of the people; and this alone is your sovereign charge, this the main point of your duty as kings."

Like her great-aunt *St. Elizabeth of Hungary, St. Elizabeth of Portugal was a royal daughter, betrothed as a child to a foreign prince for reasons of state. The daughter of the king of Aragon, she was born in 1271. At twelve she was married to King Denis of Portugal, a profligate man, who tolerated his wife's piety while making no secret of his own infidelities. Elizabeth bore two children, a son and a daughter. Her son, Alonso, would later come close to open rebellion against his neglectful father. For her role in effecting a reconciliation between father and son Elizabeth became popularly known as "the Peacemaker." But her talents as a peacemaker were exercised on an even greater level when she personally prevented a war between Portugal and Castile.

Elizabeth lived up to the public responsibilities of her office as queen. But the greater part of her time was spent in prayer and a variety of charitable projects. She established hospitals, orphanages, and religious houses throughout the kingdom, as well as halfway homes for "fallen women."

When her husband fell seriously ill in 1324 she devotedly nursed him until his death the following year. After making a pilgrimage to Compostela she put on the habit of a Franciscan tertiary and lived in the monastery of Coimbra that she had helped to found. She lived there for eleven years in poverty and prayer, emerging occasionally to intercede between rival monarchs, most of whom were relatives, either by blood or marriage. Even as she lived she was credited with numerous miracles, and she was popularly revered by the people of Portugal.

She died in 1336 and was canonized three centuries later by Pope Urban VIII, who named her the Patroness of Peace.

See: Vincent McNabb, O.P., "St. Elizabeth of Portugal," in F. J. Sheed, ed., *Saints Are Not Sad* (New York: Sheed & Ward, 1949).

July 9

Augustus Tolton
African-American Priest (1854–1897)

"I really feel that there will be a stir all over the United States when I begin my church; I shall work and pull at it as long as God gives me life, for I see that I have principalities to resist anywhere and everywhere I go."

The first black priests in the United States were a remarkable trio of brothers, the Healys, born of an Irish southerner and his slave mistress. The light-skinned boys were never treated as slaves; they were sent north and raised in freedom. Later they all three pursued vocations in the church; one of them, James Augustine Healy, became a bishop. But though they were the first to break the color barrier in the Catholic clergy, they assiduously avoided any identification with members of their race, failed to address the issue of slavery, and had no wider effect on the condition of black Catholics in America.

The next black priest in America had a different story. Augustus Tolton was born a slave in Ralls County, Missouri, in 1854. His parents, Martha and Peter Paul Tolton, met while working on adjacent plantations. Both Catholics, they were married in a local church. Augustus was their second of three children, all of whom were baptized as Catholics. Both parents took advantage of the outbreak of the Civil War to escape from their masters. Peter Paul joined the Union forces and may have died during the war. Martha Tolton took her three children to the free state of Illinois, settling in the town of Quincy. There she managed to find a Catholic school that would accept her children.

Augustus decided as a boy that he wanted to become a priest. His pastor supported his vocation but could find no seminary willing to accept him. He finally arranged for Augustus to receive private tutorials from another local priest, with whom he spent two years studying Latin, Greek, German, English, and history. Eventually he was accepted to study at Quincy College, a small Franciscan institution, where he studied for another two years until 1880.

With support from the Franciscans, Tolton won acceptance at the Urban College in Rome, a seminary attached to the missionary Congregation of the Propaganda. He diligently applied himself to his studies, expecting at the conclusion that he would be sent as a missionary to Africa. He was delighted, however, when it was decided that he should return to the United States to work among the struggling black Catholic population. He was ordained in 1886 at the age of thirty-two. Soon after, when he arrived in New York, his first Masses drew enormous crowds of cheering blacks.

Tolton continued on to his hometown of Quincy, where again he was greeted with enthusiasm. He was appointed pastor of a black parish, St. Joseph's, where he was widely loved by his congregation. His effectiveness as a preacher and spiritual leader is reflected in the fact that he began to draw a sizeable number of white parishioners. This seems to have generated resentment on the part of many of the white priests of neighboring parishes. The friendliness that had greeted his arrival steadily cooled. It was not blatant racism that he encountered so much as a sense of marginalization, as if he did not really exist. His bishop, James Ryan, reported to Rome that Tolton's troubles resulted "because he wants to establish a kind of society here that is not possible (integration)."

In 1889 Tolton managed to arrange a change of assignment to another black parish in Chicago. He enjoyed his pastoral work, but the sense of isolation remained, the burden of being the only black priest in America. A visiting nun wrote of him, "Poor Father...he is left to struggle on almost alone; in poverty and humility grappling with the giant task of founding a church and congregation in Chicago. We who come in contact with him in our labors and are the witnesses of his ardent charity and self-denying zeal feel ourselves privileged to bow the knee for his saintly blessing."

Tolton worked in Chicago for seven years, much of the time suffering in ill health and nagged by doubts about the effectiveness of his apostolate. He died on July 9, 1897, at the age of forty-three.

Augustus Tolton is remembered today as a pioneer, the first black priest in America who fully identified with and sought to represent the aspirations of African-American Catholics. A good and holy priest, he exposed the presence of racism in the church while striving to witness to an ideal of equality and reconciliation within the Body of Christ.

See: Cyprian Davis, *The History of Black Catholics in the United States* (New York: Crossroad, 1990).

Sts. Antony and Theodosius
Abbots of the Caves of Kiev (d. 1073, 1074)

"Mindful of the commandment of the good Lord, my unworthy self declares to you that it is good for us to feed the hungry and the homeless with the fruits of our labor.... If God's grace does not uphold and nourish us through the poor, what should we do with all our works?" —St. Theodosius

Antony and Theodosius were two of the original pioneers of Russian monasticism. Antony, the elder of the two, apparently spent some time in the monastery of Mt. Athos before returning to his homeland. On his return he established a hermitage in a forbidding cave overlooking the city of Kiev. There, despite his extreme austerity, he attracted followers who took up residence in neighboring caves and submitted to his authority. Eventually he retired again to his solitary life and lived on for another forty years before he finally died in 1073 at the age of ninety. In the meantime, however, he turned over the leadership of his monastery to one of his disciples, a monk named Theodosius.

Theodosius came from a prosperous family. As a young man he had scandalized his family by dressing like a serf and working in the fields. Against his mother's protests he replied, "Our Lord Jesus Christ humbled Himself and underwent degradation, and we have got to follow His example in this too." In 1032 he joined the monks in the Caves of Kiev. Soon after he succeeded Antony as abbot.

Theodosius was in every way a different type of monk and abbot than his holy predecessor. While Antony represented the ascetic style of the early desert fathers, Theodosius recalled instead the spirit of *St. Basil. Sanctification, he believed, was not to be pursued through private asceticism but through charity and the discipline of community life. He moved the monks out of their caves and forced them to live together. At the same time he insisted that the monastery should not exist for the benefit of its members alone but should serve the world. He made sure that the monastery included a hospital for the sick, a guest house for travelers, and a soup kitchen for the hungry. He was personally active in community affairs and was known as a prophetic champion of social justice, even when this brought him into conflict with the local nobility. He made himself available as a spiritual director to any lay people who sought his counsel.

In all things Theodosius tried to lead by example. This extended to his willingness to work in the kitchen and the fields and to take his turn nursing the sick brothers. For his charity, wisdom, and holiness, he was revered as much by the wider community as by his monks. He died in 1074, a year after his master Antony. They were among the first Russian saints to be canonized.

See: Louis Bouyer, *Orthodox Spirituality and Protestant and Anglican Spirituality,* A History of Christian Spirituality, vol. 3 (New York: Seabury, 1969).

St. Benedict
Monk (480–550)

*"We are about to open a school for God's service,
in which we hope nothing harsh or oppressive will be directed."*

Few saints have left such a palpable impact on the world as St. Benedict, the monk whose Rule set a standard for the Western monastic tradition. And yet the sources for his biography are limited. Virtually all that is known is contained in the brief account of his life written by *Pope Gregory the Great almost fifty years after his death.

St. Gregory records that Benedict was born in Nursia of a distinguished family and was later educated in Rome. Disgusted by the moral squalor of his fellow students he abandoned his studies, gave up his inheritance, and devoted himself to the quest for God. At first this took the form of penitential solitude in a cave at Subiaco. But gradually he attracted the attention of other spiritual seekers. He was induced, much against his will, to assume the leadership of a nearby monastic community. But apparently the monks bridled under his discipline and even tried to poison his wine. By miraculous means (a typical recourse of the narrative) Benedict foiled the plot and henceforth returned to his preferred solitude.

Still, disciples continued to seek him out. Eventually he agreed to organize them into a group of monasteries, each with its own presiding abbot. He himself assumed the leadership of one of these communities. After some time he established the famous monastery at Monte Cassino, later renowned as the birthplace of the Benedictine order. There, at some point, he wrote his monastic Rule. And there, in time, he died and was buried, beside the grave of his beloved sister, *St. Scholastica.

Gregory's account lays particular emphasis on the fantastic and miraculous, and thus gives little sense of the man behind the Rule. But if there is one personal quality to which the stories bear witness it is Benedict's extraordinary power to read and discern the souls of others. In this respect Gregory's portrait is consistent with the Rule itself, which provides ample evidence of Benedict's rare insight into human nature.

Whereas earlier monastic experiments had stressed rigorous asceticism and often superhuman self-denial, Benedict's Rule was designed for ordinary human beings. The element of discipline was shifted from externals to the interior, from the flesh to the will. His monks were not to be denied adequate food or sleep; they were in fact counseled to avoid any extraordinary or self-imposed mortifications. Their discipline was to lie in humility, obedience, a commitment to stability, and an accommodation to the requirements of community life.

Community was, in fact, the key feature of his monastic vision. Rather than writing for a collection of individuals competing against each other in their solitary quests for perfection, Benedict stressed the value of community life as a school for holiness. The community for Benedict was ideally suited to bring individuals to their highest potential. Salvation, in effect, was thus a team effort, like the performance of an orchestra under the skilled direction of a conductor.

Much depended in this scheme on the wisdom and holiness of the abbot. He must be stern, yet kind and flexible, adapting his methods to the needs of each monk and the good of all. He was eternally accountable for the salvation of his monks and he must regard them as his sons and brothers.

If this sounded like a dictatorship, there were softening features. For one thing the monastery was a place of equality; social hierarchy and distinctions between freedmen and serfs did not obtain. And in serious matters, so Benedict stressed, the whole community must be consulted — even the youngest brother.

Benedict's balance of work and prayer, his validation of community life, and his regulation of monastic discipline eventually set the pattern for Western monasticism as a whole. In part this was aided by the official sponsorship of church authorities like Pope Gregory — a monk himself, who may have had direct experience of Benedict's Rule. But a significant factor in the Benedictine success was the intrinsic attraction of the Rule itself and its underlying balance, moderation, and humanity.

Apart from its effect on the history of monasticism, Benedictine spirituality had an even wider influence on medieval society. For centuries the Benedictine monasteries presented the challenge of an alternative world, governed by the spirit of Christ. At a time of extreme social hierarchy, they presented an ideal of equality. At a time when manual labor was derided, they affirmed the spiritual value of work. During a time of cultural disintegration, they maintained islands of learning and civilization. In a time when violence was commonplace, they lived by the motto of Peace. The Benedictine monasteries represented a vision of health, wholeness, and ecology in a world badly out of kilter. To the extent that that world remains *our* world, the vision of St. Benedict retains its relevance and attraction.

See: Gregory the Great, *Dialogues, Book II: Saint Benedict,* trans. Myra L. Uhlfelder (Indianapolis: Bobbs-Merrill Educational Publishing, 1967); Joan Chittister, *The Rule of Benedict: Insights for the Ages* (New York: Crossroad 1993).

July 12

St. Veronica
(first century)

"For I was hungry and you fed me. . . .
I was a prisoner and you visited me."   —Matthew 25:35

According to pious legend, Veronica was a woman who encountered Christ as he labored under the weight of the cross on his way to Golgotha. Moved by compassion she wiped his face with her veil, which later, miraculously, bore the imprint of his features.

There is no scriptural basis for the story of Veronica. Its earliest reference occurs in the so-called Gospel of Nicodemus from the fourth century. Although various theologians have tried to identify Veronica with other unnamed women in the Gospels, it is speculated that her name is derived from the miracle itself: *vera icon* (true image).

Over time interest settled on the miracle of the veil rather than on the act of charity that preceded it. At the height of the medieval obsession with relics of Christ's passion (the True Cross, the Holy Thorn, the Holy Grail), there came to be many supposed candidates for Veronica's veil. One of these has resided in St. Peter's for many centuries, though the church now omits St. Veronica from the calendar of saints.

The story of Veronica was eventually appropriated into the stations of the cross, a devotional exercise intended to place the penitent imaginatively within the drama of Christ's passion. Veronica is the faithful disciple who ought to have been present in the gospel story. She performs the act of mercy that we *ought* to have performed, had we been there.

In fact the story of Veronica contains no indication that she was a disciple of Jesus. She was simply a woman who responded compassionately to a man in pain and anguish, a convicted felon on his way to death. Veronica wiped his face with her veil. And in the miraculous image left behind he revealed his true identity.

The story of Veronica remains a true icon — an image of the divine mystery. We need not have lived two thousand years ago to replicate her act of devotion. Every man or woman in need is an occasion to discover the meaning of Christ's words: "Inasmuch as you did this to one of the least of my brothers and sisters, you did it to me."

July 13

Bd. Jacobus de Voragine
Archbishop and Hagiographer (1230–1298)

"The Feast of All Saints was instituted for four reasons, namely, to commemorate the dedication of a temple, to supply a feast day for the saints who were omitted during the year, to expiate for negligence, and to obtain more easily the granting of our prayers."

Jacobus de Voragine was a Dominican preacher, the archbishop of Genoa, and one of the most widely read authors of the Middle Ages. He is best remembered for *The Golden Legend,* the first popular compilation of saints' lives. Drawing on traditional sources, which he freely embellished, Jacobus presented a calendar of 159 saints. These included such all but legendary figures as Sts. *Agnes and Lucy (virgin martyrs), Sebastian (riddled with arrows), Christopher (who carried the Christ child on his back), and George (who battled a dragon). By dwelling on their miraculous deeds Jacobus helped to elevate the popularity of these saints above the cult of such better-attested, if more prosaic, figures as *Augustine, *Basil, or *Ambrose.

With the rise of humanism the extravagant style of *The Golden Legend* and similar hagiographical works fell into disrepute. Rather than appreciate Jacobus's book as a work of spiritual devotion, the reformers judged it according to the emerging standards of historical science. By this measure, understandably, *The Golden Legend* was dismissed as worthless. *Erasmus was typical in derisively dismissing those fools "who love to hear or tell feigned Miracles and strange lies, and are never weary of any tale so long as it be of ghosts, spirits, goblins, or devils, or the like; which the farther they are from the truth, the more readily they are believed and the more do they tickle their hearts."

In fact Jacobus would never have conceived his task as the recording of mere historical facts. He meant to present the holy servants of God as living emblems of the gospel. In this light *The Golden Legend* has gradually earned a more devoted modern audience. Among those who have eloquently expressed their appreciation is Father Hippolyte Delehaye, a pioneer in the modern science of hagiography. Describing the motives of Bd. Jacobus, he wrote,

> In this picture God's friends are represented for us as what is greatest on earth; they are human creatures lifted up above matter and above the miseries of our little world.... The saints practice all the virtues in a superhuman degree.... They render these virtues lovable, and they urge Christians to practice them. Their life is, in truth, the concrete realization of the spirit of the Gospel, and from the very fact that it brings home to us this sublime ideal, legend, like all poetry, can claim a higher degree of truth than history itself.

See: The Golden Legend of Jacobus de Voragine, trans. Granger Ryan and Helmut Ripperger, 2 vols. (London: Longman, Green, 1941); Hippolyte Delehaye, S.J., *The Legends of the Saints* (Notre Dame, Ind.: University of Notre Dame Press, 1961).

July 14
St. Camillus de Lellis
Founder of the Ministers of the Sick (1550–1614)

"To Christ, God and Man, sick in the person of the Poor — homage of love."

The mother of St. Camillus was sixty at the time of his birth. Since his conception was nothing short of a miracle she felt it was fit that his delivery should be similarly blessed. Thus, when she went into labor during Mass, she hurried to a stable so her son, like his Savior, could be born on a bed of straw. Such a child, she believed, was destined to be a saint.

After such an auspicious beginning, it is somewhat ironic to encounter the future saint some twenty years hence, a towering man (six-foot-six), a soldier of fortune, with an irascible temper, a penchant for brawling, and a serious addiction to gambling. Camillus seems to have inherited these qualities from his father, an old soldier, considerably less pious than his wife. Together father and son went off to fight the Turks with the Venetian army. In the course of these adventures Camillus developed a hideous and painful sore on his leg, which would afflict him for the rest of his life. He was sent to the hospital of San Giacamo in Rome, where he worked as a servant while also undergoing treatment. His nursing talents were appreciated, but his temper was so intolerable that he was dismissed to return to the army.

Soon his physical suffering was compounded by the consequences of his own temperament. His gambling resulted in his losing everything, including the proverbial shirt off his back. In desperation he took a job as a builder for a Capuchin community. There his exposure to the friars awakened a dormant thirst for God and he vowed to amend his life. He sought to enter a religious community, but his ailment proved an impediment. (Sound health was required for entrants to religious orders.) Instead he returned to San Giacamo and devoted himself, in a spirit of religious discipline, to the care of the sick and dying.

Charity was not a virtue commonly associated with hospitals at the time, and healing was virtually as rare. Conditions in San Giacamo, as in most other hospitals, were appalling. Aside from the filth, the care provided by indifferent and even sadistic staff members — often recruited from the criminal class — was often more insidious than any illness. In this environment Camillus was determined to infuse an atmosphere of love. In the spirit of his newfound faith he sought to treat each sick and dying person as another Christ, a living sacrament. Before long his loving ministrations, combined with his appreciation for the value of good nutrition, cleanliness, and fresh air, produced results that appeared miraculous. The administrators of the hospital elevated him to the position of superintendent.

By this time, however, Camillus had conceived the idea of an association of similarly minded nurses, for whom care of the sick and dying would be a religious discipline. His confessor, *St. Philip Neri, encouraged him to proceed with this project. He also suggested that Camillus might be able to add the comforts of the sacraments to his nursing care should he become a priest. And so Camillus dutifully applied himself to the study of Latin and theology and received holy orders in 1584.

Soon after this he left San Giacamo with two other companions to establish a model hospital in Rome. In 1591 Pope Gregory XIV recognized Camillus and his Ministers of the Sick, allowing them to wear a religious habit adorned with a large red cross. The community grew and its members proved their mettle by volunteering for service amid outbreaks of plague. Camillus was not content to wait for the sick to come to him. He used to scour the caves and catacombs of the city to seek out any who suffered. Given the conditions under which they worked, it is no surprise that many of the ministers became sick and died.

Camillus personally founded fifteen houses of his order and eight hospitals. He himself remained in more or less unbearable pain, though to the end he insisted on providing personal care at the bedside of the most miserable cases. He eventually died in Genoa on July 14, 1614, at the age of sixty-four. He was canonized in 1746. Having known what it meant both to suffer and to provide succor, he was later declared the patron both of the sick and of nurses.

See: C. C. Martindale, *Life of Saint Camillus* (New York: Sheed & Ward, 1946).

July 15

St. Bonaventure
Franciscan, Doctor of the Church (1221–1274)

"A spiritual joy is the greatest sign of the divine grace dwelling in a soul."

Little is known of the early life of St. Bonaventure. Apparently he was born to a wealthy family in Orvieto and was inspired to become a Franciscan while studying at the University of Paris, sometime around 1238. *St. Francis had died only some dozen years before, but already his order was rapidly changing the face of the church in Europe. To Bonaventure it seemed that the Franciscan order "was not invented by human providence but by Christ. In it, the learned and the simple lived as brethren."

Bonaventure himself was most decidedly one of the learned. As such he would seem to contrast sharply with the simplicity of Francis. But in fact Francis had held learning in great esteem, as long as it was subordinated to the pursuit of holiness. In this spirit Bonaventure received the support of the order to continue his studies. In 1257, along with his Dominican counterpart *St. Thomas Aquinas, he received his doctorate in theology.

Rather than pursue the life of an academic theologian, however, Bonaventure was immediately elected at the age of thirty-six to serve as minister-general of the Friars Minor. It was a critical time for the Franciscans. Along with defending the order against its external critics, he had to contend with internal dissension between extremes within the community. On the one hand there were so-called Spirituals, who insisted on a strict adherence to Francis's spirit of poverty and who maintained a somewhat anarchistic approach to organization. On the other hand there were those who desired a much more relaxed and "practical" attitude toward property and the requirements of institutional life. Bonaventure tried to steer a middle course, establishing a balance between the radical freedom of Francis and the disciplined order of a religious community. To reinforce his moderate interpretation of the Franciscan charism he composed an influential life of St. Francis. So successful was Bonaventure in establishing the direction of the Franciscans that he was later known as the Second Founder.

Although Bonaventure's career as a theologian was sacrificed to the government of his order, he managed to write a number of important works. Among these, his most influential book was *The Journey of the Mind to God,* written during a retreat on Mt. Alvernia in 1259. It was at this site that St. Francis had received the stigmata, the mark of his identification with the crucified Christ. Bonaventure's book was an attempt to translate Francis's experience into philosophical terms. It traces the soul's journey along the path of holiness, leading from contemplation of the created world to an ever-deepening contemplation of the spiritual order, and ultimately progressing toward the goal of mystical union with God.

By all accounts, Bonaventure himself was a model of humility and charity. In 1265 Pope Clement IV wished to name him archbishop of York, an appointment he respectfully declined. In 1273, however, Pope Gregory X ordered him to accept the title of cardinal-bishop of Albano. It is said that when papal legates were sent to present him with his red hat and other insignia of office he kept them waiting while he finished washing the dishes. In a summary of his spirituality he observed, "The perfection of a religious man is to do common things in a perfect manner, and a constant fidelity in small matters is great and heroic virtue!"

Bonaventure died in 1274 during the Council of Lyons. He was canonized in 1482 and declared a Doctor of the Church in 1588. In recognition of his angelic virtue he is known as the Seraphic Doctor.

See: Etienne Gilson, *The Philosophy of St. Bonaventure* (Paterson, N.J.: St. Anthony Guild, 1965).

July 16

George Tyrrell
Modernist Theologian (1861–1909)

"There are times when a soldier is bound to disobey — if he knows his officer is drunk or mad or misinformed. If his venture succeeds he is crowned; if not, he is shot. I shall probably be shot."

George Tyrrell was one of the most prominent of those figures implicated in the so-called Modernist affair. In the encyclical *Pascendi* of 1907, Pope Pius X described Modernism as "the synthesis of all heresies," and for years its supposed proponents were branded as sinister agents of destruction. Modern historians are more likely to view the Modernists as sincere Catholics who were premature in hoping to facilitate some reconciliation between the spirit of Catholicism and the more positive features of modernity.

Tyrrell was born in Dublin in 1861 and raised in the Anglican church. At the age of eighteen he underwent a conversion to Catholicism and soon after applied for admission to the Jesuits in London. Like all theologians of the time he was forced to master the requisite course in scholastic theology. Tyrrell found it unsatisfying and ultimately inadequate to his own religious experience. After reading the church fathers and the writings of *Cardinal Newman he became convinced that the church must find a different language for expounding the faith. Part of the problem, he believed, was the church's tendency to confuse revelation (the primary content of faith), with theology — a form of secondary reflection on faith. The result was that revelation was identified with an arid system of propositional "truths," seemingly unconnected with intrinsic human experience.

> It is all but impossible to imagine the Christ of the synoptics, the advocate of the poor and simple against the intellectual tyranny of lawyers, scribes, and theologians, attaching the slightest religious value to the theologically correct formulation of the inscrutable mysteries prophetically symbolized by the Heavenly Father, the Son of Man, the kingdom of God, etc., or making salvation to depend on any point of mere intellectual exactitude.

Tyrrell's criticism extended to what he called the "dogmatic fallacy." This was the church's temptation to convert prophetic mysteries into "principles of exactly determinable intellectual value." Despite such criticisms of the church, however, he continued to conceive of himself primarily as a Catholic apologist: "What makes a Catholic is not this or that abstract theory of the church, but a belief in the historical Catholic community as the living outgrowth of the apostolic mission."

Through his writing and preaching Tyrrell gradually attracted a wide popular audience, as well as a number of devoted friends, including *Baron von Hügel and *Maude Petre. But he also attracted the negative attention of censors in Rome. He had a penchant for sarcasm and hyperbole, and his superiors ultimately charged that his writings were "offensive to pious ears." In 1906 he was expelled from the Jesuits. He remained a priest, but with no sponsoring bishop he was deprived of his priestly faculties. Petre provided him with a cottage where he continued to write.

By this time Pope Pius X had come to perceive in the work of Tyrrell and his fellow travelers a broadscale threat to the authority of the church and the integrity of Catholic truth. In 1907 he issued two sweeping condemnations of Modernism. Though the move was not unexpected, even Tyrrell was surprised by the vehemence of the pope's language and the unusually severe measures enacted. All priests were required to take an "anti-Modernist oath"; vigilance committees to root out disloyal voices were to be instituted in every diocese in the world. The effect of these decrees was to freeze the development of creative Catholic thought for decades to come.

While Tyrrell refused to recognize himself or any other person in the picture drawn by the pope, he was not unwilling to claim the name Modernist. "If we must have a sect-name, we might have a worse than one that stands for life and movement as against stagnation and death, for the Catholicism that is of every age against the sectarianism that is of one." The Modernists, he said, were those who believe as firmly as the "Medievalists" in the Catholic church, "but whose faith is not frightened but stimulated by the assured results of modern criticism." In a series of impassioned, if impolitic, letters to the *Times,* Tyrrell offered a scathing critique of *Pascendi* and the authoritarian vision it represented. He characterized the pope's attitude as being, "The church, *c'est moi.*"

The pope retaliated by ordering that Tyrrell be deprived of the sacraments. Tyrrell in turn offered to apologize for irony or sarcasm toward the Holy Father, but declared:

> If, however, my offense lies in having protested publicly, in the name of Catholicism, against a document destructive of the only possible defense of Catholicism and of every reason for submitting, within due limits, to ecclesiastical authority — a document which constitutes the greatest scandal for thousands who, like myself, have been brought into, and kept in, the Church by the influence of Cardinal Newman and of the mystical theology of the Fathers and the Saints — for such a protest I am absolutely and finally impenitent.

Tyrrell continued to insist on his loyalty to the church. But his time was running short. On March 1909 he was struck down with the first symptoms of Bright's disease and within weeks he was close to death. He died on July 15, 1909, at the age of forty-eight. Before the end he had been eager to receive the last rites of the church, to make his confession, and to receive absolution. All this was provided by a friendly priest. But he did not retract his views on the church. As a result he was denied a Catholic burial.

See: Ellen Leonard, *George Tyrrell and the Catholic Tradition* (New York: Paulist, 1982); Bernard Reardon, ed., *Roman Catholic Modernism* (Stanford, Calif.: Stanford University Press, 1970).

July 17
The Carmelite Martyrs of Compiègne
(d. 1794)

"We are the victims of the age, and we ought to sacrifice ourselves to obtain its return to God."

In 1790 a decree of the revolutionary French Republic suppressed all religious communities, save those engaged in teaching and nursing. One of the communities thus affected was a convent of Carmelite nuns in Compiègne. They were forced to relinquish their habits, to dress in secular clothes, and to abandon their convent. Nevertheless, in July 1794 sixteen nuns were arrested on the charge of continuing their illicit way of life and imprisoned in a former Visitation convent. Two weeks later they were transported to Paris. By this time, judging that the moment for compromise had passed, they resumed their religious habits and openly recited the prayers of the Divine Office.

Their trial was brief. They were convicted of having made themselves "enemies of the people by conspiring against its sovereign rule." On July 17, 1794, they were transported by open wagons to the place of execution, all the while singing the Salve Regina and the Te Deum and reciting the prayers for the dying.

These Carmelites were beatified in 1906, the first martyrs of the French terror to be so recognized. Their story has been recounted in the moving opera by François Poulenc, *Dialogues of the Carmelites,* for which *Georges Bernanos provided the libretto.

See: Terrye Newkirk, O.C.D.S., *The Mantle of Elijah: The Martyrs of Compiègne as Prophets of the Modern Age* (Washington, D.C.: ICS Publications, 1995).

July 18

Bartolomé de Las Casas
"Defender of the Indians" (1484–1566)

"Christ did not come into the world for gold."

Bartolomé de Las Casas was the most distinguished of a number of Dominican friars who raised their voices against the rapacious violence inflicted on the Indians of the Americas. Las Casas was not content to denounce the excesses of the Conquest. Reading the gospel from the perspective of what he called "the scourged Christ of the Indies," he articulated a theological understanding of religious freedom, human rights, and the relation between salvation and social justice, that was scarcely matched again in the Catholic church before the Second Vatican Council. Five hundred years after the collision of cultures in the Americas, Las Casas is chiefly recognized as a prophet, who anticipated by many centuries the church's "preferential option for the poor."

As a boy of eight, Las Casas witnessed the return of Columbus to Seville after his first voyage to the New World. He made his own first trip to Hispaniola in 1502. After studies in Rome for the priesthood he returned to the New World, where he served as chaplain in the Spanish conquest of Cuba. Though a priest, he also benefited from the Conquest as the owner of an *encomienda,* a plantation with Indian indentured laborers.

In 1514 however, he underwent a dramatic conversion, prompted by his witnessing the genocidal cruelty inflicted on the Indians. He soon joined the Dominican order and became a passionate and prophetic defender of the indigenous peoples. For more than fifty years he traveled back and forth between the New World and the court of Spain, attempting through his books, letters, and preaching to expose the cruelties of the Conquest, whose very legitimacy, and not merely excesses, he disavowed.

Although the main attraction for the Spanish in the New World was gold, the Conquest was ostensibly justified by evangelical motivations. The pope had authorized the subjugation of the Indian populations for the purpose of implanting the gospel and securing their salvation. Las Casas claimed that the deeds of the conquistadors revealed their true religion:

> In order to gild a very cruel and harsh tyranny that destroys so many villages and people, solely for the sake of satisfying the greed of men and giving them gold, the latter, who themselves do not know the faith, use the pretext of teaching it to others and thereby deliver up the innocent in order to extract from their blood *the wealth which these men regard as their god.*

Las Casas vehemently opposed the notion that the gospel could be spread through slaughter or compulsion of any kind. While others claimed that the Indians were a lesser race, he affirmed their full humanity, and thus their entitlement to all human rights. For his writings on human equality and his defense of the right to religious freedom, Las Casas deserves to be remembered as a political philosopher of extreme significance in the history of ideas.

But Las Casas's theological insights went far beyond a simple affirmation of the Indians' human dignity. Identifying the Indians with the poor, in the gospel sense, he argued that in their sufferings they represented the crucified Christ. He wrote, "I leave in the Indies Jesus Christ, our God, scourged and afflicted and beaten and crucified not once, but thousands of times."

For Las Casas there could be no salvation in Jesus Christ apart from social justice. Thus, the question was not whether the Indians were to be "saved"; the more serious question was the salvation of the Spanish who were persecuting Christ in his poor.

In 1543, with court officials in Spain eager to be rid of him, Las Casas was named bishop of the impoverished region of Chiapas in southern Mexico. There he immediately alienated his flock by refusing absolution to any Spaniard who would not free his Indian slaves. He was denounced to the Spanish court as a "lunatic" and received numerous death threats. Eventually he resigned his bishopric and returned to Spain, where he felt he could more effectively prosecute his cause. There he died on July 18, 1566, at the age of eighty-two.

See: George Sanderlin, ed., *Witness: Writings of Bartolomé de Las Casas,* 2d ed. (Maryknoll, N.Y.: Orbis, 1992); Gustavo Gutiérrez, *Las Casas: In Search of the Poor of Jesus Christ* (Maryknoll, N.Y.: Orbis, 1993).

July 19

St. Macrina the Younger
Virgin (c. 327–379)

"You who broke the flaming sword, and compassionately gave paradise back to the man crucified with You, remember me also in your kingdom, for I, too, have been crucified with You, having nailed my flesh through fear of You and having feared your judgments."

St. Macrina was the eldest child in a remarkable family. Of her nine siblings, three others became canonized saints, along with her parents, St. Basil the Elder and St. Emmelia. According to the touching memoir by her brother *St. Gregory of Nyssa, Macrina served as a spiritual fulcrum between her parents and her younger siblings, serving by her own example and exhortation to urge the rest of her family along the path to sanctity.

She was born in Caesarea in Cappadocia around 327. At her mother's insistence she received an excellent education. When she was twelve her father selected a suitable young man to whom she was betrothed. But when he died before their marriage, Macrina seized on the excuse of her betrothal to renounce all prospect of future marriage and to claim the status of a widow. She committed herself to remain at the side of her mother.

After the death of her father Macrina took special care for the education and upbringing of her younger brothers, especially *St. Basil, St. Gregory, and St. Peter of Sebatea. It was she who encouraged Peter to become a priest. She had a similar influence on Basil, weaning him from pride in his rhetorical skills and urging him to pursue instead the goal of holy wisdom. Her influence was also applied to her widowed mother. Though Macrina's father had left them considerable wealth, she persuaded her mother to dispense with all luxury and privilege and to adopt a life of prayerful simplicity. When her mother died Macrina founded a convent on the family estate. There women of all social backgrounds were drawn to consecrate their lives to prayer and God's service.

When Basil, by that time the eminent bishop of Caesarea, died in 379, Gregory returned home to find Macrina sick and lying on the two boards she used for a bed. They enjoyed a sweet reunion, conversing at length on death and the future life. Gregory, one of the outstanding theologians of all time, found himself amazed at his sister's profound insight into the mysteries of the faith. "She was uplifted as she discoursed to us on the nature of the soul and explained the reason of life in the flesh, and why man was made, and how he was mortal, and the origin of death and the nature of the journey from death to life again." She continued with her discourse until her last breath. "All this," said Gregory, "seemed to me more than human."

Gregory presided at her funeral.

See: St. Gregory of Nyssa, "The Life of St. Macrina," in *Ascetical Works* (Washington, D.C.: Catholic University of America Press, 1967).

July 20

Leo XIII
Pope (1810–1903)

"I want to see the church so far forward
that my successor will not be able to turn back."

The long reign of Pope Pius IX ended on February 7, 1878. In his thirty-two years in Rome he had managed to do more than any other pope of modern times to enhance the image and power of the papacy. But having defined the identity of the church in negative opposition to the modern age, he left little room for constructive engagement with the issues and values of the day. Since the republican capture of Rome in 1870 the pope had become a "prisoner of the Vatican" with little influence over contemporary intellectual and cultural movements. Through hostility to the principle of social change the church had become largely irrelevant to the interests of the new industrial working class. It is no wonder that by the time of Pius's death there were many in the church eager for a change of tack.

On the morning of February 20, with their third ballot, the papal conclave elected a new pope. He was sixty-eight-year-old Joachim Pecci, the cardinal archbishop of Perugia, who took the name Leo XIII. In selecting the frail and elderly Pecci it seems the conclave was anticipating a transitional pope. Pecci himself shared this expectation. As he said to friends, "If they elect me they will soon have to have another conclave." But in fact, as Pope Leo XIII, he managed to reign for twenty-five years, doing much in that time to inaugurate a new rapprochement between the church and the modern world.

In many ways Leo maintained a continuity with the conservative style of his predecessor. But having spent a good part of his career in the Vatican diplomatic service he had a far wider understanding of the world beyond Rome and a keen interest in restoring the church to a position of moral and spiritual leadership.

One of Leo's first initiatives as pope was largely symbolic. In his first appointment to the college of cardinals he bestowed the red hat on *John Henry Newman, the English priest and convert long suspected in conservative circles of harboring liberal tendencies. In other ways Leo authorized a new style of intellectual engagement. He opened the Vatican archives to scholars. He supported the foundation of the Biblical Institute in Jerusalem and in his encyclical *Providentissimus Deus* (1893) he gave the first tentative support by the Vatican to the science of modern biblical criticism.

Without a doubt, however, Leo's most significant contribution was in his pronouncements in the social realm. In particular, his encyclical *Rerum Novarum* (1891) inaugurated the modern era of Catholic social teaching. Previous Vatican pronouncements, to the extent that they addressed modern social problems, tended to concentrate on warnings against socialism and other threats to social stability. Leo was the first pope to address the problems associated with the rise of industrial capitalism and to declare the sympathy of the church with the interests of the working class.

Rerum Novarum was a reformist rather than a revolutionary manifesto. Indeed much of the document was taken up with showing why socialism was not the answer to the misery of the poor. His approach to social change relied heavily on an appeal to the conscience of the rich rather than on the empowerment of the poor. Nevertheless, the significance of the document was not so much in its recommendations as in the fact of its existence. No pope of modern times had declared as did Leo that "some remedy must be found, and quickly found, for the misery and wretchedness which press so heavily at this moment on the large majority of the very poor."

While rejecting socialism, Leo's encyclical implied a strong critique of unbridled capitalism. Most of all it declared the vital interest of the church in the social and material as well as the spiritual welfare of human beings. It articulated the church's commitment to the principles of social justice, the dignity of labor, and the defense of the poor — a commitment that would continue to unfold over the subsequent century of Catholic social teaching.

Leo died on July 20, 1903, at the age of ninety-three, the first pope whose passing was mourned not only in churches and convents but in factories and union halls.

See: Edward T. Gargan, ed., *Leo XIII and the Modern World* (New York: Sheed & Ward, 1961); Donal Dorr, *Option for the Poor* (Maryknoll, N.Y.: Orbis, 1983).

July 21
Albert Luthuli
Zulu Chief, Nobel Laureate (1898–1967)

"It is inevitable that in working for Freedom some individuals and some families must take the lead and suffer: The Road to Freedom is via the CROSS."

Among those who prepared the way to freedom in South Africa, the name of Chief Albert Luthuli is highly honored. A member of the Zulu tribe and the son of local chiefs, he was raised in Groutville, a village in a Christian mission reserve in Natal. He studied at Adams College, where he met his wife and began a career as a teacher. Eventually he was elected chief in Groutville, an office which enabled him to promote the rights of his poor and oppressed people. To the white-minority government, chiefs were principally regarded as useful intermediaries in their management and control of the black masses. Luthuli, however, had come to believe that the ultimate interests of his people could be served only by the overthrow of the system of apartheid. As a result he became active in the African National Congress (ANC), spearhead of the freedom struggle in South Africa. In 1952 the government "dismissed" him as chief of Groutville. This only freed Luthuli from tribal affairs to become fully engaged in the activity of the ANC, ultimately emerging as its national leader.

The activities of the ANC combined political education and active non-violent resistance in the form of strikes, boycotts, and civil disobedience. As a result of his work Luthuli was repeatedly arrested, "banned," and confined to house arrest. In 1955, after the Congress issued its "Freedom Charter," Luthuli and the ANC leadership were arrested en masse and charged with high treason. The charges were absurd and Luthuli was eventually freed. But the trial, in which the young Nelson Mandela conducted the defense, offered an opportunity for the ANC leaders to present their case against apartheid to the world. In 1960 Luthuli was awarded the Nobel Peace Prize.

He returned to lead a public protest against the hated passbooks — internal passports — that blacks were required to carry in South Africa. These were used to enforce restrictions on where blacks were allowed to live in their own country. Luthuli publicly burned his passbook and urged others to do the same. He was once again arrested, and then released under another five-year "banning" order.

Throughout his life Luthuli held on to the deep Christian faith in which he had been raised. This posed a conflict in the minds of some black activists. They dismissed Christianity as nothing more than the religion of the oppressors. But Luthuli disagreed: "We know Christianity for what it is, we know it is not a white preserve." Nevertheless, he challenged the churches to join in the struggle: "We do not expect to see the Church organizing political movements. But it must be *with* people, *in* their lives."

Speaking for himself he stated, "I am in Congress precisely *because* I am a Christian. My Christian belief about society must find expression here and now, and Congress is the spearhead of the real struggle....My own urge, *because* I am a Christian, is to get into the thick of the struggle with other Christians, taking my Christianity with me and praying that it may be used to influence for good the character of the resistance."

Luthuli died in a train accident on July 21, 1967. At that time the goal for which he had labored seemed impossibly far. The African National Congress had been declared illegal. Its leader, Nelson Mandela, and the rest of the ANC leadership were imprisoned on Robben Island, serving life sentences from which they were not expected to return. The system of apartheid was entrenched, and the black population seemed to be abandoned by God and the rest of the world.

And yet men and women like Luthuli, because of their faith in God, were convinced that justice would one day triumph. And so they were able to carry on the struggle, inspired by the vision of a South Africa that might one day, but did not yet, exist. So Luthuli concluded his autobiography with these hopeful words:

> The struggle must go on — the struggle to make the opportunity for the building to begin. The struggle will go on. I speak humbly and without levity when I say that, God giving me strength and courage enough, I shall die, if need be, for this cause. But I do not want to die until I have seen the building begun.
> *Mayibuye i Afrika!* Come Africa, come!

See: Albert Luthuli, *Let My People Go* (New York: McGraw Hill, 1962).

July 22

St. Mary Magdalene
Apostle to the Apostles (first century)

"I have seen the Lord."   — John 20:18

Mary Magdalene was one of the original Galilean disciples of Jesus and the most eminent among the many women who followed in his itinerant ministry. Little can be said about her origins; she is characterized simply as "a woman from whom seven demons had gone out," a statement subject to various interpretations. It was *St. Gregory the Great who identified Mary with the woman, "a sinner," who sought Jesus out in the home of a Pharisee to wash his feet with her tears and dry them with her hair. This gesture, which scandalized the other dinner guests, prompted Jesus to say, "Her sins, which are many, are forgiven, for she loved much." From this conflation, now rejected by scholars as well as the church, there came about the popular representation of Mary Magdalene as a penitent sinner or prostitute.

This image of "The Magdalene" has appealed to artists and dramatists throughout history, and it has doubtless been a comfort to many. But in attaching such a stereotypically female image to Mary Magdalene the Western fathers also helped to efface the memory of the leadership and prominence of women in the early Jesus movement. This amnesia was already well under way by the time the Gospels were written in the late first century. One of the most distinctive features of Jesus' movement was the presence of women among his intimate disciples. And yet the story and even identity of many of these women was left on the margins.

It is all the more significant when women such as Mary of Bethany, her sister Martha, or Mary Magdalene *are* named. It is a sign of just how vital a place they still occupied in the church's living memory. Mary Magdalene, in particular, was firmly associated with two vital facts: that she was a witness to the crucifixion and that she was the first witness of the Risen Lord.

All four Gospels name Mary among the women who followed Jesus to Golgotha and there witnessed his passion and death. While all the male disciples fled, it was these women who remained faithful to the end. It was also they, including Mary Magdalene, who went to his tomb on the day after the sabbath hoping to anoint his body.

Instead they found an empty tomb, guarded by an angel who revealed the astonishing news that Jesus was risen. The women were charged to tell the disciples to meet the Lord back in Galilee. In the Gospels of *John and *Matthew Mary Magdalene actually sees the Risen Lord. John provides a particularly poignant account, reflecting most clearly the special relationship that evidently existed between Mary and Jesus.

Here, after summoning *Peter and the "beloved disciple" to see the empty tomb for themselves, "Mary stood weeping outside the tomb." Suddenly she sees Jesus, but does not recognize him. Taking him to be the gardener she says, "Sir, if you have carried him away, tell me where you have laid him, and I will take him away." Jesus answers her with a single word — "Mary" — which is enough to identify him. "Rabboni!" she cries, "Teacher." He instructs her not to hold him, "but go to my brethren and say to them, I am ascending to my Father and your Father, to my God and your God." And so Mary goes out to the disciples and says, "I have seen the Lord."

Nothing else is known of Mary Magdalene. Her deeds are not reported in the Acts of the Apostles, nor does she figure in the writings of Paul. (In listing the appearances of the Risen Lord he begins with the appearance to Peter.) But the name of Mary Magdalene deserves special honor, particularly at a time when women are struggling to be heard in the church and society. It was she, the faithful disciple, who first proclaimed the good news to the Twelve. Thus she has often been called the "Apostle to the Apostles."

July 23
St. John Cassian
Abbot (360–433)

"It is a bigger miracle to eject passion from your own body than it is to eject an evil spirit from another's body. It is a bigger miracle to be patient and refrain from anger than it is to control the demons which fly through the air."

John Cassian was born somewhere in the region of Rumania around the year 360. As a young man he embarked on a great quest for spiritual wisdom. With a friend he visited the holy places in Palestine and settled there for a time as a monk. But eventually he was drawn to Egypt, home of the great and mysterious desert fathers. For ten years he traveled about interviewing these spiritual athletes. His later account of his conversations helped popularize the ascetic spirituality of these monks and hermits throughout the West. Through the endorsement of *St. Benedict, Cassian's book became one of the most influential handbooks of monastic spirituality.

At the time of Cassian's travels the movement of desert monasticism was at its zenith. This was the century in which Christianity passed from being a persecuted sect to becoming the state religion of the empire. As Christians were no longer called to battle wild beasts in the arena, the witness of martyrdom gave way to asceticism. One's own body became the arena for martyrdom, and daily life became a living sacrifice to God. At the same time a stream of spiritual pioneers fled the Christian empire to take refuge in the Egyptian wilderness. Some living alone and others in primitive monasteries, they sought a more radical form of witness to the kingdom of God, refusing to give in to the encroaching accommodation of the gospel to the world.

Ascetics like *St. Antony went into the desert to detach themselves from the values of society, to discipline their appetites and their desires, and to focus their full attention on God. The desert was a place of terrible ordeal. There one could expect to encounter hunger, thirst, and loneliness, but also the prospect of battle with one's personal demons. The goal was a perfectly integrated personality. But there was always the danger of becoming totally unhinged.

Meanwhile the world delighted in hearing of the desert fathers, of their feats of heroic self-denial, their purported miracles, and their combat with demons who might present themselves in both horrible and alluring disguise. Cassian's book, however, did not cater to such tabloid interest.

Instead he depicted these men as models of balance, wisdom, and maturity. Rather than antisocial fanatics, Cassian's desert fathers speak as masters of the spiritual life, experts in human psychology, whose wisdom is born of years of spiritual direction and disciplined introspection.

The purpose of asceticism, as Cassian learned, is not self-denial for its own sake. As one of his informants puts it, "Solitude, watches in the night, manual labor, nakedness, reading, and the other disciplines — we know that their purpose is to free the heart from injury by bodily passions and to keep it free. They are to be the rungs of a ladder up which it may climb to perfect charity." Charity — love — is the goal of the ascetic life. The various disciplines employed by the ascetic are simply the means, the "tools of the trade."

Although Cassian regarded the hermit's life as an ideal, it was not for everyone. It should certainly not be undertaken for misanthropic reasons — simply to escape the hell of other persons — and certainly it should never be worn as a mark of pride:

> If we go into the desert with our faults still hidden within us, they no longer hurt others, but our love of them remains. Of every sin not eradicated, the root is still growing secretly within. . . . If we compare our own strict discipline with the lax practices of another and feel the slightest temptation to puff ourselves, it proves that the terrible plague of pride is still infecting us. If we see these signs within, we know that it is not the desire to sin but the opportunity to sin which has vanished.

Sometime after his sojourn in Egypt Cassian was ordained a priest. He later founded monasteries in the area of Marseilles. It was there, toward the end of his life, that he recorded his *Conferences*. Cassian's own reputation was eclipsed by the success of his famous book. He found himself on the losing side of several theological controversies of his day. In one case he defended the teaching of *Origen regarding the eventual salvation of the world; at the same time, and against *Augustine's doctrine of predestination, he insisted that salvation was the fruit of cooperation between God and the human soul. Such positions are in notable contrast to the popular image of the desert hermits as world-denying extremists. If Cassian is any reflection, it seems they could more justly be accused of excessive optimism about the human condition.

See: "The Conferences of Cassian," in Owen Chadwick, ed., *Western Asceticism* (Philadelphia: Westminster, 1958); Owen Chadwick, *John Cassian* (Cambridge: Cambridge University Press, 1968).

July 24

Ammon Hennacy

"One-Man Revolution" (1893–1970)

"Love without courage and wisdom is sentimentality, as with the ordinary church member. Courage without love and wisdom is foolhardiness, as with the ordinary soldier. Wisdom without love and courage is cowardice, as with the ordinary intellectual. The one who has love, courage, and wisdom is one in a million, who moves the world, as with Jesus, Buddha, and Gandhi."

Ammon Hennacy was born on July 24, 1893, in Negley, Ohio. He was active in the radical political movements of his day and campaigned vigorously for the Socialist Party. In 1917, with America's entry into World War I, Hennacy was arrested for refusing to register for the draft. He was sentenced to five years in Atlanta Penitentiary and served two, almost half of it in solitary confinement. It was a crushing but ultimately formative experience for the young Hennacy. While in solitary, with nothing to read but the Bible, he underwent a deep religious conversion. He concluded that Jesus Christ, who sought to transform the human person from within, represented the greatest revolutionary of all time.

> Gradually I came to gain a glimpse of what Jesus meant when he said that the Kingdom of God must be in everyone.... To change the world by bullets or ballots was a useless procedure. Therefore the only revolution worthwhile was the one-man revolution within the heart. Each one would make this by himself and not need to wait on a majority.

When he was released from prison Hennacy devoted himself to realizing that ideal of the "one-man revolution." Among other sacrifices he became a vegetarian and stripped his life down to the level of bare necessities. He refused to pay taxes (which could be used in part to finance war). When withholding taxes were introduced, he deliberately worked at common day-labor — picking cotton or other field work — so that he could be paid in cash. In any case, he made it a point to subsist at a level beneath the taxable minimum.

Hennacy described himself as a Christian anarchist — a position that for him denoted the gospel call to personal responsibility, the insistence on returning good for evil, and his respect for the sovereignty of free conscience. "An anarchist," he used to say, "is someone who doesn't need a cop to tell him what to do."

In 1952 Hennacy moved to New York and joined the Catholic Worker community of *Dorothy Day. He had long been attracted to Day's commitment to nonviolence, and her paper had published a number of his articles about "life at hard labor." Both Hennacy and the Worker were permanently marked by this association. In his years in New York, Hennacy prodded the community to undertake a more active and visible stance on behalf of peace. He delighted in selling the *Catholic Worker* newspaper on street corners, an opportunity to engage in a kind of soap-box apostolate. In one of his most effective protests he organized a campaign of civil disobedience against the city's annual compulsory civil defense drills. In Hennacy's view, these drills, ostensibly intended to prepare the city for a nuclear attack, were actually exercises in folly, if not something worse. They would do nothing to save lives in the event of an attack, while such drills did have the effect of preparing the public for the inevitability of war. Hennacy felt it was the Christian's duty to refuse to collaborate with this dangerous farce. As a result, he along with Dorothy Day and others were repeatedly jailed until the drills were finally abolished.

In joining the Worker, Hennacy was at the same time moved to join the Catholic church. He was duly baptized with Dorothy Day as his godmother. Hennacy tried hard to reconcile his anarchism with the spirit of Catholicism. But he was never particularly suited to "thinking with the church," or with any other community or organization larger than himself. He was acutely sensitive to the dangers of compromise and hypocrisy, and he could not abide the spectacle of priests and bishops who casually gave their blessing to war. After fifteen years, Hennacy dropped out of the church. He remained, however, a devout "nonchurch Christian," who set a standard of obedience to gospel values that few "orthodox" Christians could hope to match.

Eventually Hennacy left New York and moved to Salt Lake City. There he opened Joe Hill House, a house of hospitality for the indigent and homeless, named after the great labor martyr who was one of his heroes. Hennacy continued his work for peace. Every August he undertook a public fast to atone for the dropping of the atomic bomb, adding an additional day of fasting for each year since 1945.

Radical that he was, Hennacy enjoyed the fantasy of one day dropping dead on a picket line. This wish was essentially fulfilled. On January 11, 1970, he collapsed with a heart attack while picketing to protest the impending execution of two convicted murderers. He died three days later.

Dorothy Day, while hurt by Ammon's defection from the church, continued to give him credit for his enormous faith, courage, and prophetic witness. She was convinced that he was "the most ascetic, the most hard working, the most devoted to the poor and the oppressed of any we had met, and that his life and his articles put us on the spot. He was an inspiration and a reproach." She regarded him as a modern day *John the Baptist, making straight the way of the Lord. Thus she found it easy to overlook his many faults, "knowing so well his own strong and courageous will to fight the corruption of the world around him."

See: Ammon Hennacy, The Book of Ammon (Ammon Hennacy, 1963); Patrick C. Coy, "The One-Person Revolution of Ammon Hennacy," in Patrick Coy, ed., A Revolution of the Heart (Philadelphia: Temple University Press, 1988).

Walter Rauschenbusch
Pastor and Theologian (1861–1918)

"The social gospel is the old message of salvation, but enlarged and intensified. The individualistic gospel has taught us to see the sinfulness of every human heart.... But it has not given us an adequate understanding of the sinfulness of the social order."

Walter Rauschenbusch was the foremost theological exponent of the Social Gospel in North America. This turn-of-the-century movement sought to relate the content of personal faith with the challenge of social justice.

Born in Rochester in 1861, the child of devout German immigrants, Rauschenbusch never had any other ambition than to be a minister. His first parish assignment came in 1886 when he became pastor of the Second German Church (Baptist) in the Hell's Kitchen neighborhood of New York City. This was a neighborhood notorious for its cramped and squalid conditions. The sights and smells of poverty, the disease and hopelessness that confronted him, left Rauschenbusch dissatisfied with the typical message of Christian piety. Under these circumstances it did not seem adequate to preach about personal salvation, conversion, or simply trusting in Jesus. Increasingly he expanded his ministry to take up social concerns and to try to awaken the conscience of the church to its responsibilities in the world. But here again Rauschenbusch felt that more was necessary than traditional forms of organized charity. He believed the gospel today required the transformation of a social system that was responsible for so much poverty and injustice. Still, he felt unsure of the theological foundation for this approach.

And then suddenly in 1891 he experienced a theological breakthrough. The key was his rediscovery of the biblical symbol of the kingdom of God, the central message that Jesus had proclaimed. It was an all-encompassing theme that included personal faith and social transformation; it related the church and the world; it connected the present and the future. It was truly "the first and most essential dogma of the Christian faith," for basically it concerned the challenge of transforming the world into conformity with the will of God. To bear witness to this kingdom Jesus was born: "All his teachings center about it. His life was given to it. His death was suffered for it. When a man has once seen that in the Gospels, he can never unsee it again."

And yet, central as this message was, it had been either forgotten or obscured in Christian history. The kingdom was identified with heaven, with individual salvation, or with the church. While it was truly concerned with all these things, he argued, the kingdom was ultimately something wider and more radical. Above all it represented the constant tension between the status quo and the world as God intended it.

To those who charged that he was reducing the teaching of Jesus, Rauschenbusch claimed, on the contrary, that he was urging a return to the real message of Jesus: "The eclipse of the Kingdom ideal was an eclipse of Jesus," he wrote. "We had listened too much to voices talking about Jesus, and not enough to his own voice."

Rauschenbusch's ideas were contained in several books, including *Christianizing the Social Order* and *A Theology for the Social Gospel*. He lectured widely, and in 1897 he accepted a teaching position at Rochester Theological Seminary. The Social Gospel of Rauschenbusch made a deep and wide impact on the Protestant churches, strongly contributing to the development of a social consciousness among Christians and boosting support for many progressive causes.

But in 1914 the outbreak of World War I posed a harsh challenge to the Social Gospelers and other liberal Christians. Their general optimism about the progress of modern civilization seemed to founder on the reality of sin and human irrationality. Rauschenbusch was actually less susceptible to such disillusionment than many of his sympathizers. He never believed that the kingdom of God was to be identified with the march of social progress. Nor, as some of his critics charged, was he oblivious to the reality of sin. His great contribution was the articulation of an understanding of "social sin," a term that has only recently resurfaced in the language of the church.

Nevertheless, sympathy for Rauschenbusch's message waned in the climate of militaristic patriotism. "Since 1914 the world is full of hate," he wrote in 1918, "and I cannot expect to be happy again in my lifetime." These words were prophetic, for he died of a brain tumor on July 25 of that same year.

It was suggested by some that Rauschenbusch died in a state of terrible disillusionment with the ideals he had served. There is no evidence for this. Instead, he seemed to hold a very realistic notion of the magnitude of the challenge and the elusive nature of his ultimate goal. As he wrote, "We shall never have a perfect life. Yet we must seek it with faith....At best there is always but an approximation to a perfect social order. The kingdom of God is always but coming. But every approximation to it is worthwhile."

See: Walter Rauschenbusch, *A Theology for the Social Gospel* (Nashville: Abingdon, 1945); Gary J. Dorrien, *Reconstructing the Common Good* (Maryknoll, N.Y.: Orbis, 1990).

July 26

Bd. Titus Brandsma
Carmelite Priest, Martyr (d. 1942)

"I see God in the work of his hands and the marks of his love in every visible thing, and it sometimes happens that I am seized by a supreme joy which is above all other joys."

Titus Brandsma was a Dutch Carmelite priest, a professor of theology, as well as a journalist. In the 1930s he was named by the bishops of Holland as spiritual advisor to the nation's several dozen Catholic newspapers. When the Nazis invaded Holland in 1940, Brandsma was at the center of an intense discussion in the church regarding the level of resistance to be offered to the new regime. Some felt that the church should be primarily concerned with maintaining the rights and security of Catholics. But Brandsma spoke for the majority who opposed any compromise with the Nazi order. His own views on Nazism were well known. For years, as a professor at the Catholic University of Nijmegen, he had delivered a popular series of lectures on the dangers of what he called "the new paganism" overtaking Germany. He had singled out for denunciation the Nazi oppression of the Jews.

In August 1941, Brandsma, as president of the Association of Catholic Secondary Schools, publicly protested a German directive requiring the prohibition of students of Jewish descent from attending Catholic schools. In December 1941 an edict of the German occupation declared that all Dutch newspapers were obliged to run Nazi advertisements and propaganda. Brandsma met personally with the editors of each Catholic newspaper to explain why it was impossible to comply with such an edict. He knew that his actions made him a marked man.

On January 19, 1942, Brandsma was arrested. After several months he ended up in the concentration camp at Dachau, home at the time to another twenty-seven hundred imprisoned clergy. There he endured several weeks of brutal treatment. All the while, according to witnesses, he maintained his prayerful equilibrium and eschewed all bitterness. "We are here," he said, "in a dark tunnel. We must pass through it. Somewhere at the end shines the eternal light."

Brandsma was already sickly before his arrest, and his health quickly deteriorated. In July he was dispatched to the hospital. In Dachau this was not a place for healing, but a center for sadistic medical experimentation. There on July 26 he was killed by a lethal injection of acid.

In 1985 Titus Brandsma was beatified by Pope John Paul II, the first victim of the Nazis to be officially declared a martyr.

See: Leo Knowles, *Candidates for Sainthood* (St. Paul, Minn.: Carillon, 1978); Kenneth Woodward, *Making Saints* (New York: Simon & Schuster, 1990).

July 27
Mechthild of Magdeburg
Beguine Mystic (1210?–1282?)

"Fish cannot drown in water,
Birds cannot sink in air,
Gold cannot perish
In the refiner's fire.
This has God given to all creatures,
To foster and seek their own nature.
How then can I withstand mine?"

Mechthild of Magdeburg, a German mystic of the thirteenth century, is known to us entirely through her book, *The Flowing Light of the Godhead*. Written in her own hand in the vernacular dialect of her native Saxony, her book is a kind of spiritual journal, a work in progress, to which she continuously returned, adding and amending, over the course of her life.

Mechthild was evidently born of a wealthy family somewhere near the town of Magdeburg in Saxony. At the age of twelve she received a mystical vision, the first of a series of "greetings of God" that would continue daily for the rest of her life. She later described the effects of such visitations: "The true greeting of God, which comes from the heavenly flood out of the spring of the flowing Trinity, has such power that it takes all strength from the body and lays the soul bare to itself. Thus it sees itself as one of the blessed and receives in itself divine glory."

Around the age of twenty Mechthild decided to leave her family and travel to Magdeburg, where she knew virtually no one. Rather than enter a convent she joined a household of Beguines. The Beguines were a movement of women who tried to fashion an independent religious life, without rules or enclosure or ecclesiastical approval. They flourished in the Low Countries and Germany in the thirteenth century and provided an attractive haven for religious visionaries like Mechthild.

Virtually nothing is known of how Mechthild spent her many years in the Beguinage, though it may be supposed that like other members of the community she passed her days in prayer, simple labor, and service to the poor. All the while she left a written trail of her inner spiritual journey. Her book combines a number of genres — mystical love poems describing the soul's communion with God, dialogues with Christ, as well as vivid accounts of her visions of paradise, hell, and the destiny of all creatures.

Among other things, Mechthild's book discloses her gift for gentle spiritual direction:

What hinders spiritual people most of all from complete perfection is that they pay so little attention to small sins. I tell you in truth: when I hold back a smile which would harm no one, or have a sourness in my heart which I tell to no one, or feel some impatience with my own pain, then my soul becomes so dark... and my heart so cold that I must weep greatly and lament pitiably and yearn greatly and humbly confess all my lack of virtue.

At the same time Mechthild turned a critical eye on what she termed "poor Christianity." "I, poor woman, was so bold in my prayer that I impudently took corrupt Christianity into the arms of my soul and lifted it in lamentation."

Sections of Mechthild's book were copied and circulated widely, apparently winning her a loyal following. At the same time her writings invited criticism from those she called "my pharisees." So vehement were her detractors that she described herself as "a post or target at which people throw stones." She was in turn unsparing in her criticism of ecclesial worldliness and corruption:

Alas! Crown of holy Church, how tarnished you have become. Your precious stones have fallen from you because you are weak and you disgrace the holy Christian faith.... Alas, crown of holy priesthood, you have disappeared, and you have nothing left but your external shape — namely, priestly power — with this you do battle against God and His chosen friends.... For our Lord speaks thus: I will touch the heart of the pope in Rome with great sadness and in this sadness I will speak to him and lament to him that My shepherds from Jerusalem have become murderers and wolves.

These were, to say the least, risky sentiments. While the Beguines afforded a certain liberty, they also provided little protection. It is therefore not surprising to learn that Mechthild eventually left her community. Sometime around 1270 she settled in the Cistercian convent at Helfta. She was by this time ill and virtually blind. Nevertheless, in that extraordinary community, which already included two other mystics, *Mechtild of Hackeborn and *St. Gertrude of Helfta, she was apparently welcomed and cared for until her death.

Mechthild's life of intimacy with God brought with it much loneliness and estrangement from the world. She accepted the price along with the rewards of her vocation:

> Ever longing in the soul,
> Ever suffering in the body,
> Ever pain in the senses...
> Those who have given themselves utterly to God
> Know well what I mean.

But for one who remained faithful, suffering was not the last word.

> See there within the flesh
> Like a bright wick englazed
> The soul God's finger lit
> To give her liberty,
> And joy and power and love,
> To make her crystal, like
> As maybe, to Himself.

See: John Howard, "The German Mystic: Mechthild of Magdeburg," in Katharina M. Wilson, ed., *Medieval Women Mystics* (Athens: University of Georgia Press, 1984); Carol Lee Flinders, *Enduring Grace: Living Portraits of Seven Women Mystics* (San Francisco: HarperSanFrancisco, 1993).

July 28

Stanley Rother
Priest and Martyr (1935–1981)

"Pray for us that we may be a sign of the love of Christ for our people,
that our presence among them will fortify them to endure these sufferings
in preparation for the coming of the kingdom."

In the early morning hours of July 28, 1981, Father Stanley Rother was murdered in the rectory of the church of Santiago Atitlán in Guatemala. Unlike some other martyred priests of Central America, this lanky Oklahoma farmboy did not pose an obvious threat to the rich and powerful. To some Father Rother might even have seemed naively detached from the social upheaval around him. But in Guatemala there were those who saw subversion in any effort to affirm the dignity of the Indian peasants. As Rother said, "To shake the hand of an Indian is a political act."

Thoughts of death were far from his mind when Rother volunteered in 1968 to serve in Santiago Atitlán. The church in this picturesque Indian town had been adopted as a mission by Rother's diocese of Oklahoma City–Tulsa. For Rother, who had nearly failed to finish seminary because of his difficulties with Latin, the first challenge was to master the Mayan dialect of the Tzutuhil Indians. Having passed this hurdle, he quickly won their trust and respect by his complete dedication to the needs of the community. The pastoral work alone was almost overwhelming — the usual cycle of baptisms, marriages, funerals, the training of catechists and eucharistic ministers, the constant visits to the sick and dying, responding to the endless stream of people at his door requiring food, medicine, or other help. Sunday Masses were attended by thirty-five hundred people.

But in the extra hours he squeezed from his days Rother could be found wielding a hoe in a farmer's cornfield, organizing weaving and food cooperatives, or performing any number of unseen acts of generosity and friendship. It is no wonder that as the years progressed, the parish church became the center of renewal in this traditional Indian town and Rother, no longer an outsider, was accepted into the inner circles of village life. The people eventually conferred on Rother a unique honor, given to no other North American priest. They gave him an Indian name: Padre A'plas. For his part, Rother felt himself so inspired by the faith, strength, and simplicity of the Tzutuhil people that he could not imagine a life apart from them.

For years Rother and his flock were untouched by the violence and repression that were a fixture of Guatemalan history. The roots of this violence extended five hundred years to the original Spanish conquest. But in recent years a succession of military governments had found in anti-communism a convenient excuse to use brutal force against any challenge to the stark inequality and injustice of the status quo. In the 1980s this violence would become a raging storm that extended for the first time to the church.

As Rother wrote to his bishop in Oklahoma City, "The country here is in rebellion and the government is taking it out on the church. The low wages that are paid, the very few who are excessively rich, the bad distribution of land — these are some of the reasons for widespread discontent. The Church seems to be the only force that is trying to do something about the situation, and therefore the government is after us."

Eventually the violence reached Santiago Atitlán, and Rother and his pastoral team could no longer avoid the need for precautions. Still, Rother resisted any suggestion that he return to the United States. "At the first signs of danger," he wrote, "the shepherd can't run and leave the sheep to fend for themselves." One day one of Rother's most experienced catechists was kidnapped by armed men in broad daylight in front of the church. For months afterward Rother was haunted by the man's desperate cries and his own inability to protect him. Then in January 1981 Rother's own name appeared on a published death list. Persuaded that his presence posed a risk to members of his pastoral team, he agreed to leave the country and returned to Oklahoma. But he could not bear to remain so far from his flock.

By Holy Week he had returned to Santiago Atitlán. Things seemed relatively calm, and he was delighted to be once more among his people, sharing with them the celebration of Christ's death and resurrection. But in the middle of the night on July 28 death came for the shepherd. Three masked men slipped into the parish rectory and found their way to Rother's room. From the struggle that ensued it appears that their intention was to kidnap the priest. But knowing that this inevitably meant torture and eventual death, Rother put up a fight. Though he never called out for help, he was heard to cry to his abductors, "Kill me here!" They complied, shooting him twice in the head.

Rother was not a priest in the prophetic mold. He was in the truest sense a pastor whose life was a constant self-giving. He could not accept that his priesthood or his American citizenship should set him apart from the risks and sufferings of his people. In laying down his life, he guaranteed that he would never leave them.

After the funeral Mass Rother's body was returned to Oklahoma for burial. But his family agreed to the request of his parish and allowed his heart to be interred in the church of Santiago Atitlán.

See: Henri J. M. Nouwen, *Love in a Fearful Land: A Guatemalan Story* (Notre Dame, Ind.: Ave Maria, 1985); Donna Whitson Brett and Edward T. Brett, *Murdered in Central America* (Maryknoll, N.Y.: Orbis, 1988).

July 29

Vincent van Gogh
Artist (1853–1890)

"I think that everything that is really good and beautiful,
of inward moral, spiritual, and sublime beauty in men and their works,
comes from God."

In the eyes of the world, and in his own eyes, Vincent van Gogh was an utter failure. Though today he is one of the most popular and beloved of all modern painters, to his contemporaries he evoked nothing but contempt. He sold nothing in his lifetime. He spent his life in squalid poverty, preferring to spend what money he could obtain on paint rather than food. But his failure never deterred him from dedicating every ounce of his strength to the expression of his personal vision. For the sake of that vision, as much as any desert father, he was prepared to sacrifice every natural happiness. His subjects were not formally religious. They included sunflowers, wheatfields, and starry night skies. But ultimately his subject was the holiness of existence. It was that vision and not the quality of his sacrifice that defined the religious dimension of his art.

Van Gogh was the son of a respected Dutch clergyman. Initially he too felt called to the ministry. But poor marks along with his coarse and disagreeable manners tended to alienate his professors. When he failed his Latin exams he remarked, "Do you seriously believe that such horrors are indispensable to a man who wants to do what I want to do: give peace to poor creatures and reconcile them to their existence on earth?" For van Gogh the ministry did not represent a respectable career but an opportunity to serve the poor. To do this, he decided, he needed no certificate or degree. And so he traveled to the desolate mining region of the Borinage, where he lived in utter poverty and tried to preach the gospel to the worn and exhausted miners and their families. His efforts ended in complete failure. The result was a personal crisis that caused him to turn his back altogether on organized religion. In a break with his family he told them he thought "their whole system of religion horrible."

In 1880, at the age of twenty-seven, he turned instead to a career as an artist. This was a surprising turn but, as *Henri Nouwen has observed, his vocation remained the same. Art became his way of expressing his solidarity and compassion for suffering humanity. As a preacher he had found that the images of poverty and misery among the miners turned his mind to God. And now through art he sought to record those impressions — not through traditional religious iconography, but by revealing the inner depths, the dimension of love, in which all reality was ultimately rooted.

What I want and aim at is confoundedly difficult, and yet I do not think I aim too high. I want to do drawings which *touch* some people....I want to progress so far that people will say of my work:

he feels deeply, he feels tenderly....What am I in most people's eyes? A nonentity, or an eccentric and disagreeable man...in short, the lowest of the low. Very well...then I should want my work to show what is in *the heart* of such a nobody. This is my ambition, which is, in spite of everything, founded less on anger than on love.

Though he pursued formal studies, Vincent remained obstinately committed to his own style and vision. For years he practiced drawing and sketching images of farmworkers and the poor, perfecting his technique before turning to painting. Nevertheless, he found no market for his work. His sole support came from his brother Theo, a successful art dealer in Paris. It was to Theo, his friend, his life-line to sanity, that he poured out his thoughts and feelings in thousands of letters.

There may be a great fire in our soul, but no one ever comes to warm himself at it, and the passers-by see only a little bit of smoke coming through the chimney, and pass on their way....Must one tend that inward fire...wait for the hour when someone will come and sit down near it — to stay there maybe? Let him who believes in God wait for the hour that will come sooner or later.

Though he was a ravening maw for human affection and understanding, van Gogh's intensity and disregard for normal courtesy deterred intimate relationships. He alienated almost everyone with whom he came into contact. Only Theo remained constant. Meanwhile he drove his mind and body to the limit with endless work, lack of sleep, and a diet consisting of little more than bread, coffee, and alcohol. His sensitivity to suffering and the miseries of life remained acute. But there were times when he hovered dangerously on the brink of madness.

While in Paris and Antwerp he developed a new appreciation for color. In February 1888 he moved to Arles in southern France. There in that sun-bathed countryside he achieved a fantastic breakthrough, producing scores of paintings that showed an exhilarating intoxication with light and life. "It is as if nature starts to burn....How beautiful is yellow!"

His portraits too reflected a different quality — not just a sensitivity to human suffering, but also something of the sacred: "I should like to paint in men and women something of that quality of eternity which was symbolized formerly by a halo and which we try to convey by the very radiance of our coloring."

But the strain of loneliness, poverty, and his own inner demons could not indefinitely be held at bay. After mutilating himself in the midst of a fit, he checked himself into a mental asylum. There he continued to paint, as much as he was able. Upon his release in May 1890 he settled in Auvers. In his last months his output was fantastic — mostly scenes of wheatfields under stormy skies. To Theo he wrote, "One does not expect out of life what one has already learned it cannot give, but rather one begins to see more and more clearly that life is only a kind of sowing time, and the harvest is not here."

On July 27, 1890, he shot himself in the stomach. When Theo heard the news he rushed to his brother's side. Vincent said, "Who could imagine that life could be so sad?" He died on July 29.

See: Henri Nouwen, "Compassion in the Art of Vincent van Gogh," *America* (March 13, 1976); Irving Stone, ed., *Dear Theo: The Autobiography of Vincent van Gogh* (New York: Doubleday, 1937).

July 30
William Wilberforce
Abolitionist (1759–1833)

"Never, never will we desist till we have wiped away this scandal [of slavery] from the load of guilt under which we at present labor, and until we have extinguished every trace of this bloody traffic which our posterity will scarcely believe had been suffered to exist so long, a disgrace and dishonor to our country."

William Wilberforce, born in Hull, England, in 1759, was an Evangelical Christian who devoted his career to abolishing the evil of slavery. He came from a wealthy and influential family; soon after graduating from Cambridge University in 1780 he entered Parliament. Around the same time he engaged in an intensive study of the New Testament, resulting in his conversion to Evangelicalism. He was acquainted with *John Wesley and his brother Charles, leaders of the Methodist movement, who encouraged him to use his office and influence to work for the moral uplift of society.

Wilberforce was convinced that there was no greater moral blight on the English conscience than the slave trade. Although slave labor was not permitted in England itself, the trafficking in African slaves and the exploitation of their labor was a mainstay of the imperial economy, particularly in the Caribbean and the southern United States. Wilberforce would not rest until his country should recognize the hideous cruelty and injustice represented by this system. Tirelessly he delivered speeches, circulated petitions, and introduced bills in Parliament calling for the immediate abolition of slavery. In the privileged circles in which he moved his position was unpopular. It was claimed that the traffic in slaves was far too profitable and the use of slave labor too indispensable to the plantation economy of the colonies to be abolished. But Wilberforce would not relent. Continuously he hammered home the fact that what was being justified in the name of profit was the brutal commerce in human life.

Finally in 1806, after twenty years of solid effort, Wilberforce won the argument. A bill in Parliament was passed outlawing slave-trading in all British colonies from the year 1807. Still the struggle continued for another twenty-five years to win the complete emancipation of all slaves in the British empire. Such a bill was eventually passed in 1833 just weeks before Wilberforce's death on July 29, 1833. Seven hundred thousand slaves were liberated.

Upon his death, Wilberforce was acclaimed as a national hero and he was buried with full honors in Westminster Abbey. In commenting on his career, one Lord said, "The wonder is that a short period in the short life of one man is, well and wisely directed, sufficient to remedy the miseries of millions for ages."

See: Eloise Lownsbery, *Saints and Rebels* (New York: Longman, Green, 1937).

July 31
St. Ignatius of Loyola
Founder of the Society of Jesus (1491–1556)

"To the greater glory of God."

Iñigo López de Loyola was born of a noble Basque family in the kingdom of Castile. The youngest of thirteen children, he spent his youth as a courtier and later a soldier in the service of the Spanish king. As such he was trained in the code of honor and chivalry, ready with his sword to avenge any slight against his dignity or the interests of his master.

In 1521 he took part in the unsuccessful defense of Pamplona against the French. During the battle he was struck in the leg by a cannonball and suffered a grievous injury. Back in his family castle, he underwent excruciating operations, followed by a prolonged convalescence. To pass the idle time he requested something to read — preferably the chivalrous romances of which he was particularly fond. Instead he had to settle for a collection of pious lives of the saints — all that could be produced. He devoured these books, at first simply as an escape from boredom. Gradually, however, he began to find them fascinating. In the long months of his recovery he started imagining what a great honor it must be to serve the glory of God. As zeal for such a life began to take hold, he resolved, upon his recovery, to reform his conduct and to imitate the example of the saints in dedication to God's service.

When he was at last well enough to walk he set off on a pilgrimage to the Catalonian shrine of Our Lady at Monserrat. After an all-night vigil at the shrine he exchanged his rich clothes with a beggar and, in a final gesture of courtly valor, laid his sword and dagger on the altar of Our Lady. Thus he became a soldier of Christ. The next day he walked to the nearby town of Manresa, where he spent several months in solitary reflection. During this time his commitment was further excited by a series of mystical visions, including the sight of a blinding light emanating from the Eucharist.

After a pilgrimage to the Holy Land, he determined to become a priest. This, however, required that he resume his education. So he applied himself diligently to the study of Latin and eventually traveled to France to study at the University of Paris. While there he began to exhort his fellow students to a life of heroic piety. Eventually he persuaded a small group of six to join him in forming a new religious order, dedicated to renewing and serving the church in any way their services might be required. This was the nucleus of what would eventually become the Society of Jesus, or the Jesuits, as they were popularly known. Their official recognition by Pope Paul III came in 1540. Ignatius was named the first superior general.

It was a period of crisis and opportunity in the Catholic church. By this time Ignatius's contemporary Martin Luther had initiated the Protestant Reformation. At the same time the voyages of Spanish and Portuguese explorers had dramatically changed the face of the known world and exposed the vast portions of the human race as yet untouched by the gospel. Ignatius's Jesuits, who took a special vow to put themselves at the service of the pope, were highly visible in rising to both these challenges. No sooner had they been established than many of the original Jesuits set out on perilous missions to Asia, New Spain, and Protestant England, in the process contributing substantially to the calendar of martyrs. Ignatius remained behind, following the progress of his sons and offering direction through voluminous correspondence. Renowned as men of action as well as learning, the Jesuits played a vital role in preserving and renewing the vitality of Catholicism in the sixteenth and subsequent centuries. At the same time, their methods and mystique aroused significant opposition. Their extreme discipline and loyalty to the Society caused friction with the secular clergy, while their commitment to social justice and their tendency to put the cause of the gospel ahead of national interests provoked the suspicions of many secular rulers.

Ignatius himself was not immune to such controversy. But ultimately the church came to recognize his substantial gifts and to draw energy from his method of "contemplation in action." Aside from founding the Jesuits, one of his great contributions was in the publication of his *Spiritual Exercises*, a manual devised for the spiritual formation of his followers. The Exercises centered around a series of guided meditations on such themes as the creation of the world, the life and ministry of Jesus, and his death and resurrection, designed to be completed in the course of a thirty-day retreat. Based on the experience of his own conversion, the Exercises were designed to facilitate "discernment." This was a process by which the retreatant might be guided in the direction of a vocation — the individual means of glorifying God by one's life.

In the fifteen years that he served as general of the order, Ignatius saw the Jesuits increase from ten members to a thousand, at the same time becoming one of the most dynamic orders in the church. Ignatius died on July 31, 1556. He was canonized in 1622.

See: The Autobiography of St. Ignatius Loyola (New York: Harper & Row, 1974); Joseph Tetlow, *Ignatius Loyola: Spiritual Exercises* (New York: Crossroad, 1992).

❦ AUGUST ❦

August 1

St. Alphonsus Liguori
Doctor of the Church, Founder of the Redemptorists
(1696–1787)

"Persecutions are to the works of God what the frosts of winter are to plants; far from destroying them, they help them to strike their roots deep in the soil and make them more full of life."

Alphonsus Liguori was born into a family of the Neapolitan nobility. His overbearing father directed him into a career in the law, but he abruptly quit this field following an embarrassing defeat in the courtroom. Instead he felt a powerful attraction to the priesthood. This caused great tension with his family. They finally relented to his vocation only upon the agreement of the bishop to let him remain living at home. He was ordained a priest in 1726 and quickly achieved fame as a popular preacher in his hometown of Naples.

Eventually Liguori undertook an ever-widening circuit of mission tours. His simple, straightforward manner of preaching ("so that the humblest peasant can understand the message") had an enormous influence on the moral and spiritual life of his listeners. Inspired by this experience, Liguori in 1732 founded the Congregation of the Holy Redeemer, an order of priests dedicated to preaching to the rural poor. His efforts to win official recognition of the order, however, became a tortuous ordeal that persisted for the remaining fifty years of his life.

In the meantime he wrote over a hundred books, the most important being his *Moral Theology*. In this work Liguori steered a moderate course between the rigors of Jansenism and the perils of laxity. With their dark view of human nature, the Jansenist confessors encouraged a morbid preoccupation with the sins of the flesh and a pessimistic outlook for salvation. On the other hand, many clergy seemed to offer a minimalist code of Catholic conduct, in which regular attendance at Mass was as much as could be expected of ordinary mortals. Liguori taught that all were called to salvation, and that the means were available to every person. But the moral life was not a matter of tortured or legalistic compliance with the law. It was essentially the life of love. Other themes stressed by Liguori were the value of human liberty and the importance of an informed individual conscience. At the same time he was a pioneer in stressing the importance of taking the concrete circumstances of a situation into account in evaluating moral conduct.

Liguori's contributions in this area generated controversy as well as admiration. Nevertheless, he was consecrated a bishop of the small diocese of Agatha dei Goti in 1762. He was an innovator in his efforts to reform the administration of the diocese and to elevate the quality and training of the clergy, but he resigned his see in 1775 as a result of increasingly poor health. He retired to his Redemptorist community and lived on for another twelve years. But they were years of acute physical suffering, compounded by private spiritual torments, the exhausting efforts to win recognition for his congregation, and the acknowledgment of bitter and nearly irreparable contentions within the congregation itself.

Along with the need for approval of his religious rule by the Vatican it was also necessary to win approval from the ruling monarch of Naples, which was now under Spanish control. Alphonsus felt his project was caught in the middle of tensions between church and state. The ultimate blow came when Alphonsus found himself expelled from the order he had founded, as a result of having failed to read a vital document before signing it. His failing health and near blindness were not accepted as excuses.

The end of these trials came only with his peaceful death on August 1, 1787, at the age of ninety. Soon after, the divisions in his beloved congregation were healed. The Redemptorists won their recognition and their numbers spread across Europe, North America, and other parts of the world. Liguori himself was canonized in 1839, and in 1871, in recognition of his contributions to moral theology, he was named a Doctor of the Church.

See: Helene Magaret, *Kingdom and a Cross: St. Alphonsus Liguori* (Milwaukee: Bruce, 1958).

August 2

St. Basil the Blessed
Holy Fool (d. 1552)

"If any one among you thinks that he is wise in this age,
let him become a fool." —1 Corinthians 3:18

While many saints have appeared eccentric to their contemporaries, the tradition of "holy fools" is nowhere so common or so revered as in the Russian Orthodox church. In this tradition the Fool for Christ is a well-established type. These vagrant ascetics, often dressed in little or nothing at all, would wear a mask of madness (in some cases, perhaps, a mask that fit all too well). They would invite ridicule and contempt with their outlandish behavior. But to the extent that their conduct suggested a divine inspiration they might also merit cautious respect. Like the "Fools" in Shakespeare, their marginal status earned them the privilege of speaking discomforting truths. Like the Hebrew prophets, who occasionally spoke by means of symbolic pantomimes, the lives of the Holy Fools often presented a prophetic judgment on their times — an expression of solidarity with the afflicted and a challenge to the rich and powerful to beware the wrath of God.

One of the most famous and widely revered of these Fools is the Muscovite Basil the Blessed, after whom the cathedral in Red Square takes its name. He used to wander naked through the streets of Moscow, whether in snow or sunshine, praying as if in church and bearing witness, by audacious gestures, to the spirit of Christ. Thus, he would often take goods from shops to distribute them to the destitute. He used to throw stones at the houses of people who made a public display of their piety, while kneeling to kiss the pavement before houses of ill repute. "Devils lay siege to those," he would say in the case of the former, whereas of the latter, "angels weep over these."

Not surprisingly, most of Basil's contemporaries liked to give him a wide berth. Yet he apparently enjoyed unimpeded access to the notorious tsar Ivan the Terrible. Once during Lent, a time when all Christians were expected to maintain a strict vegetarian fast, Basil presented Ivan with a great piece of raw meat. When the tsar protested that he did not eat meat in Lent, Basil responded, "Then why do you drink the blood of men?" Few men dared to speak so boldly to the ruthless Ivan. But so fearful was the tsar of this poor holy man that he ordered that no harm be done to him.

When Basil died in 1552, he was buried with honors beside the new cathedral in the center of Moscow. The cathedral was originally dedicated to the Mother of God, in thanks for Russia's victory over the Tartars. It is a mark of the high esteem which Basil enjoyed among his fellow Muscovites that the cathedral became better known as the site of his grave. With his canonization by the Russian church in 1580 the cathedral's name was formalized: St. Basil's it became, and so it remains.

See: Jim Forest, "Holy Foolishness," *Parabola* (Winter 1994), 22–28; Louis Bouyer, *A History of Christian Spirituality,* vol. 3 (New York: Seabury, 1969).

August 3

Flannery O'Connor
Novelist (1925–1964)

"The Catholic writer... will feel life from the standpoint of the central Christian mystery: that it has, for all its horror, been found by God to be worth dying for."

"There won't be any biographies of me," predicted Flannery O'Connor (and a good thing, too, was the implication), "because...lives spent between the house and the chicken yard do not make exciting copy."

Lacking in excitement, her short life was nevertheless marked by its own human drama. Among other things, she left behind a small output of novels and stories that assured her place among the very greatest of American writers. In her lifetime, discerning critics perceived the importance of religious themes in her work. But only with the posthumous publication of her letters in *The Habit of Being* did it become clear how much the shape of her art owed to her Catholic faith. What is more the letters revealed just how much her personal circumstances, her sharp intelligence, and her deeply held faith had combined to forge a prophetic vision of extraordinary depth.

Early in life O'Connor was diagnosed as suffering from lupus, an incurable, debilitating disease that sapped her energy and confined her to her mother's dairy farm in Milledgeville, Georgia. There she wrote as her strength permitted — two hours in the morning — and tended the menagerie of ducks, swans, and peacocks with which she surrounded herself. She disliked sentimentality and piety and reacted strongly against the temptation of critics to drag her medical history into consideration of her writing. And yet her illness imposed on her a discipline and sense of priorities that she managed to turn to the advantage of her art. From *Teilhard de Chardin she borrowed the phrase "passive diminishment" to describe a quality she admired: the serene acceptance of whatever affliction or loss no effort can change. "I have enough energy to write with and as that is all I have any business doing anyhow, I can with one eye squinted take it all as a blessing. What you have to measure out, you come to observe closer."

In her imposed confinement, she poured much energy into correspondence. Many of her letters dealt with her faith and the religious dimension of her stories. To one correspondent she wrote,

> I write the way I do because (not though) I am a Catholic. This is a fact and nothing covers it like the bald statement. However, I am a Catholic peculiarly possessed of the modern consciousness.... To possess this *within* the Church is to bear a burden, the necessary burden for the conscious Catholic. It's to feel the contemporary situation at the ultimate level.

For O'Connor the Catholic doctrines of creation, fall, and redemption were the lens through which she viewed the world. But as an artist she also valued the vivid sacramental dimension of Catholicism — the notion that grace is always mediated through nature, and mystery through manners. "I feel that if I were not a Catholic I would have no reason to write, no reason to see, no reason ever to feel horrified or even to enjoy anything." She frankly acknowledged her orthodoxy and baffled her more secular-minded friends by confessing to find in dogma a source of liberation ("it preserves mystery for the human mind").

The church, she believed, was the only thing likely to make the world endurable. She could believe this and still acknowledge the church's own sins — they were all the more painful to her. "The only thing that makes the Church endurable is that it is somehow the Body of Christ and that on this we are fed."

O'Connor saw clearly the crisis of faith in a "religionless age" — a time when it is so much easier not to believe, when "nihilism is the gas we breathe." Often, she stressed the cost of faith:

I think there is no suffering greater than what is caused by the doubts of those who want to believe. I know what torment this is, but I can only see it, in myself anyway, as the process by which faith is deepened. What people don't realize is how much religion costs. They think faith is a big electric blanket, when of course it is the cross.

Unlike most other "Catholic writers," O'Connor avoided Catholic settings in her stories. Most of her characters are a strange assortment of back-woods fanatics, secular-minded intellectuals, and self-described "good country people." Her stories are set on that contested territory where God and the devil have it out. The endings are often violent, even apocalyptic; her characters are pruned and emptied of their illusions and even their "virtues" before they can face the truth. Yet even in the darkest of her stories there is a dimension of mystery and innocence and possibility. It is the dimension of grace that heals, though first it cuts with the sword of Christ.

"All my stories," she wrote, "are about the action of grace on a character who is not very willing to support it." To the modern reader, inclined to believe that grace and faith are "twin idiocies," the point of view in her stories might seem grim and cynical. But O'Connor believed her stories were ultimately hopeful — in the same sense in which she believed that purgatory was the most hopeful doctrine of the church.

Flannery O'Connor died of lupus on August 3, 1964, at the age of thirty-nine. In her last year she completed several of her greatest stories, all written more or less *in extremis*. She had, as her friend Sally Fitzgerald observed, attained her personal form in art as well as in life. She would have been happy to be remembered for her stories. Posthumously, how-ever, she has achieved an unexpected reputation as a Christian apologist. She was able to make the life of faith seem reasonable and attractive with-out losing a sense of ambiguity. She combined detachment with a sense of the preciousness of life. She faced the horrors of history without losing sight of the resurrection. Thus, in her highly personal and modest way she exemplified the virtue and responsibility of hope.

See: Flannery O'Connor, *The Habit of Being,* ed. Sally Fitzgerald (New York: Farrar, Straus & Giroux, 1979).

St. John Vianney

Curé of Ars (1786–1859)

"To be a saint one must be beside oneself, one must lose one's head."

The early life of John Vianney contained no foreshadowing of greatness in any field. He was born to a peasant family in a village near Lyons. Though he desired nothing else but to be a priest, his humble background and lack of education made it unlikely that he could ever realize such a vocation. Nevertheless with the help of private tutoring he secured a place in seminary. His studies were interrupted when he was conscripted to serve in the army. On his way to a posting in Spain he deserted and went into hiding for several years in a neighboring village. Only with an amnesty in 1810 was he able to resume his formation.

For all his zeal, Vianney proved to be a miserable student. It was only with grave reservations that he was recommended for ordination. In the end, however, his evident piety and goodness won the day. As one of his sponsors noted, "The Church wants not only learned priests but even more holy ones." Thus he was finally ordained at the age of twenty-nine. He served for a brief time as curate in his home parish. And then in 1817 he was named the parish priest of Ars-en-Dombes, a village of 250 souls, as remote and insignificant a place as his bishop could find.

To Vianney there was nothing insignificant about his new home. The size of the village was unimportant. He regarded himself as answerable for the salvation of his flock. This was an awesome charge, which he accepted with all the determination of a soldier ordered to hold his position. Compensating for lack of learning, he girded himself for his responsibilities by ascetic zeal. This did not go unnoticed. It was said that the new curé lived on nothing but potatoes. He never seemed to sleep. When not visiting parishioners or performing the sacraments he could invariably be found in the church, fixed in silent adoration of the Eucharist.

The curé's sermons were simple and unsophisticated. His theology was rudimentary. His efforts to elevate the spiritual level of his community by combatting the evils of profanity, public dances, and work on Sunday seemed, even at the time, to verge on the naive. But what gradually dawned on his parishioners and began to work its gradual effect was the consciousness that their souls *mattered* to this holy priest and that he suffered for their sins.

For all his simplicity, there was one area in which Vianney acquired a reputation for genius: his extraordinary gifts as a confessor. It was said that he had an ability to read souls. With disarming simplicity, the Curé d'Ars was apparently able to discern the secrets of his penitents, and unlock the barriers that prevented them from knowing and loving God. This gift attracted a growing stream of penitents which gradually expanded so as to lay claim to nearly all of his waking hours. Fixed in his cramped confessional, shivering in the winter, stifling in the summer, he would sit ten, twelve, as many as eighteen hours a day.

Toward the end of his life the railroad provided special trains to accommodate the heavy traffic of pilgrims to the famous confessional in Ars. By the time of his death in 1859 Vianney was one of the most beloved figures in France. Various honors were bestowed on him. Napoleon III, in a curious gesture, sent him the medal of the Legion of Honor. Vianney refused to take it out of the box, remarking, "I don't know what I have done to deserve this except to be a deserter."

Certainly Vianney never sought or anticipated such fame. It was literally one more cross that he shouldered. Vianney could not imagine any more important calling than to serve as the parish priest of the village of Ars. This was the post where he had been placed to care for the souls of his flock, ready, like the good shepherd, to lay down his life for them, if that were required.

St. John Vianney was canonized in 1925 by Pope Pius XI. At the same time he was named patron saint of all parish priests.

See: Daniel Pezeril, *Blessed and Poor: The Spiritual Odyssey of the Curé of Ars* (New York: Pantheon, 1961); Jean de La Varende, *The Curé of Ars and His Cross* (New York: Desclée, 1959).

August 5

Bd. Mary McKillop
Foundress of the Sisters of St. Joseph
of the Sacred Heart (1842–1909)

"The Cross is my portion — it is my sweet rest and support."

With her beatification in 1995 Mary McKillop, otherwise known as Mother Mary of the Cross, became the first recognized saint of Australia. She was the foundress of a remarkable congregation, the Sisters of St. Joseph, who devoted themselves to providing free education and other services to the poor and needy.

What is most remarkable about Mary McKillop, however, is not so much the charitable work by which she expressed her faith as the utterly uncharitable treatment she received at the hands of many priests and prelates in her time. Indeed Mary McKillop might serve as the patron saint of all who have suffered the petty persecution of narrow-minded religious authorities, convinced they are acting in the place of God. That Mary remained free of bitterness, despite her ordeals, is considerable evidence of her sanctity and sufficient cause for honor.

Mary was born in Melbourne in the colony of southern Australia on January 15, 1842. Her parents were poor Scottish immigrants. While working as a governess she met a charismatic young priest, Julian Woods, who inspired her to consider a religious vocation. Together they conceived the idea of a congregation dedicated to the needs of the poor. In 1866 Mary put on a plain black dress as a sign of her dedication to religious life and the next year she took religious vows. It was the start of a new congregation, the Sisters of St. Joseph.

From the beginning Mary had given much thought to the type of congregation suited to the needs and rugged conditions of Australia. The constitutions she devised for her community had several important features. In the first place, as a congregation devoted to the poor, she felt it was essential that her Sisters themselves adhere to a strict vow of poverty. Her preference was that the congregation not own any property at all. There were also to be no social distinctions within the community between "choir" and "lay" Sisters. She insisted on radical equality.

Most important of all, however, was her insistence that the congregation be subject to "central government." This meant that instead of allowing each of her far-flung communities to be administered under the authority of a local bishop, they would be governed by an elected mother general who would answer directly to Rome. This provision proved to be the source of extreme tension between the congregation and the Australian bishops.

In almost no time Mary had attracted scores of young women to her congregation, and houses were established in a number of cities and outback missions throughout the territory. At a time when almost no public services were available for the poor, the Sisters of St. Joseph won the admiration and gratitude of Australians of all classes and religious persuasions. Many bishops were initially eager to welcome the Sisters. But inevitably they tried to interfere in the management and direction of the Sisters' work. To this Mary put up spirited resistance.

When Mary remained adamant in her commitment to central government, the bishops' support gave way to a shameless campaign of harassment and vilification. In one dramatic episode she was actually excommunicated by her local bishop. Though he later, on his deathbed, rescinded the order, she continued to operate under a cloud. Another bishop had her expelled from his diocese and refused to allow the Sisters to do any fund-raising. The bishop of Queensland sent damning letters to Rome claiming that the Sisters were "infected with fanaticism and insubordination to authority," and that Mary's aim was "to subvert the whole system here."

To shore up her position, Mary traveled to Rome and spent two years seeking authorization for her constitutions. Eventually she found an audience with Pope Pius IX. He was personally intrigued by the story of "the nun who was excommunicated." When she returned to Australia she held a papal document formally approving her congregation. Still, the persecution did not cease. A team of bishops and clerics, claiming falsely to be authorized by Rome, subjected her community to a rigorous "visitation," seizing financial records and interviewing the Sisters under a supposed "vow of secrecy" to discover scurrilous information about Mother Mary. Afterward the bishop of Adelaide leaked the slanderous story that Mary was an alcoholic and that she had misappropriated funds belonging to the congregation.

It turned out that the "visitation" had no authority from Rome. An official inquiry by Rome, provoked by this incident, completely exonerated Mother Mary. Still the harassment continued. The Australian bishops voted to overturn the constitutions of the congregation and subject the Sisters once more to diocesan control. Once more, Rome came to the rescue, nullifying the bishops' authority in the matter. The congregation would remain under central government. Mother Mary had won at last.

Although she suffered terribly from the constant attacks on her virtue and her faith, Mary never disdained the occasion to endure injustice or injury. She referred to such ordeals as "presents from God." Innocent suffering, she believed, was an opportunity to shoulder the cross and so to grow closer to God. Those who caused this suffering were thus "instruments in the hands of God"; they were, indeed, her "most powerful benefactors." Nevertheless, she acknowledged that "God's presents were often hard to understand," and that she was "too often cowardly in accepting them."

Mother Mary lived on to see her congregation firmly established throughout Australia and New Zealand. After many years of painful illness, she died on August 5, 1909. Her passing was mourned throughout Australia.

See: Lesley O'Brien, *Mary McKillop Unveiled* (Victoria, Australia: CollinsDove, 1994).

August 6

Paul VI
Pope (1897–1978)

"The Church looks at the world with profound understanding, with sincere admiration, and with the sincere intention not of dominating it, but of serving it; not of despising it, but of appreciating it; not of condemning it, but of strengthening and saving it."

Giovanni Battista Montini, archbishop of Milan, was elected pope in the conclave of June 1963. He chose to be called Paul VI. Shy and somewhat ascetic in appearance, he faced a difficult challenge in succeeding the jovial and universally beloved *Pope John XXIII. But he faced still greater challenges. It fell to Pope Paul to implement the revolutionary vision that John had unleashed with the Second Vatican Council (1962–1965). To this task Montini brought considerable diplomatic skills, gained during a lifetime of service in the Vatican Secretariat of State. Such skills would be severely taxed, as Pope Paul steered the church through one of the most turbulent decades in its history. He was buffeted by criticism from all sides, both from those who felt the church was changing too quickly as well as from those who felt the pace of change was not fast enough.

Pope Paul immediately defined his papacy in terms of continuing forward with the initiatives of his predecessor. He oversaw the final sessions of the council and approved a series of extraordinary documents that defined a new understanding of the church in relation to the Word of

God and the hopes of the wider human community. Complicating this new era for the church was the fact that it came on the threshold of a much broader cultural revolution. Old habits and values were being questioned and challenged in every corner. Traditions were being discarded, sometimes without regard for their truth or value.

While many Catholics found their faith invigorated by the spirit of renewal, others drifted away, no longer feeling the same urgency in their identity as Catholics. Priests and nuns renounced their vows in droves. Pope Paul suffered deeply over these developments and from the carping criticism of conservatives in the church — those Pope John had called the "prophets of gloom" — who blamed everything wrong in the world on the changes he had authorized. It required a deep faith for Pope Paul to maintain his confidence in the ongoing presence and guidance of the Holy Spirit amid these uncharted waters.

In 1968 Pope Paul issued his most controversial encyclical, *Humanae Vitae*. He contravened the recommendation of his own pontifical commission by upholding the church's ban on artificial contraception. Although the document reiterated traditional Catholic teaching, it appeared to put a brake on the rising tide of expectations released by the council, and so met with unprecedented public dissent. Sadly, the furor raised a divisive cloud that hovered over the remainder of Pope Paul's pontificate until his death ten years later, on August 6, 1978. In his later years Paul was often depicted as a remote figure, out of touch with the times. One of the most self-effacing of modern popes, Pope Paul disdained any cult of personality and studiously avoided the trappings of power. Though this reflected a genuine humility, it made it hard for people to feel the kind of personal bond they had experienced with the cheerful and spontaneous Pope John.

In recent years, however, there has been a steady reevaluation of Pope Paul, with a greater appreciation for both his leadership and his personal qualities. Though regarded as doctrinally conservative, Pope Paul was in his social teaching one of the most radical pontiffs in history. His encyclical *Populorum Progressio* (1967) marked the first church document to deal with the problems of the Third World, particularly the growing gap between the rich and the poor. Pope Paul addressed with urgency the sufferings of the poor and firmly committed the church to the project of authentic development, "the transition from less than human conditions to truly human ones." The most often quoted line of that encyclical was "Development is the new name for peace."

In this and subsequent documents Paul went substantially beyond any previous pope in modern history to challenge the dominant structures of the global economy and to identify with the hopes and struggles of the poor. In articulating this vision he struck a poignant note and a sense of urgency previously reserved in papal documents for the struggle against atheism itself:

> The hour for action has now sounded. At stake are the survival of many innocent children and, for so many families overcome by misery, the access to conditions fit for human beings; at stake are the peace of the world and the future of civilization. It is time for all men

and all peoples to face up to their responsibilities.... Yes, we ask you, all of you, to heed our cry of anguish, in the name of the Lord.

That anguish and pathos were part of Paul's gift to the church.

See: Peter Hebblethwaite, *Pope Paul VI* (New York: Paulist, 1993); Francis X. Murphy, *The Papacy Today* (London: Weidenfeld and Nicolson, 1981).

August 7

St. Victricius
Bishop of Rouen (c. 330–407)

"I inspired the wise with love of peace, I taught it to the teachable,
I explained it to the ignorant, I imposed it on the obstinate,
insisting on it in season and out of season."

Like his friend *St. Martin of Tours, Victricius was a Roman soldier who converted to Christianity and decided, simultaneously, that military service was incompatible with obedience to the gospel. After laying down his weapons on the parade grounds, he was arrested and charged with desertion. He was flogged and narrowly escaped execution.

Victricius traveled for some years as an itinerant preacher until 386, when he was named the bishop of Rouen. Little is known of his subsequent life in this remote mission outpost. He was greatly occupied in establishing the church in northern France and made numerous preaching tours throughout Europe. He retained his reputation as a peacemaker and was even summoned to Britain at the request of the local bishops to settle a disagreement. There and in all circumstances, according to his own words, he "did all he could, even if he did not do all that wanted doing." He died sometime around 407.

See: Ronald G. Musto, *The Catholic Peace Tradition* (Maryknoll, N.Y.: Orbis, 1986).

August 8

St. Dominic
Founder of the Order of Preachers (1170–1221)

"Fight the good fight against our ancient foe, fight him insistently with fasting, because no one will win the crown of victory without engaging in the contest in the proper way."

Dominic Guzmán was born in Spain in 1170 and became an ordained canon of the cathedral of Osma. In 1203 he accompanied his bishop on a diplomatic mission that took them through the Languedoc region of southern France. At the time the region was in the grip of Catharism, a religious cult imported from the East. Although its proponents regarded themselves as Christian, their religion was really a revival of the ancient gnostic heresy. The Cathari propounded a similar dualism, sharply distinguishing the spiritual world, which was good, from the earthly world, which was carnal and corrupt. These dimensions were, respectively, the domain of God and the devil. The object of the Cathari elite, or the *perfecti*, was to lead lives of abstemious purity and so to escape the coils of the flesh.

While lodging in an inn along the way, Dominic was horrified to discover that their very host was an adherent to these beliefs. Further probing disclosed that his heresy did not represent so much a rejection of the Catholic faith as a woeful ignorance of its essential tenets. Dominic proceeded to present the contents of the faith, and by morning's light he had convinced his host to renounce his unorthodox views. Afterward Dominic sought out the papal legates who had been appointed to combat the heresy. He found them seriously discouraged and ready to quit. But it did not take Dominic long to understand the reasons for their failure. These legates traveled like princes with a costly retinue. Their preaching was uninspired and they utterly failed to present a challenging alternative to the purity and zeal of the Cathari.

From these encounters Dominic conceived the model for a new kind of missionary, based on the pattern of the original apostles. They should travel on foot and without money, preaching wherever there was an audience and exemplifying the gospel ideals of faith and charity. They should be well trained in theology and doctrine and specially skilled in the art of communication. Dominic himself received papal authorization to under- take such a preaching mission among the Cathari, and this would in time become the foundation for a new religious congregation, the Order of Preachers (or Dominicans, as they came to be known).

With their contemporaries the Franciscans, the Dominicans introduced a new era in religious life — the age of the so-called mendicants (beggars). Rather than live within an enclosed monastery, they proclaimed the gospel on the road, open to the needs of the world. The two founders, Dominic and *Francis, had occasion to meet in Rome. They greeted one another with fraternal affection. But there were significant differences in their visions and styles. Francis was the troubadour and poet, the mystic of nature, who identified so closely with Christ that he received the marks of the stigmata. Poverty was his cherished bride, and his mission in the world, which drew him close to the sick and poor, was a witness to the spirit of the Beatitudes.

Dominic, in contrast, identified more with the missionary apostles. His order was at the service of the church and its needs. Poverty was less a spiritual than a functional virtue, allowing mobility and freedom. That they might be more effective preachers Dominic urged his friars to study theology and doctrine and to become experts in its exposition. Thus the Dominicans would produce great theologians (*Thomas Aquinas), mystics (*Catherine of Siena), and prophets (*Bartolomé de Las Casas). On the other hand, the Dominicans would later be given charge of the Inquisition, wherein some members of their order (Torquemada) would realize the consequences of a zeal for "truth" when severed from an equal regard for charity.

Dominic himself opposed the use of force in combating error. But his views did not carry the argument. In 1208 a papal legate in Toulouse was assassinated. In retaliation the pope called for a crusade to crush the Catharist heresy. Many lives were similarly crushed in the bitter and protracted war that followed.

Dominic meanwhile had extended his mission to other parts of Europe, where his methods did much to rejuvenate the church. Unlike his contemporary St. Francis, St. Dominic did not generate a rich literature of affectionate legend. He did not aspire to personify the gospel but merely to be its effective propagator. His personality, so it appears, was subsumed in his mission. And so his legacy was not in the example of his personal holiness but in the apostolic movement he initiated and inspired.

When his friars asked him to produce a formal testament, he answered, "All my children, what I leave to you: Have charity, guard humility, and make your treasure out of voluntary poverty." He died among his brethren in 1221.

See: Early Dominicans: Selected Writings, ed. Simon Tugwell, O.P. (New York: Paulist, 1982).

August 9

Franz Jägerstätter
Conscientious Objector, Martyr (1907–1943)

"Neither prison nor chains nor sentence of death can rob a man of the Faith and his own free will. God gives so much strength that it is possible to bear any suffering, a strength far stronger than all the might of the world. The power of God cannot be overcome."

In the early hours of March 1, 1943, an Austrian peasant, Franz Jägerstätter, bade farewell to his wife and home and set off by foot for the neighboring town. On a hill on the outskirts of St. Radegund, he turned one last time to take in the village of his birth, the parish church where he had served as sexton, and the fields where he had labored as a farmer. Upon recognizing him, a neighbor called out in the customary greeting, "Go with God, Franz," to which Franz answered, "You'll see no more of me."

The next day he turned himself in at the induction center in Enns, where he had been ordered to report for military service. After stating his refusal to serve in Hitler's army, he was arrested and imprisoned. He was later tried before a military court in Berlin and sentenced to death. On August 9, 1943, he was beheaded as an "enemy of the state."

To the villagers of St. Radegund, Jägerstätter's death was a sad embarrassment. But no one was surprised by his stand. It was well known that Jägerstätter had undergone a profound conversion sometime after his marriage. Once known as something of a village ruffian, Jägerstätter had returned with zeal to the Catholic faith of his upbringing. Some felt he took his piety "a bit too far," but there was nothing of the "fanatic" about him. He was known as a man of honesty and high principle, devoted to his family and to the practice of his faith. In normal times these characteristics would not have distinguished him from his neighbors, much less have hastened his death. But these were not normal times.

In 1938 Austria was invaded by Hitler and annexed into "Greater Germany." Most Austrians welcomed the *Anschluss,* which was subsequently ratified by a national plebiscite. Jägerstätter made no effort to disguise his disdain for the Nazis, and it was widely known that in the plebiscite he had cast the single "no" vote in the village. He likened that day to the original Maundy Thursday when the crowd chose the murderer Barabbas over Christ. He let it be known that whatever else might happen, he would never serve in Hitler's army.

The moment of decision came when he was served with his induction notice in 1943. Before taking his fateful stand Franz sought the counsel of his parish priest and even the local bishop. They joined his wife, family, and neighbors in trying to shake his dangerous resolution. Franz considered every argument, from the appeal to his responsibilities as a husband and the father of three daughters, to his duties to the Fatherland and his obligation to leave political judgments to those in higher authority. But no one could persuade Franz to alter his conviction that any form of service in the army would involve recognition of the Nazi cause. This, he was convinced, would be a mortal sin.

In a remarkable document written in prison, Franz described a dream he had had in 1938 in which crowds of people were struggling to board a shiny new train. At some point he heard a voice announce, "This train is bound for hell." It occurred to him afterward that this train was a symbol for the Nazi movement. Surely, he concluded, one should not board such a train; surely, having discovered its destination, one ought to jump off such a train before it reached its goal, even though it might cost one's life.

While in prison Franz continued to hear appeals from the prison chaplain, his attorney, and even the military officers before whom he was tried, urging him to renounce his conscience and save his life. But Franz was convinced that he could not prolong his life at the price of his immortal soul. In this case, obedience to Christ must mean disobedience to the state. But he took comfort in the knowledge that "not everything which this world considers a crime is a crime in the eyes of God. And I have hope that I need not fear the eternal Judge because of this crime."

For years this story was little known beyond a small circle of Jägerstätter's family and fellow villagers. It was only in the 1960s, through the work of an American scholar, Gordon Zahn, that the extraordinary story of Franz Jägerstätter and his "solitary witness" was fully documented. Since then he has been acclaimed by many in the church as one of the great saints and martyrs of our time. Nevertheless, support for his cause still encounters opposition from those who believe his beatification would reflect badly on all those of his countrymen who "did their duty" in time of war. Such attitudes, alive today, only underscore the remarkable courage of Jägerstätter's stand fifty years ago. Somehow, in contrast to virtually the entire church establishment of his country, he was able to discern how impossible it was to reconcile the evil nature of Nazism with the commandments of Christ. Nevertheless, his sacrifice, seemingly fruitless in his own time, presented an example, a beacon of conscience, that would illuminate the path of generations to come.

See: Gordon Zahn, *In Solitary Witness: The Life and Death of Franz Jägerstätter* (Springfield, Ill.: Templegate, 1964, 1991).

August 10
St. Edith Stein
Carmelite Martyr (1891–1942)

"Do you want to be totally united to the Crucified? If you are serious about this, you will be present, by the power of His Cross, at every front, at every place of sorrow, bringing to those who suffer, healing and salvation."

Edith Stein was born the eleventh child of Orthodox Jewish parents in Breslau, Germany, on October 12, 1891. Her birth fell on Yom Kippur, the Jewish Day of Atonement, a fact whose significance she later noted. Independent by nature and gifted with a prodigious intelligence, Edith had abandoned her family's faith by the time she was thirteen. She declared herself an atheist — only the first of a series of blows to her pious mother — and devoted herself to the study of philosophy. She was accepted as one of the first women students at the University of Göttingen, where she studied under the brilliant Edmund Husserl, father of phenomenology. Stein became one of his star pupils, so respected by Husserl that he invited her to become his assistant at the University of Freiburg. There she completed her doctorate at the age of twenty-three, writing a dissertation on the nature of empathy.

There was a strong ethical dimension to the phenomenological school, and a number of Husserl's disciples were professing Christians. In the years after World War I Stein herself began to feel a growing interest in religion. This culminated one night in 1921 when she happened upon the autobiography of *St. Teresa of Avila, the sixteenth-century Carmelite mystic. With fascination she read through the night and by morning concluded, "This is the truth." She was baptized as a Catholic on the following New Year's Day.

Edith's mother wept when she heard the news of her daughter's conversion. Faced with Edith's resolution, however, she had little choice but to acquiesce. Edith continued to accompany her mother to synagogue, feeling that in accepting Christ she had been reunited, by a mysterious path, with her Jewish roots.

Stein initially believed that with her conversion she should abandon thoughts of a scholarly career. For eight years she taught in a Dominican school for girls. But her study of *Thomas Aquinas eventually rekindled her interest in academic pursuits. After preparing a scholarly work integrating phenomenology with scholasticism, she obtained an academic post in Munster in 1932.

This position, however, would be shortlived. As the Nazis rose to power, Stein almost immediately felt the reverberations of anti-Semitism. With unusual foresight, she recognized the destination of this campaign of hatred. Somewhat audaciously, she wrote to seek an audience with Pope Pius XI, hoping to alert him to the peril facing the Jews. Her request was not answered. Meanwhile, with the regrets of the university administration, she was dismissed from the teaching position she had barely begun.

Already Stein understood the terrible storm that was approaching, and she felt in some way that her Jewish-Christian identity imposed a unique vocation. While praying at the Carmelite convent in Cologne, she later wrote,

> I spoke with the Savior to tell him that I realized it was his Cross that was now being laid upon the Jewish people, that the few who understood this had the responsibility of carrying it in the name of all, and that I myself was willing to do this, if he would only show me how.

For the meantime, the loss of her job enabled her to pursue her growing attraction to religious life. She applied to enter the Carmelite convent in Cologne. Once again her mother wept — this time accusing her of abandoning her people in time of persecution. It was a bitter charge, and one that would cloud their parting. After spending a final evening with her mother in the synagogue, Edith bade her farewell. None of her family was present on April 15, 1934, to witness her formal clothing in the Carmelite habit. She took as her religious name Sister Teresa Benedicta a Cruce — Blessed by the Cross. It was a name, she later explained, chosen to refer "to the fate of the people of God, which even then was beginning to reveal itself."

In 1938 the all-out war against the Jews was declared on November 8, the *Kristallnacht. Believing that her presence in the convent endangered her Sisters, Stein allowed herself to be smuggled out of the country to a Carmelite convent in Holland. She had no thought of escaping the fate of her people. In fact, she prepared a solemn prayer which she delivered to her prioress, "offering myself to the Heart of Jesus as a sacrifice of atonement" for the Jewish people, for the aversion of war, and for the sanctification of her Carmelite family. Having contemplated and faced the reality of death, she was delivered from further anxiety, and thus prepared to await the end.

In 1940 the Nazis occupied Holland. Despite her cloistered status, Stein was required to wear the Yellow Star of David on her habit. Soon the deportations began. All the while Stein hurried to finish her study of the mystical theology of *St. John of the Cross. She was consoled by the presence of her sister Rosa, who by this time had also converted and joined her in the convent as a laywoman.

The Germans had indicated a willingness to spare Jewish-Christians, provided the churches kept silent. When on July 26, 1942, a statement by the Catholic bishops of Holland denouncing the persecution of the Jews was read from pulpits throughout the country, the Nazis retaliated in rage. Within a week all Jewish Catholics, including members of religious orders, were under arrest. For Stein and her sister the end came on August 2, when the Gestapo arrived at their convent. Rosa was distraught, but Edith reassured her: "Come, Rosa. We're going for our people."

Survivors of the following days describe the nun's courage and composure despite her clear certainty of the fate that awaited her. She occupied herself with prayer while caring for the terrified children and consoling mothers separated from their husbands. Someone described her as a "Pietà without the Christ."

From a detention camp in Holland she followed the same route as millions of others: the wretched journey by sealed boxcar, the arrival half-starved at a strange camp amid snarling dogs and cursing guards, the infamous "selection," then the stripping, then the brisk walk to the shower room, from which none emerged.

Edith Stein died in the gas chamber of Auschwitz on August 9, 1942. In 1998 she was canonized as a confessor and martyr of the church by Pope John Paul II, an event that provoked considerable controversy. Many Jews complained that Stein, like six million others, had died as a Jew, and not for her Christian faith. There is a truth to this. But what is remarkable about Stein is not the manner of her death but her understanding of that death — in solidarity with her people, as an act of atonement for the evil of her time, and as a conscious identification with the cross of Christ.

See: Waltraud Herbstrith, *Edith Stein: A Biography* (New York: Harper & Row, 1983).

August 11

St. Clare
Foundress of the Poor Clares (1193–1253)

> *"Place your mind before the mirror of eternity!*
> *Place your soul in the brilliance of glory!*
> *Place your heart in the figure of the divine substance!*
> *And transform your whole being into the image*
> *of the Godhead Itself through contemplation!"*

The story of St. Clare of Assisi is inevitably linked with *St. Francis, the one she called her Father, Planter, and Helper in the Service of Christ. It was Francis who gave her a vision and enabled her to define a way of life apart from the options offered by her society. But her goal in life was not to be a reflection of Francis but to be, like him, a reflection of Christ. "Christ is the way," she said, "and Francis showed it to me."

Like Francis Clare belonged to one of the wealthy families of Assisi. Like everyone else in the town, she was aware of the remarkable spectacle that Francis had made in abandoning his respectable family and assuming the poverty of a beggar. Doubtless there were those in Assisi who respected Francis as a faithful Christian, just as there were others who believed he was a misguided fool. It was bad enough that a man of his background was tramping about the countryside, repairing abandoned churches with his bare hands and ministering to the poor and sick. But within a few years he had begun attracting some of the most distinguished young men of the town to follow him in his brotherhood.

What Clare's family thought of all this is not known. But we know what impact it had on Clare. She heard Francis deliver a series of Lenten sermons in 1212, when she was eighteen. She arranged in stealth to meet with Francis and asked his help that she too might live "after the manner of the holy gospel." On the evening of Palm Sunday, while her family and all the town slept, she crept out a back door, slipped through the gates of Assisi, and made her way through the dark fields and olive groves to a rendezvous with Francis and his brothers at the chapel of St. Mary of the Angels. Before the altar she put off her fine clothes and assumed a penitential habit, while Francis sheared off her long hair as a sign of her espousal to Christ.

It is tempting to read into this episode the romance of a spiritual elopement. To understand Clare, however, we must realize that it was not Francis whom she rushed to meet in the night. He provided the meeting place. But her assignation was with Christ.

Yet after Clare had taken the plunge of rejecting her family and her social station, it was not clear what the next step should be. Apparently neither Clare nor Francis had considered that far ahead. Although she wished to identify with Francis's community, it was not seemly that she should live with the brothers. Francis arranged for her to spend the night in a nearby Benedictine convent. There her family and a company of angry suitors tracked her down some days later in Holy Week. When pleading proved fruitless, they laid hands on her and tried to drag her out by force. She finally stopped them short by tearing off her veil and revealing her shorn head. They were too late. She was already "one of them."

Francis had long intended that a community of women, corresponding to his fraternity, should be established. In Clare he had found the partner he was seeking. She was easily persuaded to found a women's community, which was established at San Damiano. It required considerably more effort by Francis to persuade her to serve as abbess. Nevertheless, Clare quickly attracted other women. Over time these included a number of her personal relatives, including her sister Catherine and even her widowed mother. Within her lifetime additional communities were established elsewhere in Italy, France, and Germany.

Unlike the Friars, the Poor Ladies as they were originally known, lived within an enclosure. But Clare shared Francis's passionate commitment to "Lady Poverty." For her this meant literal poverty and insecurity —

not the luxurious "spiritual poverty" enjoyed by so many other convents, richly supported by gifts and endowments. To defend this "privilege of poverty" Clare waged a continuous struggle against solicitous prelates who tried to mitigate her austerity. This was the centerpiece of the rule she devised for her community. When the pope offered to absolve her from her rigorous vow of poverty, she answered, "Absolve me from my sins, Holy Father, but not from my wish to follow Christ." Two days before her death, in 1253, she enjoyed the grace of receiving from Rome a copy of her rule embellished with the approving seal of Pope Innocent IV. A notation on the original document notes that Clare, in tearful joy, covered the parchment with kisses.

It has been said that of all the followers of Francis, Clare was the most faithful. Many stories reflect the loving bonds of friendship between them and the trust that Francis placed in her wisdom and counsel. According to one story, Francis put the question to Clare whether he should preach or devote himself to prayer. It was Clare who urged him to go into the world: "God did not call you for yourself alone, but also for the salvation of others." During a period of dejection, Francis camped out in a hut outside the convent at San Damiano. It was there that he composed his exultant hymn to the universe, "The Canticle of Brother Sun." Later, when Francis received the stigmata, Clare thoughtfully made him soft slippers to cover his wounded feet.

Finally, as Francis felt the approach of Sister Death, Clare too became seriously ill. She suffered terribly at the thought that they would not meet again in this life. Francis sent word that she should put aside all grief, for she *would* surely see him again before her death. And so the promise was fulfilled, though not as she had wished. After Francis's death, the brothers carried his body to San Damiano for the Sisters' viewing. Francis's early biographer, Thomas of Celano, records that at the sight of his poor and lifeless body Clare was "filled with grief and wept aloud."

Francis was canonized a mere two years later. Clare lived on for another twenty-seven years. In her own final "Testament," written near the end of her life, Clare makes only a discrete reference to the pain of their separation and what it meant to her: "We take note . . . of the frailty which we feared in ourselves after the death of our holy Father Francis. He who was our pillar of strength and, after God, our one consolation and support. Thus time and again, we bound ourselves to our Lady, most Holy Poverty."

See: Francis and Clare: The Complete Works, trans. Regis Armstrong, O.F.M. Cap., and Ignatius Brady, O.F.M., Classics of Western Spirituality (New York: Paulist, 1982); Sister Frances Teresa O.S.C., *This Living Mirror: Reflections on Clare of Assisi* (Maryknoll, N.Y.: Orbis, 1995).

William Blake
Poet and Visionary (1757–1827)

"To see a World in a Grain of Sand
And a Heaven in a Wild Flower,
Hold Infinity in the palm of your hand
And Eternity in an hour."

William Blake, the poet and artist, was a man out of kilter with his times. Born in London in 1757, he grew up in a culture that valued reason, order, and moderation. To Blake, who from early childhood reported visions of angels, these were values to disdain. Instead of reason he prized the power of Imagination. By this, he did not mean simply creative fancy, but *insight,* the ability to see reality in its full spiritual dimension.

Blake was trained as an engraver, and by this trade he managed to support himself and his devoted wife, Catherine. But as a result of Blake's persistent habit of offending his patrons, he was often little removed from real poverty. An artist, and not simply a draftsman, he had a hard time drawing to please an audience wider than himself. For his own fantastical paintings of angels and allegorical figures there was little chance of profit. The same was true for his poetry, which was either deceptively simple or maddeningly obscure.

For Blake, his poetry and art were not intended to be "beautiful," any more than they were meant to entertain. They were the expression of his own spiritual vision — as such, a kind of protest against everything acceptable in the worlds of art and religion in his day. It is almost easier to list the things that Blake opposed than to say what he favored. He deplored the moralism that passed for virtue; the hypocrisy and dogmatism of organized religion; the ugliness and cruelty of industrialism; the hollow pedantry that substituted for insight. He was in some sense a spiritual anarchist, a kind of biblical prophet who looked at the world in light of the coming judgment.

Obsessed by the figure of Christ, he felt that the churches had emptied Christianity of its revolutionary content; they had transformed the gospel into a religion offering little alternative to the spirit-numbing values of the world. Thus, he felt forced to reinvent a kind of Christianity of his own.

This had all the dangers one might expect. Blake's "theology" was peculiar and idiosyncratic. But as refracted through his artistic lens, it could also yield moments of dazzling insight. In the words of *Thomas Merton, Blake's rebellion "was fundamentally the rebellion of the saints. It was the rebellion of the lover of the living God," a kind of "intuitive protest against Christianity's estrangement from its own eschatological ground."

From the vantage point of Imagination Blake cast his eye over the landscape of England — what seemed to many of his contemporaries to be the "best of all possible worlds" — and saw a culture of death in which all trace of the spirit was being steadily expunged.

I wander thro' each charter'd street
Near where the charter'd Thames does flow,
And mark in every face I meet
Marks of weakness, marks of woe.
In every cry of every Man,
In every Infant's cry of fear,
In every voice, in every ban,
The Mind-forg'd manacles I hear.

Blake's prophetic utterances sound no less strange today. But his warnings about "dark Satanic mills" no longer sound like the ravings of a private paranoia. In this light Blake's call for the integration of mysticism and prophecy has a more telling appeal, and many more may be persuaded to take up his challenge:

I shall not cease from Mental Fight,
Nor shall my Sword sleep in my hand
Til we have built Jerusalem
In England's green & pleasant Land.

At the very least, those who have spent much time in the company of Blake may be influenced, as was the young Thomas Merton, "to become conscious of the fact that the only way to live is to live in a world that is charged with the presence and reality of God."

Blake died on August 12, 1827.

See: William Blake, *Complete Writings,* ed. Geoffrey Keynes (London: Oxford University Press, 1971); Malcolm Muggeridge, *A Third Testament* (Boston: Little, Brown, 1976); Bro. Patrick Hart, ed., *The Literary Essays of Thomas Merton* (New York: New Directions, 1981).

August 13

St. Tikhon of Zadonsk
Bishop and Monk (1724–1783)

"All men are our brothers because they are created in the image of God, purchased by the blood of Christ, they are called to eternal salvation as members of the one Church."

This Russian saint was born to a poor family in Novgorod in 1724. A scholarship enabled him to attend the local seminary, and in 1754 he was ordained a priest. Although he desired to become a monk Tikhon was instead assigned the uncongenial task of teaching theology. In 1761, much against his desires, he was chosen to be the suffragan bishop of Novgorod. Two years later he was appointed bishop of Voronezh.

Such public responsibility was in conflict with his natural desire for solitude. Nevertheless, he was respected as an effective and holy bishop who strenuously worked to elevate the spiritual quality of the clergy and to instill in the faithful a strong sense both of the mystical and the social dimensions of the gospel. Faith, he believed, should not only reform the individual but transform society:

> No longer should our brothers be seen wandering the roads and in the squares, starving and trembling with cold, under the icy north wind, naked members of the Body of Christ.... There ought to be beggars and destitute persons no longer. All should be equal.

In 1767 Tikhon's health began to fail, and he received permission at last to retire to a monastery in Zadonsk. There he lived in a poor hut in happy isolation. Among Russian monks he was unusually receptive to Western spirituality, both Catholic and Protestant, and his voluminous writings integrated such writers as *Thomas à Kempis and the Lutheran pietist Johann Arndt with traditional Russian spirituality.

His retreat to the monastery was in some ways a new beginning of his own spiritual journey. Many of his insights came during vivid dreams in which he experienced encounters with the infant Jesus and received divine admonishment. These left him profoundly remorseful for his sins (especially his tendency to anger) and intensified his propensity for charity.

Though an intellectual, he was happiest in the company of peasants and enjoyed discussing the humble chores of country life. A strong believer in the importance of physical labor, he was determined to spend a certain portion of each day chopping wood or otherwise helping to provide for himself. His dream was "to retire to a very distant monastery, to shed not only the dignity of my office, but also my monastic habit; to work, to carry water, saw wood, sweep, bake bread."

Gradually his reputation not only for holiness but for accessibility spread. In his later years he entertained a steady stream of penitents, petitioners, and spiritual seekers, to whom he freely offered spiritual counsel and alms. His door was always open to the poor.

Tikhon died on August 13, 1783. He was officially canonized by the Holy Synod of the Russian Church in 1861.

See: Elisabeth Behr-Sigel, "Hesychasm and the Eastern Impact in Russia: St. Tikhon of Zadonsk," in Louis Dupre and Don E. Saliers, eds., *Christian Spirituality III* (New York: Crossroad, 1991).

August 14

St. Maximilian Kolbe
Francisan Priest and Martyr (1894–1941)

"These Nazis will not kill our souls, since we prisoners certainly distinguish ourselves quite definitely from our tormentors; they will not be able to deprive us of the dignity of our Catholic belief. We will not give up. And when we die, then we die pure and peaceful, resigned to God in our hearts."

On July 30, 1941, a prisoner escaped from Auschwitz, the notorious Nazi concentration camp in Poland. In retaliation the commandant of the camp lined up the inmates of cell block 14 and ordered that ten of them be selected for punishment. They would be consigned to an underground bunker and starved to death. Ten men were selected. One of them, Francis Gajowniczek, cried out in tears, "My poor wife and children! I will never see them again." At this point another prisoner stepped forward and volunteered to take his place. The commandant asked who he was. He replied, "I am a Catholic priest." The commandant accepted his offer, and so Father Maximilian Kolbe assumed his place among the condemned.

Father Kolbe was born in Zdunska Wola, Poland, in 1894. At the age of sixteen he joined the Franciscans. He was a sickly youth, prone to debilitating bouts of tuberculosis that regularly sent him to the sanatarium. Nevertheless he was animated by pious zeal which was matched by a positive genius for organization. After his ordination he formed a movement called the Knights of Mary Immaculate, which was devoted to propagating traditional Marian devotion, and launched a series of journals. One of these achieved a circulation of eight hundred thousand in Poland. He also organized a community called City of the Immaculate, which grew to include 762 Conventual friars, the largest religious community of men in the world. In the 1930s he started a similar foundation in Japan, the Garden of the Immaculate.

Kolbe was back in Poland in 1939 when the Nazis invaded. Gauging the Nazis' enmity for religion, he intuited his eventual fate and prepared himself for a time of suffering. "I would like to suffer and die in a knightly manner," he stated, "even to the shedding of the last drop of my blood, to hasten the day of gaining the whole world for the Immaculate Mother of God."

Kolbe was arrested in February 1941 and by May was on his way to Auschwitz. Ragged and hungry, suffering again from tubercular attacks, subject to beatings and other abuse, Kolbe survived for three months of hard labor. All this time he remained a beacon of faith to his fellow prisoners, encouraging them to pray and counseling them against despair.

His final passion began when he entered the death bunker in July 1941. There was nothing for the inmates to consume but their own urine. Kolbe passed the days leading his companions in prayer, preparing them for death, and keeping vigil with them as they gradually succumbed. By August 14 Kolbe and three others were still alive, at which point the Nazis grew tired of waiting any longer. The four were dispatched by injections of carbolic acid; their bodies were cremated in the camp ovens.

In 1982 Pope John Paul II who, as bishop of Cracow, had often prayed at the scene of Kolbe's death, presided over his canonization in Rome. Present for the ceremony was Francis Gajowniczek, the man in whose place Kolbe had died. The pope called Kolbe a true martyr and saint for our times whose heroic charity proved victorious over the architects of death. He cited the words from the Gospel of John: "Greater love hath no man than this: that he lay down his life for his friends."

See: Boniface Hanley, O.F.M., *Maximilian Kolbe: No Greater Love* (Notre Dame, Ind.: Ave Maria, 1982).

August 15

Catherine de Hueck Doherty
Founder of Madonna House (1896–1985)

"The hunger for God can only be satisfied by a love that is face to face, person to person. It is only in the eyes of another that we can find the Icon of Christ. We must make the other person aware we love him. If we do, he will know that God loves him. He will never hunger again."

Catherine Kolyschkine, as she was first named, was born in Russia on the feast of the Assumption in 1896. Her father, a wealthy diplomat and industrialist, was half Polish and Catholic, and so Catherine was raised in the Catholic church. When she was fifteen she married Baron Boris de Hueck, which made her a baroness. No sooner had she made this entry into the aristocracy than Russia was plunged into the First World War. While the baron served as an officer on the front, Catherine worked as a nurse. They watched as the starving and demoralized Russian army began to retreat, presaging the collapse of the tsarist empire in the October Revolution of 1917.

Though Catherine and Boris were reunited, their situation, as aristocrats, was perilous. Deprived of food rations, they came close to starving before risking a hazardous flight across the border to Finland. By 1920 they had arrived with their newborn son in Canada. Still in desperate financial straits, Catherine traveled to New York in search of work. She held a number of low-paying jobs. Finally, while working as a department store sales clerk, she was approached by a woman who asked if it was true that she was a Russian baroness, and would she be interested in lecturing about her experiences. Catherine immediately agreed, and soon she was on a lecture circuit, making $300 a week describing her harrowing escape from communism. During this time her marriage collapsed. It seemed that she had finally put the memory of poverty and hunger behind her. She had a luxurious apartment, a fancy car, and a country house in Graymore — all that communism had taken away from her. And yet her conscience was clouded by a nagging doubt, a feeling that it was just such a materialistic life and the failure of Christian values that had fed the communist revolution.

At the peak of her success she felt the pull of the gospel verse, "Go, sell what you have and give to the poor. Then come follow me." So in 1930 she gave up her worldly goods and moved into an apartment in the slums of Toronto, committed to living "the gospel without compromise." With the support of the archbishop, she came to establish Friendship House, a storefront center for the works of mercy, where the hungry were fed and the homeless were welcomed. Catherine's program of action was simple and unsystematic. It was simply a matter of living among the poor with an open door and an open heart. There was no need to seek out people in need. They came to her.

She received encouragement in these years from *Dorothy Day, whose Catholic Worker movement was operating on similar principles in New

352 ~

York's Bowery. In 1937 Catherine herself moved to New York to establish a Friendship House in Harlem. She had come to feel that the sin of racial prejudice and the consequent segregation of whites and blacks was the greatest countersign to the gospel. Friendship House was a sign of interracial justice and reconciliation.

Among those moved by her example was the young *Thomas Merton, who heard Catherine speak in 1938 and who joined her for a time in Harlem. Years later, in his autobiography, he described her message:

> Catholics are worried about Communism: and they have a right to be.... But few Catholics stop to think that Communism would make very little progress in the world, or none at all, if Catholics really lived up to their obligations, and really did the things Christ came on earth to teach them to do: that is, if they really loved one another, and saw Christ in one another, and lived as saints, and did something to win justice for the poor.

Catherine was a large woman whose bearing of authority, commanding presence, and thick Russian accent all seemed appropriate to the title of Baroness. That is indeed how most people addressed her. But to her friends she was simply "the B." She was famous for her earthy humor and her righteous anger. When a society woman sniffed contemptuously, "You smell of the Negro," Catherine retorted, "And you stink of hell!"

Nevertheless, her imperious style of leadership led to tensions. In 1946 Catherine resigned from Friendship House. By this time she had married a famous journalist, Eddie Doherty. Together they moved back to Ontario, Canada, and settled on a piece of land in the forests of Combermere. Catherine established a new community called Madonna House, which became a place of prayer and retreat. At Madonna House she returned full circle to the atmosphere of Russian spirituality she had known in her youth. Out of this came her best-selling book, *Poustinia*. The "poustinia," the Russian word for desert, is a place of silence and withdrawal from the compulsions of the world, a place to listen to God. It could be a hut in the forest, a special room in our apartment, or even a special place within our hearts, to which from time to time we might retreat. Through Madonna House and the communities it inspired around the world, Catherine promoted the two principles by which she lived — a commitment to the social apostolate in the world and the need to root such a commitment in a life of prayer and the spirit of Christ.

She died on December 14, 1985.

See: Catherine de Hueck Doherty, *Poustinia* (Notre Dame, Ind.: Ave Maria, 1975); *Fragments of My Life* (Notre Dame, Ind.: Ave Maria, 1979).

John Courtney Murray
Theologian (1904–1967)

"This Vatican Synod declares that the human person has a right to religious freedom.... This right has its foundation in the very dignity of the human person, as this dignity is known through the revealed word of God and by reason itself." — Declaration on Religious Freedom

John Courtney Murray was the most significant American Catholic theologian of the twentieth century. His writings on pluralism and "the American experiment" helped overcome nativist doubts about the place of Catholics in American democracy. In the wider church he helped to overcome ancient doubts about the separation of church and state and paved the way for a sea change in the church's attitude to religious freedom. Outwardly Murray's biography was lacking in major drama. He joined the Jesuits at the age of sixteen, went on to be ordained, and eventually received a doctorate in theology. He taught for thirty years at the Jesuit college at Woodstock, Maryland, until his death in 1967. For some years he was editor of the distinguished journal *Theological Studies*. Yet such facts alone, combined with his scholarly demeanor, conceal the quietly revolutionary impact of his contribution to Catholic thought.

The background of Murray's work was the longstanding tension between the Roman Catholic church and the culture of American democracy. Although American Catholics had attained great numbers by the twentieth century, they still tended to be viewed with prejudice by a great part of Protestant society. To some extent this attitude drew on popular disdain for "immigrants" in general. But there was also the sense that Catholics somehow deviated from the cultural "norm" and that their allegiance to a foreign pope set a limit to their loyalty as Americans. This attitude was further popularized in the 1950s by a series of books by Paul Blanshard, who argued that Catholicism was fundamentally incompatible with democracy. Blanshard was able to document his case with a rich tradition of papal pronouncements decrying the separation of church and state and denying the intrinsic rights of non-Catholics.

If American Protestants were suspicious of the Vatican, the feelings were certainly reciprocated. Conservative European prelates tended to view America as a hotbed of fanaticism. Principles of liberty and democracy, so prized in the New World, had taken a secularist and anticlerical turn in Europe. Thus when American bishops insisted that the constitutional separation of church and state was actually a great boon to the religious mission of the church, it was difficult for curial officials not to feel that their American brethren had fallen victim to a dangerous virus. It was one thing to accept the separation of church and state as a matter of necessity. But the official church continued to maintain that under ideal circumstances the state should enforce the moral truths of the Catholic religion. It was after all a commonplace of Catholic tradition that "error enjoys no rights."

Murray entered the debate only in the late 1940s. In a series of groundbreaking essays he argued that the American traditions of pluralism and religious liberty were not only compatible with Catholicism, but were a fitting reflection of the Catholic teaching on human dignity and freedom. Similarly, he argued that the separation of church and state was not simply a reality to be tolerated, but an ideal which liberated the church to pursue its genuine religious mission without danger of compromise. Published mostly in theological journals, Murray's bold thesis attracted little attention at first. But it was noticed in Rome. In 1955 Murray was ordered by the Holy Office to desist from further publication on church-state matters. He obediently complied, though such censorship simply provided more grist for the Blanshard mill.

Murray continued to write on Catholicism and American culture. In 1960 his essays were collected in *We Hold These Truths*, an unexpected bestseller. Overnight, Murray became the intellectual spokesman for the "arrival" of American Catholics in the public arena. John F. Kennedy, then planning his bid for the presidency, studied the book carefully; his advisors consulted Murray on ways to answer public concerns about the candidate's Catholicism. Drawing on this advice, Kennedy addressed the issue early on in his campaign, and effectively overcame the liability. That December Murray appeared on the cover of *Time* magazine; a separate article in *Newsweek* magazine noted, "Murray demonstrated in theory what John F. Kennedy demonstrated in practice: that Americanism and Roman Catholicism need no longer fear each other."

The election of Kennedy was a turning point in the history of American Catholicism. In Rome, with the convocation of the Second Vatican Council, an event of even wider significance for the church was about to occur. Murray was at first relegated to the sidelines. He was technically still subject to Vatican censorship. But Cardinal Spellman of New York insisted on bringing him along as his personal theologian. Before long, Murray had been entrusted with a momentous task: drafting the council's historic document on religious freedom. It was one of the last conciliar documents to be issued, finally appearing in December 1965.

In this document the church committed itself to religious freedom as a principle rooted in the dignity of the human person. Thus, the church was not simply upholding its own freedom from state interference, but renouncing any interest in imposing its faith on others: "One of the key truths in Catholic teaching . . . is that man's response to God by faith ought to be free, and that therefore nobody is to be forced to embrace the faith against his will" (Declaration on Religious Freedom II:10).

It was widely acknowledged that this document was the principal contribution of the American church to the teachings of Vatican II. With little exaggeration, it could be said that this teaching was the particular contribution of one man, John Courtney Murray, to Catholic teaching. Thus, he lived to see the complete vindication and fulfillment of his life's work. He died less than two years later on August 16, 1967.

See: John Courtney Murray, S.J., *We Hold These Truths* (New York: Sheed & Ward, 1960); Donald E. Pelotte, S.S.S., *John Courtney Murray: Theologian in Conflict* (New York: Paulist, 1976).

St. Joan Delanou

Foundress of the Sisters of St. Anne
of the Providence of Saumur (1666–1736)

"Inasmuch as you did these things
for the least of my brothers and sisters..." —Matthew 25:40

As a shopkeeper in Saumur, France, Joan Delanou was a notorious miser. She hoarded every cent she earned, angrily drove beggars from her door, and caused scandal by keeping her shop open on Sundays and feast days. Into this self-enclosed life, however, the influence of grace effected an extraordinary conversion.

It began when Joan provided lodging to a strange old woman, a widow named Frances Souchet, who spent her time traveling the countryside and visiting holy shrines. Her shabby appearance and her habit of muttering to herself led many to believe she was a bit mad. Souchet told Joan that she was sent from God. Nevertheless, she paid for her room, and that was enough reason for Joan to tolerate her company.

As time passed the presence of the old woman worked a strange influence on her landlord. Joan no longer found the same pleasure in counting her savings. She ceased to keep her shop open on Sunday, and instead she began to accompany her lodger to weekly Mass. Meanwhile Madame Souchet continued her strange pronouncements: *"He* says this..." *"He* says that..." It gradually dawned on Joan that this woman was a messenger from God sent to bear a warning and challenge: "I was hungry, and you did not feed me; thirsty, and you did not give me drink; I was a stranger, and you offered me no shelter...." At once she decided to amend her life.

She began by taking in a homeless family with six children. Others gradually found their way to her door. Her home became known as Providence House. Madame Souchet remained a welcome guest, continuing to provide her spiritual counsel. When Joan worried about how to support her groaning household, the old woman offered assurance: "The king of France won't give you his purse; but the King of kings will always keep His open for you."

Eventually she received something more precious than gold: willing helpers. She took this as a sign that she ought to found a religious congregation, dedicated to service of the poor and sick. And so on the feast of St. Anne, July 26, 1704, she and her associates took religious vows and assumed the name Sisters of St. Anne. Joan eventually became known as Sister Joan-of-the-Cross. Within a decade her community had grown and acquired several adjoining buildings with enough room for over a hundred orphans, as well as the sick and aged. Joan acquired a wide reputation for holiness. Only her confessors knew the extent of her private austerities, not to mention the physical pain and spiritual torments that regularly assailed her in later years. By the time she died on August 17,

1736, at the age of seventy, she was the best loved person in Saumur. She was canonized in 1982.

August 18
St. Jeanne de Chantal
Co-Foundress of the Order of the Visitation
(1572–1641)

"Sometimes put yourself very simply before God, certain of his presence everywhere, and without any effort, whisper very softly to his sacred heart whatever your own heart prompts you to say."

Jeanne de Chantal was born into a wealthy family in Dijon, France. At the age of twenty she married a baron, Christophe de Rabutin. It was a happy marriage, despite the fact that three of their seven children died in infancy. In 1600, however, after eight years of marriage, her husband was killed in a hunting accident. In the following years, as she struggled with her children's upbringing, dependent on her in-laws for support, her heart increasingly turned to the attractions of religious life. She vowed that she would never again marry.

In 1604 she heard a sermon preached by the bishop of Geneva, *Francis de Sales. This was a turning point in her life, the beginning of a deep spiritual friendship and partnership that would advance them both along their respective paths to sanctity. Francis was already renowned as a preacher and spiritual director. Rather than present the spiritual life as something fit only for monks and nuns, he tried to present a spirituality accessible to everyone and capable of being lived out in the world. Jeanne immediately responded to his message and asked him to become her spiritual director.

After several years, in 1610, the two of them founded the Order of the Visitation of Mary, a congregation dedicated to prayer and works of charity. Their original intention was that the order would be adapted for widows and other women who, for reasons of health or age, could not endure the rigors of enclosed life. But the plan met with such carping disapproval from ecclesiastical authorities that in the end Jeanne consented to accept enclosure. Jeanne's daughters were married by this time, but her fifteen-year-old son, Celse-Benigne, resisted his mother's plan to enter religious life. He was the occasion of a melodramatic test, for which Jeanne is especially remembered. Laying his body across the threshold of their home, he implored her not to leave. Without hesitating she stepped over him and proceeded on her way.

Jeanne proved a gifted superior, combining superb administrative skills with a profound instinct for the spiritual life. "No matter what happens," she wrote, "be gentle with yourself." In her lifetime the order grew to include eighty communities in several countries. Along the way she encountered persistent criticism from church authorities as well as internal tensions within the congregation. The order attracted many women from an aristocratic background who found it difficult to adapt themselves to the spirit of poverty and obedience. Jeanne weathered these and greater trials, including the death of her son in war, and, later, in 1622, the passing of her beloved friend, St. Francis.

She lived on for almost twenty years, dying in 1641 at the age of sixty-nine. Another holy friend, *St. Vincent de Paul, was moved to observe: "She was full of faith, and yet all her life long had been tormented by thoughts against it.... But for all that suffering her face never lost its serenity, nor did she once relax in the fidelity God asked of her. And so I regard her as one of the holiest souls I have ever met on this earth."

See: Francis de Sales, Jane de Chantal: Letters of Spiritual Direction, ed. Wendy Wright and Joseph F. Powers, Classics of Western Spirituality (New York: Paulist, 1988).

August 19

Blaise Pascal
Scientist and Apologist (1623–1662)

"The heart has its reasons of which reason knows nothing."

Blaise Pascal was a brilliant intellectual and scientist, an ornament of the dawning Age of Reason. After a profound experience of conversion he turned his genius to the defense of Christianity, convinced finally that faith gave access to a dimension of truth beyond the reach of reason.

He was born in provincial France in 1623. His mother died when he was three, and he and two sisters were raised by their father, a prosperous tax collector. As a child Pascal displayed a prodigious genius in the field of mathematics. By the time he was a teenager he had published significant studies in the geometric principles of cones, laid the foundations for calculus, conducted research on vacuums, and assembled the first mechanical calculator. Although he was nominally a Catholic, religion played little role in his early life, and as a young man he fully indulged himself in the worldly pleasures of Parisian society. Only gradually did he begin to feel that there was an emptiness to this life.

In the meantime his younger sister had become a nun in the cloistered convent of Port-Royal, center of the rigorist spirituality known as Jansenism. The Jansenists were Catholics of an intense piety and discipline who sought to purify the church of what they perceived to be the prevailing climate of moral laxity and compromise. With their strong emphasis on the wretchedness of original sin and the consequent dependence of human beings on divine grace, they were often described as Catholic Puritans.

Pascal became impressed by the piety and seriousness of the nuns, and he eventually became their devoted defender and champion. In the 1650s he wrote a series of polemical tracts, *The Provincial Letters*, aimed at their chief critics, the Jesuits. Literary masterpieces of wit and irony, the *Letters* caused a sensation. But they did not carry the day. Jansenism was eventually condemned as a heresy, and its proponents either retreated or faced excommunication.

By this time Pascal had become a completely committed Christian. The turning point was sealed in a mystical experience which occurred on the evening of November 23, 1654. That evening he recorded his impressions of the ineffable experience on a parchment which was discovered after his death to be sewn in the lining of his coat. It begins: "FIRE. 'God of Abraham, God of Isaac, God of Jacob,' not of philosophers and scholars. Certainty, certainty, heartfelt, joy, peace. God of Jesus Christ. . . . The world forgotten, and everything except God. . . . Greatness of the human soul. . . . Joy, joy, joy, tears of joy."

Pascal's last years were spent on an ambitious project, a comprehensive case for the Christian faith, to be addressed to the skeptical layperson of the modern age. The work was left unfinished at Pascal's death. And yet his fragmentary notes, later published as his *Pensées*, became the work for which he is best remembered. Indeed, it is one of the most significant and influential works in the literature of modern Christian reflection.

Pascal recognized that the age of reason was at heart an age of doubt. One could not offer a defense of Christianity that rested on the appeal to authority — whether of the church or Scripture — or on the existence of prophecies and miracles. These latter might confirm the believer's faith but they could not establish it. Nor could one follow the traditional philosophical method of arguing from nature back to first causes. This might "prove" the existence of the Deist God of mathematical truths, but not the Christian God of Love.

His approach was to begin with an examination of the human condition, the experience of what he called "inconstancy, boredom, anxiety," and then to show that Christianity offered an explanation of this predicament. With deft psychological insight, he painted a picture of the wretchedness of human existence. And yet this wretchedness is not the last word. There is simultaneously evident in human nature a greatness, a yearning for the infinite that points us in the direction of our origins. Christianity recognizes this dual aspect to human nature — poised as we are between the abyss of nothingness and the expanse of infinity to which our consciousness inclines. "Man is only a reed, the weakest in nature, but he is a thinking reed."

In Jesus Christ and the doctrines of creation and original sin we encounter an explanation of this duality. For in Jesus Christ we learn simultaneously that God exists and that we are sinners.

Pascal's *Pensées* are addressed to the Cartesian rationalist of his day, arguing for the limitations of reason and urging his famous "wager" for faith. But in his haunting introspection into the mysteries of the human heart his work belongs to a broader tradition that spans *St. Paul, *St. Augustine, and later *Kierkegaard and *Dostoevsky. He wrote, "I condemn equally those who choose to praise man, those who choose to condemn him, and those who choose to divert themselves. And I can approve only of those who seek with groans."

Pascal's last years were spent in appalling physical suffering. Meditating on the sufferings of Christ, he prayed, "I do not ask for health or sickness or life or death: I ask that You dispose of my health and sickness, my life and death, for Your glory, for my salvation, and for the use of the Church and Your Saints of which I am a part.... Give to me, take away from me; but make my will conform to Yours."

He died on August 19, 1662, at the age of thirty-nine.

See: Blaise Pascal, *Pensées* (New York: Penguin, 1966); Jean Steinmann, *Pascal* (New York: Harcourt, Brace, & World, 1965).

August 20
Geert Groote
Master of the "Modern Devotion" (1340–1384)

"Always put more hope in eternal glory than fear in hell."

Geert Groote inspired an extremely influential movement of spiritual renewal and reform that swept across the Netherlands and Germany in the fourteenth century. It was called the *Devotio Moderna;* its members were called simply the Devout, or sometimes the Brethren of the Common Life. Though their numbers were ultimately small, they exerted tremendous influence. *Thomas à Kempis, author of *The Imitation of Christ,* was one of the best-known products of the movement. The principal innovation of Groote and his followers was to stress the possibility of ardent Christian devotion "in the world," as opposed to the monastery.

Groote was born to a wealthy family in Deventer in 1340. He pursued studies in Paris where he ranged widely over a variety of disciplines and earned a master's degree by the age of eighteen. Largely through family connections he managed to obtain several church benefices, enough to provide for a comfortable existence. At the age of thirty-four, however, he experienced a sudden conversion. Committing himself heart and soul to the service of Christ, he renounced his benefices and all worldly interests. He turned his family home over to a hospice for poor women and retired to a Carthusian monastery to discern his path.

Eventually he decided his vocation lay in the world. Out of humility he declined to seek ordination. Instead he obtained a license to preach as a deacon in the diocese of Utrecht. For four years he traveled throughout the diocese spreading the fire of renewal. He emphasized the importance of inward piety rather than external exercises or rituals. He especially promoted meditation on Scripture and reflection on the life of Christ as the pattern of Christian virtue.

Communities of followers began to spring up. They were distinguished by several characteristics. One was their refusal to take vows or submit to a religious rule. Secondly, they supported themselves by common labor. The communities became particularly noted for the business of copying and binding books. Finally, there was the remarkable fact that in these communities clergy and lay people lived together in equality. All of these elements marked a departure from the patterns of medieval religious life, and they were the cause of sometimes fierce opposition from the religious orders and local bishops. At the same time Groote's outspoken criticism of the worldliness and moral failings of the clergy won him numerous enemies in the church. In 1383 the bishop revoked Groote's license to preach. He appealed this action to Rome, but died of the plague on August 20, 1384 before he could receive an answer.

See: *Devotio Moderna: Basic Writings*, ed. John van Engen, Classics of Western Spirituality (New York: Paulist, 1988); R. W. Southern, *Western Society and the Church in the Middle Ages* (New York: Penguin, 1970).

August 21

St. Abraham of Smolensk
Abbot (d. 1221)

"He slept but little; kneeling and weeping abundant tears, he beat his breast and called upon God, imploring the Lord to have mercy on His peoples and to turn away His wrath."

St. Abraham was a holy Russian monk, born sometime in the late twelfth century, whose monastic life combined both active and contemplative dimensions. He celebrated the eucharistic liturgy every day, a practice considered remarkable at the time. Otherwise he spent his days in prayer, preaching, and caring for the poor and sick in the community beyond the monastery walls.

It was Abraham's preaching that got him into trouble. His prophetic warnings about the coming judgment of God and the need for repentance provoked the resentment of both his fellow clergy as well as the rich. Things grew to the point where serious charges were leveled against Abraham, including misconduct with women, heresy, claiming to be a prophet, and "reading impious books." Abraham was arrested and publicly humiliated. Two courts, however, refused to convict him. Finally, the bishop of Smolensk examined the charges and found them completely false. Abraham was freed and installed as abbot of a small monastery in Smolensk. There he remained until his death in the year 1221.

August 22

Ignazio Silone
Novelist (1900–1978)

"In every period and in whatever society the supreme act is to give oneself, to lose oneself to find oneself. You have only what you give."

The Italian novelist Ignazio Silone represents a particular type of religious identity in our century. A self-described outsider, he confessed his disillusionment with the capacity of institutions, whether religious or political, to serve the needs of humanity. Instead, through his novels, he affirmed a perspective in which the spiritual and the political converged around the ideal of self-giving love and the imperative of human solidarity.

Silone was born in a village in the rugged Abruzzi region of Italy, a region steeped in the traditions of peasant culture and burdened with a grinding poverty — "a poverty inherited from our fathers, who had received it from their grandfathers, and against which honest work was no avail." Silone's own father was a small landowner who instilled in his son an identification with those who suffer. Later Silone recalled the sight of a convict in chains and the severe instruction his father imparted: "You must never laugh at a convict," he said, "because he can't defend himself and then because perhaps he's innocent. And in any case, he is an unhappy man."

Silone's father died when he was ten. Five years later he lost his mother in a massive earthquake that reduced much of the town to rubble. Silone received a Jesuit schooling, but he left off his studies without taking a higher degree. He also broke with the church. As he put it, the issue was not doubt or dissent about the substance of faith but a disillusionment with the church's lack of courage and credibility in facing the grave social questions of the day. In a period that saw the rise of fascism, with all its attendant crimes and violence, "the bishops' pastoral letters to the faithful went on discussing such themes as women's immodest dress, promiscuous bathing on the beaches, new dances of exotic origin, and traditional bad language."

For Silone the more vital moral question was, "Are we on the side of the men condemned to hard labor or of their keepers?" For him the answer led from the church to the Italian Communist Party, and eventually to exile in Switzerland. Meanwhile, his brother was tortured to death in a fascist prison. Silone rose to a position of leadership in the party and made several trips to Moscow. But by 1930, disillusioned with the atmosphere of repressive deceit within the Communist movement, he made "an emergency exit." Henceforth, he would be an outsider — "a socialist without a party, a Christian without a church."

While in exile Silone turned to writing, recreating in fiction the village of his youth. His first novel, *Fontamara*, tells the story of a group of peasants, their oppression by cruel exploiters, and how, through the self-sacrifice of one of their own, they learn the spirit of revolt. It was a story he retold in different ways in most of his subsequent novels. Indeed, he readily conceded that he had no interest in telling any other story: "I'm interested in the fate of a certain type of man, how a certain type of Christian fits into the machinery of the world."

In his most famous novel, *Bread and Wine*, set in 1935, a revolutionary, Pietro Spina, returns from exile disguised as a priest. Amid the common people, Spina's attachment to theories and ideology gives way to a more instinctive commitment to justice and human fellowship. The priestly disguise is ironic, for we begin to recognize the religious impulse that has ultimately motivated his revolutionary commitment, an impulse frustrated both by the church and the party. In Spina there emerge the features of a new kind of saint-revolutionary, rooted in concrete life and committed to building a new community among the poor.

After the war Silone revised some of his earlier novels to better reflect the evolution of his thinking. Characterizing the changes, *Dorothy Day, who was a particular admirer, noted, "For one thing, the emphasis was no longer on urging peasant uprising.... The emphasis now is on the individual, who conveys the message, one man to another, of man's dignity and capacity for greatness. And greatness means the overcoming of temptation and the laying down of one's life for one's fellows, in other words, the victory of love over hatred and mistrust."

One of his last projects was a play based on the life of the saintly *Celestine V, the pope who resigned his office. This gave Silone the opportunity to reflect on his own spiritual journey and the ancient tension between the gospel and the spirit of power. "I consider myself, in spite of everything, a Christian and a Socialist," he declared, noting, at the same time, that such labels settle nothing. The first Christians were considered atheists by some people "simply because they refused to follow the conventional forms of religious observance." He affirmed his loyalty to an ideal of socialism that represented devotion to the poor and an economy in the service of humanity. And he affirmed as well his abiding loyalty to Christ. "Fortunately," he noted, "Christ is greater than the church."

Silone died on August 22, 1978.

See: Ignazio Silone, *Emergency Exit* (London: Victor Gollancz, 1969), and *The Story of a Humble Christian* (New York: Harper & Row, 1970).

August 23

St. Rose of Lima
Virgin (1586–1617)

"Lord, increase my sufferings,
and with them increase thy love in my heart."

Like many another saint, St. Rose of Lima had to struggle to claim her vocation. She was born in Lima, Peru, in 1586, approximately fifty years after the arrival of the Spanish. Baptized with the name Isabel, she was called Rose on account of her extraordinary beauty. From a young age she was besieged by suitors, thus encouraging the hopes of her parents that an eventual marriage would advance the (tenuous) family fortune. But Rose had a different plan. She was determined to consecrate herself to God. Since her beauty posed an obstacle to her vocation, she deliberately disfigured herself by rubbing her face with pepper and lime.

This represented a setback to her family's ambitions. It was compounded, soon after, by the failure of a mining venture in which her father had invested heavily. Rose helped to support her family by needlework and gardening. But she longed for the day when she would live for God alone. Eventually, like her model *St. Catherine of Siena, she was allowed to join the Third Order of *St. Dominic. She spent many years as a recluse, occupying a little hut in the garden and devoting herself to constant prayer. Eventually, however, she emerged to engage in works of mercy among the poor, the Indians, and slaves. She had a strong sense of social as well as personal sin. In penance and in remembrance of Christ's crown of thorns, she wore a circlet of silver studded with sharp pricks. All who encountered her said that she seemed to glow with the love of God.

Rose's life was marked by frequent illness and periods of spiritual anguish. And yet her reputation for holiness gradually won her the reverence of the entire city. When she died on August 24, 1617, at the age of thirty-one, the dignitaries of Lima vied to pay her homage. She was the first canonized saint of the New World.

See: Frances Parkinson Keyes, *The Rose and the Lily* (New York: Hawthorne, 1961).

August 24

Simone Weil
Philosopher and Mystic (1909–1943)

"Today it is not nearly enough merely to be a saint; but we must have the saintliness demanded by the present moment, a new saintliness."

Simone Weil was born in France in 1909; her parents were well-educated, nonreligious Jews. From her early childhood she gave evidence of qualities that would characterize her later life: a brilliant mind, a steel will, and an acutely sensitive conscience. She studied philosophy at the elite École Normale Supérieur in preparation for a teaching career. But her intellectual interests ranged over many fields, including literature, history, political theory, and mathematics. For a time she was engaged in the world of radical politics. But she became strongly critical of the authoritarian tendencies of Marxism and the sectarian squabbles of left-wing intellectuals.

Weil taught in a series of high schools where she was regarded as an idiosyncratic but popular teacher. She got herself into some trouble, however, by trying to divide her time with teaching in a labor college and also engaging in trade union activity. Feeling a tremendous need to share the experience of the working class, she took a year's leave of absence from her job to work in a series of factories. In 1936 she again left her teaching to join the Republican cause in the Spanish Civil War, where she served with an anarchist brigade. Her life was probably spared by an accidental injury that forced her return to France.

Weil's life was marked by many instances of her impulse to sacrifice and to share the suffering of others. In retrospect it is possible to interpret her various intellectual and political explorations as steps on a deeply spiritual quest. Nevertheless, a significant turning point in her life came in the late 1930s through a series of experiences that brought her latent spiritual inclinations to the fore. While watching a religious procession in a Portuguese fishing village she felt the conviction arise within her "that Christianity is preeminently the religion of slaves, that slaves cannot help belonging to it, and I among others." Later in a chapel in Assisi she felt, for the first time, the compulsion to fall to her knees in prayer. And then in 1938 came the experience that "marked her forever." She was spending Holy Week at the Benedictine monastery in Solesmes, following the liturgical services. At the time she was suffering a particularly devastating round of headaches, a condition to which she was prone. In the darkness of the chapel she recited the poem "Love" by the English metaphysical poet *George Herbert, trying, through a tremendous effort of attention, to identify the pain she was suffering with the passion of Christ. In this effort she suddenly felt that "Christ himself came down and took possession of me."

From that time on her thinking became increasingly Christ-centered. She resumed her study of philosophy, history, and science, but now her angle of vision was trained on the meaning of God's intervention in history through the Incarnation and the cross. She immersed herself in the New Testament, attended Mass, studied the mystics, and brought herself, as she said, to the "threshold of the Church" — to the point, that is, of struggling for the rest of her life with the question of whether to seek baptism. And yet she did not cross the threshold.

In 1940, as a Jew, she was fired from her teaching position by the Vichy government. She went to Marseilles with her family and sought work in the countryside harvesting grapes. In 1942 she left France and made her way to America. Instantly, however, she regretted the move, feeling her place was back in France, sharing the suffering of her people. She managed to return as far as England, where she contributed her services to the Free French organization. But her efforts to find a way of getting back into occupied France were rebuffed. In the spring of 1943 she collapsed at her desk. She was hospitalized with tuberculosis, a condition that might have improved had she been willing to cooperate with her treatment. However she insisted on eating no more than was available, under rationing, to those in occupied France. She died on August 24 at the age of thirty-four.

There is no question that Simone Weil considered herself a Christian. "Nothing that is Catholic, nothing that is Christian," she wrote, was alien to her. And yet she chose not be baptized, convinced that she was thus obedient to a vocation to be a Christian outside the church — to place herself at the intersection of Christianity and all that stands outside. "I cannot help wondering whether in these days when so large a proportion of humanity is submerged in materialism, God does not want there to be some men and women who have given themselves to him and to Christ and who yet remain outside the church." She could not bear the thought of separating herself from the "immense and unfortunate multitude of unbelievers."

There were other reservations that held her back from formal conversion. At heart she was attracted to the pure spirituality she perceived in Greek philosophy and in the Hellenistic dimension of the New Testament; she was in equal measure thoroughly repulsed by everything contaminated, as she saw it, by the spirit of Imperial Rome — a territorial, legalistic, and nationalistic spirit which she detected in the Catholic church as well.

Weil was by all accounts a difficult and complex person, given to categorical and exasperating judgments. There is much in her writing that shows a distasteful disregard for bodily existence; this, and her philosophical repudiation of the Old Testament, are symptoms of a tendency to gnosticism, which has led some to question whether she was not really farther from orthodox Christianity than she even supposed.

Nevertheless, there is a rarefied integrity to Weil's life that has made her one of the most compelling religious figures of our century. She represents a type of noninstitutionally sanctioned sanctity, an engaged mysticism that takes into account the pathos of the human condition and the particular horrors of the modern age.

One thinks of her in connection with another French maid, *Joan of Arc, who also died among the English. Like Joan she defied the wisdom of the world, clinging to her vision of truth in a spirit of utter purity, obedience, and a humility so extreme that it bordered on arrogance. In any age she would have pursued her vocation with the same determination — spurred on by a private voice, her own or Another's. In any age, one feels, she would have burned at the stake, whether of her own or another's devising.

See: Simone Weil, *Waiting for God* (New York: Harper & Row, 1973); Robert Coles, *Simone Weil: A Modern Pilgrimage* (Reading, Mass.: Addison-Wesley, 1987).

August 25

St. Genesius the Actor
Martyr (no date)

"There is no other Lord beside Him whom I have seen. Him I worship and serve, and to Him I will cling, though I should suffer a thousand deaths."

According to legend Genesius was an actor, one of a company of performers hired to entertain the emperor Diocletian in Rome. Knowing of the emperor's contempt for the cult of the Christians, Genesius thought it would be amusing to mock their ceremonies. With melodramatic effect he performed a comic impersonation of a Christian catechumen. His friends played along with the jest, reenacting the ceremony of baptism. At some point, however, the attitude of Genesius changed. Whether touched by grace or moved by the pathos of his own performance, Genesius dispensed with comic exaggeration and played the part with disturbing realism. When his fellow actors, in the part of soldiers, "arrested" him and presented him before the actual emperor, Genesius spoke with unexpected feeling and declared himself a true believer in Christ.

No longer laughing, the emperor ordered Genesius to be bound and tortured. Still Genesius, in the performance of his life, continued to declaim: "No torments shall remove Jesus Christ from my heart and my mouth. Bitterly do I regret that I once detested His holy name, and came so late to His service." He continued to cry out in this fashion until he was beheaded.

August 26

Anne Hutchinson
Puritan Prophet (1591–1643)

"It was never in my heart to slight any man, but only that man should be kept in his own place and not set in the room of God."

The Puritans who settled Massachusetts in the 1630s were motivated in part by a desire to escape religious persecution. But they did not come to create a haven of religious freedom. On the contrary, they believed their holy commonwealth would stand as "a city on a hill," a beacon of purified Christianity in which biblical values of piety and sobriety would govern the conduct of its members. Severe punishment awaited those who fell short of these standards, a fate that was extended too to those who criticized the Puritan code. Rarely was there ever such a concentration of persons so godly, so sober, and so eager to cast the first stone. Among the most famous victims of Puritan justice was Anne Hutchinson, a mystic and healer, whose particular heresy was to maintain that it was a blessing and not a curse to be a woman.

Anne Hutchinson arrived in Boston in 1634, accompanied by her husband, William, a prosperous businessman, and their several children. They were committed Puritans, though of the two Anne was by far the more zealous. She was an unusually independent woman for her times, a skilled midwife with a particular gift for herbal treatments. She was also an avid student of the Bible, which she freely interpreted in the light of what she termed divine inspiration. Though she generally adhered to the principles of Puritan orthodoxy, she held extremely advanced notions about the equality and rights of women. These positions had put her in some tension not only with the established church of England but also with her own coreligionists. Nevertheless, she had decided to emigrate in the belief that New England afforded greater religious freedom as well as wider opportunities for women.

In Boston the Hutchinsons quickly achieved a prominent social position. Anne's services as a midwife were in great demand, and many a family soon found themselves in her debt. Before long she also began inviting women to join her in her home for prayer and religious conversation. In time these meetings became extremely popular, attracting as many as eighty participants a week. Hutchinson would present a text from the Bible and offer her own commentary. Often her spiritual interpretation differed widely from the learned but legalistic reading offered from the Sunday pulpit. In particular, Hutchinson constantly challenged the standard interpretation of the story of Adam and Eve. This was a vital text for the Puritans, key to the doctrine of original sin. But it was regularly cited to assign special blame to women as the source of sin and to justify the extremely patriarchal structure of Puritan society.

Increasingly, the ministers opposed Hutchinson's meetings, ostensibly on the grounds that such "unauthorized" religious gatherings might confuse the faithful. But gradually the opposition was expressed in openly misogynistic terms. Hutchinson was a modern "Jezebel" who was infecting women with perverse and "abominable" ideas regarding their dignity and rights. Anne paid no attention to her critics. When they cited the biblical texts on the need for women to keep silent in church she rejoined with a verse from Titus permitting that "the elder women should instruct the younger."

In 1637 she was brought to trial for her subversive views. She was forty-six at the time and advanced in her fifteenth pregnancy. Nevertheless she was forced to stand for several days before a board of male interrogators as they tried desperately to get her to admit her secret blasphemies. They accused her of violating the fifth commandment — to "honor thy father and mother" — by encouraging dissent against the fathers of the commonwealth. It was charged that by attending her gatherings women were being tempted to neglect the care of their own families.

Anne deftly parried and defended herself until it was clear that there was no escape from the court's predetermined judgment. Cornered, she addressed the court with her own judgment:

> You have no power over my body, neither can you do me any harm. I fear none but the great Jehovah, which hath foretold me of these things, and I do verily believe that he will deliver me out of your hands.... Therefore, take heed how you proceed against me; for I know that for this you go about to do to me, God will ruin you and your posterity, and this whole state.

This outburst brought forth angry jeers. She was called a heretic and an instrument of the devil. In the words of one minister, "You have stepped out of your place, you have rather been a husband than a wife, a preacher than a hearer, and a magistrate than a subject."

Anne was held in prison during the cold winter months. Her family and a stream of sympathizers continued to visit her, and to them she continued freely to impart her spiritual teaching. In the spring she was banished from the commonwealth along with her youngest children. After seven days of difficult travel through the wilderness they arrived in Rhode Island. There they were reunited with William Hutchinson, who had gone ahead to establish a homestead. But soon after her arrival, Anne suffered a painful miscarriage. In Boston the details were gleefully recounted by her persecutors, who saw in her misfortune a vivid confirmation of God's judgment.

In 1642 William Hutchinson died. He had been a devoted husband throughout his wife's ordeal. When the authorities had tried to pressure him to disavow his wife's teachings, he had said "he was more nearly tied to his wife than to the church; he thought her to be a dear saint and servant of God." Alone with six of her children Anne decided to leave Rhode

Island, to go as far she could from the long arm of the Massachusetts authorities. She got as far as the Dutch settlement on Long Island. There sometime in the summer of 1643 she and her children were massacred by Indians.

See: Selma R. Williams, *Divine Rebel: The Life of Ann Marbury Hutchinson* (New York: Holt, Rinehart and Winston, 1981).

August 27

St. Monica
Widow (332–387)

"Nothing is far from God."

It would be nice to suppose that behind every great saint there is a saintly mother. If so, few have been so ably memorialized by their children as St. Monica, the mother of *St. Augustine. In his *Confessions* he gives her special credit for his conversion, noting that "in the flesh she brought me to birth in this world: in her heart she brought me to birth in your eternal life."

Monica, like her son, was an African, born near Carthage of Christian parents. Though she was devout in her faith her parents arranged her marriage to a non-Christian, Patricius. It seems their relationship was marked more by mutual respect than warmth. Nevertheless, before his death, Patricius followed Monica's pious example and was received into the church. They had three children, of whom Augustine was the eldest. Augustine's account suggests that from the moment of his birth in 354 until her death thirty-three years later, Monica's relationship with her brilliant and sometimes prodigal son was the center of her life.

She had great hopes for Augustine and encouraged his academic ambitions. But her hopes extended beyond his worldly success, and she suffered greatly from the fact that he did not share her faith. Her sufferings were compounded by his amoral conduct and later by his immersion in the Manichean cult. She was consoled, however, by a prophetic vision in which an angel assured her, "Your son is with you." When she repeated this to Augustine, he replied flippantly that this might just as well foretell her own apostasy. No, she corrected, "He did not say that I was with you: he said that you were with me."

She did not cease to suffer on his behalf, praying constantly for his conversion and weeping over his sins. Finally, a sympathetic bishop reassured her: "Go now, I beg of you: it is not possible that the son of so many tears should perish."

When Augustine left for Rome to study rhetoric, Monica was determined to travel with him. Though Augustine tricked her and left without saying goodbye, Monica went in pursuit. She found him finally in Milan, where he confronted her with the joyous news that he wished to become a Christian. They both received spiritual direction from the holy bishop of Milan, *St. Ambrose. Augustine's baptism came in 387.

Soon thereafter they traveled to Ostia, awaiting a ship for their return to North Africa. Augustine describes a conversation there that lasted most of a day concerning the mysteries of faith and the joys of heaven. The beauty of the moment was such that "for one fleeting instant" they seemed to touch the eternal Wisdom for which they both longed. Monica sensed that her life was drawing to a close. She confided to her son that she found no further pleasure in this life. "There was one reason, and one alone, why I wished to remain a little longer in this life, and that was to see you a Catholic Christian before I died. God has granted my wish. . . . What is left for me to do in this world?" In fact, within days she fell mortally ill. When asked whether she did not fear dying so far from home, she replied, "Nothing is far from God."

Her death at the age of fifty-five left Augustine bereft. After describing her passing, he adds a poignant reflection on his futile effort to restrain his tears. As a Christian, he felt on one level that such an outpouring of grief was an ill reflection on his faith. But at the thought of his mother, and all she had suffered on his behalf, he could not hold back any longer: "This was the mother, now dead and hidden awhile from my sight, who had wept over me for many years so that I might live in your sight." If any reader might charge him with sin, he begs, "let him not mock at me, but weep himself, if his charity is great. Let him weep for my sins to you, the Father of all the brothers of your Christ."

See: Augustine, *Confessions*, trans. R. S. Pine-Coffin (Baltimore: Penguin, 1961).

August 28

St. Augustine
Bishop of Hippo, Doctor of the Church (354–430)

"Late have I learned to love you, Beauty, at once so ancient and so new! Late have I come to love You! You were within me, and I was in the world outside myself. . . . You were with me, but I was not with You."

St. Augustine was one of the great architects of Western thought. In the vast library of his written works he left his mark on virtually every aspect of Christian doctrine. As the bishop of Hippo in the Roman province of North Africa he was a regular hammer of orthodoxy. Indeed his engagement in a succession of bitter controversies provided the occasion and motive for much of his work. The exception was his greatest and most personal work, his autobiographical *Confessions*. If he left no other legacy, this book alone would mark him as one of the most significant figures in the history of Christian spirituality. For St. Augustine was the first Christian to regard human experience — notably his own life story — as the fit starting point for reflecting on God. The word "confession" has two meanings. Both the confession of guilt and the confession of faith are implied in the title of Augustine's memoirs. In this work he reflected on the meaning of his life in light of his most pivotal turning point: his conversion and baptism in the Catholic church. In this light he was able to discern the providential hand of God, caring for him and guiding him toward his eventual happiness, even in those times when the thought of God was far from him.

Augustine was born in 354 in the town of Tagaste in North Africa. His father Patricius was a successful businessman. His mother *Monica was an ardent Christian whose devotion to Augustine would play a critical role in his later life. Augustine himself was a brilliant student who advanced rapidly to the highest levels of academic success. By the time he was a young man he had his own school of rhetoric. Looking back on those years, however, he would see nothing but a desert of sin: pride, sensuality, and concupiscence — an anxious grasping after empty pleasure. This he later believed was the nature of all sin: a disorder in our desires that leads us to seek pleasure, beauty, and truth in creatures rather than in their Creator.

Augustine was much troubled by the mystery of evil. In seeking a solution for this problem he fell under the influence of the Manichees. This religious cult espoused a doctrine of stark dualism. They explained the existence of evil by positing a conflict between God, the cause of all good, and matter, the source of all evil. Augustine subscribed to this philosophy for a number of years, but ultimately found it dissatisfying.

In 383 Augustine left North Africa for Rome. His widowed mother Monica chose against his wishes to follow him. For years she had been weeping over his sins and praying for his salvation. Nevertheless Augustine had never felt any attraction to Christianity. He found the Bible dull and uninspiring compared to the Latin classics. While living in Milan, however, he was influenced by the saintly *Bishop Ambrose. Through his teaching Augustine began to recognize in Christian doctrine a greater depth and wisdom than he had previously supposed. In particular, he came to believe that Christianity, with its doctrines of creation, fall, and redemption, possessed a much more compelling explanation of evil and good than anything he had found among the Manichees or elsewhere.

Although he was intellectually convinced of the truth of Christianity he still held back from seeking baptism. His will remained attached to his sins, and he was loath to give them up. In the agony of his internal warfare he prayed to God, "Give me chastity and continence, but not yet." Finally, as his crisis became unbearable, he heard a voice speak to him, "Take and read." He was thus inspired to pick up the Scriptures, where he found the text, "Not in revelling and drunkenness, not in lust and wantonness, not in quarrels and rivalries. Rather, arm yourselves with the Lord Jesus Christ...." At once the storm was stilled, and his will was resolved.

Augustine was baptized by Ambrose in 387. His mother lived to see this great day but died soon after. Alone in the world, Augustine returned to North Africa with the hope of pursuing a monastic life. In 391, however, he was pressed by the local church to be ordained. Four years later, much against his will, he was chosen to be the bishop of Hippo. He remained in that post for thirty-five years until his death in 430.

In his voluminous writings, often forged in the heat of controversy, Augustine laid the foundations for much of Catholic orthodoxy. He was largely responsible for defining the theology of original sin. In this light he insisted that salvation was due to grace alone and owed nothing to human efforts. Such doctrines, accorded a lop-sided emphasis in subsequent Christian history, have left an ambiguous legacy. Other aspects of Augustine's thought have also been subject to criticism: his authorization of the use of force to compel orthodoxy; his tendency to disdain sexuality, the body, and women's bodies in particular.

Augustine was an extremely complex figure. But he was not the world-denying scourge that some have portrayed. His conversion centered on a realization that creation was fundamentally *good.* It was our sin, our disordered desires, that turned the good and beautiful things of creation into traps and snares. And if, for Augustine, sin abounded, so did grace even more abound. His *Confessions* is ultimately a hymn of praise, a love song to the God who was always closer to him than his own heartbeat. "You have made us for Yourself, and our hearts are restless until they rest in You."

See: Augustine, *Confessions,* trans. R. S. Pine-Coffin (New York: Penguin, 1961); Peter Brown, *Augustine of Hippo* (Berkeley, Calif.: University of California Press, 1967).

August 29
St. John the Baptist
Prophet (c. 30)

*"I am the voice of one crying in the wilderness,
'Make straight the way of the Lord.'"*

One of the most certain facts about the life of Jesus is that his public ministry was linked, initially, with the ministry of John the Baptist. *St. Luke claims that they were related, their mothers being cousins. The other evangelists, however, are silent on this matter. Instead they present John in somewhat mysterious terms as a kind of reprise of Elijah and the Hebrew prophets of old. Living in the wilderness, clothed in camel skins while dining on wild honey and locusts, John seems to emerge out of nowhere, warning Israel of a coming judgment and performing baptisms in the Jordan River for the forgiveness of sins. Jesus himself, according to all four Gospels, was among those who appeared among the penitents seeking baptism at John's hands.

Sin and the general need for conversion were evidently John's principal themes. By sin, however, John was not so much concerned with ritual purity or the observance of the law. The whole people stood under judgment and all were summoned to conversion. But he seems to have directed special scorn on those members of the privileged social and religious classes whom he called "a brood of vipers." His call to conversion had a distinctly social dimension: "He who has two coats, let him share with him who has none; and he who has food, let him do likewise." Baptism was not enough. It was necessary to "bear fruit that befits repentance," beginning with the practice of justice and mercy.

John did not spare the ruler of Galilee, Herod Antipas, from his sharp criticism. This Herod, like his father Herod the Great, was a brutal man who might have earned John's criticism for any number of reasons. The evangelists, however, single out the fact that Herod had divorced his first wife in order to marry the wife of his half-brother, Herodias. Apparently John rebuked Herod to his face; Herod responded by having him arrested and ultimately beheaded. The Jewish historian Josephus suggests that Herod was principally concerned that John's preaching was likely to inspire a popular uprising. In any case, this was the man with whom Jesus chose to be linked.

And yet in his message and in his style of living Jesus differed notably from John. Jesus was so far from being a fasting ascetic that he was accused of being a drunkard and glutton. There was a spirit of joyfulness among the disciples of Jesus — a group that included some of John's former disciples — that contrasted with the penitential atmosphere surrounding the Baptist. And while John's principal theme was the anger of God (typically, he employed such images as the axe at the roots, the winnowing fork, and the unquenchable fire), Jesus preferred to speak of God's mercy.

But it appears that for both John and Jesus the encounter at the Jordan marked a significant transition. Shortly afterward John was arrested, and Jesus began to preach the coming of the kingdom of God. From his prison cell John sent a message to Jesus, asking "Are you he who is to come, or shall we look for another?" To this Jesus replied: "Go and tell John what you hear and see: the blind receive their sight and the lame walk, lepers are cleansed and the deaf hear, the dead are raised up, and the poor have good news preached to them. And blessed is he who takes no offense at me."

According to the Fourth Gospel, John went to his death a happy man. As for Jesus, who could not fail to see in John's fate a foreshadowing of his own, he offered this epitaph for his cousin: "I tell you, among those born of women none is greater than John; yet he who is least in the kingdom of God is greater than he."

Bd. Jeanne Jugan
Foundress of the Little Sisters of the Poor
(1792–1879)

"Go and find Jesus when your patience and strength give out and you feel alone and helpless. He is waiting for you in the chapel. Say to him, 'Jesus, you know exactly what is going on. You are all I have, and you know all. Come to my help.' And then go and don't worry about how you are going to manage. That you have told God about it is enough. He has a good memory."

Jeanne Jugan was born to a poor family in Brittany in 1792. She spent most of her life in menial service. Poor as she was, however, she believed that God intended her for some larger purpose. In 1837, along with an older woman and a teenage girl, she rented an attic apartment in the town of Saint-Servan. The three women formed an informal community of prayer, supporting themselves by spinning and doing laundry while devoting their free time to catechizing children and assisting the poor.

It was a time of grave social upheaval. Crop failures meant widespread famine. Even provincial towns were crowded with homeless beggars. It was in this atmosphere that Jeanne conceived of her mission. In 1839, when she was forty-seven, she quit her other jobs and took to begging on behalf of the homeless old women of the town. Operating out of her own apartment she organized a hospice to care for these abandoned women. The young curate of the town, Father Le Pailleur, agreed to serve as her spiritual director.

Jeanne proved particularly talented as an organizer and fundraiser and her efforts were soon rewarded with generous support. Within a couple of years she had purchased a new building to house her charitable work. She was even recognized by the French Academy, which granted her a sizeable award. A number of women had joined her, and in 1843 they formed a religious association. Along with vows of poverty, chastity, and obedience, Jeanne added a fourth vow of hospitality. They called themselves Little Sisters of the Poor and elected Jeanne as their superior.

At this point, however, the story takes a bizarre turn. Father Le Pailleur, evidently jealous of Jeanne's success and scornful of her common origins, imposed his authority over the group and appointed one of Jeanne's associates as superior general. Jeanne remarked that he had stolen her work, but she nevertheless acquiesced without further protest.

By 1852, when the community received papal approbation, there were five hundred Sisters in the congregation working in thirty-six houses for the aged poor. Father Le Pailleur was by this time in complete control as superior general. Jeanne had for some years been permitted to continue her successful work as a fundraiser and public representative of the community. But now he decreed that she must "remain in a hidden life behind the walls of the motherhouse," supervising the manual work of the postulants. She spent the last twenty-seven years of her life in this obscure fashion.

Father Le Pailleur, in the meantime, rose to new heights of self-aggrandizement. He rewrote the history of the congregation to show that he was the true founder, with Jeanne having served simply as one of his early helpers. Jeanne, at this point better known within her congregation simply as Sister Mary of the Cross, was beloved among generations of postulants for her wisdom and loving encouragement. But none of them suspected that this humble and elderly Sister was the true foundress of their congregation.

Jeanne lived to see *Pope Leo XIII approve the constitutions for the Little Sisters in 1879. By that time they numbered twenty-four hundred. Jeanne died that same year on August 30.

Jeanne Jugan gave little importance to recognition. The success of her mission and the service of the poor were all that mattered. Nevertheless, the true story of her role as foundress was eventually recovered. She was beatified by Pope John Paul II in 1982.

See: Boniface Hanley, O.F.M., *With Minds of Their Own* (Notre Dame, Ind.: Ave Maria, 1991).

August 31

John Leary
Peacemaker (1958–1982)

"John had a sensitivity, an awareness of the pain of others that was relentless. Compassion for others had become the dominant experience of his life." —Sister Evelyn Ronan

On August 31, 1982, John Leary was jogging home from his job at the Pax Christi Center in Cambridge to Haley House, the Catholic Worker community in Boston where he lived. It was a run he made every day. But this day he did not complete the trip. Without warning he went into cardiac arrest and died almost instantly. He was twenty-four years old. In subsequent days and at his funeral at the Melkite Cathedral in Boston his friends were joined not only in sorrow at the brevity of this life cut short, but in wonder for all that he had accomplished and for the many lives he had touched in such a short time.

It was well known that John divided his time between peace work at the Pax Christi Center and his life of community among the poor at Haley House. But these were only a small part of his many activities on behalf of peace and justice. During the six years since he had arrived in Boston as a student at Harvard College he had worked with prisoners, the homeless, the elderly. He had engaged in protests over the military draft, capital punishment, and abortion. He regarded all such issues to be joined in a "seamless garment" approach to the defense of human life.

Not all agreed with his every stand. But no one who met John Leary could fail to admire his idealism and his heroic determination to put his ideals into action. Just before his death he had graduated with honors from Harvard in religious studies. To his embarrassment he had received Harvard's Ames Award for service to the greater community. But even while studying at this prestigious center of learning he had been sharing his apartment with street people and maintaining a weekly vigil at a local military research lab (for which he was twice arrested).

A mere recital of Leary's activities gives no sense of his personality and the impact he made on others. He was kind and generous in small things as well as large. There was nothing "driven" or compulsive in his efforts. On the contrary, he seemed to reflect *Chesterton's quip regarding angels, that they can fly because they take themselves so lightly. Anyone meeting Leary was struck by his joyfulness, his modesty, and a wisdom that belied his youth. According to Sister Evelyn Ronan, a Catholic chaplain at Harvard, "You could look into those eyes and see all the way, right to heaven — the goodness was so powerful and the honesty unlike anyone I've ever met."

To know John even a little was to know how deeply he drew from the traditional fonts of his Christian faith. He was raised in an Irish Catholic working-class home in New England. But from an early age his faith had widened beyond any narrow tribal identity. The turning point in his life was the discovery of Jesus' nonviolent way of the cross. Inspired by figures like *Dorothy Day and *Thomas Merton he had been drawn to the struggle to integrate the traditional disciplines of the spiritual life with compassionate engagement on behalf of a suffering world. He attended daily Mass, as well as Sunday liturgies at the Byzantine rite Melkite Cathedral; he spent long hours reading the Bible, said the rosary, and made frequent retreats at a local Trappist monastery. He revealed to a friend that while jogging he liked to recite the Jesus prayer, "Lord Jesus Christ, Son of the Living God, have mercy on me, a sinner." It is thus likely that he was reciting this prayer at the time of his death.

What was the meaning of this short life? According to a friend, the Reverend Peter Gomes of Harvard, "The difference with John was that he discovered that life had no purpose, no meaning, no direction, and no focus apart from the purpose and focus of God.... He became in his short life the complete and total man for others, and those who knew him and loved him testify to the love of Christ that shone in and through him"

See: Gordon Zahn, "John Leary: A Different Sort of Hero" (Cambridge, Mass.: Pax Christi USA Center on Conscience and War, 1983).

❦ SEPTEMBER ❦

September 1

François Mauriac
Novelist and Nobel Laureate (1885–1970)

"It is impossible for any one of those who has real charity in his heart not to serve Christ. Even some of those who think they hate Him have consecrated their lives to Him; for Jesus is disguised and masked in the midst of men, hidden among the poor, among the sick, among prisoners, among strangers."

François Mauriac, who died in 1970, was the last of the great giants of the Catholic literary revival that flourished in France between the wars. Unlike many of his contemporaries he lived well beyond the Second World War and thus faced the challenge of revisioning his traditional faith amid the ruins of the old world.

Mauriac was born in Bordeaux in 1885. His father died when he was an infant and consequently he and his four siblings were raised by their mother, a sternly religious Catholic of Jansenistic tendencies. She impressed on her children a strong sense of sin. From his bourgeois grandparents, meanwhile, he was brought up with the idea that "the most respectable thing in the world is money honestly earned by a businessman who has started out with nothing, who owes nothing to anyone, and who has acquired the right to marry into an old family." The combination of these outlooks — a type of religious phariseeism on the one hand, and the values of bourgeois respectability on the other — provided the background to many of his later novels.

Mauriac was deeply inspired by the work of *Blaise Pascal (1623–1662). He once suggested that his own work was reflected in the title that Pascal had proposed for a chapter in his unfinished apologetics: "Misery of the world without God." In a series of dark, pessimistic novels such as *The Desert of Love* and *Woman of the Pharisees*, Mauriac explored a world in which human beings were warped and distorted by frustrated hopes, pride, avarice, and the failure to connect with other persons in love. And yet his characters were not drawn in spite. For one thing, he had too much respect for the complexity of the human soul to paint anyone as purely villainous. Ultimately, he believed that within each person there were the outlines of the fully realized human being, the saint, which he or she was called to become. "For Sartre hell is other people; but for us, others are Christ."

One of his most famous characters was the protagonist of his novel *Thérèse Desqueyroux* (1926). She is a notorious sinner, an embittered wife who rebels against the entrapment of her unloving marriage by attempting to poison her husband. Behind her shocking actions, Mauriac tried to suggest the uncompromising spirit which might, under the influence of grace, propel Thérèse to holiness. She is a woman who typifies "that power, granted to all human beings — no matter how much they may seem to be slaves of a hostile fate — of saying 'No' to the law which beats them down."

In his *Viper's Nest* (1932) Mauriac portrayed a family enclosed behind a mask of pious respectability that hides the swamp of hatred and sin within. The hero of the novel is the family's much-despised patriarch, a man who spends his time plotting ways of depriving his children of his fortune. His life, as we learn, has been fatally derailed by the mistaken (as it turns out) belief that his wife never loved him. When he learns the truth, it is the beginning of his conversion and salvation.

Mauriac was deeply affected by the tragedy of World War II and the experience of the Occupation. He was haunted by the moral failure that allowed his fellow citizens to collaborate in the deportation of French Jews and by the capacity of so many Christians to look the other way. His writing took on a steadily deeper concern for social issues, reflecting his conviction that Christianity must incarnate the values of the gospel in history. As he wrote, "Our hidden life with Christ ought to have some bearing on our lives as citizens. We cannot approve or practice publicly in the name of Caesar what the Lord condemns, disapproves, or curses, whether it be failure to honor our word, exploitation of the poor, police torture, or regimes of terror."

Increasingly Mauriac was recognized not only as a religious artist but as a voice of conscience within the church and French society. Although this embroiled him in controversy, his contributions were recognized in many public honors, including the Nobel Prize for Literature in 1952.

Mauriac's earlier work had tended to focus more on the vertical relationship between God and the individual soul. In his later life he became more concerned with the implications of the Incarnation and its meaning for our encounter with God in other people. One of his last books was entitled *The Son of Man*, a meditation on the humanity of Jesus. In this work he pondered the significance of the fact that God chose to be incarnate as a poor man, a worker, and a Jew. What would our world look like if Christians gave proper credit to these facts? For Mauriac this insight was the foundation for a profound Christian humanism: "All tyrannies are founded upon contempt for man. When this temptation to contempt overcomes us, we must remember that Christ was a man like us and that He loved us. If He was one of us, then every man, no matter how miserable he be, has a capacity for God."

Mauriac died at the age of eighty-five on September 1, 1970.

See: François Mauriac, *The Son of Man* (New York: Collier, 1961); Sr. Annita Mazrie Caspary, I.H.M., *François Mauriac*, The Christian Critic Series (St. Louis: B. Herder, n.d.).

September 2

Bd. John du Lau and Companions
Martyrs of Paris (d. 1792)

"No church or parish of France, and no French citizen, may, under any circumstances or on any pretext whatsoever, acknowledge the authority of an ordinary bishop or archbishop whose see is established under the name of a foreign power" —Civil Constitution of the Clergy, Paris, 1790

The martyrs commemorated on this day were 191 priests and bishops who were massacred in September 1792 during the Terror of the French Revolution. It was two years after the Constituent Assembly had passed a civil constitution, subjecting the clergy to secular authority. These measures were accompanied by a mandatory oath which all but four of France's bishops and most of the clergy refused to take. Those who refused the oath were to be deported from the country as enemies of the Revolution.

In Paris on September 2, 1792, a riotous mob, enraged by reports that a foreign invasion was imminent, stormed the prisons in search of counter-revolutionary priests. One of their first stops was the Carmelite church on the Rue de Rennes, where over 150 bishops and priests and one layman were being held while awaiting deportation. Encountering Mgr. John du Lau, the archbishop of Arles, they asked him, "Are you the archbishop?" When he answered yes, they cut him down with their swords and pikes. This initiated a killing frenzy that lasted for many hours. The prisoners were gathered together and interrogated two by two. Upon their refusal to take the oath they were directed down a narrow stairway to the garden where executioners were waiting to hack them to pieces. Toward evening the name of the bishop of Beauvais, Francis de La Rochefoucauld Maumont, was called. An invalid, he replied from his pallet, "Here I am at your disposal, gentlemen, ready to die, but I cannot walk. Will you please be so kind as to carry me where you wish me to go." He was carried and presented to the "court." When he refused the oath he met the same fate as his brothers.

These martyrs were beatified in 1926.

September 3

St. Gregory the Great
Pope and Doctor of the Church (540–604)

"I remember with sorrow what I once was in the monastery, how I rose in contemplation above all changeable and decaying things and thought of nothing but the things of heaven.... But now, by reason of my pastoral care,

I have to bear with secular business.... And when I recall the condition of my former life, I sigh as one who looks back and gazes on the shore he has left behind."

St. Gregory brought to the papacy an unusual combination of managerial genius and personal holiness. While the once-glorious Roman empire fell into decay and ruin, he steered the church with a wise and steady hand, concerning himself with all matters large and small, and thus establishing the church as the great stable institution of the Middle Ages.

In a sense, Gregory was born for this role. He came from a patrician Roman family that had provided two previous popes to the church. After an excellent classical education, he embarked on a career in the civil service, attaining, by the age of thirty, the office of prefect of Rome. The city was not what it had been. Sacked four times within a century, its great buildings were largely in ruins. Gregory's deft administration under these circumstances won the admiration of the entire city.

When his father died in 575 Gregory seized the opportunity to put aside "worldly" concerns. He turned his family home into a monastery and used his patrimony to establish six other monasteries. The next years were the happiest of his life. But in 579 he was called to serve the church in a number of sensitive positions, including papal ambassador to the imperial court in Constantinople. In 590 Pope Pelagius II succumbed to an outbreak of plague, and Gregory, who was still warmly remembered by the people of Rome, was chosen as his successor.

Gregory was mortified by his selection. His fondest wish had been to return to his monastery. Reluctantly, he yielded to the call of duty. But his letters contain many poignant references to the sacrifice this entailed. Henceforth, his personal challenge was to find a balance between the inner spiritual life and the responsibilities of ecclesial office.

Quickly Gregory established his leadership over the local and universal church. With the civil administration of Rome in a state of collapse he assumed de facto authority over Rome and much of Italy, responsible for meeting successive onslaughts of war, famine, and plague. At the same time he left his mark on the spiritual life of the church through his regulation of the liturgy and his promotion of plainsong choral music (later known as Gregorian chant). Probably his greatest legacies, however, were the flowering of monasticism and the successful Christian mission to England.

As the first monk to become pope, Gregory used his office to encourage and regularize the development of monasticism. His major work, the *Dialogues,* which includes an entire book devoted to the life of *St. Benedict, did much to extend the popularity of the great father of Western monasticism.

Gregory, however, was concerned not only with consolidating the church but also with spreading the gospel. His most successful effort in this regard was the commissioning of a party of forty monks under the leadership of Augustine to bring Christianity to England. Apparently his commitment to this project preceded his papal election. According to the story recounted by *Bede, Gregory was in the marketplace in Rome one day when he noticed some fair-haired British slaves. When he asked of their nationality he was told, "They are Angles." "They are well named," he replied, "for they have angelic faces and it becomes such to be companions with the angels in heaven." Bede documents Gregory's great personal interest in the conduct of the British mission. When Augustine's party halted in Gaul, frightened by reports of the savagery of the English, Gregory exhorted them to continue: "My very dear sons, it is better never to undertake any high enterprise than to abandon it when once begun. So with the help of God you must carry out this holy task.... And although my office prevents me from working at your side... I hope to share in your joyful reward."

Augustine continued to write back for instructions, receiving replies in Gregory's own hand. Among the new bishop's questions: What exactly are the functions of a bishop? What punishment should be awarded to those who rob churches? Is it permissible for two brothers to marry two sisters? May an expectant mother be baptized, and may a woman receive communion during her menstrual periods? On such matters as these, Augustine wrote, "These uncouth English people require guidance."

Gregory's answers reflect his characteristic wisdom, but also his humane flexibility in responding to new problems. Thus, in punishing those who rob churches care must be taken to determine the motivation for the crime, whether malice or poverty. Regarding brothers who wish to marry sisters: "There is nothing in holy Scripture that seems to forbid it." As for the final questions: "Why should not an expectant mother be baptized? — it is no offense in the sight of Almighty God to bear children." And if a woman who suffered an issue of blood could touch the hem of the Lord's robe, "Why may not one who suffers nature's courses be permitted to enter the church of God?"

Bede spoke for the entire English church in paying tribute to Gregory: "For while other popes devoted themselves to building churches and enriching them with costly ornaments, Gregory's sole concern was to save souls." Though as pope he never traveled from Rome, Bede proudly claimed him as "our own apostle ... and we are the seal of his apostleship in the Lord." In light of his many accomplishments, the church later appended the honorific title "Magnus" — the Great — to his name. Gregory himself preferred to be known as "Servant of the servants of God." He died in 604. (On this date the church commemorates the translation of St. Gregory's relics.)

See: Bede, *A History of the English Church and People,* trans. Leo Sherley-Price (Baltimore: Penguin, 1955); Jeffrey Richards, *Consul of God: The Life and Times of Gregory the Great* (London: Routledge & Kegan Paul, 1980).

September 4

Albert Schweitzer
Missionary Doctor and Nobel Laureate (1875–1965)

"It's not enough merely to exist. It's not enough to say, 'I'm earning enough to live and support my family. I do my work well. ... I'm a good churchgoer.' That's all very well, but one must do something more. Seek always to do some good somewhere. Every man has to seek in his own way to make his own self more noble."

Albert Schweitzer was born in 1875 in the region of Alsace, the contested province along the border of France and Germany. In his youth he was torn between the lure of scholarship and the impulse to serve, like his father, as a simple Protestant minister. He ended up earning doctorates in both theology and philosophy. Yet at the same time, he served as a village curate, preaching each Sunday to a congregation in Günsbach. He kept this up even when he held a prestigious university chair in theology.

To note that Schweitzer was a distinguished scholar is a considerable understatement. It is more accurate to say that through his book *Quest of the Historical Jesus* (1905) he emerged as one of the foundational figures of twentieth-century theology. He was responsible for recognizing the centrality of eschatology in the preaching of Jesus. On the basis of his critical examination of the Gospels he argued that Jesus operated within an expectation of the imminent end of the world. This assessment contrasted sharply with the traditional image of Jesus as founder of the church, but it also confounded the image of the "liberal Jesus" depicted in scores of nineteenth-century "lives of Jesus." Schweitzer's work sent a generation of scholars back to reexamining the meaning of Jesus' proclamation of the kingdom of God.

Having achieved renown (and in some quarters notoriety) for his theology, Schweitzer managed, astonishingly, to win equal fame in an entirely different arena. He was perhaps the world's foremost authority on the music of *J. S. Bach. Himself an organist of international repute, he edited the first great modern edition of Bach's works and wrote a six-hundred-page study of the composer that was simultaneously published in French and German.

Such achievements would have been the proud legacy of any of Schweitzer's contemporaries. But he felt called to an even more extraordinary path. One day, after chancing upon a notice in the magazine of the Paris Missionary Society about the need for doctors in Africa, he decided to leave behind his previous accomplishments and to answer this appeal. When he announced to his friends and colleagues that he intended to become a doctor in Africa they thought he was mad. As one of them put it, it was like a general deciding to take up a rifle and fight in the trenches. But his mind was made up, and he was able to convince his new fiancée, Helene Bresslau, the Jewish daughter of one of his professors, to join him on this venture.

The first step was to earn a medical degree with a specialty in tropical disease. Having accomplished this, all the while continuing his teaching duties, he presented himself to the Paris Missionary Society, only to be rejected. The conservative evangelical board of the Society, familiar with his controversial theology, feared that he would undermine their mission efforts. Undeterred, he went about raising sufficient funds to underwrite his own hospital, and then presented himself again. On the condition that he would stick to medicine and not interfere with Sunday school classes the Society accepted his offer.

So Schweitzer and his wife embarked for Lambaréné, an outpost in French equatorial Africa on the Ogowe River in what is now Gabon. The hospital had to be built from scratch. Schweitzer himself took part in the design and construction of the buildings. It was his preference that the hospital compound preserve a truly African village feeling. Thus, families camped out on the preserve, cooking their own meals for the patients. Animals wandered freely among the buildings. Many European visitors were shocked by the "primitive" atmosphere that Schweitzer maintained, even years later when the means existed to achieve some degree of modernization. But Schweitzer insisted that the purpose of the hospital was to reduce pain and prolong life, not to create an outpost of "modern civilization."

If anything, Schweitzer's presence in Africa was an effort to "atone" for the sins of European civilization. White Christians, he believed, had a limitless debt to pay for the history of colonialism. His life and service in the hospital were his way of paying up personally. Aside from his medical work, he continued to develop and articulate the philosophical position he called "Reverence for Life." Believing that Christian ethics was improperly confined to the realm of the human, he tried to relate Christianity to the sacredness of life in all its forms. It was a perspective that found support in elements of African spirituality, though certain orthodox critics charged that he was veering into some kind of pantheism.

Over the years the fame of Lambaréné traveled throughout the world. Many distinguished persons made the arduous and uncomfortable pilgrimage by boat and canoe to visit the famous doctor. Photographs of Schweitzer with his trademark white suit, pith helmet, and remarkable moustache became a familiar image of the true modern hero. Honors proliferated, among them the Nobel Peace Prize, which he won in 1958. Schweitzer used the occasion to warn against the evils of nuclear weapons. And yet with fame there also came criticism. Many accounts described his autocratic management of the hospital and his supposedly paternalistic manner of relating to Africans. Was he perhaps a living anachronism in the era of postcolonial nationalism — as someone put it, "The Last of the Great White Fathers"?

But Schweitzer had not gone to Africa to become famous or to win the world's admiration. Rather, he was motivated by the scriptural verse, "Seek ye first the kingdom of God.... " In such a quest it was the pursuit and not the attainment that mattered. Schweitzer lived to the age of ninety and died in his hospital on September 4, 1965.

See: George Marshall and David Poling, *Schweitzer: A Biography* (Garden City, N.Y.: Doubleday, 1971).

September 5

Bd. Ramón Lull

Missionary and Martyr (1232–1316)

"The one and only method of teaching persons the true religion was estab-
lished by Divine Providence for the whole world, and for all times, that is,
by persuading the understanding through reason, and by gently attracting
or exhorting the will."

Ramón Lull was one of the most remarkable missionaries in the history
of Christianity. Others before him had certainly shared his zeal to witness to the gospel and make disciples of all nations. He lived in the
great era of the Franciscan and Dominican friars who would eventually
spread to all corners of the known world. In contrast, there is no evidence that Lull, a layman, ever converted a single soul. His distinction
was to be the first to develop a systematic theory and method of Christian
mission.

He was born in Majorca in 1232, the son of one of the Catalan military chiefs who had only recently reconquered the island from Muslim
Saracens. His early life was spent in the frivolity of court life. Despite
a wife and child he was, by his own account, something of a wastrel,
more inclined to amorous pursuits than to any serious occupation. But
at the age of thirty, prompted by a recurrent vision of Jesus on the
cross, he underwent a dramatic and total conversion. Afterward he gave
up all his property to his family and the poor and determined to devote his life to God's cause. In particular, he felt called to bring the
gospel to the Muslims — a vocation, he was sure, that would cost him
his life.

Lull prepared himself for this mission with extraordinary zeal. For over
a decade he applied himself to rigorous study, mastering Latin and Arabic and immersing himself — to a degree quite remarkable for his day —
in the literature of Muslim religion and philosophy. Lull believed, naively,
that the superiority of Christianity could be demonstrated through reason and open debate. But this required that the missionary be fully
knowledgeable about the beliefs of those he wished to convert.

Heretofore, the primary locus of Christian-Muslim encounter had been
the battlefields of the Crusades. To most Christians of Lull's day, the Muslims were irredeemable heretics whose slaughter brought glory to God.
The Crusades were not even ostensibly concerned with the conversion of
Muslims; their object was simply to drive the "infidels" from the Holy
Land, a sacred cause which justified any means. A bright exception to this
attitude was reflected in *St. Francis of Assisi. In his missionary forays
into Morocco and Egypt, Francis set an example of Christian piety that
won the respect, if not the conversion, of the Muslims.

Lull himself, at the age of sixty, became a Franciscan tertiary. It must
be acknowledged, however, that his vision never advanced so far as to
denounce all recourse to force in the service of the gospel. In this he
was all too much a man of his times. But in his essential respect for

the intelligence and good faith of non-Christians and his belief in the need to encounter them on their own terms he introduced a remarkably progressive path.

Lull had few occasions to test his theories. He traveled incessantly throughout Europe, lecturing in Paris, lobbying for his missionary ventures before a series of popes and princes, and seeking sponsors for his ambitious projects. These included a proposal for a series of missionary colleges where the best preachers of the world would study the languages and cultures of the non-Christian world. Such plans largely came to naught. In contrast, Lull's literary output was nothing short of spectacular. He was the author of at least several hundred major works — some thousands of pages long — ranging from philosophical treatises (written in Latin, Catalan, and Arabic) as well as mystical poetry and allegorical romances about the Christian life. A Christian troubadour in the Franciscan mold, he has been called "the Catalan *Dante."

Lull made three trips to North Africa. Each time he was arrested shortly after his arrival. On the first and second occasions he endured long periods of imprisonment and harsh treatment before being expelled. On at least one occasion he had the opportunity to engage in debate with Muslim scholars in the court of the caliph, but there was little to show for his sufferings. In 1316 he made his third and final trip to North Africa. In Tunisia, while preaching in a marketplace, he was accosted by a violent mob and stoned to death. Lull had foreseen this fate from the outset of his vocation. As he wrote, "Missionaries will convert the world by preaching, but also through the shedding of tears and blood and with great labor, and through a bitter death."

The life and teachings of Ramón Lull are not without their problematic areas. Certainly he espoused the triumphalistic and exclusivistic theology of his day, convinced that those who died outside the church were doomed to perdition. This helped him justify his acceptance of force as a last resort. And yet it was a passionate love of Christ and a concern for the salvation of others that motivated his tireless efforts to spread the gospel. For this love he was prepared to lay down his life, armed with nothing other than his faith and his "hunger for souls." Had his method of evangelization, rather than the Crusades, typified the encounter between Christianity and Islam, the balance of the faithful might not be any different today; but the history of the church would not be stained with so much blood and a legacy of enmity and suspicion would have been avoided.

See: E. Allison Peers, *Fool of Love: The Life of Ramon Lull* (London: SCM, 1946).

Charles Péguy
French Poet (1873–1914)

"There have been saints of all sorts,
but today perhaps there is need for a new kind of saint."

The poet Charles Péguy struggled hard to reconcile the principles of his Catholic faith with the republican spirit of liberty — thus contributing, in some measure, to the healing of deep wounds within the heart of France. His idiosyncrasies made it difficult for him to win full acceptance in either camp. But his death on a battlefield of the Great War enhanced his image as a tragic champion of all that was noble and true.

Péguy was born in Orleans. His father died when he was an infant, and he was raised in poverty by his mother. She supported her family by recaning chairs. Péguy did well in school and managed to win a place in the university. But he never forgot his kinship with the poor, and he was determined not to allow his education to turn him into a bourgeois.

Early in life he exchanged his religious faith for the creed of socialism. Therefore it came as something of a surprise to his friends when he withdrew from the university to write a play about *St. Joan of Arc. Though she appeared in his early work as an embodiment of the heroic spirit of France, the figure of Joan would continue to haunt his imagination. Over time he returned repeatedly to her story, each time plumbing deeper into the mystery of her sanctity. She was the counterpoint to his own personal struggle to integrate the "temporal and the eternal."

Péguy married the widow of one of his socialist comrades. Together they sank her savings into a bookstore on the Left Bank. There in the evenings, they hosted soirees to discuss literature, politics, and the issues of the day. In lieu of benches, the patrons were seated on piles of unsold copies of Péguy's play.

By this time the notorious Dreyfus Affair had come to dominate the attention of France. The case centered around the conviction of Alfred Dreyfus, a French officer and a Jew, accused of espionage and treason. Ultimately it was proved that he had been falsely charged and that the military command had preferred to sacrifice an innocent man to preserve the honor of the army. But while his case dragged on for ten years, the affair came to epitomize the violent contradictions in French society.

Péguy was an ardent and tireless supporter of Dreyfus. He devoted scores of essays to the case and continued to obsess about its meaning for years after most partisans considered the matter closed. Péguy believed that both sides had used the case to promote their own agendas and that few had comprehended the full moral character of the affair. The case of Dreyfus, he charged, was ultimately about whether France would perish in a state of mortal sin.

Many of Péguy's socialist comrades began to find his constant moralizing tiresome or irrelevant. Péguy countered that "the revolution will be moral or there will be no revolution." The problem with history was that *mystique* — the animating spirit of life, the dimension of the heroic — too often ended in mere *politique,* where winning and holding power were everything. What was needed was a political morality that retained its sense of spirituality and its concern for ultimate ends.

By 1908 Péguy had alienated most of his political allies. His bookstore was a failure. At this point he confided to a friend that he had regained his Catholic faith. The word spread quickly. Catholic friends, like the philosopher *Jacques Maritain, were delighted. Others were astounded. The church, after all, was the friend of the rich, the ultimate refuge of the anti-Dreyfusards.

Péguy did not dispute the charge. He remained an outspoken critic of the church's clericalism, its alliance with the rich, and its otherworldly spirituality. And yet he felt himself irresistibly drawn to the church of Christ, the church of St. Joan, despite the fact that it so often betrayed its master. Realizing, finally, that he was himself nothing but a "good sinner," he felt there was nowhere else but the church where he felt so much at home.

And yet this confession brought him no peace but a sword. His wife was a committed freethinker. She would have no part in his conversion and recoiled at the thought of a church-sponsored marriage or the baptism of their children. Péguy would take no step that would alienate him from his family. And so he felt called to remain at the threshold of the church, outside its sacraments, in solidarity with all those others who remained outside the door. It was a spirit of solidarity informed not only by his socialist convictions, but in a peculiar sense by his understanding of the communion of saints: "We must be saved together," he said. "We cannot go to God alone; else He would ask, 'Where are the others?'"

To his Catholic friends his scruples were incomprehensible. But it was clear to all that Péguy was a man in deep anguish. When one of his children became seriously ill, he reached deep into the roots of his peasant faith and undertook a pilgrimage by foot to the Cathedral of Chartres. There he prayed to the Virgin: "Mother of God, I can bear no more.... I have suffered enough.... I cannot cope with it all.... My little ones are unbaptized. It is for Thee to see to the matter. I have not the time. I do not know what to do about it. Take the children. I hand them over to you."

Immediately he was overcome by an experience of grace, a confidence that whatever the peculiarities of his situation or the struggles he endured to reconcile his faith and his convictions, God would accept the sacrifice. In the following years Péguy turned to writing the poetry that would eventually win him fame. Among other projects, he undertook a completely new version of his life of Joan. He worked feverishly, as if he understood that little time was left him. For years he had anticipated a cataclysm that would expose the true character of the modern age — a world without Christ. His prophecy was fulfilled in 1914 in the outbreak of war.

Péguy was quickly mobilized and was sent to the front in August. Within weeks, in early September, he had fallen at the battle of the Marne.

See: Alexander Dru, *Péguy* (New York: Harper & Bros., 1956); Marjorie Villiers, *Charles Péguy: A Study in Integrity* (New York: Harper & Row, 1965).

September 7

E. F. Schumacher
Economist (1911–1977)

"Out of the whole Christian tradition there is perhaps no body of teaching which is more relevant and appropriate to the modern predicament than the marvelously subtle and realistic doctrines of the Four Cardinal Virtues — prudentia, justitia, fortitudo, *and* temperantia.*"*

E. F. Schumacher was a prophet in the guise of an economist. He spent a lifetime mastering the principles of growth, savings, and the "invisible hand" of the market. Yet ultimately he became one of its most effective critics, alerting the world to the catastrophic consequences of the Western experiment in materialism. He wrote, "In the excitement over the unfolding of his scientific and technical powers, modern man has built a system of production that ravishes nature and a type of society that mutilates man." And yet he was not content to denounce. He inspired hope that it was not too late to fashion an alternative society modeled on the human scale and responsive to the moral, aesthetic, spiritual, as well as material needs of human beings.

Schumacher was born in Germany in 1911. In the 1930s he went to England as a Rhodes Scholar and was detained there as an enemy alien during World War II. He spent the war working on a farm in the north of England, an experience of common productive labor that played an important role in his formation. He also became a Roman Catholic. After the war he worked as an economic advisor to the British Control Commission in Germany. For twenty years he was the top economist and head of planning at the British Coal Board.

Through these experiences he came to believe that traditional economics, despite its scientific pretensions, was really a kind of religion, and an inferior one at that. It was based on a materialistic view of reality in which growth, efficiency, and production were the ultimate measures of value. In this fashion economists ignored the spiritual dimensions of human beings while promoting a civilization headed for catastrophe.

In the 1960s and 1970s Schumacher began to publish his "heretical" opinions in obscure alternative publications. But in 1973 he achieved wide recognition with the publication of his work *Small Is Beautiful*, subtitled, "Economics as if People Mattered." The book caused an appropriately modest sensation, arriving just at the time when ecological consciousness was beginning to catch up with the deadly perils of pollution, unbridled growth, and the depletion of the earth's nonrenewable resources.

One of the most popular essays in the book was called "Buddhist Economics," which reflected Schumacher's experience as an advisor to the government of Burma. Most economists, he claimed, were utterly unaware of the degree to which their programs for economic "development" reflected Western metaphysical presuppositions. In this essay he imagined what an economy would look like that reflected the Buddha's idea of "Right Livelihood." In describing an economy regulated by concern for permanence, equality, the reduction of desires, the alleviation of suffering, respect for beauty, and the dignity of work, he implicitly called into contrast an economic system sustained by waste, short-term savings, and the stimulation of avarice and envy. (He later observed that he might just as well have written an essay called "Christian Economics," but then "no one would have read it.")

In his second book, *A Guide for the Perplexed*, Schumacher was even more explicit about the spiritual and theological concerns behind his work. He traced the problems of our civilization to a failure of metaphysics, the loss of a "vertical dimension," which meant that while we have the answers to all kinds of technical questions we no longer know how to answer the question, "What am I to do with my life?" Science, he argued, cannot produce the ideas by which we can live. "The task of our generation, I have no doubt, is one of metaphysical reconstruction."

Not everyone could follow Schumacher's erudite appeal to the wisdom of *Thomas Aquinas. But his lucid writings and speeches on the virtues of decentralization, appropriate technology, renewable resources, and "economics on a human scale" made eminent sense to a wide audience. In fact, one of his frequent themes was the idea that we are approaching a Great Convergence — that is, a convergence between the practical imperatives of planetary survival and the great, though unheeded, wisdom of our prophets and sages. The current logic of our civilization, he said, indicated a "violent attitude to God's handiwork instead of a reverent one." If this did not change, the human species would simply not survive.

Schumacher's ideas quickly entered the permanent vocabulary of the modern ecology movement. But his own presence was short-lived. Only four years after the appearance of his famous book, he died on September 4, 1977.

See: E. F. Schumacher, *Small Is Beautiful: Economics As If People Mattered* (New York: Harper & Row, 1973); Schumacher, *A Guide for the Perplexed* (New York: Harper & Row, 1977).

Bd. Frédéric Ozanam
Founder of the St. Vincent de Paul Society
(1813–1853)

"We are here below in order to accomplish the will of Providence."

Nineteenth-century France was a society rent by the continuing reverberations of the Revolution. The church, which had suffered not only the loss of property and power but also many martyrs, tended to regard the Revolution as an unmitigated disaster. By and large, the hierarchy allied itself with the conservative cause, a stance that incurred the distrust of the working class and the disdain of those intellectuals who embraced the republican spirit of liberty. One man who tried to bridge this gap was a Catholic layman and scholar, Frédéric Ozanam.

In 1831 when Ozanam arrived at the University of Paris to study law, he was appalled to encounter such an atmosphere of bitter hostility to Christianity. With a number of his fellow students he formed a study circle to present a positive intellectual witness to their faith. He and his friends engaged in endless debates and public controversies on behalf of Christianity. But finally Ozanam was stung by one student's derisive challenge: "You Christians are fine at arguing, but what do you ever *do?*" In that instant he was struck by a fundamental insight: that Christianity is not about ideas but about deeds inspired by love. There was no credibility to his fine arguments as long as they were not reflected in his life. So Ozanam resolved to start a fellowship of Christian lay people who would immerse themselves in the world of the poor, performing acts of charity at a personal sacrifice. This became the *St. Vincent de Paul Society.

In these early years of the industrial era the poor of Paris and other cities inhabited a world of unbelievable squalor. These were the people whom Victor Hugo immortalized as "Les Misérables" — eking out a miserable existence in overcrowded, disease-ridden slums. A report of the time estimated the average lifespan of the child of a factory worker to be nineteen months. In entering this world Ozanam and his companions were not simply "crossing the tracks" — they were crossing a divide of bitter class hatred, entering a world as little known to most clergy as it was to the bourgeois intellectuals so enamored with "liberty, equality, and fraternity." Ozanam had no program of social reform. Indeed, there was little that his program of charity could do to change the fundamental conflicts in society. But his experience did allow him to see beneath the surface and to understand the underlying issues at stake. As he wrote, "It is the battle of those who have nothing and those who have too much; it is the violent collision of opulence and poverty which makes the earth tremble under our feet."

Ozanam's response, if not his solution, was Christian charity. If only privileged Christians could act on the mandate of their faith, they might mediate and reconcile the antagonistic interests of rich and poor and so avert the coming catastrophe. His concern was not only the welfare of the poor but the credibility and integrity of the gospel. The poor, he said, are "messengers of God to test our justice and our charity, and to save us by our works."

Ozanam's work with the St. Vincent de Paul Society was only one of his many projects. Having earned doctorates in both law and literature he became a distinguished and popular professor at the Sorbonne, lecturing on the Catholic interpretation of history. His main intellectual interest was the task of reconciling the church and the best features of the modern age — especially the values of liberty and democracy. With other liberal Catholics he believed that the church must overcome its attitude of defensive isolation and nostalgia for a bygone era. Nevertheless, his writings in this area drew widespread criticism and questions about his orthodoxy. Conservatives were particularly offended by an article in which he compared the present age to the fifth century when the church had faced the challenge of the fall of Rome. As it had done then, so it was time now, he said, for the church to "pass to the side of the barbarians" — that is, to go over to the people. "The Church would do better to support herself upon the people, who are the true ally of the church, poor as she, devout as she, blessed as she by all the benedictions of the savior."

In 1848 the explosion that Ozanam had feared and anticipated finally occurred. The workers threw up barricades and turned Paris into a battle zone. The uprising was suppressed at terrible cost. For most Catholics the events simply confirmed their conservatism, their distrust for the lower classes, and their commitment to "law and order." Ozanam believed this was shortsighted. Though he deplored the violent means of the workers, he defended the justice of their cause and insisted that there was no solution that did not address the underlying social misery that gave rise to violence.

His stance increased the suspicions of his fellow Catholics and left him isolated and discouraged. His great hope of reconciling the church with the spirit of liberty seemed a goal far beyond his abilities. Broken in health, if not in spirit, he resigned from teaching and public activity. He died soon after, on September 8, 1853, at the age of forty. Ozanam was beatified in 1997.

See: Thomas E. Auge, *Frederic Ozanam and His World* (Milwaukee: Bruce, 1966); James Patrick Derum, *Apostle in a Top Hat* (St. Clair, Mich.: Fidelity, 1960).

September 9

St. Peter Claver
Missioner to Slaves (1581–1654)

"Deeds come first, then the words."

Peter Claver was a Spanish Jesuit who was sent to Cartagena (now in Colombia) in 1610. Cartagena was then a great port of entry for African slaves. Ten thousand arrived every year to work in the mines (work considered too onerous for the native Indians). The conditions of their journey in this "middle passage" were unspeakably atrocious. The slaves were packed in dark holds like cordwood, chained together, lying in their own filth, fed no more than was sufficient to keep them alive. Perhaps a third of all those who embarked from Africa failed to survive the journey. To the wretched souls who remained Peter Claver devoted his life.

With news of the arrival of each fresh slave ship, Claver would make his way to the dock and talk his way past the captain to gain access to the "cargo." There he would move among the dazed and half-dead Africans, treating their wounds and distributing food and drink. With the help of interpreters and pictures, he would also try to communicate something of the principles of Christianity. How this was received is difficult to imagine, given that Christianity was ostensibly the religion of the slave masters. Nevertheless, Claver tried to instill in the slaves a sense of their human dignity and their preciousness in the eyes of God. This in itself represented a subtle subversion of the principles of the slave trade. Claver often confronted angry opposition from business and civil authorities who suspected that his ministry was undermining their lucrative commerce. Claver was tireless in his efforts. It is reported that during a career of forty years, he baptized over three hundred thousand slaves. He tried as best he could to follow them to the mines and the plantations, where he continued to intercede for them and to look after their material and spiritual welfare. At one point he called himself "the slave of the Negroes forever."

In 1650 Claver was struck by an outbreak of plague. He survived, but was left physically helpless. He remained in his cell, virtually alone and in a shocking state of neglect. He died on September 8, 1654. The city and the church, which had treated him with some reserve (if not disdain), now competed to honor his memory. He was canonized by Pope Leo XIII in 1888. His feast is celebrated on this day.

See: C. C. Martindale, S.J., "St. Peter Claver," in F. J. Sheed, ed., *Saints Are Not Sad* (New York: Sheed & Ward, 1949).

September 10

Bd. (Mother) Mother Teresa of Calcutta
Founder of the Missionaries of Charity (1910–1997)

*"To show great love for God and our neighbor we need not do great things.
It is how much love we put in the doing that makes our offering
something beautiful for God."*

On September 10, 1946, the woman who would become Mother Teresa was traveling on a train to Darjeeling, a hill station in the Himalayas. At the time she was simply Sister Agnes, a thirty-six-year-old Loreto Sister of

Albanian extraction, who had spent the past twenty years teaching in her order's schools in India. Though she was a devoted nun, beloved by her mostly middle-class students, there was nothing to suggest that she would one day be regarded as one of the most compelling Christian witnesses of the twentieth century. But on this day she received "a call within a call." God, she suddenly felt, wanted something more from her: "He wanted me to be poor with the poor and to love him in the distressing disguise of the poorest of the poor."

So, with the permission of her congregation, she left her convent. In place of her traditional religious habit she donned a simple white sari with blue border and went out to seek Jesus in the desperate byways of Calcutta. Eventually she was joined by others — including many of her former students. They became the Missionaries of Charity. And she became Mother Teresa.

With time Mother Teresa would establish centers of service around the globe for the sick, the homeless, the unwanted. But she was particularly identified with her home for the dying in Calcutta. There, destitute and dying men and women, gathered off the streets of the city, were welcomed to receive loving care and respect until they died. Those who had lived like "animals in the gutter" were enabled, in Mother Teresa's home, to "die like angels" — knowing that they were truly valued and loved as precious children of God.

It was not Mother Teresa's way to change social structures. "We are not social workers," she said, but "contemplatives in the heart of the world. For we are touching the body of Christ twenty-four hours a day." It was this mystical insight, which she obviously lived, that made Mother Teresa such a widely inspiring figure. She did not simply practice charity; she embodied it.

> God has identified himself with the hungry, the sick, the naked, the homeless; hunger, not only for bread, but for love, for care, to be somebody to someone; nakedness, not of clothing only, but nakedness of that compassion that very few people give to the unknown; homelessness, not only just for a shelter made of stone, but that homelessness that comes from having no one to call your own.

For many years Mother Teresa toiled in obscurity. But eventually she was "discovered" by the world. She became the subject of documentary films and biographies; she received honorary degrees from prestigious universities and countless honors, including the Nobel Peace Prize for 1979. Widely regarded as a "living saint," she nevertheless remained remarkably unburdened by such adulation. Nor did she have any exalted sense of her own vocation. "We can do no great things," she said, "only small things with great love." Often when people begged to join her in her "wonderful work" in Calcutta she would respond gently but firmly: "Find your own Calcutta!" As she explained,

> Don't search for God in far lands — he is not there. He is close to you, he is with you. Just keep the lamp burning and you will always

see him. Watch and pray. Keep kindling the lamp and you will see his love and you will see how sweet is the Lord you love.

In later life Mother Teresa traveled widely around the world. In the affluent West she had no trouble finding poverty — both the material kind and a no less destructive impoverishment of the spirit. The answer in both cases was love, a love that would begin with persons and ultimately transform the world. But before we tried to love the entire world, we should start by trying to love one other person — someone apparently unlovable, unwanted, or rejected. "You can save only one at a time. We can love only one at a time." That, she believed, is what we were put on earth to do: "Something beautiful for God." Mother Teresa died on September 5, 1997.

See: Eileen Egan, *Such a Vision of the Street* (New York: Doubleday, 1985); Mother Teresa of Calcutta, *My Life for the Poor* (New York: Harper & Row, 1985).

September 11

Vinoba Bhave
Apostle of Nonviolence (1895–1982)

"All revolutions are spiritual at the source.
All my activities have the sole purpose of achieving a union of hearts."

Vinoba Bhave was widely regarded as the spiritual heir of *Mahatma Gandhi in India. He was born on September 11, 1895, to a devout Brahmin family near Bombay. As a youth he felt torn between the desire to spend his life as a spiritual seeker in the Himalayas or to join in a violent revolution against the oppressive British colonial rule of his country. The dilemma was resolved in 1916 when Vinoba first encountered Gandhi. He realized that in this poor, half-naked prophet, armed only with the power of truth and a simple spinning wheel, he had found a model of holiness in the pursuit of social transformation.

Among Gandhi's disciples, it was Vinoba who best appreciated the spiritual dimension of Gandhi's vision. He understood that Gandhi aimed at something greater than independence from Britain — nothing less than the kingdom of God. While resistance had its place in the struggle, Gandhi believed that colonialism must also be uprooted from within. It was necessary to overcome the cultural and spiritual habits of dependence, fear, and division that were the footholds of foreign oppression. That was the logic behind the spinning wheel. Not only did the production of homespun cloth withdraw the market for imported British fabric, but it affirmed social equality, simplicity, native culture, and the dignity of common labor.

In 1940 it was Vinoba whom Gandhi selected to initiate a great campaign of civil disobedience in his struggle against the British. Vinoba was arrested and spent five years in prison. Soon after the war came independence, followed shortly by Gandhi's assassination. Though grief-stricken, many of Gandhi's comrades felt by this point that the victory of independence had been achieved. But Vinoba vowed to carry on the struggle for Gandhi's wider goal — *Sarvodaya* — a nonviolent society dedicated to "the welfare of all." As he traveled the country Vinoba perceived that for the majority of India's poor the achievement of formal independence had not altered their oppression. This was especially so for the vast number of the rural poor who had no access to land. In 1951 while visiting a village in Telengana, Vinoba was presented with an appeal for help by a group of landless peasants. Vinoba was suddenly inspired to address the village and ask whether there was not someone present who could help. At once a prosperous farmer stepped forward and offered to donate a hundred acres of his own land.

In this gesture of individual generosity, Vinoba conceived of what became known as the Bhoodan (land-gift) movement. Vinoba went on to travel by foot from village to village asking for contributions of land for the poor. His efforts met with extraordinary success. Within seven weeks he had collected over twelve hundred acres. Co-workers, extending his travels, collected another hundred thousand acres. By 1954 the sum had grown to 2.5 million acres, far exceeding any land reform achieved by the government. Vinoba did not believe that the donation of a few acres of land would solve all of India's problems. It was the underlying spiritual revolution, reflected in the gift, that would make all the difference. "We do not aim at doing mere acts of kindness," he wrote, "but at creating a Kingdom of Kindness."

By this time Vinoba had inaugurated a new phase of his movement, the Gramdan (village-gift) movement. Having started by gathering land, he began to seek out whole villages willing to commit themselves to the ideals of Sarvodaya. Gramdan villages took a pledge to hold all land in trust for the benefit of the community. Again the movement met with astonishing success. By 1970 160,000 villages — almost a third of all the villages in India — had responded to his appeal. It seemed that the Gandhian revolution might actually be achieved.

By the mid-1970s, however, the movement had begun to founder against the limits of its utopian promise. Much of the donated land was unusable. In other cases landowners reneged on their promises. The structures of poverty and oppression were deeper than could be reached entirely through Vinoba's appeal to love for neighbor. But Vinoba resolutely refused to combine his moral appeal with a campaign of active resistance. In this, it was commonly observed, Vinoba differed from the Mahatma.

In later years Vinoba devoted himself more exclusively to prayer, disillusioned by the divisiveness and rancor that had entered into the Gandhian movement itself. He died in 1982 at the age of eighty-seven.

Measured against the goal of ending poverty his movement must ultimately be judged as a heroic but failed experiment. Vinoba, however, was not so much a social activist as a man of prayer and a poet of deeds. Through the power of his personal faith he unlocked the consciences of countless persons, and so provided a glimpse of what it would look like if a society were organized around the systematic appeal to human goodness and solidarity rather than the narrow instincts for self-preservation and greed.

See: Lanza del Vasto, *Gandhi to Vinoba: The New Pilgrimage* (New York: Schocken, 1974); Mark Shepard, *Gandhi Today: A Report on Mahatma Gandhi's Successors* (Arcata, Calif.: Simple Productions, 1987).

September 12
Stephen Biko
South African Martyr for Freedom (1946–1977)

"The sense of defeat is what we are fighting against. People must not just give in to the hardship of life. People must develop a hope. People must develop some form of security to be together to look at their problems, and people must, in this way, build up their humanity. This is the point about Black Consciousness."

At the time of his death in 1977 South African opinion about Steve Biko was sharply divided, a reflection of the vast racial divide imposed by the system of apartheid. As the leader of the Black Consciousness movement, Biko was the outstanding intellectual conscience of the freedom struggle — a man who had emerged to fill the void left by the imprisonment of Nelson Mandela and the exile or death of so many other heroes of the movement. To the white authorities, of course, he represented the face of the enemy — a figure all the more sinister since he did not fight with weapons of violence but with more subtle means. James Kruger, the Minister of Security, called him "the most dangerous man in South Africa."

In fact, most whites actually knew little more of Biko than the caricature drawn by his enemies. For four years he had been officially "banned" — a unique South African punishment intended to render its subjects into "nonpersons." It made it illegal for his picture or his words to be published in South Africa; it required him to report constantly to the police; it prohibited any travel from his hometown or any meeting with more than two other people at any time. But despite these obstacles, Biko continued to behave like a free man, circulating clandestine literature, visiting the clinics and other black self-help institutions he had organized, and slipping his watchdogs in order to meet with friends and allies. It was during one such outing on August 18, 1977, that he was discovered at a roadblock by security police. Three weeks later it was announced that he had died in custody at the age of thirty.

Stephen Biko was born in 1946 in King William's Town. He was raised in the Anglican church and educated at a Catholic school before studying at the University of Natal. Initially he wished to study medicine. But he was gradually drawn into the political struggle by means of the South African Student Association, of which he was the leader. Biko became the foremost exponent of Black Consciousness in South Africa. While the white government portrayed this as an ideology of hatred and racism, in fact the movement was an effort to foster a spirit of pride, self-reliance, and resistance among the oppressed.

All overt political activity by black opponents of apartheid being completely outlawed, Biko believed that a primary focus of the struggle should be on the level of consciousness. Apartheid was based on an ideology of white racial superiority and black inferiority. It functioned not only through overt repression but through the colonization of consciousness — training black people to see themselves through white eyes and thus to accept their own helplessness and sense of inferiority. It was on this level that Biko operated. The effect of such organizing was evident in the 1976 Soweto uprising, when black school children sparked a revolt against their compulsory education in Afrikaans, the language of their white oppressors. It was the most serious challenge to the system in a generation, and it was put down only at the cost of thousands of lives. Many later believed that this revolt marked the beginning of the end of apartheid.

Biko was not directly active in the church, though he acknowledged the influence of his Christian upbringing on his later commitment to social justice. At the same time he issued a challenge to black Christians in South Africa to acknowledge the ambiguities of their Christian heritage. "We as blacks cannot forget the fact that Christianity in Africa is tied up with the entire colonial process." He called for the development of a "black theology" that would not "challenge Christianity itself but its Western package, in order to discover what the Christian faith means for our continent."

Biko's friends were not unduly alarmed when they heard of his arrest in August 1977. He had been arrested before and had always emerged intact. Although the South African security police were notorious for their brutality, they were regarded as smart enough to take care of such a prominent prisoner. Nevertheless, Biko died on September 12 after twenty-six days of detention. The authorities first attributed his death to the effects of a hunger strike or self-inflicted injuries. But an official inquest yielded different answers, in the process providing a rare inside glimpse of the quality of South African justice.

It was determined that Biko died of brain injuries sustained sometime on September 7 or 8, presumably as a result of beating during his interrogation. Despite the seriousness of his injuries for days he was kept naked in his cell, shackled in leg irons, lying on a mat in his own urine. When it was finally determined that he needed medical attention, he was not taken to a nearby hospital. Instead it was decided to transport him in the back of a Land Rover, still naked and in shackles, to a prison hospital in Pretoria, 750 miles away. He died within hours of his arrival.

After determining these facts, the inquest judge nevertheless ruled that there was no government responsibility in the death of Stephen Biko. It seemed at that point that the day of freedom for which Biko had struggled was impossibly distant. But it was not so. In only a dozen years, Nelson Mandela, free at last, stood before a cheering crowd of black and white supporters. In 1994, at his inauguration as the first black president of South Africa, he recited the names of fallen heroes and martyrs of the struggle who had not lived to see this day, but whose hopes and sacrifices had helped to make it possible. In the hearts of millions of South Africans that day, Stephen Biko was present.

See: Donald Woods, *Biko* (New York: Paddington, 1978).

September 13

Dante Alighieri
Poet (1265–1321)

"Midway in our life's journey, I went Astray from the straight road and woke to find myself alone in a dark wood."

Dante Alighieri, one of the great literary geniuses of all time, was also a man of action, committed to social justice and the affairs of his native Florence. But he was at the same time a man of deep faith, a visionary and prophet, who judged the world and the church by the light of the gospel and the radiance of eternity. All these factors combined in *The Divine Comedy* to create at once a literary and spiritual masterpiece.

In his autobiographical *Vita Nuova*, Dante described the impact on his life of a beautiful girl named Beatrice, whom he first sighted when they were both children. Although Dante later married another, Beatrice remained for the rest of his life the object of an idealized and unattainable love. Her death at the age of twenty-five provoked in Dante a spiritual crisis. Close to despair he turned desperately to the study of philosophy and theology. Finally he experienced a miraculous vision in which Beatrice appeared to him as a purified representative of all that was good and holy. It was an experience that freed him to return to the world while at the same time inspiring him to achieve a new poetic voice.

Toward the end of the thirteenth century Dante became engaged in the tempestuous political scene in Florence. The city was bitterly divided between rival factions, one favoring the temporal influence of the pope and the other committed to the autonomy of the city. Dante favored the latter. Influenced by the radical Spiritual Franciscans, Dante bitterly opposed the papal claims to temporal power, favoring a return to the evangelical ideals of poverty and simplicity. He was openly contemptuous of the reigning pontiff, Boniface VIII, a master of the game of power politics. Boniface had imprisoned his predecessor, the saintly *Celestine V, and he felt no compunction in turning the sword on his enemies. In the *Paradiso* Dante would allow *St. Peter to denounce among his papal successors such "wolves dressed as shepherds":

> We never meant ... that the keys consigned into my hand
> should fly as emblems from a flag unfurled
> against the baptized in a Christian land.

> Nor that my head should, in a later age,
>   seal privilege sold to liars. The very thought
>   has often made me burn with holy rage!

In 1300 Dante was elected one of the six governing magistrates in Florence. Two years later, however, the tide had so shifted to favor the papal party that Dante was forced to flee. His enemies invented charges of corruption and he was sentenced, in absentia, to be burned at the stake should he ever return. As a result, he spent the last twenty years of his life in lonely exile. As he later wrote, "I have been truly a ship without sail or rudder, carried to many ports and straits and shores by the dry wind blown by grievous poverty."

It was in these years that Dante conceived and wrote *The Divine Comedy*, the record of an imaginative pilgrimage from the depths of Hell, up the mount of Purgatory, and finally to the ethereal rapture of Paradise. He himself is the narrator/pilgrim who finds himself, at the age of thirty-five (as Dante was in the year 1300), at a point of crisis midway through the journey of his life. He is joined by the Roman poet Virgil, an emissary of the sainted Beatrice, who guides him on a tour through the circles of Hell and up to the top of Purgatory. There Beatrice herself assumes the role of guide, continuing the journey through the ascent of Paradise.

At each step along the way Dante encounters figures from history, literature, or his own contemporaries, and sees how their earthly sins, weaknesses, and errors, have shaped their eternal destiny. Popes and bishops, as well his own political rivals, appear among the landscape of the damned. But at the same time the poet's journey involves his own progressive conversion, preparing him to endure the increasingly rarefied atmosphere along his spiritual path. His love for Beatrice, transfigured and purified, is the lure that draws him ultimately to the source of Love.

As he passes by the realm of the saints, encountering such figures as *St. Benedict, the apostles, and finally St. Bernard, he approaches an experience of enlightenment to which words are ultimately inadequate:

> What then I saw is more than tongue can say.
>   Our human speech is dark before the vision.
>   The ravished memory swoons and falls away.
> I saw within Its depth how It conceives
>   all things in a single volume bound by Love,
>   of which the universe is the scattered leaves.

Dante died in September 1321. We know little of his final years or the ultimate conclusion of his earthly pilgrimage. Thus his last recorded words remain the abrupt conclusion of his great Comedy:

> Here my powers rest from their high fantasy,
>   but already I could feel my being turned —
>   instinct and intellect balanced equally
> as in a wheel whose motion nothing jars —
>   by the Love that moves the Sun and the other stars.

See: Dante, *The Divine Comedy*, trans. John Ciardi, 3 vols. (New York: New American Library, 1970); George Holmes, *Dante* (New York: Hill and Wang, 1980).

September 14

Martyrs of Birmingham

(d. 1963)

"These children — unoffending; innocent and beautiful — were the victims of one of the most vicious, heinous crimes ever perpetrated against humanity."   — Martin Luther King, Jr.

On the morning of September 15, 1963, someone tossed a packet of dynamite sticks through the basement window of the Sixteenth Street Baptist Church in Birmingham, Alabama. Moments later an explosion took the lives of four young girls and seriously injured twenty others. The slain children were Addie Mae Collins, Carole Robertson, and Cynthia Wesley, all fourteen, and Denise McNair, eleven. At the moment of the blast they had just finished their Sunday school lesson and were changing into their choir robes in the basement changing room.

The church bombing was a terrible rejoinder to the uplifting spectacle, only weeks before, of the March on Washington where *Martin Luther King, Jr., had delivered his famous speech, "I Have a Dream." But in Birmingham it also followed an intense summer of demonstrations and civil disobedience. The aim of this campaign, much of it organized in churches like the one on Sixteenth Street, was to challenge the rigidly enforced policies of racial segregation in this city, known as the "Johannesburg of the South." Scenes of fire hoses and attack dogs set upon nonviolent demonstrators had dramatized to the nation both the reality of racism and the hateful violence untapped by the peaceful cry for justice.

All this seemed to culminate in the explosion on this Sunday morning. The terrible symbolism of such a massacre in church, and the innocence of the young victims, seemed to underscore the spiritual character of the forces engaged in the Birmingham struggle — literally a battle between the Children of Light and the Children of Darkness. Martin Luther King delivered a eulogy at the funeral for the girls. He called them "martyred heroines of a holy crusade for freedom and human dignity." He expressed the hope that their deaths would awaken the conscience of Birmingham and the nation and so douse the flames of hatred and division. "God still has a way of wringing good out of evil," he said hopefully. "History has proven over and over again that unmerited suffering is redemptive." To the parents of the four girls he addressed these words of comfort:

> Your children did not live long, but they lived well. The quantity of their lives was disturbingly small, but the quality of their lives was magnificently big. Where they died and what they were doing when death came will remain a marvelous tribute to each of you and an eternal epitaph to each of them. . . . They died within the sacred walls of the church after discussing a principle as eternal as love.

See: Henry Hampton and Steve Fayer, *Voices of Freedom* (New York: Bantam, 1990); James M. Washington, ed., *Testament of Hope: Essential Writings of Martin Luther King, Jr.* (San Francisco: Harper & Row, 1986).

St. Catherine of Genoa
Mystic (1447–1510)

"All goodness is a participation in God and His love for his creatures."

Catherine of Genoa was a mystic and the author of several spiritual classics. She spent much of her days and nights in ardent prayer, in which, it is said, she experienced the burning flame of God's presence in her heart. What is more remarkable, however, is that this contemplative life was not spent in a convent. Catherine remained a laywoman, immersed in hands-on nursing care for the sick and dying poor. She helped to found and maintain the first hospital in Genoa, at various times performing every type of work from the most menial to the office of director. It is this extraordinary combination of action and contemplation that has made her one of the most compelling figures in the history of Christian spirituality. But this exquisite spiritual balance was not achieved at once. It was the fruit of a long and costly struggle.

Catherine was born into one of the great aristocratic families of Genoa. Her desire from a young age was to enter a religious order. But at the age of fifteen, before she could realize her dream, she was married to a young man, Julian Adorno. He came from a rival family, and the marriage was evidently arranged by the two families as an act of reconciliation. Unfortunately the matchmakers gave little heed to the obvious fact that Catherine and her husband were singularly unsuited for one another. While she aspired to religious life, Julian, as her biographer notes, was "entirely the opposite of herself in his mode of life." It appears that Julian lived his own quite separate and notorious life and that Catherine quickly sank into a state of chronic depression. This lasted for five years. For another five years she tried to engage in the frivolous diversions of society life. But this only left her all the more empty and melancholy.

At the age of twenty-five she uttered a desperate prayer for some relief from the torment of her existence, even praying that some illness might send her to bed "for three months." Instead, on March 22, 1473, while kneeling for confession, she was suddenly overcome with an infusion of divine love which impressed her simultaneously with the immensity of her sins and with the goodness of God. "No more world," she was heard to utter, "no more sins." The well-justified resentments and the petty bitterness that had steadily cramped her spirit were discarded, and from that moment she began to live a new life.

With newfound faith she also found new purpose for her existence. Immediately she threw herself into hospital work — hardly the normal profession for a woman of her social standing. Forcing herself to overcome her fastidious nature, she deliberately took on the most filthy and even repulsive cases. The miracle was that as she grew in the practice of love so also she found herself growing in her capacity for happiness.

Coincidentally, it was also at about this time that Julian's extravagant tastes finally reduced the couple to bankruptcy. They gave up their grand house and moved into a simple cottage, much more to Catherine's tastes. Eventually — perhaps through her example — Julian himself underwent a conversion and became a Franciscan tertiary. They then moved into the hospital, where, after many years of work, Catherine eventually assumed the job of director.

In running the hospital, it is said that Catherine was able to account for every farthing. But she was particularly renowned for her devoted care of the sick. During the plague of 1493, which killed four-fifths of those who remained in the city, Catherine stayed at her post. She herself became ill and nearly died after kissing a dying woman. She recovered. But that same year she had occasion to nurse Julian during a fatal illness. He had caused her much suffering over the years, but before he died, she confided, "My sweet Love [that is, Christ] assured me of his salvation."

In her later years Catherine drew a devoted circle of disciples, attracted not only by the opportunity to work beside her in her charitable work, but by the chance to benefit from her spiritual wisdom. Her most famous work is her mystical treatise on purgatory, based on her own experience of divine love. Rather than stressing the misery and suffering of souls in purgatory, Catherine describes this state as a kind of antechamber to paradise, the state in which the soul is stripped and purified so as to be able to bear the light of divine love. While we are still attached to our sins the flame of love burns us. But the pain is endurable because, unlike the pains of hell, it has a limit, and each moment brings the soul nearer to union with the Beloved.

> There is no joy save that in paradise to be compared to the joy of the souls in purgatory. This joy increases day by day because of the way in which the love of God corresponds to that of the soul, since the impediment to that love is worn away daily. This impediment is the rust of sin. As it is consumed, the soul is more and more open to God's love.... The more rust of sin is consumed by fire, the more the soul responds to that love, and its joy increases.

In her final years Catherine often experienced mystical ecstasies. It was said that she conversed with angels. And yet this profound "otherworldliness" was combined with fastidious attention to practical detail and constant availability to the needs of others. In 1510 she became very ill. After much physical suffering she died on September 15. She was canonized in 1733.

See: Catherine of Genoa, *Purgation and Purgatory, The Spiritual Dialogue,* Classics of Western Spirituality (New York: Paulist, 1979).

James "Guadalupe" Carney
Priest and Revolutionary (1924–1983)

"To be a Christian is to be a revolutionary."

In 1983 Father James Carney asked his brother and sister to meet him in Nicaragua. He explained that he was planning soon to cross over the border into Honduras. In that poor country he had spent twenty years of his life until 1980, when he was denounced as a subversive and forcibly expelled. It was understood that he was going back to die. Before parting Carney entrusted them with the manuscript of his recently completed autobiography, "The Metamorphosis of a Revolutionary." In his own words, it was "the history of an American reared and educated to be a Catholic, bourgeois 'gringo,' but who little by little was transformed by the Spirit of Jesus, using the experiences of his soul in contact with the world around him."

Carney's book describes a fairly typical American upbringing in his large Catholic family in the Midwest: altar boy, high school football hero, fun-loving college student. As with many of his contemporaries, his untroubled youth was interrupted by the call to military service during World War II. Carney served in the Army Corps of Engineers during the invasion of France. After the war he studied engineering at the University of Detroit, a Jesuit school. But the war had forced him to think hard about the meaning of life, and he could no longer be content with simply earning a living. He wanted more. He decided to become a Jesuit.

The training of a Jesuit is exceptionally long, requiring many years of philosophy and theology, all of it, in those days, in Latin. Carney was not a particularly avid scholar. But he was driven by the desire to become a missionary priest and to serve among those in greatest need. He was ordained in 1961 and immediately received the assignment he had hoped for — a Jesuit mission in Honduras. Carney asked to be known as Padre Guadalupe, an expression of his deep devotion to Our Lady of Guadalupe.

At first Carney's work was filled with traditional pastoral and sacramental duties: saying Mass on Sundays, preaching, preparing children for first communion. Insofar as he failed to address the social world of the people, he later recognized "that this was an alienating kind of religion: drawing the people to Jesus in the Blessed Sacrament instead of teaching them to imitate Jesus of Nazareth, the Liberator of the oppressed."

The most striking reality in Honduras was the extreme poverty of the rural peasants. Increasingly Carney felt compelled to leave the comfortable security of the priestly world to identify more deeply with the world of the poor. Reform was surely needed to lift the masses from their misery, and Carney lent his support to many social projects. But gradually he concluded that this poverty was the fruit of injustice and that nothing less than the empowerment of the poor and radical social transformation would bring relief.

Over the next decade Carney became increasingly committed to peasant struggles for land and justice. The grossly inequitable distribution of land left the majority of the rural population in the status of indentured servants — hungry, illiterate, living in shacks, resigned to watching their children die of malnutrition and disease. Meanwhile, the owners of the haciendas made a show of their Catholic faith, appealing to the bishops to bless the status quo and to denounce communism. But when the bishops began to talk about social justice, then the rich spoke of betrayal, heresy, communist subversion! Carney was a particularly useful scapegoat.

With his public ministry and his close identification with the struggling peasants union, Carney had became an increasingly visible irritant to the oligarchy. But he never abandoned his pastoral work. Indeed he worked tirelessly to raise the religious as well as social consciousness among the campesinos, awakening them to a sense of their dignity and rights as children of God. Wearing khaki pants and the cotton blouse of a peasant, he traveled throughout the countryside, sleeping on hammocks or earthen floors in the homes of the poor. "If I love the Honduran poor," he said, "I have to share their life as much as possible." Eventually this meant renouncing the security of his U.S. passport and becoming a Honduran citizen. What got Carney into trouble was his conviction that it was not enough to share the life of the poor; if one truly loved them one must try to eliminate their poverty.

By the 1970s Carney described himself as a "Marxist-Christian." Christianity supplied the motive of love; Marxist analysis, he believed, provided the tools for rendering that love socially effective. He was convinced that his role should be to add a Christian dimension to the revolutionary struggle.

In 1980 the Honduran government arrested Carney, stripped him of his Honduran citizenship, and forcibly expelled him from the country. For three years he worked in Nicaragua, recently liberated from dictatorship by the successful Sandinista insurrection. He was inspired by this experience of living in a revolutionary society. But all the time his heart remained in Honduras.

In mid-July 1983 he slipped across the border with a small band of Honduran guerrillas. "If the armies of the capitalist bourgeoisie can have their chaplains," he reasoned, "with much more right the people's army of liberation should have its priest chaplains." But dreams of a popular uprising were unrealistic. Within weeks the guerrilla band had been tracked down and eliminated.

As for Padre Guadalupe, the army claimed, implausibly, that he had starved to death in the wilderness. Years later army deserters disclosed how Carney had been captured with the rest of his band. He was interrogated and tortured. On September 16 he was taken up in an army helicopter and hurled out, alive, to die on the mountainside below. His remains were never recovered.

In the manuscript he had handed to his brother and sister, Carney had written, "Since my novitiate, I have asked Christ for the Grace to be able to imitate him, even to martyrdom, to the giving of my life, to being killed for the cause of Christ. And I strongly believe that Christ might give me this tremendous Grace to become a martyr for justice."

See: To Be a Revolutionary: The Autobiography of Father James Guadalupe Carney (New York: Harper & Row, 1987); Donna Whitson Brett and Edward T. Brett, *Murdered in Central America* (Maryknoll, N.Y.: Orbis, 1988).

September 17

St. Hildegard of Bingen
Abbess and Visionary (1098–1179)

"In the year 1141...a fiery light, flashing intensely, came from the open vault of heaven and poured through my whole brain. Like a flame that is hot without burning, it kindled all my heart and all my breast, just as the sun warms anything on which its rays fall. And suddenly I could understand what such books as the Psalter, the Gospel and the other Catholic volumes both of the Old and New Testament actually set forth."

St. Hildegard was by any standard one of the remarkable figures of her age: abbess and foundress of a Benedictine religious community; author and theologian; prophet and preacher; musician and composer; poet and artist; doctor and pharmacist. She had visions in which the word of God — both in Scripture and in the book of nature — was revealed to her. Yet for eight hundred years she remained in relative obscurity. Only in recent decades has she emerged into the light, partly thanks to contemporary interest in the role of women in history. But increasingly Hildegard is honored not only as an outstanding woman of history but as a visionary whose ecological and holistic spirituality speaks prophetically to our time.

Hildegard was born in 1098 in the German province of Rheinhessen, the tenth child of noble parents. When she was eight she was given to the care of a holy anchoress, Bd. Jutta, who lived in a cottage attached to a nearby Benedictine abbey. Jutta raised the child and educated her until the age of eighteen, when Hildegard put on the habit of a Benedictine nun. By this time a monastic community had gathered about Jutta. When the old woman died in 1136 Hildegard became prioress.

Up to this point it seems that Hildegard was an unexceptional nun. Only to Jutta had she confided the secret of the visions which, as she later wrote, she had enjoyed since the age of three. "These visions which I saw I beheld neither in sleep nor dreaming nor in madness nor with my bodily eyes or ears, nor in hidden places; but I saw them in full view and according to God's will, when I was wakeful and alert, with the eyes of the spirit and the inward ears."

After she became prioress her visions pressed upon her with greater urgency until she eventually described them to her confessor. She was bidden to write them down, and the text was presented to the archbishop of Mainz. He in turn read them and had them examined by a team of theologians who certified their orthodoxy. Henceforth she was provided with a monk as secretary and with his help she began her major work, *Scivias* (Know the Ways), which occupied her efforts over the next ten years. Eventually Pope Eugenius III himself read her book and authorized her to continue to write.

Her *Scivias* is the record of a series of visions concerning the relation between God, humanity, and the cosmos. With extraordinary symbolic paintings that accompany the text, Hildegard presents a picture of human beings and the cosmos as emanations from God's love, "living sparks" or "rays of his splendor, just as the rays of the sun proceed from the sun itself." She shows the effects of sin in rupturing creation, and the drama of redemption that ultimately restores the world to its intended state, purified of its infirmities and reconciled with the divine energy of its origins.

About this time Hildegard received a divine call to move her community to a new site on the Rupertsberg, a hill above the Rhine, near Bingen. This involved an ordeal with the monks and the town of her original foundation, who depended on the traffic of pilgrims and thus adamantly opposed her plan. But after she became deathly ill — a frequent occurrence when Hildegard's will was crossed — she had her way.

Between 1152 and 1162 Hildegard made numerous preaching tours through the Rhineland. Her authority as a holy preacher was widely recognized, and her reputation extended far beyond her native Germany. She corresponded with kings, popes, and other figures of note, sharing her spiritual insights but also freely dispensing criticism where she felt it was needed. Besides her religious writings, she wrote extensively on medicine and physiology. She avidly studied the use of medicinal herbs and seems to have anticipated the principles of homeopathy. In addition she composed religious music of haunting beauty and originality; music, she wrote, was a symbol of the harmony that Satan disturbed.

There are many elements to Hildegard's visions which speak to our ecological age. She had a wide understanding of the cosmos as a whole and of the human place in it. Human beings, she wrote, are the universe in microcosm, made of the same elements that constitute the world. But within the great cosmos human beings are the thinking heart, called to be co-creators with God in shaping the world. Through human sin the entire world was fractured and fell out of harmony with the Creator. But this sin does not erase the original goodness and blessing of creation. Through Christ — first fruits of a new creation — the cosmos and human beings find their way back to their original destiny. Constantly Hildegard refers to God as "Living Light," and she employs a remarkable word — "greenness" (*viriditas*) — to describe the animating energy or grace of God that shines forth in all living things. For this holistic vision Hildegard has been particularly celebrated by proponents of "creation spirituality."

Toward the end of her life Hildegard ran afoul of local church authorities after she allowed a young man who had been excommunicated to be buried in the monastery cemetery. She was ordered to have the body disinterred. This Hildegard refused, insisting that before dying the youth had been reconciled with the church and received the sacraments. Nevertheless, the bishop had the convent placed under an interdict, forbidding the celebration or reception of the Eucharist. It was a terrible sanction, and Hildegard protested bitterly. Eventually the interdict was lifted, but she lived on only a few months longer. She died on September 17, 1179.

See: Hildegard of Bingen: Mystical Writings, ed. Fiona Bowie and Oliver Davis (New York: Crossroad, 1995); Hildegard of Bingen, *Illuminations,* with commentary by Matthew Fox (Santa Fe: Bear, 1985).

September 18
Dag Hammarskjöld
Secretary General of the U.N. (1905–1961)

"In our era, the road to holiness necessarily passes through the world of action."

On September 18, 1961, a plane crash in central Africa took the life of Dag Hammarskjöld, secretary general of the United Nations. At the time he was attempting to negotiate a cease-fire between the government of the Congo and secessionist rebels in Katanga. It was a quixotic mission, like many he had undertaken in his eight years as secretary general. But it was typical of his deep commitment to the cause of peace and his willingness to undertake the greatest personal sacrifice on its behalf. He was universally mourned as a man who combined the roles of public servant and global leader.

But it was only after his death that the world learned of the private faith that had guided his public role. There was found in his apartment a manuscript, apparently completed shortly before his final trip, with a cover letter authorizing its publication. Based on journal entries and poems written over a period of several decades, it was published under the title *Markings.*

It was an oddly personal testament from an extremely public man. Consisting of short, aphoristic reflections — some evidently referring to issues so private as to be nearly incomprehensible to an outside reader — the book represented what he called the story of "my negotiations with myself and with God." Whatever meaning it might have for others, it revealed Hammarskjöld's lifelong struggle with God, Christ, and such issues as the relation between faith and duty, self-doubt and pride, the meaning of existence, and the deep isolation and loneliness that were evidently the price of his vocation.

Hammarskjöld came from a wealthy and eminent Swedish family; his father was a former prime minister. As a young man he studied law and economics and served in a variety of high-ranking government positions before accepting the post of Swedish ambassador to the relatively new organization of the United Nations. Outwardly he appeared to be the consummate diplomat, suave, charming, skilled at subordinating his personal opinions to the responsibilities at hand. Few of his closest friends had any notion of his religious preoccupations. Nevertheless, he occasionally let drop a hint, as in his remarks to an interviewer:

> From generations of soldiers and government officials on my father's side I inherited a belief that no life was more satisfactory than one of selfless service to your country — or humanity.... From scholars and clergymen on my mother's side I inherited a belief that... all men were equals as children of God, and should be met and treated by us as our masters.

The journals reveal his deep attraction to such figures as *Pascal, *Buber, *Meister Eckhart, and *Thomas à Kempis. Likewise biblical citations fill his pages. In contrast, there are virtually no references to the public responsibilities or world events in which he was outwardly immersed. It has been left to his biographers to correlate his "markings" with external events. Thus, the only record of his election to the post of secretary general is the brief phrase, "Not I, but God in me."

The central concerns of Hammarskjöld's writing are not abstract theological reflections, but concrete issues posed by the challenges of his own lonely path in life:

> What I ask for is absurd: that life shall have a meaning. What I strive for is impossible; that my life shall acquire a meaning.

> *

> Pray that your loneliness may spur you into finding something to live for, great enough to die for.

> *

> The best and most wonderful thing that can happen to you in this life is that you should be silent and let God work and speak.

> *

> Long ago you gripped me, Slinger. *Now* into the storm. *Now* towards your target.

> *

> Do not seek death. Death will find you. But seek the road which makes death a fulfillment.

There is no reason to believe that Hammarskjöld had any special presentiment of his death in 1961. But it is clear that he lived day by day in a very conscious confrontation with the Absolute. It is difficult if not impossible to discern the exact threads of the development, if such there was, in Hammarskjöld's spiritual path. But it does seem that over time he had come to some sense of inner resolution, and that at some point he managed to calm his tendency to scrupulosity and doubt. Some months before his death, he wrote,

> I don't know Who — or what — put the question, I don't know when it was put. I don't even remember answering. But at some moment I did answer *Yes* to Someone — or Something — and from that hour I was certain that existence is meaningful and that, therefore, my life, in self-surrender, had a goal.... I came to a time and place where I realized that the Way leads to a triumph which is a catastrophe and

to a catastrophe which is a triumph, that the price for committing one's life would be reproach, and that the only elevation possible to man lies in the depths of humiliation. After that, the word "courage" lost its meaning, since nothing could be taken from me.

With his tragic death at the age of fifty-six the world lost a great servant of peace. He was an example of that rare person for whom public service is not simply a career or a means to power, but a religious vocation, a way of being faithful to God. He had sought and found the road that makes death a fulfillment.

See: Dag Hammarskjöld, *Markings,* trans. Leif Sjöberg and W. H. Auden (New York: Alfred A. Knopf, 1964); Henry P. Van Dusen, *Dag Hammarskjöld: The Statesman and His Faith* (New York: Harper & Row, 1967).

September 19

St. Martin I
Pope and Martyr (d. 655?)

"I am wasting away and frozen through with dysentery.... At this time of bitter need I have nothing whatever to strengthen my broken and unhappy body, for the food that is given me is disgusting. But God sees all things, and I trust in him, hoping that when he shall have taken me out of this world he will enlighten my persecutors, that thus they may be led to repentance and better ways."

St. Martin, a native of Umbria, became pope in 649. He presided over a council at the Lateran which condemned the doctrine of "Monothelitism," the claim that in Christ there is only one divine will. The language of Monothelitism had been proposed as a compromise to reconcile adherents of Monophysitism (who held that in Christ there was only one nature, the divine). Martin and the orthodox bishops held that Monothelitism still departed from the teaching of Chalcedon (451), which affirmed the full co-presence of human and divine natures in Christ.

So divisive was this issue that Emperor Constans II had issued an edict banning any further discussion of the issue. When he learned that his edict had been ignored by the council he was furious and dispatched troops to Rome to arrest the pope. Martin was seized in the Lateran Basilica and transported in chains on a long voyage to Constantinople. He arrived at the capital on September 17, 653, bedridden and suffering from dysentery and gout. After three months of solitary confinement he was tried and convicted of treason against the emperor. He was deposed of his office, publicly flogged, and sentenced to death, a sentence subsequently commuted to exile in the Crimea.

When Martin arrived in his place of exile he found the region in the grips of famine. But apart from physical hardship, he suffered greatly from the sense of having been forgotten by the church of Rome. It pained him to learn that in his absence the church had elected a successor as pope. He was truly alone. In a poignant letter to friends, he wrote, "I am surprised at the indifference of those who used to know me but have now so completely forgotten me that they apparently do not know that I am still alive.... As for this wretched body of mine, God will look after it: he is near at hand, so why should I be anxious? I hope that in his mercy he will not prolong my course."

Martin's hope in God's mercy was soon fulfilled. He died in 655. The church that had quickly abandoned him was also quick to venerate him as a martyr, the last pope, so far, to have earned this crown. (His feast in the East is celebrated on September 20.)

See: Donald Attwater, ed., *Martyrs* (New York: Sheed & Ward, 1957).

September 20

Henri Nouwen
Priest and Spiritual Guide (1932–1996)

"Dear Lord, I will remain restless, tense, and dissatisfied until I can be totally at peace in your house.... There is no certainty that my life will be any easier in the years ahead, or that my heart will be any calmer. But there is the certainty that you are waiting for me and will welcome me home when I have persevered in my long journey to your house."

At the time of his death in 1996, Henri Nouwen was one of the most popular and influential spiritual writers of his time. Through dozens of books he invited countless persons to enter more deeply into the spiritual life — intimacy with Jesus and solidarity with a wounded world. Much of his impact came from his frank willingness to confide his own woundedness. This confessional honesty was a central feature of his message. The spiritual life, he insisted, was not simply intended for saints or "perfect people." Instead, the call of Jesus was addressed to the lame and halt, ordinary people, all of us in our brokenness and humanity: "We have been chosen to make our own limited and very conditional love the gateway for the unlimited and unconditional love of God." It was a call to conversion, to healing, a call to come home.

The search for his true home was a constant motif of Nouwen's life and writings. Born in Holland where he was ordained a priest, Nouwen spent the better part of his life in the United States. He taught at a number of prestigious American universities, including Notre Dame and Yale Divinity School. It was during these years in the 1970s that he began to emerge as the popular author of such books as *Reaching Out*, *Intimacy*, and *The Wounded Healer.* Though he quickly won a devoted following, Nouwen experienced a constant restlessness and anxiety about his place in the world. He was afflicted by an inordinate need for affection and affirmation; there was a depth within, it seemed, that God alone could fill.

In 1974 Nouwen took a year off to live in the Trappist Abbey of the Genesee. It was not enough simply to teach spirituality; he felt he must cultivate some deeper spiritual center of his own. His subsequent *Genesee Diary* offered a moving account of this monastic retreat, while at the same time opening a window on his spiritual struggles: "What was driving me from one book to another, one place to another, one project to another?" He returned to Yale. But in 1981 he left for a different kind of retreat, this time among the poor of Latin America. Living with missioners in the poor barrios of Bolivia and Peru, he wondered whether God was calling him to some kind of ministry in Latin America. Ultimately he returned to the United States, convinced that his vocation was to help serve as a bridge between the oppressed but faithful people of Latin America and Christians in the North.

In 1982 he accepted an invitation to teach at Harvard Divinity School. His lectures attracted enormous crowds. But this only underlined his abiding sense of loneliness and isolation. Later he wrote with feeling about the temptations that Christ suffered in the desert: to be "relevant, powerful, and spectacular." He was no longer satisfied with the glittering stimulation of university life. But neither monastic solitude nor Third World mission seemed to answer his heart's desire. At this point there came a great turning point in his life.

Over the years Nouwen had visited a number of L'Arche communities in France and Canada. In these communities mentally handicapped persons lived in community with able helpers. In 1986 Daybreak, the L'Arche community in Toronto, formally invited Nouwen to join them as their pastor. As he later observed, it was the first time in his life that he had received such a formal call. Having lived for many years among the "best and brightest," he wondered whether it might be among the "poor in spirit" that he would finally find what he was seeking. With trepidation, he accepted the call and Daybreak became his home for the rest of his life.

It was a different life than what he had known before. Aside from his pastoral duties, Nouwen lived like all other members of the community in a house with handicapped people. He was assigned to care for the most severely handicapped adult in the community, a young man named Adam, who could not talk or move by himself. Nouwen spent hours each morning simply bathing, dressing, and feeding Adam. He found it an occasion of deep inner conversion. Adam was not impressed by Nouwen's books or his fame or his genius as a public speaker. But through this mute and helpless man, Nouwen began to experience a sense of what it means to be "Beloved" of God.

This was not, however, the end of his struggles. After his first year at Daybreak he underwent a complete emotional breakdown — doubtless the culmination of long suppressed tensions. For months he could barely talk or leave his room. Now he was the helpless one, mutely crying out to God for some affirmation of his existence. With the support and prayers of his friends he was able to break through, to emerge more at peace with himself. To this trauma there was added a nearly fatal accident that impressed him further with a sense of his own mortality and a deeper appreciation for the preciousness of life. These insights were expressed in his subsequent books. He described a sense of "being sent: sent to make the all-embracing love of the Father known to people who hunger and thirst for love." Increasingly, his writings reflected a sense of urgency, as if he sensed how little time there was to share all he wanted to say.

In a series of books he reflected on the challenge of befriending our death as an event that gives ultimate meaning to our lives. "The main question is not, How much will we still be able to do during the few years we have left to live? But rather, How can we prepare ourselves for our death in such a way that our dying will be a new way for us to send our own and God's spirit to those whom we loved and who have loved us?"

In the summer of 1996 Nouwen worked hard, completing five books. To many friends he seemed happier and more at peace than they had ever seen him — talking with great enthusiasm of his coming sixty-fifth birthday. Thus it came as a great shock when he suddenly died of a heart attack on September 21. Death came as he was passing through his native Holland, on his way to Russia to work on a film about his favorite painting, Rembrandt's *Return of the Prodigal Son*. His body was returned for burial among his Daybreak family and friends.

He left many books in production. One of them, published on the day he died, concluded with these words: "Many friends and family members have died during the past eight years and my own death is not so far away. But I have heard the inner voice of love, deeper and stronger than ever. I want to keep trusting in that voice, and be led by it beyond the boundaries of my short life, to where Christ is all in all."

See: Henri Nouwen, *The Return of the Prodigal Son* (New York: Doubleday, 1992); *The Road to Daybreak: A Spiritual Journey* (New York: Doubleday, 1988).

September 21

St. Matthew
Evangelist (first century)

"As Jesus passed on from there, he saw a man called Matthew sitting at the tax office; and he said to him, 'Follow me.' And he rose and followed him." —Matthew 9:9

This brief verse supplies the extent of our knowledge of the disciple traditionally identified as St. Matthew the Evangelist. Was he a tax collector, as the parallel texts in Mark and Luke indicate? If so he would have been despised by his fellow Jews as a collaborator with the Roman occupation. It was for consorting with such public sinners that Jesus himself earned a certain opprobrium. But whatever Matthew's former life he apparently recognized that in order to follow Jesus he must leave the past behind.

Scholars doubt that the Gospel of Matthew, which appears to date from the end of the first century, could have been written by any of Jesus' original disciples. It does seem, however, that the author of Matthew's Gospel was a Greek-speaking Jewish Christian, determined to affirm, in the face of rejection by his fellow Jews, that Jesus was the Messiah, the fulfillment of the Scriptures and messenger of a new law. It is also likely that Matthew wrote for a community accustomed to affluence. His Gospel extols an attitude of spiritual poverty and counsels his readers that their salvation depends on the quality of their mercy toward the poor. All this is certainly consistent with the attitude of a reformed tax collector.

Matthew attributes to Jesus several long discourses that summarize his essential spirituality. These include the Sermon on the Mount, which begins with the sublime litany of the Beatitudes:

> Blessed are the poor in spirit, for theirs is the kingdom of heaven.
> Blessed are those who mourn, for they shall be comforted.
> Blessed are the meek, for they shall inherit the earth.
> Blessed are those who hunger and thirst for righteousness, for they shall be satisfied....
> Blessed are the peacemakers, for they shall be called sons of God....

Later Matthew records the great parable about the Last Judgment, when "the Son of man comes in his glory," to separate "the sheep from the goats." To those he blesses he will say, "For I was hungry and you gave me food, I was thirsty and you gave me drink, I was a stranger and you welcomed me, I was naked and you clothed me, I was sick and you visited me, I was in prison and you came to me." "When did we do these things?" they will ask. He will answer, "Truly, I say to you, as you did it to one of the least of these my brethren, you did it to me."

St. Matthew is the great patron of the church's mission. Called in his own life to follow Jesus, he closes his Gospel with Jesus' Great Commission to his followers, "Go therefore and make disciples of all nations," and concludes with words that speak to our time and every time: "And lo, I am with you always, to the close of the age."

See: Michael H. Crosby, O.F.M. Cap., *Spirituality of the Beatitudes: Matthew's Challenge for First World Christians* (Maryknoll, N.Y.: Orbis, 1980).

September 22

St. Maurice and Companions
Martyrs of the Theban Legion (c. 287)

"We cannot dip our hands into the blood of innocent persons."

There was a Roman legion recruited from Thebes in Upper Egypt which consisted entirely of Christians. In 287 they were mobilized to assist in putting down an uprising among the rebellious Gauls. When the Theban Legion arrived at Martigny near the lake of Geneva, they were ordered to join with the assembled army, on the eve of battle, in offering a sacrifice to the gods. The Theban Legion refused to take part. When they persisted in their insubordination, they were sentenced to decimation: One out of every ten men, chosen by lots, was to be put to death. Still they refused to obey. A second lottery was taken. Still the soldiers refused to obey.

The early chronicle of this incident, which is reproduced in Butler's *Lives of the Saints,* leaves some ambiguity as to the supposed cause of the rebellion. Was the issue simply the idolatrous oath, or were there also reservations about the justice of the cause? The latter is suggested in the statement which the Thebans' officer, St. Maurice, made on behalf of his men:

We are your soldiers, but we are also servants of the true God. We owe you military service and obedience; but we cannot renounce Him who is our Creator and Master, and also yours, even though you reject Him. In all things which are not against His law we most willingly obey you, as we have done hitherto. We readily oppose all your enemies, whoever they are; but we cannot dip our hands into the blood of innocent persons. We have taken an oath to God before we took one to you; you can place no confidence in our second oath if we violate the first. You command us to punish the Christians; behold, we are such. We confess God the Father, author of all things, and His Son, Jesus Christ. We have seen our companions slain without lamenting them, and we rejoice at their honor. Neither this nor any other provocation has tempted us to revolt. We have arms in our hands, but we do not resist because we would rather die innocent than live by any sin.

The legend records that the entire Theban Legion — a total of sixty-six hundred men — was subsequently slaughtered without putting up resistance. Among the troops charged with executing this slaughter there were several non-Christians who refused to take part. Their blood too was added to the holocaust.

September 23
St. (Padre) Pio
Capuchin Friar and Mystic (1887–1968)

"I need to love You more and more, but I don't have any more love in my heart. I have given all my love to You. If You want more, fill my heart with Your love, and then oblige me to love You more and I will not refuse You."

Padre Pio was forced to carry a double cross. On the one hand he bore the painful, bleeding wounds that marked his body with the passion of Christ. At the same time he endured the burden that came from being popularly acclaimed as a living saint. It is hard to say which was the heavier burden.

A Capuchin friar of peasant background, Padre Pio spent virtually his entire life in a monastery in the Apulian region of southern Italy. In appearance and in his preaching he was indistinguishable from the other friars. But for some mysterious purpose Padre Pio was set apart. For the thousands of pilgrims who flocked to hear him say Mass, or to have him hear their confessions, or simply to rest their gaze on his bandaged hands, he was a living proof for the existence of God. Needless to say, this was a difficult and unsolicited responsibility.

Like his spiritual father *St. Francis, Padre Pio was a stigmatic; he bore on his hands, feet, and side the wounds of Christ's sufferings. These mysterious open wounds, for which no natural explanation could be determined, appeared on his body in 1910. They remained until some months before his death over fifty years later, continuously bleeding, and causing great suffering. But this was only the beginning of his wonders. He was credited with literally thousands of miracles, including such feats as restoring sight to a man born with no pupils. He had frequent mystical colloquies with Jesus, Mary, and the saints. As a confessor he was said to have the gift of "reading hearts," knowing the secrets of penitents whom he had not previously met. It is even said that he had the rare gift of bilocation — the ability to be in more than one place at the same time. In other words he was endowed with a full repertoire of the supernatural gifts which commonly adorned the lives of medieval saints. But this was a man living under the full glare of twentieth-century skepticism, an era when the miraculous was more likely to cause embarrassment than wonder.

Padre Pio was capable of extraordinary prophecies. In 1947, when he heard the confession of a young Polish priest, Karol Wojtyla, he made the astonishing declaration that this priest would one day be pope. Not surprisingly, Pope John Paul II is considered a strong proponent of his canonization. Nevertheless, and despite the fact that he so closely conforms to traditional models of the wonder-working saint, the cause of Padre Pio has proceeded with exceptional caution. In part, this seems to reflect the Vatican's desire to discourage the widespread "cult of personality" that surrounded Padre Pio even during his life. At the same time there is evidently a desire to discourage the notion that "miracles" are per se synonymous with holiness.

If and when Padre Pio is formally canonized the decree will rest not only on his authenticated miracles but also on the way he coped with the suffering caused by his special gifts. This suffering was only partly physical (including bouts with demons that often left him bruised and bloodied). There was also the burden of his celebrity, the constant press of pilgrims and penitents who never left him. And finally, there was the suffering he endured at the hands of his own church officials.

Vatican experts scoffed at reports of Padre Pio's wounds. Disturbed by his popularity, they instructed him for a number of years not to say Mass publicly — an order that caused him great spiritual pain. They suggested that his stigmatic wounds were a result of psychosomatic stress, caused by too much concentration on the passion of Christ. To this Padre Pio responded, "Go out to the fields and look very closely at a bull. Concentrate on him with all your might. Do this and see if horns grow on your head!"

What was the purpose of all this suffering? Padre Pio said it was the answer to his prayer — so that sinners might believe in God and that the world might be saved. He died on September 23, 1968. (Padre Pio was beatified in 1999.)

See: Rev. John A. Schug, *Padre Pio* (Huntington, Ind.: Our Sunday Visitor, 1976); Kenneth Woodward, *Making Saints* (New York: Simon and Schuster, 1990).

Margery Kempe
Mystic and Pilgrim (1373–1438?)

"And this creature wept and sobbed as plenteously as though she had seen our Lord with her bodily eyes suffering His Passion at that time."

Margery Kempe was born in 1373 to a well-to-do family in King's Lynn, Norfolk. When she was twenty she married John Kempe and within a year bore the first of her fourteen children. This birth precipitated a grave spiritual crisis, approaching madness, which lasted more than six months. She emerged only after experiencing a visitation by Christ, who spoke to her these comforting words: "Daughter, why have you forsaken me, and I never forsook you?"

Afterward Margery recovered her wits, but her heart remained fixed in the world. She dressed in finery, boasted of her social standing, and went in for the business of brewing beer. Evidently her failure in this venture convinced her that God had other plans for her. One night soon after, as she lay in bed with her husband, she seemed to hear a sweet music and immediately jumped up, saying, "Alas that ever I sinned! It is full merry in heaven." It was at this moment that she experienced a dramatic conversion, dedicating herself to a life of prayer, penance, and service of God. She also committed herself to celibacy. Unfortunately, her husband did not immediately share this commitment, a source of ongoing marital discord that lasted throughout many years and the birth of many more children.

Meanwhile Margery began adopting a rigorous penitential discipline. She also began to experience frequent conversations with Christ, his Father, his Mother Mary, and many of the saints. Through these "dalliances," reported in her autobiography in the same matter-of-fact way she uses to describe encounters with her contemporaries, she received assurance of her vocation as a penitent, as well as the extraordinary assurance of her own salvation.

While all this was going on within, externally Margery was most conspicuous for her "gift" of tears. She wept loudly throughout much of the day, especially when she came near a church or happened upon any scene that reminded her of the love of God and the sufferings of Christ. Under certain circumstances, Margery's "gift" inspired wonder and admiration. But by and large it attracted ridicule and contempt.

Margery wandered widely in England, seeking interviews with religious authorities and spiritual guides. Some, like *Dame Julian, the holy anchoress of Norwich, approved her spiritual vocation. Others were plainly at a loss to make sense of her.

England at the time was in the throes of religious turmoil, stirred up by the Lollard heretics. These followers of the reformer John Wycliffe championed a simplified biblical faith in place of all priestly religion. Margery, with her frequent recourse to confession and weekly communion, was clearly not a Lollard. Nevertheless, the epithet was regularly hurled at her by clerics and other citizens scandalized by her unregulated enthusiasm. It was a dangerous charge, which could lead to imprisonment or death at the stake. Fortunately, Margery was always able to demonstrate her orthodoxy. But this did not prevent certain clerics from wishing she would "go to sea in a bottomless boat."

Actually, the clergy of her acquaintance differed widely in their estimation of Margery. There were certainly some, especially those whose sermons she interrupted with her uncontrollable weeping and screams, who considered her a holy nuisance. But many others became convinced of the genuineness of her vocation. Among these she eventually found willing scribes to whom she dictated her autobiography, The Book of Margery Kempe.

When she was about forty she finally won her husband's consent to accept a mutual vow of chastity. At about the same time she widened the scope of her pilgrimage, beginning with a trip to the Holy Land. Her fellow pilgrims quickly tired of her incessant weeping and became openly rude in their efforts to keep her at bay and even to lose her along the way. Nevertheless, she completed the journey, and among the holy shrines she found an even more vivid reference for her constant meditations on the life and passion of the Lord. Her weeping was now punctuated by unbidden "cries," which if anything only added to her strangeness. As Margery notes, "The crying was so loud and so amazing that it astounded people."

Along with the usual curses and rude accusations, Margery's behavior won a certain respect, and many were impressed with the edifying power of her public contrition. When once a priest said to her, "Woman, Jesus is long since dead," she replied: "Sir, his death is as fresh to me as if he had died this same day, and so, I think, it ought to be to you and to all Christian people. We ought always to remember his kindness, and always think of the doleful death that he died for us."

From her autobiography, the single manuscript of which was discovered only in the twentieth century, Margery Kempe emerges as one of the most vivid personalities of the Middle Ages. Scholars, like her contemporaries, have been divided in their opinion of her. There is no doubt as to her eccentricity; even she refers to herself as a "singular lover of God." But what stands out is Margery's bold determination to live out a unique spiritual vocation, in full public view, even in the face of ridicule and persecution. It is clear that the purpose of her public spectacle was not to draw attention to herself or to inspire imitators of her extreme spirituality. Rather, she hoped to inspire others to share just a small portion of her contrition for their sins and a small measure of her emotion at the thought of Christ's sufferings. In one of her mystical colloquies, the Lord told her: "I have ordained you to be a mirror amongst [your fellow Christians], to have great sorrow, so that they should take example from you to have some little sorrow in their hearts for their sins, so that they might through that be saved."

See: The Book of Margery Kempe, trans. B. A. Windeatt (New York: Penguin, 1985); Clarissa W. Atkinson, Mystic and Pilgrim: The Book and the World of Margery Kempe (Ithaca, N.Y.: Cornell University Press, 1983).

St. Sergius of Radonezh
Russian Abbot (1314–1392)

"Not without temptations is God's Grace given;
but we must expect joy after sorrow."

St. Sergius, a fourteenth-century monk and abbot, is one of the most popular saints of the Russian Orthodox church. He is also one of a few Russian saints who appear on the Catholic calendar. He epitomizes the ideal of the Russian monk through whose transparent holiness an entire age is illuminated.

Sergius was born in Rostov. Although he was the son of noble parents, as a child he and his family were uprooted and impoverished by civil war. Hence, they settled in Radonezh, a town near Moscow, where they were forced to live as peasants. After the death of his parents Sergius felt called to a life of prayer and dedication to God. With his brother Cyril he withdrew to an isolated hermitage in the forest. There, like the ancient desert fathers, they embraced cold, hunger, and other privations, all the while battling with "the devil in various forms and apparitions." Gradually as fellow seekers came to join them, they received permission to establish a monastery, over which Sergius consented to serve as abbot.

The story of this band of brothers, living in the wilderness, recalls the tales of *St. Francis of Assisi. There is a similar joyfulness about the community, with many stories of Sergius's celebration of poverty and of his communion with nature and its wild beasts. His dress was shabby and his appearance was evidently rough. Once a visitor came seeking the holy Sergius. When he was presented with the abbot he recoiled with surprise: "I have come to see a prophet," he said, "and you show me a beggar!"

Gradually the fame of the monastery of the Holy Trinity spread, and a well-worn path brought a constant flow of penitents and spiritual seekers. Sergius received all visitors with courtesy. For the poor, however, he felt a special warmth and affection, and his reputation for charity endeared him far beyond the monastery walls. To this was added a reputation as a national liberator after he encouraged Prince Dimitry of Moscow in his successful resistance to Tartar invaders.

Sergius performed many miraculous healings, and it was said that he enjoyed mystical visions of the Holy Mother. He died in his monastery on September 25, 1392. His biographer notes, "The face of the saint gleamed like snow, not like the face of a dead man, but with a living radiance, or like the face of an angel, thus manifesting the purity of the saint's soul and the reward of God for his labor."

See: "The Life of St. Sergius," in G. P. Fedotov, ed., *A Treasury of Russian Spirituality* (London: Sheed & Ward, 1950).

Jeremiah
Prophet (sixth century B.C.E.)

"The word of the Lord came to me saying,
'Before I formed you in the womb I knew you,
And before you were born I consecrated you;
I appointed you a prophet to the nations.' "

Jeremiah received his call to be a prophet in the year 625 B.C.E. His career was played out against the final years of the southern kingdom of Judah and continued for some time after the destruction of Jerusalem in 587 and the great exile to Babylon. His message was directed against the elite, the monarchy, the priests, and the official cult prophets who clung to the false assurance that nothing could happen to Judah so long as the Ark was safe in the Temple. Like other prophets before him, Jeremiah was sensitive to a deeper contradiction in the heart of Israel. The people had failed to comprehend that true faithfulness to God must be reflected in mercy and justice. To Jeremiah the gap between the rich and poor of the land was a yawning gap in the covenant between the people and Yahweh. Under these circumstances the official cult of Yahweh had become a form of idolatry. Short of some drastic signs of public conversion, destruction was inevitable.

Jeremiah preached this message for forty years. It didn't win him many friends. In good times he seemed like a harmless crank, but when conditions became ominous Jeremiah's message sounded like treason or blasphemy. He was forced for long periods to go underground; he was flogged and put in the stocks by the head priest of the Temple; he narrowly survived various assassination plots, one involving his own family. Once he was nearly killed after being tossed into an empty well.

Ultimately Jeremiah's message went unheeded and indeed his worst fears were realized. In 587 the Babylonians laid siege to Jerusalem for six months. Terrible famine befell the people. It all ended with a massacre of the royal family, the destruction of the Temple, and the burning of Jerusalem. Most of the population was carted into exile in Babylon, leaving only a few peasants to till the land. Our last glimpse of Jeremiah sees him being kidnapped by a band of renegades, a hostage to some petty intrigue. How and where he died is not recorded.

Most of the Hebrew prophets remain relatively anonymous figures. Few biographical details are included in their writings, and their personalities are shrouded in the wrath or pathos of God. This is not so with Jeremiah, a man in whose experience and consciousness the tragedy of the nation met full force with the tragedy of God:

> My grief is beyond healing,
> 　my heart is sick within me....
> For the wound of the daughter of my people
> 　is my heart wounded.

His original call was marked by extreme reluctance. He experienced continuing tension throughout his life between his prophetic commission and the natural impulses of his heart. It gave him no pleasure to prophesy the destruction of Jerusalem. His suffering was compounded by the derision and persecution which greeted his pessimistic oracles. At the same time, extremely sensitive as he was to the "feelings" of God, he was haunted by the people's willful disobedience in the face of a disaster which he could foresee, but which he was powerless to avert. In Jeremiah words became flame. He could curse the day of his birth and wish that his mother's womb had been his grave. Against the apathy of the people his own pathos strained the limits of tolerance.

And yet his commission as a prophet was not simply to "overthrow and destroy" but to "build up and plant." After the worst had happened, Jeremiah felt liberated at last to speak tenderly of hope and consolation. He wrote to the exiles in Babylon urging them to survive their captivity and to look forward to their eventual return. Transmitting the word of Yahweh he said,

> The people who survived the sword found grace in the wilderness.
> . . . I have loved you with an everlasting love; there I have continued
> my faithfulness to you, again I will build you, and you shall be built,
> O Virgin Israel.

Israel would not be destroyed. The people's relationship with God would not depend on the Temple or the monarchy or the city of Jerusalem but on faith, love, and obedience. What is more, Jeremiah prophesied the coming of a new covenant with the people of Israel, not like the old covenant written on tablets: "I will put my law within them, and I will write it upon their hearts, and I will be their God, and they shall be my people."

Jeremiah was powerless to avert the destruction and the exile. But he did plant the seeds of hope and a new understanding of faith that allowed the coming generation to endure and survive.

See: Abraham Heschel, *The Prophets: An Introduction* (New York: Harper & Row, 1963); William Holladay, *Jeremiah: Spokesman Out of Time* (Philadelphia: United Church Press, 1974).

September 27

St. Vincent de Paul
Founder of the Vincentians (1580–1660)

"I am for God and the poor."

Vincent de Paul was born to a peasant family in Gascony. Though he later achieved fame for his dedication to the poor, his early life was spent in a determined struggle to escape his humble roots. His family shared this ambition, hoping that a career in the priesthood would better the family fortune. Thus, as a boy, he was entrusted to the Franciscans and was eventually ordained at the remarkably young age of nineteen. It appears that Vincent's early attitude toward his vocation was no less worldly than that of his parents. The priesthood was a way to escape the farm. Once, in the seminary, he was visited by his father, but was so ashamed by the old man's shabby peasant clothes that he refused to receive him.

After his ordination, Vincent applied himself to securing a series of lucrative benefices. It was not long before he had risen to become a chaplain in the service of Queen Margaret of Valois. His charm and social skills gained him entry into the highest levels of society. Eventually he served as family tutor and chaplain to one of the wealthiest families of Paris, the Gondis. Thus he might have passed his life as one of the worldly and entitled clerics of pre-Revolutionary France, living off of benefices and enjoying the stimulating table-talk of the salons.

In mid-life, however, Vincent underwent a great transformation. The occasion was a summons to hear the dying confession of a peasant on the estate of the Gondis. After he had received absolution, the man happened to remark that he might well have perished in a state of mortal sin had the priest not heard his confession. Vincent was struck as never before by the seriousness of his vocation. He determined that henceforth his priesthood would be dedicated to service of the poor.

A number of concerns competed for his attention in the years that followed. Vincent was concerned about the spiritual impoverishment of the rural masses and about the poor formation of the clergy. He founded a mission congregation — a society of secular priests, later known as the Vincentians — devoted to the training of parish clergy and to mission work in the countryside. At the same time he utilized his extensive contacts in the court and high society to organize a wide range of charitable endeavors. He was particularly adept at attracting the services of aristocratic women. He convinced a number of them to don gray habits and to undertake a personal ministry to the poor and destitute. One exceptional woman, a widow, *Louise de Marillac, became a particularly close companion in his work. With her able help he founded the Daughters of Charity, an unenclosed congregation of women devoted to serving the poor and the sick. In describing what was at that time a revolutionary model of religious life, he wrote, "Their convent is the sickroom, their chapel the parish church, their cloister the streets of the city."

There were few charitable projects in which Vincent was not engaged. He founded hospitals and orphanages, as well as homes for the humane care of the mentally infirm. He had a personal ministry to prisoners and galley slaves and also raised money for the ransom of Christian slaves held captive in North Africa. Already in his lifetime Monsieur Vincent, as he was widely known, became something of a legend. The rich and powerful vied to endow his projects, while the poor accepted him as one of their own. His spirituality was based on the encounter with Christ in the needs of one's poor neighbors. As he instructed his priests and Sisters, "The poor are your masters and you are their servants."

Love of the poor did not mean sentimental adoration. He was scornful of those who liked to remain in the realm of imaginary acts of charity. Our love of God must be "effective," he wrote. "We must love God.... But let it be in the work of our bodies, in the sweat of our brows. For very often many acts of love for God, of kindness, of good will, and other similar inclinations and interior practices of a tender heart, although good and very desirable, are yet very suspect when they do not lead to the practice of effective love."

Vincent's last years were spent in painful illness. In approaching the hour of his death his prayer was, "We have done what you commanded; do now what you have promised." He died on September 27, 1660, at the age of eighty. His canonization followed in 1737. Later, Pope Leo XIII named him patron of all charitable societies. These included the movement dedicated to his name, the St. Vincent de Paul Society, founded in 1833 by *Frédéric Ozanam.

See: Jacques Delarue, *The Holiness of Vincent de Paul* (New York: P. J. Kenedy & Sons, 1960).

September 28

St. Lioba
Nun and Missionary (c. 700–780)

"I send you this little gift, not because it is worth your consideration but simply so that you may have something to remind you of my humble self, and so not to forget me when you are so far away; may it draw tighter the bond of true love between us forever." — St. Lioba to St. Boniface

The chronicles of early Christian mission tend to focus on the adventures of monks and priests, with less attention paid to the holy women who often accompanied them. One of these early pioneers was St. Lioba, the friend and companion of *St. Boniface. Lioba was an English nun in the abbey of Wimborne in Dorsetshire and a distant relative of Boniface. When word traveled back to England about his exploits as a missionary in Germany she made bold to initiate a correspondence. She began her charming letter,

> To the most reverend Boniface, bearer of the highest dignity and well-beloved in Christ, Liobgetha [Lioba], to whom he is related by blood, the least of Christ's handmaids, sends greetings for eternal salvation.

From this beginning there bloomed a devoted friendship. After corresponding for a full twenty years, Boniface requested of the abbess of Wimborne that Lioba and a group of other nuns be sent to join him in his mission and to establish monastic centers for women in Germany. Lioba was delighted to answer this invitation. With a group of thirty nuns she made her way to Germany, there meeting for the first time her friend and mentor. He provided them with a monastery in Mainz, where he was now the bishop. With Lioba in charge, this community prospered and soon established sister communities throughout Germany.

Lioba was renowned for her wisdom and piety, as well as for her pleasant disposition. Many well-born persons, including the wife of the emperor, sought her out for spiritual counsel and learned conversation.

In 754 Boniface resigned his see and undertook his final perilous mission to non-Christian Frisia. In parting from Lioba he expressed his respect and affection and noted his desire that after her death she might be buried with him "so that their bodies might wait the resurrection and be raised together in glory to meet the Lord and be forever united in the kingdom of His love." It was their last meeting. Soon after, Boniface fell a martyr.

In years to come Lioba made frequent trips to his grave at the abbey of Fulda. She lived on for more than twenty years, and with her monastery she continued to serve the steady Christianizing of Germany that Boniface had started. When she died in 780 her body was indeed buried in the abbey-church of Fulda, according to their common wishes, a short distance from the bones of Boniface.

See: Rudolf, Monk of Fulda, "The Life of St. Lioba," in *The Anglo-Saxon Missionaries in Germany,* ed. D. H. Talbot (New York: Sheed & Ward, 1954).

September 29

Bd. Richard Rolle
Mystic (1300–1349)

"My heart Thou hast bound in love of Thy Name,
and now I cannot but sing it!"

Richard Rolle was the first of the great mystics who thrived in fourteenth-century England. It seems he was born to a prominent family in Yorkshire in 1300. He studied at Oxford but left early at the age of nineteen. Borrowing a gown from one of his sisters, he fashioned for himself a rough tunic, renounced all interest in his family's property, and adopted a solitary life of prayer and devotion. His physical austerities, especially in the early years, were apparently extreme. His family thought him mad. But he gradually won the support of patrons who set him up in a simple hermitage and who in turn received his spiritual counsel.

Rolle wrote a number of books describing his experience of mystical rapture. For Rolle this was an experience of ardent love, characterized in terms of "warmth, song, and sweetness." In one of his early experiences he described how, while sitting in church contemplating the love of God, he felt his breast infused with a divine fire or "inward music." Afterward his prayers spontaneously turned to song.

> In the beginning truly of my conversion and singular purpose I thought I would be like the little bird that for love of its lover longs; but in her longing she is gladdened when he comes that she loves. And joying she sings, and singing she longs, but in sweetness and heat.

Rolle's writings exemplify the positive and affirmative style of English mysticism. But he was capable of acerbic criticism of conditions in the church and society. He challenged the worldliness prevalent among many clergy, and he seems to have espoused an ideal of apostolic poverty. This caused him difficulties with the local bishop. But he maintained that "the more men have raved against me with words of backbiting, so much the more I have grown in spiritual profit."

Despite his solitary life, Rolle was no gloomy misanthrope. He exemplified that "mirth in the love of God" which he credited to the saints. Having perfected his capacity for contemplation, he found himself equally capable of encountering God among other people or in nature as in solitude. As he wrote, "If our love be pure and perfect, whatever our heart loves, it is God."

Rolle died on September 29, 1349, a victim of the Black Death.

See: Richard Rolle, *The English Writings,* ed. Rosamund S. Allen, Classics of Western Spirituality (New York: Paulist, 1988).

September 30
St. Jerome
Monk and Doctor of the Church (331–420)

"Christ is our all; whoever has given up everything for Christ's sake will find Him alone in exchange for all else, and can boldly cry, 'My inheritance is the Lord!'"

St. Jerome was one of the first great scholars of the Christian church. He was born in Aquilea of Christian parents, but received his schooling in Rome. Learning, indeed, was the first passion of his life, as later it would be his path to sanctity. But in his youth he cared far more for classical poetry than he did for the vulgar Greek of the Gospels. So it was that one night, as a young man, he had a significant dream in which the Great Judge asked him what condition he was. When he answered "A Christian," the Judge responded: "You lie. You are a Ciceronian, not a Christian. Where your treasure is, there is your heart." On waking Jerome was stricken with remorse. He resolved to make a break with the world, to retire to the life of a desert hermit, and thus to devote himself strictly to the study of God's books.

In the wilderness he adopted a regime of great austerity. In one respect, however, he differed from the typical hermit. He took care to bring his library with him. So he made use of his solitude to intensify his studies. In particular, he undertook the study of Hebrew, an unusual pursuit among the early Latin fathers. Few Christians by this time shared his ability to read the Old Testament in its original language. In 382 Jerome returned to Rome, where he was employed as a secretary to Pope Damasus. The pope was intrigued by Jerome's skills and gave him an important assignment. At the time the church had access to the Scriptures only through the Greek Septuagint translation of the Hebrew Bible as well as the original Greek version of the New Testament. But since Greek had by this time given way to Latin as the common language of the church, the pope directed Jerome to prepare a Latin translation of the whole. Rather than simply translate the Septuagint into Latin, Jerome went back to the original Hebrew. It was an overwhelming project for any single man, and it was to occupy him for the rest of his long life. At the same time he became attracted to a community of holy Christian women, particularly Sts. *Marcella and *Paula, to whom he provided instruction and spiritual direction.

Otherwise Jerome was disgusted by the luxury and corruption of Rome, and he was not sparing of his frank criticism when he felt it was warranted. Indeed, the extensive correspondence of Jerome displays an unseemly pleasure in the sport of controversy. To this pursuit he brought vast rhetorical skills, a capacity for intellectual overkill, and a taste for personal sarcasm. Of one of his enemies he offered this opinion: "If he will only conceal his nose and keep his tongue still he may be taken to be both handsome and learned." These qualities earned him many enemies, and he was frequently the subject of malicious gossip. But as long as Damasus lived, he was unassailable.

With the death of his patron, however, he felt it wise to depart from Rome. He made for the Holy Land, where he was joined by Paula. The two of them founded a pair of monasteries in Bethlehem, one for men and the other for women. Jerome also founded a free hospice for pilgrims, so that it might never again be said that the Mother of God had to sleep in a stable. Jerome himself fashioned a study in a cave near the site of the Nativity. There he continued his translation, continuing his study of Hebrew under the tutelage of friendly rabbis, as well as learning the ancient language of Aramaic. Paula remained at his side, assisting him in his work. Medieval artists, perhaps sharing the scandal of some of Jerome's contemporaries over his close association with women, obliterated the role of Paula, replacing her instead with the companionship of a lion. When she died in 404 Jerome was devastated. "All of a sudden," he said, "I have lost her who was my consolation."

In 410 Jerome, along with every imperial subject, was shocked by news of the sack of Rome. Truly it was as if the entire world had come to an end. Within a short time a stream of refugees began to arrive on the distant shores of Egypt and the Holy Land. They included aristocrats, now reduced to beggars, who brought heart-rending stories of famine and cannibalism in the former capital of the world.

Jerome paused from his studies to undertake relief work. "Today," he noted, "we must translate the words of the Scriptures into deeds, and instead of speaking saintly words we must act them." Before long, however, he returned with zeal to his twin passions of scholarship and controversy. In 416 he wrote proudly, "I never spared heretics and have always done my utmost that the enemies of the Church should be also my enemies." But as the editors of Butler's Lives note, "It seems that sometimes he unwarrantably assumed that those who differed from himself were necessarily the Church's enemies." A later Renaissance pope, looking upon a painting of Jerome in the desert striking his breast with a stone, re-marked: "It is a good thing for that stone, or you would not be counted as a saint today!"

In fact, Jerome is remembered neither for his self-mortification nor for the mortification he heaped on others, but for his diligent service as a scholar. Few remember his position on the Origenist controversy. But his translation of the Scriptures, the Vulgate Bible, was the official text of the church for over fifteen hundred years. Jerome died in Bethlehem on September 30, 420. He was buried under the Church of the Nativity, close to the grave of Paula.

See: J. N. D. Kelly, *Jerome: His Life, Writings, and Controversies* (New York: Harper & Row, 1975).

☙ OCTOBER ❧

October 1

St. Therese of Lisieux
Doctor of the Church (1873–1897)

"I am only a very little soul,
who can only offer very little things to our Lord."

The story of St. Therese is lacking in outward drama. She was born in 1873 to a middle-class family in Lisieux, a small town in Normandy. Her mother died when she was four, and Therese and her four older sisters were left in the care of their father, a watchmaker and a man of marked piety. Therese, it seems, was his favorite child. When she was fifteen she received a special dispensation (in light of her young age) to enter the Carmelite convent of Lisieux, where two of her sisters had already preceded her. The rest of her short life was spent within the cloister of this obscure convent. She died of tuberculosis on September 30, 1897, at the age of twenty-four. It might be supposed that the memory of such a short and uneventful life would remain within the walls of the convent. Instead, her name quickly circled the globe. In response to popular acclamation, her canonization was processed with remarkable speed. She was declared a saint in 1925. Her feast is on October 1.

What lay behind these developments was the posthumous publication of her autobiography, *The Story of a Soul,* in which she described her experience and her distinctive insights into the spiritual life. It is a book that might well have been subtitled "The Making of a Saint," for essentially it is about the path to holiness in everyday life. Despite the somewhat cloying and sentimental style of her provincial piety, Therese presents herself as a woman possessed of a will of steel. As a child she had determined to set her sights on the goal of sanctity, and she went on to pursue this objective with courageous tenacity. She called her method of spirituality "the Little Way." Simply put, this meant performing her everyday actions and suffering each petty insult or injury in the presence and love of God.

As a teenager she had literally stormed heaven to win acceptance into the Carmelite convent. Once inside, as her book reveals, she was not content merely to fulfill the letter of her religious rule. Seemingly driven by an inner sense that little time was available, she tried to accelerate the process of sanctification. Devoting herself body and soul to Christ she offered her life as a victim of love for the salvation of souls. So acute was her belief in the Mystical Body of Christ that she believed each act of devotion, each moment of suffering patiently endured, might be credited to other souls in greater need.

Therese considered herself to be of little account — literally a "Little Flower" — though for this reason no less precious in the eyes of God. She also called her Little Way the way of spiritual childhood. But she believed that this way might transform any situation into a profound arena for holiness, and that one might thus, through the effect of subtle ripples, make a significant contribution to transforming the world.

Therese writes of her feeling that she was called to all vocations. She felt a powerful vocation to be a priest — but also a warrior, an apostle, a Doctor of the Church, and a martyr. "I would like to perform the most heroic deeds. I feel I have the courage of a Crusader. I should like to die on the battlefield in defense of the church. If only I were a priest!" The passage of time has not dulled the challenge of this heartfelt confession. But ultimately Therese came to realize that her vocation was nothing less than Charity itself, a virtue embracing every other vocation. "My vocation is love!... In the heart of the Church, who is my Mother, *I will be love*. So I shall be everything and so my dreams will be fulfilled!" At another point she described her mission as simply "to make Love loved."

In 1894 Therese woke on the morning of Good Friday to find her mouth filled with blood. She rejoiced privately in the thought that she might soon be on her way to heaven. "I was absolutely sure that, on this anniversary of His death, my Beloved had let me hear His first call, like a gentle, far-off murmur which heralded His joyful arrival." But instead this sign simply heralded the onset of a protracted period of agonizing pain as well as spiritual desolation. Before the end her sufferings would constitute a virtual crucifixion.

Therese wrote her autobiography in obedience to the request of her superior. The last chapters were literally written *in extremis*. During this time her physical torment was aggravated by periods of intense spiritual suffering. Her consciousness was flooded with terrifying images and at times she came close to despair. By continuing to pray and to hold fast to the image of Christ she eventually passed through this dark night. When she died, surrounded by her Carmelite Sisters, her last words were, "Oh, I love Him!...My God...I love you."

The publication of Therese's autobiography immediately struck a responsive chord, especially among the "simple faithful." Few are they who are called to do great things, to witness before kings and princes, or to shoulder the cross of martyrdom. And yet, as Therese demonstrated, there is a principle of continuity between our response to the everyday situations in which we find ourselves and the "great" arenas in which the saints and martyrs have offered their witness. According to Therese, each moment, accepted and lived in a spirit of love, is an occasion for heroism and a potential step along the path to sanctity.

In the years following her death, Therese was credited with an extraordinary number of miracles. It was remembered that she had once said,

"After my death I will let fall a shower of roses. I will spend my heaven in doing good upon earth."

See: *The Autobiography of St. Therese of Lisieux: The Story of a Soul* (Garden City, N.Y.: Image, 1957); Dorothy Day, *Therese* (Springfield, Ill.: Templegate Publishers, 1960).

October 2
The Pilgrim
(nineteenth century)

"By the grace of God I am a Christian man, by my actions a great sinner, and by calling a homeless wanderer of the humblest birth who roams from place to place. My worldly goods are a knapsack with some dried bread in it and in my breast-pocket a Bible. And that is all."

So begins *The Way of a Pilgrim,* the extraordinary narrative of a religious seeker, which was published in Moscow in 1884 and appeared in English in 1930. The identity of the Pilgrim is never disclosed, and apart from his own account, apparently written sometime in the mid-1800s, nothing is otherwise known of his life. He was apparently born of peasant origins, a fact that would inspire wonder on the part of many of his acquaintances on the road. He owed his ability to read and write to the care of a grand-father who raised him and who evidently inspired his lifelong passion for holiness. The Pilgrim had a withered arm, which prevented him from working. Nevertheless, a modest inheritance allowed him to marry and buy a small house. But he was soon struck by a double misfortune, first in a fire that left him penniless; then in an illness that took his wife. Bereft, he abandoned his village and assumed the life of a wanderer. Carrying no possessions but his Bible and a sack of dried bread, he undertook a fantastic journey, traversing the whole of Russia and Siberia on foot.

One day in church he was struck by the reading from Scripture: "Pray without ceasing." Troubled by these words, he became obsessed with dis-covering their meaning. In his quest he sought spiritual advice from many quarters. Finally he encountered a holy monk who introduced him to the ancient Byzantine tradition of *hesychia* (stillness or rest in God) and to the Jesus Prayer that lies at the heart of this spirituality. He was instructed to repeat the words, "Lord Jesus Christ, have mercy on me." The monk also introduced him to a collection of writings on hesychasm by the Greek fa-thers, the *Philokalia* ("Love of Beauty"). This, along with the Bible, became the focus of his daily meditation and reflection.

The Pilgrim began by reciting the Jesus Prayer three thousand times a day. At first this required considerable effort. But within weeks he had in-creased this to six thousand and then twelve thousand times a day. Soon, he wrote,

My whole desire was fixed upon one thing only — to say the Prayer of Jesus, and as soon as I went on with it I was filled with joy and relief. It was as though my lips and my tongue pronounced the words entirely of themselves without any urging from me. I spent the whole day in a state of the greatest contentment....I lived as though in another world.

The Prayer became his constant companion as he performed his daily routines and continued on his solitary way. Eventually he had the impression that the Prayer had passed from his lips to his heart. He had no further need to repeat the words; they now coincided with the rhythm of his own breathing and the beating of his heart.

The rest of his book describes his wanderings and his encounters with a rich assortment of Russian characters — soldiers, peasants, criminals, beggars, and holy monks. Sometimes he encounters ill treatment, as when he is accosted by robbers who refuse to believe that he carries no money. Other times he is received with pious reverence as a messenger of God. For the Pilgrim, good fortune and bad are alike. Every encounter is an opportunity to extol the power of prayer and the beauty of the gospel.

Despite the poverty and hardships of his life, the Pilgrim finds that through his unceasing prayer of the heart he is enabled to see the world in the light of the transfiguration. Not only does he feel that he is the happiest person on earth, "but the whole outside world also seemed to me full of charm and delight. Everything drew me to love and thank God; people, trees, plants, animals. I saw them all as my kinsfolk, I found on all of them the magic of the Name of Jesus."

By the end of his book the Pilgrim is still on his way, his destination unknown, his ultimate fate untold. But through his story his beating heart continues to reverberate.

See: The Way of a Pilgrim and The Pilgrim Continues His Way, trans. R. M. French (New York: Harper & Brothers, 1952).

October 3

Agneta Chang
Maryknoll Sister and Martyr (d. 1950)

"I have tried innumerable times to write to you but I cannot say how many times I took up my pen to begin a letter only to find that all turned black before me and I could not hold back the tears that blinded me."
—Sister Mary Peter Kang, O.L.P.H.

With these words a Korean nun began her account of the final days of Sister Agneta Chang, a Korean-born Maryknoll Sister who died among her people in 1950.

From the early years of their foundation, the American-based Maryknoll Sisters welcomed foreign vocations. Agneta Chang and a younger cousin were among the first Korean Sisters to join in 1921. In her application to Maryknoll, Sister Agneta, answering a question about her reason for applying to a religious community, wrote, "In order to become holy and then to help my country and people." Agneta came from a prominent and devoutly Catholic family in Korea. Two of her older brothers were priests; a younger brother would later become Korean ambassador to the United States.

After spending her novitiate in the Maryknoll motherhouse in New York, Agneta was assigned to her own country. There she spent many peaceful years in catechetical and parish work before the outbreak of World War II. When the American Sisters were imprisoned by the Japanese and then repatriated, Sister Agneta stayed behind to help develop the first Korean women's congregation, the Sisters of Our Lady of Perpetual Help (O.L.P.H.). For the duration of the war she and the small community of twenty-nine young Korean women were cut off from the rest of the world.

When the war ended and communication was resumed it was hoped that Sister Agneta would be reunited once again with her Maryknoll community. But it was not to be. Korea was divided at the 38th Parallel, trapping Sister Agneta and the novitiate in the Soviet-occupied North. By the time Russian troops departed in 1949 leaving Korean Communists in control, the situation had became particularly grave. Soon it was no longer possible even to smuggle messages to the outside. Many priests and even bishops were arrested and killed. After the government ordered the disbanding of all religious communities Sister Agneta and a companion, Sister Mary Peter, found refuge in a Catholic village.

For years Agneta had worn a back brace, the result of an old injury. She was in constant pain, and by now virtually bedridden. Nevertheless, she received word to report for mandatory civil defense work. When she could not comply, soldiers came looking for her. They ordered her neighbors to carry her outside and place her in a waiting ox cart. She made no complaint, but only exclaimed, "Lord, have mercy on us." It was October 4, 1950, the last time Sister Agneta was seen alive. As Sister Mary Peter described the scene,

> The time was about eight in the evening. The world was wrapped in dusk. The only sound was that of the ox cart jogging down the quiet mountain trail together with the groaning and sound of her prayers. Oh miserable night! My heart seemed to shatter and break into a thousand pieces and it seemed pitiless to me that the ground did not cleave open.

While Sister Mary Peter and some other O.L.P.H. Sisters eventually made their way to the South, another twelve remained in the North, where their fate was never learned. Word was later received that Sister Agneta Chang and a number of other women had been shot. Their bodies were buried in a nearby ditch.

See: Penny Lernoux (with Arthur Jones and Robert Ellsberg), *Hearts on Fire: The Story of the Maryknoll Sisters* (Maryknoll, N.Y.: Orbis, 1993).

October 4

St. Francis of Assisi
Founder of the Friars Minor (1182–1226)

"We have no right to glory in ourselves because of any extraordinary gifts, since these do not belong to us but to God. But we may glory in crosses, afflictions and tribulations, because these are our own."

St. Francis was born in the Umbrian city of Assisi about the year 1182. His parents were Pietro di Bernardone, a wealthy cloth merchant, and Pica, his French-born wife. Francis was one of the privileged young men of Assisi, attracted to adventure and frivolity as well as tales of romance. When he was about twenty he donned a knight's armor and went off, filled with dreams of glory, to join a war with the neighboring city-state of Perugia. He was captured and spent a year in prison before being ransomed. Upon his return he succumbed to a serious illness from which his recovery was slow. These experiences provoked a spiritual crisis which was ultimately resolved in a series of dramatic episodes.

Francis had always been a fastidious person with an abhorrence for paupers and the sick. As he was riding in the countryside one day he saw a loathsome leper. Dismounting he shared his cloak with the leper and then, moved by some divine impulse, kissed the poor man's ravaged face. From that encounter Francis's life began to take shape around an utterly new agenda, contrary to the values of his family and the world.

While praying before a crucifix in the dilapidated chapel of San Damiano, Francis heard a voice speak to him: "Francis, repair my church, which has fallen into disrepair, as you can see." At first inclined to take this assignment literally, he set about physically restoring the ruined building. Only later did he understand his mission in a wider, more spiritual sense. His vocation was to recall the church to the radical simplicity of the gospel, to the spirit of poverty, and to the image of Christ in his poor.

To pay for his program of church repair, Francis took to divesting his father's warehouse. Pietro di Bernardone, understandably enraged, had his son arrested and brought to trial before the bishop in the public marketplace. Francis admitted his fault and restored his father's money. And then in an extraordinary gesture, he stripped off his rich garments and handed them also to his sorrowing father, saying, "Hitherto I have called you father on earth; but now I say, 'Our Father, who art in heaven.'" The bishop hastily covered him with a peasant's frock, which Francis marked with a cross. And so his transformation was complete.

The spectacle which Francis presented — the rich boy who now camped out in the open air, serving the sick, working with his hands, and bearing witness to the gospel — attracted ridicule from the respectable citizens of Assisi. But gradually it held a subversive appeal. Before long a dozen other young men had joined him. They became the nucleus of his new order, the Friars Minor. The beautiful *Clare of Assisi was soon to follow, slipping through the city walls in the middle of the night to join the waiting brothers. Francis personally cut off her hair, marking her for the life of poverty and her consecration to Christ.

The little community continued to grow. In 1210 they made a pilgrimage to Rome and won the approval of Pope Innocent III. Some of the pope's advisors warned that Francis's simple rule, with its emphasis on material poverty, was impractical. But the worldly pope was apparently moved by the sight of the humble friar and perceived in this movement a bulwark against more radical forces.

Francis left relatively few writings, but his life — literally the embodiment of his message — gave rise to numerous legends and parables. Many of them reflect the joy and freedom that became hallmarks of his spirituality, along with his constant tendency to turn the values of the world on their head. He esteemed Sister Poverty as his wife, "the fairest bride in the whole world." He encouraged his brothers to welcome ridicule and persecution as a means of conforming to the folly of the cross. He taught that unmerited suffering borne patiently for love of Christ was the path to "perfect joy."

But behind such holy "foolishness" Francis could not disguise the serious challenge he posed to the church and the society of his time. Centuries before the expression became current in the church, Francis represented a "preferential option for the poor." Even in his life the Franciscans themselves were divided about how literally to accept his call to radical material poverty. In an age of crusades and other expressions of "sacred violence," Francis also espoused a radical commitment to nonviolence. He rejected all violence as an offense against the gospel commandment of love and a desecration of God's image in all human beings.

Francis had a vivid sense of the sacramentality of creation. All things, whether living or inanimate, reflected their Creator's love and were thus due reverence and wonder. In this spirit he composed his famous "Canticle of Creation," singing the praises of Brother Sun, Sister Moon, and even Sister Death. Altogether his life and his relationship with the world — including animals, the elements, the poor and sick, as well as princes and prelates, women as well as men, represented the breakthrough of a new model of human and cosmic community.

Ultimately Francis attempted no more than to live out the teachings of Christ and the spirit of the gospel. His identification with Christ was so intense that in 1224, while praying in his hermitage, he received the "stigmata," the physical marks of Christ's passion, on his hands and feet. His last years were marked at once by excruciating physical suffering and spiritual happiness. "Welcome Sister Death!" he exclaimed at last. At his request he was laid on the bare ground in his old habit. To the friars gathered around him he gave each his blessing in turn: "I have done my part," he said. "May Christ teach you to do yours." So he died on October 3, 1226. His feast is observed on October 4.

See: Regis J. Armstrong, ed., *St. Francis of Assisi: Writings for a Gospel Life* (New York: Crossroad, 1994); *The Little Flowers of St. Francis,* trans. Raphael Brown (Garden City, N.Y.: Image, 1958).

October 5

Jonathan Edwards
Puritan Theologian (1703–1758)

*"Holiness... made the soul like a field or garden of God,
with all manner of pleasant flowers, enjoying a sweet calm,
and the gently vivifying beams of the sun."*

The notoriety of Jonathan Edwards's extraordinary sermon of 1741, "Sinners in the Hands of an Angry God," has served to link the name of one of America's greatest theologians with a morbid and possibly neurotic brand of religiosity. Edwards's famous depiction of a God who holds human beings "over the pit of hell, much as one holds a spider, or some loathsome insect over the fire," has served to characterize everything dismal about Puritan theology and its legacy. In the case of Edwards such a reputation is undeserved. Though he certainly shared the Puritan conviction that fallen human nature is corrupt and worthy of punishment, he was equally concerned with the signs of God's remarkable mercy. His most consistent theme was not the anger of God, but God's beauty, or — to use his favorite expression — God's *excellence.*

Edwards was born on October 5, 1703, in East Windsor, Connecticut. After studies at the newly established Yale College, he followed the path of his father and grandfather by studying for the ministry. Eventually he was ordained as a pastor in Northampton, Massachusetts, in 1727.

Edwards was a faithful representative of Puritan theology, with its strong emphasis on original sin and predestination. But he believed the essence of religion was not so much a matter of doctrines and beliefs but of *experience,* or what he called "affections." In his famous "Personal Narrative" Edwards described how he arrived at this insight through his own experience of conversion.

In this text Edwards recounts how in his life an early flush of childish piety had gradually given way to a dry and "miserable" approach to religious duties. In particular he resented the doctrine of God's sovereignty, which ascribed to God the power to choose whom He liked for eternal salvation or damnation. To the young Edwards this seemed "like a horrible doctrine." But eventually he resolved his difficulties — not through any intellectual rationale, but by the mysterious acquisition of "a sense of the heart," a new means of apprehension that brought him to a "delightful conviction" of the justice and reasonableness of God's sovereignty. It was a matter of moving from a "natural" recognition of God's power and might to a "supernatural" appreciation for God's beauty and love.

This "sense of the heart" was God's own gift. It enabled the difference between "having an opinion that God is holy and gracious, and having a sense of the loveliness and beauty of that holiness and grace," or — to cite one of his most characteristic analogies — the difference between "a rational judgment that honey is sweet, and having a sense of its sweetness."

Having arrived at this sense of divine things, Edwards was simultaneously sensitized to the divine aspect of "ordinary" reality:

The appearance of every thing was altered; there seemed to be, as it were, a calm, sweet cast, or appearance of divine glory, in almost every thing. God's excellency, his wisdom, his purity and love, seemed to appear in every thing; in the sun, moon, and stars; in the clouds and blue sky, in the grass, flowers, trees; in the water, and all nature.

After this, for Edwards, creation became the language of the Divine Spirit.

This was hardly the standard fare of Puritan preaching. But it had a powerful and surprising effect on Edwards's congregation. Soon his pulpit became the focus of an astonishing religious revival. On one Sunday alone a hundred new converts applied for membership in his church. But the effects of the revival proved ephemeral. The mighty sentiments stimulated on a Sunday were not necessarily sustained in the workaday world. Eventually, when he tried to uphold strict conditions for full church membership, Edwards faced dissension. In 1750 the congregation finally rebelled and dismissed him as pastor.

Edwards took his family to Stockbridge to work for six years as a missionary among the Housatonic Indians. There he managed to write some of his most significant theological works. In 1757 he was called to serve as president of the new Princeton College in New Jersey. He had barely arrived when he succumbed to an epidemic of smallpox and died on March 22, 1758. So he went to what he called "the day of the infallible and unalterable sentence."

For Edwards the beauties of this world were "images of divine things." So great was his appreciation for these beauties that he lived in eager anticipation of the vision to come. How ironic that he should be remembered as a preacher of fire and brimstone and not as the author of these words:

Hence the reason why almost all men, and those that seem to be very miserable, love life, because they cannot bear to lose sight of such a beautiful and lovely world. The ideas, that every moment whilst we live have a beauty that we take not distinct notice of, bring a pleasure that, when we come to the trial, we had rather live in such pain and misery than lose.

See: Ola Elizabeth Winslow, ed., *Jonathan Edwards: Basic Writings* (New York: New American Library, 1966).

October 6

St. Hugh

Bishop of Lincoln (1140–1200)

"If all the prelates of the church were like him, there is not a king in Christendom who would dare to raise his head in the presence of a bishop."
—King Richard I

From the era of Robin Hood and "Bad King John," the story of St. Hugh recalls the witness of a real-life defender of the poor and champion of justice. Born in Burgundy, he passed his life until the age of forty as a Carthusian monk in the order's motherhouse, the famous Grande Chartreuse. The Carthusians, an order founded by St. Bruno, were hermit-monks devoted to silence and a life of contemplation. This was a life apparently well-suited to Hugh's angelic disposition. But in 1180 he accepted a request from King Henry II of England for a monk to assume leadership of a Carthusian monastery in Witham. (Henry's sponsorship of this pious project was part of his penance for the murder of *St. Thomas Becket.)

Upon arriving in England, Hugh discovered (contrary to his previous understanding) that the monastery had yet to be built. More alarming still was the discovery of deep local resentment against the whole project. It seems that the foundation of the monastery would displace scores of peasants. Hence, Hugh refused to have anything to do with the monastery until these people were justly compensated by the king. Hugh's resistance proved effective, and it immediately endeared him to the local population.

In 1186 Hugh was elected bishop of Lincoln, a see which had remained vacant for eighteen years. He resisted this preferment, yielding only to the insistence of his community. As bishop, Hugh enjoyed equal distinction for his wise administration, his pastoral gifts, and his self-effacing personality. He was well known for his affection for animals, as reflected in his habit of feeding birds and squirrels from his own hand. While a bishop, he kept a pet swan who guarded him during the night and would set forth a piercing shriek if anyone approached. Hugh showed comparable devotion to the poor and sick of his diocese and made it a point to wait personally on lepers. When reminded that *St. Martin's kisses were said to have healed lepers, Hugh replied, "With me it is the other way; the lepers' kisses heal my sick soul."

Despite his meekness, Hugh was fully prepared to stand up for principle. At a time when enthusiasm for the Crusades had a tendency to ignite spontaneous assaults on the Jewish ghetto, Hugh was resolute in his defense of the rights and dignity of the Jews. On several occasions he placed himself in the way of angry mobs and so defused their hateful zeal. Hugh showed similar courage in opposing King Richard I ("the Lionhearted") when he tried to raise money for the Crusades by taxing the church. Hugh refused to comply, an act which resulted for a time in the confiscation of all church property in the diocese. Ultimately the king capitulated in the face of Hugh's defiance, the first recorded instance of deliberate tax resistance against the crown.

In 1200 Hugh returned to France for a tour of the great monasteries. Aside from his old home, the Grande Chartreuse, he visited Cluny, Cîteaux, and Clairvaux, before setting off for the return to England. On the way home he fell ill and died on November 16. A long procession carried his body back to Lincoln, where his burial was attended by King John of England and King William of Scotland, as well as by fourteen bishops and more than a hundred abbots. The streets were lined with mourners, including the poor of Lincoln as well as the Jewish community, whose rights and lives he had defended and championed.

St. Hugh was canonized twenty years after his death. His feast is celebrated on November 16, with a celebration on October 6 for the translation of his relics.

See: E. I. Watkins, *Neglected Saints* (New York: Sheed & Ward, 1955); Joseph Clayton, *St. Hugh of Lincoln* (New York: P. J. Kenedy & Sons, 1932).

October 7
John Woolman
Quaker (1720–1772)

"It requires great self-denial and resignation of ourselves to God to attain that state wherein we can freely cease from fighting.... Whoever rightly attains to it, does in some degree feel that Spirit in which our Redeemer gave his life for us."

John Woolman was an American Quaker born in Rancocas, New Jersey, twenty miles east of Philadelphia. He was married and earned his living as a tailor. A man of extreme integrity, his life was spent in a continuous effort to heed the dictates of Christ and to apply them in all areas of his life. Above all, he took it as a personal charge to do all in his power to oppose the evil institution of slavery. His conscience was particularly offended by the knowledge that many of his fellow Quakers saw no harm in this practice. To Woolman's mind, "The only Christian way to treat a slave is to set him free."

He began speaking on this question in his local Quaker meeting and then took up a series of ever-widening journeys, on foot, to admonish slave-owning Quakers, journeys that extended to the South and throughout New England. Believing that "conduct is more convincing than language," he refused to accept hospitality in the home of slave owners.

This was only one of his principled stands. During the time of the French and Indian War he refused to pay a war tax, preferring instead to be fined for disobedience. His typical Quaker simplicity of life was reinforced by a conviction that the craving for luxuries and unnecessary possessions was the root of all oppression and war. Thus, he also resolved not to eat anything made with sugar or molasses, as these were the products of slave labor in the West Indies. For similar reasons he disdained dyed clothes. He was determined not simply to avoid all direct oppression of his fellow humans, but to root out any indirect enjoyment of exploited labor. In his "Plea for the Poor," he wrote: "May we look upon our treasures and the furniture of our houses and the garments in which we array ourselves and try whether the seeds of war have any nourishment in these our possessions, or not."

During a time of violent tensions with Indians on the Pennsylvania frontier, Woolman felt called to undertake a peacemaking mission to the Indian territory, "that I might feel and understand their life and the spirit they live in, if haply I might receive some instruction from them, or they have in any degree helped forward by my following the leadings of Truth amongst them." In several peaceful encounters, he managed to sit with the Indians and experienced a silent communion.

In 1772 Woolman felt moved to journey all the way to England to bear witness to Quakers there about the evils of slavery and the temptations of commerce and prosperity. He arrived in June and traveled widely, speaking at Quaker Meetings in a number of cities. In York he caught smallpox and died on October 7, 1772.

Woolman's journal, published after his death, is a classic expression of Quaker spirituality. In its self-effacing and matter-of-fact chronicle of his adventures in applied Christianity, it exemplifies the ideal Quaker integration of the prophetic and the mystical. As Douglas Steere has noted, "Woolman's *Journal* is not only the story of a 'collected' man but it is the recounting of the way in which a Quaker 'concern' may unfold within a man's heart, and if attended to and followed out, may not only reshape his own life as its vehicle but spread to others, and become a transforming power in the history of his time."

See: *The Journal of John Woolman,* ed. Janet Whitney (Chicago: Henry Regnery, 1950); Douglas Steere, ed., *Quaker Spirituality: Selected Writings,* Classics of Western Spirituality (New York: Paulist, 1984).

October 8

Penny Lernoux
Journalist (1940–1989)

"You can look at a slum or peasant village . . . but it is only by entering into that world — by living in it — that you begin to understand what it is like to be powerless, to be like Christ."

In the 1970s Christians around the world become aware of two extraordinary and related stories unfolding in Latin America. One was about the spread of terror and repression wrought by brutal military dictatorships throughout the continent. The other story concerned the transformation of the Latin American church. Traditionally a conservative institution allied with the rich and powerful, the church was being renewed as a prophetic force, a champion of human rights and the cause of the poor. These stories converged in the imprisonment, torture, and martyrdom of countless Christians, guilty only of professing the gospel message of justice and peace.

One woman who helped to tell these stories to the world was Penny Lernoux, an American journalist based in Latin America. Lernoux first went to Latin America in 1962. Though born a Catholic, she had drifted away from the church, disillusioned in part by its conservatism and seeming irrelevance. In the early 1970s, however, she came into contact with priests and missioners who were living out a different model of the church in solidarity with the poor. The encounter renewed her faith at the same time as it affected her mission as a journalist. As she later wrote,

It was through them that I became aware of and entered into another world — not that of the U.S. Embassy or the upper classes, which comprise the confines of most American journalists, but the suffering and hopeful world of the slums and peasant villages. The experience changed my life, giving me new faith and a commitment as a writer to tell the truth of the poor to the best of my ability.

While other American journalists were covering the repression in Latin America in terms of a war against communism, Lernoux told the story from the standpoint of the poor. Through her writings, especially her landmark history of the suffering church of Latin America, *Cry of the People,* she became a critical link between the churches and peoples of North and South America. It was clear that her writing was rooted in something deeper than professional commitment; her writing was itself an expression of her faith. She became a witness, a voice for the voiceless, a hero to many who depended on her courage in reporting the truth.

In the church of Latin America she had seen the promise of renewal and reform for the world church. In later years she was saddened by Vatican policies aimed at curbing the influence of this church, the silencing and scorn directed at many of its most prophetic ministers and theologians. Her last book, *People of God,* was a study of the struggle between contending models of world Catholicism, "the church of Caesar, powerful and rich, and the church of Christ—living, poor, and spiritually rich."

Penny Lernoux died on October 8, 1989, one month after being diagnosed with cancer. At the time she was working on a history of the Maryknoll Sisters, the repayment of a debt she felt to the Sisters she had known in Latin America and through whom she had regained her faith. In the end the Maryknoll Sisters took her in, giving her a home in their center in Ossining, New York. It was an unexpected turn in her journey, but one that was mysteriously illuminated in the light of faith. Two weeks before her death she wrote,

I feel like I'm walking down a new path. It's not physical fear or fear of death, because the courageous poor in Latin America have taught me a theology of life that, through solidarity and our common struggle, transcends death. Rather, it is a sense of helplessness — that

I who always wanted to be the champion of the poor am just as helpless — that I, too, must hold out my begging bowl; that I must learn — am learning — the ultimate powerlessness of Christ. It is a cleansing experience. So many things seem less important, or not at all, especially the ambitions.

Penny often quoted the saying in the Latin American church, that "we make our path by walking it." For Penny, it was finally a path that led full circle. She was buried in the cemetery of the Maryknoll Sisters.

See: Tom Fox, "Penny Lernoux: Faithful to the Truth," in Jim Wallis and Joyce Hollyday, eds., *Cloud of Witnesses* (Maryknoll, N.Y.: Orbis, 1991); Penny Lernoux, *Cry of the People* (New York: Doubleday, 1980).

October 9
Mollie Rogers
Foundress of the Maryknoll Sisters (1882–1955)

"There is nothing more astonishing than life, just as it is, nothing more miraculous than growth and change and development, just as revealed to us. And as happens so often when we stop to regard God's work, there is nothing to do but wonder and thank Him, realizing how little we planned, how little we achieved, and yet how much has been done."

Mollie Rogers dated the beginning of her vocation to a summer evening at Smith College when a crowd of her fellow students rushed outdoors singing "Onward Christian Soldiers." They had just signed the Student Volunteer pledge to go to China as Protestant missionaries. Mollie shared their exhilaration, mixed with a certain regret that there was no similar Catholic mission group that she could support. She made her way to the parish church and there, "before Jesus in the tabernacle, I measured my faith and the expression of it by the sight I had just witnessed. From that moment I had work to do, little or great, God alone knew."

There was no immediate issue from this resolution. But several years later in 1905 Mollie, now an instructor at Smith, sought out Father James Anthony Walsh, local director of the Society for the Propagation of the Faith in Boston. He immediately enlisted her help with *Field Afar,* a new journal aimed at stimulating mission awareness in the U.S. church.

Walsh, an Irish-American priest in his thirties, was at the time collaborating with Father Thomas Price from North Carolina on a plan to establish an American foreign mission society. Their objective: the great expanse of China. It is hard today to appreciate the magnitude of this vision. Until 1908 the United States was itself designated as a mission territory. America was still in the midst of a massive influx of European immigrants, and a good number of the Catholic priests serving in the country were themselves foreign born. Overseas mission at the time was considered a Protestant enterprise, while the Catholic church had its hands full dealing with more pressing needs at home. Nevertheless in 1911 Walsh and Price won support from the American bishops to establish a mission seminary. This was the origin of the Catholic Foreign Mission Society of America, soon to be known as Maryknoll.

Mollie was one of a small group of women who volunteered to join the priests in Ossining, New York, to help with the launching of this project. Their work was mostly confined to secretarial work on *Field Afar*. But as the Society took shape Mollie became more and more convinced that the women had a wider role to play than as mere helpers to the priests. Why, she asked, shouldn't women also serve as overseas missionaries? She won over Walsh and Price to her project. They perceived the advantage of women missioners who could more easily relate to the women of China. But to pursue this plan it was necessary that they form a religious congregation. Mollie had felt no special call to become a nun, but if that is what it took to become a missioner she was game.

This plan encountered resistance from Vatican officials who doubted that women were suited to the rugged demands of mission. The congregation that Rogers envisioned also represented a departure from the conventional model of religious life. She wished her Sisters to live amid the people — not cooped up in monastic enclosures, but able to move freely about to bear witness to the gospel. Despite reservations, the Vatican in 1920 granted approval. A year later Mollie Rogers and twenty-one other women made their formal religious vows as Maryknoll Sisters of St. Dominic.

The Sisters were helped in their early formation by members of other religious congregations. But Mollie Rogers, or Mother Mary Joseph as she was now known, found it difficult to adjust to the discipline and spirituality of these nuns, rooted in the traditions of the old world. Rogers was interested instead in adapting religious life to the needs of mission. Refusing "to be hampered by an over-regimented and parceled-out prayer life," she fought hard to impress on the congregation the importance of flexibility and individuality. Describing the ideal Maryknoll Sister, she said,

> I would have her distinguished by Christ-like charity, a limpid simplicity of soul, heroic generosity, selflessness, unfailing loyalty, prudent zeal, gracious courtesy, an adaptable disposition, solid piety, and the saving grace of a kindly humor.

The first mission of the Maryknoll Sisters was among Japanese immigrants on the West Coast. But soon Rogers's dream was fulfilled when the first Maryknoll Sisters were sent to China. Again, as she had hoped, the Sisters branched out beyond the work of support for the priests or traditional works of charity. In China, and eventually elsewhere, Maryknoll Sisters went out into the countryside to befriend the poor and to engage in the direct work of evangelization. Other missions followed in Korea, the Philippines, and eventually throughout the world.

Rogers followed the work of her Sisters with maternal pride and made several trips overseas to survey their progress. But it was not her vocation to join them. Instead she remained at the motherhouse directing the congregation until she retired from office in 1950. At the time of her death on October 9, 1955, there were eleven hundred Maryknoll Sisters serving worldwide.

In years to come the Maryknoll Sisters would achieve a heroic image for their exploits in the jungles of Africa and Latin America, and for their sufferings during World War II and under Communist persecution in China. Later still, beginning in the 1960s, their commitment to social justice and their "option for the poor" would entail a different type of heroism. But as the congregation grew and evolved over time the Sisters continued to draw inspiration from the vision and personality of Mollie Rogers, who once wrote, "Love, work, prayer, and suffering will sustain us in the future as they have in the past. All who are here now, all who will come after us, will have no other tools than these with which to build."

See: Penny Lernoux (with Arthur Jones and Robert Ellsberg), *Hearts on Fire: The Story of the Maryknoll Sisters* (Maryknoll, N.Y.: Orbis, 1993).

October 10

Alban Butler
Priest and Hagiographer (1710–1773)

"Though we cannot imitate all the actions of the saints, we can learn from them to practice humility, patience, and other virtues in a manner suiting our circumstances and state of life."

Alban Butler, an English priest, did more than any modern writer to stimulate devotion to the saints. His *Lives of the Saints,* published in the mid-1700s, was for its time the most thorough review of the topic undertaken since the far more credulous *Golden Legend* by *Jacobus de Voragine in the thirteenth century. Though subsequent revised editions bear scant resemblance to Butler's original text, *Butler's Lives* remains the standard English guide to the calendar of saints.

Butler himself lived a good but relatively unremarkable life. He was born in Northamptonshire on October 10, 1710. Later, like other Catholics wishing to avoid the penal laws in force in England, he studied at Douai in France. There he was ordained in 1735 and afterward remained on as a professor of theology. He returned to England in 1749, serving as chaplain to the duke of Norfolk. More inclined to scholarship than pastoral work, however, he happily returned to France in 1766 to assume the post of president of the English College of Saint-Omer. He remained there until his death in 1773.

His great work, originally entitled *Lives of the Primitive Fathers, Martyrs, and Other Principal Saints*, appeared in four volumes between 1756 and 1759. With long essays on approximately sixteen hundred saints, it was a prodigious achievement, the product of thirty years of work. It was not, unfortunately, the product of literary genius. Even his greatest admirers were forced to note Butler's verbose and prolix style. This defect has been removed by his modern editors, Father Herbert Thurston and Donald Attwater. But if the modern edition does not retain Butler's actual words it maintains his animating hope, that sustained reflection on the lives of the saints might provide spiritual benefit to his readers.

Much traditional interest in saints focused on their miraculous power and the benefits of their spiritual patronage. Butler was more interested in the saints as exemplars of faith, hope, and charity. He believed that in studying the saints and learning of their individual struggles, readers might be inspired to strive for greater holiness in their own given circumstances.

> They were once what we are now, travellers on earth: they had the same weaknesses which we have. We have difficulties to encounter; so had the saints.... The saints are a "cloud of witnesses over our head," showing us that a life of Christian perfection is not impossible.

Butler was less interested in the saints as powerful intercessors in heaven than as examples of the gospel, "clothed as it were with a body":

> In the lives of the saints we see the most perfect maxims of the gospel reduced to practice, and the most heroic virtue made the object of our senses, clothed as it were with a body, and exhibited to view in its most attractive dress.... Whilst we see many sanctifying themselves in all states and making the very circumstances of their condition... the means of their virtue and penance, we are persuaded that the practice of perfection is possible also to us.

All who have benefitted from Butler's faithful labor should venerate his memory.

See: Butler's Lives of the Saints, ed. Herbert Thurston, S.J., and Donald Attwater (London: Burns and Oates, 1956).

October 11
João Bosco Bournier
Jesuit Martyr of Brazil (1917–1976)

"The history of salvation is nothing more than the accumulation of the responses of individual men and women to the call of their baptism."

For most of his career as a priest Father João Bosco Bournier made little impression on his confrères. It was only toward the end of his life, when he had been planted in a wasteland, that his true talents found the opportunity to bloom.

Born in Brazil, Bournier entered the Jesuits at the age of nineteen. When he was ordained in 1946 he dreamed of serving in the overseas mission, but instead he was assigned to various administrative duties, including nine years in the central office of the Jesuits in Rome. He spent nearly thirty undistinguished years in tasks that brought him little sense of fulfillment or reward. What is more, he found himself bewildered by the changes introduced by Vatican II. The debates between proponents of the "old way" and the "new way" left him cold. He prayed for some deliverance. This came at last in 1966 when he received a new assignment, to be a missionary at last — not overseas, but in the frontier region of Mato Grosso. Though not exactly a coveted assignment, for Bournier it was the answer to a prayer.

Mato Grosso was a newly created region carved out of the Amazon jungle in central Brazil. Developers had pushed back the jungle and cleared the forests and swamps to create enormous plantations, some as large as a quarter of a million acres. For the wealthy cattle barons there were fortunes to be made. But for landless peasants who provided the labor, their existence was little removed from bondage. A step below them were the Indians, regarded as less-than-human and simply one more obstacle to be cleared from the land. Any effort to challenge this lawless system was met with brutal force, administered either by the police or by the hired thugs of the owners.

This was the world that Father Bournier encountered when he arrived to begin his duties as pastor. It was not long before he found himself rethinking everything he had ever understood and learned about theology. This was not under the influence of the new post–Vatican II theology from France or Germany. It was a matter of reflecting on the meaning of faith in light of the social reality surrounding him. What was the meaning of the gospel in a situation where life was counted cheap? Bournier soon concluded that the role of a priest in such a place was not simply to administer the sacraments. The priest's job was to represent the interests of human dignity and justice and to make it clear that God was not indifferent to the fate of the poor.

Bournier found himself especially drawn to the Indians, the least among the poor, who otherwise had no friends or advocates. In doing so he found himself further exploring the need to adapt the faith to the culture of the people: "We must adapt ourselves to the culture of the Indian in order to transmit the gospel, or to discover within the life of the Indians the gospel values." It was a hard and demanding assignment. But for the first time in his life Bournier felt genuinely happy in his priesthood.

He was fortunate to find in his local bishop, Dom Pedro Casaldáliga, one of the true prophets and heroes of the Latin American church. Spurning all episcopal privileges, Dom Pedro lived in a humble shack and dressed like a peasant. For his tireless defense of the poor, Casaldáliga had endured continuous harassment and persecution from the military government and the local landowners. They called him a communist. He well understood what Bournier was facing. He said, "The humblest and most difficult job for a Brazilian priest is in Mato Grosso, working for a people dragged and carried along on a wave of poverty, solitude, and crime. Mato Grosso is still a land without law.... The peasant's life is to be born and to die, to be killed without fundamental rights — in the Mato Grosso, these words go together with a stupefying naturalness."

In October 1976 Bournier attended a church meeting in São Felix and then enjoyed the great privilege of accompanying Bishop Casaldáliga on a visit to some of the remote villages in his far-flung diocese. On October 11 they arrived at the small town of Ribeirão Bonito. Toward the evening they learned that two peasant women were being held and tortured in the local jail. The bishop at once set off to intercede for the women. Bournier accompanied him.

Outside the jail they confronted the police and demanded that the women be released. The officers were abusive, contemptuously addressing the bishop and priest as "commies." When Bournier threatened to report them to their superiors, a police corporal struck him across the face with his gun. Possibly by accident, the gun discharged and Bournier was shot in the head.

As the priest lay dying Casaldáliga administered the last rites. Bournier remained conscious for some while. "Whatever suffering I have," he said, "I would like to offer to God that the Indian Commission could help these poor people. They are so anonymous." Finally, as his life poured out, he whispered, "I've finished my course. *Consummatum est.*" And then, "Dom Pedro, we've come to the end of the job together."

As the fruit of his priesthood Bournier had wished above all to restore a sense of dignity to the poor of Mato Grosso. This he accomplished above all by his willingness to lay down his life. In his many years in the Jesuits he had left few lasting monuments. But at the site of his death the peasants erected a cross with the inscription: "On 11 Oct 76 in this place of Ribeirão Bonito, Mato Grosso, was assassinated Father João Bosco Bournier, for defending the liberty of the poor. He died, like Jesus Christ, offering his life for our liberation."

See: William J. O'Malley, S.J., *The Voice of Blood* (Maryknoll, N.Y.: Orbis, 1980).

October 12
Elizabeth Fry
Quaker Reformer (1780–1845)

"My mind is in a state of fermentation.
I believe I am going to be religious or some such thing."

Elizabeth Fry was raised in a prosperous Quaker family, the Gurneys of Norwich, England. Her family represented the more "lax" end of the Quaker spectrum; thus, the children were allowed to sing and dance and wear bright clothes to Meeting. As Elizabeth grew up, however, she was increasingly attracted to the more austere devotional habits of the "Plain Quakers." When she was seventeen an encounter with a Quaker abolitionist from the United States stimulated her desire to pursue a path of godly service. Afterward she wrote in her journal, "I wish the state of enthusiasm I am now in may last, for today I *have felt* there is a *God. I have been devotional,* and my mind has been led away from the follies that it is mostly wrapt up in."

Within two years she was married to Joseph Fry, and her life was subsequently absorbed in the responsibilities of a growing family. Ultimately, she bore eleven children over a period of twenty-one years. This life was not without its rewards. But after twelve years of marriage, she felt that she was missing out on her true vocation. In her diary she wrote, "I fear that my life is slipping away to little purpose."

It was soon afterward that she accepted the invitation of another Quaker to visit the infamous Newgate prison. There she witnessed conditions which filled her with shame and indignation. Women and their young children were crowded into fetid cells, "tried and untried, misdemeanants and felons" together, "in rags and dirt . . . sleeping without bedding on the floor." In one cell she saw two women strip the clothing off a dead baby to dress another infant.

This was the beginning of a cause, public and private, that Fry pursued for the rest of her life. She began by returning to the prison with clean clothing and straw for the women to lie on. Although the jailers tried to obstruct her efforts, claiming that the women were incorrigible savages, Fry was determined to respond to them in a manner befitting their humanity. When she asked them whether they would like her to provide instruction to their children, they responded eagerly, with many of the illiterate women pressing in to benefit from her lessons.

With the support of a committee of other Quaker women Fry launched a campaign for general prison reform. This achieved many results, including provisions for larger living quarters, better food, fresh air, and the supply of sewing materials to provide the women with some occupation and a means of earning money. Over the years Fry was tireless in her efforts, which eventually extended throughout England and Scotland. There were some who criticized her on the grounds that her devotion to this cause entailed the neglect of her family. She too upbraided herself at times. As she wrote in her journal in 1817,

My mind too much tossed by a variety of interests and duties — husband, children, household, accounts, Meetings, the church, near relations, friends, and Newgate — most of these things press a good deal upon me. I hope I am not undertaking too much, but it is a little like being in the whirlwind and in the storm.

Her efforts also elicited public opposition from those who felt that to humanize the prisons was to undermine their deterrent value, thus "removing the dread of punishment in the criminal classes." But Fry was motivated by the conviction that prisoners, regardless of their crimes, were human beings who bore within them the spark of the divine image. It was sacrilege to treat them with no more than punitive cruelty. Fry continued to live in the whirlwind and pressed on with her cause, in season and out, until the end of her life on October 12, 1845.

See: D. Elton Trueblood, *The People Called Quakers* (New York: Harper & Row, 1966); George Anderson, "Elizabeth Fry: Timeless Reformer," *America* (October 14, 1995).

The Syrophoenician Woman
Faithful Witness (first century)

"But immediately a woman, whose little daughter was possessed by an un-
clean spirit, heard of him, and came and fell down at his feet."

—Mark 7:25

The Gospels record numerous occasions in which Jesus confronted his disciples and others with the liberating implications of his message. But there is at least one story in which the challenge was reversed. The story of an unnamed gentile woman, identified only by her Syrophoenician origins, recalls an instance in which it was Jesus himself who was moved to act upon the universal logic of the gospel.

As related by *Mark, this woman accosted Jesus in a private home, begging him to cast out a demon from her sick daughter. Surely she knew that her action seriously violated the social and religious codes of Jewish society. If so, she was probably better inured than the modern reader to Jesus' insulting rebuff: "Let the children first be fed for it is not right to take the children's bread and throw it to the dogs." Rather than take offense, however, she persisted in her request, cleverly returning Jesus' words with a challenge he could not resist: "Yes, Lord; yet even the dogs under the table eat the children's crumbs."

There are few encounters in which Jesus does not have the last word. But this is one. Apparently persuaded by the woman's claim he answers her request: "For this saying you may go your way; the demon has left your daughter."

The unnamed Syrophoenician woman deserves to be remembered as one of the foremothers of the gentile church who intuited, even while Jesus lived, that his gospel was for everyone. She may also be honored as an example of the countless women who, having refused to accept their marginalization as the final word, have challenged the church to comprehend the universal and liberating logic of salvation.

St. Callistus
Pope and Martyr (d. 222)

"We should not do unto others what we would not
that they should do unto us." —Motto of St. Callistus

St. Callistus traveled a great distance to reach the chair of *St. Peter. He began life as the slave of a Christian. He fled his master, following the failure of a financial enterprise with which he had been entrusted. Apprehended, he was sent to the Sardinian mines, where he languished for some years. After his release he found a position with Pope St. Zephyrinus as superintendent of a Christian cemetery on the Appian Way. Zephyrinus ordained him a deacon and made him a trusted advisor.

In 217 the pope died, and Callistus was elected to replace him. His election prompted bitter opposition from Hippolytus, a priest of Rome and a rival candidate. Hippolytus's opposition became even more outspoken in the face of Callistus's style of leadership. Hippolytus represented a rigorist vision of the church. He resented what he deemed the overlaxity or mercifulness of Callistus's approach to sinners. The pope admitted murderers and adulterers back to communion after they had performed public penance. Hippolytus believed they should be permanently excommunicated. Callistus allowed priests to marry and ordained twice- and even thrice-married men to the clergy. He recognized the marriage between free women and slaves, a violation of Roman law. He welcomed converts from heretical or schismatic sects into the church. All this offended Hippolytus's image of the church as the ark of the saints. He could not abide Callistus's model of the church as the loving home for saints and sinners alike.

Though Hippolytus was unremitting in his attacks on the pope, Callistus never tried to silence him. He remained tolerant even when Hippolytus, believing that the church had fallen into apostasy and sin, went so far as to have himself consecrated as a rival pope.

The reign of Callistus was short — only five years. He was apparently killed in a riot, and so is included in the list of papal martyrs.

October 15

St. Teresa of Avila
Mystic, Doctor of the Church (1515–1582)

"Let nothing disturb you, nothing dismay you. All things are passing, God never changes. Patient endurance attains all things. . . . God alone suffices."

By any standard, Teresa of Avila is one of the towering figures in Christian history. In a time and place (sixteenth-century Spain) which paid little attention to the voice of any woman, Teresa managed to outshine nearly all her contemporaries. She was a mystic, a religious reformer, the foundress of seventeen convents, the author of four books, and one of the outstanding masters of Christian prayer. In light of these accomplishments it is not surprising to learn that she possessed a vivid and charismatic personality. She could be at turns charming, imperious, irreverent, and impossible, depending on the circumstances and the provocation. But there was little doubt among any she encountered that her courage and wisdom were rooted in a special relationship with God.

Teresa was born in the fortress city of Avila in 1515. Her father, a wealthy merchant, had married into the aristocracy. Nevertheless, the family's social standing was tenuous. Teresa's grandfather was a *converso*, one of the many Spanish Jews who converted to Christianity under threat of exile. In later years such a pedigree reinforced the suspicions of those otherwise inclined to fault her program or her leadership. Teresa's mother died when she was fourteen, and her father arranged for her education in a local convent. By the time she was twenty she had decided to become a nun, a vocation motivated, she later recognized, much more by the fear of purgatory than by the love of God. Her father opposed this plan, but Teresa, with characteristic willfulness, disobeyed his wishes and ran off to the Carmelite convent in Avila. Within a year she had become so ill that her father came to take her home. Her condition deteriorated to the point that she fell into a coma and was thought to be dead. Although she recovered, her convalescence was long and painful. For three years she was virtually paralyzed from the waist down. Eventually she was well enough to return to her monastery, but her spiritual life had grown tepid and superficial.

Her progress was not helped by the lax conditions of the convent. The strictness of the original Carmelite rule had been so mitigated over the years that the convent in Avila had come to resemble a boarding house for wealthy maidens more than a house of prayer. The enclosure was not seriously maintained, and the nuns spent much of their time in the parlor entertaining visitors and gentlemen callers. In this atmosphere Teresa's natural charm and extroverted personality brought her much attention.

At the age of thirty-nine, however, Teresa had an experience of conversion. It was sparked when she happened to glance, one day, at an image of the suffering Christ on the cross. Instantly she was filled with loathing for the mediocrity of her spiritual life, and she determined to devote herself more seriously to a life of prayer. Almost immediately upon this resolution she began to experience the sensation of God's love, transforming her from within. She decided to establish a new reformed Carmelite house, returning to the spirit of the original primitive rule of Carmel. After strenuous lobbying she finally won permission to undertake this initiative. Her new convent was founded in Avila in 1562.

Her new community was known as the Discalced (shoeless) Carmelites. In fact the nuns wore hemp sandals, but their name referred to the strict poverty that was a feature of Teresa's reform. Her nuns were to seek no endowments but to live entirely by alms and their own labor. A strict enclosure was to be maintained, along with a vegetarian diet and a rigorous schedule of prayer.

From Avila Teresa went on to establish sixteen other convents in Spain. In the meantime she had to endure opposition from within her Carmelite family, suspicion from members of the hierarchy, and eventually formal investigation by the dreaded Spanish Inquisition. Not so many years had passed since the Spanish victory over the Moors and the expulsion of the Jews in 1492. Spain at this time was exultantly and aggressively Catholic. Along with this came a fanatical suspicion of anything that smacked of Protestantism. As a woman and reformer, who based her authority on private visions, Teresa's activities entailed considerable risk. Her confessor and colleague, *John of the Cross, with whom she helped to inspire a male branch of the Discalced Carmelites, had a direct taste of these dangers when he was for a time imprisoned in the dungeon of the "Calced" Carmelite monastery in Toledo.

Teresa blithely surmounted all obstacles in her path. When asked how she intended to found a monastery with only a handful of ducats in her purse, she answered, "Teresa and this money are indeed nothing; but God, Teresa and these ducats suffice." The Inquisition was not her only concern. She also endured sickness, hunger, and poverty along the way. A particular mortification was the misery and hazards of travel at a time when donkey carts were the standard mode of transportation. One time her cart overturned, throwing her into a muddy river. When she complained to God about this ordeal, she heard a voice from within her say, "This is how I treat my friends." "Yes, my Lord," she answered, "and that is why you have so few of them."

Teresa's public accomplishments are all the more remarkable in light of the intensity of her life of prayer. Among all the saints there are few to rival the variety and depth of her mystical experiences. As she advanced in life she experienced frequent ecstasies in which it seemed her heart had been pierced by God's love. She described this and other experiences in great detail in her autobiography, along with several other volumes on prayer and mystical spirituality. And yet for someone who had achieved a virtually unique degree of communion with God, she remained fully able to speak in common terms: "Prayer, in my view, is nothing but friendly intercourse, and frequent solitary converse, with Him Who we know loves us." Having achieved the most rarefied heights of spiritual wisdom Teresa retained the ability to counsel "everyday" Christians. In a maxim she left for her Sisters she wrote, "Remember that you have only one soul; that you have only one death to die; that you have only one life, which is short and has to be lived by you alone; and that there is only one glory, which is eternal. If you do this, there will be many things about which you care nothing."

Teresa died in 1582. She was canonized forty years later. In 1970 she was the first woman to be named a Doctor of the Church.

See: *The Life of Teresa of Avila*, ed. E. Allison Peers (Garden City, N.Y.: Image, 1960); Tessa Bielecki, ed., *Teresa of Avila: Mystical Writings* (New York: Crossroad, 1994); John Beevers, *St. Teresa of Avila* (Garden City, N.Y.: Doubleday, 1961).

October 16

Cardinal Gaspar Contarini
Catholic Reformer (1483–1542)

"If we wish to put an end to the Lutheran errors and troubles we need not muster against them heaps of books, Ciceronian orations, or subtle arguments: let us rely on the probity of our lives and a humble spirit, desiring nothing but the good of Christ and our neighbors."

Before the irreparable hardening of those divisions that separated the Protestant Reformers from the Catholic church, there were Catholic voices who remained hopeful that the breach might still be repaired. Gaspar

Contarini, a lay theologian and later cardinal, was the leader of this doomed cause.

He was born on October 16, 1483, to a noble family in Venice and later studied philosophy at the University of Padua. Several of his closest friends from the university entered religious orders. But Contarini, though deeply pious, believed that his vocation was to serve the cause of Christ while remaining in the secular world. He entered the diplomatic service of Venice, serving in the court of Emperor Charles V and later as ambassador to the Vatican.

Even before Luther posted his famous ninety-five theses, Contarini was an advocate of church reform. In 1510 he published a tract critical of the worldliness of many bishops. While in Germany he studied the writings of Luther and wrote a critical, though in many respects sympathetic, review of his theological positions. In 1529, during an audience with Pope Clement VII, he advised the pope to give less regard to the management of the Papal States and to think of ways of heading off the impending divisions within Christendom. When the pope, a true Medici, replied that the world respected only power, Contarini insisted, "If your Holiness were to consider all the contents of Holy Scripture, which cannot err, he would see that nothing is stronger and more vigorous than truth, virtue, goodness, and right intention."

In 1534 a new pope, Paul III, was receptive to the need for church reform. He named Contarini, while still a layman, to the college of cardinals and placed him in charge of a commission to investigate reform. The commission's report, issued after three months, presented a scathing inventory of corruption and abuses, mostly emanating from the sale of church benefices and the consequent elevation of unworthy bishops. When the report was leaked and found its way to Luther, he promptly published it as a confirmation of the Protestant critique of Rome.

One of the last hopes for reconciliation between the church and the Protestants occurred at a conference in Regensburg, convened in 1541 by the emperor. A number of the more moderate Protestant spokesmen were present, and hopes were elevated when Contarini was appointed as the papal legate. Contarini was eager to seek areas of agreement rather than to focus exclusively on points of conflict. Instead of simply issuing condemnations, he believed it would be more fruitful to meet the Lutheran "troubles" in a spirit of understanding and charity. "I believe it is our part to strive, by goodwill and well-doing, to put our opponents to shame of themselves for separating from brethren who are filled with love."

In a short time Contarini was able to work through agreement on a number of points, including the nature of original sin and a compromise language on the nature of justification by faith. When word of this leaked out, both sides reacted with angry condemnations. On the Roman side, there were already serious doubts about the wisdom of dialogue with the Lutherans. Now Contarini was denounced as a crypto-Protestant. Soon word returned that the Vatican had rejected the new language on justification. By that time, however, the conference had already dissolved in failure.

Thereafter, leadership of the church reform was taken up by Cardinal

Carafa, a hardliner, who was vehemently opposed to dialogue. In 1542 he was authorized to establish the Inquisition. Later, as Pope Paul IV, he would remark, "Even if my own father were a heretic, I would gather wood to burn him." By that time the possibility of reconciliation had passed. And so had Contarini. He died of a fever on August 24, 1542.

See: David C. Steinmetz, *Reformers in the Wings* (Philadelphia: Fortress, 1971).

October 17

St. Ignatius
Bishop of Antioch, Martyr (c. 107)

"Now is the moment I am beginning to be a disciple."

St. Ignatius became bishop of Antioch in Syria toward the end of the first century. It appears that he was arrested during the persecution of Christians under the emperor Trajan and condemned to fight with wild beasts in Rome. He was transported in chains in the company of a squad of soldiers who took an overland route through Asia Minor. Stopping periodically along the way, he was able to meet with representatives from the local churches, some of whom traveled great distances to pray or celebrate the Eucharist with this servant of God.

Most of our knowledge of the saint is derived from seven letters which he composed along the way. They provide an unusually intimate portrait of Ignatius and his struggles to interpret his impending martyrdom in the light of Christ's passion and death.

On the surface the letters are marked by a kind of bravado, a *longing* for martyrdom and a fear that influential friends in Rome may intercede for him and thus deprive him of his victory crown.

> Let me be fodder for wild beasts — that is how I can get to God. I am God's wheat and I am being ground by the teeth of wild beasts to make a pure loaf for Christ. I would rather that you fawn on the beasts so that they may be my tomb and no scrap of my body be left.... Then I shall be a real disciple of Jesus Christ when the world sees my body no more. Now is the moment I am beginning to be a disciple. May nothing seen or unseen begrudge me making my way to Jesus Christ. Come fire, cross, battling with wild beasts, wrenching of bones, mangling of limbs, crushing of my whole body, cruel tortures of the devil — only let me get to Jesus Christ!

This apparent appetite for martyrdom strikes a rather distasteful chord for the modern reader who is liable to shrink from the suggestion that only violent death is the mark of authentic Christian discipleship.

However, closer reading of these letters suggests that Ignatius's words are not so much self-congratulation as self-exhortation. Rather than boasting in his courage, he is steeling himself against his fears — not only the fear of physical pain, but fear that in the end he will not be able to see the race to the finish and that he will scandalize his flock. "If, when I arrive, I make a different plea, pay no attention to me. Rather heed what I am now writing to you. For though alive, it is with a passion for death that I am writing to you."

And in this context Ignatius's affirmation of theological orthodoxy takes on a more personal aspect. The meaning of his coming sacrifice and death, and thus the meaning of his life, depends on the truth of the claims of faith: that Jesus truly died and was resurrected. "If what our Lord did is a sham, so is my being in chains. Why, then, have I given myself up completely to death, fire, sword, and wild beasts? For the simple reason that near the sword means near God."

Ignatius believed strongly that his life and death did not belong to himself alone. It was his responsibility as a bishop to strengthen the faith of his flock, and his ultimate concern was that he not give scandal by doubting the teaching of the resurrection. "We have not only to be called Christians, but to *be* Christians," he wrote. The intense conviction that death suffered for the sake of Christ would lead to eternal life helped sustain Ignatius as he made his journey to Rome. In the end, Ignatius was not impeded from fulfilling his hopes. He was consumed by lions in the amphitheater in Rome in the year 107. It is said that he died well.

See: "The Letters of Ignatius, Bishop of Antioch," in Cyril C. Richardson, ed., *Early Christian Fathers* (New York: Macmillan, 1970).

October 18

St. Luke
Evangelist (first century)

"It seemed good to me also...to write an orderly account for you, most excellent Theophilus, that you may know that truth concerning the things of which you have been informed."

St. Luke was the author of one of the four Gospels as well as the Acts of the Apostles. From references in the letters of *St. Paul it is supposed that he was a gentile Christian who accompanied Paul on many of his journeys and who attended him faithfully during his final days of imprisonment. In his letter to the Colossians Paul refers to "Luke, the beloved physician," a phrase which has prompted the traditional depictions of Luke as a doctor. Support for this tradition may perhaps be found in the clinical detail with which Luke ornaments his stories of illness and healing. But as Joseph Donders has observed, Luke's greater concern is with Jesus as the "healer of a broken world."

Luke's Gospel is marked by a special concern for the poor, the marginalized, women, and social outcasts. His account of the Nativity, with its stress on the faith of Mary, emphasizes the humbleness of Jesus' birth and its significance in fulfilling the hopes of the poor. He has Jesus announce his mission in the synagogue in Nazareth with the text from *Isaiah, "The

Spirit of the Lord is upon me, because he has anointed me to preach good news to the poor,... to proclaim release to the captives and recovery of sight to the blind, to set at liberty those who are oppressed, to proclaim the acceptable year of the Lord." In Luke's version of the Beatitudes, Jesus proclaims, "Blessed are you poor, for yours is the kingdom of God." And it is in Luke's Gospel that we find the parable of the rich man and the poor beggar, Lazarus, that offers such a striking image of the relation between mercy and justice in this life and in the life to come.

Throughout history Luke's Gospel has held special meaning for those Christian movements inspired by the poverty of Jesus and his ministry among the poor. It is significant, however, that Luke never met Jesus. His knowledge of Jesus came only from his encounter with the Risen Lord, present in the Christian communities he described in Acts. Of all the evangelists, Luke had the most vital sense of God's presence in ongoing history. That is why his story does not end with the resurrection of Jesus but continues with Pentecost and the ongoing story of Christ's presence in the life of the church and in the midst of the world. That story, which is partly Luke's legacy, continues still.

See: Richard J. Cassidy, *Jesus, Politics, and Society: A Study in Luke's Gospel* (Maryknoll, N.Y.: Orbis, 1978); Joseph Donders, *Risen Life: Healing a Broken World* (Maryknoll, N.Y.: Orbis, 1990).

October 19
St. Isaac Jogues
Jesuit and North American Martyr (1607–1646)

*"My hope is in God, who has only us with whom to fulfil his plans.
It is for us to be faithful and not to spoil his work by our cowardice."*

Early one winter morning in 1644, a gaunt and ragged figure knocked at the door of the Jesuit house in Paris asking to see the Father Rector. When he was presented, the visitor announced that he had news from New France. Intrigued, the priest asked whether he knew the Jesuits in Canada. "Oh, yes," answered the stranger, "I know them well." And what of Father Isaac Jogues, a young priest who had been captured by the Iroquois, who was horribly tortured, and was presumed dead? "He is not dead," answered the mysterious visitor. "He stands before you." As proof, he held out his hands, from which one of his thumbs and several fingers had been severed. "Dear God in heaven!" exclaimed the Father Rector, before grasping Father Jogues in his arms.

Within days this dramatic scene was known throughout France, and Jogues was a national hero and celebrity. He was ordered to appear before the queen to recount the details of his mission to the Huron and Mohawk Indians in Canada, of his ordeal as a prisoner and slave, and of his daring escape. But for Jogues the publicity and the acclaim were no more than a second ordeal to be escaped. There was talk among the Jesuits of putting him on a lecture circuit. His heroic exploits and the marks of his suffering might inspire new vocations and support for the missions. But his superiors left the decision to him. His choice was to return to the Mohawks, to carry on the work of winning souls and, God willing, to offer his life for their salvation. The Jesuits acceded to this wish and obtained for him a special gift: a papal dispensation from the canonical rubrics, allowing him to celebrate Mass despite his mutilated fingers. As Pope Urban VIII remarked, "It would be shameful that a martyr of Christ be not allowed to drink the Blood of Christ."

Jogues had first arrived in New France in 1636, one of a company of Jesuits who undertook the perilous mission among the Indians. Like their confrères in India and China, these Jesuits sought, as much as possible, to eschew the European enclaves and to immerse themselves in the life of the people. Their mission was complicated not only by the difficulties of language, the harshness of the environment, and the Indians' understandable distrust of the European invaders. They also found that the Indians of the region — the Algonquins, Hurons, and Iroquois — were in a state of perpetual warfare among themselves. It was difficult to be immersed in this culture while remaining aloof from such deep-rooted animosities.

Of the three groups, the Jesuits found their most hospitable welcome among the Hurons. Not that many converts were found, but the Jesuits — or Blackrobes as they were called on account of their soutanes — were at least tolerated in the Hurons' villages and allowed to share their way of life. There was little preparation in seminary for the hardships to be endured: cold, starvation, hard labor, and illness. But despite the primitive conditions, the letters of the Jesuits recounted their deep respect for the Indians and for their innate spirituality. Rather than impose Western civilization as a prerequisite for evangelization, the Jesuits were determined to seek out and build on the already-present seeds of God's revelation within Indian culture and religion. There were other features of Indian culture more difficult to comprehend. Soon after his arrival among the Hurons, Jogues was witness to the brutal torture of several Iroquois prisoners. He was shaken by the experience, but remained firm in his determination, at all costs, to proclaim the gospel of love. In 1642 he was captured by a war party of Mohawks, a tribe within the Iroquois confederation. His party was subjected to excruciating tortures over a period of days; one of his companions was summarily killed after making the sign of the cross over an infant. Jogues was kept alive as a slave for many months, but finally escaped, with the help of Dutch merchants, and made his way back to France.

In 1644 he returned to Quebec, where he found the French forces engaged in an effort to negotiate a truce among the warring tribes. With his knowledge of Mohawk, Jogues agreed to travel as a French ambassador. Thus, he voluntarily returned to the village where he had been held captive. He was received respectfully. But he discovered, to his horror, that under secret terms of the agreement between the Iroquois and the French, the Indians had committed themselves only to refrain from violence against *Christians*. Such an agreement, Jogues believed, would not only fail to reduce the level of violence, but it would fatally compromise the Jesuits' mission. It would seem to the Indians that the Blackrobes' only concern was for the welfare of *their own.* He immediately set off for Montreal to protest this policy and to resign from any further diplomatic role. But as a sign of his commitment to return again *as a priest,* he left in the village a box containing his materials for Mass. The box was to be the cause of his martyrdom.

After his departure the village suffered a terrible crop failure, followed by a deadly epidemic. These misfortunes were attributed to evil spirits in the Blackrobe's box. Unaware of these developments, Jogues returned to the village some months later. As he neared the village, he was beset by Mohawk braves. Again he was put through the gauntlet. Knowing that he would not escape death this time, he prayed that his life might be offered for the salvation of his assailants.

Word of his death traveled slowly. Some time later the very Mohawk brave who had delivered Jogues's mortal blow came to the Jesuits, seeking refuge from the revenge of Christian Hurons. He provided details of the priest's death and also recalled the substance of his earlier Christian teaching. He asked to be baptized. For his Christian name he chose to be called Isaac Jogues.

See: Glenn D. Kittler, *Saint in the Wilderness: The Story of St. Isaac Jogues and the Jesuit Adventure in the New World* (Garden City, N.Y.: Doubleday, 1964); James T. Moore, *Indian and Jesuit: A Seventeenth-Century Encounter* (Chicago: Loyola University Press, 1982).

October 20

Jerzy Popieluszko
Priest and Martyr of Solidarity (1947–1984)

"At this time, when we need so much strength to regain and uphold our freedom, let us pray to God to fill us with the power of His Spirit, to reawaken the spirit of true solidarity in our hearts."

The end of the communist era in Eastern Europe began in June 1979 when John Paul II, the newly elected Polish pope, returned to his homeland for the first of three visits. As the communist authorities stood helplessly by, millions of Poles provided the pontiff with an ecstatic welcome. His message was ostensibly spiritual, but in officially atheistic Poland the spiritual inevitably carried the weight of social criticism. There was no escaping the import of the pope's message when he proclaimed, "Do not be afraid to insist on your rights. Refuse a life based on lies and double thinking. Do not be afraid to suffer with Christ." Within a year of his visit the militant Solidarity trade union movement was born.

At the time of the pope's visit Father Jerzy Popieluszko was living in Warsaw and working as a chaplain to the university medical students. Born in 1947 to a peasant family, he belonged to the generation that had grown up under communism. But while he shared with most Poles a disdain for the communist system, he had never before taken an active part in political discussions. His role in the Solidarity movement came about almost by accident. When the Gdansk ship workers went on strike in August 1980, steelworkers in Warsaw joined them in solidarity. They sent a request to the chancery for a priest to come and celebrate Mass at the factory. Father Jerzy, who happened to be on hand at the time, volunteered.

The Mass in front of the factory, where the workers had erected an enormous cross, was an extraordinary turning point in the young priest's life. At once he realized that the workers' struggle for justice and freedom was truly a spiritual struggle. It was entirely appropriate and vital that the church bear witness in the midst of this struggle. And so, with his bishop's consent, he became a chaplain to the striking workers.

In December 1981 the government declared martial law, and thousands of Solidarity members and their supporters were arrested. At this point Father Jerzy's pastoral duties expanded to include visiting the prisoners and organizing support for their families. At the same time, through his "patriotic sermons," which drew enormous crowds, he underlined the moral and spiritual dimensions of the Solidarity cause. It was a struggle for freedom and independence against foreign-imposed totalitarianism. But it was also a struggle to affirm the spiritual nature of the human person and to reject a culture built on hatred, lies, and fear.

Though the government claimed that this was no business for the church, Father Jerzy proclaimed, "It is not only the hierarchy but the millions of believers who in the broadest sense embody the church. So when people suffer and are persecuted the church also feels the pain. The mission of the church is to be with the people and to share in their joys and sorrows." As for his own vocation, he said, "To serve God is to seek a way to human hearts. To serve God is to speak about evil as a sickness which should be brought to light so that it can be cured. To serve God is to condemn evil in all its manifestations."

As his popularity grew, the government sought ways to silence him. He was subjected to countless forms of petty harassment. He was followed wherever he went. His Masses were often interrupted by provocateurs. In the most ominous attack, a bomb was hurled against his apartment. Still, he refused to be paralyzed by fear: "The only thing we should fear is the betrayal of Christ for a few silver pieces of meaningless peace."

In 1984 the pressures increased. Between January and June he was brought in for interrogation thirteen times. In July he was indicted on the charge of "abusing freedom of conscience and religion to the detriment of the Polish People's Republic." The charge provoked a storm of protest, and he was quickly offered an amnesty in honor of the fortieth anniversary of communist Poland. The workers themselves, fearful for his safety, requested that the cardinal send him abroad for study. But Father Jerzy would not consider any appearance of abandoning the workers in their time of need. He understood the risks but insisted that "if we must die it is better to meet death while defending a worthwhile cause than sitting back and letting an injustice take place. . . . The priest is called to bear witness to the truth, to suffer for the truth, and if need be to give up his life for it. We have many such examples in Christianity. From them we should draw conclusions for ourselves."

On the night of October 19, Father Jerzy was abducted by three men who stuffed him in the trunk of their car and sped off. His driver managed to escape and report the incident. Masses were said throughout the country for the priest's safe deliverance. But it was already too late. The government, facing a propaganda debacle, launched an immediate investigation and subsequently arrested four members of the security police who led them to the priest's body. They confessed that in the early morning hours of October 20, after savagely and repeatedly beating Father Jerzy, they had tied him up, weighted his body with stones, and tossed him, still alive, into a reservoir. Those who killed Father Jerzy had wished to still his voice. But it only reverberated the louder. It was clearly heard five years later when, in the first free elections in postwar Poland, the people peacefully threw out the communist regime and elected a Solidarity government.

See: Grazyna Sikorska, *Jerzy Popieluszko: A Martyr for the Truth* (Grand Rapids: Eerdmans, 1985).

October 21
St. Malchus
Monk (fourth century)

"Pass this story on to posterity, so that all may know that in the midst of swords, and deserts, and beasts, chastity is never a captive, and that a man consecrated to Christ may die, but can never be conquered."
—St. Jerome

St. Malchus was born in Nisibis (Syria), the only child of his prosperous parents. They wished him to marry and carry on the family line. But he was determined to become a monk. So one night he stole away and ran off to a community of hermits in the wilderness of Khalkis. Although he was content with the monastic life, he was disturbed, after some years, to receive news that his parents had died, leaving him a great inheritance. Despite the warnings of his abbot, he was drawn by an irresistible desire to return home to claim his property.

While traveling with a caravan his party was attacked by Bedouin marauders. They took Malchus and another young woman as slaves and carried them deep into the desert. There for some years Malchus was forced to endure harsh conditions while laboring in the service of his master. Strangely, he did not find the experience entirely disagreeable. While tending the flocks he was able to spend much of his time in prayer and reflection. Thus he maintained his monastic identity.

Eventually, however, his master wished to reward his service by giving him in marriage to the woman who had shared his abduction. The prospect filled him with dread. Not only would it violate his monastic vow of celibacy, but the woman still had a husband living. On the night of his forced wedding Malchus prepared to take his own life. At this point, however, the woman revealed herself to be a Christian who shared his desire for chastity. "Take me, therefore, as a spouse in chastity," she said, "and love the bond of the soul rather than that of the body. Let our masters believe you a husband; Christ will know the brother."

This conceit left everyone satisfied. But eventually Malchus began to pine for his old monastery. When he disclosed his feelings to his "wife" they formed a plan to escape. Hoarding enough food and drink to last them for three days, they made their escape in the dark of night. They managed to travel for three days across the open desert before their master and another servant, following their trail in the sand, caught up with them on camel-back. The terrified runaways hid themselves in the mouth of a cave, prepared at that moment to meet their deaths. Instead a lioness leapt from the cave and slew the two pursuers. Now with the help of the camels and fresh supplies Malchus and his companion were able to cross the rest of the desert and find their way to help.

Malchus returned to his monastery. His companion, finding that her husband had died, settled nearby among a community of Christian women. But the intimacy born of their common faith and adventures remained intact with the passage of years. It was in a village near Antioch in Syria that their biographer, *St. Jerome, encountered them. He described them as "another Zachary and Elizabeth" from the gospel. When he asked about them "and wondered just what was the bond between them — whether of wedlock, of blood, or of the spirit," their neighbors "answered promptly and unanimously that they were a holy pair, pleasing to God."

See: St. Jerome, "Life of Malchus," in Roy J. Deferrari, ed., *Early Christian Biographies,* Fathers of the Church 15 (New York: Fathers of the Church, 1952).

October 22
Maura O'Halloran
Christian Zen Monk (1955–1982)

*"Suddenly I understood that we must take care of things
just because they exist."*

In a Buddhist monastery in northern Japan there is a statue of a young Irish-American woman whose memory is revered by many pilgrims. How a Catholic woman came to be honored as a Buddhist saint is an interesting story of "interreligious dialogue." But it also says something about the convergent paths of holiness and their capacity to meet in a spirit of compassionate awareness.

Maura O'Halloran was born in Boston, the daughter of an Irish father and American mother. When she was four the family moved to Ireland, where she was educated in convent schools and later graduated from

Trinity College, Dublin. Her father died when she was fourteen, and she played a large role in the upbringing of her four younger siblings.

From a young age, Maura displayed a deep awareness of human suffering. After college she spent time working in soup kitchens and traveled widely in Latin America. Her concern for social justice was accompanied by a serious attraction to the spiritual life. After experimenting for some years with various methods of prayer and meditation, she decided to explore the wisdom of the East.

In 1979 she flew to Japan and applied for admission to a traditional Buddhist monastery in Tokyo. Many Catholics, and even Jesuit priests, have undergone training in Zen meditation in Japan, finding no inherent conflict between their Christian faith and the principles of Zen. But at the time of Maura's arrival there were few Western women who had been accepted into the very male world of a Zen monastery. Maura was admitted, and so she embarked on the rigorous training of a monk.

Her journals offer an unusual record of her experience, which included sustained periods of meditation, arduous manual labor, and an ascetic discipline of mind and body. Under the guidance of her Roshi (master), she struggled to solve her assigned *koans,* the famous Zen riddles designed to free the mind of dualistic illusions and lead the novice on the path to enlightenment. In the cold of winter she joined the other monks on an annual begging expedition in the North. With her shaved head and monk's robe, wearing only straw sandals in the snow and sleet, she would join the other monks as they passed through the streets, ringing a bell and holding out their bowls for alms and donations of food.

After six months of intensive training, Maura experienced an ecstatic breakthrough. While being interrogated by her Roshi she was suddenly overcome by tears and laughter. "It is enlightenment!" her Roshi cried. Afterward, when she went outside, she was overcome with a feeling of compassion for everything in existence.

This was not the end of her training. In the months that followed she concentrated more energy than ever on her meditation and her self-discipline. By the next year her Roshi made her an extraordinary offer. If she would agree to marry a fellow monk, he would entrust his temple to her. Torn between the desire to obey her Roshi and a conviction that this was not where she was intended to remain, she experienced a strange physical collapse. Her Roshi at this point accepted her plan to leave the monastery at the conclusion of her training. Some months later, Maura reflected on her vocation:

I'm twenty-six and I feel as If I've lived my life. Strange sensation, almost as if I'm close to death. Any desires, ambitions, hopes I may have had have either been fulfilled or spontaneously dissipated. I'm totally content. Of course I want to get deeper, see clearer, but even if I could only have this paltry, shallow awakening, I'd be quite satisfied.... So in a sense I feel I've died. For myself there is nothing else to strive after, nothing more to make my life worthwhile or to justify it. At twenty-six, a living corpse and such a life!... If I have another fifty or sixty years (who knows?) of time, I want to live it for other people. What else is there to do with it? ... So I must go deeper and deeper and work hard, no longer for me, but for everyone I can help.

As this reflection makes clear, Maura did not consider enlightenment something to be grasped for herself alone. Rather, she wished to empty herself to serve others in the way of compassion. This was Maura's wish. But it was not her karma. Instead, after leaving the monastery on her way back to Ireland, she was killed in a bus accident in Thailand on October 22, 1982. She was twenty-seven.

In a letter of condolence to her mother her Roshi wrote,

> She had achieved what took the Shakuson [Shakyamuni Buddha] eighty years in twenty-seven years. She was able to graduate Dogen's thousand-day training. Then she left this life immediately to start the salvation of the masses in the next life! Has anyone known such a courageously hard working Buddha as Maura? I cannot possibly express my astonishment.

Through a memoir published by her mother in a Catholic journal and the later publication of her journals, Maura's story has earned a devoted following among Christians as well as Buddhists. Her short road to holiness in a Zen monastery has been compared to the compressed career of *Therese of Lisieux, the French nun who set out as a child to become a saint. Both young women, having accomplished their spiritual business in this world, promptly departed. It is certain that Maura would have identified with the words of Therese, who said she hoped to spend her heaven doing good on earth.

See: Pure Heart, Enlightened Mind: The Zen Journals and Letters of Maura "Soshin" O'Halloran (Boston: Charles E. Tuttle, 1994); Ruth L. O'Halloran, "In Twenty-Seven Short Years," *Commonweal* (February 28, 1992).

October 23
St. Boethius
Philosopher (480–524)

"O God, whoever You are who joins all things in perfect harmony, look down upon this miserable earth! We men are no small part of Your great work, yet we wallow here in the stormy sea of fortune. Ruler of all things, calm the roiling waves and, as You rule the immense heavens, rule also the earth in stable concord."

Socrates said that the purpose of philosophy is to learn how to die. In *The Consolation of Philosophy* by Severinus Boethius, we are afforded some insight into the way Philosophy helped one Christian to meet his fate with grace and courage.

Boethius was born in 480 to one of the most prominent families of Rome. He was the son of a former consul of Rome, an office that he himself would later occupy, along with the even more prestigious post of

Master of the King's Offices. Aside from his public service, Boethius dedicated himself to the study of philosophy. An expert on the classics, he composed translations of Aristotle and Plato and wrote books on a wide range of topics, including logic, mathematics, and astronomy, as well as several volumes on Christian theology. It seemed as if Boethius was a man on whom fortune smiled. But all this would fall away when he dared to intercede on behalf of an innocent man accused of conspiring against the emperor. Boethius himself was arrested. He was accused not only of treason but of the impious study of philosophy and astronomy. He was stripped of his honor and possessions and thrown into prison for nine months before he was ultimately tortured and executed. It was during these months in prison that he composed his *Consolation.*

In this work he imagines a conversation with the female personification of Philosophy, who attempts to comfort her disciple in his present sufferings. When he asks Lady Philosophy what she is doing in prison, she answers, "How could I desert my child, and not share with you the burden of sorrow you carry, a burden caused by hatred of my name?" Philosophy counsels him to become detached from worldly cares and to focus his attention on the only supreme good, God, the Creator of all things. In such a mind his peace and equilibrium will not be determined by outward circumstances.

Many critics, observing the lack of any specific Christian reference in the *Consolation,* have wondered if Boethius still regarded himself as a Christian at the time of its writing. In commending a path to liberation from the turning wheel of fortune, Boethius's philosophy bears a strong resemblance to the Buddhist way of detachment. It seems clear, however, that Boethius, like earlier apologists, saw no contradiction between the eternal wisdom of pagan philosophers and the wisdom of Christ, the incarnate "Logos."

Though his death was not the product of his faith so much as a miscarriage of justice, the piety and courage with which Boethius endured his fate were so widely recognized by the church in Rome that he was quickly acclaimed as a saint and martyr. How much actual consolation Boethius derived from his reflections cannot be known. But his book went on to become one of the most widely read and influential works of the Middle Ages. It is a reflection of its power to speak to those *in extremis,* even under vastly different circumstances, that the book was translated in England in 1650. It was used to encourage Catholics struggling to hold up under persecution and the threat of death.

See: Boethius, *The Consolation of Philosophy,* trans. Richard Green (Indianapolis: Bobbs-Merrill, 1962).

Fritz Eichenberg
Quaker Artist (1901–1990)

"It is my hope that in a small way I have been able to contribute to peace through compassion and also to the recognition, as George Fox has said . . . 'That there is that of God in everyone,' a conception of the sanctity of human life which precludes all wars and violence."

At the time of his death at the age of eighty-nine Fritz Eichenberg was widely acknowledged as one of the modern masters of the wood engraving. He was famous for his illustrations of literary classics by *Dostoevsky, *Tolstoy, and the Bronte sisters, and his work was featured in galleries and museums around the world. But through his association with *Dorothy Day and the *Catholic Worker*, he achieved recognition among a different audience. His wood engravings could be found printed on fading newsprint, taped to the walls of a coal miner's home in West Virginia or a farmworker's shack in California. In over a hundred works, some reprinted so often as to assume the status of Catholic Worker icons, he was able to summarize in simple images the moral and spiritual perspective which the editors otherwise strove to communicate in words and deeds.

Eichenberg was born in Cologne on October 24, 1901. He underwent formal training as an artist, choosing wood engraving as his special medium. But his heroes were artists like *Kollwitz, Daumier, and Goya, who had put their talents at the service of their moral and social convictions. With the rise of Hitler, Eichenberg, who came from an assimilated Jewish background, decided that he had no future in Germany. In 1933 he managed to get his family out of the country and to emigrate to the United States. In 1938 the tragic death of his wife prompted an emotional breakdown. Afterward he found solace in his conversion to Quakerism. In the Society of Friends he was attracted by the spirit of simplicity and stillness, the quest for the Peaceable Kingdom, and the conviction, in the words of *George Fox, "that there is that of God in everyone."

A major event in his life occurred in 1949 when Eichenberg was introduced to Dorothy Day, editor of the pacifist *Catholic Worker* newspaper. By this time Eichenberg had achieved some renown for his illustrations of the Russian classics, a passion for which he shared with Day. There was an instantaneous communion of spirits between the two, and Eichenberg gladly responded to Day's invitation to contribute his art to her paper. Day felt strongly that images could touch people emotionally and communicate the Catholic Worker spirit to people who, perhaps, could not read the articles. For his part, Eichenberg felt that in this Catholic newspaper, with its emphasis on the works of mercy and the witness for peace, he had found the expression of his own spiritual and moral convictions.

Eichenberg's first contributions were depictions of the saints. Whether it was a *Benedict, a *John of the Cross, or his personal favorite, *St. Francis of Assisi, Eichenberg's saints were men and women of flesh and blood, fully engaged in the struggle to follow Christ in their own time, challenging his viewers to do the same in their own circumstances. Soon canonical saints were joined by an ecumenical parade of other holy witnesses: *Tolstoy, *Erasmus, and *Mahatma Gandhi, as well as modern-day heroes like *Thomas Merton, *Cesar Chavez, and *Lanza del Vasto.

His most poignant and powerful images, however, were drawn from the life of Christ. In Nativity scenes set in a war zone or an urban slum, in his Black Crucifixion — drawn during the height of the civil rights struggle — and in a haunting Pietà, he evoked not only Jesus' humanity but his familiarity with the common world of the working poor, the refugee, the outcast, the prisoner. Two of his most successful images directly connected the life of Christ to the world of the Catholic Worker. "Christ of the Breadlines" (1953) shows a ragged line of men and women waiting their turn for a handout of bread — an image literally inspired by the breadline that daily formed outside the Catholic Worker house of hospitality. In the midst of the line, however, is the unmistakable silhouette of Christ, awaiting his turn among the hungry. Similarly, in "Christ of the Homeless" (1982), two homeless figures huddle in the cold of night with a third, Jesus, crouched in between. Thus, Eichenberg illustrated one of the central inspirations of the Catholic Worker and its commitment to the works of mercy: that Christ comes to us disguised in the need of our neighbor, so that what we do for the poor we do directly for him.

Eichenberg's art was a faithful reflection of his own spirit and the ideals by which he hoped to live. Often he expressed his regret that he did not have the temperament to live in a Catholic Worker house of hospitality or, like the young peacemakers he admired, to go to jail in obedience to conscience. Yet he struggled through his work to communicate a compassionate vision of the world and an affirmation of the sanctity of life that he dared to hope might affect his viewers for the better. In this he identified with the words of Dostoevsky, which Dorothy Day often repeated: "The world will be saved by beauty."

Fritz Eichenberg died of Parkinson's disease on November 30, 1990.

See: Fritz Eichenberg: Works of Mercy, ed. Robert Ellsberg (Maryknoll, N.Y.: Orbis, 1993).

October 25

St. Edmund Campion
Jesuit Priest and Martyr (1540–1581)

"In condemning us you condemn all your own ancestors, all the ancient bishops and kings, all that was once the glory of England.... God lives. Posterity will live. Their judgment is not so liable to corruption as that of those who now sentence us to death."

From the time he arrived at Oxford at the age of fifteen, Edmund Campion showed signs of extraordinary promise. A brilliant scholar and orator, within two years he was appointed a junior fellow at St. John's College, where he attracted his own circle of devoted pupils. In 1569 he was ordained a deacon in the Anglican church, another step up the ladder of social advancement. But his ambition faced a formidable obstacle. He found himself increasingly gripped by the conviction that he should become a Catholic. In Elizabethan England such a move would surely entail professional ruin if not also the risk of life itself. In 1571, his doubts resolved, he abandoned his home and friends, crossed the Channel for the English College at Douai, and there was formally reconciled with the Roman Catholic church.

Two years later he moved to Rome and entered the Society of Jesus. He was ordained in 1578. There being no English province of the Jesuits at that time Campion was assigned to the Czech province. By the next year, however, he was one of the first group assigned the perilous mission of returning to England. He landed in Dover in 1580. After establishing contact with the renegade Catholic community, he set about his underground ministry.

Through its spies the government was soon aware of his arrival. Nevertheless, he managed successfully to elude capture through the use of clever disguises and with the help of ingenious hiding places in the homes of great recusant families. All the same, in anticipation of his eventual arrest, Campion composed a short address to the Royal Privy Council, later known as "Campion's Brag." In case his captors should deny him an opportunity to defend himself or should circulate lies about his true intentions, he declared in advance his eagerness to debate doctrine with any appointed team of Anglican divines. His mission was simply "of free cost to preach the Gospel, to minister the Sacraments, to instruct the simple, to reforme sinners, to confute errors — in brief, to crie alarme spiritual against foul vice and proud ignorance, wherewith many of my dear Countrymen are abused." He concluded with an eloquent affirmation of the Jesuit cause:

> Be it known to you that we have made a league — all the Jesuits in the world... — cheerfully to carry the cross you shall lay upon us, and never to despair your recovery, while we have a man left to enjoy your Tyburn, or to be racked with your torments, or consumed with your prisons. The expense is reckoned, the enterprise is begun; it is of God, it cannot be withstood. So the faith was planted: so it must be restored.

After his friends saw to the publication of this document, Campion became England's most famous — and most wanted — Catholic. With the help of bribes and informers, his arrest was not long delayed.

Campion was confined in the Tower of London. For the first four days his cell was the terrible "Little Ease," so called because its dimensions made it impossible either to stand erect or to lie down. Straight upon this ordeal he was brought before Queen Elizabeth herself. He had first met her at Oxford, under happier circumstances, when he had been elected by the university to make a speech in her honor. Now, on his knees, he acknowledged her temporal authority, but would not recognize her authority in matters of religion. Still, she offered him a full pardon if he would return to the Protestant ministry. When he refused this offer he was returned to the Tower.

Campion was charged along with a number of others with having come to organize a seditious rebellion against England. There was some semblance of a trial, in which Campion defended himself and his companions. Though he was fresh from torture on the rack and unable to stand or lift his arms, he brilliantly refuted the false testimony presented in evidence and showed effectively that the only crime uniting the defendants was their Catholic faith. Nevertheless, they were all found guilty.

On December 1, 1581, Campion was executed at the gallows at Tyburn. Among the witnesses was one Henry Walpole, a student from Cambridge. As Campion was being drawn and quartered — part of the ghoulish ritual of execution — some of his blood apparently splashed on Walpole's coat. This had such a grave impact on the young man that his life was forever changed. He too crossed the Channel, became a Jesuit, and returned to England to face the identical fate as the martyr Edmund Campion. They were both canonized in 1970 by Pope Paul VI. Their feast is celebrated on October 25 among the "Forty Martyrs of England and Wales."

See: Evelyn Waugh, *Edmund Campion* (New York: Sheed & Ward, 1935).

October 26

Noah

A Righteous Man

"Noah was a righteous man, blameless in his generation;
Noah walked with God." —Genesis 6:9

The story of Noah and his ark is sufficiently familiar as to require no rehearsal. The charming spectacle of the animals proceeding two by two is one of the most beloved images from Scripture. It nearly overshadows the grislier aspect of the story: God's determination, on account of human wickedness, to "make an end of all flesh" on the earth.

The story of Noah and the flood has offered a persistent field of battle between those committed to fundamentalist interpretations of Scripture and those who believe the Bible's message is often communicated through fiction and myth. An inordinate amount of energy has been spent on such debates as whether or not a great flood ever occurred, whether Noah himself ever existed, and to what extent his story is indebted to other creation myths of the Ancient Near East. Our interest lies elsewhere.

Among other things, Noah signifies the importance of the holy remnant. One does not "walk with God" for oneself alone. The call to righteousness carries with it a responsibility for the entire globe and all its inhabitants. Thus, Noah represents an ethic and spirituality concerned with the preservation of the earth and the survival of endangered species and cultures; he might well serve as a patron of ecological stewardship.

Through Noah's faithfulness God makes a universal and unconditional covenant with every living creature: "Never again shall all flesh be cut off by the waters of a flood, and never again shall there be a flood to destroy the earth again." God's covenant with Noah extends to his descendants "and with every living creature that is with you, the birds, the cattle, and every beast of the earth with you." This is a universal covenant that precedes the specific covenant with Abraham, Moses, and the children of Israel. Its sign is the rainbow.

But the fact that God has vowed never again to destroy the earth by means of a flood offers no grounds for complacency. The earth and all flesh are now, as never before, threatened by human wickedness, greed, and carelessness. The challenge for Noah's descendants is not "survivalism" but defense of our common planet and its delicate ecology. For the earth itself, as we now know, is a fragile ark. If it becomes uninhabitable there will be no other lifeboats.

October 27

Desiderius Erasmus
Christian Humanist (1466–1536)

"When faith came to be in writings rather than in hearts . . . contention grew hot and love grew cold. . . . That which is forced cannot be sincere, and that which is not voluntary cannot please Christ."

Desiderius Erasmus was the foremost representative of the ideals of Christian humanism. As a priest and scholar, his greatest wish was to see the church restored to the simplicity and holiness of the Gospels. He prized the values of charity, tolerance, and moderation and sought to conduct every controversy in such a way as never to lose a friend. But he lived in a time when such values were in short supply, and his dream of a reformation without violence or schism proved impossible to realize.

Erasmus was born in Rotterdam, Holland, on October 27, 1466. The illegitimate son of a priest, he was raised under the care of the Brethren of the Common Life (see *Geert Groote). In 1487 he entered the Augustinian monastery at Steyn, though it seems he had no special attraction to monastic life. After five years he was ordained a priest and later received a dispensation to leave the confines of his monastery. He never returned. Instead, he studied theology in Paris and afterward embarked on a peripatetic career as a scholar and author, living in many European countries. A self-described "citizen of the world," he spurned national ties, preferring to identify himself with the universal guild of scholars and the universal Christian church.

In the spirit of Renaissance humanism, Erasmus believed strongly in the power of human reason and dialogue to resolve conflicting interests. He valued learning, especially the wisdom of classical sources, and he strongly opposed the spirit of superstition, fanaticism, and obscurantism. One of the foremost masters of classical Greek and Latin, he published critical editions of the church fathers, including *Jerome, *Origen, and

*Augustine. But his most significant contribution was a new Greek edition of the New Testament, accompanied by his own translation and commentary in Latin.

Erasmus befriended many of the leading intellectuals and reformers of his day. During a stay in England he found a particular soul-mate in *Thomas More, to whom he later dedicated his masterpiece, *Praise of Folly* (1511). In this and other satirical works, Erasmus chose the weapon of wit to confront the laxity, hypocrisy, and corruptions that he beheld in the church of his day.

Aside from his treatment of superstitious monks, money-hungry prelates, and nit-picking theologians, Erasmus also trained his critical eye on social injustices. A passionate defender of peace, he entitled one essay, "War Is Sweet to Those Who Have Not Tried It." He excoriated theologians who tried to justify war on the ground that Christ said, "Let him who has no sword sell his mantle and buy one." "As if Christ, who taught nothing but patience and meekness, meant the sword used by bandits and murderers rather than the sword of the Spirit. Our exegete thinks that Christ equipped the apostles with lances, crossbows, slings, and muskets."

Christians, he believed, had greater need of the spirit of the Gospels and should put less emphasis on laws, prohibitions, and dogmas. The latter fed intolerance, vanity, and sterile knowledge, while Christ had come to teach humility, charity, and the folly of the cross. Above all, Erasmus could not abide the effort to reconcile violence with the spirit of Christ. "How can you say *Our* Father if you plunge steel into the guts of your brother? Christ compared himself to a hen: Christians behave like hawks. Christ was a shepherd of sheep: Christians tear each other like wolves." Little did he then know that the battle had scarcely begun.

In 1515 a young Augustinian monk named Martin Luther posted a notice of "Ninety-Five Theses against Indulgences." Few could guess that this was to be the opening salvo in a campaign leading to the wholesale rupture of Christendom. Erasmus studied the manifesto with sympathetic interest and sent a copy to his friend More. It contained many points he had made himself. Indeed, it was commonly said that "Luther hatched the egg that Erasmus laid."

Erasmus defended Luther against the charge of heresy, a term he believed was all too readily invoked by partisans on either side. In any case, he felt that the spirit of dialogue and Christian charity should be the first recourse in entering controversy: "Why do we prefer to conquer than to cure?" As the battle intensified, Erasmus continued to affirm the truth and justice in many of the Reformers' complaints. This put him in a difficult spot. Why, the Lutherans asked, did he then remain attached to the church? Church authorities, meanwhile, challenged him to declare himself clearly. If he was an orthodox Catholic, then he must prove it by condemning Luther.

Erasmus tried to find a neutral spot above the fray, hoping that the church could be peacefully reformed from within. But his nature recoiled from the idea that theological "obscurities" were any reason to divide the Body of Christ. He did engage in a protracted polemical exchange with

Luther over the question of freedom of the will. This did not satisfy his Catholic critics, who felt he conceded all too much to Luther's doctrine of salvation by grace. For his part Luther angrily concluded that Erasmus was a hypocrite and a coward. Erasmus retorted, "I would be glad to be a martyr for Christ, but I cannot be a martyr for Luther."

Sadly Erasmus watched his longed-for goal of Christian renewal degenerating into unprecedented violence and factionalism. The church was wonderful at condemning heresy but less effective at promoting charity. The Reformers for their part were quick to smash statues and stained-glass windows, but where was the much-vaunted increase in evangelical virtue? "The world is full of rage, hate, and wars. What will the end be if we employ only bulls and the stake? It is no great feat to burn a little man. It is a great achievement to persuade him." Both sides had their martyrs. Among them he mourned his English friend Thomas More, beheaded by Henry VIII. "By his death I feel myself to be dead," he remarked on hearing the news. What he had hailed as the dawn of a golden age had become the "very worst century" since the days of Jesus Christ.

His last years were spent in the Protestant city of Basle. He suffered from kidney stones and other ailments. His famous wit was silent. He prayed for a quick death. The end came on July 12, 1536. His last words were, "O Jesus have mercy."

See: Erasmus, *Praise of Folly,* trans. Betty Radice (New York: Penguin, 1971); Roland H. Bainton, *Erasmus of Christendom* (New York: Charles Scribner's Sons, 1969).

October 28

St. Jude
Apostle (first century)

"To those who are called, beloved in God the Father and kept for Jesus Christ: May mercy, peace, and love be multiplied in you."

Of all the original twelve apostles St. Jude is perhaps the most commonly invoked in prayer. This is an ironic compensation for his obscurity in the Gospels. Aside from the citation of his name in listings of the Twelve, St. Jude is quoted only once. This occurs in the Gospel of John (14:22) when he interrupts a disquisition by Jesus at the Last Supper to ask, "Lord, how is it that you will manifest yourself to us, and not to the world?" This question evokes the answer of Jesus: "If a man loves me, he will keep my word, and my Father will love him, and we will come to him and make our home with him. He who does not love me does not keep my words; and the word which you hear is not mine but the Father's who sent me."

This Jude is also the supposed author of the shortest book of the New Testament, "The Letter of Jude," which in its twenty-five verses warns against the dangers of false teachers who divide the church and lead many astray. While a number of the epistles are thought to be pseudony-mous, it is very possible that this letter was indeed written by Jude. One of the arguments in favor of its authenticity is the unlikelihood that any pseudonymous author would have attributed the letter to such an obscure figure.

Apart from this, St. Jude enjoys widespread fame as the "patron of hopeless causes." Perhaps this is due to the similarity of his name to that of the traitor Judas Iscariot. For a long time this evidently inhibited sup-plicants from invoking the name of St. Jude. It might be supposed that this had the effect of storing up a good deal of efficacious power, now available for even the most desperate cases.

According to legend, St. Jude was martyred in Persia.

October 29

Clarence Jordan
Founder of Koinonia Farm (1912–1969)

"Jesus has been so zealously worshiped, his deity so vehemently affirmed, his halo so brightly illumined, and his cross so beautifully polished that in the minds of many he no longer exists as a man.... By thus glorifying him we more effectively rid ourselves of him than did those who tried to do so by crudely crucifying him."

Clarence Jordan was born in rural Georgia and studied agriculture at the University of Georgia before attending Southern Baptist Theological Sem-inary in Louisville. Though he earned ministerial credentials as well as a doctorate in New Testament studies, he chose, instead of a career in min-istry or academe, to pursue the less common vocation of discipleship to Jesus Christ.

In 1942, with his wife, Florence, and a couple of other families, he founded Koinonia Farm, an experiment in communal Christian living, near Americus, Georgia. Koinonia was the Greek word used in the book of Acts to describe the early church community in which resources were shared in an atmosphere of reconciliation and partnership. Jordan be-lieved that the most vital need for reconciliation in the South was between whites and blacks. It was this conviction that drove a wedge between Koinonia and its neighbors. In the South of that time, even talk of recon-ciliation between the races was dangerously radical. Jordan and his family were expelled from the local Baptist church. However, the community's troubles really began in the mid-1950s after the Supreme Court's ruling on school desegregation inflamed the passions of white segregationists. Koinonia was subjected to a campaign of violent persecution — shootings, bombings, and vandalism. An economic boycott of the community was so vigorously enforced that they managed to hold on only by developing a mail-order business in pecans.

In the 1960s Clarence began a new project, a vernacular translation of the New Testament that he called his "Cotton Patch version." The Cotton Patch Gospels emphasized the humanity of Jesus, setting him and his companions "along the dusty rows of cotton, corn, and peanuts" in rural Georgia. As his Gospel of *Matthew began, "When Jesus was born in Gainesville, Georgia, during the time that Herod was governor, some scholars from the Orient came to Atlanta and inquired, 'Where is the one who was born to be governor of Georgia?'"

Jordan believed that the problem with Christianity today stemmed from the fact that most Christians preferred to picture Jesus enthroned in heaven or safely confined to distant "Bible times." Thus they missed the radical and disturbing challenge of the Incarnation. It was important to realize that "the resurrection places Jesus on this side of the grave, here and now, in the midst of life. The Good News of the resurrection is not that we shall die and go home with him but that he is risen and comes home with us, bringing all his hungry, naked, thirsty, sick, prisoner brothers with him."

An inspired preacher, Jordan liked to read and translate freely from his well-worn Greek New Testament. Customarily dressed in overalls, his hands worn and soiled from work in the fields, Jordan had a power to inspire or disturb that was rooted in his radical witness to the Incarnation and his simple conviction that the values of God's reign were meant to be lived out here and now.

After one sermon before a southern congregation, an elderly woman approached Clarence and said, "I want you to know that my grandfather fought in the Civil War, and I'll never believe a word you say." Clarence returned her steely glare with a gracious smile and replied, "Ma'am, your choice seems quite clear. It is whether you will follow your granddaddy or Jesus Christ."

The chronicles of Jordan's famous wit constitute a veritable book of parables. One time a minister was giving Jordan a tour of his church, showing off with pride the church's imported pews and other costly accouterments. Outside the church the minister pointed to a huge cross on top of the steeple. "That cross alone cost us ten thousand dollars," he boasted. "You got cheated," Jordan answered. "Times were when Christians could get them for free."

Clarence Jordan died in his writing shack on October 29, 1969, at the age of fifty-seven. On his desk before him was the unfinished Cotton Patch version of the Gospel of *John.

See: Dallas Lee, *The Cotton Patch Evidence: The Story of Clarence Jordan and the Koinonia Farm Experiment* (New York: Harper & Row, 1971); Joyce Hollyday et al., "The Legacy of Clarence Jordan," *Sojourners* (December 1979).

Fyodor Dostoevsky
Russian Novelist (1821–1881)

"The world will be saved by beauty."

Few writers have matched Dostoevsky's appreciation for the pathos and misery of human existence. Drawing on his own sufferings, he depicted the depths of evil and psychological anguish with vivid, if not morbid, realism. At the same time, drawing also on his own deep, if anguished, faith, Dostoevsky wrote about the meaning of grace, conversion, and the possibility of salvation. Indeed, it is the dialectic between sin and salvation that provides the theme of many of his greatest novels.

Dostoevsky was born in Moscow on October 30, 1821. At the age of sixteen he was enrolled in the school of military engineering in St. Petersburg. It was an uncongenial environment from which his principal escape came in reading novels. After graduation he decided to pursue a literary career. In 1846 he published his first story, *Poor People,* which reflected his lifelong concern for the sufferings of common people. It was an immediate success.

Nevertheless, in 1849 Dostoevsky's literary promise was nearly extinguished when he was arrested and charged with participation in an underground socialist study circle. After some period in prison he was condemned to death. He was actually tied to a post and came within minutes of meeting the firing squad when the execution was halted by an imperial reprieve. Psychologically, it was a shattering experience that left a permanent mark on his soul. His sentence was reduced to four years of hard labor in a Siberian prison camp. He passed the time among common criminals, an experience that proved invaluable to his later work as a writer. But this period was also the forge of his spiritual convictions. His only book in prison was a copy of the New Testament. From long contemplation on this text he imbibed such themes as the common human solidarity in the sin of the world, the redemptive meaning of suffering, and the power of Christ's love.

Upon his release from prison Dostoevsky still had to serve several years in a regiment on the Siberian border. There he married a young widow whom he treated disdainfully, only to be racked by guilt after her premature death. He suffered from epileptic seizures. He was a compulsive gambler, and his addiction contributed to his lifelong penury. Nevertheless, in the midst of these circumstances he managed to write with a feverish intensity, producing in a short period such novels as *Crime and Punishment, The Idiot,* and *The Possessed.* In 1867 he married his stenographer, Anna Snitkina, whose love and support provided some balance to his overwrought sensibility. They had four children, of whom two died.

All of Dostoesvky's great novels were marked by a powerful understanding of human psychology and an obsession with certain great spiritual themes. Among these were the nature of evil, the condition of humanity in rebellion against God, and the meaning of salvation. In *Crime and Punishment* his protagonist, Raskolnikov, murders an old pawnbroker simply to test his theory that for superior human beings — as he deems himself to be — the ordinary moral code does not apply. Ultimately he cannot run from his guilt. He confesses his crime and must serve his sentence in Siberia. He is followed into exile by a saintly prostitute in whose love and faith reside the possibility of his final redemption.

In his last and greatest work, *The Brothers Karamazov*, Dostoesvky gave particular vent to his religious concerns. The character Ivan Karamazov espouses an intellectually inclined form of nihilism. He rejects the existence of God because of the suffering of the innocent. At the same time he holds that "if God does not exist everything is permissible" (only to be appalled when someone else enacts the logic of this creed). His brother Alyosha, on the other hand, is a novice at the local monastery, a disciple of the saintly Father Zossima, whose story and discourses offer a distillation of the gospel according to Dostoevsky.

Zossima's great theme is the centrality of love, a message that many of his penitents and some of his own monks consider all too simple. Among those seeking his spiritual counsel is a proud rich woman. Zossima counsels her that the solution to her spiritual problems is "active love." "Strive to love your neighbors actively and indefatigably. And the nearer you come to achieving this love, the more convinced you will become of the existence of God and the immortality of your soul." The woman responds that she already *does* love humanity, so much so that she sometimes dreams of giving up everything to become a hospital nurse, a dream she would surely fulfil if it weren't for the abhorrent prospect of having to deal with human *ingratitude*. In a memorable phrase, Zossima responds that "love in action is a harsh and dreadful thing compared to love in dreams."

Despite his youthful dalliance with socialism, Dostoevsky became deeply suspicious of revolutionary politics. In *The Possessed* he displayed with uncanny prescience the totalitarian tendencies that may cloud the best humanitarian impulses. He anticipated the oppressive effect of any effort to achieve a utopia apart from God. For Dostoevsky authentic community and human fellowship could be founded only on a living faith in Christ.

After years of ill health Dostoevsky died of a hemorrhage on January 28, 1881, at the age of sixty.

Despite his conservative views, Dostoevsky's work remained in the canon of Soviet literature throughout the communist era. Many credited his novels with preserving a space for spirituality in the midst of the official culture of atheism. He had anticipated that the effort to create heaven on earth, at the expense of love, would end by creating hell. Nevertheless, his prophecy for Russia was ultimately hopeful: "God will save Russia as he has saved her many times. Salvation will come from the people, from their faith and their weakness."

See: Hutterian Brethren, eds., *The Gospel in Dostoyevsky* (Farmington, Pa.: Plough Publishing House, 1988); A. Boyce Gibson, *The Religion of Dostoevsky* (Philadelphia: Westminster, 1973).

St. Alphonsus Rodriguez
Jesuit Lay Brother and Porter (1533–1617)

"To try to know oneself is the foundation of everything. He who knows himself despises himself, while he who does not know himself is puffed up."

St. Alphonsus is proof of Milton's line, "They also serve who only stand and wait." For forty years Alphonsus served as a porter at the Jesuit College in Majorca. He embraced this humble job as seriously as any mission assignment, determined to welcome each caller as if he were Christ himself. So deeply did the porter's faith and love shine through his daily occupation that many of the students who passed through his doorway ended up applying for his spiritual direction. These included the famous *St. Peter Claver, later the apostle to the slaves in Cartagena, who regarded Alphonsus as his spiritual mentor.

Most of the students and professors at the college knew little of Alphonsus's background. Although he was always prepared to talk about Christ and his Holy Mother, he was reluctant to speak of himself and the sad story that preceded his religious vocation. He had been the son of a prosperous wool merchant in Segovia, Spain. He had studied at a nearby Jesuit college, but had been forced to break off his studies in 1545 when his father died. Although he was little more than a boy, his mother had called him home to take up the family business. About 1560 he married a devout young woman, María Suárez, who bore him two children. But soon there came a series of terrible tragedies, beginning with the death of his wife in childbirth, followed by the death of both his children, his mother, and the failure of his business — all within the space of a few short years.

Shattered by these misfortunes, Alphonsus chose to devote the rest of his life to God. He wished to enter the Jesuits, but his application was denied. Not only was he nearly forty, but he had almost no education. So importunate was he, however, that he was eventually admitted as a lay brother in 1571. He was sent to Majorca and given the job as hall porter of the Jesuit College. He made his final vows in the Society in 1585.

No great events marked the rest of his life. Alphonsus spent forty years at his post and left no special writings or distinctive teachings — just the impact of his personality on the countless people he met. He had responded to tragedy by opening his broken heart to God. Henceforth he encountered God in each person who passed through his open door. He performed his tasks with such infinite love that the act of opening the door became a sacramental gesture.

Alphonsus died on October 31, 1617, at the age of eighty-four. His funeral was attended by the Spanish viceroy and the local nobility, as well as by crowds of the poor and sick to whom his holiness and his reputation for miracles were well known. He was canonized in 1888.

❧ NOVEMBER ❧

November 1

All Saints

"Around your throne the saints, our brothers and sisters,
sing your praise forever.
Their glory fills us with joy,
and their communion with us in your church
gives us inspiration and strength
as we hasten on our pilgrimage of faith, eager to meet them.
With their great company and all the angels
we praise your glory as we cry out with one voice:
'Holy, holy, holy...'"
— Preface for the feast of All Saints

Since the early centuries of the church the liturgical calendar has reserved one day to honor, collectively, all the saints, both those officially recognized and those known only to God. Thus we are reminded that the true company of saints is far more numerous than the list of those who have been formally canonized. There are many anonymous saints who nevertheless form part of the great "cloud of witnesses," surrounding us with their faith and courage and so participating in the communion between the living and the dead.

This collective feast, All Saints, is also an occasion to acknowledge the varieties of holiness. Though they share a certain family resemblance, the saints are not formed in any particular mold. Some are renowned for contemplation and others for action; some played a public role while others spent their lives in quiet obscurity. Some demonstrated the vitality of ancient traditions while others were pioneers, charting new possibilities in the spiritual life. Some received recognition and honor within their lifetimes, while others were scorned or even persecuted.

The feast of All Saints does not honor a company of "immortals," far removed from the realm of ordinary human existence. The saints were not "super" human beings but those who realized the vocation for which all human beings were created and to which we are ultimately called. No one is called to be another *St. Francis or *St. Teresa. But there is a path to holiness that lies within our individual circumstances, that engages our own talents and temperaments, that contends with our own strengths and weaknesses, that responds to the needs of our own neighbors and our particular moment in history. The feast of All Saints strengthens and encourages us to create that path by walking it.

See: Karl Rahner, "All Saints," in *Theological Investigations* 8 (New York: Seabury, 1977).

November 2
Léon Bloy
Pilgrim of the Absolute (1846–1917)

"There is only one sorrow—not to be a saint."

The novelist Léon Bloy was more than simply a man of letters. To his friends he was a prophet, a "pilgrim of the absolute," a man on fire with zeal for the justice and love of God. To his critics he was a man blinded from staring too long at the sun. He was in any case one of those who helped stimulate the extraordinary revival of French Catholic literature in the early twentieth century.

Bloy, who had little formal education, spent most of his youth drifting aimlessly from job to job. His relations with the church reflected a similar inconstancy, his flirtations with piety alternating with crude rebellion. The turning point in his life came with his attraction to an impoverished prostitute, Veronique. Convinced that she possessed a spark of greatness Bloy dedicated himself to her "rescue." She was soon caught up in a religious conversion so dramatic that it pulled Bloy himself along in its wake. Sadly, her religious exaltation eventually gave way to madness, and the poor woman spent the rest of her life in an asylum. Bloy was left on the edge of despair, but with his faith intact, along with a new and unshakable sense of his vocation. He would be a writer.

Bloy later married and had four children. But his life remained marked with affliction. He managed to publish dozens of books, but few of them ever sold more than a thousand copies. As a result he and his family were consigned to atrocious poverty. Many winters were spent close to literal starvation, with his wife burning books and furniture to provide a little heat. Two of his children died in infancy from the effects of their deprivation.

Arguably, there were alternatives to such misery. But Bloy seemed to feel, with a kind of religious certainty, that he was meant to devote himself to his literary witness and to trust himself entirely to the providence of God. At the same time he felt it was his vocation to identify with those who had nothing and so to bear witness to the beatitude of poverty: "One does not enter into paradise tomorrow, nor in ten years; one enters it today, when one is poor and crucified." The mystical dignity of the poor as ambassadors of God was one of the principal themes of his novels. Another was the spiritual value of suffering: "In his poor heart man has places which do not yet exist and suffering enters in order to bring them to life." Elsewhere he wrote, "Suffering...is that holy veil imprinted with the bleeding Face of our gentle crucified Savior....A heart without affliction is like a world without revelation; it sees God only in the faint gleam of twilight. Our hearts are filled with angels when they are full of afflictions."

The other side of Bloy's pathos was a capacity for holy rage over the materialism and injustice of modern society. He loathed the bourgeois spirit — the love of success and comfort and the idolatry of money. When he saw these values accepted within the church he responded with prophetic wrath. He recalled that Jesus himself had paired his "Blessed are you poor" with "Woe to you rich!" With scathing invective he calumniated against those who dined on the blood of the poor. For the sins of the world and the failings of Christians he prophesied a coming cataclysm. As early as 1893 he wrote, "Pity cannot extinguish my anger, for my anger is the daughter of infinite foreboding. I am devoured by the need for justice as though by a dragon famished since the days of the Deluge. My anger is the effervescence of my pity."

Among other evils of the day he devoted considerable attention to the rise of Christian anti-Semitism. Like few of his Catholic contemporaries, Bloy had a deep veneration for the Jewish roots of the church. Among all his books he particularly favored one called *Salvation from the Jews*. There he wrote, "Anti-Semitism is the most horrible blow which Our Lord has received in His Passion that continues forever; it is the most bloody and the most unpardonable, because He receives it *upon the face of His Mother* and from the hands of Christians."

Bloy received little recognition from the church. Within the literary world he tended to be dismissed as a Catholic fanatic. Yet his works attracted a certain number of devoted readers, many of whom became his friends. Among these were a young couple, *Jacques and *Raïssa Maritain. They were inspired by his writings and his friendship to enter the Catholic church. Bloy served as their godfather, a privilege he prized before any other honor. That the Maritains had been led to Christ through his writings, he believed, signified a confirmation from the Holy Spirit that his vocation was true.

With the coming of World War I Bloy fell into increasing melancholy. For many who had placed their faith in progress the war brought a shattering disillusion. But for Bloy, who had never entertained such false faith, the horrors of the war were only a forewarning of even more terrible and apocalyptic suffering to come. At the time Raïssa Maritain wondered whether he was not like the prophet Jonah, so unbalanced by righteous anger as to despair of God's excessive mercy. In later years, however, she could only marvel at the perspicacity of his warning.

But if Bloy was hard on the world he was no kinder to himself. "The worst evil is not to commit crimes," he wrote, "but to have failed to do the good one might have done." Constantly at prayer he fell to tears at the thought of his failings. Toward the end of his life he wrote a friend,

> God has given me the sense, the need — I don't know how to put
> it — the instinct for the Absolute as he gave the hedgehog its prickles

and the elephant its trunk. It is an extremely rare gift of which I have been aware from my childhood, a more dangerous faculty and more pregnant with suffering than genius even. For it involves an insatiable and ravenous hunger for what the earth does not contain and its effect upon its possessor is an unbounded loneliness. I might have become a saint and a worker of miracles. I became a man of letters!

He died on November 3, 1917.

See: Léon Bloy, *Pilgrim of the Absolute,* ed. Raïssa Maritain (New York: Pantheon, 1947); Raïssa Maritain, *We Have Been Friends Together* (New York: Longman, Green, 1942).

November 3
St. Martin de Porres
Dominican Lay Brother (1579–1639)

"He was a man of great charity, who being in charge of the infirmary not only healed his brother religious when they were sick but also assisted in the larger duty of spreading the Great Love of the world. For this they knew him as their father and consolation, calling him father of the poor."

— A contemporary witness

Martin de Porres was born in Lima, Peru, in 1579. His father was a Spanish nobleman who later became governor of Panama. His mother, however, was a free black woman named Anna. Martin apparently took after his mother in appearance, and his father refused to acknowledge his "mulatto" child until many years later. Martin was apprenticed to a barber, a profession which at the time combined hair-cutting with surgical and medical skills. Martin quickly mastered his trade, but at the age of fifteen he applied for admission to a Dominican monastery. Rather than enter as a lay brother, he applied for the lowliest position as a *donado* or lay helper, responsible for such menial tasks as sweeping the cloister and cleaning the latrines. He was accepted, and so assumed the habit of white linen, black scapular, and black cloak.

Despite his extreme humility, Martin could not long disguise his talents and abilities, especially his medical skills. Before long he was given charge of the monastery infirmary. Through his ingenious knowledge of herbal remedies and homemade medicines Martin earned a wide reputation as a gifted healer. But his medical protocol was reputedly supplemented by miraculous healing powers. Many stories were told of his mysterious diagnostic abilities and his power to heal illnesses by his mere touch or presence.

Martin did not confine his healing ministry to the monastery. He cared for the sick and injured wherever he found them, especially the wretched poor who lived in the streets of Lima with no one to care for them. Martin was apt to carry them back to his cell and lay them in his own bed. At one point his superior ordered him to desist from this practice. When he was found to have transgressed the command, he was severely upbraided, but meekly answered: "Forgive my mistake, and please be kind enough to instruct me. I did not know that the precept of obedience took precedence over that of charity." Henceforth, Martin was given liberty to act according to his lights. But it was not the only time Martin's holy simplicity put his superiors to shame. Once when the monastery was in debt he offered himself to be sold as a slave. The prior was deeply moved. "Go back to the monastery," he told Martin. "You are not for sale."

Martin's charity was poured out on all those who were counted as nothing — Indians, the poor, the sick. He had a special ministry to African slaves, to whom he would deliver gifts of food and drink, healing their sick, consoling them in their miserable bondage. But even animals were the objects of his loving service. He treated sick animals with the same devotion he extended to humans. Sick and hungry dogs, donkeys, and turkeys were among his patients. And it is said that he was able to communicate with such creatures. When the monastery was once infested with mice, Martin caught one and exhorted it respectfully to lead its fellows out of the monastery and into the garden where he would personally provide for their needs. Within minutes, a horde of mice abandoned the monastery, just as he had requested. Ever after, Martin kept his side of the bargain, bringing food and leaving it for them. Once, in the kitchen, one of the monks was surprised to discover a dog, a cat, and a mouse, all eating simultaneously from the same bowl that Martin had provided — an image of the "peaceable kingdom" that flourished in his presence.

After nine years Martin's superiors finally prevailed upon him to become a full lay brother. It was recognized by all his brothers in the monastery, and before long throughout Lima, that Martin was one of God's special friends. His humility, piety, and prodigious charity were all the theme of countless stories, many of which circulated even during his life. Innumerable witnesses later testified to his supernatural gifts. These included the power of levitation during prayer, the gifts of healing, of miraculous learning, and of clairvoyance, and the power to pass through locked doors and to become invisible at will. As if these abilities were not sufficient, it was also claimed that Martin had the gift of bilocation — the ability to be in more than one place at the same time. Witnesses frequently claimed to have met him in distant corners of the globe — China, Mexico, North Africa — when all the time he had never left Lima.

On both the natural and moral planes, Martin seemed in so many ways to exceed the limits of the possible. His piety was fueled by an equally extreme asceticism. He subsisted almost entirely on bread and water. He slept on the ground, wore a hair shirt, and generally treated his body with contempt. The accounts of his nightly rituals of self-flagellation are particularly painful to read. When questioned about such practices, which were considered wildly excessive even by the prevailing standards of a sixteenth-century monastery, Martin could only mumble something about the immensity of sins to be atoned for. What sins could afflict the conscience of this holy brother? Slavery, the scorn heaped on the poor and the Indians, the existence of so much injustice in a supposedly Christian society. . . . Martin did not set himself apart from the sins of his age, and he punished himself accordingly.

There is much that seems strange and extreme in the life of Martin de Porres. Like *St. Francis he was a living parable of the reign of God. The certified facts as well as the myriad legends that surround his life all reflect a witness to God's predilection for the "little ones" of the world, the poor, the weak, the powerless, the offscouring of an ostentatiously Catholic society.

Martin de Porres died on November 3, 1639. All Lima, from the viceroy to the beggars in the street, mourned the passing of a saint. Formal canonization was slow in coming. In declaring him a saint in 1962 *Pope John XXIII also named him the patron of all who work for social justice.

See: Stanislas Fumet, *Life of St. Martin de Porres* (Garden City, N.Y.: Doubleday, 1964); Giuliana Cavallini, *St. Martin de Porres* (St. Louis: B. Herder, 1963).

November 4
Raïssa Maritain
Poet and Contemplative (1883–1960)

"It is an error to isolate oneself from men. . . . If God does not call one to solitude, one must live with God in the multitude, make him known there and make him loved."

The life of Raïssa Maritain was inextricably intertwined with that of her husband, *Jacques, the renowned Catholic philosopher. In their long life together they were united not only by bonds of matrimony but by "holy friendship," a union in which God remained an intimate third partner.

Raïssa and Jacques met as students at the Sorbonne. Raïssa had been born in Russia. Her parents, Orthodox Jews, had moved to France to seek better educational opportunities for their gifted daughters. Raïssa had advanced so quickly in her studies, despite having to learn a new language, that she was admitted to the university at the age of sixteen.

She met Jacques Maritain when he solicited her signature on a petition protesting the treatment of socialist students in tsarist Russia. The attraction between them was immediate, and they were soon inseparable. They were married in 1904. Raïssa and Jacques shared a passion for poetry, art, and social justice. But they soon found another bond — a common obsession with the question of truth and a need to discover the meaning of life. Though neither had much religious training, they found it intolerable to imagine that existence might be absurd. They made a vow that if they had not, within a year, found an answer to their quest they would end their lives.

Soon after this they began to attend the lectures of the philosopher Henri Bergson. From him they acquired a sense of the Absolute. They were led in turn to the novelist *Léon Bloy. He was not only a devout Catholic but a prophet, whose writings celebrated God's predilection for the poor, while excoriating the sins of bourgeois Christianity. From their friendship with Bloy the Maritains were introduced to the world of Catholicism but also to Holy Scripture. Raïssa was particularly moved by Bloy's writings on the Jews, chosen by God for a special role in the history of salvation. Within a year of their first meeting with Bloy the Maritains were baptized in 1906. Bloy was their godfather.

Having found their way to the church, Raïssa and Jacques ever after conceived of their lives in religious terms. They took vows as Oblates of *St. Benedict and soon after made a vow of perpetual celibacy. Despite this private commitment, they felt strongly that they were not meant for monastic life, but were called to live out their faith in the midst of the intellectual and artistic circles in which they were immersed.

In the first volume of her memoirs, *We Have Been Friends Together*, Raïssa described the early years of their marriage almost entirely in terms of their relationships with such figures as Bloy, the artist *Georges Rouault, and the poet *Charles Péguy. Throughout their life together the Maritains' salon was the center of an extraordinary Catholic intellectual revival. Jacques became the most eminent Catholic philosopher of the twentieth century. Raïssa was also recognized through the publication of several volumes of poetry and prose. But otherwise she remained more in the background, the intimate collaborator in her husband's work. He later said that her aid and inspiration had penetrated everything he wrote: "Every good thing comes from God. But as an intermediary on earth everything good has come to me from her."

Raïssa died on November 4, 1960. It was only then that Jacques discovered her private journals and so realized the depth of spirituality that had remained hidden even from him. Later published, the journals reflected Raïssa's intense life of prayer and her understanding of her vocation as a contemplative "on the roads of the world." Indeed, on the basis of these writings, *Thomas Merton called her "perhaps one of the great contemplatives of our time."

In one of her entries she had written: "I have the feeling that what is asked of us is to live in the whirlwind, without keeping back any of our substance, without keeping back anything for ourselves, neither rest nor friendships nor health nor leisure — to pray incessantly...in fact to let ourselves pitch and toss in the waves of the divine will till the day when it will say: 'That's enough.'"

See: Raïssa Maritain, *Raïssa's Journal* (Albany, N.Y.: Magi, 1974); *We Have Been Friends Together* (London: Longman, Green, 1942).

St. Hilda of Whitby
Abbess (610–680)

"All that knew her called her Mother."   —St. Bede

St. Hilda was one of the great lights of the early Anglo-Saxon church. According to *Bede, whose *History* is the principal source for her life, she was the great niece of St. Edwin, king of Northumbria. With the rest of her family she was baptized by St. Paulinus when she was thirteen. Says Bede, "She spent thirty-three years most nobly in secular occupations" before deciding to "serve God alone." Hilda spent time in a number of monasteries in East Anglia before returning home to found a new monastery at Whitby. This would remain her home for the rest of her life, and under her leadership it would become an important center for the spread and consolidation of the Christian faith in England.

Whitby was a double monastery — that is, one comprising both men and women who lived separately but gathered together to chant the office. In the tradition of Celtic monasticism, in which Hilda was formed, it was not unusual for a woman to preside over such a mixed community. Hilda set a standard for holiness, wisdom, and scholarship, promoting through her example "the observance of righteousness, mercy, purity, and other virtues, but especially in peace and charity." Bede observes that in her monastery "no one there was rich or poor, for everything was held in common, and none possessed any personal property."

Hilda also served as a spiritual director, serving not only her monastic children but the wider community. "So great was her prudence that not only ordinary folk, but kings and princes used to come and ask her advice in their difficulties." Five of her monks went on to become bishops. She was also influential in encouraging the gifts of *St. Caedmon, the cowherd and poet who became a monk of Whitby.

As a reflection of the prestige of Whitby, the monastery was chosen as the site for the important church synod of 664. The synod was called, ostensibly, to resolve disagreements about the correct day for observing Easter. But this issue was symptomatic of deeper tensions between those favoring the Roman model of authority, rooted in the episcopal hierarchy, and those inclined to the more monastic model characteristic of the Celtic church. Hilda favored the latter, but the synod decided otherwise.

Hilda's last years were spent in painful illness. She never retired from her office nor did she ever fail to give thanks to God. By her own example she instructed her flock "to serve God rightly when in health, and to render thanks to him faithfully when in trouble or bodily weakness." Her last counsel to her community was to "maintain the gospel peace among yourselves and with others." She died on November 17, 680, and her feast is observed on that date.

See: Bede, *A History of the English Church and People* (Baltimore: Penguin, 1955).

Little Sister Magdeleine of Jesus
Foundress of the Little Sisters of Jesus (1898–1989)

"As you work, as you come and go, as you pass among the crowds, to be a contemplative will mean simply that you try to turn to Jesus within you and enter into conversation with him, as with the one you love most in the world."

While growing up in France, Madeleine Hutin felt a powerful devotion to Jesus, but she could find no religious congregation that reflected her sense of vocation. Then, in her twenties, she happened upon a biography of *Charles de Foucauld, the French explorer, priest, and finally desert father who died in North Africa in 1916.

Foucauld had envisioned a new kind of contemplative life, rooted in the world of the poor and based on the "hidden years" that Jesus spent as a carpenter in Nazareth. In his hermitage in the Sahara, he had conceived of a "fraternity" of men and women who would live among their Muslim neighbors as brothers and sisters, embracing poverty, manual labor, and a spirit of prayer. Thus, they would proclaim the gospel, not with their words, "but with their lives." For many years Foucauld had patiently prepared the way for followers who never came. In the end he died alone, his message bequeathed to the appreciation of a later generation. Decades later, it was discovered, among others, by Madeleine Hutin. Upon reading his biography she determined immediately to adopt Foucauld as her spiritual guide and to make his vision her own.

Because of poor health and family obligations, Hutin was not able to make a beginning until 1936 when, at the age of thirty-eight, she finally set sail for Algiers. She embarked with few if any plans, determined to trust herself entirely to providence. Soon she was introduced to Father René Voillaume, who had been converted by the same biography of Foucauld and whose Little Brothers of Jesus had been living in the desert since 1933. When she had confided to him her sense of vocation he responded with encouragement as well as invaluable assistance in obtaining the support of local church authorities. In 1939 the new congregation, the Little Sisters of Jesus, was finally established under the leadership of Little Sister Magdeleine, as she was henceforth known.

The word "Little" had special meaning for Magdeleine. During the early years of her vocation she had experienced a number of intense visions inspired by her meditations on the Infant Jesus. The humility, weakness, and vulnerability of a baby were the disguises under which the world's savior first appeared. And it seemed appropriate to her that this baby should also be the inspiration and model for those who wished to bear witness to divine love among the poorest and most powerless of the world.

It was years before the congregation was fully recognized by Rome. Along the way it was necessary to overcome many doubts and criticisms arising from the originality of Magdeleine's vision. Her Little Sisters were neither enclosed contemplatives nor were they engaged in traditional apostolic activities. They lived in small "fraternities," some consisting of no more than a couple of Sisters. While maintaining an intense commitment to contemplative prayer, they endeavored to enter fully into the life and culture of their poor neighbors. Among other things this meant supporting themselves by common labor. Instead of a traditional habit, they wore a simple denim habit adorned with a cross. What was essential to the Little Sisters was that wherever they lived they should find themselves among the very poor. As for misunderstandings, she noted that "the world looks for efficiency more than for the unobtrusiveness of the hidden life." Thus, "Bethlehem and Nazareth will always remain a mystery to it."

In the beginning, basing her vision on the literal model of Brother Charles, Magdeleine had conceived of the mission of the Little Sisters exclusively in relation to the Muslims of North Africa. It was there that the congregation took root and flourished. But gradually Magdeleine enlarged her vision to conceive of a universal mission. Hence the fraternities spread throughout the world, attracting women of all races and nationalities.

By the time of her death there were 280 fraternities with 1,400 Little Sisters from 64 different countries. These included Little Sisters who traveled with gypsy caravans in Europe, who lived with nomadic circus troupes, and who even volunteered as prisoners. There were communities among the pygmies of Cameroon, in remote Eskimo villages in Alaska, among boat people in Southeast Asia, and in the slums of London, Beirut, and Washington, D.C. In her later life Magdeleine felt a special call to bear witness in the communist countries of the Eastern bloc. Driving in a converted minivan, she made dozens of trips throughout Eastern Europe, including eighteen trips to Russia. Quietly she was able to establish fraternities in a number of these countries. Whatever the setting, the aim of the Little Sisters was not to evangelize in a formal sense but to serve modestly as a kind of leaven in the midst of the world, imparting a spirit of love.

In 1949 Little Sister Magdeleine formally relinquished leadership of the congregation. She preferred to play an informal role as mother to her Sisters, traveling constantly around the globe rather than confining herself to the administration of a growing congregation. Although she had been sickly in her youth, she remained remarkably robust into her old age, continuing to do manual labor well into her eighties and undertaking her final exhausting trip to the Soviet Union at the age of ninety-one. She died later that year on November 6, 1989.

See: Kathryn Spink, *The Call of the Desert: A Biography of Little Sister Magdeleine of Jesus* (London: Darton, Longman and Todd, 1993).

Albert Camus
Novelist and Nobel Laureate (1913–1960)

"What the world expects of Christians is that Christians should speak out, loud and clear,... that they should get away from abstractions and confront the blood-stained face history has taken on today. The grouping we need is a grouping of men resolved to speak out clearly and to pay up personally."

Albert Camus, the French novelist and philosopher, was, in the strict sense, an "unbeliever." And yet, arguably, he represented a type of moral engagement, in the face of doubt, that is one of the characteristic forms of religious witness in our age.

Camus was born in Algeria on November 7, 1913. Raised in poverty, he studied philosophy before deciding on a career as a writer. In 1934 he briefly joined the Communist Party but otherwise remained aloof from organizations of any kind. During World War II he wrote for the Resistance newspaper *Combat* and afterward served as its editor. In this role, with his strong defense of social justice and human values, he acquired a reputation as an exacting moralist, indeed as a public conscience.

Camus achieved wide fame through a series of essays and novels, including *The Stranger* and *The Plague,* which reflected his philosophical interests: the absurdity of human existence and the obligation, nevertheless, to offer resistance to evil. In a famous lecture at a Dominican monastery in 1948, Camus described the moral challenge of his generation: "If not to reduce evil, at least not to add to it." Elsewhere he observed, "Perhaps we cannot prevent this world from being a world in which children are tortured. But we can reduce the number of tortured children." Camus won the Nobel Prize in 1957. On January 4, 1960, he died in a car accident at the age of forty-six.

Among modern writers, Camus commanded unusually respectful attention from Christian readers. At times this bordered on the proprietary. Several of his works prompted anticipation of the author's imminent conversion. His untimely death did nothing to silence the rumors that he had been secretly receiving instruction in the Catholic faith. All this was ironic tribute to a man whose philosophy began with the assumption that God does not exist.

Nevertheless, the fact remains that there is much in Camus's work for Christians to admire and learn from without trying to convert him into something he was not. His importance to Christians is not that he almost became a Christian but that, while rejecting Christianity, he remained in dialogue with it and defined the terms for any future dialogue between Christians and nonbelievers. That dialogue, he believed, must involve the search for common cause in the struggle for life and against the forces of death.

Camus's work was marked by the theme of exile. While for Christianity this metaphor served to describe the human estrangement from God, in the case of Camus it referred to the condition of humanity in the absence of God. It was an image of exile without remedy, since there was no memory of a lost home or any hope of a promised land. The solution for Camus was not a leap into the absurd, but revolt. In a world without ultimate meaning human beings must create their own meaning by revolting against their condition, refusing to reconcile themselves to their fate. In this stance they discovered a certain greatness, for they were stronger than their condition.

Camus's hero was the mythical Sisyphus, condemned to push an enormous boulder up a hill only to watch it roll back down again. Camus imagined a Sisyphus who was conscious of his condition, who was free from hopeful illusions about the future, and who, in his contempt for the forces that condemned him, took possession of his existence. And so, although his condition was tragic, Camus invited us to imagine Sisyphus as happy.

In one of his most powerful novels, *The Plague*, Camus describes the collective experience of a modern port city in Algeria as it is besieged by an epidemic of bubonic plague. The disease becomes a symbol for the human condition. According to Camus, such a world imposes a solemn duty of revolt, the refusal to consent to a condition which tortures innocents and reduces the life of each person to absurdity.

The heroes of this novel are those who resist the plague. But for Camus the plague has a spiritual counterpart. This consists of giving consent to murder or consenting to principles that must end in murder. Camus counted Christians among the latter. This was not because they actively support evil, but because, Camus believed, their ability to render complete resistance is restricted by the fact that ultimately their hope is in another world. Their belief in an omnipotent God makes them more acquiescent to their fate, no matter how unjust. By failing, in Camus's opinion, to live life with sufficient passion they become implicit collaborators with the forces of death. The Christian may protest this characterization. In the end, however, the charge that Christianity makes human beings unconscious collaborators with evil cannot be refuted by dogmatic assertions but only by actions.

Despite his protests, many have suggested that Camus's position was not so far removed from Christianity as he supposed. The number of those who serve Christ is not confined to self-professed Christians. Paradoxically, Camus served the Truth by keeping faith with his conscience and denying God. The alternative for him would have been to "love a scheme of things in which children are put to torture." This, to his credit, he would not do. Instead he spent his life among those who "intercede almost everywhere and ceaselessly for children and for men," a cause in which he did not despair of Christian support.

See: Albert Camus, *Resistance, Rebellion and Death* (New York: Alfred A. Knopf, 1960); Jean Onimus, *Albert Camus and Christianity* (University, Ala.: University of Alabama Press, 1970).

Bd. John Duns Scotus
Franciscan Theologian (1266–1308)

*"In paying homage to Christ I would rather go too far
than not far enough to give him the praise that is due him."*

John Duns, later known as the Subtle Doctor, was called Scotus on account of his birth in the Scottish county of Roxborough. Educated by the Franciscans, he entered the order at the age of fifteen and was later ordained a priest. He studied at Oxford and Paris and later occupied teaching chairs in Paris and Cologne. There he died on November 8, 1308, at the age of forty-two. Although his thought was eventually overshadowed by the Dominican followers of his rival, *Thomas Aquinas, he was one of the greatest of the scholastic theologians. His mystically charged theology held a particular charm for the Franciscans, rendering in philosophical terms the highly affective and creation-centered spirituality of their holy founder.

Scotus addressed many of the same themes as Aquinas and his scholastic forerunner *St. Anselm. Like Anselm he tried to present a philosophical "proof" for the existence of God. But rather than focus on the grammatical implications of the word "God," he began with the observation that all things require some prior cause for their existence. From this he predicated the existence of a primary infinite cause which owes its existence to itself alone. Yet he differed from some scholastic theologians in drawing a distinction between what could be "proved" through reason and what could be known only through revelation, and hence by faith. There was a difference between a rational knowledge of the existence of God and a saving knowledge of the *Love* of God.

The definition of God as infinite Love was a particularly important theme for Scotus. He disagreed with Anselm, who understood the Incarnation as a necessary payment for sin. He also disagreed with Thomas, who argued that the Incarnation, though willed by God from eternity, was made necessary because of the existence of sin. For Scotus the Incarnation was willed through eternity as an expression of God's love, and hence God's desire for consummated union with creation. Our redemption by the cross, though caused by sin, was likewise an expression of God's love and compassion rather than an appeasement of God's anger or a form of compensation for God's injured majesty. Scotus believed, in turn, that knowledge of God's love should evoke a loving response on the part of humanity: "I am of the opinion that God wished to redeem us in this fashion principally in order to draw us to his love." Through our own loving self-gift, he argued, we join with Christ in becoming "co-lovers" of the Holy Trinity.

Unlike philosophers in the line of Plato, Scotus did not value the ideal at the expense of the real. Created things pointed to their Creator not only by their conformity to an ideal pattern but by their individuality and uniqueness — what he termed their "thisness" (*haecceitas*). Thus, the path to contemplation of God should proceed not only through the mind but through the senses. This insight of Scotus especially endeared him to the most highly distinctive of Catholic poets, the Jesuit *Gerard Manley Hopkins. He paid tribute to the Subtle Doctor in one of his poems: "Of realty the rarest-veinèd unraveller; a not / Rivalled insight, be rival Italy or Greece." John Duns Scotus was beatifed in 1992.

See: David Knowles, *The Evolution of Medieval Thought* (New York: Vintage, 1962); Etienne Gilson, *History of Christian Philosophy in the Middle Ages* (London: Sheed & Ward, 1955).

November 9

Kristallnacht Martyrs
(1938)

"I would like to say that I would not like to be a Jew in Germany now."
— Reichsmarshall Hermann Göring

Before the Nazis implemented their plan to exterminate the Jewish people they advertised their intentions through a number of public spectacles. The most dramatic of these occurred on the night of November 9, 1938, when Nazi storm troopers throughout Germany mounted a terrible, coordinated assault on the Jewish community. One hundred and ninety-one synagogues were burned to the ground. Seventy-five hundred Jewish-owned shops were destroyed. Because of the shattered windows the pogrom became known as the *Kristallnacht,* or Crystal Night. In addition twenty thousand Jewish men were arrested and placed in "protective custody," with half of them shipped to the Buchenwald concentration camp. Nearly one hundred Jews were killed.

The following day there was little protest, either in Germany or abroad. Notes from a meeting of the top-ranking Nazi officials indicate that they considered the night's activities a tremendous success.

November 10

St. Gertrude the Great
Mystic (1253–1302)

"Inscribe with your precious blood, most merciful Lord, your wounds on my heart, that I may read in them both your sufferings and your love."

Of the birth and background of St. Gertrude there is no record. When she was five she was given to the nuns of the monastery at Helfta in Saxony, and within the walls of that enclosure she remained for the rest of her life. This monastery was one of the great religious communities of its time, distinguished by women of great learning as well as a number of famous mystics. One of them, *St. Mechthild (d. 1295), was put in charge of the girl and oversaw her education and upbringing. Their relationship remained particularly intimate.

When she came of age Gertrude was professed as a nun. The religious life was all she had ever known. Nevertheless she truly owned her vocation only at the age of twenty-five. The turning point came one evening as she was preparing for bed. Suddenly she experienced a vision of Christ in the form of a young man. He spoke to her and said, "Fear not. I will save and deliver you." The figure was bathed in a dazzling light which emanated from his five wounds. He went on to say, "You have licked the dust with my enemies and sucked honey from thorns. Now come back to me, and my divine delights shall be as wine to you."

For the rest of her life Gertrude enjoyed frequent mystical revelations, often couched in dialogues with Christ, her Beloved Spouse. Believing these revelations were not for her own sake alone she forced herself to record them in a book, *The Herald of Divine Love,* a work combining great theological sophistication with mystical ardor. Nearly all the themes of Catholic theology are treated in her book, though the principal theme is God's love for his creatures. Gertrude had a special devotion to the Sacred Heart of Jesus, the point where human and divine love are most intimately joined.

Gertrude was often in poor health. Once when she was too sick to attend a sermon the Lord spoke to her: "Would you like me to preach to you, my dearest?" When she assented, "the Lord made her lean against his heart, with the heart of her soul close to his divine heart. When her soul had sweetly rested there awhile, she heard in the Lord's heart two wondrous and very sweet pulsations." He told her that the first pulse was for the salvation of sinners, the second for the salvation of the just.

Gertrude served her community as a spiritual director and was frequently called upon to lead the community in prayer. When another of Helfta's mystics asked the Lord what he most liked about Gertrude, he answered: "Her freedom of heart." She died on November 17, 1302. Her feast day is observed on November 16.

See: Gertrude of Helfta: The Herald of Divine Love, ed. Margaret Winkworth, Classics of Western Spirituality (New York: Paulist, 1993).

November 11

Søren Kierkegaard
Philosopher (1813–1855)

"What the age needs is not a genius but a martyr."

Søren Kierkegaard made no pretense of being a saint. He hardly dared to call himself a Christian. But he claimed to know, with an uncommon clarity, what it means to *be* a Christian. This knowledge imposed the thankless but nevertheless sacred duty of exposing official Christianity for what he believed it to be: a counterfeit and a fraud. Thus, indirectly, he hoped to bear witness to the truth.

Kierkegaard was born in Copenhagen, Denmark, in 1813. His father was a dour and puritanical figure who bequeathed to Søren, the child of his old age, his own melancholy disposition. Even as a child Søren affected the mannerisms of an old man. This was compounded by a childhood accident that left him with a limp and a crooked spine. His plan was to go into the Lutheran ministry. But several significant episodes steered him on a different course.

The first great turning point was the breaking of his engagement to a young woman named Regina. Although his love was apparently genuine, something convinced him that the path of worldly happiness was not his calling. Believing that Regina could not understand his true motives he contrived to let her believe that he was simply a cad. Though Regina did in fact go on to marry another, Kierkegaard's reputation in Copenhagen society would suffer. He spent the rest of his life scrutinizing and justifying his motives.

It may be said that Kierkegaard elevated introspection to a fine art. This he distinguished from the endless "reflection" that deadlocks action. What he favored was a type of "inwardness" that was the precondition for any passionate commitment. Sadly, he believed, the capacity for such inwardness was becoming increasingly scarce in "the present age."

There was nothing Kierkegaard despised more than the "modern" addiction to novelty, news, and gossip. All this typified the superficiality and "leveling" of a mass society which preferred to experience life at "second-hand." A tawdry scandal sheet called the *Corsair* was the particular object of his contempt. In hopes of igniting a moral uprising, Kierkegaard publicly offered himself as a victim of the journal's ridicule. The editors obliged him, attacking him so mercilessly for most of a year that for a long time afterward the very name "Søren" became synonymous with fool.

Now something of a social pariah, Kierkegaard easily concluded that a career in the ministry was not for him. Instead, with the support of a sizeable inheritance, he chose to devote himself to writing, a task he pursued with extraordinary concentration. In a few short years he produced a whole library of works on philosophy, ethics, psychology, and theology. This work would eventually secure his reputation as one of the most significant figures in the history of Western thought. But such acclaim would come only many generations after his death.

The underlying thrust of Kierkegaard's work was to show just what it means to become and to be a Christian. This was an ironic task, given that he lived in the midst of an officially Christian country. But for Kierkegaard this was the very point. Insofar as the church permitted people to believe that being a Christian was nothing more than a matter of being born in a Christian state, the church authorities insured that nobody would ever feel challenged to *become* a Christian. The result was Christendom: a species of baptized paganism in which every respectable citizen could pass for a disciple.

This harm was compounded, in Kierkegaard's eyes, by the professors and theologians who tried to turn Christianity into a system of ideas. Christianity could not be comprehended as the object of thought; its central truth — that God became a human being in history — was an absolute offense to reason. It could be apprehended only by a leap of faith, a passionate commitment, a decisive interest of the kind that academic study normally discouraged. The problem of Christianity was ultimately not *objective* ("What is Christianity?") but *subjective:* "How do I *become* a Christian?"

Through most of his work Kierkegaard assumed an attitude of "indirect communication," devising ingenious "pseudonymous" voices to reflect the various stages of religious development. But in his later years he spoke more directly, writing sermons and devotional writings of sublime loveliness. By the end of his life, however, he had returned to the barricades for his most audacious campaign.

For Kierkegaard the gauntlet was cast at his feet in 1854 when Bishop Mynster of Copenhagen died and was eulogized by a prominent theologian as "a genuine witness to the truth," part of "the holy chain of witnesses which stretches back to the days of the Apostles." To Kierkegaard the bishop had been a well-intentioned and decent fellow. But to call him a "witness" or to invoke the apostles was simply indecent, if not blasphemous. He responded with a series of articles which cut to the heart of his dispute with Christendom. Compared with the spirit of the New Testament, he charged, official Christianity was simply a form of play-acting. To participate in such Christianity was to betray the spirit of Christ as surely as any Judas.

Kierkegaard carried on this campaign for most of a year. If he expected that his articles would bring martyrdom he was disappointed. For the most part the official church chose simply to ignore him. But at least he satisfied himself that he had fulfilled his task as an "auditor." (As he put it, "an apostle proclaims the truth, an auditor is responsible for discovering counterfeits.")

On October 2, 1855, Kierkegaard collapsed in the street. He was carried to the hospital where he remained for the last month of his life, paralyzed and unable to leave his bed. Visitors remarked that his face reflected a great calm and peace in the face of death, though he made a show of refusing any ministration by the clergy: "I have made my choice. The parsons are royal functionaries, and royal functionaries are not related to Christianity." He died on November 11 at the age of forty-two.

See: Søren Kierkegaard, *Attack upon Christendom* (Boston: Beacon, 1956); Walter Lowrie, *A Short Life of Kierkegaard* (Princeton: Princeton University Press, 1942).

Sor Juana Inés de la Cruz
Poet and Scholar (1651–1694)

"From the moment I was first illuminated by the light of reason, my incli-nation toward letters has been so vehement that not even the admonitions of others . . . nor my own meditations . . . have been sufficient to cause me to forswear this natural impulse that God placed in me."

Sor (Sister) Juana Inés de la Cruz was a seventeenth-century nun, the first great poet of Latin America, and one of the earliest champions of equality for women in the church. She has been called a genius, a saint, a heretic, and an early feminist. The degree to which she may have reconciled these various identities is the source of her attraction and, ultimately, her mystery.

Juana was born on November 12, 1651, in Mexico, then called New Spain, in a small town not far from Mexico City. Raised by her mother's family — her parents were evidently unmarried — she displayed from her earliest childhood an extraordinary passion for knowledge. She learned to read and write by the time she was four and mastered Latin after only twenty lessons. As she recalled of her childhood, "In me the desire for learning was stronger than the desire for eating." By the time she was six-teen her reputation for brilliance, augmented by her famous beauty, had brought Juana to the attention of the viceregal court. She lived there for several years as a lady-in-waiting and became a popular member of elite society. But then suddenly, at the age of nineteen, she turned her back on the court and entered the Convent of St. Jerome in Mexico City.

There is no evidence that she was motivated by great piety. In fact she was later frank in describing her repugnance for "certain conditions" of convent life. Nevertheless, she said, "given the total antipathy I felt for marriage, I deemed convent life the least unsuitable and the most honor-able I could elect if I were to insure my salvation." No doubt it was in part the name of *St. Jerome, translator of the Bible and patron of all scholars, that dictated her choice of a convent.

Happily, the convent lived up to the promise of its name. Within the cloister she was able to amass one of the great personal libraries of her day — several thousand volumes — and to indulge her voracious appetite for learning of every sort. She could discourse intelligently on history, rhetoric, philosophy, art, architecture, geometry, astronomy, and many other fields. At the same time she wrote volumes of poems — passion-ate love poems, religious allegories, historical odes. These constitute one of the great literary outputs of the baroque era. She wrote plays, musi-cal librettos, and scholarly monographs. All these were well known in the viceregal court, and her fame extended to Spain.

The watershed in her life occurred in 1690 when she first ventured to write on matters of theology. She was moved to cross this threshold by reading a forty-year-old sermon by a famous preacher which struck her as idiotic. In response she wrote a long and brilliant critique, certainly the first theological work by a woman in the New World. This elicited an open letter from the bishop of Puebla, who praised her orthodoxy and her insight, but then condescendingly urged her to restrict herself to activities more becoming to a member of her sex.

This released a tightly wound coil in Sor Juana. After several months she responded with a lengthy treatise. In this letter, composed with devastating irony and self-restraint, she defended her compulsion to learn as a God-given calling, one that she was powerless to deny. Even if she were deprived of books, she said, all the world was her university: "There is no creature, however lowly, in which one cannot recognize that *God made me*; there is none that does not astound reason if properly meditated on." At the same time she championed the equal rights of women to learning with an erudite appeal to Aristotle and Cicero, Scripture, her patron St. Jerome, his holy helper, *St. Paula, and all other learned women saints. "You foolish men," she wrote, "accusing women for lacking reason when you yourselves are the reason for the lack."

It was a bold and unprecedented manifesto. In the eyes of many church authorities it was also outrageously presumptuous. What happened next is not in doubt, though the meaning of it is open to interpretation. After Sor Juana's "Response," her confessor would have no more to do with her. Soon after she made a public renewal of her vows and consecrated herself to the Immaculate Conception of the Virgin Mary — a document she signed with her own blood. She then dispersed her famous and beloved library, distributing the proceeds among the poor. She wrote no more. In 1694, while nursing her sister nuns during a virulent outbreak of plague, she succumbed to the dread disease and quickly died on April 17.

Some critics have seen in Juana's last years the marks of a profound conversion; her silence is akin to that of *Thomas Aquinas, when he realized that all his great words were as straw. The proof is in the mystical charity she displayed in her final days. Others, including Octavio Paz, see her actions as a humiliating exercise in self-abnegation, an expression of her powerlessness as a woman. Just as her options dictated that she enter the convent in order to be a scholar, so her options as a woman religious dictated that she renounce her learning — renounce herself — in order to stay alive. The issue was not her orthodoxy. The issue was her gender. The alternative was the Inquisition.

Still, the mystery lingers. Though not conventionally pious, Juana embraced the religious life as a means of pursuing the call to learning — a vocation she believed to come from God. Ultimately it proved difficult, if not impossible, to negotiate the claims of these vocations. And so the question remains: Did Sor Juana's elected silence represent an act of faithful submission or a betrayal of herself, her true vocation, and thus of God? Which was ultimately the greater rebellion: to stand up to church authorities or to submit? Her only answer is silence. No one can answer the riddle of Sor Juana who has not tried to walk her path.

See: A Woman of Genius: The Intellectual Autobiography of Sor Juana Inés de la Cruz (Salisbury, Conn.: Lime Rock, 1982); Octavio Paz, *Sor Juana* (Cambridge, Mass.: Harvard University Press, 1988).

November 13

Cardinal Joseph Bernardin
Archbishop of Chicago (1928–1996)

"The truth is that each life is of infinite value.... My final hope is that my efforts have been faithful to the truth of the gospel of life and that you ... will find in this Gospel the vision and strength needed to promote and nurture the great gift of life God has shared with us."

On August 12, 1996, Cardinal Joseph Bernardin, archbishop of Chicago, announced the formation of what he called the Catholic Common Ground Project. This, he said, was an effort to address the increasing polarization within the American Catholic church. In the face of such division, particularly between conservatives and liberals, he called on all members of the church to approach the situation "with fresh eyes, open minds, and changed hearts."

Bernardin's initiative was widely applauded, but it also invited criticism from both sides of the ideological divide. For Bernardin this was not an unfamiliar position. So many times in his career as a bishop he had played the role of peacemaker, the one who struggled to negotiate a path to common ground. Nevertheless, Bernardin's project assumed a more poignant urgency when in another press conference, two weeks later, he announced that a previously treated pancreatic cancer had spread to his liver. He had been told he had less than a year to live. Even with such a personal matter, Bernardin was once again characteristically forthright. "I can say in all sincerity that I am at peace," he declared. "As a person of faith I see death as a friend, as the transition from earthly life to life eternal."

So began the final journey for a man many regarded as the leader of the American Catholic church. He was named a bishop in 1966, and his career had coincided with the heady and turbulent post–Vatican II era. Thirty-eight at the time of his consecration, he represented a new generation of bishops inspired by the council's spirit of collegiality and determined to apply the gospel to questions of public policy and the common good. The church was emerging from the Catholic ghetto and entering into the mainstream of American life. In effect, Bernardin, the son of Italian immigrants, was one of those who helped to shepherd the American church into the postimmigrant era.

Bernardin served as the first general secretary and later as president of the National Conference of Catholic Bishops. He came into public prominence in the early 1980s when, as archbishop of Cincinnati, he oversaw the drafting of "The Challenge of Peace," the bishops' pastoral letter on nuclear war. It was the most significant statement ever issued by the bishops on public policy, and it raised much controversy for its strong condemnation of nuclear war and its critical treatment of American military policies. Bernardin's leadership was later exhibited in a significant speech in which he enunciated what he called a "consistent ethic of life." According to Bernardin, the church's commitment to the sacredness of life was a "seamless garment" that integrated opposition to abortion with opposition to capital punishment and euthanasia, concern for peace and social justice, and a commitment to the poor and the most helpless persons in society. His approach established a wider framework for the bishop's pro-life stance, and it was widely adopted.

By this time, in 1982, Bernardin had been named archbishop of Chicago, an appointment followed by his elevation to the college of cardinals. Such an appointment, at the age of fifty-four, was the enviable cap to a distinguished episcopal career. But inwardly he had embarked on a different journey.

Some years before, challenged by a group of trusted priests, he had faced the realization that his life was focused on the church rather than on Christ. It was the beginning of a quiet process of conversion, marked by prayer and reflection on the cross that transformed a successful churchman into a man of God and prepared him for the trials that were to come.

In the early 1990s a number of persons came forward with shocking revelations about their experience as children of being sexually abused by priests. Bernardin was a leader among the bishops in establishing procedures in his archdiocese for addressing such cases. Then in November 1993 a young man under treatment by an unlicensed hypnotist claimed to remember that, while a seminarian in Cincinnati, he had been molested by Archbishop Bernardin. Bernardin vehemently denied the charges. But rather than lodge a defensive counterattack, he insisted that his case be submitted to the same process of investigation he had established for such allegations. He refused to impugn the man's character or do anything that might discourage other victims of abuse from coming forward.

The charges against Bernardin were widely publicized. Doubtless there were many who privately sneered at his humiliation, clucking smugly at the sight of yet another hypocrite unmasked. But the story took a different turn, three months later, when the accuser abruptly withdrew his charges. Acknowledging that his memories were "unreliable," he apologized to Bernardin. Bernardin met privately with the young man, who was dying of AIDS, and forgave him. Publicly he acknowledged the painfulness of his ordeal, but he insisted that his own experience of false accusation would not undermine his determination to reach out to the victims of abuse.

Bernardin's courage and grace throughout this ordeal were underlined only a few months later with the announcement that he was suffering from cancer. He received aggressive treatment and resumed his pastoral ministry, to which he now added considerable time with others who were sick and dying. He was determined to impart something of his abiding belief in the sacredness of life and his faith and hope in God's promises. Finally in 1996 came the announcement of his limited prognosis. In a speech in September he said,

> As a bishop I have tried...to shape a moral message about the unique value of human life and our common responsibilities for it. As my life slowly ebbs away, as my temporal destiny becomes clearer

each hour and each day, I am not anxious, but rather reconfirmed in my conviction about the wonder of human life, a gift that flows from the very being of God and is entrusted to each of us.

In his last weeks, as his candle burned visibly shorter, Bernardin received a great outpouring of affection and admiration, not simply from his fellow Catholics. His courage and tranquility, up to the end, bore a powerful witness to his faith in God and his commitment to the cause of reconciliation. He died on November 14, 1996.

See: Cardinal Joseph Bernardin, *The Gift of Peace* (Chicago: Loyola University Press, 1997).

November 14

St. Gregory Palamas
Monk and Mystical Theologian (1296–1359)

"This is the nature of prayer, that it raises one from earth to heaven, higher than every heavenly name and dignity, and brings one before the very God of all."

St. Gregory Palamas spent most of his life as a monk and hermit of Mt. Athos. Located on a peninsula in Thessalonica, Mt. Athos was virtually a republic of eastern monasticism, a network of dozens of independent communities and hundreds of hermitages where monks and hermits practiced the "hesychastic" spirituality, of which Gregory was the most famous advocate. "Hesychia," the Greek word for quietude, was here applied to a spiritual discipline of interior prayer and rest in God. The hesychasts took to heart *St. Paul's admonition to "pray without ceasing." By constantly repeating the name of Jesus or the "Jesus prayer" ("Lord, Jesus Christ, Son of the Living God, have mercy on me, a sinner"), sometimes coordinated with the rhythm of their breathing, the monks entered into a state of extreme concentration on spiritual reality. In such a state they liked to say that the Holy Spirit was praying through them. By such constant prayer, Gregory taught, the Christian might latch onto the divine nature, much like a rope flung over a rock, and so pull free of worldly attachments and draw nearer to God. The ultimate goal of this ascetic life was a vision of the divine light, witnessed by the disciples on Mt. Tabor when they beheld Christ in his transfigured state.

Gregory spent many years as a hermit, remaining alone in prayer for five days of the week, emerging only on Saturdays and Sundays to participate in the divine liturgy. His later preeminence is due to his role in defending hesychast spirituality against the attacks of a Calabrian monk named Barlaam. Barlaam took violent exception to the notion that humans could achieve direct knowledge of the nature of God. He called the hesychasts "navel-gazers," because of the attitude which many of the monks assumed in prayer. Gregory countered that while it was impossible to have direct knowledge of God's "essence" it was possible to have direct experience of God's "energies." He strongly championed the traditional Orthodox position that the goal of the Incarnation was "deification," the restoration of human beings to their intended condition in the image and *likeness* of God.

The battle between Barlaam and the Palamites was bitter and protracted, extending over a series of special synods in Constantinople. A synod in 1350 upheld the orthodoxy of Gregory. Gregory spent his last years as archbishop of Thessalonica and died in 1359. He was canonized by the Byzantine church in 1368.

See: Gregory Palamas: The Triads, ed. John Meyendorff, Classics of Western Spirituality (New York: Paulist, 1983).

November 15
St. Roque Gonzalez and Companions
Jesuit Martyrs of Paraguay (d. 1628)

"God does not command the Gospel of Our Lord Jesus Christ to be preached with the noise of arms and with pillage. What He rather commands is the example of a good life and holy teaching."

Much legend and controversy surround the famous Jesuit "reductions" of Paraguay. For 160 years a network of utopian communities was organized by Jesuit missionaries in the vast jungle region of the Guarani Indians. The Jesuits were authorized to establish these experimental colonies as a means of Christianizing the Indians. But there is no question that they also offered a measure of protection to the Indians from the more brutal exploitation of the Spanish *encomiendas* and the slave traders.

One of the early pioneers of the reductions was a second-generation Paraguayan, Roque Gonzalez. The son of a Spanish nobleman, he was born in Asunción in 1576. He was ordained a priest at the age of twenty-three, and ten years later entered the Society of Jesus, attracted by the Jesuits' heroic missionary work among the Indians. He was already well-prepared for such work by his knowledge, from childhood, of the difficult Guarani language.

Leaving behind the security of the colonial enclaves, Gonzalez and his fellow Jesuits set out for unexplored territories, braving hunger, disease, and the threat of death with each fresh encounter with one of the scattered Indian communities along the Paraná and Uruguay Rivers. Carrying no weapons, they often heralded their presence by playing musical instruments, which fascinated and charmed the native peoples. Having piqued their interest, the Jesuits tried to convey to the Indians a sense of the Christian faith but also to encourage them to abandon their nomadic existence in favor of farming in organized settlements. Their efforts met with surprising success. Between 1610 and 1623 twenty-three settlements were established with a combined population of one hundred thousand.

Only a small percentage of this number was formally baptized. More were apparently attracted by the protection which the Jesuits offered from the direct encroachment of colonial rule. Though indirectly the Indians were subjects of the Spanish crown, the reductions represented in effect a parallel society, organized on communitarian principles far different from the feudal world of the colonial settlements. There the Indians were treated as serfs, if not less than human. The reductions, in contrast, were based on respect for the dignity and independence of the Indians and their human rights as children of God.

The reductions, however, were not universally admired. Many of the colonists were furious at the Jesuits for their criticism of the *encomienda* system and for their success in effectively closing off a vast pool of potentially exploited labor. The secular church resented the Jesuits for their supposed arrogance in turning their backs on the needs of the colonial society. Meanwhile the Jesuits had to defend their communities from marauding slave traders and the colonial government, which wanted to appoint civil administrators over the reductions. It was difficult under these circumstances for the Jesuits completely to disassociate themselves from the imperial culture of the Europeans. Though they won the affectionate devotion of many Indians, there were others who challenged the legitimacy of the enterprise. To them the white priests represented nothing but a more benign form of colonial exploitation.

In the fall of 1628 one of these hostile chiefs gave an order to kill Father Gonzalez and his Jesuit companions. A party of assassins was dispatched to carry out this order. On November 15 they attacked Gonzalez and hacked him to death with a stone hatchet. They also killed his fellow Jesuit Alonso Rodriguez. Two days later they killed a third priest, Father Juan de Castillo, who was stationed at a nearby mission.

The murder of these priests did not stop the encroachments of the Europeans. If anything, the Indians had lost courageous and effective defenders. A similar fate awaited the reductions themselves. In 1773 political and ecclesial rivalries in Europe prompted Pope Clement XIV to suppress the Jesuits. Thousands of missionaries were forced to abandon the field, among them the fathers of the Paraguayan reductions. The Society of Jesus would later rise from the ashes. But the reductions were finished. Within a few years the neat rows of houses, the paved avenues, and the baroque stone churches had been reclaimed by the verdant jungle.

In 1934 Gonzalez was the first American-born martyr to be beatified. His canonization followed in 1988, with a feast day established for November 16.

See: C. J. McNaspy, S.J., *Conquistador Without Sword: The Life of Roque Gonzalez, S.J.* (Chicago: Loyola University Press, 1984).

November 16

Ignacio Ellacuría and Companions
Jesuit Martyrs of San Salvador (d. 1989)

"What is it to be a companion of Jesus today? It is to engage, under the standard of the cross, in the crucial struggle of our time: the struggle for faith and that struggle for justice which it includes."

On the morning of November 16, 1989, news photographers in El Salvador recorded a scene of abomination: the bodies of six Jesuit priests strewn across the garden lawn of the University of Central America. Those seeking a meaning for their deaths could look to the Latin American church's option for the poor or to the Jesuits' commitment to social justice. Indeed, they could look to the Sermon on the Mount. But the immediate context was the fratricidal war in El Salvador, which in November 1989 had reached a critical stage. For several weeks, the capital city of San Salvador was swept up in the most serious rebel offensive of the ten-year civil war. As fighting spread to the formerly insulated neighborhoods of the rich, the military responded with panic and desperation.

On the evening of November 15, in a meeting of top military commanders (as investigations would later disclose), the order was given to eliminate all suspected sympathizers with the leftist rebels and to wipe out their "command centers" in the city. One of those present was Colonel Guillermo Alfredo Benavides. Within his sector of command lay the Jesuit-run Central American University.

Later that night, in the early morning hours of November 16, a unit of the Atlacatl Battalion, an elite "antiterrorist" force notorious for its record of human rights abuses, stole onto the campus of the university. The troops had been told that the targets of their operation were the intellectual authors of the uprising. After locating Father Ignacio Ellacuría, rector of the university, along with five other Jesuits asleep in their community residence, the troops forced the priests outside, had them lie on the lawn, and then scattered their brains with machine-gun fire.

Aside from Father Ellacuría, fifty-nine, the other priests were Ignacio Martín-Baró, forty-seven, a psychologist and vice-rector of the university; Juan Ramón Moreno, fifty-six, a theologian; Amando López, fifty-three, a theologian; Segundo Montes, fifty-six, superior of the community; and Joaquin López y López, seventy-one, national director of the "Faith and Joy" catechetical movement. Unexpectedly, the troops also discovered a housekeeper, Elba Ramos, and her sixteen-year-old daughter, Celina. Ironically, the two women, frightened by the street fighting outside, had chosen to remain in the supposed safety of the university. They were also murdered.

For years the Jesuits of the university had been a thorn in the side of the military and the ruling elite. This was not because they supported the rebels, but because they had consistently denounced the injustice and repression that fed the bitter war, and because they had sought to promote a negotiated settlement to the conflict. The Spanish-born Ellacuría had emerged as a particularly effective and eloquent advocate of national dialogue. But he was also outspoken in criticizing the injustices endemic to Salvadoran society, and he had earned the enmity of the military command with his frequent denunciation of their reign of terror. As a result, he was often identified by name in right-wing propaganda as the intellectual "brains" of the "communist" movement.

Ellacuría and his fellow priests were no communists. They were priests who had struggled hard to live out the church's proclaimed "option for the poor." More specifically they had committed themselves to the vision of the Jesuits' 1975 General Congregation, which defined the Society's mission in terms of "service of faith and promotion of justice." As intellectuals, as well as priests, they had committed the university itself to this mission, believing that in a world of conflict a Christian university must stand for truth and with the victims of violence. Because of this stand, the university had become a frequent target of bombs and right-wing terror.

Ellacuría, the theologian, was increasingly moved to articulate the meaning of faith and the gospel from the perspective of the suffering poor. In an arresting phrase, he liked to speak of the "crucified peoples" of history. Thus, he compared the poor with Yahweh's Suffering Servant. In their disfigured features he discerned the ongoing presence and passion of Christ — suffering because of the sins of the world. In this light, the task of the Christian was not simply to contemplate the mystery of suffering, but to "take the crucified down from the cross" — to join them in compassion and effective solidarity.

Thus, the decade that began with the assassination of *Archbishop Romero ended in this savage bloodletting. Romero had said, "I am glad that they have murdered priests in this country, because it would be very sad if in a country where they are murdering the people so horrifically, there were no priests among the victims." Friends of the slain Jesuits felt it was significant that in their death they were joined by two humble Salvadoran women, representatives of the more than seventy thousand victims, mostly poor and anonymous, who had already died in that decade of war. So in their deaths they joined their features to the face of the crucified people — victims of the same sin, witnesses to the same hope.

Segundo Montes had spoken for all his brothers when he explained to an interviewer his decision to remain in El Salvador: "This is my country and these people are my people.... The people need to have the church stay with them in these terrible times — the rich as well as the poor. The rich need to hear from us, just as do the poor. God's grace does not leave, so neither can we."

See: Jon Sobrino et al., *Companions of Jesus: The Jesuit Martyrs of El Salvador* (Maryknoll, N.Y.: Orbis, 1990).

St. Elizabeth of Hungary
Franciscan Queen (1207–1231)

"We must give God what we have, gladly and with joy."

St. Elizabeth was the daughter of Hungarian royalty. At the age of four, in a politically arranged match, she was betrothed to the future landgrave (prince) of Thuringia in southern Germany. So she was sent away from her family to live in the castle of her future husband, Ludwig, at the time a boy of nine. It may be supposed that such matches seldom tended to genuine romance. In this case however, it appears that the two children developed an intimate friendship which eventually blossomed into loving devotion. This endured the growing disapprobation of Ludwig's family as Elizabeth's piety steadily transgressed the boundaries of what was considered good taste. The young princess dressed too simply, it was said; she was inordinate in her prayer and profligate in her almsgiving. Ludwig, however, rejected any suggestion of returning her to Hungary; he declared that he would sooner part with a mountain of gold than be parted from the woman he affectionately called his "dear sister."

In due time they were married amid much ceremony. Elizabeth gave birth to three children in quick succession, and she rejoiced that as landgravine of Thuringia, she now had much greater scope for her charitable activities. She established several hospitals for the indigent and aroused scandal by nursing the sick and even lepers with her own hands. Her instinctive spiritual poverty was only magnified with the arrival of the first Franciscan missionaries in Germany. She was captivated by the story of *Clare and *Francis (from whom she received the gift of his cloak) and she eventually embraced the rule of a Franciscan tertiary.

In all her piety and service to the poor, Elizabeth received the loyal support of her husband. When famine struck the kingdom, while Ludwig was away, Elizabeth took it upon herself to open the royal granaries to the poor. Many lives were spared through her generosity. Nevertheless, upon his return Ludwig was shocked to discover that his wife had become an object of scorn among the rich and elite members of the court. Aside from her charity, they were offended by a personal discipline she had imposed on herself never to eat any food that might be the fruit of injustice or exploitation.

In 1227 Ludwig revealed that he had accepted command of a force of Crusaders bound for the Holy Land. Elizabeth, who was pregnant, felt a terrible premonition that they would not meet again and their parting was a scene of heartbreak. Some months later the news returned that Ludwig had died of plague on his journey. In a paroxysm of grief, Elizabeth cried, "The world is dead to me, and all that was joyous in the world."

Shocking developments followed. Without Ludwig to shield her from the resentment of her in-laws, Elizabeth was banished from the castle. She left in a winter night, leaving her few belongings and carrying nothing but her newborn child. She who had embraced the spirit of poverty now found herself happy to accept shelter in a pig-shed, for no reputable home would take her in. Eventually the scandal of her impoverishment was too much for her relatives to bear, and she was provided with a simple cottage in Marburg. Aside from her virtue, Elizabeth was equally admired for her "dark beauty." Her fall from grace did not prevent Emperor Frederick II, whose wife had recently died, from making inquiries regarding her marriageability. But she insisted that she was determined to remain a widow and devote herself to prayer and service of the poor.

Meanwhile, behind these public sufferings, Elizabeth had another cross to bear. Before her husband's death, she had accepted from Pope Honorius III the services of a spiritual director, Conrad of Marburg, who exacted from Elizabeth a vow of unquestioning obedience. This priest's most recent service had been as an Inquisitor of heretics, an experience he applied to his new undertaking. Ostensibly his aim was to advance Elizabeth's sanctification by weaning her of any vestige of attachment to the world. Thus, he cruelly upbraided her and even beat her with a stick for any infraction of his rules. He forced her to part with her two closest friends, the ladies-in-waiting who had accompanied her from Hungary as a child, and he replaced them with two "harsh females" who spied and reported on her activities. Escaping their attentions was one of the benefits of her exile from the court. Despite such treatment she maintained her gentleness of spirit and even responded to these cruelties with subversive humor, evidence, if any were needed, of how little encouragement her sanctity required.

In the meantime Elizabeth's reputation for holiness began to take root. The spectacle of this princess working at a spinning wheel or nursing the sick in their homes or in the hospices she had endowed inspired the grudging respect of those who had persecuted her, as well as the devoted affection of the poor and common folk. When not at prayer or engaged in other service, she liked to go fishing in nearby streams, selling her catch to provide alms.

In 1231 she fell ill and announced calmly that she would not recover. She died on November 17, at the age of twenty-four. Her confessor, Master Conrad, worked energetically (and with ill-concealed self-interest) to promote her cause. It was easy to assemble a dossier of reputed miracles and other documentation of her sanctity. His efforts were rewarded with her canonization a mere three years after her death — an event, however, which he did not live to witness. For many years the remains of Elizabeth, buried in the church in Marburg, were the object of pilgrimage until, during the Protestant Reformation, a future landgrave of Thuringia had her body removed to an unknown location.

See: Nesta de Robek, *Saint Elizabeth of Hungary: A Story of Twenty-Four Years* (Milwaukee: Bruce, 1954).

November 18

Jacques Maritain
Philosopher (1882–1973)

*"If Christians were to renounce ... the desire for sanctity ...
this would be an ultimate betrayal against God and against the world."*

Jacques Maritain, the foremost Catholic philosopher of the twentieth century, was born in Paris on November 18, 1882. He was raised in a liberal Protestant home. By the time he arrived as a student at the Sorbonne, however, he had succumbed to the pervasive attitude of agnosticism. Still, something within him could not be reconciled to the possibility of a world without transcendent meaning. In his spiritual restlessness he soon found a soulmate among his fellow students. She was *Raïssa Oumensoff, a young Jewish emigrant from Russia, who would become his wife and his lifelong companion in the spiritual journey.

Early in their intense relationship they agreed on a kind of mutual suicide pact if, in the space of a year, they could not "find meaning for the word 'truth.'" Happily, through the lectures of Henri Bergson they were led to apprehend a "sense of the absolute." Later they befriended the novelist *Léon Bloy, through whom they discovered the world of Catholicism. A year later, in 1906, they were received into the Catholic church, with Bloy as their godfather.

From that time on Jacques and Raïssa regarded themselves as living at the service of God and the church. Soon after their conversion they made a private vow of perpetual chastity. Nevertheless, they remained thoroughly devoted to one another, convinced that they were joined by God in order to assist one another along the path to holiness. Jacques completed his degree in philosophy and became a professor at the Institut Catholique in Paris, a position he held until 1939. Along the way he discovered the work of *Thomas Aquinas, a discovery that would determine the shape of his future work.

Although Thomistic scholasticism had for some time been the prescribed method of Catholic philosophy, it was Maritain who led the way in creatively applying Thomist principles to the modern world. Among the many topics he addressed were art and culture, democracy, and human rights. In the thought of Aquinas Maritain found a philosophy that was comprehensive in its integration of faith and reason, that was open to all aspects of culture, and that provided principles of government and social action rooted in an equal respect for the individual and the requirements of the common good.

For a time Maritain maintained a friendly relationship with the right-wing, ostensibly Catholic movement Action Française. When the movement was condemned by the Vatican in 1926 Maritain became intensely self-critical for having failed to perceive the movement's errors. Afterward he became an ardent proponent of democracy and earned the ire of conservatives when he refused to endorse the cause of Franco in the Spanish Civil War.

Jacques and Raïssa were in the United States in 1940 when Germany invaded France. They were not able to return for five years. Jacques taught at several universities, all the while writing extensively on philosophy and moral issues. Among other topics, he devoted extensive attention to a critique of Christian anti-Semitism.

By this time Jacques was widely recognized as the world's preeminent Catholic lay intellectual. Aside from the revival of Thomism he was identified with what he called "integral humanism" — the task of infusing the world with Christian values. This task called for a new type of "lay spirituality," which Jacques and Raïssa, with their intense commitment to prayer and the church and their equal engagement in the intellectual and cultural affairs of their day, very much exemplified.

After the war Jacques served for several years as the French ambassador to the Vatican. He became friends with the papal nuncio in France, Archbishop Roncalli, later to become *Pope John XXIII. Maritain contributed to the development of the United Nations and had a hand in drafting the U.N. Universal Declaration of the Rights of Man. In 1948 the Maritains returned to the United States, where Jacques took a position at Princeton University. He remained there until 1960, when Raïssa died.

Jacques and Raïssa had always said that should one of them die the other would enter a religious order. Despite his advanced age Jacques honored this commitment. But his choice of communities surprised those friends who imagined him in the elite company of the Jesuits or Dominicans. Instead he entered the novitiate of the Little Brothers of Jesus, the fraternity inspired by the modern desert father *Charles de Foucauld. He lived out his remaining days with the Little Brothers in a slum neighborhood in Toulouse.

In 1965 Maritain was summoned to Rome at the close of the Second Vatican Council. *Pope Paul VI personally presented him with the document on the Church in the Modern World and publicly recognized all that he had done to contribute to the renewal of Catholic intellectual life. Afterward Maritain returned to Toulouse. He took his vows as a Little Brother in 1970 and died three years later, on April 28, 1973, at the age of ninety-one.

See: Julie Kernan, *Our Friend, Jacques Maritain* (Garden City, N.Y.: Doubleday, 1975); James Bacik, "Jacques Maritain: Developing a Christian Humanism" (Chicago: Thomas More Association, 1987).

St. Mechtild of Hackeborn
Nun and Mystic (1241–1298)

"She gave teaching with such abundance that such a one has never been seen in the monastery and we fear, alas, will never be seen again."
—St. Gertrude

St. Mechtild was one of a trio of extraordinary mystics who inhabited the same Benedictine convent in Saxony in the late thirteenth century. Aside from Mechtild of Hackeborn, who first came to the convent of Helfta when she was seven, there was also the ex-Beguine *Mechthild of Magdeburg and the younger *Gertrude the Great. None of these women held any notable office in their community and yet they exerted spiritual authority far beyond the convent as a result of their visions and their wide reputation for holiness.

Mechtild of Hackeborn and Gertrude were particularly close. Gertrude had been donated to the convent at the age of five, and Mechtild, fifteen years her senior, had been largely responsible for her upbringing. As nuns and mystics they both developed a similar spirituality, emphasizing an affective devotion to the humanity of Christ and a strong focus on the Eucharist.

In the case of Mechtild, her first mystical vision occurred while receiving communion. Christ appeared to her, held her hands, and left his imprint on her heart "like a seal in wax." Christ furthermore presented his own heart to her in the form of a cup and said, "By my heart you will praise me always; go, offer to all the saints the drink of life from my heart that they may be happily inebriated with it."

Mechtild had a great devotion to the humanity of Christ, for this humanity was the "door" by which human beings and, indeed, all creation entered into union with divinity. In one extraordinary vision she perceived that "the smallest details of creation are reflected in the Holy Trinity by means of the humanity of Christ, because it is from the same earth that produced them that Christ drew his humanity."

As a result of her visions, Mechtild wielded tremendous authority within her community and beyond. She was regarded as a prophet, teacher, and counselor, "a tender mother of the unfortunate by her continual prayers, her zealous instruction, and her consolations." The teachings and visions of St. Mechtild were carefully recorded by her spiritual daughter and lifelong friend, St. Gertrude, in a work entitled the *Book of Special Grace*. She died on November 19, 1298.

See: Caroline Walker Bynum, *Jesus as Mother: Studies in the Spirituality of the High Middle Ages* (Berkeley: University of California Press, 1982).

Leo Tolstoy
Novelist and Moralist (1828–1910)

"Man gives himself to the illusion of egoism, lives for himself — and he suffers. It suffices that he begin to live for others, and the suffering becomes lighter, and there is obtained the highest good in the world: love of people."

Count Leo Tolstoy was born in 1828 to a wealthy and aristocratic family. By the age of sixteen he had abandoned the Orthodox faith of his childhood. By his own account, his youth was largely spent in the pursuit of pleasure, sensual gratification, and vain distractions. After serving as a military officer in the Crimean War and traveling abroad, he settled with his wife, Sonya, on his family estate, Yasnaya Polyana. There he set himself to the writing that would earn him fame and even greater wealth. His *War and Peace* and *Anna Karenina* were immediately acclaimed as works of genius, among the greatest novels ever written.

And yet despite his success Tolstoy was haunted by an underlying dis-ease, a yearning to find some deeper meaning to life. He was struck by a longstanding suspicion that such feelings of emptiness were unknown among the peasants. By emulating their life of poverty, work, and simple faith, he hoped to find the secret of happiness that otherwise seemed to elude the members of his privileged class.

Thus, Tolstoy publicly professed his return to the Orthodox faith. This was reflected immediately in the nature of his writing. No longer did he feel it appropriate to write "vain" novels. His future writing would serve his religious convictions. But he also became steadily embroiled in personal and public tensions and controversies, beginning in his family life. Sonya, the mother of his thirteen children, who had faithfully served as his literary assistant as well as devoted wife, found it impossible to sympathize with his religious obsessions; it seemed to her that Tolstoy was recklessly disregarding the welfare and interests of his own family.

This discord was only an intimate reflection of a struggle internal to Tolstoy himself. This struggle, to achieve a consistency between his ideals and his life, continued unabated for the rest of his days. His study of the Gospels led him increasingly to the conviction that the true essence of Christianity had become fatally encrusted by dogmatism, ritual, and subservience to secular authority. The heart of the gospel, in his opinion, was to be found in the Sermon on the Mount, with such themes as the presence of the kingdom of God within each soul, the counsel of voluntary poverty and nonresistance to evil, and the "law of love." He attacked the Orthodox church for neglecting these principles; in return he was excommunicated in 1901.

Tolstoy turned over his estate to his children and gave away the rights to his religious writings. He dressed as a peasant and took to working several hours a day in the fields. In his work *What Is to Be Done?* he had articulated his philosophy of bread labor, the conviction that each person should perform some physical labor to support his or her existence.

Philanthropy was not enough. This was comparable, he said, to a man sitting upon an overtaxed horse who tries to lighten the beast's burden by removing a few coins from his purse when the essential thing is to dismount.

Tolstoy wrote extensively on the philosophy of nonviolence and civil disobedience. Among his avid readers was a young Indian lawyer in South Africa, *Mohandas Gandhi, who would become, arguably, his most effective disciple and interpreter. For himself, Tolstoy remained haunted by the notion that he was merely play-acting as a Christian.

On October 28, 1910, at the age of eighty-two, Tolstoy ran away from home, accompanied only by his family physician. In a note to Sonya he wrote, "I am doing what people of my age often do — giving up the world in order to spend my last days alone and in silence." The strange flight to solitude did not take him far. On November 10 he fell ill while traveling by train. He stopped at Astapova and was taken to the station-master's house. There his identity was quickly discovered. Within days a crowd of disciples, curiosity seekers, journalists, and family members had converged on this obscure town to be present near the deathbed of a great man. His last words were, "To seek, always to seek." He died on November 20.

See: Leo Tolstoy, *My Religion* (London: Walter Scott, 1899); *The Kingdom of God Is within You* (New York: Farrar, Straus and Giroux, 1961).

November 21

St. Columbanus
Irish Abbot (530?–615)

"The true disciples of the crucified Christ follow him with a cross....
In it are hidden all the mysteries of salvation."

Within a generation of *St. Patrick the church in Ireland was firmly established. One of the distinctive features of the Irish church was an enthusiasm for the monastic ideal. So numerous and large were these monasteries that they soon began overflowing their native country. For a good part of the Middle Ages monks and saints were the principal export of Ireland. As missionaries spread throughout the British Isles and on to the Continent, Irish monks played an important role in stabilizing the primitive civilization of Europe, offering, through their monasteries, a safe haven for learning and culture.

One of the greatest of these Irish missionaries was St. Columbanus. He was born around 530 to a prosperous family in Leinster. As a young man, disturbed by the temptations of the world, Columbanus fled to a remote monastery in Bangor. There he lived for many years until he received an inspiration to reverse the missionary venture of Patrick and carry the gospel to foreign lands. With twelve companions he embarked for Gaul. He established a monastery in Burgundy which quickly attracted such large numbers that he was forced to found several other monasteries in the area.

Despite growing popularity, Columbanus came in for criticism from the local bishops, who objected to his severe Celtic spirituality. He also ran afoul of the royal family and was ordered to leave Burgundy with all his Irish monks. Columbanus made his way to Austria and Switzerland, everywhere establishing new monasteries. He finally crossed the Alps and settled in Milan, where he established yet another monastery and became embroiled in debate with exponents of the Arian heresy. He died in 615.

Columbanus did much to extend and popularize the monastic movement in Europe. He also devised an influential monastic rule, notable for its heavy emphasis on discipline. Ultimately it was eclipsed in popularity by the relatively clement Rule of *St. Benedict, which eventually came to dominate Western monasticism.

See: Vincent McNabb, O.P., "St. Columbanus," in F. J. Sheed, ed., *Saints Are Not Sad* (New York: Sheed & Ward, 1949).

November 22

Eberhard Arnold
Founder of the Bruderhof (1883–1935)

"In the name of Jesus Christ we can die, but not kill. This is where the Gospel leads us. If we really want to follow Christ, we must live as He lived and died. But this will not be clear to us until we understand how final His words are: You cannot serve God and mammon."

During the Reformation there were those who believed that Luther and Calvin and the churches they founded did not go far enough in recovering the radical spirit of Christianity. For one thing, they did not differ from the body of Christendom in their justification of violence, nor was there any appreciable difference in their attitude toward property. The so-called Radical Reformers, in contrast, wished to remake Christianity in the image of the Gospels and the early apostolic church. They stressed community, simplicity of life, and an uncompromising commitment to gospel nonviolence. As a result they suffered persecution at the hands of Catholics and Protestants alike. Nevertheless, their spirit took root in such Anabaptist communities as the Hutterites and Mennonites, which continue to this day. And their ideals, though never in the mainstream, have shown the capacity to send occasional sparks flying across time and space.

One of those sparks landed on Eberhard Arnold, a young theologian in Germany in the 1920s. He was the son of a professor of church history who had been persuaded to follow a similar course of studies at the university. Though more inclined to study medicine, he had followed his father's wishes and eventually earned a doctorate from the University of Erlangen. Well might he have pursued a career as a professor of theology — a vocation which in Germany, more than most places, confers considerable prestige. Eberhard's only problem was that he took the gospel too seriously. He believed that before "professing" theology, it was more important to *be* a Christian. His study of the New Testament and Christian origins, furthermore, had led him to question the legitimacy of the state church. Increasingly he was attracted to the pure message of the Sermon on the Mount, which seemed to contain the essence of the gospel.

World War I, with its suicidal indulgence of nationalism and militarism, followed by the crippling postwar depression, impressed Arnold as a sign of the great gulf between the spirit of Jesus and the spirit of the times. Through lectures and writing he began to attract similar seekers. They formed a Bible study group that earnestly searched the Scriptures for answers about how to live a life of faithful discipleship. What would it mean to live by the Sermon on the Mount in the world today? Would it be possible really to live a life given over to the love of neighbor? To live in a spirit of poverty, to love one's enemies, to accept insecurity like the birds in the air, the lilies of the field? Gradually the idea formed of a new Christian community of families sharing all things in common, attempting to live the spirit of the Beatitudes in the world.

These were the origins of the *Bruderhof* (meaning "a place where brothers live"). Eberhard, his wife, Emmy, and their children, along with half a dozen other individuals, formed the nucleus of the original community. Rediscovering, in effect, the spirit of the sixteenth-century Anabaptists, the Bruderhof practiced adult baptism of believers. Members lived together, shared all property in common, and adhered to a code of peace and nonviolence. Inevitably, the community endured birth pangs. Not all were suited to such a radical commitment. At one point nearly everyone left and the community was again reduced to seven individuals. But by the early 1930s the community, based in a settlement in the Rhön mountains, had grown to over a hundred people. In 1930 they affiliated with the Hutterites in North America, a group that was in certain respects more conservative than the German Bruderhof, but with whom they felt a deep spiritual bond.

By this time Germany was experiencing the rise of National Socialism. To Arnold and his companions there could be no doubt of the evil tendencies unleashed with Hitler's rise to power. Members of the Bruderhof were immediately conspicuous for refusing to offer the obligatory salutation, "Heil Hitler." Clearly the spirit of the Bruderhof was fundamentally incompatible with the forces driving Germany.

On November 16, 1933, the Bruderhof community was surrounded by 140 armed men, including SS officers and the Gestapo. The community was thoroughly searched, and great quantities of books and writings were seized for examination. It was the beginning of a time of continuous scrutiny and harassment. The community was forbidden to receive overnight guests or to publish books or journals. An order was issued to close the Bruderhof school unless they accepted a government-appointed principal. Rather than comply, the community decided to smuggle all the school children out of the country to Switzerland. Next there arose the question of military service. Should young draft-age men stay in Germany and accept imprisonment for their pacifist stand? Or was it better to abandon Germany altogether? Ultimately, the community chose the latter. Otherwise, no doubt, they would have all eventually faced extermination.

Eberhard did not make the move. For some time he had been crippled by a badly broken leg. In November 1935 he went into the hospital for surgery. Complications set in and he died some days later, on November 22, 1935.

This was not the end of the Bruderhof. Having survived sojourns in England and Paraguay, they went on to thrive in a network of communities in the United States. Supporting themselves by the manufacture of toys and equipment for the physically handicapped and by their publications, members of the Bruderhof continue to bear witness to the reign of God and to offer a window on a life patterned on the Sermon on the Mount.

See: The Hutterian Brethren and John Howard Yoder, eds., *God's Revolution: The Witness of Eberhard Arnold* (Farmington, Pa.: Plough Publishing House, 1984); Emmy Arnold, *Torches Together: The Beginning and Early Years of the Bruderhof Communities* (Rifton, N.Y.: Plough Publishing House, 1964).

November 23

Bd. Miguel Pro
Jesuit and Martyr (1891–1927)

"Let me spend my life at your side, my Mother, the companion of your bitter solitude and your profound pain. Let my soul feel your eyes' sad weeping and the abandonment of your heart."

In 1926 Father Miguel Pro landed at the Mexican port of Veracruz, the starting point for his journey to the capital. During his Jesuit formation in Europe he had always worn the distinctive black cassock of a priest. But now in his native country he was forced to travel in disguise. Mexico was passing through a period of violent anti-Catholic repression, and to be identified as a priest would mean instant arrest. Father Pro's mission was simple: to serve the Catholic people, to strengthen their faith, to celebrate the sacraments, and to elude arrest as long as possible.

It was not so many years since the Revolution of 1910 when armies of landless peasants had marched under the banner of Our Lady of Guadalupe. Now under President Plutarco Calles the heroic ideals of "Land and Liberty" had been largely reduced to a campaign against Catholicism, which Calles blamed for all the country's woes. But though repressive laws had driven the faith underground, it was not uprooted. As soon as Father Pro arrived in Mexico City, he quickly made contact with a thriving underground church.

Since childhood Pro had been famous for his irreverent humor. Now his letters to the Jesuits reflected his characteristic bravado and a playful spirit of adventure. He delighted in wearing disguises and in his ability to pass undetected under the noses of the police. But it was a serious business. He spent his days hearing confessions, performing clandestine baptisms, distributing communion to those who could not attend Mass. There were spies everywhere, but also, it seemed, an inexhaustible supply of loyal Catholics, prepared to undergo terrible risks to assist a priest on the run.

Some went further than offering prayers. The atmosphere of repression provoked the famous Cristero Rebellion, a defense of the church, but also, in the eyes of many of its partisans, a defense of the lost ideals of the Revolution. Pro's own brothers were members of the Religious Defense League, which challenged the regime through symbolic gestures. On one occasion they released hundreds of balloons that dropped religious leaflets over the city. But others took more drastic actions. After an assassination attempt on the ex-president, the police undertook a full-scale sweep with orders to round up suspected Catholics and their leaders.

Father Pro slipped through the net several times. But eventually he was captured along with his brothers and charged with participation in the murder plot. Pro denied any knowledge of the plot, and later evidence confirmed that the police were aware of his innocence. Nevertheless, it was thought expedient to make an example of this priest. President Calles personally ordered his execution.

Since arriving in Mexico Pro had foreseen the likelihood of his martyrdom. Before his arrest he had prayed at Mass that God might accept the sacrifice of his life for the salvation of his country and for the benefit of his fellow priests. He closed his last letter with the words, "*Adios.* Remember me to all, never forget me, and any time you lack someone for whom to say an Ave Maria, know that I shall accept it with the greatest pleasure."

Pro was held for several days in a cramped dungeon, uncertain of his fate. He was never formally sentenced. But on the morning of November 23, 1927, he was taken to the police firing range. A crowd of reporters as well as a delegation of the top military authorities had been summoned to witness his death.

Pro was asked if he had any last requests. He asked to be permitted to pray. When he had finished he stood and held out his arms in the form of a cross — by this gesture making a silent allusion to the meaning of his sacrifice. As the firing squad took aim, he spoke in a soft voice the words, "Viva Cristo Rey."

So ended the life of Father Pro. But if the president had hoped Pro's death would put an end to further Catholic resistance, he had not reckoned on the power of martyrdom. Father Pro was instantly acclaimed by the people as a saint. The photographs of his execution became holy cards, eagerly distributed among the faithful. Miguel Pro was beatified as a martyr by Pope John Paul II in 1988.

See: Fanchón Royer, *Padre Pro* (New York: P. J. Kenedy & Sons, 1954).

John LaFarge
Priest and Champion of Interracial Justice
(1880–1963)

"The Negro brings to the Church something that is in danger of disappearing from its life in this country, and thereby putting American Catholicism out of touch with the rest of the great universal suffering world — a keen sense of social justice."

John LaFarge hailed from one of America's most distinguished families. His father, also John, was a famous painter and master of stained glass. His mother was a Catholic convert who had received instruction from *Isaac Hecker. It was said of the younger John that, from his birth in Newport, Rhode Island, he was enrolled in both the Catholic church and the Social Register. After studying classics at Harvard he decided to become a priest, and so traveled to the Jesuit school at Innsbruck, Austria, to study theology. As he embarked his mother cried out to him (for no particular reason that she could later remember), "Whatever you do, don't become a Jesuit!" "You needn't worry!" he shouted back. But several years later a Jesuit he became.

One of his first assignments as a priest was to serve as chaplain in the hospital and prison on Blackwell's Island in New York City. This experience first awakened his commitment to the social dimensions of the gospel, a commitment that was further intensified with his assignment as part of a parish team in Leonardtown, Maryland. The parish was largely black, and it was the first time that the privileged Father LaFarge had been truly exposed to the bleak marginalization of blacks in American society and in the church. He determined to dedicate his priesthood to awakening the conscience of America to this reality.

In 1926 he moved back to New York to join the staff of *America* magazine, a Jesuit journal. LaFarge spent the rest of his life at the magazine. Through his editorials, articles, and columns, he gradually gained a reputation as the premier Catholic champion of what he called "interracial justice," a cause not shared by many Catholics until the rise of the civil rights movement several decades later.

In the 1930s LaFarge, along with others including *Dorothy Day, helped found the Catholic Interracial Council. He also wrote several books on the issue of racism and social action. One of them fell into the hands of Pope Pius XI. In 1938, during a papal audience, Pius asked LaFarge to draft an encyclical on racism. "Say simply," the pope said, "what you would say to the whole world if you yourself were pope." LaFarge was overwhelmed by the challenge, but he complied, drafting a powerful statement of the church's attitude toward the "sin" and "heresy" of racism. It is tempting to imagine the possible impact such a document might have made in the impending struggle against Nazism. Sadly, it was never published. Soon after LaFarge had finished his draft, the pope passed away and the encyclical was shelved by his successor.

LaFarge continued in his own voice to challenge the church and American society. Racial prejudice and injustice, he believed, exposed the hypocrisy of America's profession of democracy. To the extent that the church failed to address this sin, it undermined the credibility of its witness to the universal love of Christ. The persistence of racism was a powerful challenge not only to the social conscience of the church but to the fulfillment of its true mission and reason for being.

LaFarge lived to see a new dawn for his ideals in the Second Vatican Council and the rise of the black freedom struggle. In August 1963 *Martin Luther King delivered his "I Have a Dream" speech in Washington, D.C. On November 24, at the age of eighty-three, John LaFarge died peacefully in his sleep.

See: Edward St. Stanton, "John LaFarge," in John J. Delaney, ed., *Saints Are Now* (Garden City, N.Y.: Doubleday, 1981); *A John LaFarge Reader,* ed. Thurston N. David, S.J., and Joseph Small, S.J. (New York: America Press, 1956).

November 25

St. Catherine of Alexandria
Martyr (date unknown)

"Come my beloved, my spouse, behold the door of heaven is opened to thee; and to those that shall celebrate the memory of thy passion with devout minds I promise the protection of heaven!"

In the aftermath of Vatican II a reform of the calendar led the church to disavow a number of popular but, in all likelihood, nonexistent saints. St. Catherine of Alexandria, one of the most popular of all saints, was among these demobilized from active service. Though her cult had flourished since at least the tenth century, there was little to connect her to her supposed adventures in Roman times, and it was reluctantly determined that no such person ever existed.

Nevertheless, for centuries her "remains" attracted pilgrims to a monastery on Mt. Sinai. What is more, hers was one of the heavenly voices that supposedly spoke to *St. Joan of Arc, thus empowering the peasant maid to defy every authority of her age. For refusing to disavow her voices Joan went to the stake, and for the same holy disobedience she was later canonized. It is a case that brings to mind *Karl Barth's famous dictum, when asked by a student whether he really believed a snake spoke to Eve in the Garden: "The important thing is not whether or not a snake could talk; the important thing is what he said."

According to what the editors of *Butler's Lives* call "her completely worthless *acta,*" St. Catherine was supposed to be the daughter of a patrician family in Alexandria, Egypt, sometime in the Roman era. Through her study of philosophy she became convinced of the truth of Christianity and converted to the illicit faith. When she sought to convert the emperor himself, he had her examined by fifty of the leading philosophers of the court. Unable to refute her arguments they were all in fact persuaded to convert. (Consequently, they were all also burned to death.) The emperor was so impressed by Catherine's beauty, if not her brilliance, that he tried to induce her to be his consort. This offer she declined, preferring instead to be imprisoned and tortured. While in prison, however, she successfully converted the emperor's wife, her jailer, and two hundred of the imperial guards. All these too were consequently slain. Enraged, the emperor condemned her to be tortured on a spiked wheel (hence the "catherine wheel" that is her famous emblem). But the machine miraculously broke apart and killed many onlookers. At this point, and before she could perform any more mischief, the exasperated emperor had this dangerous woman put to the sword.

In removing Catherine of Alexandria from the canon of saints, the church has indicated that the minimal requirement for the legitimate cult of a saint is that such a person actually existed. But it is not this minimal requirement that has strengthened the faith and inspired the imitation of subsequent generations. More important, in many cases, is the meaning which Christians find in the stories of the saints, in short, what they "say" to us.

St. Catherine of Alexandria, a saint who never was, served for centuries as "the patroness of maidens and women students, of philosophers, preachers and apologists, of wheelwrights, millers and others" (*Butler's Lives*). She may continue to represent the subversive power of women's wisdom, a voice which many would like to silence lest it subvert the whole world with its irrefutable logic. So Catherine continues to inspire and illuminate us with her edifying story, like the light emanating from a distant star which no longer exists.

See: The Golden Legend of Jacobus de Voragine (London: Longman, Green, 1941).

November 26

Sojourner Truth
Abolitionist Preacher (1797–1883)

"What we give the poor, we lend to the Lord."

Sojourner Truth was born a slave in Hurley, New York, around the year 1797 (her master did not record the exact date of her birth). Her parents named her Isabella, a name she abandoned at the age of forty-six when she took up her calling as a prophet and preacher.

Her first language was Dutch, the language of her master. It marked her English with a strong accent, just as her back ever bore the mark of beatings she received as a child of bondage. In her youth she was bought and sold a number of times. Some of her owners were relatively benign, while others were harsh and cruel. She was the ninth child born to her parents, but she never knew her brothers and sisters — all of them sold away to different owners.

Despite Isabella's sufferings, her mother raised her to believe in "a God who hears and sees everything you think and do." Her mother told her, "When you are beaten or cruelly treated, or you fall into any kind of trouble, you must ask his help. He will always hear you and help you." Indeed, throughout her life Isabella carried on a continuous conversation with God. Later she used to begin her speeches with the phrase, "Children, I speak to God and God speaks to me." She poured out her sufferings to God, and God told her that she would be free.

As a young woman Isabella was given in marriage to an older slave, with whom she bore five children. But early one morning in 1826 she walked away from her master's farm and stole herself from slavery, taking only her infant daughter and leaving her other four children behind.

She worked as a servant in and about New York City for a number of years. But by 1843 Isabella became convinced that God was calling her to some greater mission. So she set off on foot and left New York, carrying her few possessions in a pillow case, unsure about her destination, determined to be a preacher. With her new freedom she felt it was time to replace her slave name. After appealing to God for inspiration, she chose the name Sojourner Truth, which reflected her calling to travel "up and down the land, showing the people their sins and being a sign unto them."

As Sojourner Truth she commenced an itinerant ministry of the word, preaching from the Scriptures she had practically learned by heart and delivering God's judgment against the evils of slavery. Her autobiography, *The Narrative of Sojourner Truth,* which she dictated and published in 1847, became a powerful weapon in the abolitionist cause. Yet, as eloquent and effective a speaker as she was in the antislavery movement, Truth divided her energies with the growing movement for women's rights. Many abolitionists were wary of the feminist movement, worried about compromising the struggle against slavery by linking it with another unpopular cause. But Truth insisted that there was no separating the issues. "If colored men get their rights, and not colored women," she said, "colored men will be masters over the women, and it will be just as bad as before."

In a time when the country was increasingly divided over the issue of slavery, Truth's appearances were often met with violent mobs. She never let fear or conflict silence her. More than once she tamed a hostile audience with her disarming wit. When an angry heckler once declared, "Old woman, I don't care any more for your talk than I do for the bite of a flea," she replied, "The Lord willing, I'll keep you scratching."

She never doubted that the end of slavery would come at last. When the great abolitionist Frederick Douglass once ended a speech on a discouraging note, Truth interjected with forthright confidence, "Frederick, is God dead?" In the end, however, the conflict over slavery led to bloody civil war. Truth lent her energies to supporting the war effort, especially by visiting black troops who were fighting in the Union Army. In 1864 she traveled to Washington to meet Abraham Lincoln and to encourage him in the struggle. Moved by the sufferings of the many ex-slaves who had crowded into squalid refugee camps in Washington, she decided to stay on in the capital and minister to their needs. She was there when the war ended at last, and on December 12, 1865, when Congress ratified the Thirteenth Amendment to the Constitution, abolishing slavery in the United States.

She continued to struggle for freedom and equality until the day she died on November 26, 1883, at the age of eighty-six. She was widely acclaimed as one of the most influential women of her day: an illiterate black woman, a political activist without office, a preacher without credentials save for her penetrating and holistic vision of God's justice.

In one of her most famous speeches, she rose in a women's rights meeting to respond to those men who had spoken with patronizing solicitude of women's weakness and consequent subordination to men:

> I have plowed and planted and gathered into barns, and no man could head me — and ain't *I* a woman? I have born'd five childrun and seen 'em mos' all sold off into slavery, and when I cried out with mother's grief, none but Jesus heard — and ain't *I* a woman?...Den dat little man in black dar, he say women can't have as much rights as man, 'cause Christ warn't a woman. Whar did your Christ come from? *Whar did your Christ come from?* From God and a woman! Man had nothing to do with him!

A few days before she died, Truth said to a friend, "I'm not going to die, honey. I'm going home like a shooting star." Her star still shines.

See: Joyce Hollyday et al., "'Ain't I a Woman?' Sojourner Truth," special issue of *Sojourners* (December 1986); Peter Krass, *Sojourner Truth* (New York: Chelsea House, 1988).

November 27

Sts. Barlaam and Josaphat
Monks (no date)

"This city is the world, and the citizens are the princes of darkness.... Then death comes upon us unexpectedly and we are submerged in the place of darkness. But by the hands of the poor we can store up riches in eternity."

According to legend, St. Josaphat was the son of an Indian king who had persecuted his Christian subjects. When a seer foretold that Josaphat himself would one day become a Christian, the king had him locked up in seclusion. Eventually, however, the young man was converted by Barlaam, a wandering monk of Mt. Sinai, who approached him in the guise of a merchant offering to sell "a pearl of great price." After receiving baptism, Josaphat renounced his throne and all worldly wealth. Instead he retired to the desert with Barlaam to pursue his ongoing quest for moral and spiritual truth.

This story, which was long attributed to St. John of Damascus, had a long and extremely influential life in the Christian East and West, especially in the Middle Ages. In recent times it has been traced to a Georgian monk on Mt. Athos in the eleventh century, from which source it was circulated in Latin as well as Greek versions, but also in many Slavonic and vernacular translations.

The story is clearly legendary. What is especially interesting is the complicated religious history of the tale. Scholars have shown that the Christian legend was a translation of an Islamic version, which had in turn been taken from Manichean sources in Western Asia. Going back further, the story is ultimately traced to Siddhartha Gautama, the Hindu prince who renounced his family, wealth, and worldly power to seek the path of enlightenment. Sitting under the Bo tree he became the future Buddha, or "Bodhisattva." In the transmigration of the story this word became Bodisaf (Manichee), Yudasaf (Arabic), Lodasaph (Georgian), Ioasaph (Greek), and finally Josaphat (Latin).

Wilfred Cantwell Smith has offered this story as an illustration of the principle that every religious tradition has developed in interaction with others. After tracing the above-noted prehistory of the story, he proceeds to look at its ongoing effects. He notes that *Tolstoy cited this story in his *Confessions* and described the effect it had in prompting his own conversion. It was largely by reading Tolstoy that the Indian *Mohandas Gandhi was converted to the message of nonviolence (and incidentally rediscovered the spiritual traditions of his homeland). It was in turn by reading Gandhi that *Martin Luther King, Jr., discovered the methods of nonviolence which he applied in the United States.

At various turns we find the power of a story of religious conversion — specifically an impulse to turn away from the worldly agenda of wealth and power — serving as a catalyst in the spiritual awakening and conversion of others. So by this curious route, the Buddha became a Christian saint who inspired later generations of Christians to pursue the path of enlightenment. Rather than disavow Sts. Barlaam and Josaphat as figures of legend, it might be better to celebrate them as patron saints for an age of interreligious dialogue.

See: The Golden Legend of Jacobus de Voragine (London: Longman, Green, 1941); Wilfred Cantwell Smith, *Towards a World Theology: Faith and the Comparative History of Religion* (Philadelphia: Westminster, 1981).

November 28

St. Joseph Pignatelli
Jesuit (1737–1811)

"Why should ours be the hearts to bleed in this affliction? Why should ours be the eyes to weep in sorrow? We know that we have committed no fault in all this unhappy business.... The time will come when they will cry out for these Fathers to return to them but their cry will be in vain; they shall not find them."

After midnight on April 2, 1767, the Jesuit house in Saragossa, Spain, was surrounded by soldiers. When the rector answered a knock on the door he was confronted by a military commander who rudely insisted that the entire Jesuit community be roused and gathered to hear an edict from His Majesty King Charles. When all the priests were present they heard the astonishing news that "for grave reasons" which "by their nature must remain unrevealed in our royal bosom" the king had ordered the immediate expulsion from Spain of all members of the Society of Jesus. An identical message was at that same moment being delivered in Jesuit houses throughout Spain.

Thus began the most terrible ordeal in the history of the Jesuits, a wholesale assault aimed at their eradication. This concerted effort was mounted by Bourbon princes throughout Europe who saw in the powerful Jesuits an obstacle to their control over the church. Certainly among the instigators of this persecution were the ruling elites in the New World colonies who bitterly resented the Jesuits' defense of the Indians and the poor. But ultimately the assault was unsuccessful. The Jesuits survived. Among those especially credited with this feat was a Spaniard, St. Joseph Pignatelli, whom Pius XI acclaimed as a "Second Founder" of the Society.

Pignatelli, the son of Spanish nobles, was among those present in the Saragossa house the night of the infamous decree. Because of his royal blood he was offered the choice of remaining in Spain. He chose, however, to accompany his brothers. The next day they were ignominiously transported by oxcart to the Catalan border, where similar convoys of Jesuits, five thousand altogether, were arriving from across Spain. Pignatelli was put in charge of the Spanish exiles, a charge he would honor for the rest of his life.

For three weeks, on crowded boats, the Jesuits sailed from port to port in search of a receptive home. On principle, the pope refused them entry into the Papal States, not wanting to recognize Spain's illegal actions. Finally the priests settled in Corsica. Pignatelli immediately organized a house of studies to continue the training of the novices. But within months, after Corsica fell to France, the Jesuits were once again expelled and once again forced to resume their search for safe haven.

Similar expulsions had occurred from France and Portugal. But the worst was yet to come. In 1769 Pope Clement XIV, under unremitting pressure from the Bourbon princes, agreed to suppress the Society altogether. When the papal brief was read aloud the Jesuits submitted with characteristic obedience. At once twenty-three thousand Jesuit priests were dispensed from their religious vows. Pignatelli settled in Bologna, where he continued his studies and remained an unofficial leader among his dispersed fellow Jesuits, all the while maintaining constant faith in the providence and justice of God.

There was, however, an anomaly in the Society's brief of suppression, namely, that in order to be put into effect it had to be officially delivered to each local community. For her own reasons of state, Empress Catherine the Great refused to allow the bishops in White Russia to deliver the brief. Thus, at least in this corner of Europe, the Jesuits remained in official existence.

When Father Pignatelli learned of this, he wrote to the superior in Russia and asked to be affiliated with this province. Permission was granted.

And so without ever setting foot in Russia Pignatelli renewed his vows and quietly became the only Jesuit in Italy. With verbal permission from the pope he organized a novitiate at Colorno. In 1804 Pope Pius VII approved the reestablishment of the Society in Naples. Pignatelli was named provincial, an authority that was eventually extended to all of Italy.

Pignatelli did not live to see the full restoration of the Society, which took place in 1814. He died on November 11, 1811, and was canonized in 1954. His feast day is November 28.

See: Mons. D. A. Hanley, *Blessed Joseph Pignatelli* (New York: Benziger Bros., 1937).

November 29

Dorothy Day
Co-Founder of the Catholic Worker (1897–1980)

"Whatever I had read as a child about the saints had thrilled me. I could see the nobility of giving one's life for the sick, the maimed, the leper.... But there was another question in my mind. Why was so much done in remedying the evil instead of avoiding it in the first place? ... Where were the saints to try to change the social order, not just to minister to the slaves, but to do away with slavery?"

When Dorothy Day died in 1980 at the age of eighty-three it was observed that she was "the most influential, interesting, and significant figure" in the history of American Catholicism. This was an extraordinary statement on behalf of someone who occupied no official position in the church — indeed, someone whose ideas were almost universally rejected throughout most of her life. The Catholic Worker, a lay movement she founded in 1933 and oversaw for nearly fifty years, was an effort to show that the radical gospel commandment of love could be lived. She understood this challenge not just in the personal form of charity (the works of mercy) but in a political form as well, confronting and resisting the social forces which gave rise to such a need for charity. She represented a new type of political holiness — a way of serving Christ not only through prayer and sacrifice but through solidarity with the poor and in struggle along the path of justice and peace.

As a result some people called her a communist. She was shot at, jailed, and investigated repeatedly by the F.B.I. She was not seriously disturbed by criticism. "The servant is not greater than his master," she liked to quote. On the other hand there were many who liked to call her saint. That was another matter. "When they call you a saint," she often said, "it means basically that you're not to be taken seriously." She regarded it as way of dismissing her challenge: "Dorothy can do that; she's a saint!" The implication was that hard decisions must have come easily for her. Actually, no one knew as well as she how dearly she had paid for her vocation: "Neither revolutions nor faith is won without keen suffering.

For me Christ was not to be bought for thirty pieces of silver but with my heart's blood. We buy not cheap in this market."

Day was born in Brooklyn in 1897. Though she was baptized as an Episcopalian she had little exposure to religion. By the time she was in college she had rejected Christianity in favor of the radical cause. She dropped out of school and worked as a journalist in New York with a variety of radical papers and took part in the popular protests of her day. Her friends were communists, anarchists, and an assortment of New York artists and intellectuals, most of the opinion that religion was the "opium of the people."

A turning point in her life came in 1926 when she was living on Staten Island with a man she deeply loved. She became pregnant, an event that sparked a mysterious conversion. The experience of what she called "natural happiness," combined with a sense of the aimlessness of her Bo-hemian existence, turned her heart to God. She decided she would have her child baptized as a Roman Catholic, a step she herself followed in 1927. The immediate impact of this was the painful end of her common-law marriage. The man she loved had no use for marriage. But she also suffered from the sense that her conversion represented a betrayal of the cause of the poor. The church, though in many ways the home of the poor, seemed otherwise to identify with the status quo. So she spent some lonely years in the wilderness, raising her child alone, while praying for some way of reconciling her faith and her commitment to social justice.

The answer came in 1932 with a providential meeting. *Peter Maurin, an itinerant philosopher and agitator, encouraged her to begin a news-paper that would offer solidarity with the workers and a critique of the social system from the radical perspective of the Gospels. The *Catholic Worker* was launched on May 1, 1933. Like a true prophet, Maurin was concerned not simply to denounce injustice but to announce a new social order, based on the recognition of Christ in one's neighbors. In an effort to practice what they preached, Day converted the office of the Catho-lic Worker into a "house of hospitality" — the first of many — offering food for the hungry and shelter for the tired masses uprooted by the Depression.

But Day's message did not end with the works of mercy. For her the logic of the Sermon on the Mount also led to an uncompromising com-mitment to nonviolence. Despite widespread criticism she maintained a pacifist position throughout World War II and later took part in numer-ous civil disobedience campaigns against the spirit of the Cold War and the peril of nuclear war. Later, in the 1960s, when social protest became al-most commonplace, Day's peacemaking witness—rooted in her daily life among the poor and sustained by the discipline of liturgy and prayer — retained a particular credibility and challenge.

The enigma of Dorothy Day was her ability to reconcile her radi-cal social positions (she called herself an anarchist as well as a pacifist) with a traditional and even conservative piety. Her commitment to pov-erty, obedience, and chastity was as firm as any nun's. But she remained thoroughly immersed in the secular world with all the "precarity" and disorder that came with life among the poor. Her favorite saint was

*Therese of Lisieux, the young Carmelite nun whose "little way" indicated the path to holiness within all our daily occupations. From Therese Day drew the insight that any act of love might contribute to the balance of love in the world, any suffering endured in love might ease the burden of others; such was the mysterious bond within the Body of Christ.

In combining the practice of charity and the call to justice Day represented a type of holiness not easily domesticated, but perhaps of special relevance to our times. She called on the church to recover its identity as an offense and mystery in the eyes of the world. Her life was a living parable, focused on what she called the mystery of the poor: "that they are Jesus, and what you do for them you do to Him." She died on November 29, 1980.

See: Robert Ellsberg, ed., *Dorothy Day: Selected Writings* (Maryknoll, N.Y.: Orbis, 1992); Jim Forest, *Love Is the Measure: A Biography of Dorothy Day* (Maryknoll, N.Y.: Orbis, 1993).

November 30

Etty Hillesum
Mystic of the Holocaust (1914–1943)

"God is not accountable to us, but we are to Him. I know what may lie in wait for us.... And yet I find life beautiful and meaningful."

Little is known of the external life of Etty Hillesum, a young Jewish woman who lived in Amsterdam during the Nazi occupation and who died as one of the millions of victims of the Holocaust. This obscurity is in contrast with her well-documented internal life. From the day when Dutch Jews were ordered to wear a yellow star up to the day she boarded a cattle car bound for Poland, Etty consecrated herself to an ambitious task. In the face of her impending death, she endeavored to bear witness to the inviolable power of love and to reconcile her keen sensitivity to human suffering with her appreciation for the beauty and meaning of existence. For the last two years of her life Etty kept a meticulous diary, recording her daily experiences and the unfolding of her interior response. Published four decades after her death, this book was quickly recognized as one of the great moral documents of our time.

Etty maintained a clear sense of solidarity with the Jewish people. But her personal reflection was nourished by an eclectic range of sources, including Rilke, the Bible, *St. Augustine, and *Dostoevsky. When a friend exclaimed indignantly that her attitude on the love of enemies sounded like Christianity, she responded, "Yes, Christianity, why ever not?" But in fact she had little interest in organized religion of any kind. In a time when everything was being swept away, when "the whole world is becoming a giant concentration camp," she felt one must hold fast to what endures — the encounter with God at the depths of one's own soul and in other people.

There is an earthy and embodied dimension to Etty Hillesum's spirituality. She described her romantic adventures with no more reticence than she reserved for descriptions of her prayer. For Etty, everything — the physical and the spiritual without distinction — was related to her passionate openness to life, which was ultimately openness to God.

In the meantime her life was unfolding within the tightening noose of German occupation. Etty's effervescence might seem to resemble a type of manic denial. The fact is, however, that she seems to have discerned the logic of events with uncommon objectivity. In this light, her determination to affirm the goodness and beauty of existence becomes nothing short of miraculous. Her entry for July 3, 1942, reads:

> I must admit a new insight in my life and find a place for it: what is at stake is our impending destruction and annihilation. . . . They are out to destroy us completely, we must accept that and go on from there. . . . Very well then . . . I accept it. . . . I work and continue to live with the same conviction and I find life meaningful. . . . I wish I could live for a long time so that one day I may know how to explain it, and if I am not granted that wish, well, then somebody else will perhaps do it, carry on from where my life has been cut short. And that is why I must try to live a good and faithful life to my last breath; so that those who come after me do not have to start all over again.

For Etty, this affirmation of the value and meaning of life in the face of overwhelming evidence to the contrary became her guiding principle. In the midst of suffering and injustice, she believed, the effort to preserve in one's heart a spirit of love and forgiveness was the greatest task that any person could perform. This, she felt, was her vocation.

With increasing regularity, Etty described her compulsion to drop to her knees in prayer. Toward the end of her journals, God had become the explicit partner of her internal dialogue:

> God take me by Your hand, I shall follow You faithfully, and not resist too much, I shall evade none of the tempests life has in store for me, I shall try to face it all as best I can. . . . I shall try to spread some of my warmth, of my genuine love for others, wherever I go. . . . I sometimes imagine that I long for the seclusion of a nunnery. But I know that I must seek You amongst people, out in the world. And that is what I shall do. . . . I vow to live my life out there to the full.

Etty worked for a while as a typist for the Jewish Council, a job that delayed her deportation to the transit camp at Westbork. Eventually she renounced this privilege and volunteered to accompany her fellow Jews to the camp. She did not wish to be spared the suffering of the masses. In fact, she felt a deep calling to be present at the heart of the suffering, to become "the thinking heart of the concentration camp."

Her sense of a call to solidarity with those who suffer became the specific form of her religious vocation. But it was not a vocation to suffering as such. It was a vocation to redeem the suffering of humanity from within, by safeguarding "that little piece of You, God, in ourselves."

I know that a new and kinder day will come. I would so much like to live on, if only to express all the love I carry within me. And there is only one way of preparing the new age, by living it even now in our hearts.

On September 7, 1943, Etty and her family were placed on a transport train to Poland. From a window of the train she tossed out a card that read, "We have left the camp singing." She died in Auschwitz on November 30. She was twenty-nine.

See: An Interrupted Life: The Diaries of Etty Hillesum, 1941–1943 (New York: Pantheon, 1983).

❧ DECEMBER ❧

December 1

Charles de Foucauld
Little Brother of Jesus (1858–1916)

"I no longer want a monastery which is too secure. I want a small mon-astery, like the house of a poor workman who is not sure if tomorrow he will find work and bread, who with all his being shares the suffering of the world."

Charles de Foucauld was born into an aristocratic family in Strasbourg in 1858. An indifferent student and evidently possessed of a weak character, he sought a career in the army but was dismissed in 1881 as a result of his scandalous behavior. The saving benefit from his military service was a fascination with the North African desert, to which he returned under the aegis of the French Geographical Society to undertake a dangerous exploration of Morocco. It was there that the experience of Muslim piety helped prompt in Charles a dramatic recovery of his Catholic faith, chang-ing his character and his life forever. "As soon as I believed that there was a God," he later wrote, "I understood that I could not do anything other than live for him. My religious vocation dates from the same moment as my faith."

A pilgrimage through the Holy Land, following the footsteps of Jesus in the actual towns and countryside where he had walked, made a pro-found impact. Afterward Foucauld entered the Trappists and spent a number of years in a monastery in Syria. But conventional monastic life did not satisfy him. If there is an essential insight which impressed Fou-cauld it was the fact that Jesus, the Son of God, had been a poor man and a worker. As a carpenter in Nazareth Jesus had, in these lowly cir-cumstances, embodied the gospel message in its entirety, before ever announcing it in words.

Having achieved this insight, Foucauld set about trying to put it into practice — at first rather literally. For three years he worked as a servant at a convent of Poor Clares in Nazareth itself. But eventually he realized that "Nazareth" might be any place. And so, after seeking ordination, he returned to Algeria, to the oasis of Béni-Abbès on the border of Morocco. His goal was to develop a new model of contemplative religious life, a community of Little Brothers, who would live among the poor in a spirit of service and solidarity. In the constitutions he devised for his planned order, Foucauld wrote, "The whole of our existence, the whole of our lives should cry the Gospel from the rooftops...not by our words but by our lives."

Foucauld spent fifteen years in the desert. When he found the remote Béni-Abbès becoming too congested, he sought greater solitude in Tamanrasset, a small outpost in the rugged Hoggar. It was there on December 1, 1916, that he met his death, killed by Tuareg rebels.

Foucauld had spent many years conceiving and preparing the way for followers who never arrived, and he might well have died with little sense of accomplishment had his spirituality not trained him to look beyond outward appearances. In his famous Prayer of Abandonment he had written: "Father, I abandon myself in Your hands, do with me what You will. For whatever You may do, I thank you. I am ready for all, I accept all, let only Your will be done in me, as in all Your creatures."

Ultimately, however, the reverberations from Foucauld's solitary witness achieved considerable effect. In 1933, long after his death, René Voillaume and four companions left France for the Sahara. They became the core of the Little Brothers of Jesus. Several years later they were joined by the Little Sisters of Jesus. Both fraternities gradually spread throughout the world, their small communities taking up life among the poor and outcast, first in the Sahara desert, but eventually in many obscure corners of the globe.

Alone, a seeming failure by the end of his life, Foucauld was to become one of the most influential spiritual figures of the twentieth century. He was responsible for reviving the tradition of desert spirituality in our time. Rather than a retreat from humanity, he believed, the experience of being alone with God made us truly available to encounter and love our neighbor as ourselves. In contrast with triumphalistic models of mission, Foucauld exemplified an evangelism of presence, an encounter with people of other faiths on a basis of mutual respect and equality. Furthermore, he pioneered a new model of religious life, patterned after the life of Jesus himself, whose only cloister was the world of the poor.

Shortly before his death Foucauld summarized his spirituality in a brief testament:

Jesus came to Nazareth, the place of the hidden life, of ordinary life, of family life, of prayer, work, obscurity, silent virtues, practiced with no witnesses other than God, his friends and neighbors. Nazareth, the place where most people lead their lives. We must infinitely respect the least of our brothers...let us mingle with them. Let us be one of them to the extent that God wishes...and treat them fraternally in order to have the honor and joy of being accepted as one of them.

See: Robert Ellsberg, "Charles de Foucauld," in Susan Bergman, ed., *Martyrs* (San Francisco: HarperCollins, 1996); *Silent Pilgrimage to God: The Spirituality of Charles de Foucauld* (Maryknoll, N.Y.: Orbis, 1974).

Maura Clarke and Companions
Martyrs of El Salvador (d. 1980)

"One cries out, 'Lord, how long?' And then too what creeps into my mind is the little fear or big, that when it touches me very personally, will I be faithful?" —Maura Clarke

On a December morning in 1980 a small assembly of priests, nuns, and peasants gathered in a cow pasture in El Salvador to witness the exhumation of four North American women. One by one their broken and disheveled bodies were dragged from the shallow grave: Maura Clarke and Ita Ford, both Maryknoll Sisters; Dorothy Kazel, an Ursuline Sister, and Jean Donovan, a lay missioner, both from Cleveland. They had been missing since December 2 when Dorothy and Jean, in their distinctive white minivan, had left for the airport to pick up Maura and Ita on their return from a meeting in Nicaragua. Two days later some peasants alerted church authorities and led them to the site of this hasty burial.

Each woman had followed a different path. Maura and Ita had spent many years in mission in Nicaragua and Chile. Dorothy Kazel was the longest in El Salvador. Jean Donovan, only twenty-seven, had wrestled with the possibility of marriage and the security of a lucrative career before choosing, instead, to remain in El Salvador. But for each one, called by Christ to live out her faith in solidarity with the poor, the path had led to the same cow pasture.

It was a possibility they had all wrestled with and faced up to. After all, they had all to one extent or another been touched by the witness of *Archbishop Oscar Romero, assassinated only nine months before. In words which Ita Ford quoted on the night before she died, he had said, "One who is committed to the poor must risk the same fate as the poor. And in El Salvador we know what the fate of the poor signifies: to disappear, to be tortured, to be captive, and to be found dead."

The death of the four women had an enormous effect on the North American church, galvanizing opposition to U.S. funding for the Salvadoran government. But at the same time, the deaths provoked a backlash on the part of apologists for these policies. As one American official noted, "The nuns were not just nuns, the nuns were also political activists... on behalf of the Frente [the guerrillas]." The U.S. secretary of state went so far as to describe a "prominent theory" that the churchwomen may have been killed "in an exchange of fire" after they were believed to be running a roadblock.

This "prominent theory" had little to do with the readily determined facts of the case: that the four women were targeted for assassination by Salvadoran officers; that soldiers, dressed in civilian clothes for a "special assignment," had followed the Sisters on their way home from the airport; that the women were killed many hours later in a different place; that they were shot in the head at close range; and that before being killed two of them were raped.

In fact the four women were anything but "political activists." Their work, in support of the Salvadoran church, involved ministering to the needs of refugees; shepherding priests on the run; delivering supplies; offering solace to isolated and terrified catechists. These were nightmare years in El Salvador. The women's work confronted them with scenes from hell. They saw villages where the security forces had committed massacres and then refused to allow the survivors to bury the dead. "The other day," wrote Maura, "passing a small lake in the jeep I saw a buzzard standing on top of a floating body. We did nothing but pray and feel." They each had identified with the church's "preferential option for the poor," believing that the effective witness to the gospel was inseparable from the witness to life and solidarity with the oppressed. In El Salvador this was enough to label one a subversive.

And yet in bearing witness to the cross they were also witnesses to the resurrection. Among the believing poor of El Salvador there was not only death, but a faith and a stubborn hope that inspired them to carry on — or at least, kept them from fleeing. As Ita wrote to her sixteen-year-old niece:

> This is a terrible time in El Salvador for youth. A lot of idealism and commitment are getting snuffed out here now. The reasons why so many people are being killed are quite complicated, yet there are some clear, simple strands. One is that people have found a meaning to live, to sacrifice, struggle, and even die. And whether their life spans sixteen years, sixty or ninety, for them their life has had a purpose. In many ways, they are fortunate people.
>
> Brooklyn is not passing through the drama of El Salvador, but some things hold true wherever one is, and at whatever age. What I'm saying is that I hope you can come to find that which gives life a deep meaning for you, something that energizes you, enthuses you, enables you to keep moving ahead.

Jean Donovan, at twenty-seven, was the youngest of the four, and the only laywoman among them. From a privileged background, with a degree in business and a promising career, she had been drawn to the mission in El Salvador and stayed on even when the risks became clear. Two weeks before her death she wrote, "Several times I have decided to leave — I almost could except for the children, the poor bruised victims of adult lunacy. Who would care for them? Whose heart would be so staunch as to favor the reasonable thing in a sea of their tears and loneliness? Not mine, dear friend, not mine."

The history of the church is written in the blood of martyrs. But these four women represented a different kind of martyrdom, increasingly common in our time. Their murderers dared to call themselves Christians, indeed defenders of Christian values. And they died not simply for clinging to the true faith but for clinging, like Jesus, to the poor.

See: Donna Whitson Brett and Edward T. Brett, *Murdered in Central America* (Maryknoll, N.Y.: Orbis, 1988); Penny Lernoux (with Arthur Jones and Robert Ellsberg), *Hearts on Fire: The Story of the Maryknoll Sisters* (Maryknoll, N.Y.: Orbis, 1993).

St. Francis Xavier
Jesuit Missionary (1506–1552)

"The dangers to which I am exposed and the tasks I undertake for God are springs of spiritual joy, so much so that these islands are the places in all the world for a man to lose his sight by excess of weeping: but they are tears of joy."

Francis Xavier was one of the original company of six who joined with *St. Ignatius Loyola in taking vows in the Society of Jesus. Francis met Loyola, a fellow Basque, while he was studying at the University of Paris in the 1530s. In 1541, armed with a papal decree naming him apostolic nuncio to Asia, he embarked for a perilous journey to Portuguese Goa. It was the beginning of one of the greatest of all missionary journeys, lasting eleven years, and one from which he would never return. In his parting letter to Ignatius, he wrote, "For what is left of this life, I am well assured, it will be by letter only that we shall be together — in the other we shall embrace face to face."

Francis arrived in Goa after a fifteen-month voyage. Christianity of a sort had already been established there by the Portuguese, but the church was in a deplorable condition. He immersed himself in the local languages and used this port as a base for travels along the southern coasts of India. Through his preaching he won many conversions, almost all among poor, tribal, and lower-caste peoples. But he was constantly frustrated by the immorality, greed, and violence of the European colonists, which undermined the credibility of Christianity.

In 1546 Francis explored other islands in southern Asia. But by this time he had begun to receive reports of the highly advanced kingdom of Japan, as yet unknown to Westerners. Determined to make Japan his next mission field, he eventually landed there, after many adventures, on August 15, 1549. Fortunately for Francis, his arrival came at a time of great political instability in Japan; 250 local rulers controlled the country, none able to achieve ultimate power. This left the country unusually open to the arrival of foreigners.

Francis quickly recognized the sophistication of Japanese culture, and realized that special methods would be needed in order to preach the gospel to such a people. As he wrote to Ignatius,

It seems to me that we shall never find...another race to equal the Japanese. They are a people of very good manners....They are men of honor to a marvel, and prize honor above all else in the world....They like to hear things propounded according to reason; and, granted that there are sins and vices among them, when one reasons with them, pointing out that what they do is evil, they are convinced by this reasoning.

The experience of Japanese culture induced a change in Francis's approach to mission. Whereas before he had tended to see himself as building on barren ground, now he felt a need to comprehend the local culture, to discover its latent strengths and virtues and to find ways of connecting these with the gospel message.

Francis remained in Japan for twenty-seven months, long enough to establish several small groups of converts. It was only a beginning, but his work prepared the ground for the wave of Jesuits who would follow — many to lose their lives during later persecution. In the meantime, however, Francis had set his sights on yet another great, and as yet virtually unknown, frontier: China.

At that time China remained closed to foreigners. Nevertheless Francis believed that this would be the grand prize of all his missionary endeavors. But this prize would elude him. In 1552, after finally finding a ship to take him to China, he became seriously ill. He was taken off the ship on the unpopulated island of Sancian near the Chinese coast. His condition deteriorated, and he died on December 3 at the age of forty-six.

Xavier was canonized in 1622. In 1927 he was named, along with *St. Therese of Lisieux, patron of foreign missions.

See: Jean-Marc Monguerre, *St. Francis Xavier* (Garden City, N.Y.: Doubleday, 1963); Andrew Ross, *A Vision Betrayed: The Jesuits in Japan and China, 1542–1742* (Maryknoll, N.Y.: Orbis, 1994).

December 4

St. Clement of Alexandria
Christian Apologist (c. 150 – c. 215)

"Even if Greek philosophy does not comprehend the truth in its entirety... yet at least it prepares the way for the teaching which is royal in the highest sense of the word, by making a man self-controlled, by molding his character, and by making him ready to receive the truth."

The city of Alexandria, founded by Alexander the Great on the Mediterranean coast of Egypt, was a center of Hellenistic culture. Jews, pagans, and eventually Christians lived side by side, each with their schools and centers of training. Clement was the eminent director of the Christian school, and in this position he was enormously influential in his efforts to interpret the gospel in terms of Greek philosophy. Little is known of his life. He was apparently born in Athens and traveled widely in his youth, seeking wisdom from teachers of many schools before converting to Christianity. As a Christian philosopher he strenuously opposed the anti-intellectual bias of many Christians. "What has Jerusalem to do with Athens?" asked his contemporary and fellow North African Tertullian. Clement's answer was that "Greek philosophy, as it were, provides for the soul the preliminary cleansing and training required for the reception of the faith, on which foundation the truth builds up the edifice of knowledge." Clement believed that God's wisdom had been communicated in some form to every people. The task of the Christian apologist was to seek out that primordial wisdom in the culture of a people — Greek philosophy in this case — and to build on this foundation in expounding the gospel.

In synthesizing the gospel with Greek philosophy there was loss as well as gain. The translation encouraged a preoccupation with doctrine and eternal truths, in place of the concrete and ethical thrust of the Gospels. Indeed, within a century of Clement it had become difficult for the church to understand the gospel otherwise than in terms of Hellenistic thought. Clement, of course, cannot be blamed for this extreme.

While Clement pioneered the adaptation of the gospel to the positive features of his culture, he was adamant in opposing those gnostic Christians for whom the gospel was entirely subordinated to Greek philosophy. In contrast he affirmed the value of the created world, defended the role of free will, and expounded the virtues of Christian marriage. As a pioneer in what would today be called inculturation, his example might encourage the efforts of contemporary theologians to express the gospel in terms of other cultural horizons.

See: Clement of Alexandria, in Henry Chadwick, ed., *Alexandrian Christianity* (Philadelphia: Westminster, 1954).

December 5

Wolfgang Amadeus Mozart
Composer (1756–1791)

"I never lie down at night without reflecting that — as young as I am — I may not live to see another day. Yet no one of all my acquaintances could say that in company I am morose and disgruntled. For this blessing I daily thank my Creator and wish with all my heart that each one of my fellow-creatures could enjoy it."

Wolfgang Amadeus Mozart was, arguably, the greatest classical composer of all time. Was he also some kind of a saint? Judging by his personal piety and character the answer would probably be no. Although he was a baptized Catholic and wrote much of his music for liturgical occasions, he was also attracted to the philosophy of Freemasonry and was inclined to a fairly cynical attitude toward the church (which he had experienced in a fairly decadent form). In temperament he was either childlike or immature, depending on one's point of view, given by turns to sulking, giddy humor, and profanity.

But then there was his music. The writer George Bernard Shaw, hardly noted for his piety, once called Mozart's music "the only music yet written that would not sound out of place in the mouth of God." The great Protestant theologian *Karl Barth, only one of the modern theologians to take a professional interest in Mozart, wrote of his certainty "that when the angels go about their task of praising God, they play only Bach." But he was sure "that when they are together *en famille* they play Mozart and that then too the good God listens with special pleasure."

Mozart was born in Salzburg, Austria, in 1756. His prodigious musical talent was evident from early childhood. By the age of five he was writing minuets for the harpsichord. By the time he was six his father was conducting him on performing tours through most of the royal courts of Europe. In 1770 he performed at the Vatican for Pope Clement XIV, after which he was rewarded with a papal knighthood.

Mozart's fame as a composer quickly surpassed his reputation as a performer. He wrote in almost every genre, from Masses and Oratorios, to chamber music, symphonies, and secular operas. Still he spent much of his life in financial insecurity, depending on the fickle support of patrons in the church and the royal courts. His short life ended in poverty and protracted illness. In 1791 a mysterious stranger commissioned a Requiem. Mozart worked feverishly on the composition, convinced that he was writing for his own funeral. It was his last and one of his most sublime works. He finally collapsed of exhaustion and died just a few days later on December 5, 1791.

Those who consider Mozart a great religious artist are not interested simply in his extensive body of religious music. They argue that in all his work there is a delight in creation, a balance, a sense of order, an affirmation of light and the final triumph of life over death and darkness. Barth claimed to find in Mozart more than any other person "an art of playing" which presupposes "a childlike awareness of the essence or center — as also the beginning and the end — of all things." In listening to Mozart, he wrote, one is "transported to the threshold of a world which in sunlight and storm, by day and by night, is a good and ordered world."

Mozart had a great capacity to enjoy the pleasures of life. But it is striking, in light of the "life-affirming" qualities of his music, to consider how deeply preoccupied he was with the subject of death. Through constant meditation on this, "the true goal of our existence," he had come to the conclusion that death is the "best and truest friend of mankind, that his image is not only no longer terrifying to me, but is indeed very soothing and consoling. And I thank my God for graciously granting me the opportunity...of learning that death is the *key* which unlocks the door to our true happiness."

So Mozart, after a life of phenomenal industry, achieved his true happiness at the age of thirty-five. He was buried in a pauper's grave in Vienna.

Barth once had a dream in which he was given the task of examining Mozart on various points of theology and dogmatics. Although Barth deliberately tried to pitch easy questions, Mozart gave him no answer. The great theologian offered no interpretation of this dream. But perhaps it says something about Mozart as a religious artist. For him the Holy Mystery was a reality best conveyed not in dogmas but in music. In any case, Barth confessed that if he ever arrived in heaven he would "first of all seek out Mozart" before inquiring after his fellow theologians.

See: Karl Barth, *Wolfgang Amadeus Mozart* (Grand Rapids: Eerdmans, 1986). Hans Küng, *Mozart: Traces of Transcendence* (Grand Rapids: Eerdmans, 1991).

December 6

St. Nicholas
Bishop of Myra (fourth century)

"So famous and renowned did he quickly become not only among the faithful but among many of the infidels as well that in all peoples' minds he was admired beyond the power of words."

It is hard to reconcile the extraordinary influence and appeal of St. Nicholas with the paucity of established facts about his life. He is the patron of Russia and Greece, as well as of many classes of people, including children, sailors, pawnbrokers, and prostitutes. Many hundreds of churches are named after him, and his feast day is an occasion for ardent celebration in many parts of the globe. But as for his biography, it may be summarized — with little danger of elision — in the simple statement that he served as bishop of Myra, a provincial capital in Asia Minor, sometime in the fourth century.

The most curious development in the cult of St. Nicholas has been the amalgamation of this fourth-century bishop with the features of a Scandinavian elf. The transfiguration of St. Nicholas into Santa Claus has been traced to Dutch Protestants living in New Amsterdam. As the story made its way back to England the familiar features of Father Christmas gradually took shape until he had achieved his eventual iconographic status.

In Holland it is still St. Nicholas himself who delivers presents to deserving children on his feast day. In America and England, where, on Christmas Eve, young ears are attentive for the sound of reindeers' hooves, we are at least several steps further removed from the original bishop of Myra. And yet in linking the hopes of children with the memory of St. Nicholas there is some faint echo of an ancient cult.

St. Nicholas was the hero of several legends involving children. To be sure, they reflect an image of childhood that has little to do with "sugar-plums." In one story Nicholas rescued three young girls whose father, for want of a dowry, was about to sell them into prostitution. Nicholas tossed three bags of gold through an open window, enough to pay the dowry of each of the sisters. In another story these three bags of gold (with which the saint is often depicted) became the heads of three little boys who were murdered by an evil maniac. The holy bishop not only uncovered the crime but restored the children to life.

It is common and appropriate to decry the commercialization of the Christmas season. There are fewer voices raised to mourn the trivialization of St. Nicholas. Well does he deserve to be the patron of children, and well might they delight in his name. But he might be remembered not only as the jolly source of toys and treats but also as the protector of those whose lives and innocence remain threatened today, as they were in the time of St. Nicholas, by violence, poverty, and exploitation.

See: The Golden Legend of Jacobus de Voragine (London: Longman, Green, 1941).

St. Ambrose

Bishop of Milan, Doctor of the Church (339-397)

"An emperor should not abolish liberty, even in the case of those who owe him a military obedience. The difference between good and bad rulers is that the good love freedom, the bad slavery."

Ambrose was the son of a high-ranking Roman official. He too pursued a career in the civil service and rose to become the provincial governor of Aemilia-Liguria in northern Italy. His headquarters was in Milan, imperial capital of the Roman empire. In 374 the bishop of Milan died leaving the church bitterly divided between Catholic and Arian factions, and thus unable to choose a successor. When violence threatened to erupt, Ambrose went to the basilica in his civil capacity and exhorted the assembly to conclude their deliberations in a peaceful manner. Suddenly a voice rose up, "Ambrose for bishop!" This cry was quickly taken up by the entire assembly. Ambrose was horrified. Not only was he a layman — he was not even baptized. Fleeing the basilica, he went into hiding to evade the importunate crowd. But when he was finally cornered, he acquiesced to what was evidently the will of God. So within a week he was baptized, was confirmed, received holy orders, and was consecrated bishop of Milan.

Despite his lack of preparation for the office, Ambrose quickly made up for lost time. If he was going to be a bishop he believed in doing it properly. Thus he gave away all his property, embraced a severe standard of austerity and daily prayer, and immersed himself in the study of Scripture and theology. He became the protector of the poor and opened his door to all in need. He made a practice of preaching every Sunday in the basilica and personally oversaw the preparation of catechumens and the training of clergy. In all this he quickly established a reputation as a model bishop.

Among those affected by his wisdom and holy example was *St. Augustine, who, as a young man living in Milan, was baptized under the bishop's instruction in 386. In his *Confessions* there is a touching description of Augustine's wonder at coming upon Ambrose silently reading the Bible. It was the custom of those times to read aloud, and Augustine was moved to speculate on the meaning of this silence: Was it to avoid the need to explain an obscure passage to a curious passerby? Was he trying to spare his voice? "Whatever his reason, we may be sure it was a good one."

Though he wrote many books, Ambrose is remembered less for his teaching than for his deft leadership of the church in a tumultuous era. The church was deeply divided by Arianism, a christological heresy that denied the full divinity of Christ. Though already condemned at the Council of Nicea (325) the Arian doctrine continued to enjoy wide support throughout the fourth century. Among its proponents was the mother of the emperor Valentinian. In an effort to establish civic harmony he ordered Ambrose to cede one of his churches for the use of the Arians. Ambrose, the former imperial official, stoutly refused the emperor's command. The conflict escalated to the point that imperial troops surrounded the basilica with the bishop and his congregation inside. For some days it appeared that there might be bloodshed. As Ambrose defined the issue: "The emperor is *in* the church, not *over* it." Eventually the emperor backed down.

Ambrose's other great confrontation with imperial power came in 390, when Emperor Theodosius authorized a shocking massacre in Thessalonica. In retaliation for a riot resulting in the death of the governor, imperial troops set upon an unrelated crowd, killing as many as seven thousand people in a matter of hours. Ambrose addressed an extraordinary letter to the emperor, insisting that he do penance and barring him from communion until he had received absolution:

> What has been done at Thessalonica is unparalleled in the memory of man.... You are human, and temptation has overtaken you. Overcome it. I counsel, I beseech, I implore you to penance. You, who have so often been merciful and pardoned the guilty, have now caused many innocent to perish. The devil wished to wrest from you the crown of piety which was your chiefest glory. Drive him from you while you can.

Theodosius did as he was told and was duly reconciled with the church. "I know no one except Ambrose," he reportedly said, "who deserves the name of bishop." St. Ambrose died on Good Friday, April 4, 397, at the age of fifty-seven. His feast day is December 7.

See: Maisie Ward, *Saints Who Made History* (New York: Sheed & Ward, 1959); Ambrose, in S. L. Greenslade, ed., *Early Latin Theology* (Philadelphia: Westminster, 1956).

December 8

Walter Ciszek
Jesuit Priest and Confessor (1904–1984)

"For each of us, salvation means no more and no less than taking up daily the same cross of Christ, accepting each day what it brings as the will of God, offering back to God each morning all the joys, works, and sufferings of that day."

In 1947 the Jesuits in New York said a memorial Mass for Father Walter Ciszek, one of their priests missing in the Soviet Union for seven years and presumed dead. As a young seminarian he had volunteered to study Russian in hopes of a possible mission to the Soviet Union. But when that possibility remained closed, he was sent to a Jesuit mission in eastern Poland in 1938. He was there a year later when Red Army troops invaded. In the confusion and disruption of war, Ciszek saw the hand of providence. Disguised as a worker he joined with Polish refugees being transported to labor camps in Russia, thus hoping to carry on some kind of clandestine ministry. For two years he worked in a lumber yard. Then in 1941 he was arrested by the Soviet secret police. As far as the outside world was concerned, he disappeared without a trace. But in fact he remained very much alive within the enclosed system of the Soviet Gulag.

Ciszek was held for five years in solitary confinement in the notorious Lubianka prison in Moscow. It was known that he was a Catholic priest of Polish-American descent. But the secret police were determined to prove that he was also a spy. In his later books Ciszek described in detail the terrible psychological ordeal of his confinement. He was kept day and night in his cell, except for the periodic interrogation sessions that were his only opportunity for human contact. To keep his wits intact he adopted a daily routine of spiritual exercises, all based on what he could remember from his Jesuit formation. The day began with morning prayers and an examination of conscience. Then came the Mass, all enacted mentally. The noon bells in Red Square signaled the Angelus, followed by the rosary and meditation on the Scriptures. Each day ended with another examination of conscience. So the solitary days, weeks, and years were passed. And so he could later observe, "Lubianka, in many ways, was a school of prayer for me."

In the beginning Ciszek assumed that he would eventually satisfy the concerns of the police. But eventually he became resigned to the fact that there was nothing he could do or say that would win his freedom. Finally exhausted with the charade of interrogation and at the limits of his endurance, he agreed to sign a confession. On the basis of this he was sentenced to fifteen years of hard labor in Siberia.

In all that befell Father Ciszek over the years he remained confident that with sufficient faith he could discern the will of God in his circumstances. He found that as long as he tried to struggle and resist his destiny he was exhausted and miserable. But to the extent that he abandoned himself to providence, convinced that in every situation he was exactly where God wanted him to be, he felt a sense of freedom and peace.

This confidence survived the horrifying experience of his transport to Siberia, surrounded by the brutality of hardened criminals. In the prison camp in Siberia he faced backbreaking work, shoveling coal or working in mines. When prisoners learned he was a priest, he found himself serving as an unofficial chaplain in the camps. Bread and wine were smuggled in, making it possible even to say Mass. Thus he found the grace to carry on, convinced that it was possible with faith to redeem these terrible circumstances: "For I was Christ in this prison camp." Even nonbelievers sought him out for counsel and encouragement, and he could not help but see in each encounter with every prisoner an opportunity to do the work of God. Simply by refusing to succumb to bitterness or despair Ciszek felt that he had a most vital spiritual witness to share. He also felt, as a priest, that by "offering up" his sufferings he might help others to discover or preserve the faith.

Apart from the crushing slave labor, the famous Siberian cold, the experience of hunger and illness, Ciszek also had to resign himself to constant insecurity. Once after a prison revolt, he and other prisoners were taken out before a firing squad. He fully expected that he would die on the spot and struggled to remember how to make an Act of Contrition. At the last moment the execution was halted. But by this time he had moved beyond the fear of death; he was fully open to whatever God might send him. And this essential freedom of the soul, the ability to give his consent to God, was the constant reminder of his dignity as a human being and a child of God. "I realized that true freedom meant nothing else than letting God operate within my soul without interference."

Finally after he had served and survived his entire sentence, Father Ciszek was freed. But it was a relative freedom. As a convicted felon he was restricted to living in towns in Siberia, where he continued to be subject to constant surveillance and harassment by the secret police. He worked in various kinds of menial labor. Once again, when his identity was discovered, he found great demand for his service as a priest. But invariably, when he became too popular, this would be the signal for the KGB to banish him to another town.

So his life continued on for several years. He was eventually able to write letters home, informing his astonished Jesuit family that he remained alive. In 1963 he was summoned without warning to Moscow and put on a plane to the West to be exchanged for a couple of Soviet spies. He arrived in New York on October 12 after twenty-three years in the Soviet Union.

Ciszek lived on for another twenty years. He remained extraordinarily free of bitterness toward the land of his captivity. He believed that the spiritual lessons he had discovered during his ordeal were applicable to all people, whatever their circumstances. To those who asked for the secret of his survival, he always answered, "God's providence." Pressed further, he repeated the question of *St. Paul: "If God is for us who can be against us?" Father Ciszek died on December 8, 1984, at the age of eighty.

See: Walter Ciszek, S.J., *He Leadeth Me* (Garden City, N.Y.: Doubleday, 1973) and *With God in Russia* (New York: McGraw-Hill 1964).

December 9

St. Juan Diego
Witness to Our Lady of Guadalupe
(sixteenth century)

"My dear Lady, . . . this I beg you, entrust your mission to one of the important persons who is well known, respected, and esteemed so that they may believe him. You know that I am nobody, a nothing, a coward, a pile of old sticks. . . . You have sent me to walk in places where I do not belong. Forgive me and please do not be angry with me, my Lady and Mistress."

On the morning of December 9, 1531, a Christian Indian named Juan Diego was on his way to Mass. As he passed a hill at Tepeyac, not far from present-day Mexico City, he heard a voice calling him by name. Looking up he was surprised to see a young Indian maiden. She instructed him to go to the bishop and tell him to construct a church on this hill, the site of an ancient Nahuatl shrine to the mother goddess. Juan faithfully carried out the assignment, but the bishop paid him no attention. In a subsequent showing the maiden charged him to try again, this time identifying herself as the Mother of God. Again the bishop scoffed. At a third audience with the Lady, she instructed Juan Diego to gather a bouquet of roses which were growing, unseasonably, at her feet. Juan gathered the roses in his *tilma*, or cape. Having gained another audience with the bishop, who had demanded some kind of sign, Juan Diego opened his tilma to present the flowers. To his astonishment, he discovered a full-color image of the Lady mysteriously imprinted on the rough fabric.

So was born the cult of Our Lady of Guadalupe (as the Indian name of the Lady was rendered in Spanish). But in a deeper sense this apparition marked the birth of the Mexican people — a fusion between the Spanish and the indigenous races and cultures. The apparition to Juan Diego occurred only ten years after the conquest of Mexico, a time when the native Indians were languishing under the impact of their cultural decimation. The conquerors had brought with them the new Christian religion, but under such circumstances that it posed little attraction.

All this changed after Guadalupe. The image of the Lady had dark skin and Indian features. The style and colors of her clothing, her blue mantle covered with stars, her depiction as standing on a crescent moon held aloft by an angel, all these features had deep symbolic references to the Indian religion and culture. She spoke to Juan Diego in his own Nahuatl language — not in Spanish — and presented herself not in terms of power and domination but in terms of compassion and solidarity with the poor. She called herself the "Mother of the true God through whom one lives" and stated her wish to see a temple built at that site so that she could "show and give forth all my love, compassion, help, and defense to all the inhabitants of this land ... to hear their lamentations and remedy their miseries, pain, and sufferings."

If all this was significant to the Indians, there was also a message to the Spanish. Previously the Spanish had seen no conflict between the mission of conquest and the mission of evangelization. But here a divine message was delivered to the bishop — the official representative of the Spanish church — by means of a humble Indian. In effect, Juan Diego was chosen to be the agent of the bishop's — and the church's — conversion. The message was clear: the church must not serve as the religious arm of colonial oppression. Instead it must be rooted in the experience of the poor and become a vehicle for their cultural and spiritual survival.

Within six years of the apparition nine million Aztecs were baptized. The official church went on to build a rich basilica at Tepeyac and to sponsor the official cult of Our Lady of Guadalupe. Still, in succeeding centuries the image of Guadalupe remained a source of special pride and devotion among the poor, a symbol of God's special love for the oppressed, and of the compassionate face of God revealed in his Mother.

Apart from the official cult, the image of Guadalupe would resurface regularly in more militant and "unauthorized" contexts. Banners with her image were carried by the peasant army of Emiliano Zapata during the Mexican Revolution. *Cesar Chavez, leader of the United Farmworkers Union in the United States, carried her image on the picket line. In 1993 Indian peasants supporting the Zapatista uprising in Chiapas, Mexico, marched beneath her banner. The image of Guadalupe continues to hold a special meaning for the humble and oppressed peoples of the Americas. For others she is a potent symbol of the church of the future — a church that celebrates diversity, empowers the poor, and speaks with the voice of compassion. Where such a church lives, roses bloom in December.

See: Jeanette Rodriguez, *Our Lady of Guadalupe* (Austin: University of Texas Press, 1994); Virgil Elizondo, *Guadalupe: Mother of the New Creation* (Maryknoll, N.Y.: Orbis, 1997).

December 10
Thomas Merton
Trappist (1915 – 1968)

"The Christian life — and especially the contemplative life —
is a continual discovery of Christ in new and unexpected places."

In 1949 a surprising title made its way onto the best-seller lists. *The Seven Storey Mountain* was not a mystery or a tale of alpine adventure. It was the autobiography of a clever young man named Thomas Merton who had turned his back on the modern world to adopt the austere, medieval regime of a Trappist monk. What made the book so fascinating was that Merton appeared to be, as he described himself, "the complete twentieth-century man." He had enjoyed a life of freedom, excitement, and pleasure only, in the end, to reject it all as an illusion.

Merton told a story — by turns funny and sad — of the search for his true identity and home: of his orphaned childhood, his education in France, England, and Columbia University, of the pride and selfishness that brought nothing but unhappiness to himself and others. And he told of how his search had led him ultimately to the Catholic church and finally, on the eve of World War II, to the Trappist Abbey of Gethsemani in Kentucky. On viewing the silent monks, dressed in their white habits and kneeling in prayer in the chapel, Merton had exclaimed, "This is the true center of America."

It was in some respects a classic tale of conversion. And yet for many readers, encountering Merton's book in the postwar years, his story struck a very contemporary note. It fed a widespread hunger for spiritual values in a world poised between war and the empty promise of "happy days." Suddenly Merton was the most famous monk in America. The irony was not lost on him. He had become a Trappist in part to escape the claims of ego, the anxious desire to "be somebody." And yet his superiors felt his writing had something to offer the world and they ordered him to keep at it. And so he did. Yet for all the books he would go on to produce, he remained firmly identified with his autobiography. It became a painful burden. *"The Seven Storey Mountain* is the work of a man I never even heard of," he would later protest.

One aspect of the book that he particularly came to regret was the attitude of pious scorn directed at "the world" and its citizens. He had seemed to regard the monastery as a haven set apart from the *massa damnata*. Only with time had he realized that "the monastery is not an 'escape' from the world. On the contrary, by being in the monastery I take my true part in all the struggles and sufferings of the world."

In one of his journals he recorded a moment of mystical insight that marked a critical turning point in his life as a monk. It occurred during an errand in Louisville, "at the corner of Fourth and Walnut, in the center of the shopping district."

> I was suddenly overwhelmed with the realization that I loved all those people, that they were mine and I theirs, that we could not be alien to one another even though we were total strangers. It was like waking from a dream of separateness, of spurious self-isolation in a special world, the world of renunciation and supposed holiness.

Merton suddenly experienced a sense of solidarity with the human race — not simply in sin, but in grace. "There is no way of telling people that they are all walking around shining like the sun. . . . There are no strangers! . . . The gate of heaven is everywhere."

For years Merton had devoted creative thought to the meaning of monastic and contemplative life. But from this point on he became increasingly concerned with making connections between the monastery and the wider world. Scorn and sarcasm gave way to compassion and friendship. This was reflected in his writing. Along with the more traditional spiritual books there appeared articles on war, racism, and other issues of the day. Long before such positions were commonplace in the church he was a prophetic voice for peace and nonviolence. In fact, his writings were so controversial that for some years he was ordered to remain silent on "political" topics. Only after the Second Vatican Council was he freed from such censorship.

Ironically, this increasing engagement with the secular world and its problems was accompanied by an increasing attraction to an even more total life of contemplation. In 1961 he was given permission to move into a hermitage on the monastery grounds. There he continued to perfect the delicate balance between contemplative prayer and openness to the world that had become the distinctive feature of his spirituality.

Merton maintained a wide circle of friends. Many of them knew something of the tensions which at times characterized relations with his religious superiors. In the spirit of the 1960s some of them frankly questioned whether his vocation wasn't an anachronism and challenged him to "get with it." In fact, Merton's personal temptations were all in the direction of even greater solitude among the Carthusians or in some other remote setting. But in the end he always returned to the conviction that his best service to the world lay in faithfulness to his monastic vocation, and that his spiritual home was at Gethsemani.

In his last years a more liberal abbot did encourage Merton to venture forth. In 1968 he accepted an invitation to address an international conference of Christian monks in Bangkok. Merton was particularly excited about the prospect of exploring his deep interest in Eastern spirituality. In this respect, as his journals show, the trip marked a new breakthrough, another encounter with the "gate of heaven" that is everywhere.

On December 10 he delivered his talk and afterward retired to his room for a shower and nap. There he was later found dead, apparently electrocuted by the faulty wiring of a fan. For all his restless searching he had ended exactly as he had foreseen in *The Seven Storey Mountain*. The book had concluded with a mysterious speech in the voice of God:

> I will give you what you desire. I will lead you into solitude.... Everything that touches you shall burn you, and you will draw your hand away in pain, until you have withdrawn yourself from all things. Then you will be all alone.... That you may become the brother of God and learn to know the Christ of the burnt men.

See: Lawrence S. Cunningham, ed., *Thomas Merton: Spiritual Master* (New York: Paulist, 1992); Jim Forest, *Living with Wisdom: The Life of Thomas Merton* (Maryknoll, N.Y.: Orbis, 1991).

December 11

Martyrs of El Mozote
El Salvador (d. 1981)

"I was afraid that I would cry out, that I would scream, that I would go crazy. I couldn't stand it, and I prayed to God to help me. I promised God that if He helped me I would tell the world what happened here."

— Rufina Amaya

On December 10, 1981, scores of Salvadoran troops, part of the elite, U.S.-trained Atlacatl Battalion, entered the town of El Mozote, a small hamlet in the Salvadoran province of Morazán. Their mission was code-named "Rescue." Its objective was to pursue guerrilla troops, cut off their supply lines, and eliminate suspected subversives.

No one had ever accused the people of El Mozote of being subversives. They were, in fact, something of an anomaly in this province, otherwise largely under guerrilla control. More than half of the townspeople were born-again evangelicals, a fact which may have accounted for their determination to remain neutral in the ongoing civil war in El Salvador. On the day of Operation Rescue the town was in fact swollen with refugees from the countryside, drawn by the belief that El Mozote would provide a safe haven amid the encircling fighting. They were wrong.

On the first day the soldiers gathered the townspeople and roughly interrogated them for information about the guerrillas. The people had no information to give. At some point the decision was made simply to destroy the town. For the next two days the soldiers systematically gathered the townspeople into small groups of men, women, and children and massacred the lot of them. It was exhausting work, carried out with extraordinary brutality. All the while the air was filled with screams and cries, punctuated by bursts of gun fire. Having begun the task, the soldiers were determined to leave no survivors. But they failed.

A peasant woman, Rufina Amaya, was put at the end of a line of women taken out to be executed. She had already seen her husband decapitated. When she arrived at the site where she was to be killed, Rufina fell to her knees: "I was crying and begging God to forgive my sins. Though I was almost at the feet of the soldiers I wasn't begging them — I was begging God." But in a moment when the soldiers weren't looking she seized the opportunity to crawl away and hide herself in some bushes. She remained there for days — shivering, thirsty, bleeding — watching and listening as the soldiers completed their mission. The children were the last to go. Rufina had to listen to the sounds of her own children being killed, biting her tongue to keep from screaming.

That night she overheard some of the soldiers discussing the faith of the people they had killed. One young girl in particular remained on their minds. While they had raped her repeatedly she had continued to sing hymns. Even after they shot her in the chest she sang. They shot her again, and still she sang. And then "their wonder began to turn to fear — until finally they had unsheathed their machetes and hacked through her neck, and at last the singing stopped."

Rufina alone survived to tell the world what had happened at El Mozote, where as many as a thousand people were killed. It was the largest massacre in modern Latin American history.

For more than a decade, years after the end of the civil war, the town of El Mozote remained abandoned. In the meantime forensic investigators, sponsored by a U.N. Truth Commission, sifted through the gruesome evidence, confirming Rufina's account of the terrible events she had witnessed. Eventually people began to return and rebuild. But not Rufina. She could not bring herself to return. She lived on in a nearby town, where she remarried and bore new children. But despite the pain of her memories she kept her pledge to recount the story of the massacre to any who asked.

A memorial in the town square of El Mozote bears the inscription: "They did not die, they are with us, with you, and with all humanity."

See: Mark Danner, "The Truth of El Mozote," *The New Yorker* (December 6, 1993).

December 12

Sister Alicia Domon

Martyr (d. 1977)

*"I didn't come here [to the shantytown] to tell people what they had to do
but in order that we could help each other and share life's joys and sorrows,
here where we take each other for what we are. I have probably received more
than I have given."*

During the period of 1976 to 1983 a military dictatorship in Argentina
conducted a "dirty war" against "subversives" and dissidents. Advocates
of human rights and social justice for the poor were among the special
victims of the repression. At least four thousand civilians were killed.
Another ten thousand were "disappeared" — abducted by the military,
never to be seen again. Two French nuns, Sisters Alicia Domon and Léonie
Duquet, were among them.

They were both members of the Toulouse Institute of the Sisters of Foreign Mission. Alicia Domon arrived in Argentina in 1967, part of the great
wave of foreign religious who flocked to Latin America in the years after
Vatican II. At first they engaged in more traditional apostolates. Alicia
worked with mentally retarded children, helping them prepare for their
first communion. By 1969, however, she and other members of her congregation had moved out of their convent to take up residence in an urban
shantytown. Alicia supported herself by working halftime as a household
servant while otherwise ministering as a friend and sister to her poor
neighbors.

In the following years she spent much time in the countryside, becoming acquainted with the struggles of landless peasants and lending
support to their efforts to organize. It was a time of rising hopes in the
possibility of peaceful social change. In the 1970s, however, such efforts
and hopes were brutally suppressed.

Back in Buenos Aires, Sister Alicia became closely involved with a
courageous organization of women, the so-called Mothers of the Disappeared, who gathered in the central plaza each day, dressed in black and
bearing photographs of their missing children. This mute but eloquent
protest was for many years the only visible sign of dissent in Argentina.
The conservative hierarchy of the Catholic church remained largely silent,
when not actually endorsing the military's defense of "law and order."

For Christmas 1977 Alicia had prepared a retreat for the Mothers. On
the evening of December 8, however, after leaving a planning meeting of
the group, Sister Alicia and twelve other women were seized by armed
men in civilian clothing. Two days later, Sister Léonie Duquet was also
abducted, apparently because she shared a residence with Alicia Domon.
None of them was ever seen again, nor was there ever any official news
of their fate.

In subsequent years jokes circulated among the military about the
"flying nuns." This was taken to be a reference to rumors that the disappeared were routinely tossed out of airplanes over the Atlantic Ocean. In

1995 these rumors were confirmed by a retired Navy commander, Adolfo Scilingo, who described his own part in two "death flights" in 1977.

According to his account, "At first it didn't bother me that I was dumping these bodies into the ocean because as far as I was concerned they were war prisoners. There were men and women, and I had no idea who they were or what they had done. I was following orders." At some point, however, "It hit me exactly what we were doing. We were killing human beings. But still we continued." Afterward, when he confessed his actions to a military priest, he was told the killings "had to be done to separate the wheat from the chaff."

Asked to describe another mission in December of 1977, Scilingo became distraught and said he could not bear to discuss the details. Despite having received absolution at the time, Scilingo said that in subsequent years, "I have spent many nights sleeping in the plazas of Buenos Aires with a bottle of wine, trying to forget. I have ruined my life. . . . Sometimes I am afraid to be alone with my thoughts."

In her death Sister Alicia attained her most intimate union with the poor and rejected to whom she was drawn. After her disappearance the police who requisitioned her house were surprised to discover that, like the poorest peasant, she did not own so much as a change of clothes. Several months before her disappearance she had written to the archbishop of Toulouse, "I would ask you not to do anything to save me which could endanger others. I have already made the sacrifice of my life."

See: Martin Lange and Reinhold Iblacker, *Witnesses of Hope* (Maryknoll, N.Y.: Orbis, 1980); "Argentine Tells of Dumping 'Dirty War' Captives into Sea," *New York Times* (March 13, 1995).

December 13

Micah
Prophet (eighth century B.C.E.)

*"They shall sit every man under his vine and under his fig tree,
and none shall make them afraid."*

The prophet Micah was a younger contemporary — perhaps even a disciple — of the prophet *Isaiah. Like Isaiah he operated in the southern kingdom of Judah in the late eighth century B.C.E. Unlike Isaiah, who sprang from the priestly elite of Jerusalem, Micah came from a small village in the countryside. He identified with the poor of the land, those who bore the burden of the city folk with their privileges and their greed. The rich, he said, were like cannibals feeding off "the flesh of my people." In harsh tones he denounced those who "abhor justice and pervert all equity":

> They covet fields, and seize them;
>   and houses, and take them away;
> they oppress a man and his house
>   a man and his inheritance.

The northern kingdom of Israel had fallen to Assyria. Micah warned that the same fate awaited Judah. In another departure from Isaiah, he would not spare Jerusalem itself from the heat of divine judgment to come. The corruption had gone too far; the wound was "incurable."

And yet what Yahweh sought from Judah was correction and not destruction. Micah proclaimed the preservation of a saving "remnant" from which a new nation would emerge. There would be a lasting era of peace and justice. War would be no more. Justice would reign. The God who brought Israel out of bondage in Egypt would see to it.

What, in return, did Yahweh require? Not burnt offerings, lavish sacrifices, or elaborate worship. In words of sublime simplicity Micah proposed this definition of true religion:

> He has showed you, O man, what is good;
> and what does the Lord require of you
> but to do justice, and to love kindness,
> and to walk humbly with your God?

December 14

St. John of the Cross
Mystic and Doctor of the Church (1542–1591)

"Where there is no love, put love, and you will draw love out."

St. John of the Cross has been acclaimed as one of the church's great mystics — indeed, a genius of mystical theology. For this he was not merely canonized but proclaimed a Doctor of the Church. In light of this solid recognition, it is important to recall that such approval came only after his death. In life, his spiritual insights were forged in the experience of persecution and suffering, trials inflicted not simply by his own church but by the members of his own house.

Juan de Yepes grew up in poverty. His father, a nobleman by birth, had been disinherited for marrying a "common girl" and died several months after Juan's birth, leaving the family in desperate straits. Nevertheless, Juan received an education and pursued his religious inclinations. At the age of twenty-one he became a Carmelite friar, Juan de la Cruz — John of the Cross.

Of the prominent religious orders in Spain, the Carmelites were known for their special commitment to interior prayer and the spiritual life. But by John's day they had become lax and complacent. The great turning point in John's life came in 1567, the year of his ordination, when he was introduced to *Teresa of Avila, leader of a Carmelite reform movement and one of the great religious personalities of the sixteenth century. At that time she was fifty-two while John was twenty-five. And yet from the start they both recognized an extraordinary spiritual affinity. Teresa had been seeking a man to initiate a parallel reform to her so-called Discalced (barefoot) Carmelites. In John she recognized that man. At the same time he was greatly attracted by her efforts to restore the Carmelites to a simpler and more deeply spiritual standard. He became her confessor and also the prior of the first community of Discalced friars in Duruelo. Later, when Teresa became prioress of a convent at Avila, she asked him to serve as spiritual director.

Spiritual innovation was a dangerous matter in sixteenth-century Spain. This was the era of the notorious Spanish Inquisition, which thrived on the detection of heresy and nonconformity. Teresa herself was always conscious of the Inquisitor's long arm. And yet much of her greatest opposition came from the traditional wing of her own Carmelite order. John, too, fell a victim to this internecine rivalry. In 1577 he was kidnapped and taken to an unreformed Carmelite monastery in Toledo. He was held there in penal confinement, sustained on bread and water, and taken out regularly to be beaten and abused. This lasted for nine months. Finally, at a point close to death, he managed to make a most miraculous escape by dark of night (an incident which supplied one of his potent metaphors for the spiritual life.)

Although he made it back to his Discalced community, John's sufferings were not over. He continued to find himself in the middle of petty divisions, which only intensified after the death of Teresa in 1582. He was systematically stripped of any position of leadership in the order by jealous rivals determined to belittle his extraordinary gifts. John endured all this treatment without a murmur of complaint. All the time he was writing the mystical treatises that would ensure his later fame. But none of this work was valued while he lived. He died after a long illness on December 14, 1591, alone and virtually ignored in the congregation he had helped to found.

There is a clear relation between John's spirituality and the harshness and sufferings of his life. His mystical theology treats the path by which the soul is united in love with God. Like any great love affair, the relationship is marked by periods of joy as well as desolation. John was particularly acute in his analysis of what he called "the dark night," when God appears hidden and the soul endures the interminable suffering of dryness and abandonment. But to the person who seeks holiness, this suffering is simply one of the aspects of love, rather than its absence. If endured, it may lead the soul to the ecstatic breakthrough of union with God.

John's theology was written in the form of commentary on his own mystical poems. His greatest work, *Dark Night of the Soul*, is based on a poem he composed while a prisoner in Toledo. It describes the soul, like a lover, slipping out in the night to keep a rendezvous with its Beloved. John proceeds in his commentary to present a scientific discourse on the way of purgation, a stripping of ego and self-delusion to be achieved not only by means of our own asceticism but with the assistance of involuntary humiliations. John is devastatingly astute in unmasking the psychological devices that impede and distract our efforts at spiritual growth. But ultimately, he writes, the pain we experience is directed to a goal. Just as the burning of a log transforms the wood into fire, so the stripping away of our imperfections prepares us for the embrace of God.

It is difficult to read the life of Juan de la Cruz without wincing at the cruelties inflicted by his brothers in Christ. And yet in the midst of his ordeal, one can imagine a secret smile on John's face, undetected by his enemies. They could not suspect that by their petty persecutions they were only hastening the saint's reunion with his Beloved. As he wrote in one of his poems,

> I will mourn my death already,
> Lament the life I live, as long
> As misdeed, sin and wrong
> Detain it in captivity.
> O my God, when will it be?
> The time when I can say for sure,
> At last I live: I die no more.

See: St. John of the Cross, *Dark Night of the Soul,* trans. E. Allison Peers (Garden City, N.Y.: Image, 1959); Gerald Brenan, *St. John of the Cross: His Life and Poetry* (Cambridge: Cambridge University Press, 1973).

December 15

St. Nino
Slave and Evangelist (fourth century)

"It is not my work, but Christ's;
and He is the Son of God who made the world."

According to early legends, St. Nino was a slave-girl who was responsible for the evangelization of the kingdom of Georgia. A foreign captive, most likely from Armenia, she attracted attention as a result of her virtue and her habit of spending much of the night in prayer. When anyone questioned her, she answered that she worshiped Christ as God. Offering blessings in Christ's name, she was credited with a number of miraculous healings. On one occasion the Georgian queen was herself a beneficiary of Nino's gifts. This led to an interview with the king in which she once again attributed all her powers to Christ. Both the king and queen begged Nino to instruct them in the Christian faith. This she did. Later she oversaw the construction of the first church in Georgia, an accomplishment attended by further miracles.

As often happened in such cases, the conversion of the king led the way to the wholesale conversion of his kingdom. This created a widespread demand for religious instruction, which the king answered by entreating Emperor Constantine to send clergy. As for Nino, having won her freedom she retired to a remote cell in the mountains where she spent the rest of her life in prayer.

Maude Dominica Petre
Catholic Modernist (1863–1942)

"The church has lighted my way. Instead of struggling through a wilderness I have had a road — a road to virtue and truth. Only a road — the road to an end, not the end itself — the road to truth, not the fullness of truth itself. . . . In one word, she has taught me how to seek God."

Throughout the nineteenth century a number of Catholic intellectuals sought a way to reconcile the church with the positive features of modernity. By and large their efforts were scorned. By the turn of the century, faced with the rising tide of liberal and secular modes of thought, the church had come to define itself against the dominant social and political values of the age. With a state-of-siege mentality, many church leaders felt compelled to define their mission largely in terms of condemning error and asserting their authority.

The Modernist movement at the turn of the century was the most serious challenge to this mentality. To speak of a "movement" is a somewhat misleading reference to a handful of formally unrelated scholars working in various European countries. In general they sought to interpret and present the faith in terms of modern historical consciousness, critical biblical study, and an apologetic method rooted in philosophy's "turn to the subject." The seriousness of their challenge evoked an unusually severe response from the Vatican — a condemnation so vehement that it was many decades before any Catholic scholar could safely refer to their work without evincing horror.

Among this group the English writer Maude Petre was the lone woman. She outlived the other protagonists of the affair by many years. But she is otherwise distinguished, alone among them all, for having remained a loyal member of the church while also proudly and without repentance owning the epithet of Modernist.

Maude Petre grew up in a Catholic household. Although she belonged for some years to a community of vowed religious, she felt her contribution to the church would be in the intellectual realm. She pursued theological studies in Rome, and so became one of the first Catholic women theologians in modern times.

A great event in her life came in 1900 when she became acquainted with *George Tyrrell (1861–1909), a charismatic Jesuit theologian, who was to figure as a principal actor in the Modernist drama. A deep intellectual and spiritual bond quickly developed between Petre and Father Tyrrell, and she devoted herself wholeheartedly to his cause and his struggles. Tyrrell's work challenged the extrinsic and rationalistic mode of Catholic teaching. Instead of the appeal to dogmatic authority, he emphasized the affective and mystical dimension of Christianity and its appeal to human experience. In her own books Petre did not so much address such theological matters as defend the principle of freedom within the church to raise the kinds of questions posed by Tyrrell and his friends.

She later compared her efforts with the famous motivation for World War I: to make the world — in this case the church — safe for democracy.

The response of the Vatican was swift and furious. In 1907 Pope Pius X issued the encyclical *Pascendi* condemning the errors of "Modernism" in sweeping terms. The Modernists were depicted as archenemies of the faith to be combatted by extraordinary measures. These included an anti-Modernist oath to be sworn by all clergy as well as the establishment of vigilance committees in every diocese to watch out for signs of the heresy. The irony was that the cause of the Modernists — whatever their errors — was not intended as an attack on Catholicism but as an effort to affirm and defend the relevance and vitality of Catholicism in the modern world.

In the aftermath of the encyclical Tyrrell and several others were excommunicated and their works banned. Tyrrell died two years later, still protesting his faith and loyalty to the church. Petre, who regarded her friend as a saint and martyr, assumed the role of his literary executor. She oversaw the editing and publication of his autobiography and a series of other posthumous books. This was regarded as a sign of defiance by her bishop, who insisted that she too swear the "anti-Modernist" oath. As a laywoman, Petre refused to comply with this extraordinary command, arguing that such an oath would accord equal authority to these papal documents and the Nicene Creed. "If I am wrong," she wrote, "then I am so deeply, fundamentally wrong, that only God can prove it to me. If I am right, then He will make good to me what I have forfeited before men." As a result, her bishop announced that she too was formally excommunicated in that diocese.

Nevertheless, she did not cease to regard herself as a faithful Catholic. Indeed, she later moved to the diocese of Westminster in London, where she maintained her practice of daily communion. She lived on for three decades, publishing historical and critical reflections on the Modernist controversy and its principal figures. Late in her long life, she described herself as "a solitary marooned passenger, the sole living representative of what has come to be regarded as the lost cause of Modernism in the Catholic Church." While she never compromised her principles, she likewise never wavered in her loyal commitment to the church. Thus, she might be said to exemplify a spirituality of loyal dissent.

Toward the end of her life, in an assessment of the Modernist cause, she wrote:

> Nothing can alter the radical aspirations of the human heart, and it was for these that the Modernist contended, and for the sake of which he endured the cramping torture of ecclesiastical institutions, because in spite of their limitations, he found in them a support in the passage through this dark and troubled life; he found through them, the grace to live, the courage to die.

Maude Petre died on December 16, 1942. She was buried in the Anglican cemetery in Storrington, one grave removed from Father Tyrrell.

See: M. D. Petre, *My Way of Faith* (New York: E. P. Dutton, 1937); Clyde F. Crews, *English Catholic Modernism: Maude Petre's Way of Faith* (South Bend, Ind.: University of Notre Dame Press, 1984).

Dom Bede Griffiths
Monk and *Sannyasi* (1906–1994)

"The call of the Church today is to transcend the limits of the institutional structures and to open itself to the presence of the Spirit in the Church and in every Christian."

Bede Griffiths's journey to God was a classic story of the spiritual encounter between East and West. In his old age he looked every bit the part of an Indian holy man — with long beard, flowing white hair, and saffron robe. But while he felt equally at home in the Vedas and Upanishads as in the Christian Scriptures, he remained thoroughly rooted in the church. He had come to the point where all religions, indeed all creation, spoke to him of Christ.

He began life as Alan Richard Griffiths, born into a middle-class English family on December 17, 1906. In 1925 he went up to Oxford, where he studied literature and moved within a circle of self-described "aesthetes." His tutor at Magdalen College was C. S. Lewis, later to become famous as a Christian writer, though at the time neither of them felt any strong religious inclination.

It was after his graduation that Griffiths began to explore the world of faith, stimulated at first through his reading of *Dante, *St. Augustine, and the Bible. Living in a cottage in the Cotswolds, he gradually adopted an ascetic life, experimenting with fasting and other disciplines while passing his days in rigorous sessions of prayer and reflection. Without any particular deliberation, he found himself reinventing for himself a kind of monastic spirituality. What was missing in all this, he came to realize, was the monastery. Eventually he visited Prinknash Priory, a Benedictine monastery, where he believed he had found his true home. There on Christmas Eve 1932 he was received into the Roman Catholic church and soon after formally applied for admission to the priory. Upon receiving the robe of a novice he took the name Bede and went on to spend the next twenty years in conventional monastic life.

In 1955, however, everything conventional in Griffiths's life would be left behind. An invitation arrived to help establish a Benedictine monastery in southern India, and Griffiths impulsively volunteered. Some instinct had made him believe that in India he would discover what he called "the other half of my soul."

India at the time was only newly independent and struggling to define itself as a modern country. But what struck Griffiths, apart from the staggering poverty, was the profoundly religious atmosphere — what he later called "a sense of the sacred" — that seemed to permeate the air. He had come in some sense as a missionary — to help implant and witness to the gospel in a non-Christian culture. But he soon came to believe that the secularized West had much to learn from India. Increasingly, his mission was to witness to the "marriage of East and West" — attempting to facilitate an encounter between Western rationality and the intuitive spirituality that remained so much a part of the Indian soul.

In Kerala Griffiths helped to establish a monastic ashram — a community faithful to the monastic tradition, while adapting its form to Indian culture. Thus Griffiths and the other monks adopted the appearance of *sannyasi,* or Hindu holy men. Instead of the traditional Benedictine habit, they donned the saffron robes of Indian monks, went barefoot, and like all poor Indians sat and slept on the floor and ate with their hands. Griffiths accompanied these formal experiments in inculturation with efforts to bring the dialogue between East and West to a deeper level.

He experimented with yoga, meditation, and other Indian spiritual disciplines. He also immersed himself in the study of Vedanta and the Hindu religious classics. His study confirmed his faith that Christ represented the fulfillment of the religious quest. But just as the church had discerned the mystery of Christ hidden in the religious history of Israel, so it was possible and necessary to discover the face of Christ hidden within all the religions of the world. Christ, he believed, was already present in the Hindu soul, waiting to be discovered. This was Griffiths's life project and his passion.

At the same time, Griffiths believed, the Hindu world had much to teach the West. India had preserved a religious depth, an appreciation for interiority, that was so often effaced in Western culture. A true dialogue between East and West would help seekers in both cultures to travel "upstream," to find their way to a deeper dimension of reality in which all religious paths might ultimately converge.

In 1968 Griffiths helped establish Saccidananda Ashram, a new monastic community which was even more radical in its synthesis of Eastern and Western spirituality. Liturgies combined Christian prayers and reading from the Bible with readings from the *Vedas* and the *Bhagavadgita.*

Griffiths, meanwhile, produced a stream of books which brought wide attention to his monastic experiments. In his later years he also began to travel throughout the world, sharing the wisdom of his experience in India and seeking to recall Christians to a more mystical and contemplative brand of spirituality. His travels brought him into contact with the monastic tradition of the Camaldoli, whose combination of solitary and community life he found attractive. In 1980 he formally affiliated with this order.

In an age of "interreligious dialogue," Griffiths stood in a category of his own. He represented an image of the monk as holy man, a living bridge between different cultures and religious paths. Rooted in the Christian tradition, he witnessed to a Truth, he believed, that was the object of all religious striving. To the East he represented the face of a Christianity stripped of the trappings of Western culture. To the West he issued a challenge to recover the contemplative and mystical dimensions of Christian faith.

Griffiths died on May 13, 1994, at the age of eighty-eight.

See: Kathryn Spink, *A Sense of the Sacred: A Biography of Bede Griffiths* (Maryknoll, N.Y.: Orbis, 1989).

Isaac Hecker

Founder of the Paulist Fathers (1819–1888)

"One may be right, and by contradiction and condemnation
open the way to the success of the truth."

The decades prior to the American Civil War were a time of spiritual upheaval and enthusiastic revival. The early life of Isaac Hecker shared something of that restless confusion. Born to German immigrants in New York City on December 18, 1819, Hecker in his youth undertook a wide-ranging spiritual journey that led him from the Methodist church to experiments with Unitarianism, Mormonism, and the famous Transcendentalist communities at Brook Farm and Fruitlands.

In 1844, however, at the age of twenty-five, he entered the Roman Catholic church. This was hardly a typical destination for the spiritual seekers of his generation. The year 1844, in fact, marked the worst outbreak of anti-Catholic violence in ten years. In Philadelphia nativist mobs burned two churches to the ground; similar violence was avoided in New York only through the deployment of armed guards. This resurgent anti-Catholicism combined the revivalists' theme of America as a beacon of purified Protestant faith with resentment against immigrants in general. Catholicism, on both counts, was an easy target, the ideal symbol of foreign ideas and foreign workers.

Through massive European immigration the Catholic church was in process of becoming the single largest denomination in America. The hierarchy was divided over the best pastoral strategy for protecting the immigrants' faith amid a hostile culture while also serving their social advancement. Conservatives emphasized the need to nurture the immigrants' faith by preserving separate cultural institutions. Liberals favored assimilation.

Hecker viewed the issue in a different light. Not only did he believe that Americanism and Catholicism were compatible. He believed that they were complementary. It was in this light that he viewed the issue of "Americanization." Only by divesting itself of its European appearance could the church fulfil its ultimate mission: the conversion of America to Catholicism.

After his baptism Hecker was ordained in the missionary Redemptorist order, ministering to the German immigrant population. Increasingly, however, he felt that his mission was to minister to the non-Catholic, to convert the Protestant, and speed the "Catholicization" of America. Naturally, this led to tensions with his German superiors. Thus, in 1856 he traveled to Rome and received permission from Pope Pius IX to establish a community in the United States devoted to the conversion of Protestants, the Congregation of St. Paul the Apostle.

This was a considerable achievement. If most Americans harbored suspicions regarding Catholicism, the Vatican maintained a corresponding distrust of American culture. Apart from the issue of Protestantism,

American democracy and the separation of church and state were ideals that directly contradicted Catholic principles of the time. Hecker addressed these concerns, arguing that there was a natural compatibility between the Catholic doctrine of human nature and the institution of democracy. As for the separation of church and state, far from limiting the freedom of the church, this provision of the Constitution was ideally suited to the purpose of spreading the faith. The founding fathers had "made it unlawful for Congress to interfere with the divine prerogative of true religion — the freedom to exercise its divine mission over the whole face of the globe." The church was thus unhindered in ministering to its own flock, but it also enjoyed an unequaled opportunity to win the souls of those outside the fold. Hecker believed not only that the Catholic church had something to offer America, but that "America is the future hope of the church."

Hecker and his Paulist Fathers traveled throughout the country, lecturing to Protestant audiences on the compatibility between Catholic faith and the principles of American democracy. Rather than base his apologetic arguments on history, Scripture, or dogmatic authority, he appealed to his listeners' desire to know the truth, showing how Catholic faith corresponded to the "cravings of the heart." Hecker's belief in democracy marked his own community. The Paulists were not to take vows. He believed the internal discipline of the order should arise as much as possible from remaining open and responsive to the promptings of the Holy Spirit: "One of the natural signs of the true Paulist is that he would prefer to suffer from the excesses of liberty rather than from the arbitrary actions of tyranny."

After his death in 1888 Hecker's name became both a rallying cry and target in the battle to define the church's attitude toward the modern world. To liberals he represented a pioneer in the task of what today might be called inculturation — in this case into the culture of modern pluralistic democracy. In the eyes of conservatives he embodied a range of subversive tendencies.

Hecker's prophecy of the imminent conversion of America to Catholicism was not realized. What did come to pass would have seemed equally utopian to Hecker's contemporaries — that the Catholic church would come to recognize the principles of democracy, the separation of church and state, and religious pluralism, not simply as tolerable facts of life but as desirable ideals. This was the distinctive contribution of the American church to Catholic teaching at Vatican II. It was an achievement grounded, in turn, in the contribution of Isaac Hecker and his followers to the American church.

See: John Farina, *An American Experience of God: The Spirituality of Isaac Hecker* (New York: Paulist, 1981); Vincent Holden, C.S.P., *The Yankee Paul: Isaac Thomas Hecker* (Milwaukee: Bruce, 1958).

Isaiah
Prophet (eighth century B.C.E.)

"I was ready to be sought by those who did not ask for me;
I was ready to be found by those who did not seek me.
I said, 'Here am I, here am I,' to a nation that did not call on my name."

It is very likely that Isaiah began his career as a priest in the Temple in Jerusalem. It was there that he received his prophetic call. It began with a vision: "I saw the Lord sitting upon a throne, high and lifted up, and his train filled the temple." When the prophet bewailed his "unclean lips," an angel flew down and touched his mouth with a burning coal, thus burning his sins away. "And I heard the voice of the Lord saying, 'Whom shall I send, and who will go for us?' Then I said, 'Here am I! Send me.'"

Isaiah's career as a prophet took place against a bewildering backdrop of international politics. Caught between mighty empires, the rulers of Jerusalem sought to maintain the kingdom's independence by striking a series of opportunistic alliances, first with one foreign power, then another. Isaiah believed that by trusting in such military alliances — in essence, by trusting in swords — Israel was losing sight of its ultimate dependence on God. The result would be disaster.

Isaiah's oracles are filled with painful references to the disobedience, apostasy, and hypocrisy he perceived around him: The poor are oppressed; the nation bows down to idols of security and affluence. Under these circumstances all the fine sacrifices in the Temple have become an abomination. Rather than offer prayers with bloody hands, the people had better wash themselves, "cease to do evil, learn to do good; seek justice, correct oppression; defend the fatherless, plead for the widow." In other words, Isaiah called for a return to Israel's primitive trust and faith in Yahweh, a faith expressed in humility and the works of justice and mercy. His hope was that the people would see the light and embrace this course voluntarily. Failing that, he made the extraordinary claim that Assyria and Israel's enemies would be God's instruments for chastising and correcting an errant nation.

Yet along with his grave warnings and denunciation, Isaiah's message was marked by a strong current of annunciation. He believed that destruction would not be the last word. Though it would be cleansed and purified through suffering, the nation would not be destroyed. God's promises would be fulfilled, if only through a remnant of survivors. He even named his son She-ar-jashub, meaning "a remnant shall return."

Isaiah leavened his message with the promise of a future Messiah and a vision of the peaceable kingdom to come. Later Christians would seize on these prophecies as references to Jesus:

> The people who walked in darkness
> have seen a great light;
> those who dwelt in a land of deep darkness,

on them has light shined. . . .
For to us a child is born,
to us a son is given;
and the government will be upon his shoulder,
and his name will be called
"Wonderful Counselor, Mighty God,
Everlasting Father, Prince of Peace."

It is difficult for Christians to read these words without hearing the joyous strains of Handel's *Messiah*. If so, it is important to recall how much of Isaiah's hope remains to be fulfilled. In the messianic age which he prophesied,

They shall beat their swords into plowshares
and their spears into pruning hooks;
One nation shall not raise the sword against another,
nor shall they train for war again.

In that age,

The wolf shall be the guest of the lamb
and the leopard shall lie down with the kid;
The calf and the young lion shall browse together,
with a little child to guide them.

Isaiah's active mission lasted at least forty years, from 742 B.C.E. to about 701, and possibly longer. So influential was his voice that he inspired a tradition of ongoing reflection that would continue in his name for another two hundred years.

The later prophets who wrote in his name applied Isaiah's perspective to the events of their day — the fall of Jerusalem, the exile to Babylon, and the eventual return. In the light of the sufferings and humiliation of Israel they dispensed with the oracles of destruction and gave even greater emphasis to Isaiah's consoling vision of the messianic age.

Thus, Israel is compared to a "suffering servant" who by his vicarious suffering serves to reconcile a sinful humanity to God:

Surely he has borne our griefs
and carried our sorrows . . .
But he was wounded for our transgressions,
he was bruised for our iniquities;
upon him was the chastisement that made us whole,
and with his stripes we are healed.

The book of Isaiah ends with a vision of cosmic fulfillment: "a new heaven and a new earth," wherein justice and peace shall dwell. It is an open vision that still retains its hope and challenge.

See: Abraham Heschel, *The Prophets* (New York: Harper & Row, 1962).

December 20
Raoul Wallenberg
Righteous Gentile (1912–?)

"I think I may have been forgotten by Sweden, and the rest of the world.
I wonder if any of the people I saved still remember?"

Among the list of Righteous Gentiles — Christians who undertook the rescue of Jews from Nazi extermination — the name of Raoul Wallenberg is the most highly honored. Born to a life of privilege, a member of one of Sweden's most distinguished families, he volunteered in the midst of the war for a hazardous diplomatic mission in Budapest for the purpose of rescuing Hungarian Jews.

By the time he arrived in Budapest in July 1944 half a million Jews had already been deported to death camps in Poland. Additional transports were leaving every few days. Under the cover of his diplomatic status, Wallenberg immediately went to work distributing Swedish passports to Hungarian Jews. Despite the brazen audacity of his operation, he managed to browbeat the Hungarian authorities, working under the thumb of the Nazis, to respect the protected status of these "subjects" of a neutral state.

That fall the Nazis finally swept away the fiction of Hungarian autonomy and took charge of the deportations. Adolf Eichmann, Hitler's notorious overseer of the "Final Solution," was himself in Budapest. He believed that the extermination of Hungarian Jewry would be his proudest, and perhaps final, legacy. The Red Army was by this time steadily advancing. It was clear the war's end could not be far behind. Still the Nazis applied themselves to their genocidal task with single-minded devotion.

As the months passed, it seemed that Eichmann and Wallenberg were locked in a personal contest to see whether the Nazi's passion for killing would triumph over the Swede's passion for life. By this time there were over a hundred thousand Jews left in the ghetto of Budapest. Wallenberg had managed to have as many as thirty thousand of them segregated into a special preserve for "protected foreign nationals." He had become the Jews' last and only hope. He would typically appear at the train station, alerted that a shipment of Jews was heading out, bluster his way past the Nazi guards with an imperious shout, "I am Wallenberg! I insist that all Swedish citizens be removed from this transport immediately!" Before the astonished guards could react he would hustle the children and anyone able to wave a piece of paper — a driver's license, a library card — onto his waiting trucks.

He could not save them all. But there was always the hope that by trying harder, with a bit more finagling, with a little less sleep, with a few more bribes or brash threats, he might save just one more. As the end of the war came steadily closer, the race against death became more heated. He took to reminding the Nazis and their local collaborators of the fate that awaited war criminals. It was not too late to give it up. Wallenberg put the argument to Eichmann himself over a bizarre dinner engagement not long before the end. "Your genocide plans were doomed from the start. Why not leave now, while you still can?" But Eichmann was determined to see it through to the end. "When the Russians come, I know they'll shoot me," he said. "I'm ready."

The Russian siege of Budapest began on December 8, 1944. The rest of the diplomatic corps abandoned the city. Eichmann, in fact, chose to run. But in spite of the dangers, Wallenberg insisted on remaining to protect "his Jews" and to oversee relief work after the armistice. He was now a man marked by the remaining Nazis; his diplomatic cover would no longer protect him. Yet he managed to survive, and with him nearly a hundred thousand Jews. For them the nightmare was over. For Wallenberg it was only the beginning.

On January 16 Wallenberg surrendered to Red Army troops and insisted on being taken to headquarters. From there he disappeared into the silence of the Soviet Gulag, one of the first casualties of the new Cold War. Apparently the Soviets suspected that the rich Swedish capitalist, funded by overseas Jewish organizations and somehow able to manage an enormous underground operation under the noses of the Nazis, must be some kind of foreign spy. Within days Wallenberg had been conveyed to Moscow, where he was held in the infamous Lubianka Prison of the secret police.

Inquiries by the Swedish government were simply ignored. Then the Soviets claimed he had died in the battle of Budapest. Finally, in the 1950s, as pressure mounted, it was claimed that he had died of a heart attack in Soviet custody in 1947. That remained the official Soviet story. And yet reliable witnesses continued to report chance encounters with Wallenberg in prisons throughout the Soviet Union as late as the 1960s. Although he was constantly moved through the penal system and kept in careful isolation, there were occasional mistakes, an opportunity to entrust a short message to a fellow prisoner: "Tell them you met a Swede from Budapest."

The exact fate of Wallenberg remains unknown. Perhaps in his cell in a remote prison, or in a hospital, or even in a mental asylum in the company of other special prisoners, he eventually passed from this world. Under other circumstances he might well have lived to see the collapse of communism, as he had witnessed the collapse of the Nazi empire. He would have been seventy-seven in 1989. But many others lived to see that day because of his efforts, and they are only a small fraction of those who revere the name and memory of Raoul Wallenberg.

Aside from the mystery of his fate there remains a deeper enigma. Unlike many other rescuers, Wallenberg left no record of soul-searching, conversion, or even profound reflection on the meaning of his efforts. He did not come from a particularly religious family, and his privileged upbringing had fairly insulated him from much contact with suffering. He simply rose to the ethical demands of the situation as though it were the self-evident duty of a human being. He did what needed to be done. The Nazis did not know what to make of this. More than once it seems they put the question to him: "Why would a Christian go to such trouble to save some Jews?" There is no record of his ever having dignified the question with a reply.

See: Kati Marton, *Wallenberg* (New York: Random House, 1982).

December 21
St. Peter Canisius
Doctor of the Church (1521–1597)

"The fear of many people is greater than necessary, because they look for human and not for divine help; they act in despair instead of praying with holy confidence for the oppressed Church."

Peter Canisius, one of the first Jesuits, played a vital role in the renewal and reformation of the Catholic church in Central Europe. He was among those who believed the church's best response to the Protestant challenge was to cleanse its own house, present the faith in a clear and attractive form, and offer the living witness of evangelical piety.

Born in Holland, Canisius studied in Louvain before joining the Society of Jesus. He was the eighth Jesuit to make his solemn profession of vows. Afterward he became an almost ubiquitous figure in the campaign of Catholic renewal. He served in Sicily, Rome, Bavaria, and Vienna before being named as the first Jesuit provincial of South Germany. For his successful service in this post he was later called by *Pope Leo XIII "the second apostle of Germany, after *Boniface." It is estimated that in the course of his career he traveled up to twenty thousand miles on horseback and foot. In 1580 he was assigned to the Catholic city of Fribourg. There he founded the famous university and almost singlehandedly preserved the Catholic presence in Switzerland. He died in 1597.

Two features of Peter Canisius are particularly memorable. The first was his determination to affirm the gospel in a positive and noncontroversial light. At a time when malicious defamation was commonly traded between opposing sides of the Reformation, Canisius tried to maintain a tone of charity and generosity toward his opponents. In 1555 he published his *Catechism,* a fantastically successful work that went through two hundred editions and was translated into fifteen languages during his lifetime. He presented the faith with no mention of his opponents and thus managed to earn appreciative notice from a number of Protestant divines.

The second great contribution of Canisius was in his role as the first patron of Catholic publishing. While Martin Luther had quickly perceived the potential power and significance of printed media, the Catholic reformers were slower to seize on this technological revolution. Canisius was in this respect a leader. In the words of a fellow Jesuit, "Canisius held that to defend the Catholic truth with the pen was just as important as to convert the Hindus." Not only did he himself write scores of books, both for scholars and for a general audience, but in every city where he worked he was active in obtaining church support for Catholic printers and publishers. This contribution was especially emphasized by Pope Pius XI when in 1925 Canisius was canonized and named a Doctor of the Church.

See: William Reany, *A Champion of the Church* (New York: Benziger Brothers, 1931).

December 22
Chico Mendes
Rubber Worker and Martyr (d. 1988)

"If a messenger from heaven would guarantee that my death would strengthen our struggle, it might be worthwhile. But experience teaches us the opposite, so I want to live."

Chico Mendes, who was assassinated in 1988, was the leader of a movement linking the defense of the Amazon region with justice for the poor who lived there. Living in the state of Acre in the Amazonian region of Northwest Brazil, he organized a union of the region's rubber tappers and other poor families who earned their meager living by extracting the renewable resources of the rainforest. Mendes was himself the son of tappers who arrived in the Amazon to take advantage of the rubber boom between the two World Wars. In more recent years the fate of such workers was threatened by big landowners and ranchers who preferred to burn and clear the forests to make way for cattle.

Mendes began organizing the rubber workers in 1977. At first his aim was simply to protect their rights and livelihood. But he gradually expanded his concerns to encompass a wider ecological vision. The burning of the forest contributed to the "greenhouse effect." It ruined the land and ultimately threatened the survival of the whole planet. Thus, he made the connection between the "cry of the poor" and the "cry of the Earth."

The owners resorted to threats and brutal violence to break the will of the union. But the nonviolent tactics of Mendes and his supporters began to attract international support. Mendes himself was repeatedly threatened with death. According to his wife, Ilza, "Sometimes I'd say to Chico, 'Chico, they're going to kill you! Why don't you take care of yourself and go away?' But Chico wasn't afraid of death. He told me that he would never stop defending the Amazon forest — never!"

In 1987 Mendes was awarded the United Nations' Global 500 Award for Environmental Protection. He was called "the *Gandhi of the Amazon." Soon after this the government of Brazil granted reserve status to four areas of the rainforest. But this was not enough to protect the life of Chico Mendes. On December 22, 1988, he was shot and killed by a rancher and his son.

His widow observed, "Chico had a lot of faith. When he died, I was filled with despair. But God comforted me and inspired me to work alongside others to carry on Chico's work. They killed him, but they didn't kill his ideals or crush the struggle."

See: Mev Puleo, "The Struggle Continues," *Maryknoll* Magazine (January 1990).

December 23
Rabbi Abraham Heschel
Teacher and Prophet (1907–1972)

"I did not ask for success; I asked for wonder. And You gave it to me."

Abraham Heschel was born in Warsaw in 1907. Descended from a long line of Hasidic rabbis, it was his destiny to take his place among them. Nevertheless, he resisted the will of his family when he chose to leave his enclosed community to explore the wisdom of the outside world. He studied philosophy in Warsaw and then at the University of Berlin, where he received a doctorate in 1933. Though he was never again at home in the Jewish ghetto, he did not dispense with his Orthodox faith. Rather, he believed it was his special vocation to connect two worlds: the mystical world of Hasidic Judaism and the modern world of "man in search of meaning."

Heschel succeeded *Martin Buber in his chair at Frankfurt. But in 1938, as a foreign Jew, he was expelled from Germany and forced to return to Warsaw. He was fortunate to escape the city just weeks before the Nazi invasion in 1939. He made his way to London and eventually to the United States, where he remained for the rest of his life, teaching in a series of Jewish as well as Christian seminaries. Though he wrote relatively little about the Holocaust, his writing was deeply affected by his brush with this modern manifestation of evil. As he wrote, "I am a brand plucked from the fire, in which my people was burned to death."

Through a series of books published in the 1950s Heschel emerged as one of the significant religious voices of his time. His writings contributed greatly to the spiritual renewal of Judaism. "A Jew," he wrote, "is asked to take a leap of action rather than a leap of thought. He is asked to surpass his deeds, to do more than he understands in order to understand more than he does." But Heschel exerted an almost equal influence on Christians, so much that he was called another "apostle to the gentiles." His writings recalled Christians to their Jewish roots and their common faith in the God of Israel.

Heschel was a passionate champion of interfaith dialogue and cooperation. "No religion," he wrote, "is an island. We are all involved with one another." And "God is greater than religion." Heschel was particularly influential in challenging the Catholic church to overcome the harmful legacy of anti-Semitism. He met with Popes *John XXIII and *Paul VI and was an official observer at the Second Vatican Council. There his influence was felt in the council's historic statement on the church's kinship with Judaism.

With his bushy beard and aura of holiness, Heschel gave the vivid appearance of a biblical prophet. Indeed, his study *The Prophets* is a modern classic. He emphasized in that work that the prophet was not a fortuneteller but someone who identified with and communicated the pathos of God. In the 1960s Heschel's vocation as a prophet was tested against the challenges of war and social justice. He was a close friend of *Martin Luther King, Jr., and took a prominent place in the protest against racism. He was also an early critic of the Vietnam War, noting, "To speak about God and remain silent on Vietnam is blasphemous." Explaining his engagement in political issues, he referred to the lessons he had learned from the prophets: "that, morally speaking, there is no limit to the concern one must feel for the suffering of human beings, that indifference to evil is worse than evil itself, that in a free society, some are guilty, but all are responsible."

Faithful to his Hasidic roots, Heschel managed to communicate to a largely secular world a sense of "the holy dimension of all existence." He had a poetic knack for communicating whole volumes in a single phrase: "To pray is to dream in league with God, to envision His holy visions." Heschel's religion did not represent an escape to another world but a deep sense of responsibility to this world and its questions and needs. "We are not asked to abandon life and to say farewell to this world, but to keep the spark within aflame, and to suffer His light to reflect in our face."

He had written of the prophets that because they are ultimately motivated by love, their message often begins with denunciation but concludes with hope. This too characterized Heschel's message. Shortly before his death he taped a television interview, which he concluded with some words for young people: "Remember that there is meaning beyond absurdity. Know that every deed counts, that every word is power.... Above all, remember that you must build your life as if it were a work of art."

Heschel died on December 23, 1972.

See: Abraham Heschel, *I Asked for Wonder: A Spiritual Anthology,* ed. Samuel H. Dresner (New York: Crossroad, 1993); Franklin Sherman, *The Promise of Heschel* (Philadelphia: J. B. Lippincott, 1970).

December 24
The Anointer of Bethany
(first century)

"Truly, I say to you, wherever the gospel is preached in the whole world, what she has done will be told in memory of her."

One of the great women of the Gospels is remembered by her deed alone; her name is totally lost. *St. Mark relates that as Jesus sat at table in Bethany an anonymous woman proceeded to anoint his head with precious oil. As a gesture of hospitality, the deed itself provokes no comment. What gives rise to grumbling is the extraordinary value of the oil expended — virtually the equivalent of a year's wages. Could not the money have been spent on the poor?

But Jesus stills the complainers and accepts the woman's gesture. In fact he does more. He underscores the prophetic timeliness of her deed and so names it as one of the exceptional and defining moments of the gospel. A similar moment occurred with *Peter's famous confession: "You are the Christ [the Messiah/Anointed One]." In that episode and elsewhere, however, Jesus had shown a determination to correct the disciples' understanding of what it means to be God's Anointed One: he will have to suffer and die. The pattern of this interaction is repeated several times. Jesus is acclaimed as the Messiah; this is misunderstood by his disciples in terms of simple power and glory; Jesus redefines his identity in terms of suffering and death.

As he approaches Jerusalem the way is strewn with portents of his messianic authority: the waiting colt, the entry into the royal city with its overtones of the coronation of Solomon. Now in the climax of his ministry he is anointed with oil. The extravagance of the gesture points to its prophetic-symbolic significance. Once again the exchange between master and disciples echoes previous controversies: Jesus the Anointed is anointed; the disciples do not comprehend the action, or comprehend it falsely (a waste of precious oil); Jesus accepts the form of this symbolic acclamation, but uses the situation once again to reinterpret the meaning of his Messiahship — his mission — in terms of suffering and death. "She has done what she could; she has anointed my body beforehand for my burial."

Thus, Jesus accepts the import of the woman's "christological" gesture in a way that he could not, without qualification, accept the naive confession of Peter. In her wordless act of compassion she has recognized in Jesus, the Poor Man par excellence, the Christ who is about to die. She alone has responded appropriately. Though her name would be forgotten Jesus holds her forth as the faithful disciple whose deed should be remembered wherever the gospel is preached.

See: Mark 14:3–9; Elisabeth Schüssler Fiorenza, *In Memory of Her* (New York: Crossroad, 1983).

December 25

Bd. Jacopone of Todi
Franciscan poet (1230–1306)

"Now, a new creature, I in Christ am born,
    The old man stripped away; — I am new-made;
And mounting in me, like the sun at morn,
    Love breaks my heart, even as a broken blade:
Christ, First and Only Fair, from me hath shorn
    My will, my wits, and all that in me stayed,
    I in His arms am laid,

> I cry and call —
> 'O Thou my All,
> O let me die of Love!' "

Jacopone Benedetti was born in the Umbrian town of Todi, the region that gave birth to *St. Francis and that had but recently mourned his passing. Jacopone's early life was unaffected by this atmosphere of spiritual renewal. Everything in his background — his wealthy and well-connected family, his training in the law, and finally his happy marriage to a beautiful young woman, Vanna di Guidone — all pointed to a future of worldly success and happiness.

But all this changed overnight. While attending a wedding party, a balcony upon which a number of guests were seated suddenly collapsed. Vanna, his bride of only a year, was fatally injured. As she died before his eyes, Jacopone's terrible loss was compounded by the belated discovery of his wife's piety. Loosening her gown he was surprised and deeply moved to find that she wore a secret hair shirt, a penance which he believed she must have undertaken to atone for his own sins.

His world in ruins, the emptiness of his ambitions laid bare, Jacopone was literally undone. In subsequent days he quit his profession, gave away all his belongings, and became a public penitent or, to all appearances, a kind of wandering fool. With the passage of time the pity which his tragic condition at first evoked gradually turned to ridicule.

For ten years he maintained this life of aimless poverty and penance. At the age of forty-eight, however, he knocked on the door of the Franciscans and applied for admission to the brotherhood. Thus, as Brother Jacopone, he found a more socially acceptable way to express his contempt for the world. What is remarkable is that in joining the Franciscans he also found his voice as a poet, indeed one of the great lyric poets of the Middle Ages. In the passionate language of love, his mystical poems describe the soul's yearning for Christ. But unlike the poems of his master, Francis of Assisi, they retain a mournful undertone, the accent of a faith born in loss. This is evident in the most famous poem with which he is credited, the *Stabat Mater Dolorosa*, a heartbreaking meditation on the sorrows of Mary as she stands at the foot of the cross.

> At the cross her station keeping,
> Stood the mournful Mother weeping,
>   Close to Jesus to the last:
> Through her heart, His sorrow sharing,
> All His bitter anguish bearing,
>   Now at length the sword had passed.

Jacopone soon emerged as a leader of the Spirituals, a party among the Franciscans who represented the most radical commitment to apostolic poverty. The Spirituals received some support from the saintly *Pope Celestine V, but this policy did not survive his unexpected resignation and the election of the controversial Pope Boniface VIII. The Spirituals directly challenged the legitimacy of Boniface's election. They especially deplored Boniface's imprisonment of his predecessor. Jacopone addressed a savagely bitter manifesto to the pope, with the result that he too landed in a dungeon. There he remained for five years, still writing his sorrowful love poems, until Boniface's death in 1303 brought his release.

Jacopone retired to a hermitage near Orvieto and later lived at a Poor Clare convent near Todi. There he died in the early morning hours of Christmas Day, 1306. On his tomb an inscription was placed: "Here lie the bones of Blessed Jacopone dei Benedetti da Todi, Friar Minor, who, having gone mad with love of Christ, by a new artifice deceived the world and took heaven by violence."

See: Ray C. Petry, ed., *Late Medieval Mysticism,* Library of Christian Classics (Philadelphia: Westminster, 1967).

December 26
St. Stephen
Deacon and Martyr (c. 34)

"Lord, Jesus, receive my spirit."

St. Stephen is remembered as the Proto-Martyr of the church, the first disciple to shed his blood in witness to Christ. As such, his story, as re-counted in the Acts of the Apostles, became a prototype for subsequent accounts of Christian martyrdom.

St. Stephen, evidently a Hellenistic Jew, was one of the first seven dea-cons ordained in the church of Jerusalem. Nothing is recorded of his conversion or early life, but we are told that he was "full of grace and power" and did great wonders and signs among the people. Apparently he also liked to engage his fellow Jews in public disputation over the life and teachings of Christ, and for this he was denounced before the Jewish Sanhedrin.

As the story is recounted in Acts, Stephen was interrogated before the high priest. Responding to the charge of blasphemy, he delivered a long sermon chronicling the history of God's covenant with his servants Abra-ham and *Moses before rising to a shocking rhetorical climax. In a bold charge, he turned the accusations against the Jewish leaders themselves:

> You stiff-necked people, uncircumcised in heart and ears, you al-ways resist the Holy Spirit. As your fathers did, so do you. Which of the prophets did not your fathers persecute? And they killed those who announced beforehand the coming of the Righteous One, whom you have now betrayed and murdered, you who received the law as delivered by angels and did not keep it.

His audience responded with predictable outrage. Stephen was driven from the city and stoned to death. But he did not die before receiving a vision of the open heavens with "Jesus standing at the right hand of God," and before praying for the forgiveness of his murderers.

The death of Stephen marked a new foundation for the early church. Jesus' proclamation of the reign of God had given way to the proclamation of Jesus himself. But the continuity was underlined in the fact that the disciple met the same fate as his Master. Dying, like Jesus, with words of forgiveness on his lips, the martyr was vouchsafed a vision of Christ in his glory, a pledge of the reward that awaits all who remain faithful to the end.

See: Acts 6:1–8:1.

December 27

St. John
Apostle (first century)

"For God so loved the world that he gave his only Son,
that whoever believes in him should not perish but have eternal life."

St. John figures in all four Gospels as one of the earliest of the twelve apostles. He and his brother James, both Galilean fishermen, were called by Jesus "sons of thunder." John was a privileged witness of many significant moments in Jesus' life, including the raising of Jairus's daughter, the transfiguration, and the agony in the Garden. By tradition, John is also identified as the author of the Fourth Gospel, written most likely toward the end of the first century. If not actually written by his hand, the Fourth Gospel is certainly the product of a community that traced its identity and spirituality to the apostle John, referred to throughout the Gospel as "the disciple whom Jesus loved."

The Gospel of John includes many references to the affectionate relationship between Jesus and the "beloved disciple." The latter is described as resting his head on Jesus' breast during the Last Supper. He alone among the Twelve is described as a witness to the crucifixion. There, among his parting words, Jesus takes care to entrust the disciple and his mother to one another's care: " 'Woman, behold, your son!' Then he said to the disciple, 'Behold, your mother!' and from that hour the disciple took her to his own home."

John's Gospel, far more than the other Gospels, emphasizes Jesus' human affections — especially for John himself, but also for *Mary Magdalene, for Mary of Bethany and her sister Martha, and for their brother Lazarus, whose death causes Jesus to weep. Indeed, John's Gospel alone records that Jesus addressed his disciples as friends:

"Greater love has no man than this, that a man lay down his life for his friends. You are my friends if you do what I command you. No longer do I call you servants, for the servant does not know what his master is doing; but I have called you friends."

For the community that honored the "beloved disciple" the gospel message is succinctly summarized in the charge to love one another as Jesus loved us. In John's account of the Last Supper he provides a striking example of such love when, after supper, Jesus lays aside his garments, girds himself with a towel, and proceeds to wash the feet of his disciples. Ultimately the power of God is revealed in loving service.

According to tradition John outlived the rest of the Twelve. He escaped martyrdom and was sent into exile on the island of Patmos. Later he retired to Ephesus, where he presided over the local church until the end of his days. He was supposedly known for delivering the same short sermon, regardless of the occasion or circumstances: "Brothers and sisters, love one another." When members of his congregation asked whether they couldn't, sometime, hear a different message, he answered: "When you have mastered this lesson we can move on to another."

See: Wes Howard-Brook, *Becoming Children of God: John's Gospel and Radical Discipleship* (Maryknoll, N.Y.: Orbis, 1995).

December 28

Holy Innocents
(first century)

"Rise, take the child and his mother, and flee to Egypt and remain there till I tell you; for Herod is about to search for the child, to destroy him."
— Matthew 2:13

It is the constant fear of every tyrant that somewhere, perhaps in an obscure village, perhaps at that very moment, there is a baby born who will one day signal the end of his power. According to the Gospel of *Matthew, this fear was realized for King Herod when wandering wise men from the East came to Jerusalem asking, "Where is he who has been born king of the Jews?"

By all accounts, Herod was a man of extreme brutality. He conceived of a simple plan: Rather than sit and wait anxiously for the day of reckoning with this future "king," why not simply kill the babe before he could grow and pose a threat? But when the wise men failed to cooperate with his plan, Herod simply ordered his troops to the village of Bethlehem, there to kill every male child under the age of two. The order was given and it was dutifully carried out.

But the reader knows, as Herod does not, that the massacre is pointless. *Joseph, forewarned in a dream, has taken his family into exile in Egypt. The child lives.

This terrible story, omitted from the typical Christmas pageant, is a vivid reminder of the violent world into which Jesus was born. There were certainly those for whom the coming of the Messiah represented anything but good news. Did Jesus at some point learn the story of his birth and of the children who had perished in his place? If so, that chapter in his education is reserved for his "hidden years," beyond the scope of the Gospel narratives. From the early centuries, however, the church has commemorated the feast of these Holy Innocents. Unlike traditional martyrs who would later die bearing witness to Christ, these little ones died unwittingly in the place of Christ. They were killed by the same interests that would later conspire in the death of Jesus and for the same reasons — to stifle from birth any hope that the world might be changed.

In our own time whole villages have been massacred on the basis of similar reports: "In such-and-such-a-hamlet the peasants have formed a cooperative.... It is said that in such-a-village poor families are gathering at night to read the Bible and other subversive literature.... It is well known where this is likely to lead.... Advise that appropriate action be taken before the danger spreads."

The feast of the Holy Innocents is not simply a memorial to those who died before their time. These infants represent all those cut down to prevent the seed of liberation from taking root and growing. They are those who die in the dream of a different future, hoping but never knowing that their redeemer lives. In remembering the feast of the Holy Innocents the church commemorates these victims of Herod's rage. But it also celebrates his failure.

His power is doomed. The child lives.

December 29

St. Thomas Becket
Archbishop and Martyr (1118–1170)

"I commit myself and my cause to the Judge of all men.
Your swords are less ready to strike than is my spirit for martyrdom."

The murder of Archbishop Thomas Becket in Canterbury Cathedral is one of the most celebrated episodes in medieval history. Within days of his death in 1170 there were reports of miracles at his grave, and his canonization followed only two years later. Becket's death was but one episode in a longstanding struggle to define the respective jurisdictions of the church and the crown. But it was also the culmination of a complicated relationship between two men, Thomas Becket and King Henry II.

Thomas was born in England, the son of well-born Norman parents who arranged for him to serve in the household of Theobold, archbishop of Canterbury. Thomas proved so capable in this service that he became the archbishop's favored protégé. Eventually he was named archdeacon of the cathedral. At some point his reputation reached the young King Henry and there began an unusually close and devoted friendship between them. As a seal of their friendship Henry named Thomas his chancellor, the second most powerful office in the realm.

In this role, which entailed responsibility for the finances of the kingdom, Thomas was an effective and devoted servant of the king's interests. Thus, upon the death of Archbishop Theobold, Henry perceived an excellent opportunity to extend his power by appointing his friend Thomas to the vacant see. Thomas demurred, sensing that this would be the end of their friendship. But ultimately he yielded to Henry's wishes. He was ordained a priest and thereafter he was consecrated archbishop of Canterbury with great pomp and ceremony.

Henry's intentions were not terribly subtle, and the canons of the cathedral were less than enthusiastic about this imposition of the "king's man." Nevertheless, Thomas began at once to define his independence by renouncing the office of chancellor. This was not part of the script that Henry had devised. But it was only the first of many signs that Thomas intended to take his office seriously. He began fasting and keeping nightly prayer vigils. He wore a secret hair shirt and practiced other mortifications.

Of more serious issue, Thomas began resisting various encroachments on the independence and prerogatives of the church which his respected predecessor had tolerated. Henry was in many ways a modern monarch who wished to claim absolute jurisdiction over all affairs in his domain. He instituted a new code of law and various reforms in civil administration, many of which served the cause of justice. Furthermore, he wished to go farther than any of his predecessors in asserting the jurisdiction of the crown over members of the clergy. This meant challenging the institution of separate ecclesial courts for clergy accused of violating civil law, and it meant asserting the ultimate authority of the king rather than the pope in such cases. In these matters Thomas stood adamantly opposed.

Eventually things came to such a pass that Thomas was forced to flee England for exile in a Cistercian monastery in France. He submitted himself to the will of the pope, but the pontiff's support was tepid. Though he appreciated Thomas's stand, he was involved in his own struggles against a rival antipope, and he had no interest in feeding the antagonism of the King of England.

Many overtures to reconciliation were tested and failed. Henry intensified the crisis by arranging for the coronation of his son by the archbishop of York, thus defying ancient custom that reserved this privilege to the primate of England. He also allowed various barons to steal property from the see of Canterbury. Thomas responded by issuing excommunications on his enemies.

In July 1170 Henry and Thomas met on the beach in Normandy and both seemed eager to patch up their differences. Thomas returned to Canterbury, where he was greeted, after an absence of six years, by an outpouring of popular joy. But there would be no peace. The underlying conflicts remained, intensified now by the excommunications that remained in force against many of Henry's closest allies. In his Christmas sermon, Thomas told the congregation that their bishop might soon be taken from them.

Within days Henry flew into an uncontrollable rage and uttered, in the presence of several of his loyal barons, the fateful words that would be a death sentence for his one-time friend: "What a set of idle cowards I keep in my kingdom who allow me to be mocked so shamefully by a low-born clerk." The four knights, fully comprehending their lord's meaning, immediately departed for Canterbury. On December 29, they accosted Thomas inside the cathedral as he prepared for evening vespers. Thomas made no effort to resist their assault. In a fury they struck him down with their swords and scattered his brains on the stone floor. Before he died he cried out, "Into thy hands, Lord, I commend my spirit."

All of Europe was horrified by this wanton deed. Thomas was immediately acclaimed as a saint by the common people of England. Perhaps not all could comprehend the constitutional issues at stake in the archbishop's conflict with the king. Indeed, from the modern perspective, Becket's commitment to the autonomy of ecclesiastical courts seems a somewhat antiquated principle, which even then had little apparent relevance to the lives of most citizens. But the people understood, on some level, that Becket had stood in the way of the total self-aggrandizement of the state, and that he had died finally in defense of the principle that there is a higher authority than the king.

Henry himself was forced to acknowledge as much when he fasted for forty days, walked barefoot to Becket's grave, and submitted himself to a scourging by the cathedral canons. Becket was canonized in 1173. His tomb at Canterbury became one of the most frequented pilgrimage sites in Europe.

See: David Knowles, *Thomas Becket* (Stanford, Calif.: Stanford University Press, 1970).

December 30

John Main
Monk and Master of Christian Meditation
(1926–1982)

"All Christian prayer is a growing awareness of God in Jesus. And for that growing awareness we need to come to a state of undistraction, to a state of attention and concentration — that is, to a state of awareness. And as far as I have been able to determine ... the only way ... to come to that quiet, to that undistractedness, to that concentration, is the way of the mantra."

In 1959 at the age of thirty-three John Main entered Ealing Abbey in London and became a monk in the Order of *St. Benedict. This marked the resolution of one question — whether he was meant to live a married life or to become a monk. He had previously had a wide range of experience "in the world," as a soldier, a lawyer, and a civil servant in the British Overseas Service in Malaya. Ultimately he had felt called to a life of prayer and total dedication to God. But becoming a monk only opened the door on a different kind of spiritual search to find the contemporary relevance of monastic life to the needs of the world today.

After fifteen years as a monk, mostly spent teaching in Benedictine schools in London and Washington, D.C., Main was increasingly struck by the great spiritual hunger afflicting the modern world. He was convinced that part of this reflected the loss of a spiritual dimension to life and that the answer to this was prayer. But what kind of prayer? What was needed, he believed, was a form of prayer adapted to the demands of life in the world.

Main remembered a friendship he had enjoyed years before with a Hindu swami in Malaya. The swami had contrasted the verbosity and self-consciousness of Christian prayer with the simplicity of the mantra — the repetition of a word or phrase — that was a common method of prayer in the East. This memory led Main to return to the pre-Benedictine sources of monasticism, the spirituality of the desert fathers described by *John Cassian. Cassian had recommended just such a discipline, the constant repetition of certain sacred words, as a way of emptying the mind of concepts and rooting oneself in the divine mystery. Cassian had suggested, as an example, the ancient Aramaic prayer *Maranatha* — "Come Lord Jesus" — and Main later adopted this for his personal use.

In 1975 Main organized a small prayer group at Ealing Abbey to experiment with this new form of Christian meditation. As he later explained, "To meditate means to live out of the center of our being." Through imageless prayer and the repetition of the mantra, he taught, one might move away from the surface of consciousness to penetrate the silent place where Jesus lives and prays within us.

Many lay people were attracted to Main's circle, confirming his belief that he had rediscovered a way of prayer widely accessible and meaningful to ordinary people. This led Main to ponder the possibility of a new type of monasticism in which monks, nuns, and lay people might be able to share a common life of prayer and work together.

In 1977, an invitation from the bishop of Montreal provided an opportunity to launch the kind of experimental monastic community that he had envisioned. The Benedictine priory in Montreal became a center that attracted seekers from around the world — both monks and lay people. Gradually the influence of this school of spirituality spread far and wide, as local prayer circles inspired by Main's writings began to form. This again confirmed Main's conviction that prayer, far from being a solipsistic activity, was the rich soil of community. From many parts of the globe countless numbers of people began to describe the ways that their lives were turning around through the simple discipline of sitting in meditation for half an hour, once or twice a day.

While remaining intensely focused on Christ, Main's approach to prayer also fostered dialogue with people of other faiths. After a visit by the Dalai Lama, he described how they had meditated together:

> We meditated together in absolute openness to love and to the Lord of love. We were not trying to convert one another. Our challenge as Christians is not to try to convert people around us to our way of belief but to love them, to be ourselves living incarnations of what we believe, to live what we believe and to love what we believe.

Little time was given to Main to develop his experimental monastery. In 1982 he was discovered to be in a state of advanced lung cancer. His last months were spent in terrible pain and debilitating treatments, yet few apart from his closest friends were aware of the seriousness of his condition. Until the end he continued to write and give conferences. In his last major talk he spoke at length on "the inner journey":

> The inner journey is a way of union. Firstly, it unites us to ourselves. Then (as our personal fulfillment is found beyond ourselves) it unites us to others. And then (as union with others opens up the heart of the mystery of love to us) it unites us with God, so that God may be all in all.

He died in Montreal on December 30, 1982.

See: Neil McKenty, *In the Stillness Dancing: The Journey of John Main* (London: Darton, Longman and Todd, 1986); John Main, *Word into Silence* (New York: Paulist, 1981).

December 31

St. Melania the Younger
(383 – 439)

"The Lord knows that I am unworthy, and I would not dare compare myself with any good woman, even of those living in the world. Yet I think the Enemy himself will not at the Last Judgment accuse me of ever having gone to sleep with bitterness in my heart."

St. Melania was one of the great women of the early church. In a life of unusually varied experience she passed through many roles — as wife and mother, monk and hermit, pilgrim and spiritual director — all united in an underlying call to the spiritual life.

She began life as the daughter of a wealthy Christian family in Rome. (She was named for her grandmother, St. Melania the Elder.) Despite a professed desire to consecrate herself to God, her family forced her to marry at the age of fourteen. After the death in infancy of her first two children, however, she won the consent of her husband, Pinian, and her widowed mother to follow her vocation. What is more, she convinced them also to adopt her life of prayer and pious works. And so she and her husband divested themselves of their fabulous wealth. They set eight thousand slaves at liberty and distributed the proceeds from their many estates to the poor.

In 406 she and her family fled Rome to escape the invasion of the Goths. They went first to North Africa, settling in Tagaste in Numibia. Melania and Pinian were a great adornment to the local church, and they counted such figures as *St. Augustine among their friends and admirers. Melania established two monasteries, one for men and the other for women, among whom she lived, supporting herself by the transcription of manuscripts (she was fluent in Latin and Greek).

In 417 Melania, still accompanied by her mother and husband, moved on to the Holy Land, where she settled in Jerusalem. Inspired by the fathers of the Egyptian desert, she resolved to live a life of solitude and prayer. Nevertheless, she became closely acquainted with the community in Bethlehem that included *St. Paula and *St. Jerome. After fourteen years her mother and husband died. She buried them on the Mount of Olives and established a cell nearby that became the center of a large convent of women.

In 439 she went to celebrate Christmas in Bethlehem with her friend Paula. There she became seriously ill. Sensing that her life was ending she sent for her Sisters and bade them farewell, "for I am going to the Lord." On Sunday, December 31, she attended Mass and spent the rest of the day receiving visitors. Finally she asked for leave to rest. She died after uttering her final words: "As the Lord willed, so it is done."

STUDY GUIDE

Questions for discussion

1. *All Saints* assembles an inclusive calendar of "saints, prophets, and witnesses for our time." What is the rationale for combining officially recognized saints with figures who are not candidates for official canonization? How does this approach affect your understanding of saints and the "call to holiness"?

2. Alban Butler said that in the lives of the saints we see the gospel "clothed as it were with a body." What does this mean? To what extent do saints also illuminate "forgotten" aspects of the gospel? Consider the subjects of radical poverty, nonviolence, the rights of conscience, ecology, or the dignity and equality of women. Who are some of the saints who exemplify these principles? Are there prophets and holy men and women today who "remind" us of other gospel truths?

3. Some saints were revered while they lived. But for many others veneration came long after they died. While they lived they were scorned, ignored, or even subject to persecution. Consider the stories of St. John of the Cross, St. Elizabeth of Hungary, Bd. Mary McKillop, St. Peter Claver, St. Joan of Arc, and St. Celestine V. To what extent is this a common motif in the lives of saints and prophets? Can you think of other modern prophets or holy people who might fit this rule?

4. Many of the great saints founded religious orders. Thus, we tend to remember them as "institutional types." Yet in their lives they were actually great innovators. Finding no available outlets for their particular vocations, they invented something new. In this light, consider the stories of St. Benedict, St. Francis and St. Clare, St. Teresa of Avila, St. Angela Merici, St. Ignatius, St. Dominic, St. Jeanne de Chantal, and St. Louise de Marillac. Compare these with George Fox, John Wesley, Mother Teresa, Molly Rogers, Mary Ward, Eberhard Arnold, Dorothy Day, Charles de Foucauld, and Isaac Hecker.

5. The word "conversion" often signifies a change in religious affiliation or identity, such as when someone becomes a Catholic. Among the "converts" in this book are such figures as St. Augustine, St. Edith Stein, Gerard Manley Hopkins, Thomas Merton, and Dorothy Day. But is it possible to consider conversion in a wider sense? How does it apply to the stories of Oscar Romero, Mother Teresa, Charles de Foucauld, St. Teresa of Avila, or St. Francis of Assisi?

6. As with most people, the lives of the saints were often marked by suffering. In some cases this played an important role in the discernment of their vocation or the shaping of their spirituality. Consider the role of suffering in the following saints: St. John of God, St. Ignatius of Loyola. St. Camillus de Lellis, St. Therese of Lisieux, Bd. Damien of Molokai, Padre Pio, Jacopone de Todi, Julian of Norwich, and St. Patrick. Consider also Job, Cardinal Joseph Bernardin, Mother Maria Skobtsova, Flannery

O'Connor, Simone Weil, and Walter Ciszek. In what ways might their experience help us cope with our own suffering?

7. The cult of saints has its basis in the early veneration of martyrs (see St. Stephen, St. Polycarp, St. Ignatius of Antioch, and Sts. Perpetua and Felicity). Famous martyrs of other ages include St. Thomas Becket, St. Thomas More, St. Isaac Jogues, and Bd. Miguel Pro. What aspects of martyrdom have remained constant throughout history? In what ways has it changed? Compare the early Roman martyrs with Franz Jägerstätter, Dietrich Bonhoeffer, Maximilian Kolbe, Stanley Rother, Oscar Romero, Jerzy Popieluszko, Alexander Men, Christian de Chergé, Father Engelmar Unzeitig, Felix and Mary Barreda, Hans and Sophie Scholl.

8. The official calendar of saints abounds in examples of what could be called "clerical styles" of holiness (see St. Alphonsus Liguori, St. Vincent de Paul, St. John Vianney, St. Maximilian Kolbe, or Bd. John XXIII); likewise, there are abundant representatives of monastic, religious, and ascetic styles. In contrast, there are relatively few canonical saints who exemplify the challenge of lay holiness. What accounts for this imbalance? Does this reflect on the process of canonization, or does it also reflect traditional understandings of holiness? Among the non-canonized figures in this book are there any who might suggest the dimensions of such "lay holiness"?

9. Apart from biblical figures (Noah, Hagar, Rahab, Job, and the Hebrew prophets), *All Saints* includes a number of non-Christians. Among them are Jews (Anne Frank, the Baal Shem Tov, Martin Buber, Etty Hillesum, and Abraham Heschel), Hindus (Vinoba Bhave, Mohandas Gandhi), and non-believers (Albert Camus, for one). In addition, there are numerous figures who lived out their faith on the boundaries of organized religion (see, for example, Etty Hillesum, Simone Weil, Vincent van Gogh, Gustav Landauer, Henry David Thoreau, William Blake, Steve Biko, Oskar Schindler). What is the basis for inserting such figures in a Christian calendar of holy people?

10. The story of each saint is also, to some extent, a story about God. Many of the saints, beginning with St. Augustine, studied their own "stories" in this light. Others in this tradition might include St. Patrick, St. Therese of Lisieux, Dorothy Day, Thomas Merton, Henri Nouwen, Blaise Pascal, and St. Teresa of Avila. By reading their stories, and other lives of the saints, what lessons might we learn about how to "read" our own stories?

11. The official calendar includes many women saints — though not nearly as many as men. Some of the best known are Mary the Mother of Jesus, St. Mary Magdalene, St. Agnes, Sts. Perpetua and Felicity, St. Catherine of Alexandria, St. Brigid, St. Rose of Lima, St. Catherine of Siena, St. Teresa of Avila, St. Clare, St. Louise of Marillac, St. Jeanne de Chantal, St. Joan of Arc, St. Therese of Lisieux, and St. Edith Stein. But even as the church celebrates such lives it often depicts female sanctity according to a few stereotypical models. Traditional stories about women saints

often emphasize such virtues as virginity, obedience, humility, and patient suffering. How do the examples above support or challenge such assumptions?

12. Are there distinctively female styles of holiness? Beyond the examples cited above, consider the stories of Mev Puleo, St. Scholastica, St. Elizabeth of Hungary, St. Catherine of Genoa, Thea Bowman, Mother Maria Skobtsova, Hadewijch, Julian of Norwich, Rose Hawthorne, Cornelia Connelly, Heloise, Bd. Mary McKillop, Mother Teresa, St. Hildegard of Bingen, Sor Juana Inés de la Cruz, Margery Kempe, Maura O'Halloran, Dorothy Day, Maura Clarke, Anne Hutchinson, and Etty Hillesum. Whether canonized or not, what do these examples add to our understanding of holiness and of the role of women?

13. The history of Christianity can be told in terms of the constant interaction between the gospel and new cultural horizons. This is clearly true in the case of the early apologists who translated the gospel into the terms of Hellenistic thought (see St. Justin, Origen, St. Clement of Alexandria), or the early missionaries who brought the gospel to the tribes of Europe (see St. Patrick, St. Bede, St. Boniface). It is clearly the case with later missionaries like St. Francis Xavier, Mateo Ricci, or Roberto de Nobili. But might we also extend this model to those who tried to broker a dialogue between the church and modernity (see Henri Dominique Lacordaire, John Lord Acton, Baron von Hügel, Pierre Teilhard de Chardin, Karl Rahner) or to cross over into the world of the poor and oppressed (see Frederic Ozanam, Ignacio Ellacuría, Sister Alicia Domon, Henri Perrin), or to comprehend their faith in terms of other religious traditions (Bede Griffiths, Sadhu Sundar Singh, Maura O'Halloran). What new cultural, intellectual, or religious horizons confront us today? What are some of the areas in which this new "missionary" encounter might occur?

14. Simone Weil wrote, "Today it is not nearly enough merely to be a saint; but we must have the saintliness demanded by the present moment." What are some of the characteristics of the saintliness needed today? Who are some of the people who embody such saintliness, whether represented in this book or otherwise?

Themes

1. Consider the theme of social justice through the following: Moses, St. James, St. Basil, Bartolomé de Las Casas, Bd. Frédéric Ozanam, Pope Leo XIII, Pedro Arrupe, Dom Helder Camara, Fannie Lou Hamer, Oscar Romero, Cesar Chavez, Albert Luthuli, William Wilberforce, Martin Luther King, Jr., Pope Paul VI, Steve Biko, James Carney, Jerzy Popieluszko, Walter Rauschenbusch, Harriet Tubman, Dorothy Day, Rutilio Grande, Ignacio Ellacuría, and Chico Mendes.

2. St. Aelred of Riveaulx said that "Friendship is God." Simone Weil described friendship as one of the "implicit forms of the love of God."

Consider the role of friendship in the lives of these men and women: Sts. Francis de Sales/Jeanne de Chantal; Sts. Jerome/Paula/Marcella; Sts. Benedict/Scholastica; Sts. Perpetua and Felicity; Sts.Vincent de Paul/ Louise de Marillac; George Tyrrell/Maud Petre; Peter Maurin/Dorothy Day; Sts. Boniface/Lioba; Sts. Francis/Clare; St. Teresa of Avila/John of the Cross; Raïssa and Jacques Maritain; Sts. Gertrude/Mechtild of Hackeborn.

3. Consider the theme of tolerance and the practice of dialogue through the following: Cardinal Gaspar Contarini; Yves Congar; Erasmus; Sebastian Castellio; John Woolman; John Courtney Murray; George Fox; C. F. Andrews, St. Francis de Sales; Charles de Foucauld; Henri Perrin; Christian de Chergé; John Wesley, Sadhu Sundar Singh; Mohandas Gandhi; Maura O'Halloran; Etty Hillesum; Thomas Merton; Bede Griffiths; Martin Buber; John Main; Cardinal Joseph Bernardin.

4. Consider the theme of peace and nonviolence through such classic saints as St. Maximilian, St. Martin of Tours, and St. Francis. Compare their message with the vision of modern peacemakers such as Martin Niemöller, A. J. Muste, Mohandas Gandhi, Martin Luther King, Jr., Ben Salmon, Max Metzger, Franz Jägerstätter, John Leary, Dorothy Day, Ammon Hennacy, Lanza del Vasto, Andre Trocmé, and Eberhard Arnold.

5. Consider the various styles of mysticism in the following lives: St. Angela of Foligno; Julian of Norwich; Takashi Nagai; Bd. Henry Suso; Meister Eckhart; Moses; Hadewijch of Brabant; Pierre Teilhard de Chardin; St. Catherine of Siena; St. Osanna of Mantua; Sadhu Sundar Singh; The *Cloud* Author; Mechthild of Magdeburg; Simone Weil; St. Catherine of Genoa; St. Hildegard of Bingen; Dag Hammarskjöld; Padre Pio; Bd. Richard Rolle; St. Therese of Lisieux; The Pilgrim; St. Francis; St. Teresa of Avila; St Gertrude; St. Mechtild of Hackeborn; Etty Hillesum; St. John of the Cross; Thomas Merton.

6. St. Francis of Assisi has been named the patron saint of ecology. For others concerned with the divine presence in nature and the cosmos, see: St. Seraphim of Sarov; Galileo Galilei; Giordano Bruno; Meister Eckhart; Pierre Teilhard de Chardin; Henry David Thoreau; Bd. Julian of Norwich; St. Isidore the Farmer; Chief Seattle; Vincent van Gogh; William Blake; Jonathan Edwards; Noah; E. F. Schumacher; Chico Mendes.

Icons

1. Saints have been described as "icons" or images of God. For icons of divine compassion, see: St. Camillus de Lellis; St. Catherine of Genoa; Bd. Damien of Molokai; Dorothy Day; Rose Hawthorne; Etty Hillesum; Albert Schweitzer; Julian of Norwich; St. Therese of Lisieux; Maura O'Halloran; Bd. Frédéric Ozanam; Mev Puleo; Oskar Schindler; Raoul Wallenberg; John Howard Griffin; Mother Maria Skobtsova; Mother Teresa; Father Engelmar Unzeitig; St. Maximilian Kolbe.

2. For "icons" of divine wisdom, see: St. Francis de Sales; St. Thomas Aquinas; Cardinal John Henry Newman; Meister Eckhart; Pierre Teilhard de Chardin; Origen; St. Bonaventure; St. Augustine; St. Hildegard of Bingen; St. Catherine of Alexandria.

3. For icons of divine forgiveness: St. Patrick; St. Isaac Jogues; Cardinal Joseph Bernardin; St. Catherine of Genoa; Etty Hillesum; Walter Ciszek; Bishop James E. Walsh; St. Callistus; St. John Vianney; St. Alphonsus Liguori; St. Josephine Bakhita; St. Germaine Cousin; Christian de Chergé; Vinoba Bhave.

4. For icons of divine humility, see: St. Seraphim of Sarov; Brother Lawrence; St. John of God; St. Josephine Bakhita; Bd. Damien of Molokai; St. Benedict Joseph Labre; Woman with a Flow of Blood; Peter Waldo; Brother Juniper; St. Isidore the Farmer; St. Celestine V; Job; St. Basil the Blessed; St. John Vianney; Bd. Jeanne Jugan; St. Therese of Lisieux; St. Francis of Assisi; St. Alphonsus Rodriguez; St. Elizabeth of Hungary; Charles de Foucauld; St. Juan Diego; St. Martin de Porres.

5. For defenders of liberty, religious freedom, and the rights of conscience, see: Cardinal John Henry Newman; Felix Varela; John Courtney Murray; John Lord Acton; Fannie Lou Hamer; Harriet Tubman; Marc Sangnier; Isaac Hecker; Henri Dominique Lacordaire; Gustav Landauer; Jerzy Popieluszko; William Wilberforce; Sebastian Castellio; Henry David Thoreau; St. Thomas More; Franz Jägerstätter.

6. For icons of divine justice, see: Dom Helder Camara; Rutilio Grande; Fannie Lou Hamer; Oscar Romero; Harriet Tubman; Amos; Martin Luther King Jr.; Cesar Chavez; Leon Bloy; Bartolomé de Las Casas; Walter Rauschenbusch; William Wilberforce; Bd. Frédéric Ozanam; Jeremiah; Isaiah; Micah; John Woolman; Jerzy Popieluszko; Ignacio Ellacuría.

7. For those men and women who died in isolation or obscurity, their gifts and vision bequeathed to a more sympathetic generation, see: Mary Ward; Giordano Bruno; Marc Sangnier; Pierre Teilhard de Chardin; Henri Perrin; Anne Frank; Peter Waldo; St. Joan of Arc; Gerard Manley Hopkins; William Blake; Wolfgang Amadeus Mozart; Sor Juana Inés de la Cruz; Antonio Rosmini; Sebastian Castellio; Jan Hus; Vincent van Gogh; Cardinal Gaspar Contarini; Charles de Foucauld; Matteo Ricci; Franz Jägerstätter; Ben Salmon; Søren Kierkegaard; Bartolomé de Las Casas; Anne Hutchinson.

Index

ROBERT ELLSBERG was born in 1955 and raised in Los Angeles. He graduated from Harvard College with a degree in religion and literature and later studied theology at Harvard Divinity School. From 1975 to 1980 he was a member of the Catholic Worker community in New York City, serving for two years (1976–78) as managing editor of *The Catholic Worker* newspaper. Since 1987 he has served as editor-in-chief of Orbis Books. He has written or edited a number of books, including *Dorothy Day: Selected Writings* (Christopher Award), *Fritz Eichenberg: Works of Mercy* (Christopher Award, Catholic Book Award), *Gandhi on Christianity, Carlo Carretto: Selected Writings,* and *The Saints' Guide to Happiness.* With Tom Cornell and Jim Forest he co-edited *A Penny a Copy: Readings for The Catholic Worker.* With Penny Lernoux and Arthur Jones he wrote *Hearts on Fire: The Story of the Maryknoll Sisters* (Catholic Book Award). In 1998 he received a third Christopher Award for *All Saints* and the Veritas Medal of Dominican College for service to peace and justice. In 2002, Ellsberg was named a recipient of Harvard Divinity School's First Decade Award. He lives in Ossining, New York, with his wife and their three children.

Of Related Interest

Robert Ellsberg
TODOS LOS SANTOS

The Spanish translation of the best-selling *All Saints!* This masterpiece is a beautiful collection of daily reflections on saints, prophets, and witnesses of our time.

"A great treasure."
— Henri Nouwen

0-8245-1911-6, $24.95 paperback

Andrew Seddon
WALKING WITH THE CELTIC SAINTS
A Devotional

This light and enjoyable book is a series of stories and reflections on the Celtic saints. Each of the fifteen chapters begins with a semi-fictional story or event from the life of a saint, showing some characteristic quality for which the saint is known. This is followed by a reflection that combines history and inspiration. Then comes a short original poem, scripture, meditation, and a blessing. A website connected with the book will offer fully arranged original hymns to accompany the poems.

0-8245-2264-8, $16.95 paperback

Frederick Quinn
AFRICAN SAINTS
Saints, Martyrs, and Holy People
from the Continent of Africa

"The official calendar of the saints has long been weighted toward the West. But in this era of the 'world church' it is more important than ever to draw on the inspiration and challenge of holy people from other parts of the world. This important book reminds us of the vital contributions of the African church, greatly expanding that 'cloud of witnesses' who inspire and challenge us on our path to holiness."
— Robert Ellsberg, Editor-in-Chief of Orbis Books,
and author of *All Saints*

0-8245-1971-X, $22.95 paperback

crossroad

Of Related Interest

Rudolf Stertenbrink
THE WISDOM OF THE LITTLE FLOWER
Thérèse of Lisieux — Bearer of Modern Spirituality

Beloved Saint Enters the Mainstream!

Millions of people around the world, including the pope, are devoted aficionados of a modest young nun who died early last century. What is the secret of Thérèse of Lisieux, who is one of only three women to be awarded the exclusive title of "Doctor of the Church?"

St. Thérèse of Lisieux believed that what matters most in life is not high theology, but hope against all adversity. In this engrossing book, Stertenbrink unearths the more thoughtful side of this simple nun. In doing so, he quotes from Dostoyevsky, Kierkegaard, Cardinal Newman, and Edith Stein, among others. The result is a direct encounter with Thérèse. The book comprises short essays that can be read one at a time — before bed or on the train — or straight through for a compelling narrative.

0-8245-1983-3, $17.95, paperback

Please support your local bookstore,
or call 1-800-707-0670 for Customer Service.

For a free catalog, write us at

THE CROSSROAD PUBLISHING COMPANY
16 Penn Plaza, 481 Eighth Avenue
New York, NY 10001

Visit our website at
www.crossroadpublishing.com
All prices subject to change.

crossroad